Internet of Things and Network Infrastructure

Internet of Things and Network Infrastructure

Edited by **Anthony Rocus**

WILLFORD **P**RESS
New York

Published by Willford Press,
118-35 Queens Blvd., Suite 400,
Forest Hills, NY 11375, USA
www.willfordpress.com

Internet of Things and Network Infrastructure
Edited by Anthony Rocus

International Standard Book Number: 978-1-68285-213-2 (Hardback)

Printed in the United States of America.

Contents

Preface VII

Chapter 1　MediaWise cloud content orchestrator 1
Rajiv Ranjan, Karan Mitra and Dimitrios Georgakopoulos

Chapter 2　Consumer-centric resource accounting in the cloud 15
Ahmed Mihoob, Carlos Molina-Jimenez and Santosh Shrivastava

Chapter 3　A DDS-based middleware for scalable tracking, communication and collaboration of mobile nodes 31
Lincoln David, Rafael Vasconcelos, Lucas Alves, Rafael André and Markus Endler

Chapter 4　PolyViNE: policy-based virtual network embedding across multiple domains 46
Fady Samuel, Mosharaf Chowdhury and Raouf Boutaba

Chapter 5　Replica placement to mitigate attacks on clouds 69
Filipe Araujo, Serhiy Boychenko, Raul Barbosa and António Casimiro

Chapter 6　PAMPA in the wild: a real-life evaluation of a lightweight ad-hoc broadcasting family 82
Christopher Winstanley, Rajiv Ramdhany, François Taïani, Barry Porter and Hugo Miranda

Chapter 7　Radiator - efficient message propagation in context-aware systems 98
Pedro Alves and Paulo Ferreira

Chapter 8　AppaaS: offering mobile applications as a cloud service 116
Khalid Elgazzar, Ali Ejaz and Hossam S Hassanein

Chapter 9　Quality-of-service in cloud computing: modeling techniques and their applications 128
Danilo Ardagna, Giuliano Casale, Michele Ciavotta, Juan F Pérez and Weikun Wang

Chapter 10　On middleware for emerging health services 145
Jatinder Singh and Jean M Bacon

Chapter 11　*Flux*: a quality-driven dataflow model for data intensive computing 164
Sérgio Esteves, João Nuno Silva and Luís Veiga

Chapter 12   **PaaSHopper: Policy-driven middleware for multi-PaaS environments**   **187**
Stefan Walraven, Dimitri Van Landuyt, Ansar Rafique, Bert Lagaisse and
Wouter Joosen

Chapter 13   **Partitioning of web applications for hybrid cloud deployment**   **201**
Nima Kaviani, Eric Wohlstadter and Rodger Lea

Chapter 14   **Dioptase: a distributed data streaming middleware for the
future web of things**   **218**
Benjamin Billet and Valérie Issarny

Chapter 15   **Mapping virtual networks onto substrate networks**   **237**
Gustavo P Alkmim, Daniel M Batista and Nelson LS da Fonseca

Permissions

List of Contributors

Preface

Every book is a source of knowledge and this one is no exception. The idea that led to the conceptualization of this book was the fact that the world is advancing rapidly; which makes it crucial to document the progress in every field. I am aware that a lot of data is already available, yet, there is a lot more to learn. Hence, I accepted the responsibility of editing this book and contributing my knowledge to the community.

Internet of things is a relatively new concept which has gained significance in the past few years. The applications of this concept are rapidly expanding and opening doors for more and more innovative research. This extensive book focuses primarily on the current status of internet of things by exploring its models, theories and future implications. Also elaborated in this book are network infrastructures and protocols for a better understanding of the given concepts. It aims to fuel the growth of this discipline and keep the readers updated with the latest research in the field.

While editing this book, I had multiple visions for it. Then I finally narrowed down to make every chapter a sole standing text explaining a particular topic, so that they can be used independently. However, the umbrella subject sinews them into a common theme. This makes the book a unique platform of knowledge.

I would like to give the major credit of this book to the experts from every corner of the world, who took the time to share their expertise with us. Also, I owe the completion of this book to the never-ending support of my family, who supported me throughout the project.

Editor

MediaWise cloud content orchestrator

Rajiv Ranjan*, Karan Mitra and Dimitrios Georgakopoulos

Abstract

The growing ubiquity of Internet and cloud computing is having significant impact on media-related industries. These industries are using the Internet and cloud as a medium to enable creation, search, management and consumption of their content. Primarily, Content Delivery Networks (CDNs) are deployed for distributing multimedia content to the end-users. However, existing approaches to architecting CDNs have several limitations. Firstly, they do not harness multiple public cloud services for optimizing cost to performance ratio. Secondly, they lack support for dynamic and personalized content creation and distribution. Finally, they do not support end-to-end content lifecycle operations (production, deployment, consumption, personalization, and distribution).

To overcome these limitations, in this paper, we propose, develop and validate a novel system called MediaWise Cloud Content Orchestrator (MCCO). MCCO expands the scope of existing CDNs with novel multi-cloud deployment. It enables content personalization and collaboration capabilities. Further, it facilitates do-it-yourself creation, search, management, and consumption of multimedia content. It inherits the pay-as-you-go models and elasticity that are offered by commercially available cloud services.

In this paper, we discuss our vision, the challenges and the research objectives pertaining to MCCO for supporting next generation streamed, interactive, and collaborative high resolution multimedia content. We validated our system thorugh MCCO prototype implementation. Further, we conducted a set of experiments to demonstrate the functionality of MCCO. Finally, we compare the content orchestration features supported by MCCO to existing CDNs against the envisioned objectives of MCCO.

Keywords: Content delivery network, Cloud computing, Media management, Media delivery, Media consumption, Personalization, Quality of service

1. Introduction

Internet is having a significant impact on the media-related industries which are using it as a medium to enable delivery of their content to end-users. Rich web pages, software downloads, interactive communications, and ever-expanding universe of digital media require a new approach to content delivery. Size and volume of multimedia content is growing exponentially. For example, more than 30 billion pieces of content such as web links, news stories, blog posts, notes, and photo albums are shared each month on Facebook. On the other hand, Twitter users are tweeting an average 55 million tweets a day that includes web links and photo albums. Web pages and other multimedia content are being delivered through content delivery networks (CDN) [1] technologies. These technologies optimize network usage through dedicated network links, caching servers and by increasingly using peer-to-peer technologies. The concept of a CDN was conceived in the early days of Internet but it took until the end of 1990's before CDNs from Akamai and other commercial providers managed to deliver Web content (i.e., web pages, text, graphics, URLs and scripts) anywhere in the world and at the same time meet the high availability and quality expected by their end users. For example, Akamai [2] delivers between fifteen to thirty percent of all Web traffic, reaching more than 4 Terabits per second. Commercial CDNs achieved this by deploying a private collection of servers and by using distributed CDN software system in multiple data centres around the world.

A different variant of CDN technology appeared in the mid 2000's to support the streaming of hundreds of high definition channels to paid customers. These CDNs had to deal with more stringent Quality of Service (QoS) requirements to support users' experience pertaining to high definition video. This required active management

* Correspondence: rajiv.ranjan@csiro.au
CSIRO ICT Centre, Canberra, Australia

of the underlying network resources and the use of specialized set-top boxes that included video recorders (providing stop/resume and record/playback functionality) and hardware decoders (e.g., providing MPEG 4 video compression/decompression). Major video CDNs where developed by telecommunications companies that owned the required network and had Operation Support Systems (OSSs) to manage the network QoS as required by the CDN to preserve the integrity of high definition video content. Just like the original CDNs, video CDN also utilize a private collection of servers distributed around the network of video service provider. The first notable CDNs in this category include Verizon's FiOS and AT&T's U-verse. Some CDN providers such as Limelight Networks invested billions of dollars in building dedicated network links (media-grade fiber-optic backbone) for delivering and moving content from servers to end-users.

A more recent variant of video CDNs involves the caching video content in cloud storage and the distribution of such content using third-party network services that are designed to meet QoS requirements of caching and streaming high definition video. For example, Netflix's video CDN has been developed on top of Amazon AWS. CloudFront is Amazon's own CDN that uses Amazon AWS and provides streaming video services using Microsoft Xboxes. While Cloud-based CDNs [3,4] have made a remarkable progress in the past five years, they are still limited in the following aspects:

- CDN service providers either own all the services they use to run their CDN services or they outsource this to a single cloud provider. A specialized legal and technical relationship is required to make the CDN work in the latter case.
- Video CDNs are not designed to manage content (e.g., find and play high definition movies). This is typically done by CDN applications. For example, CDNs do not provide services that allow an individual to create a streaming music video service combining music videos from an existing content source on the Internet (e.g., YouTube), his/her personal collection, and from live performances he/she attends using his/her smart phone to capture such content. This can only be done by an application managing where and when the CDN will deliver the video component of his/her music program.
- CDNs are designed for streaming staged content but do not perform well in situations where content is produced dynamically. This is typically the case when content is produced, managed and consumed in collaborative activities. For example, an art teacher may find and discuss movies from different film archives, the selected movies may then be

edited by students. Parts of them may be used in producing new movies that can be sent to the students' friends for comments and suggestions. Current CDNs do not support such collaborative activities that involve dynamic content creation.

In [5], we proposed the MediaWise cloud which facilitates the collaborative content production and deployment using public clouds. This paper builds on [5]. However, compared to [5], in this paper, we propose, develop and validate the MediaWise Cloud Content Orchestrator (MCCO). MCCO is an enabler for MediaWise cloud facilitating content orchestration operations (e.g., content production and deployment) across cloud service layers [3] including Software as a Service (SaaS), Platform as a Service (PaaS) and Infrastructure as a Service (IaaS) layers. MCCO aims to address the shortcomings of current CDN technologies. Compared to [5], we perform extensive experiments to validate MCCO. MCCO [a] aims to address the shortcomings of current CDN technologies. In particular, MCCO makes the following contributions:

- Unlike existing commercial CDN providers such as Limelight Networks and Akamai, MCCO eliminates the need to own and manage expensive infrastructure while facilitating content owner requirements pertaining to price, SLA, privacy and QoS. Instead, it can utilize the cloud storage and CPU resources from virtually any public cloud provider. This provides additional flexibility for meeting QoS requirements (e.g., by staging content in public cloud storage "closer" to its consumers and by choosing the most cost-effective combination of public cloud providers to deliver short term and long term content delivery services).
- We describe and discuss sample application domains (education, news and entertainment) which will benefit by using MCCO.
- We present design and prototype implementation of MCCO and conduct experiments to show its effectiveness.

To the best of our knowledge, we are first to clearly articulate the major research challenges involved with designing next generation media management CDNs. The rest of this paper is organised as follows: Section 2 articulates the sample media applications that will benefit from MCCO innovations. Section 3 presents the research vision, challenges, and objectives of designing MCCO. Section 4 describes the design, architecture and implementation of MCCO. Section 5 presents the early performance evaluation study of MCCO. Finaly, we discuss the conclusion and future work in section 6.

2. MediaWise innovations and sample applications

In the following sections, we discuss three interactive applications that will be demonstrated and used in the rest of this paper to help explain the planned innovations of our research regarding MCCO and illustrate its benefits. After discussing these applications, we will introduce the technical research areas of the MCCO Project that constitute its major functions. Finally, we outline the innovations of MCCO project, categorized by technical research areas, using examples from the application areas. Figure 1 shows the innovation areas of the MCCO project as intersections of the project's research and functional areas, the roles users play in producing, managing, and consuming multimedia content, and related application areas.

2.1 Applications and impact areas

In the following paragraphs, we describe the specific application areas we plan to use to demonstrate the impact of the MCCO project. Having specific applications and developing demonstrations that illustrate the benefits of this technology will provide focus in our research and facilitate adoption of MCCO.

2.1.1 Virtual classroom

A virtual classroom is a crucial component of an e-learning system. It requires two main capabilities:

- *synchronous communication and collaboration* for interactive teaching, questioning and answering, allowing class discussions, and supporting team work; and
- *asynchronous web-based knowledge management and dissemination* for making class-related material available to students, performing and submitting homework, and compiling with grading.

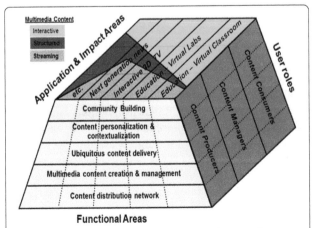

Figure 1 MCCO research areas organized by functional areas, applications, and user roles.

The MCCO project will develop and demonstrate a next generation virtual classroom. Synchronous communication and collaboration will be supported by a high resolution (100 M pixels) immersive videoconference environment that will be integrated with various state of the art tele-presence and shared workspace tools that are appropriate for remote teaching and class work. Provided workspace tools will include a virtual blackboard, screen sharing and co-browsing tools, as well as tools for scientific instrument sharing (e.g., virtual microscopy). Classroom tele-presense will be supported via low cost commercially available devices such as Microsoft's Kinect. It can achieve automatically tracking of the physical activities of all those in a virtual class room. For example, Kinect may be deployed at students' homes to track when two or more students raise their hands to ask or respond to a question. Automatic tracking of such activities can be used to make the virtual classroom more responsive (e.g., notify the remote teacher that a student has a question or requests permission to speak) and to improve classroom fairness (e.g., by automatically queuing and responding to student requests in the order they are manifested by a physical activity).

Next generation asynchronous web-based knowledge management and dissemination will be provided via scientific wikis. Surprisingly, by looking at current practices in many fields of asynchronous web-based, collaborative, distributed knowledge production and dissemination (ranging from community-managed web repositories to complex software development), it is easy to observe that *innovative forms of scientific publications are still lagging behind*, and that the world of scientific publications has been largely oblivious to the advent of the Web and to advances in ICT. Scientific knowledge dissemination is still based on the traditional notion of "paper" publication. In this application area, we want to explore the MCCO approach and how lessons learned from the social Web can be applied to provide a radical paradigm shift in the way scientific knowledge is created, disseminated, and maintained. We argue that novel technologies can enable a transition of "books" and "scientific publications" from its traditional "solid" form, (i.e. a crystallization in space and time of a scientific knowledge artifact) to a more fluid form (hereafter, what we call *Multimedia Scientific Knowledge Objects or MSKOs*), that can take multiple shapes, evolves continuously in time, and is enriched by multiple sources. Conceptually, this application area is a multimedia counterpart of the traditional notion of scientific publications based on emerging and mature Web 2.0 services. We view the Multimedia Scientific Wiki service as a software application that manages MSKOs embodying a novel form of multimedia publications lifecycle. We consider MSKOs as being intrinsically:

- multi-media, i.e., they support different kinds of content, such as text, images, videos, slides, case studies, experimental datasets, and also include reviews and feedback by the community;
- multi-version, i.e., MSKOs and their constituents evolve over time as people contribute knowledge to them. They exist in multiple, incremental versions;
- multi-author, i.e., they enable the collaboration and contribution of a number of interested and expert authors on a specific MSKO, with different levels of "ownership" and control of the MSKO, and each able to claim credit and responsibility for the contribution; and
- multi-publication, i.e., they support the creation of new MSKOs by composing (and extending) existing ones.

Additional multimedia content in MSKOs includes video captures of demonstrations, experiments, and presentations, and other supplemental material that is essentially the complements of a publication, like experimental data, spatial and temporal information, etc., as well as the opinion and feedback of people in the community. All of these are part of the knowledge associated to an MSKO – and hence contribute to the creation of multimedia knowledge – as it facilitates the understanding of the authors' original contribution. MSKOs evolve in time as scientific knowledge progresses, and have many actors contributing to their creation and evolution, according to various lifecycle processes. Authors progressively add knowledge (delta-increments) to multimedia content. The community – including other teachers and students, progressively validates the quality of multimedia publications and adds value to it in the form of comments and feedback. Evolution of a publication is not conceived as a novel publication to be created, evaluated, and published anew (with significant loss of time for the community), but rather as the evolution of an existing MSKO, possibly by different authors, with each able to claim credit and responsibility for their contribution.

The paradigm we want to explore in this application is similar to what started to happen twenty years ago in software engineering with the progressive adoption of more agile and iterative development processes, from the spiral model to extreme programming up to "social", open source development. Furthermore, the open source and web communities teach us how to perform a "validation" and "credit attribution" of the work (which is key to people's careers and goals, and their continued participation) that is fair, relatively accurate, allows for high-quality artefacts to be generated, but is also lightweight (relative to peer review today) in terms of reviewing time requirements.

Besides supporting MSKOs and their lifecycle, the Multimedia Scientific Wiki service will involve the development of a prototype of a publication centre, i.e., a set of tools that manage the entire lifecycle of MSKOs and its continuous evolution.

2.1.2 Virtual labs

Today's Internet-based learning systems can be successfully applied to teach theoretical knowledge presented in the form of structured multimedia content. However, this form of presentation is often insufficient to teach practical skills. Serious games involving Virtual Labs provide users with interactive virtual reality environments, where they can collaboratively work on performing practical tasks and experiments. Serious games bring users exceptional freedom of experimentation. In a game environment, users can interact with virtual objects in a Virtual Lab similarly to the ways they would interact with real objects. For example, they can be confronted with interactive simulations of situations that they may not be able to experience in the real world. Another significant advantage is safety since unskilled learners are able to explore potentially dangerous situations without any risk of harm to themselves or damage to expensive equipment. Serious games may be particularly useful for presenting phenomena, which are:

- potentially dangerous (e.g., chemical or radioactivity experiments);
- macroscopic or microscopic (e.g., astronomical events and molecular movements);
- very fast or very slow (e.g., explosions and continental drift);
- normally hidden from view (e.g., inner workings of machines, human anatomy);
- normally inaccessible (e.g., a nuclear reactor, undersea life); or involve
- abstract concepts (e.g., magnetic fields, molecular forces).

There are many examples of subject domains where serious games have been used for educational purposes, e.g., geography, astronomy, chemistry, and physics. The level of success of applying serious games largely depends on the flexibility of learning environments to match particular user needs. The presented multimedia content can be tailored to the age, learning styles, and performance characteristics of users. Consequently, when users are provided with such highly-customized multimedia content, they become more interested and more engaged in the games and the degree of their satisfaction from the experience increases.

Serious games can serve as the focal point of vibrant eLearning communities. Multimedia content for learning may be created by content producers around the world that join together in communities working on a particular game. An example of a game community may consist of a user playing the role of an instructor, two advanced players, and several beginners. Within such a community two teams may be created. Each team is a sub-community, which must be composed of an advanced player, who is a team leader, and several beginners. The instructor may manage the way the game develops over time, and may judge the competitors and evaluate the achieved results.

In some serious games, player communities may be dynamic. Players may join or leave teams, and move from one team to another, if their profile fits requirements of a destination community. For example, a community may try to outbid another one for the best specialists by offering them better positions. The game provides additional interactive capabilities that help build gaming communities. When a player logs in, the game helps him/her find and re-join his/her team, or search for other gaming friends so he/she can create/join a new team.

There are several scenarios related to possible serious game environments. In one scenario the game may be immersed in a purely virtual environment, where multimedia content is presented in a 3D virtual space. In another scenario, the game may be located in an augmented reality environment, where multimedia content is displayed in real environments of the players. Augmented reality environments combine video streams presenting views of real environments with digital interactive multimedia content. Players using mobile devices could play an interesting variation of a serious game over physical terrain. In this case, the game environment includes real landmarks and real obstacles. A game may rely on searching for some real objects hidden in a real building or discovering some knowledge based on the information derived from the environment. This location-based variation of serious games fosters dynamic formation of location-based teams that are associated by physical proximity.

2.1.3 Ubiquitous news
There are several variations of this application. One variation revolves around a clearinghouse service for video and audio news. Creation of such multimedia news content would be performed by individuals that happen to be present in an event and use personal devices, such as video cameras and cell phones for multimedia capture. This multimedia news content is consumed by users that search the new clearinghouse service for the news they need. Another variation of this news service may allow consumers to request news, even in situations where the event of interest is current but no multimedia news

content is being collected or where there is no content because the news request is for a future event. To satisfy such consumer needs, the news service must obtain news content by communicating and negotiating with other users that may be willing to serve as news content creators. To address these diverse requirements, the news clearinghouse service indexes and stores old content, streams new content from current events, and facilitates collaboration between content creators and consumers to obtain new multimedia content. In one version of the news service, multimedia content is not managed in any way (i.e., is raw audio and video that is not combined with other content or adapted for its consumers). In a more traditional multimedia news service, that content will be managed (e.g., enhanced with titles and narrative, and adapted to fit a specific spot in the news program).

Such content management may be performed by more specialized users that participate in another collaborative workflow that assembles a news program for consumers. When multimedia content is uploaded to the clearinghouse, contextual information (such as time and location) is automatically attached to the content. By using the clearinghouse the group is able to compose joint products, such as a "group trip report." These products also may be posted to a structured multimedia service that permits easy viewing by the family back home for multimedia content performed by more specialized users that participate in another collaborative workflow that assembles a news program for consumers. Another variation of ubiquitous news may involve location-based indexing and search capabilities for multimedia content. Such a service may allow a group of people (e.g., tourists or a school class on a field trip) to make movies and record narratives describing the points of interest

3. Research vision, challenges and objectives of MCCO
This section summarizes the research vision, challenges, and objectives of designing MCCO. Table 1 presents a comparative study of the existing CDN services against the research objectives of MCCO.

3.1 Content creation and management
Users and organizations involved in the creation of multimedia content play the role of content producers. The content they produced can be requested by and delivered to users playing the role of content consumers. Existing models of multimedia content creation are usually one-to-many (i.e., they involve one producer and many consumers) [6,7]. Content producers perform digital capture of multimedia data, and use software tools to perform multimedia post-production (e.g., to add graphics, audio, and titles to raw video clips), and finally produce a

Table 1 A comparative study of the existing CDN services against the research objectives of MCCO

CDN Application Provider	Content creation and management	Ubiquitous content delivery	Content indexing	Content personalization and contexualization	Community building	Quality of service optimization
Limelight Networks [25]	Browser based interface to upload static content; supports multiple media types; do not support dynamic content creation	Dependent on private Limilight networks backbone for content delivery; supports bitrate streaming as configured by content user; only limelight audio/video player supported	Title and Keyword based	No	No	Handled behind the scenes; content providers have no control over QoS; best effort QoS at network layer
Oyala [26]	Browser-based interface to upload static content. Dynamic content creation is not supported.	Yes, to multiple devices using multiple formats	Title and Keyword based	Personalization is partially supported based on the type of devices to be used for media streaming	No	Yes, based on different CDN providers such as Akamai,
NetFlix [27]	N/A	Yes, to multiple devices using multiple formats	Title and Keyword based	Personalization is partially supported based on the type of devices to be used for media streaming	No	Yes, based on different CDN providers such as Akamai and now their own.
Akamai (Sola) and Ultraviolet [28]	Content can be managed partially, only for purchased content such as movies.	Yes, to multiple devices using multiple formats.	Title and Keyword based	Personalization is partially supported based on the type of devices to be used for media streaming	No	Yes, via Akamai. The content providers have no control over QoS provisioning.
MetaCDN [29]	Content cannot be created but can only be managed using pre-defined emplates	Yes, to multiple devices using multiple formats.	No	No	No	Yes but content providers have no control over QoS provisioning.
Rackspace [30]	Mainly content storage and provisioning	Yes, based on Akamai CDN	No	No	No	Yes, using Akamai. However, content providers have no control over QoS provisioning.

media product (e.g., a TV program, a podcast, or a set of structured multimedia web pages that link text, pictures, video and music content). The MCCO research will focus on many-to-many models for creating novel forms of expressive and interactive content. In particular, as a starting point, MCCO will utilize existing Web 2.0 technologies for creating structured multimedia content (i.e., tools allowing users to create web pages linking video, pictures, audio, text, and graphics), but broaden existing Web 2.0 strengths with new technologies for creating novel forms of interactive multimedia content (e.g., as discussed earlier, our research will consider interactive content involving virtual and augmented reality). In particular, novel research in the MCCO will focus on the following three content creation and management areas:

3.1.1 Novel types of multimedia content
Existing Web 2.0 technologies currently support the authoring of *structured multimedia content* (e.g., web pages linking images, sounds, videos, and animations). The MCCO will extend and broaden existing Web 2.0

strengths with a new environment aimed at supporting the creation and consumption of interactive multimedia content (e.g., interactive audio and video), as well as other novel forms of multimedia content (e.g., *virtual* and *augmented reality*) that are currently not supported by existing Web 2.0 technologies and tools.

3.1.2 Advanced content management services
Multimedia content management includes the creation, adaptation, and composition of *content management* (CM) services. Basic CM services package multimedia content together with functionality that manipulates it. Examples of basic content services include functions for storing, indexing, and searching multimedia content [8]. CM services may be adapted for a specific purpose, or personalized for individual users or communities. Creation, adaptation, and composition of CM services are accomplished by (possibly collaborating) users that play the role of *content managers*. Complex CM services may be created by adapting or composing simpler CM services. For example, a basic content management service

may index movies, TV programs and news for future search. A complex content management service may provide an interactive TV guide and its functionality may use the basic indexing service.

The MCCO research will develop and demonstrate complex content management services for learning, news and entertainment applications. For example, we will build a software tool that allows users to collaboratively create non-linear multimedia presentations. For example, a teacher may create a new project. Teams of students can play the role of content creators and upload new content to the common project in the form of photos as well as audio and video recordings from mobile and desktop devices. Other students can become content managers and create a joint presentations by defining the relations (e.g., temporal, geographical, or topical) between these multimedia objects. Moreover we want to enhance Web 2.0 with novel technologies (for storing, indexing, searching, adapting, composing, and consuming streamed and interactive multimedia content) as well as innovative tools for collaborative editing, trends/hot topics/historical patterns identification and metadata feature management. The interactive video production will be further optimized by removing the redundant information that may introduced by multiple users. The redundant multimedia parts that are same in content are identified by incorporating the advanced near duplicate multimedia content detection techniques [9]. MCCO research in collaborative multimedia content management will provide next generation CM services for these functions; as well develop technologies for automating the adaptation and composition of CM services. Our research in MCCO will also develop a novel environment for automating the adaptation and composition of CM services.

3.1.3 Collaborative content management workflows

The research in MCCO will develop novel technology for supporting collaborative workflows that manage the lifecycle (i.e., the creation, management, and consumption) of complex multimedia content. In particular, we will research a wide range of user collaboration styles, develop novel technology for collaborative workflows managing the orchestration of services and human activities for multimedia content creation, management, consumption, and determine how to achieve greater collaboration scale, user participation, and efficiency. Collaborative workflows for multimedia content creation, management, and consumption may range from structured to unstructured. As an example of structured workflow that manages the lifecycle of multimedia content, consider the production of a web-based news program. The production of such a news program follows an established workflow process that involves the following steps: (1) capture and post-process

new video clips of a newsworthy event, (2) search video archives for related video clips, (3) create/edit audio annotations for the new and possibly old video clips, (4) save the new video clips/audio annotations and enable future content-based search, (5) capture the video or audio presentation of a news script by a news anchor, (6) post all products on a website, and (7) enable both linear and non-linear viewing of the news products. At the other end of the spectrum, ad hoc multimedia content creation involves no explicit control flow or coordination between multimedia content producers or mangers. Consider an existing Web 2.0 service that allows users to post video clips of events they consider to be newsworthy. This involves unconstrained uploading and sharing of multimedia content. MCCO will develop new technologies that accommodate these and any style of work or user preferences ranging from ad hoc to highly-structured activities for collaborative content creation and management. We will focus particularly on identifying, modelling, and automating collaboration patterns that increase the scale, user participation, efficiency, and automation of collaborative media creation and management activities.

3.2 Ubiquitous content delivery

Multimedia content can be subscribed to or requested by *content consumers*. The goal of multimedia content delivery is to provide a seamless multimedia experience to users. In its simplest form, this involves rendering the multimedia content to deal with the constraints of the network that carries the multimedia content and the characteristics of the specific device a user utilizes to receive the content and interact with it. Advanced multimedia delivery involves the development of *content delivery* services (CD). CD services will interact with the network and appropriately adjust its QoS as needed to deliver specific multimedia content to a specific user. In particular, we will focus on research that will lead to the development of CD services. When given a specific content and a specific content consumer, these CD services will adjust QoS characteristics based on content requirements for maintaining its integrity, the device the user is using, his/her location, and the service contract. We will research content transformation to meet target device and network constraints. Another related research objective of MCCO is to provide ubiquitous content delivery between producers/managers that may be distributed across many states or nations. The research in MCCO will develop technology for ubiquitous content delivery accommodating desktop users as well as mobile users who may meet in a coffee shop.

3.3 Flexible content storage, compression, and indexing

Cloud storage resources allow content producers to store content on virtualized disks and access them anytime from any point on the Internet. These storage resources are different from the local storage (for example, the local hard drive) in each CPU resource (e.g., Amazon EC2 instance types), which is temporary or non-persistent and cannot be directly accessed by other instances of CPU resources. Multiple storage resource types are available for building content Orchestrator. Naturally, the choice of a particular storage resource type stems from the format (e.g., structured vs. unstructured) of the content. For instance, Azure Blob [10] and Amazon S3 [11] storage resources can hold video, audio, photos, archived email messages, or anything else, and allow applications to store and access content in a very flexible way. In contrast, NoSQL (Not Only SQL) storage resources have recently emerged to complement traditional database systems [12]. They do not support ACID transaction principles, rather offer weaker consistency properties, such as eventual consistency. Amazon SimpleDB [13], Microsoft Azure Table Storage, Google App Engine Datastore [14], MongoDB [15], and Cassandra are some of the popular offerings in this category. For example, in Amazon CloudFront [16], CDN contents are organized into distributions.

A distribution specifies the location of the original version of contents. The distribution can be hosted on cloud storage resources such as Amazon S3 or Amazon EC2 CPU resources. With an increase in the scale and the size of content distribution, efficient indexing and storage become a critical issue. The challenge is further aggravated in case of live and interactive content, where size of distribution (hence the indexing complexity) in not known in advance. Though cloud environments are decentralized by nature, existing application architecture tends to be designed based on centralized network models. To support efficient content production and consumption on scale of TeraBytes or PetaBytes, it is mandatory to design decentralized content indexing algorithm to enable access and search over large-scale database. It is worth noting that none of the existing cloud storage resources exposes content indexing APIs. It is up to the CDN application designer to come-up with efficient indexing structure that can scale to large content sizes. To help end-users find and retrieve relevant content effectively and to facilitate new and better ways of media delivery using cloud resources, advanced distributed algorithms need to be developed for indexing, browsing, filtering, searching and updating the vast amount of information available in multimedia content.

3.4 Content personalization and contextualization

We are just beginning to realize the power of location-aware services, especially for mobile devices, that aid users in their interaction with their immediate physical environment. Location-aware services allow users to become aware of physically proximate resources that they might not otherwise know about, provide convenience in finding and interacting with those resources, and enable interpersonal networking that takes physical location as well as ad-hoc community-building in account. Imagine young people planning their weekend meetings within a connected infrastructure which is location-aware: the group of young people meet ad-hoc, are aware of each other's locations and create media content using video cameras or chatting (through typing or directly through voice messages).

MCCO will also support additional contextual information, including users' resources and capabilities for networking and computing, their work and leisure activities, their preferences, and the communities to which they belong. For the user, the benefits of content awareness, convenience, and community-building will be enabled by each such context. For the content producers, context can be viewed as a mechanism for mass customization that better meshes the needs and interests of each user with the multimedia capabilities at his/her disposal. MCCO will support models of users profiles which will store contextual information, including users resources and capabilities for networking and computing, their work and leisure activities, their preferences, and the communities to which they belong. For a user, the benefits of content awareness, convenience, community searching and community building will be enabled by each such a user profile. For the content producers, this contextual information can be viewed as a mechanism for mass customization that better meshes the needs and interests of each user with the multimedia capabilities at his/her disposal. In addition, models of users' profiles will include the specification of competences, skills of users, and evaluation of users' former activities, *potentially in other communities*. Additionally the storage of profiles of content creators and managers is especially important to find users which fulfil the requirements of a given community.

In this part of the work, research objectives within the MCCO include the following: (1) *Semi-automatic contextualization* – the automatic construction and maintenance of context of MediaWise content users through mechanisms including user-modelling and data mining, but augmented with more interactive mechanisms such as knowledge elicitation. (2) *Personalization* – capturing the needs of users related to their evolving context so as to maximize the benefit to each user. (3) *Adaptation* – customizing content and services based on context to better meet the needs of users who ultimately pay for them. (4) *Community building* – which extends personalization to groups of users with various commonalities. (5) Finally, *cross-community aspects of users' profile* – modelling aspects of users' profiles which are relevant for various communities to which they belong, such as skills and competences, as well as aspects of users' profiles related through their activities in other communities, such as level of involvement.

3.5 Community building

The concept of community is at the core of the Web 2.0 [17]. In most applications of the Web 2.0, the structures of communities in terms of members' competences are pre-defined, e.g. on flickr.com, users may publish their pictures to predefined groups: family members, friend or others. In current Web 2.0 applications, a user cannot tailor a community to his/her own needs, for instance defining an editor, a graphic designer and 5 journalists for a newspaper edition community. Nor can users easily find communities to which they may contribute, depending on their competencies, skills and centres of interest. Currently, users enter and leave communities in a chaotic way, depending mostly on recommendations of other users or links they may find while navigating.

Our research in MCCO intends to provide users with tools for community-building, based on a new model of communities and users' profiles. The proposed model of communities will integrate the concepts of competences and skills to specify the requirements of a community to be built. The model of users' profiles will support, on the one hand, the specification of competences and skills of users and, on the other hand, evaluation of users' former activities, potentially in other communities. The latter information will be obtained via: (1) real time monitoring of events (e.g., initiation and completion of user activities) that create, manage, and consume multimedia content, and (2) tracing such events involving one or more users to user communities. Based on the models of communities and users' profiles, new algorithms matching community specifications with users' profiles will be proposed for 1) identification of communities of interest, and 2) creation of new communities. Finally, as the requirements of a given community may evolve through time, the proposed model of communities will support adaptation of community specifications during the lifetime of a given community. Similarly, the profile of a given user will evolve in time along with the evaluation of his/her former activities. Therefore, tools supporting community management will take into account the high dynamics of communities and users' profiles.

3.6 Quality of service optimizer

It has been shown that one of the challenges in orchestrating cloud resources for managing CDN application is uncertainty. Resource uncertainty arises from a number of issues including user location, content type, malicious activities and heterogeneity. In some cases, media content delivery application may face with failure of resources or sometimes it may suffer from lack of sufficient resources. In this project, we will investigate the following issues for ensuring end-to-end QoS fulfilment in content production, consumption, and delivery.

3.6.1 Optimizing cloud resource selection

There are two layers in cloud computing as shown in Figure 2: a) service layer (e.g., Google App Engine, 3Tera Applogic, BitNami), where an engineer builds applications using APIs; and b) infrastructure layer (e.g., GoGrid, Amazon EC2), where an engineer runs applications inside CPU resources, using APIs provided by their chosen guest operating systems. Optimal CDN application performance demands bespoke resource configuration, yet no detailed, cost, performance or feature comparison of cloud providers exists. This complicates the choice of cloud providers.

The diversity of offering at this layer leads to a practical question: how well does a cloud provider perform compared to the other providers? For example, how does a CDN application engineer compare the cost/performance features of CPU, storage, and network resources offered by Amazon EC2, Microsoft Azure, GoGrid, FelxiScale, TerreMark, and RackSpace. For instance, a low-end CPU resource of Microsoft Azure is 30% more expensive than the comparable Amazon EC2 CPU resource, but it can process CDN application workload twice as quickly. Similarly, a CDN application engineer may choose one provider for storage intensive applications and another for computation intensive CDN applications. Hence, there is need to develop novel decision making framework that can analyse existing cloud providers to help CDN service engineers in making optimal selection decisions.

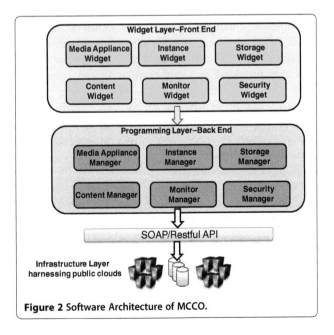

Figure 2 Software Architecture of MCCO.

3.6.2 Adapting to Dynamic CDN workload

Media delivery CDN applications must accommodate highly transient, unpredictable users behaviour (arrival patterns, service time distributions, I/O system behaviours, user profile, network usage, etc.) and activities (streaming, searching, editing, and downloading). Yet many cloud providers contract service-level agreements which stipulate specific QoS targets, such as how fast a web page is served. It is therefore important to all parties that highly variable spikes in demand, caused by large number of simultaneous requests for a shared CDN service, do not degrade QoS [18,19].

It is critical that MCCO is able to predict the demands and behaviours of hosted media applications, so that it can manage resources. Concrete prediction or forecasting models must be built before the demands and behaviours of a CDN application can be predicted accurately. The hard challenge is to accurately identify and continuously learn the most important behaviours and accurately compute statistical prediction functions based on the observed demands and behaviours such as request arrival pattern, service time distributions, I/O system behaviours, user profile, and network usage. The challenge is further aggravated by statistical correlation (such as stationary, short- and long-range dependence, and pseudo-periodicity) between different behaviours and activities of CDN application.

3.6.3 Adapting to uncertain cloud resource environment

The availability, load, and throughput of hardware resources (CPU, storage, and network) can vary in unpredictable ways Thus, ensuring that CDN applications achieve QoS targets can be difficult. Worse still, hardware resource status can be changed intentionally through malicious external interference. The recent high-profile crash of Amazon EC2 cloud which took down many applications is a salient example of unpredictability in cloud environments. Theoretically, the elasticity provided by cloud computing can accommodate unexpected changes in capacity, failure, adding hardware resources when need, and reducing them during periods of low demand, but the decision to adjust capacity must be made frequently, automatically, and accurately to be cost effective.

3.7 Other research objectives

The objective of our research in MCCO is to provide for *agility* in the creation, management, and consumption of content by small groups of users. For large groups of users and massive content, we will focus on providing maximum *efficiency*. Specifically, it should be noted that our research intends to specifically address scalability, reliability and flexibility issues. While scale may be defined in a variety of ways (e.g., by the number of end-to-end users involved in various content production, management and consumption roles, the number or sources and size of multimedia content, the group sizes of collaborating content producers and managers, the size of consumer communities, etc.), scale issues impact all functional areas and user roles as illustrated in Figure 1. Reliability is achieved through the fault-tolerance feature of a system in the face of sudden load spikes such as flash crowds. Flexibility of the system can be realized through the ease of use, integration to existing system and on-demand deployment. We intend to test selected scenarios within a mobile city environment so that local, as well as mobile, scenarios can actually be explored.

4. MediaWise cloud content orchestrator: design and architecture

As mentioned earlier, we developed a cloud-based generic and scalable software framework called MCCO [20] for supporting the end-to-end lifecycle operations required for managing content via clouds and the Internet. The MCCO exploit public clouds for offloading computing, storage, network, and content distribution functionalities in a cost effective manner. Cloud computing [3,4] assembles large networks of virtualized services: hardware resources (CPU, storage, and network) and software resources or appliances (e.g., databases, message queuing systems, monitoring systems, load-balancers). Cloud providers including Amazon Web Services (AWS), Microsoft Azure, Salesforce.com, Google App Engine, and others give users the option to deploy their application over a network of infinite resource pool with practically no capital investment and with modest operating cost proportional to the actual use.

MCCO offers enhanced flexibility and elasticity as it inherits pay-as-you-go model from public cloud resources. MCCO content orchestration operations include: (i) production: create and edit; (ii) storage: uploading and scaling of storage space; (iii) keyword-based content tagging and searching and (iv) distribution: streaming and downloading. At Cloud service level, MCCO capabilities span across a range of operations such as selection, assembly, deployment of cloud resources to monitoring their run-time QoS statistics (e.g., latency, utilization, and throughput). MCCO orchestrate public cloud resources via open-source RESTFul APIs. It supports deployment, configuration and monitoring of content and cloud resources using Web-based widgets. These widgets hide the underlying complexity related to cloud resources and provide *an easy do-it-yourself* interface for content management. The high level architecture of MCCO is shown in Figure 2. The Widget layer presents a unified front end for end users to perform aforementioned content orchestration operations. It hides the complexities related to all these operations by using a plethora of in-house and open source APIs. These APIs are implemented at the Programming layer and manage operations for Infrastructure layer. For example, starting and stopping a virtual machine.

4.1 Infrastructure layer

This layer provides cloud-based hardware resources such as CPU, storage, routers and switches that hosts the media appliances such as streaming server, indexing server, and editing server. Hardware resources expose certain configuration that can be allocated to media appliances. For example, a streaming server appliance available from Wowza [21] can be assigned following Amazon EC2 CPU configurations: 7.5 GB memory, 4 EC2 Compute Unit, 850 GB instance storage, 64-bit addressing and moderate I/O. More details on optimal hardware and appliance selection can be found in the following paper [22]. In general, cloud providers manage resources at infrastructure layer through hardware virtualization technologies [23] such as Xen, Citrix, KVM (open source), VMWare and Microsoft Hyer-V. Virtualization allows providers to get more out of hardware resources by allowing multiple instances of virtual resources to run at the same time. Each virtual resource believes it has its own hardware. Virtualization isolates the resources from each other, thereby making fault tolerant and isolated security behaviour possible.

4.2 Programming layer

This layer implements the logic for interfaces exposed by widget layer. For example, the Media Appliance Manager implements Cloud resource API that allows Appliance Widget to list the set of media appliances (e.g., streaming, indexing and editing servers) associated with owner's account. Programming Layer is also designed to allow engineers to plug-in different Cloud service APIs. Notably, each of the managers at this layer has to perform certain orchestration operation on infrastructure layer cloud resources, such as provisioning of a streaming server appliance over an Amazon EC2 or indexing of contents over Amazon S3. Currently, our implementation works with Amazon Web Service (AWS) and is being extended to support other Cloud providers.

4.3 Widget layer

Widget Layer encapsulates user interface components in the form of six principle widgets including Media Appliance, Instance, Storage, Monitor, Content, and Security. Next, we provide the brief details about each widget.

- Media Appliance Widget: It lists the set of media appliances associated with content owner's account. In general, an appliance [24] is pre-configured, self-contained, virtualization-enabled, and pre-built software resource unit (e.g., streaming, indexing and

editing servers) that can be integrated with other compatible appliances for architecting complex applications such as video-on-demand CDN.
- Instance Widget: Content owners are required to describe the media appliances' deployment configurations that will affect and drive its instance's placement and performance. Configuration parameters include number of instances, their types, security setting, and monitoring preference. In context of Amazon's EC2, different instance types provide different minimum performance guarantees depending on their memory, storage, and processor configurations. Additionally, content owners or CDN administrators can also consider non-functional attributes related to deployments such as hosting cost, latency, throughput, scalability, and availability. The discussion of algorithms that consider optimization of these attributes is beyond the scope of this paper.
- Storage Widget: It allows content owners to upload content and media appliances to storage service (e.g., Amazon S3). Cloud storage resources provide a highly durable and available storage for a variety of content types, including web applications and multimedia files.
- Content Widget: It enables the functionality for tagging, indexing, and personalizing content with metadata. It exposes a drag and drop interface for mapping of an audio/video content from cloud storage to a media appliance. Content can be tagged with one or more keywords.
- Monitor Widget: It supports monitoring the status of media appliance instances, network and storage services. Monitored data such as media appliance throughput, utilization, disk I/O are made available in form of two-dimensional charts
- Security Widget: It manages all the authentication and authorization credentials related to orchestrating content (e.g. content access secret key) and cloud resources (access key and secret key). MCCO includes security credentials provided by Amazon EC2 which is read directly from a file stored in a web folder. In future, we will implement more security mechanisms to better manage the security credentials from different cloud providers.

4.4 Implementation

Although the design of MCCO is generic and extensible, our current implementation is specific to supporting orchestration of do-it-yourself CDN using public cloud resources. However, we believe the system is mature enough for validating the overall idea and vision. The system is entirely written in Java and makes use of number of open-source libraries:

- GWT and SmartGWT, to build basic user interfaces.
- Amazon's EC2 API, for implementing appliance life cycle operations (start, stop, suspend, and delete).
- Amazon's S3 API, for implementing data copy operation across S3 and media appliances.
- Amazon's CloudWatch API, for collecting performance data from CPU resource instances.
- JQuery, for interactive charting function.
- Apache Commons File Upload, for implementing upload function.
- JSch, for implementing secure communication channel to access the appliance instance environment.

MCCO supports adapter and factory design fattern to provide clear mechanisms for designing flexible software architecture that are highly adaptable and extendable.

5. Early experiments and preliminary results

Although we are actively working towards the implementation of MCCO, it is still a work-in-progress. Hence, in this section, we present our experiments and evaluation that we undertook for studying the feasibility of the proposed research vision.

5.1 Testbed setup

5.1.1 Media appliance configuration

The MediaWise testbed setup is shown in Figure 3. To stream audio and video content, we leverage the streaming media appliance provided by Wowza Media Systems [21]. In the current release, Wowza media appliance support following streaming protocols: Flash (RTMP and HTTP), Microsoft Silverlight, QuickTime/3GPP (RTSP/RTP). The Wowza appliance is deployed on Ubuntu operating system (ami-d7a273be).

For Wowza appliance to work properly, it has to be a properly integrated with content storage resource. As mentioned previously, cloud storage resources do not expose any content indexing API. Hence, we created our own appliance that supports keyword-based content indexing. This appliance had the following software configuration: a RESTFul indexing web service hosted on 32Bit Java Virtual Machine version 1.6 and Glassfish application server on a Windows 7. At the deployment phase, we created multiple instances of the streaming appliance and one instance of indexing appliance.

The indexing appliance stores the content URL in the MySQL in the format: http://[IP address]/vods3/_definst_/mp4:amazons3/[S3 Bucket name]/[File name]. At run time, the indexing appliance fetches the URL of end-user requested contents from storage resources to Wowza appliance.

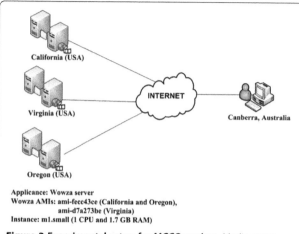

Appliance: Wowza server
Wowza AMIs: ami-fecc43ce (California and Oregon),
         ami-d7a273be (Virginia)
Instance: m1.small (1 CPU and 1.7 GB RAM)

Figure 3 Experimental setup for MCCO project. Media server appliances are hosted at three locations across USA. A user in Australia then deploys appliances' and uploads and downloads the media content through MCCO.

5.1.2 Hardware resource (Infrastructure) configuration

We tested our implementation of MCCO in experiment where it was hosted on a 32Bit Java Virtual Machine version 1.6 and Glassfish application server on a Windows 7 with an Intel Core 2 Duo 2.5 Ghz CPU and 2 GB of RAM. We configured the MCCO with security credentials required for orchestrating Amazon EC2 and Amazon S3 resources hosted in US Oregon, US North California, and US Virginia availability zones. We hosted both media appliances using an Amazon EC2 large instance across these availability zones. By default, a large instance has the following hardware configuration: 7.5 GB of main memory, 4 EC2 Compute Unit (i.e. 2 virtual cores with 2 EC2 Compute Unit), 850 GB of local instance storage, and a 64-bit platform.

5.2 Results and discussions

For results validation, we considered two metrics, , average upload throughput and average upload delay. The choice of these metric were based on the fact that MCCO enables content creation and its timely sharing. This requires timely content availability to end users. In cloud systems, content can be geographically located around the globe. Usually, content is placed at the location closest to the user for QoS maximization. In this section, we estimate the aforementioned metrics by uploading the content to three different US-based Amazon S3 datacenters in Oregon, California and Virginia. These experiments were conducted from Canberra, Australia.

Figure 4 shows the graph for Wowza instance startup time based on three different availability zones across USA. It can be observed that the instance startup time can vary from around 1 minute to 3 minutes. We consider these times to be sufficient if there comes a need

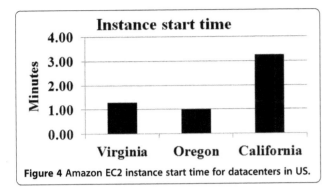

Figure 4 Amazon EC2 instance start time for datacenters in US.

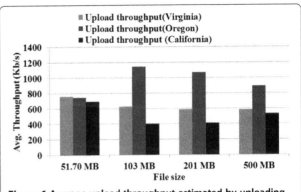

Figure 6 Average upload throughput estimated by uploading files of various sizes to three Amazon S3 datacenters in US.

to deploy more media appliances to manage varying access load.

Figures 5 and 6 shows the graph for average upload delay and average upload throughput estimated by MCCO by uploading video file content various file sizes to three different US-based Amazon S3 datacenters. We considered video file sizes of 51.70 MB, 103 MB, 201 MB and 500 MB. From these results, we concluded that average upload delay and throughout varies from one avaliabiity zone to another. In particular, we conclude that Oregon datacenter provided best network delay and throughput followed by Virginia and California data centers.

Figure 7 shows the content access delay which is the time difference between a button pressed by a user in application to the time video is rendered on the users screen. It can be concluded that content access delay, if high, a user has to wait for several seconds for video to start. This might not be optimal for users' viewing experience. Thus, the videos need to be hosted at and streamed from a location closest to the end user. From these experiments we concluded that MCCO can be used to deploy media appliances and host content across different geographical locations. It can be noted that content originating from Oregon datacenter started much earlier than California and Virginia.

6. Conclusions and future work

The growing ubiquity of the Internet and cloud computing is having significant impact on the media-related industries, which are using them as a medium to enable creation, search, management, and consumption of their contents online. We clearly articulate the architecture of MediaWise Cloud, its service components and associated research challenges, wherever applicable. Arguably, this paper is the first attempt at capturing the research and development challenges involved with engineering next-generation, *do-it-yourself CDN platform* using public cloud resources.

Our future work includes monitoring and learning of QoS-related performance of virtually all available public cloud services, and using this information for on demand prediction of expected QoS for media delivery requests. Other innovations will include providing seamless and personalized user experience,and allowing users to collaborate in creating, managing, and consuming multimedia content virtually from anywhere and whichever means available to them. To achieve seamless and personalized user experience, we will develop sophisticated context-aware, location-dependent media-related services. We will develop technologies that will present each user with media choices appropriate for his/her

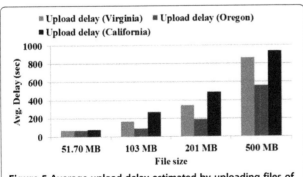

Figure 5 Average upload delay estimated by uploading files of various sizes to three Amazon S3 datacenters in US.

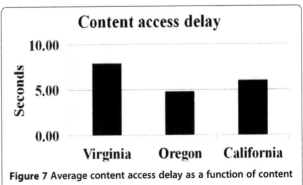

Figure 7 Average content access delay as a function of content location.

situation (i.e., location, task at hand, resources, skills, past activities, etc.). For seamless multimedia content experience, we will provide novel solutions for rendering such content to address network and user device constraints. To improve scale and efficiency of collaborative media creation and management activities, we will enhance user coordination by capturing and automating efficient collaboration patterns, activities, and processes. Further, MCCO will be used to develop and demonstrate three innovative applications in the areas of education, news and entertainment.

Interaction with cloud resources can be done through Application Programming Interface (API) in specific programming languages such as Java, C#, Python and Ruby on Rails. Unfortunately, most of the existing APIs supported by cloud providers (e.g., Amazon, Microsoft Azure, GoGrid and Ninefold) are not compatible with each other. These providers tend to have their own proprietary APIs which are not explicitly designed for cross-cloud interoperability. To tackle such heterogeneities, there is a design requirement to enforce standardization across service implementations. In future, we will take advantage of recent developments in the context of standardized cloud APIs including Simple Cloud, Delta Cloud, JCloud, and Dasein Cloud, respectively. These APIs simplify the cloud programming task by implementing single API that abstracts multiple heterogeneous APIs exposed by cloud providers.

Endnotes
[a]In rest of this paper, we address to the terms MCCO and MCCO project interchangeably.

References
1. Buyya R, Pathan M, Vakali A (2008) "Content Delivery Networks", Lecture Notes in Electrical Engineering (LNEE), vol 9. Springer, Germany. ISBN 978-3-540-77886-8
2. BigData & CDN, http://www.slideshare.net/pavlobaron/bigdata-cdn-oop2011-pavlo-baron, [ONLINE], Access date: 03/07/2012
3. Wang L, Ranjan R, Chen J, Benatallah B (eds) "Cloud Computing: Methodology, Systems, and Applications,". CRC Press, Taylor and Francis Group, p 844, Publication Date: October 03, 2011. ISBN 9781439856413
4. Armbrust M et al (2010) "A view of Cloud Computing,". Communications of the ACM Magazine 53(4):50–58. doi:10.1145/1721654.1721672, ACM Press
5. Georgakopoulos D, Ranjan R, Mitra K, Zhou X (2012) "MediaWise – Designing a Smart Media Cloud", in Proceedings of the International Conference on Advances in Cloud Computing (ACC 2012), Banglore, India [Keynote paper]
6. Bianchi M (2004) "Automatic Video Production of Lectures Using an Intelligent and Aware Environment". Proceedings of the third international conference on Mobile and ubiquitous multimedia: 117–123
7. Laibowitz M, Gong N-W, Paradiso JA (2010) "Multimedia Content Creation Using Societal-Scale Ubiquitous Camera Networks and Human-Centric Wearable Sensing". in ACM Multimedia: 571–580
8. Prabhakaran B (1997) "Multimedia Database Management Systems"
9. Zhou X, Chen L (2010) "Monitoring near duplicates over video streams". in ACM Multimedia: 521–530

10. AzureBlob, http://cloud-computing.learningtree.com/tag/azure-storage-blobs/ [ONLINE], Access date: 8/06/2012
11. AmazonS3, http://aws.amazon.com/s3/, [ONLINE], Access date: 8/06/2012
12. NoSQL, http://nosql-database.org/, [ONLINE], Access date: 8/06/2012
13. AmazonSimpleDB, http://aws.amazon.com/simpledb/, [ONLINE], Access date: 8/06/2012
14. GoogleAppEngineDatastore, https://developers.google.com/appengine/docs/python/datastore/, [ONLINE], Access date: 8/06/2012
15. MongoDB, http://www.mongodb.org/, [ONLINE], Access date: 8/06/2012
16. AmazonCloudfront, http://aws.amazon.com/cloudfront/, [ONLINE], Access date: 8/06/2012
17. Web2.0, http://en.wikipedia.org/wiki/Web_2.0, [ONLINE], Access date: 8/06/2012
18. Wada H, Suzuki J, Oba K (2009) "Queuing Theoretic and Evolutionary Deployment Optimization with Probabilistic SLAs for Service Oriented Clouds". In: Proc. of IEEE ICWS International Workshop on Cloud Services. IEEE Computer Society, Los Angeles, CA
19. Calheiros RN, Ranjan R, Buyya R (2011) "Virtual Machine Provisioning Based on Analytical Performance and QoS in Cloud Computing Environments", 40th International Conference on Parallel Processing (ICPP 2011). IEEE Computer Society, Taipei, Taiwan
20. Ranjan R, Mitra K, Saha S, Georgakopoulos D, Zaslavsky A (2012) "Do-it-Yourself Content Delivery Network Orchestrator". Web Information System Engineering-WISE 2012, 789-791
21. Media Server & Video Streaming Server, Wowza Media Systems, http://www.wowza.com, [ONLINE], Access date: 5/07/2012
22. Menzel M, Ranjan R (2012) "CloudGenius: Decision Support for Web Server Cloud Migration", In Proceedings of the 21st international conference on World Wide Web (WWW '12). ACM, New York, NY, USA, pp 979–988
23. Barham P et al (2003) Xen and the Art of Virtualization. Proceedings of the 19th ACM Symposi-um on Operating Systems Principles. ACM Press, New York
24. Ranjan R, Benatallah B "Programming Cloud Resource Orchestration Framework: Operations and Research Challenges"., p 19, Technical report, arXiv:1204.2204, Published Online on 10 April 2012
25. Limelight Networks, http://www.limelight.com/ [ONLINE], Access date: 07/06/2012
26. Ooyala, http://www.ooyala.com/, [ONLINE], Access date: 07/06/2012
27. Netflix, http://www.netflix.com, [ONLINE], Access date: 07/06/2012
28. Akamai, http://www.akamai.com/html/solutions/sola-solutions.html, [ONLINE], Access date: 07/06/2012
29. MetaCDN, http://www.metacdn.com/, [ONLINE], Access date: 07/06/2012
30. Rackspace, http://www.rackspace.com/cloud/, [ONLINE], Access date: 07/06/2012

2

Consumer-centric resource accounting in the cloud

Ahmed Mihoob, Carlos Molina-Jimenez and Santosh Shrivastava[*]

Abstract

"Pay only for what you use" principle underpins the charging policies of widely used cloud services that are on offer. Ideally for these services, consumers should be in a position to verify the charges billed to them. However, unlike traditional utility services such as gas and electricity, no consumer–trusted metering services are available for cloud services, so consumers have no choice but to rely on the usage data made available by the providers. In light of this, the paper proposes the notion of Consumer–centric Resource Accounting Models for cloud resources. An accounting model is *strongly consumer–centric* if all the data that the model requires for calculating billing charges can be collected independently by the consumer (or a trusted third party, TTP); in effect, this means that a consumer (or a TTP) should be in a position to run their own measurement service. With this view in mind, the accounting models of some widely used cloud services are examined and possible sources of difficulties in data collection are identified, including causes that could lead to discrepancies between the metering data collected by the consumer and the provider. The paper goes on to suggest how cloud service providers can improve their accounting models to make them consumer-centric.

Keywords: Cloud resource consumption, Storage resource, Computational resource, Resource metering, Accounting models, Amazon web services

1 Introduction

Cloud computing services made available to consumers range from providing basic computational resources such as storage and compute power (infrastructure as a service, IaaS) to sophisticated enterprise application services (software as a service, SaaS). A common business model is to charge consumers on a pay-per-use basis where they periodically pay for the resources they have consumed. Needless to say that for each pay-per-use service, consumers should be provided with an unambiguous resource accounting model that precisely describes all the constituent chargeable resources of the service and how billing charges are calculated from the resource usage (resource consumption) data collected on behalf of the consumer over a given period. If the consumers have access to such resource usage data then they can use it in many interesting ways, such as, making their applications billing aware, IT budget planning, creating brokering services that automate the selection of services in line

with user's needs and so forth. Indeed, it is in the interest of the service providers to make resource consumption data available to consumers; incidentally all the providers that we know of do make such data accessible to their consumers in a timely fashion.

An issue that is raised is the *accountability* of the resource usage data: who performs the measurement to collect the resource usage data - the provider, the consumer, a trusted third party (TTP), or some combination of them[a]? Provider-side accountability is the norm for the traditional utility services such as for water, gas and electricity, where providers make use of metering devices (trusted by consumers) that are deployed in the consumers' premises. Currently, provider-side accountability is also the basis for cloud service providers, although, as yet there are no equivalent facilities of consumer-trusted metering; rather, consumers have no choice but to take whatever usage data made available by the provider as trustworthy.

In light of the above discussion, we propose the notion of a Consumer–centric Resource Accounting Model for a cloud resource. We say that an accounting model is

*Correspondence: santosh.shrivastava@ncl.ac.uk
School of Computing Science, Newcastle University, Newcastle upon Tyne, NE1 7RU, UK

weakly consumer–centric if all the data that the model requires for calculating billing charges can be queried programmatically from the provider. Further, we say that an accounting model is *strongly consumer–centric* if all the data that the model requires for calculating billing charges can be collected independently by the consumer (or a TTP); in effect, this means that a consumer (or a TTP) should be in a position to run their own measurement service. We contend that it is in the interest of the providers to make the accounting models of their services at least weakly consumer–centric. Strongly consumer–centric models should prove even more attractive to consumers as they enable consumers to incorporate independent consistency or reasonableness checks as well as raise alarms when apparent discrepancies are suspected in consumption figures; furthermore, innovative charging schemes can be constructed by consumers that are themselves offering third party services. Strongly consumer–centric accounting models have the desirable property of openness and transparency, since service users are in a position to verify the charges billed to them.

As a motivating example, consider a consumer who rents a storage service to run an application shown in Figure 1. The storage is consumed by the consumer's application and by applications hosted by other users ($user_1$, $user_2$, etc.) that access the storage service at the consumer's expense. An example of this case is a consumer using a storage service to provide photo or video sharing services to other users. The ideal scenario is that the consumer is able to instrument the application to collect all the necessary storage consumption data and use the accounting model of the provider to accurately estimate the charges, and use that information to provide competitively priced service to users.

Since cloud service providers do publish their charging information, it is worth investigating whether their information matches the proposed notion of accounting models that are consumer–centric. With this view in mind, we studied the accounting models of various service providers for two basic resource types, storage and processor. We concluded that the models of the leading provider, Amazon Web Services, can be taken as the representative class. We therefore concentrate most on

their models. We performed a detailed evaluation of the accounting models of two cloud infrastructure services from Amazon (Simple Storage Service, S3, and Elastic Compute Cloud, EC2) and Cloud Storage Network (CSN) from Nirvanix, a service that is similar to S3.

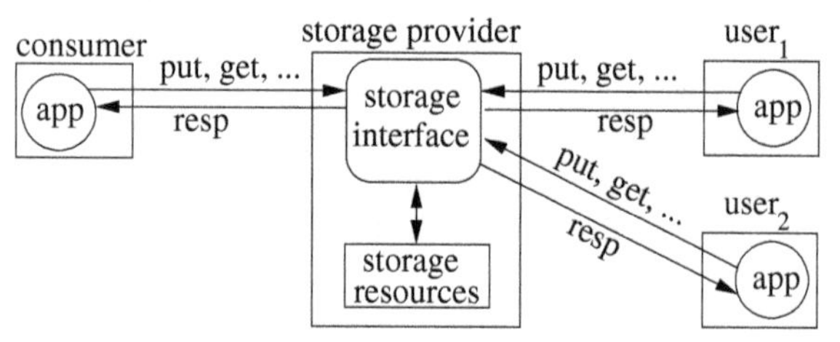

We began by independently collecting (by examination of requests and responses) our own resource usage (consumption) data for S3 and compared it with the provider's data. Our investigations indicate that even though it is conceptually a very simple service, the accounting model description of S3 nevertheless suffers from ambiguities and incompleteness with the result that the resource usage data that the model requires for calculating billing charges as collected by a consumer can turn out to be different from that collected by Amazon. A similar evaluation of Nirvanix CSN and EC2 also revealed a few shortcomings.

Service providers can learn from our evaluation study to re-examine their accounting models. In particular, we recommend that a cloud provider should go through the exercise of constructing a third party resource accounting service, and based on that exercise, perform any amendments to the model so as to remove potential sources of ambiguities and incompleteness in the description of the model, so that as far as possible, consumers are able to collect with ease their own usage data that matches provider side data with sufficient precision[b].

The paper reports the results of our work and makes the following contributions:

> – it presents a systematic way of describing resource accounting models so that they can be understood and reasoned about by consumers;
> – it precisely identifies the causes that could lead to discrepancies between the resource usage data collected by the provider and the consumer, and whether the discrepancies can be resolved; and
> – it presents ideas on how an accounting model should be constructed so as to make it consumer–centric.

We begin by presenting the related work in this area; the following section (Section 3) presents the relevant background information on resource accounting. Section 4 presents a systematic way of describing resource accounting models. Sections 5 to seven examine respectively the accounting models of S3, SDN and EC2 from the point of view of consumer–centric resource accounting and identify causes that could lead to discrepancies between resource consumption figures independently collected by providers and consumers. Learning from this exercise, Section 8 presents the way forward: how should resource accounting models be made consumer–centric. Section 9 illustrates how consumer–centric models can form the basis for creating tools for consumers that automate the

Figure 1 Provider, consumer and users of storage services.

task of computing billing charges. Concluding remarks are presented in Section 10.

2 Related work

An architecture for accounting and billing in cloud services composed out of two or more federated infrastructures (for example, a storage and computation providers) is discussed in [1]. The architecture assumes the existence of well defined accounting models that are used for accounting resources consumed by end users and for accounting resources that the cloud provider consumes from the composing infrastructures. This issue is related to the scenario that we present in Figure 1. In [2], the author discuss the requirements for accounting and billing services, but within the context of federated network of telecommunication providers. A detailed discussion of an accounting system aimed at telecommunication services is also provided in [3]. These papers overlook the need to provide consumers with means of performing consumer–side accounting.

In [4], the authors observe that "the black–box and dynamic nature of the cloud infrastructure" makes it difficult for consumers to "reason about the expenses that their applications incur". The authors make a case for a framework for *verifiable resource accounting* such that a consumer can get assurances about two questions: (i) *did I* consume what I was charged? and (ii) *should I* have consumed what I was charged? Verifiability is clearly closely related to the notion of consumer–centric resource accounting developed in this paper.

Our concept of consumer–centric resource accounting is similar in spirit to that of monitorability of service level agreements, discussed in [5]; in this work, the authors point out that service level agreements signed between clients and providers need to be precise and include only events that are visible to the client and other interested parties.

In [6], the authors develop a model in which the consumer and provider independently measure resource consumption, compare their outcomes and agree on a mutually trusted outcome. The paper discusses the technical issues that this matter involves, including consumer side collection of metering data, potential divergences between the two independently calculated bills, dispute resolution and non–repudiable sharing of resource usage records. Naturally, a starting point for such a system will be consumer–centric accounting models of cloud resources.

Good understanding of cloud resource accounting models is essential to consumers interested in planning for minimisation of expenditures on cloud resources. The questions raised are what workload to outsource, to which provider, what resources to rent, when, and so on. Examples of research results in this direction are reported in

[7-9]. In [8], the authors discuss how an accounting service deployed within an organisation can be used to control expenditures on public cloud resources; their accounting service relies on data downloaded from the cloud provider instead of calculating it locally. In [10], the authors take Amazon cloud as an example of cloud provider and estimate the performance and monetary–cost to compute a data–intensive (terabytes) workflow that requires hours of CPU time. The study is analytical (rather than experimental) and based on the authors' accounting model. For instance, to produce actual CPU–hours, they ignore the granularity of Amazon instance hours and assume CPU seconds of computation. This work stresses the relevance of accounting models. The suitability of Amazon S3, EC2 and SQS services as a platform for data intensive scientific applications is studied in [11]; the study focuses on performance (e.g. number of operations per second), availability and cost. It suggests that costs can be reduced by building cost–aware applications that exploit data usage patterns; for example, by favouring data derivation from raw data against storage of processed data. These arguments support the practical and commercial relevance of our study of resource accounting models.

3 Background

For resource accounting it is necessary to determine the amount of resources consumed by a given consumer (also called client and consumer) during a given time interval, for example, a billing period. *Accounting systems* are composed of three basic services: *metering, accounting* and *billing*.

We show a typical consumer side accounting system in Figure 2. We assume that resources are exposed as services through one or more service interfaces. As shown in the figure, the metering service intercepts the message traffic between the consumer application and the cloud services and extracts relevant data required for calculating resource usage (for example, the message size which would be required for calculating bandwidth usage). The metering service stores the collected data for use by the accounting service. The accounting service retrieves the metering data, computes resource consumption from the data using its *accounting model* and generates accounting data that is needed by the billing service to calculate the billing data.

Accounting models are provider–specific in the sense that the functionality of an accounting model is determined by the provider's policies. These policies determine how the metrics produced by his metering service are to be interpreted; for example, 1.7 GB of storage consumption can be interpreted by the provider's accounting model either as 1 or 2 GB. The accounting models of cloud providers are normally available from their web pages and in principle can be used by a consumer to perform

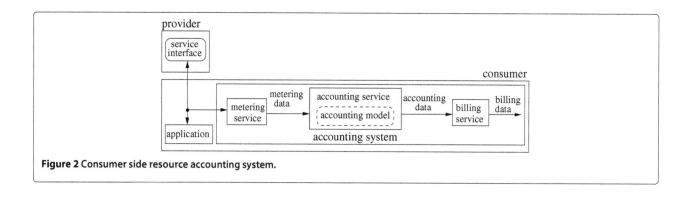

Figure 2 Consumer side resource accounting system.

their own resource accounting. The difficulty here for the consumer is to extract the accounting model from their online documentation as most providers that we know of, unnecessarily blur their accounting models with metering and billing parameters. A structured description using a generic model, as suggested next, would be a great help. In the following discussion we gloss over the fine details of pricing, but concentrate on metering and accounting aspects.

4 Abstract resource

We suggest a systematic way of describing resource accounting models so that they can be understood and reasoned about by consumers. The key idea is very simple: first define a set of "elementary" chargeable resources and then describe the overall resource consumption of a given resource/service in terms of an aggregation of the consumption of these elementary resources. With this view in mind, we present the resource consumption model of an *abstract resource*.

With some small resource specific variations, the accounting models of resources such as S3, CSN and EC2 and other infrastructure level resources can be represented as special cases of the abstract resource accounting model, and therefore can be understood and reasoned about in a uniform manner.

We consider a typical configuration where a *server (cloud) resource* and a *client resource* interact with each other by means of requests/responses (req/res) sent through a communication channel (see Figure 3).

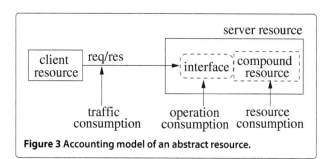

Figure 3 Accounting model of an abstract resource.

As shown in the figure, the *client resource* uses the interface of the *server resource* to place its requests and collect the corresponding responses. This deployment incurs three types of consumption charges: *traffic consumption, operation consumption* and *resource consumption*. Traffic consumption represents the amount of traffic (for example in MBytes) generated by the requests and responses on the communication channel. Operation consumption captures the activities generated by the client resource on the interface such as the the number of requests (also called operations) and the number of responses produced. Finally, resource consumption represents the actual consumption of the resource measured in units that depend on the specific nature of the resource, for example, in units of volume (for example, MBytes), time or a combination of them (for example, MBytesHours).

As the figure suggests, the accounting model for a given resource is an aggregation of three elementary models: a model for traffic consumption, a model for operation consumption and a model for resource consumption. In particular, the accounting model of a particular resource will be strongly consumer–centric if all the three of its elementary models are strongly consumer-centric. These elementary models operate independently from each other, thus they can be specified and examined separately.

Using the abstract resource model as the basis, we now evaluate the accounting models of the three resources indicated earlier to see to what an extent they match our notion of consumer-centric accounting. In particular, for each resource we determine if there are causes that could lead to discrepancies between the metering data collected by the provider and the consumer.

5 S3 accounting model

An S3 space is organised as a collection of buckets which are similar to folders. A bucket can contain zero or more objects of up to 5 terabytes of data each. Both buckets and objects are identified by names (keys in Amazon terminology) chosen by the customer. S3 provides SOAP and RESTful interfaces. As per the abstract model, an

S3 customer is charged for: a) *resource:* storage space consumed by the objects that they store in S3; b) *traffic:* network traffic generated by the operations that the customer executes against the S3 interface; and c) *operations:* number of operations that the customer executes against the S3 interface.

5.1 Storage resource

The key parameter in calculation of the storage bill is number of byte hours accounted to the customer. *Byte Hours* (ByteHrs) is the the number of bytes that a customer stores in their account for a given number of hours.

Amazon explains that *the GB of storage billed in a month is the average storage used throughout the month. This includes all object data and metadata stored in buckets that you created under your account. We measure your usage in TimedStorage–ByteHrs, which are added up at the end of the month to generate your monthly charges.* Next, an example that illustrates how to calculate your bill if *you keep 2,684,354,560 bytes (or 2.5 GB) of data in your bucket for the entire month of March* is provided. In accordance with Amazon the total number of bytes consumed for each day of March is 2684354560; thus the total number of ByteHrs is calculated as $2684354560 \times 31 \times 24 = 1997159792640$, which is equivalent to 2.5 GBMonths. At a price of 15 cents per Giga Bytes per month, the total charge amounts to 2.5 × 15 = 37.5 cents.

They further state that *at least twice a day, we check to see how much storage is used by all your Amazon S3 buckets. The result is multiplied by the amount of time passed since the last checkpoint.* Records of storage consumption in ByteHrs can be retrieved from the Usage Reports associated with each account.

From the definition of ByteHrs it follows that to calculate their bill, a customer needs to understand 1) how their byte consumption is measured, that is, how the data and metadata that is uploaded is mapped into consumed bytes in S3; and 2) how Amazon determines the number of hours that a given piece of data was stored in S3 —this issue is directly related to the notion of a checkpoint.

Amazon explains that each object in S3 has, in addition to its data, system metadata and user metadata; furthermore it explains that the *system metadata* is generated and used by S3, whereas *user metadata* is defined and used only by the user and limited to 2 KB of size [12]. Unfortunately, Amazon does not explain how to calculate the actual storage space taken by data and metadata. To clarify this issue, we uploaded a number of objects of different names, data and user metadata into an equal number of empty buckets. Figure 4 shows the parameters and results from one of our upload operations where an object named *Object.zip* is uploaded into a bucket named *MYBUCKET*, which was originally empty.

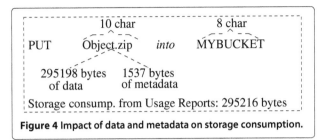

Figure 4 Impact of data and metadata on storage consumption.

Notice that in this example, the object and bucket names are, respectively, ten and eight character long, which is equivalent to ten and eight bytes, respectively.

The object data and metadata shown in the figure correspond to information we extracted locally from the PUT request. In contrast, the storage consumption of 295216 bytes corresponds to what we found in the Usage Reports. The actual Usage Reports show storage consumption per day in ByteHrs; the value shown is the result of its conversion into bytes. Notice that this storage consumption equals the sum of the object data, the length of the object name and the length of the bucket name: $8+10+295198 = 295216$.

Three conclusions can be drawn from these experiments: first, the mapping between bytes uploaded (as measured by intercepting upload requests) and bytes stored in S3 correspond one to one; second, the storage space occupied by system metadata is the sum of the lengths (in Bytes) of object and bucket names and incur storage consumption; third, user metadata does not impact storage consumption. In summary, for a given uploaded object, the consumer can accurately measure the total number of bytes that will be used for calculating ByteHrs.

Next, we need to measure the 'Hrs' of 'ByteHrs'. As stated earlier, Amazon states that at least twice a day they check the amount of storage consumed by a customer. However, Amazon does not stipulate exactly when the checkpoints take place.

To clarify the situation, we conducted a number of experiments that consisted in uploading to and deleting files from S3 and studying the Usage Reports of our account to detect when the impact of the PUT and DELETE operations were accounted by Amazon. Our findings are summarised in Figure 5. It seems that,

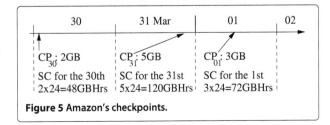

Figure 5 Amazon's checkpoints.

currently, Amazon does not actually check customers' storage consumption twice a day as they specify in their Calculating Your Bill document, but only once. From our observations, it emerged that the time of the checkpoint is decided randomly by Amazon within the 00:00:00Z and 23:59:59Z time interval[c].

In the figure, CP stands for checkpoint, thus $CP_{30} : 2GB$ indicate that CP_{30} was conducted on the 30th day of the month at the time specified by the arrow and reported that at that time the customer had 2 GB stored in S3. SC stands for Storage Consumption and is explained below.

As shown in the figure, Amazon uses the results produced by a checkpoint of a given day, to account the customer for the 24 hrs of that day, regardless of the operations that the customer might perform during the time left between the checkpoint and the 23:59:59Z hours of the day. For example, the storage consumption for the 30th will be taken as $2 \times 24 = 48$ GBHrs; where 2 represents the 2GB that the customer uploaded on the 30th and 24 represents the 24 hrs of the day.

5.2 Traffic

Amazon explains that *DataTransfer–In* is the network data transferred from the customer to S3. They state that *Every time a request is received to put an object, the amount of network traffic involved in transmitting the object data, metadata, or keys is recorded here.* *DataTransfer–Out* is the network data transferred from S3 to the customer. They state that *Every time a request is received to get an object, the amount of network traffic involved in transmitting the object data, metadata, or keys is recorded here.* By here they mean that in the Usage Reports associated to each account, the amount of DataTransfer–In and DataTransfer–Out generated by a customer, is represented, respectively, by the DataTransfer–In–Bytes and DataTransfer–Out–Bytes parameters.

Amazon use an example to show that if *You upload one 500 MB file each day during the month of March* and *You download one 500 MB file each day during the month of March* your bill for March (imagine 2011) will be calculated as follows. The DataTransfer–In would be $500MB \times (1/1024) \times 31 = 15.14GB$. At a price of 10 cents per Giga Bytes, the total charge would be $15.14 \times 10 = 151.4$ cents. In a second example they show that if *You download one 500 MB file each day during the month of March* the total amount of DataTransfer–Out would be 15.14 GB which charged at 15 cents per GB would amount to 227 cents.

It is however not clear from the available information how the size of of the message is calculated. To clarify the point, we uploaded a number of files and compared information extracted from the PUT operations against bandwidth consumption as counted in the Usage Report.

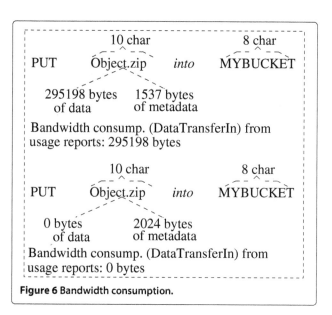

Figure 6 Bandwidth consumption.

Two examples of the experiments that we conducted are shown in Figure 6: we used PUT operations to upload an object into a bucket. The data and metadata shown in the figure represent the data and metadata extracted locally from the PUT requests.

As shown by the *Bandwidth consump.* parameters extracted from the Usage Reports, only the object data consumes DataTransfer–In bandwidth; neither the metadata or the object or bucket names seem to count as overhead. This observation refers to RESTful requests. In contrast, for SOAP messages, the total size of the message is always used for calculating bandwidth consumption.

5.3 Operations

It is straightforward for a consumer to count the type and number of operations performed on S3. To illustrate their charging schema Amazon provide an example in the Amazon Simple Storage Service FAQs where You transfer 1000 files into Amazon S3 and transfer 2000 files out of Amazon S3 each day during the month of March, and delete 5000 files on March 31st. In this scenario, the total number of PUT request is calculated as $1000 \times 31 = 31000$, whereas the total number of GET requests is calculated as $2000 \times 31 = 62000$. The total number of DELETE requests is simply 5000 though this is irrelevant as DELETE requests are free. At the price of one cent per 1000 PUT requests and one cent per 10000 GET requests, the total charge for the operations is calculated as $31000 \times (1/1000) + 62000 \times (1/10000) = 37.2$ cents.

We note that an operation might fail to complete successfully. The error response in general contains information that helps identify the party responsible for the failure: the customer or the S3 infrastructure. For example, *NoSuchBucket* errors are caused by the customer when they try to upload a file into a non-existent bucket; whereas an *InternalError* code indicates that S3 is experiencing internal problems. Our understanding is that the consumer is charged for an operation, whether the operation succeeded or not.

To offer high availability, Amazon replicates data across multiple servers within its data centres. Replicas are kept weakly consistent and as a result, some perfectly legal operations could sometime fail or return inaccurate results (see [12], Data Consistency Model section). For example, the customer might receive a *ObjectDoesNotExist* as a response to a legal GET request or an incomplete list of objects after executing a LIST operation. Some of these problems can be corrected by re-trying the operation. From Amazon accounting model, it is not clear who bears the cost of the failed operations and their retries.

We executed a number of operations including both valid and invalid ones (for example, creation of buckets with invalid names and with names that already existed). Next we examined the Usage Reports and as we expected, we found that Amazon counted both successful and failed operations. Figure 7 shows an example of the operations that we executed and the bandwidth and operation consumptions that it caused in accordance with the Usage Reports.

Thus, the failed operation to create that bucket consumed 574 bytes for DataTransfer–In and and 514 bytes for DataTransfer–Out. These figures, correspond to the size of the SOAP request and response, respectively. As shown in the figure, we also found out that the failed operation incurred operation consumption and counted by the RequestTier2 parameter in the Usage Reports.

5.4 Potential causes of discrepancies
5.4.1 Storage
Since, for the calculation of ByteHrs, the time of the checkpoint is decided randomly by Amazon within the 00:00:00Z and 23:59:59Z time interval, the time used at the consumer's side need not match that at the provider's side: a potential cause for discrepancy. This is illustrated with the help of Figure 8.

CREATE MYBUCKET // *MYBUCKET already exists*

Response: Error:BucketAlreadyExists

Bandwidth consump. (DataTransferIn) from usage reports: 574 bytes

Bandwidth consump. (DataTransferOut) from usage reports: 514 bytes

Operation consump. (RequestTier2) from usage reports: 1

Figure 7 Bandwidth and operation consumption of failed operations.

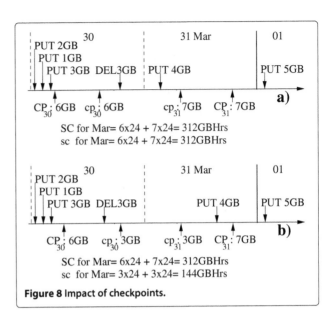

Figure 8 Impact of checkpoints.

The figure shows the execution time of four PUT and one DEL operations executed by an S3 consumer during the last two days of March. The first day of April is also shown for completeness. For simplicity, the figure assumes that the earliest PUT operation is the very first executed by the consumer after opening his S3 account. The figure also shows the specific points in time when checkpoints are conducted independently by two parties, namely, Amazon and a consumer. Thus, CP and cp represent, respectively, Amazon's and the consumer's checkpoints; the Giga Bytes shown next to CP and cp indicate the storage consumption detected by the checkpoint. For example, on the 30th, Amazon conducted its checkpoint about five in the morning and detected that, at that time, the customer had 6 GB stored ($CP_{30} : 6GB$). On the same day, the consumer conducted his checkpoint just after midday and detected that, at that time, he had 6 GB stored ($cp_{30} : 6GB$). SC and sc represent, respectively, the storage consumption for the month of March, calculated by Amazon and consumer, based on their checkpoints.

The figure demonstrates that the storage consumption calculated by Amazon and consumer might differ significantly depending on the number and nature of the operations conducted within the time interval determined by the two parties' checkpoints, for example, within CP_{31} and cp_{31}.

Scenario a) shows an ideal situation where no consumer's operations are executed within the pair of checkpoints conducted on the 30th or 31st. The result is that both parties calculate equal storage consumptions. In contrast, b) shows a worse–case scenario where the DEL operation is missed by CP_{30} and counted by cp_{30} and the

PUT operation is missed by cp_{31} and counted by CP_{31}; the result of this is that Amazon and the consumer, calculate SC and sc, respectively, as 312 GB and 144 GB.

Ideally, Amazon's checkpoint times should be made known to consumers to prevent any such errors. Providing this information for upcoming checkpoints is perhaps not a sensible option for a storage provider, as the information could be 'misused' by a consumer by placing deletes and puts around the checkpoints in a manner that artificially reduces the consumption figures. An alternative would be to make the times of past checkpoints available (e.g., by releasing them the next day).

5.4.2 Impact of network and operation latencies

In the discussion concerning calculation of ByteHrs (illustrated using Figure 8), we have implicitly assumed that the execution of a PUT (respectively a DELETE) operation is an atomic event whose time of occurrence is either less or greater than the checkpoint time (i.e., the operation happens either before or after the checkpoint). This allowed us to say that if the checkpoint time used at the provider is known to the consumer, then the consumer can match the ByteHrs figures of the provider. However, this assumption is over simplifying the distributed nature of the PUT (respectively a DELETE) operation.

In Figure 9 we explicitly show network and operation execution latencies for a given operation, say PUT; also, *i, j, k and l* are provider side checkpoint times used for illustration. Assume that at the provider side, only the completed operations are taken into account for the calculation of ByteHrs; so a checkpoint taken at time *i* or *j* will not include the PUT operation (PUT has not yet completed), whereas a checkpoint taken at time *k* or *l* will. What happens at the consumer side will depend on which event (sending of the request or reception of the response) is taken to represent the occurrence of PUT. If the timestamp of the request message (PUT) is regarded as the time of occurrence of PUT, then the consumer side ByteHrs

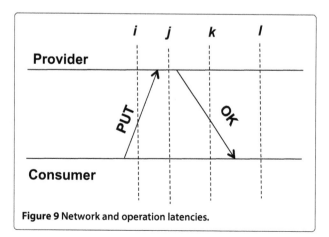

Figure 9 Network and operation latencies.

calculation for a checkpoint at time *i* or *j* will include the PUT operation, a discrepancy since the provider did not! On the other hand, if the timestamp of the response message is regarded as the time of occurrence of PUT, then a checkpoint at time *k* will not include the PUT operation (whereas the provider has), again a discrepancy. In short, for the operations that occur sufficiently close to the checkpoint time, there is no guarantee that they get ordered identically at both the sides with respect to the checkpoint time. Assuming checkpoint times are known to a consumer, then any discrepancies can be resolved at the consumer side by examining the storage consumption figures of the provider and working out the place of the operations that happened around the checkpoint times.

5.4.3 Operations

Earlier we stated that it is straightforward for a consumer to count the type and number of operations performed on S3. There is a potential for discrepancy caused by network latency: operations that are invoked 'sufficiently close' to the end of an accounting period (say i) and counted by the consumer for that period, might get counted as performed in the next period (say j) by the provider if due to the latency, these invocation messages arrive in period j. This will lead to the accumulated charges for the two period not being the same. This is actually not an issue, as the Amazon uses the timestamp of the invocation message for resolution, so the consumer can match the provider's figure.

One likely source of difficulty about the charges for operations is determining the liable party for failed operations. Currently, this decision is taken unilaterally by Amazon. In this regard, we anticipate two potential sources of conflicts: DNS and propagation delays. As explained by Amazon, some requests might fail and produce a Temporary Redirect (HTTP code 307 error) due to temporary routing errors which are caused by the use of alternative DNS names and request redirection techniques [13]. Amazon's advice is to design applications that can handle redirect errors, for example, by resending a request after receiving a 307 code (see [12], Request Routing section). Strictly speaking these errors are not caused by the customer as the 307 code suggests. It is not clear to us who bears the cost of the re–tried operations.

5.5 Summary

In summary, we can say that the models of the two elementary resources for traffic and operation consumption can be considered strongly consumer-centric, but suffer form incompleteness and ambiguities (that we have pointed out) and the model for storage resource consumption is weakly consumer–centric (checkpointing event is not observable), making the overall model weakly consumer–centric.

6 CSN accounting model

A Nirvanix CSN space is organised as a collection of folders that support nesting. A folder can contain zero or more subfolders and files of up to 250 GB [14]. Both folders and files are identified by names chosen by the customer. Nirvanix CSN uses accounting model concepts that are almost the same as those used by Amazon S3; however, compared to Amazon, information about pricing and the charging schema used to calculate the customers bill is sparsely documented. Of the three elementary chargeable resources identified for the abstract resource, a CSN customer is charged only for the consumption of storage and traffic (there is no charge for operation consumption). We performed resource consumption measurements for storage and network traffic using the same kinds of experiments as described for S3.

Like Amazon, for storage, Nirvanix uses GB/Month to calculate the bill, so a customer needs to understand: 1) how their GB consumption is measured, that is, how the data and metadata that is uploaded is mapped into consumed bytes; and 2) how Nirvanix determines the number of hours that a given piece of data was stored in CSN (how frequently and when checkpoints are taken). Concerning 1), our experiments show that the mapping between bytes uploaded by PUT requests and bytes stored in CSN is one-to-one; secondly, user and system metadata do not impact storage consumption. Concerning 2), although Nirvanix does not provide any details about when their checkpoints take place, our experiments revealed that Nirvanix computes storage consumption at the start point of each 24 hour consumption interval (at 00:00:00 GMT). Concerning traffic charges, experiments revealed that only the size of the data counted and neither the metadata nor the file or folder names contributed to charges.

Thus, given the above information, a consumer can accurately measure their storage consumption figures and traffic charges; hence we consider the model strongly consumer–centric.

7 EC2 accounting model

EC2 is a computation service offered by Amazon as an IaaS [15]. The service offers raw virtual CPUs to consumers. A consumer is granted administrative privileges over his virtual CPU, that he can exercise by means of sending remote commands to the Amazon Cloud from his desktop computer. For example, he is expected to configure, launch, stop, re–launch, terminate, backup, etc. his virtual CPU. In return, the consumer is free to choose the operating system (eg Windows or Linux) and applications to run. In EC2 terminology, a running virtual CPU is called a *Virtual Machine Instance (VMI)* or just an *instance* whereas the frozen bundle of software on disk that contains the libraries, applications and initial configuration settings that are used to launch an instance is called an *Amazon Machine Image (AMI)*.

Currently, Amazon offers six types of instances that differ from each other in four initial configuration parameters that cannot be changed at running time: amount of EC2 compute units that it delivers, size of their memory and local storage (also called ephemeral and instance storage) and the type of platform (32 or 64 bits). An EC2 compute unit is an Amazon unit and is defined as the equivalent CPU capacity of a 1.0–1.2 GHz 2007 Opteron or 2007 Xeon processor. Thus Amazon offer small, large, extra large and other types of instances. For example, the default instance type is the *Small Instance* and is a 32 bit platform that delivers 1 EC2 compute unit and provided with 1.7 GB of memory and 160 GB of local storage. These types of instances are offered to consumers under several billing models: *on–demand instances, reserved instances* and *spot instances*. In our discussion we will focus on on–demand instances.

Under the on–demand billing model, Amazon defines the unit of consumption of an instance as the *instance hour (instanceHr)*. Currently, the cost of an instance hour of a small instance running Linux or Windows, is, respectively, 8.5 and 12 cents. On top of charges for instance hours, instance consumers normally incur additional charges for data tranfer that the instances generates (*Data Transfer–In* and *Data Transfer–Out*) and for addtional infrastructure that the instance might need such as disk storage, IP addresses, monitoring facilities and others. As these additional charges are accounted and billed separately, we will leave them out of our discussion and focus only on instance hours charges.

The figures above imply that if a consumer accrues 10 instanceHrs of a small instance consumption, running Linux, during a month, he will incur a charge of 85 cents at the end of the month.

In principle, the pricing tables publicly available from Amazon web pages should allow a consumer to independently conduct his own accounting of EC2 consumption. In the absence of a well defined accounting model this is not a trivial exercise.

Insights into the EC2 accounting model are spread over several on–line documents from Amazon. Some insight into the definition of instance hour is provided in the *Amazon EC2 Pricing* document [16] (see just below the table of *On–demand Instances*) where it is stated that *Pricing is per instance–hour consumed for each instance, from the time an instance is launched until it is terminated. Each partial instance–hour consumed will be billed as a full hour.* This statement suggests that once an instance is launched it will incur at least an instance hours of consumption. For example, if the instance runs continuously for 5 minutes, it will incur 1 instanceHrs; likewise, if the instance runs continuously for 90 minutes, it will incur 2 instanceHrs.

The problem with this definition is that it does not clarify when an instance is considered to be launched and terminated. Additional information about this issue is provided in the *Billing* section of FAQs [17], *Paying for What You Use* of the *Amazon Elastic Compute (Amazon EC2)* document [15] and in the *How You're Charged* section of the User Guide [18]. For example, in [15] it is stated that *Each instance will store its actual launch time. Thereafter, each instance will charge for its hours of execution at the beginning of each hour relative to the time it launched.*

From information obtained from the documents cited above it is clear that Amazon starts and stops counting instance hours as the instance is driven by the consumer, through different states. Also, it is clear that Amazon instance hours are accrued from the execution of one or more individual sessions executed by the consumer during the billing period. Within this context, a *session* starts and terminates when the consumer launches and terminates, respectively, an instance.

Session–based accounting models for resources that involve several events and states that incur different consumptions, are conveniently described by Finite State Machines (FSMs). We will use this approach to describe the EC2 accounting model. Others, for example RightScale (a broker of cloud services), have also taken this approach [19].

7.1 States of an instance session

The states that an instance can reach during a session depend on the type of memory used by the AMI to store its boot (also called root) device. Currently, Amazon supports S3–backed and EBS–backed instances. EBS stands for Elastic Block Store and is a persistent storage that can be attached to an instance. The consumer chooses between S3 or EBS–backed instances at AMI creation time.

Unfortunately, the states that an instance can reach during a session are not well documented by Amazon. Yet after a careful examination of Amazon's online documentation we managed to build the FSM shown in Figure 10a).

The FSM of an Amazon instance includes two types of states: *permanent and transient states*. Permanent states (represented by large circles, e.g. *running*) can be remotely manipulated by commands issued by the consumer; once the FSM reaches a permanent state, it remains there until the consumers issues a command to force the FSM to progress to another state. Transient states (represented by small circles, e.g. *stopping*) are states that the FSM visits temporarily as it progresses from a permanent state into another. The consumer has no control over the time spent

in a transient state; this is why there are no labels on the outgoing arrows of these states.

We have labeled the transitions of the FSM with *event/action* notations. The *event* is the cause of the transition whereas the *action* represents the set (possibly empty) of operations that Amazon executes when the event occurs, to count the numbers of instance hours consumed by the instance.

There are two types of events: consumer's and internal to the FSM events. The consumer's events are the commands (*launch, application commands, reboot, stop* and *terminate*) that the consumers issues to operate his instance; likewise, internal events are events that occur independently from the consumer's commands, namely, *timer = 60min* and *failure*. A discussion on all the permanent and some of the transient states depicted in the FSM follows.

- **AMI configured:** is the initial state. It is reached when the consumer successfully configures his AMI so that it is ready to be launched.
- **Running:** is the state where the instance can perform useful computation for the consumer, for example, it can respond to application commands issued by the consumer.
- **Terminated:** is the final state and represents the end of the life cycle of the instance. Once this state is reached the instance is destroyed. To perform additional computation after entering this state the consumer needs to configure another AMI. The terminated state is reached when the subscribed issues the *terminate* command, the instance fails when it is in running state or the instance fails to reach running state.
- **Pending:** is related to the instantiation of the instance within the Amazon cloud. *Pending* leads to *running* state when the instance is successfully instantiated or to *terminated* state when Amazon fails to instantiate the instance.
- **Shuttingdown:** is reached when the consumer issues the *terminate* command.
- **Stopped:** this state is supported only EBS–backed instances (S3–backed instances cannot be stopped) and is reached when the user issues *stop* command, say for example, to perform backup duties.
- **Rebooting:** is reached when the consumer issues the *reboot* command.

7.2 States and instance hours

In the figure, *NinstHrs* is used to count the number of instance hours consumed by an instance during a single session. The number of instance hours consumed by an instance is determined by the integer value stored in *NinstHrs* when the instance reaches the *terminated* state.

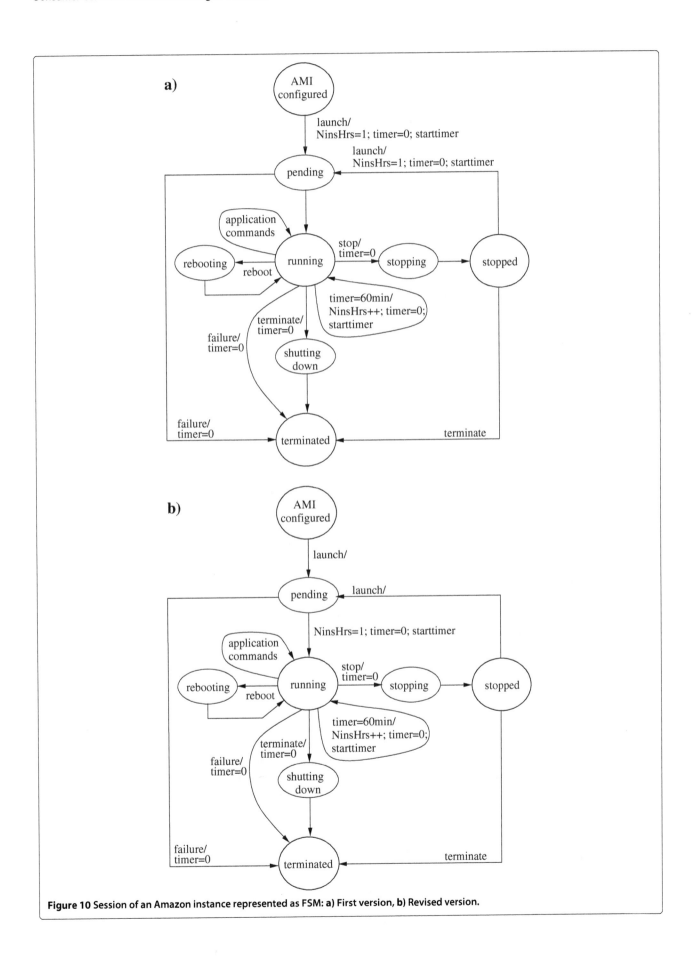

Figure 10 Session of an Amazon instance represented as FSM: **a)** First version, **b)** Revised version.

timer is Amazon's timer to count a 60 minutes interval; it can be set to zero (*timer* = 0) and started (*starttimer*).

In the FSM, the charging operations are executed as suggested by the Amazon's on line documentation. For example, in *Paying for What You Use* Section of [15], Amazon states that the beginning of an instance hour is relative to the launch time. Consequently, the FSM sets *NinstHrs* = 1 when the consumer executes a launch command from the *AMI configured* state. At the same time, *timer* is set to zero and started. *NinstHrs* = 1 indicates that once a consumer executes a launch command, he will incur at least one instance hour. If the consumer leaves his instance in the *running* state for 60 minutes (*timer* = 60*min*) the FSM increments *NinstHrs* by one, sets the timer to zero and starts it again. From *running* state the timer is set to zero when the consumer decides to terminate his instance (*terminate* command) or when the instance fails (*failure* event). Although Amazon's documentation does not discuss it, we believe that the possibility of an instance not reaching the *running* state cannot be ignored, therefore we have included a transition from *pending* to *terminated* state; the FSM sets the timer to zero when this abnormal event occurs.

As explained in *Basics of Amazon EBS–Backed AMIs and Instances* and *How You're Charged* of [18], a running EBS–backed instance can be stopped by the consumer by means of the *stop* command and drive it to the *stopped* state. As indicated by *timer* = 0 operation executed when the subscribed issues a *stop* command, an instance in *stopped* state incurs no instance hours. However, though it is not shown in the figure as this is a different issue, Amazon charges for EBS storage and other additional services related to the stopped instance. The consumer can drive an instance from the *stopped* to the *terminated* state. Alternatively he can re–launch his instance. In fact, the consumer can launch, stop and launch his instance as many times as he needs to. However, as indicated by the *NinstHrs* + + , *timer* = 0 and *starttimer* operations over the arrow, every transition from *stopped* to *pending* state accrues an instance hour of consumption, irrespectively of the time elapsed between each pair of consecutive *launch* commands.

7.3 Experiments with Amazon instances

To verify that the accounting model described by the FSM of Figure 10a) matches Amazon's description, we (as consumers) conducted a series of practical experiments. In particular, our aim was to verify how the number of instance hours is counted by Amazon.

The experiments involved 1) configuration of different AMIs; 2) launch of instances; 3) execution of remote commands to drive the instances through the different states shown in the FSM. For example, we configured AMIs, launched and run them for periods of different lengths and terminated them. Likewise, we launched instances and terminated them as soon as they reached the *running* state.

To calculate the number of instance hours consumed by the instances, we recorded the time of execution of the remote commands *launch, stop, terminate* and *reboot*, and the time of reaching both transient and permanent states. For comparison, we collected data (start and end time of an instance hour, and number of instance hours consumed) from Amazon EC2 usage report.

A comparison of data collected from our experiments against Amazon's data from their usage report reveals that currently, the beginning of an instance hour is not the execution time of the consumer's *launch* command, as documented by Amazon, but the time when the instance reaches the *running* state. These findings imply that the current accounting model currently in use is the one described by the FSM of Figure 10b). As shown in the figure, the *NinstHrs* is incremented when the instance reaches the *running* state.

7.4 Potential causes of discrepancies

The mismatch between Amazon's documented accounting model and the one currently in use (Figure 10a and b, respectively) might result in discrepancies between the consumer's and Amazon's calculations of instance hours. For example, imagine that it takes five minutes to reach the *running* state. Now imagine that the consumer launches an instance, leaves it running for 57 minutes and then terminates it. Assuming consumer side is using the FSM of Figure 10a), the consumer's *NinstHrs* will be equal to two: *NinstHrs* = 1 at launch time and then *NinstHrs* is incremented when *timer* = 60*min*. In contrast, to the consumer's satisfaction, Amazon's usage records will show only one instance hour of consumption. One can argue that this discrepancy is not of the consumer's concern since, economically, it always favours him.

More challenging and closer to the consumer's concern are discrepancies caused by failures. Amazon's documentation does not stipulate how instances that fail accrue instance hours. For example, examine Figure 10a) and imagine that an instance suddenly crashes after spending 2 hrs and 15 min in *running* state. It is not clear to us whether Amazon will charge for the last 15 min of the execution as a whole instance hour. As a second example, imagine that after being launched either from *AMI configured* or *stopped* states, an instance progresses to *pending* state and from there, due to a failure, to *terminated*. It is not clear to us if Amazon will charge for the last instance hour counted by *NinstHrs*.

We believe that, apart from these omissions about failure situations, the accounting model of Figure 10a) can be implemented and used by the consumer to produce accurate accounting. A salient feature of this model is that all the events (*launch*, *stop* and *terminate*) that impact the *NinstHrs* counter are generated by consumer. The only exception if the *timer* = 60*min* event, but that can be visible to the consumer if he synchronises his clock to UTC time.

The accounting model that Amazon actually uses (Figure 10b) is not impacted by failures of instances to reach *running* state because in this model, *NinsHrs* is incremented when the instance reaches *running* state. However, this model is harder for the consumer to implement since the event that causes the instance to progress from *pending* to *running* state is not under the consumer's control.

7.5 Summary

In summary, the accounting model of EC2 is weakly consumer–centric: the traffic consumption and operation consumption models are strongly consumer–centric (operation consumption model is precisely specified – there is no charge!), but the resource consumption model is weakly consumer–centric because, as we explained with respect to Figure 10b, the event that causes a virtual machine instance to progress from pending to running state is not visible to the consumer.

8 Developing consumer–centric models

Strongly consumer–centric accounting models have the desirable property of openness and transparency, since service users are in a position to verify the charges billed to them. Our investigations revealed the causes that could lead to discrepancies between the metering data collected by the consumer not matching that of the provider. Essentially these causes can be classed into three categories discussed below.

1. Incompleteness and ambiguities: It is of course necessary that consumers are provided with an unambiguous resource accounting model that precisely describes all the constituent chargeable resources of a service and how billing charges are calculated from the resource usage (resource consumption) data collected on behalf of the consumer over a given period. We pointed out several cases where an accounting model specification was ambiguous or not complete. For example, for S3, regarding bandwidth consumption, it is not clear from the available information what constitutes the size of of a message. It is only through experiments we worked out that for RESTful operations, only the size of the object is taken into account and system and user metadata is not part of the message size, whereas for SOAP operations, the total size of the message is taken into account. Failure handling is another area where there is lack of information

and/or clarity: for example, concerning EC2, it is not clear how instances that fail accrue instance hours.

2. Unobservable events: If an accounting model uses one or more events that impact resource consumption, but these events are not observable to (or their occurrence cannot be deduced accurately by) the consumer, then the data collected at the consumer side could differ from that of the provider. Calculation of storage consumption in S3 (ByteHrs) is a good example: here, the checkpoint event is not observable.

3. Differences in the measurement process: Difference can arise if the two sides use different techniques for data collection. Calculation of BytHrs again serves as a good example. We expect that for a checkpoint, the provider will directly measure the storage space actually occupied, whereas, for a given checkpoint time , the consumer will mimic the process by adding (for PUT) and subtracting (for DELETE) to calculate the space, and as we discussed with respect to Figure 9, discrepancies are possible.

Issues raised above can be directly addressed by the providers wishing to build consumer–centric models. They should use the abstract resource model as a basis for constructing the accounting model of a service as it will introduce much needed structure into the specification intended to describes all the constituent chargeable resources. For services that go through several state transitions (like EC2), providers should explicitly give FSM based descriptions. Further, they should ensure, as much as possible, that their models do not rely on unobservable (to consumer) events for billing charge calculations. Finally, the provider should go through the exercise of constructing a third party measurement service to see whether the necessary metering data can be collected with ease and that it matches the provider side data with sufficient precision. Any discrepancies that get introduced unintentionally (e.g., due to non identical checkpoint times) can be resolved by consumers by careful examination of corresponding resource usage data from providers. Those that cannot be resolved would indicate errors on the side of consumers and/or providers leading to disputes.

9 Estimating and verifying billing charges

We note that many cloud service providers make available manual bill calculators for estimating charges for using their cloud resources. AWS Simple Monthly Calculator [20] is a good example. We believe that the abstract resource accounting model provides a good starting point for developing an automatic cost–estimation tool that can take information on resources and the way they have been connected and configured and use that information for estimating charges for specific usage patterns.

Such a tool can be used by consumers for obtaining cost–effective resource configurations before actually deploying them in the cloud. The tool can be integrated with consumer side resource accounting system of the type depicted in Figure 2 for verifying billing charges during run time. Further enhancements are possible by incorporating dynamic adjustment of resource capacity throughout the life cycle of the cloud based application to stay within the bounds of some pre–determined cost. We suggest these as directions for future work, and use the hypothetical deployment shown in Figure 11 to highlight some of the technical issues involved.

The deployment of Figure 11 involves the client's application that is making use of three types of Amazon basic resources: S3 storage, EC2 VMIs and Elastic Block Storage (EBS) volumes.

A few words on EBSs: these are persistent block storage volumes frequently used for building file systems and databases. They support two interfaces: a Web service interface and a block–based input/output interface. The Web service interface can be used by the client to issue (for example, from his desktop application) administration operations, such as *create volume, delete volume, attach volume, detach volume*, etc. The block–based input/output interface can be used by EC2 VMIs and becomes available upon attaching the EBS to the VMI. A consumer of EBS is charged for operation consumption (measured as the number of input/output operations that the EC2 VMI places against the EBS) and resource consumption (GB-months, where the duration is determined as the time that elapses between the creation and deletion of the EBS).

For calculation of billing charges, some pertinent information on the physical structure of the provider's cloud and charging policies are required. Taking Amazon as a case, their cloud is divided into *regions* which are physical locations geographically dispersed (e.g. US–East in Northern Virginia, US–West in Northern California, EU in Ireland). The EC2 cloud is divided in *zones* which are failure–independent data centres located within Amazon regions and linked by low latency networks.

Concerning pricing, in general, Amazon charges for traffic in and out (Data Transfer–In and Data transfer–Out respectively) of the Amazon cloud and for traffic in and out of the EC2 cloud. However, Amazon does not charge for traffic between a VMI and another resource (say S3) located within the same region. Neither do they charge for traffic between two VMIs located within the same availability zone. However, Amazon charges for inter–region traffic between a VMI and another resource (for example, S3) located within a different region. In these situations, the sender of the data will be charged for Data Transfer–Out whereas the receiver will be charged for Data Transfer–In.

The deployment shown in Figure 11 involves two Amazon regions (US East and US West) and two availability zones (av–zoneA and av–zoneB) located within the US West region. The arrowed lines represent bi–directional communication channels. Omitted from the figure are the communication channels used by the client to issue administrative commands to the VMIs (*launch, stop, reboot*, etc.) and the EBS (*create volume, attach volume*, etc.).

We open this discussion with a study of the charges that apply to EBS_1 and EBS_2. Imagine for the sake of argument that they are volumes of 50 GB and 100 GB, respectively. Of concern to us here is the operation consumption and time consumption of the EBSs. EBS_1 will be charged for the number of input/output operations that the VMI_1 places against the EBS_1 interface and also for the period of time of usage of the allocated 50 GB. Being currently detached, the charges for EBS_2 are simpler to calculate, consisting only of the time consumption for 100 GB.

With these pricing policies in mind, let us study the charges for VMI_1. Of concern to us here is traffic consumption and resource consumption. VMI_1 will be charged for inter–region traffic (Data Transfer–In and Data Transfer–Out) consumed on the channel that links it to S3. In addition, VMI_1 will be charged for traffic (Data Transfer–In and Data Transfer–Out) consumed on the channel that links VMI_1 to the client application, as the latter is outside the Amazon cloud. There are no charges for the traffic consumed by the interaction against EBS_1 as the traffic consumed by the interaction between VMIs and EBSs is free. Neither are there charges for traffic

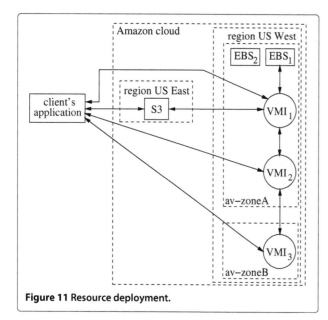

Figure 11 Resource deployment.

consumed by the interaction against VMI_2 since VMI_1 and VMI_2 share availability zone A. Resource consumption of VMI_1 will be counted as the number of hours that this instance is run.

In the similar vain, the charges for VMI_2 will take into account traffic consumption and resource consumption. The traffic consumed will be determined by the amount of Data Transfer–Out and Data Transfer–In sent and received, respectively, along two channels: the channel that leads to the client's application and the one that leads to VMI_3. There are no charges for traffic consumed on the channel that leads to VMI_1 because the two instances are within the same availability zone. Again, resource consumption will be counted as the number of instance hours of VMI_2. The charges for VMI_3 can be calculated similarly to VMI_2.

We can visualise that S3 will incur charges for traffic consumed on the channel that links it to VMI_1 and on the channel that links it to the client's application. In addition, S3 charges will account for operation consumption counted as the aggregation of the number of operations placed against S3 by the client's application and VMI_1. In addition, the charges will take into consideration resource consumption (storage space consumed) measured in storage–time units. This will be counted as the aggregated impact of the activities (*put, get, delete*, etc.) performed by the client's applications and VMI_1.

We anticipate that the cost–estimation tool will need a formal description language for expressing both the deployment description of the consumer's application and the provider's pricing policies. Deployment description will need to include information such as the constituent resources and their connectivities, geographical location of the resources, amount of input and output data, number of users to support and so forth. Pricing policy description will need to take into account the particularities of the provider, such as for Amazon, there are no charges for VMI to VMI traffic within a single availability zone. Development of such as language is suggested as a topic for further research.

10 Concluding remarks

'Pay only for what you use' principle underpins the charging models of widely used cloud services that are on offer. Unlike traditional utility services such as gas and electricity, no consumer–trusted metering services are available for cloud services, so consumers have no choice but to rely on the usage data made available by the providers. This situation motivated us to propose the notion of a consumer centric resource accounting model. An accounting model is said to be weakly consumer-centric if all the data that the model requires for calculating billing charges can be

queried programmatically from the provider. An accounting model is said to be strongly consumer-centric if all the data that the model requires for calculating billing charges can be collected independently by the consumer (or a TTP); in effect, this means that a consumer (or a TTP) should be in a position to run their own measurement service. We evaluated infrastructure level resource accounting models of prominent cloud service providers and found that the accounting model of SDN is strongly consumer–centric and those of S3 and EC2 are weakly consumer–centric.

Our investigations indicate that because accounting model descriptions of service providers lack clarity and completeness, collecting metering data is fraught with difficulties even for infrastructure level services that are conceptually quite simple. We suggested a systematic way of describing resource accounting models so that they can be understood and reasoned about by consumers. We presented ideas on how accounting models should be constructed so as to make them strongly consumer–centric. Direction for further research for the development of cost-effective cloud based applications were also suggested.

Service providers can learn from our evaluation study to re-examine their accounting models. In particular, we recommend that a cloud provider should go through the exercise of constructing a third party measurement service, and based on that exercise, perform any amendments to the model, remove potential sources of ambiguities in the description of the model, so that as far as possible, consumers are able to collect with ease their own usage data that matches provider side data with sufficient precision.

Endnotes

[a] A note on terminology: 'accountability' refers to concepts such as responsibility, answerability, trustworthiness; not to be confused with 'resource accounting' that refers to the process concerned with calculating financial charges.

[b] This paper combines and extends the material presented in two conference papers [21,22].

[c] S3 servers are synchronised to the Universal Time Coordinated (UTC) which is also known as the Zulu Time (Z time) and in practice equivalent to the Greenwich Mean Time (GMT).

Competing interests
The authors declare that they have no competing interests.

Authors' contributions
The experimental work reported here was carried out by AM as a part of his doctoral studies jointly supervised by CM and SS. All authors read and approved the final manuscript.

Acknowledgements
The first author was funded by a grant from the Libyan Government; the
second author was funded by EPSRC grant KTS-EP/H500332/1.

References
1. Elmroth E, Marquez FG, Henriksson D, Ferrera DP (2009) Accounting and
   billing for federated cloud infrastructures. In: The Eighth Int'l Conf. on Grid
   and Cooperative Computing, Aug 27–28, Lanzhou, Gansu, China, pp
   268–275
2. Bhushan B, Tschichholz M, Leray E, Donnelly W (2001) Federated
   accounting: service charging and billing in a business-to-business
   environment. In: Proc 2001 IEEE/IFIP Int'l Symposium on Integrated
   Network Management VII, pp 107–121. IEEE, Piscataway, NJ, USA
3. de Leastar E, McGibney J (2000) Flexible multi-service
   telecommunications accounting system. In: Proc. Int'l Network Conf.
   (INC'00). University of Plymouth, School Of Computing, Communications
   And Electronics, Plymouth, UK
4. Sekar V, Maniatis P (2011) Verifiable resource accounting for cloud
   computing services. In: Proc. 3rd ACM workshop on Cloud computing
   security workshop (CCSW'11), pp 21–26. Association for Computing
   Machinery, Inc., New York, NY
5. Skene J, Raimondi F, Emmerich W (2010) Service-level agreements for
   electronic services. IEEE Trans Software Eng 36(2): 288–304
6. Molina-Jimenez C, Cook N, Shrivastava S (2008) On the feasibility of
   bilaterally agreed accounting of resource consumption. In: 1st Int'l
   workshop on enabling service business ecosystems (ESBE08), Sydney,
   Australia. pp 170–283
7. Wang H, Jing Q, Chen R, He B, Qian Z, Zhou L (2010) Distributed systems
   meet economics: Pricing in the cloud. In: Proc. 2nd USENIX workshop on
   hot topics in cloud computing (HotCloud'10). USENIX Association,
   Berkeley, CA 94710
8. den Bossche RV, Vanmechelen K, Broeckhove J (2010) Cost-optimal
   scheduling in hybrid iaas clouds for deadline constrained workloads. In:
   Proc IEEE 3rd Int'l Conf. on cloud computing(Cloud'10), pp 228–235. IEEE
   Computer Society, Los Alamitos, CA
9. Suleiman B, Sakr S, Jeffery R, Liu A (2011) On understanding the
   economics and elasticity challenges of deploying business applications
   on public cloud infrastructure. J Internet Serv Appl 3(2): pp 173–193.
   doi:10.1007/s13174-011-0050-y
10. Deelman E, Singh G, Livny M, Berriman B, Good J (2008) The cost of doing
    science on the cloud: The montage example. In: Proc. Int'l Conf. on High
    Performance Computing, Networking, Storage and Analysis (SC'08). IEEE,
    Piscataway, NJ, USA
11. Palankar M, Iamnitchi A, Ripeanu M, Garfinkel S (2008) Amazon s3 for
    science grids: a viable solution? In: Intl Workshop on Data–Aware
    Distributed Computing (DADC'08), Jun 24, Boston, USA, pp 55–64
12. Amazon (2006) Amazon simple storage service. developer guide, API
    version 2006–03–01. [Online]. Available: aws.amazon.com/
    documentation/s3/
13. Murty J (2008) Programming Amazon Web Services. O'Reilly. ISBN-10:
    0596515812, O'Reilly Media, Sebastopol, CA 95472
14. Nirvanix (2012) Nirvanix cloud storage network. [Online]. Available www.
    nirvanix.com
15. Amazon (2011) Amazon elastic compute cloud (amazon ec2). [Online]
    Available: aws.amazon.com/ec2/
16. Amazon ec2 pricing (2011). [Online]. Available aws.amazon.com/ec2/
    pricing
17. Amazon ec2 faqs (2011). [Online]. Available aws.amazon.com/ec2/faqs
18. Amazon elastic compute cloud user guide (api version 2011–02–28)
    (2011). [Online]. Available docs.amazonwebservices.com/AWSEC2/latest/
    UserGuide/
19. RightScale (2011) Rightscale server management. [Online]. Available
    support.rightscale.com/12-Guides/Lifecycle_Management
20. Amazon (2012) How aws pricing works. [Online]. Available http://
    calculator.s3.amazonaws.com/calc5.html
21. Mihoob A, Molina-Jimenez C, Shrivastava S (2010) A case for
    consumer–centric resource accounting models. In: Proc. IEEE 3rd Int'l
    Conf. on Cloud Computing (Cloud'10), IEEE Computer Society, California,
    pp 506–512
22. Mihoob A, Molina-Jimenez C, Shrivastava S (2011) Consumer side
    resource accounting in the cloud. In: Proc. 11th IFIP WG 6.11 Conf. on
    e-Business, e-Services, and e-Society (I3E 2011), IFIP AICT 353, Springer,
    Heidelberg. pp 58–72

3

A DDS-based middleware for scalable tracking, communication and collaboration of mobile nodes

Lincoln David[*], Rafael Vasconcelos, Lucas Alves, Rafael André and Markus Endler[*]

Abstract

Applications such as transportation management and logistics, emergency response, environmental monitoring and mobile workforce management employ mobile networks as a means of enabling communication and coordination among a possibly very large set of mobile nodes. The majority of those systems may thus require real-time tracking of the nodes and interaction with all participant nodes as well as a means of adaptability in a very dynamic scenario. In this paper, we present a middleware communication service based on the OMG DDS standard that supports on-line tracking and unicast, groupcast and broadcast with several thousand mobile nodes. We then show a Fleet Tracking and Management application built using or middleware, and present the performance results in LAN and WAN settings to evaluate our middleware in terms of scalability and robustness.

Keywords: Mobile communication; Middleware; Adaptability; DDS; Collaboration; Scalable communication

1 Introduction

Advances in mobile communication, GPS positioning and sensor technology networks are some of the driving forces pushing computing to mobile-networked systems, enabling new services and applications. Many current distributed systems such as transportation and logistics, emergency response, environmental monitoring, homeland security and mobile workforce management employ mobile networks as a means of enabling communication, collaboration and coordination among the mobile nodes, which might be people, vehicles [1,2] or autonomous mobile robots [3,4]. With the rapid increase of embedded mobile devices, many such applications are faced with the challenge of supporting several thousands of nodes, requiring both real-time tracking of their context/location information and efficient means of interaction among all nodes. Moreover, in many of these applications, the set of participating mobile nodes can vary constantly, as nodes may join and leave the system at any time, either due to application-specific circumstances or because of intermittent wireless connectivity. Such large-scale mobile systems thus require a scalable communication infrastructure that supports reliable and almost instantaneous data and context dissemination

between all mobile nodes [5] as well as monitoring and dynamic adaptation capabilities that enable automatic adjustment of the infrastructure to the very dynamic load demand caused by the mobile nodes. In this paper, we present a scalable communication middleware that addresses most of these requirements. We also present a Fleet Tracking and Management application built using our middleware and show performance results of our middleware for thousands of mobile nodes, both for Local Area and Wide Area Network settings.

A common characteristic of the distributed mobile applications considered in our work is that the mobile nodes periodically produce data about them, i.e., context information probed from sensors. Examples of produced context information may include the node's position, speed, and ambient temperature. These produced data are then published to be processed or visualised by other nodes, which can be either stationary or mobile. We also assume that each mobile node has some wireless network interface that is capable of running the IP protocol, which in fact most current wireless networks do. In these applications, the main requirement is that if the mobile node has connectivity and is generating context data or other application messages, this data should be delivered to all other interested nodes almost instantaneously, i.e., with minimum delay. Moreover, all messages

* Correspondence: lnsilva@inf.puc-rio.br; endler@inf.puc-rio.br
Department of Informatics, Pontifícia Universidade Católica do Rio de Janeiro (PUC-Rio), Rio de Janeiro, Brazil

addressed to the connected mobile nodes should also be delivered reliably and with minimum delay.

In the past, much research has been performed in Publish/Subscribe (Pub/Sub) [6-10], but only a few support large-scale mobile networks and simultaneously offer QoS (Quality of Service) guarantees for the mobile communications, especially the aforementioned reliability and low-latency message delivery [11-13]. On the other hand, the OMG's Data Distribution Service for Real-time Systems (DDS) standard [14,15] offers high-performance communication capabilities and is currently used for several real-world distributed mission-critical applications. DDS specifies a decentralised (Peer-to-Peer) scalable middleware architecture for asynchronous, Publish-Subscribe-like data distribution, supporting several QoS policies (e.g., best effort or reliable communication, data persistency, data flow prioritisation, and several other message delivery optimisations). Unlike traditional Publish-Subscribe middleware, DDS can explicitly control the latency and efficient use of network resources through fine-tuning of its network services, which are critical for soft real-time applications (e.g., its QoS policies deadline, latency budget or transport priority) [16]. Moreover, because Publish-Subscribe communication is widely acknowledged as being one of the most suitable paradigms for mobile systems, we were sure that DDS would be very appropriate for large-scale mobile applications.

However, despite its advantages, DDS cannot be efficiently deployed directly on mobile nodes or in wide-scale wireless networks [17-19], where the obtainable performance may become unpredictable [20]. The main reasons for this problem are the extensive use of IP multicast in DDS domains, the lack of proper mechanisms to handle intermittent connectivity and IP address variability, and the that resource-limited (mobile) devices cannot perform well as DDS peers because they must cache and route data for other peers. These mobile-specific limitations of DDS motivated us to design and implement a middleware that extends DDS' high-performance communication capabilities to wireless-connected mobile devices. Another limitation of current DDS implementations is their poor support for deployment and efficient data exchange among nodes in Wide-Area-Network (WAN) settings, which is the predominant scenario in current cellular network services. As the most important requirements of our middleware, we considered scalability, simplicity and high communication performance, even in the presence of intermittent connectivity, handovers and slower wireless communications.

The main contributions of this paper are the following:

1. We present our DDS-based communication middleware, give evidence of its scalability, and show how it supports efficient and reliable unicast, groupcast and broadcast message delivery to mobile nodes regardless of IP address changes, temporary disconnections, and Firewall/NAT traversal.

2. We describe support for two types of node groups, explicit and implicit, or context-defined groups, and we show how the latter are efficiently computed/updated in our middleware.

3. We show how the communication workload can be balanced among Gateways that are special DDS nodes responsible for acting as a bridge between the DDS domain and the mobile communication protocol. We also show how the system supports reliable message delivery, even in the presence of frequent handovers of mobile nodes among the Gateways.

4. We also present the results of several performance tests made in LAN and WAN settings, showing the apparent suitability of our middleware for context information distribution and communications in large-scale mobile applications with thousands of nodes.

This work is part of a larger project called ContextNet [21,22], which aims to develop middleware for (soft)-real-time communication, coordination and collaboration in large-scale distributed mobile applications. Within the scope of this project, the middleware presented in this paper is the basic layer for communication and context information sharing. This middleware, called the Scalable Data Distribution Layer (SDDL), is available for download at www.lac-rio.com/sddl.

Paper outline: In the next section, we present the goals and the main characteristics of the SDDL communication layer. In section 3, we describe a Fleet Tracking and Management application, and in section 4 we present results on performance tests. Section 5 discusses related work on scalable middleware for such mobile systems, and in section 6 we argue the benefits of our system. Finally, in section 7 we draw conclusions and point to future work.

2 Overview of the Scalable Data Distribution Layer (SDDL)

Scalable Data Distribution Layer (SDDL) is a communication middleware that connects stationary DDS nodes in a wired "core" network to mobile nodes with an IP-based wireless data connection. Some stationary nodes are information and context data processing nodes, others are gateways for communication with the mobile nodes, and yet others are control nodes operated by system managers. A control node (or Controller) is used to display all the mobile nodes' current positions (or any other context information), manage groups of nodes, and send unicast, broadcast, or groupcast messages to the mobile nodes (MNs). Figure 1 shows these types of nodes within the context of an implemented Fleet Management Application.

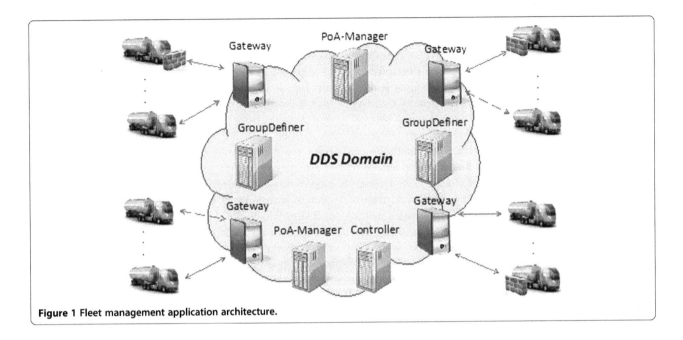

Figure 1 Fleet management application architecture.

The Scalable Data Distribution Layer (SDDL) employs two communication protocols: DDS' Real-Time Publish-Subscribe RTPS Wire Protocol [16] for wired communication within the SDDL core network, and the Mobile Reliable UDP protocol (MR-UDP) for inbound and outbound communication between the core network and the mobile nodes. The core elements rely on the DDS Data Centric Model, where DDS Topics are defined to be used for communication and coordination between these core nodes. The MR-UDP protocol will be explained in section 2.1. As part of the core network, there are three types of SDDL nodes with distinguished roles:

The *Gateway (GW)* defines a unique Point of Attachment (PoA) for connections with the mobile nodes. The Gateway is thus responsible for managing a separate MR-UDP connection with each of these nodes, forwarding any application-specific message or context information into the core network and, in the opposite direction, converting DDS messages to MR-UDP messages and delivering them reliably to the corresponding mobile node(s). Being the handler of connections to the mobile nodes (MNs), the Gateway is also responsible for notifying other SDDL core network nodes when a new MN becomes available or when MNs disconnect from it. This information is necessary for implementing other SDDL core nodes, such as nodes that cache messages addressed to temporary offline mobile nodes for later delivery.

The *PoA-Manager* is responsible for two tasks: to periodically distribute a list of Points of Attachments (PoA-List) to the MNs and to eventually request that some MNs switch to a new Gateway/PoA. The PoA-List is always a subset of all available Gateways in SDDL, and the order in the list is relevant, i.e., the first element points to the preferred Gateway/PoA and so forth. By having an updated PoA-List, an MN may always switch its Gateway if it detects a weak connection or a disconnection with the current Gateway. Moreover, by distributing different PoA-Lists to different groups of mobile nodes, the PoA-Manager is able to balance the load among the Gateways as well as announce to the mobile nodes when a new Gateway is added to or an existing Gateway is removed (or failed) from the SDDL core.

GroupDefiners are responsible for evaluating group-memberships of all mobile nodes. To do so, they subscribe to the DDS topic where any message or context update is disseminated (e.g., those sent by mobiles and forwarded by the corresponding Gateway), and they map each node to one or more groups according to an application-specific group membership processing logic. This group membership information is then shared with all Gateways in the SDDL core network using a specific DDS Topic for control, to which all Gateways subscribe so they can update their cached mobile node's membership information. Whenever a new message is sent to a group, each Gateway queries its group-to-MN mapping to know to which of the connected MNs it must send the message. The current groups of a node can be determined, for example, by its node ID, its current position (e.g., if it is inside some region), or by any other attribute/field of its context information (e.g., a node's energy level). In any case, it is important to note that the logic to define the groups is always application-specific, is to be implemented by the application developer and is added to the GroupDefiner as a *Group-selection module* plug-in.

Figure 2 shows all the types of SDDL nodes and the communication protocols they use. On the mobile side, a mobile client app – currently, we support only Android mobile apps - uses a ClientLib (CNCLib) for establishing and managing MR-UDP connections and sending and receiving application-specific messages to/from a Gateway or other mobile node. At the SDDL core network side, all nodes use a DDS implementation-independent Universal DDS Interface (UDI), whose API classes and methods are mapped to the different primitives for setting up and configuring the communication entities of each DDS product, which in turn uses the DDS standard, high-performance RTPS protocol. The Gateways are the only nodes in the SDDL core that also use the CNCLib to manage (an arbitrary number of) mobile connections. As seen, the GroupDefiners, PoA-Manager and Gateways are all Publishers and Subscribers of several DDS Control or Application Topics, by which they are able to interact with each other for processing and classifying data transmitted to/ from the mobile nodes. The *Controller* is a Java Applet that interacts with a JavaScript for displaying all MNs' current locations on a map using a Web browser window. The Web browser also displays the current groups of MNs (which can be defined and managed by the user) and supports operations to send (uni-/group-/broadcast) messages to, as well as receive text messages from, the MNs. Most of the elements shown in Figure 2 will be explained in mode detail in the remainder of this section.

2.1 MR-UDP

The Mobile Reliable UDP (MR-UDP)[a] protocol is the basis for the Gateway-mobile node interaction. This protocol implements TCP-like functionality at the top of UDP and has been customised to handle intermittent connectivity, Firewall/NAT traversal and robustness to changes of IP addresses and network interfaces. Each message, in either direction, requires an acknowledgement that, if not received, causes each transmission to be retried several times before the connection is considered broken. In addition, MR-UDP implements the following optimisations: a reduced number of connection-check packets; the transparent continuation of an MR-UDP connection regardless of IP address changes; a small number of connection maintenance packets for Firewall/NAT traversal; and simple data-flow control. Because the mobile device has its own restrictions, such as limited battery life, it is also important that the communication protocol not use too much processor resources. These optimisations are very important because cellular wireless networks are not fully reliable everywhere, and resources must be used wisely and only when truly necessary. For example, when a mobile node connected to a Gateway enters an area with no, or weak, connectivity, it may suffer a temporal disconnection; and when the signal comes back, the device will most likely have obtained a new IP address. In our MR-UDP implementation, the previous connection to the mobile node will be maintained, and all buffered UDP packets will be delivered in the original order if the disconnection time is shorter than a threshold timeout.

2.2 Handling mobile node handover

A Handover (HO) happens when a mobile node connected to a Gateway drops or loses its connection and connects itself to a different Gateway. SDDL supports

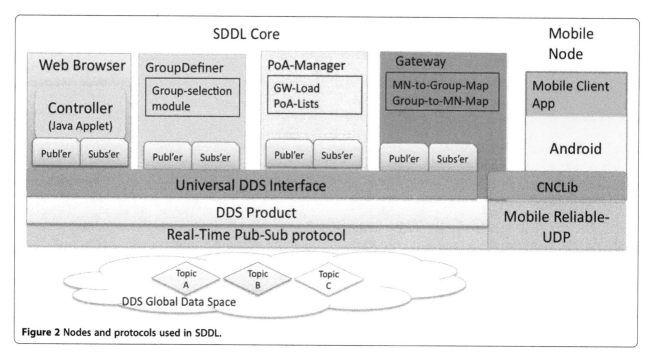

Figure 2 Nodes and protocols used in SDDL.

both Core-initiated Handover, i.e., when a mobile node is requested by the PoA-Manager to connect to a new GW, and Mobile-initiated Handover, i.e., when the mobile node spontaneously decides to connect to a new GW. In either case, it is the mobile node that actually chooses another PoA from its PoA-List and reconnects to the corresponding GW.

While performing a handover between Gateways, i.e., during the period when the node is temporarily disconnected, it is possible that some messages will fail to be delivered to it. To enable the reliable delivery of messages during a handover (a.k.a. *smooth handover*), SDDL also supports the *Mobile Temporary Disconnection* (MTD) Service, which can run on any node(s) of the SDDL core network.

The MTD Service is responsible for listening to *disconnected-MN* messages produced by Gateways and, thereafter, to collect all messages that could not be delivered to the mobile node during its HO or offline period. However, as soon as the node is connected to a new GW, which will also be announced by the corresponding GW, the MTD Service will resend all the buffered messages through the DDS domain to deliver them to the node through the new GW. Because not all applications require such reliable delivery, the MTD service is optional in SDDL, and of course, the buffering capacity of MTS is limited by the amount of memory allocated to it at deployment time. Thus far, we have not implemented any specific garbage-collection algorithm for minimising message loss due to buffer overflow.

2.3 Node Ids and message delivery

In SDDL, each mobile node and each Gateway has a unique identifier (ID). While MR-UDP messages carry only the mobile node's ID, the ID of the GW currently serving the mobile node is automatically attached to any message (or context update) entering the SDDL core network. Thus, any corresponding node can learn which is the mobile's current GW, and most messages addressed to a mobile node will thus also carry a Gateway ID, allowing them to be directly routed only to the corresponding Gateway via DDS content filtering. However, if the mobile node suddenly becomes unreachable/disconnected, its most recent Gateway will notify all other nodes in the SDDL core network of this issue; thus, the Gateway ID will be omitted in future messages to the mobile node. However, in cases where the current Gateway of a mobile node is not known or specified, messages addressed to the mobile node will still be delivered because they will be received by all Gateways.

As part of SDDL's basic functionality, it is possible to send two types of messages: unicast messages to a specific node or broadcast messages to all active nodes. Messages can be sent by a SDDL-specific node within the core network, by an arbitrary application node in the core network, or by any mobile node. The communication from a mobile node to another mobile node is achieved by using the mobile nodes´ GWs as *brokers* to deliver the message from the sender to the receiver through the SDDL core. SDDL was designed to be a robust, high-performance message exchange middleware even under high load periodic context/location update messages from all mobile nodes. The main goal is to offer a scalable communication infrastructure for the development of collaborative mobile applications.

Applications developed using SDDL can also include groupcast communication, whose group-definition logic is processed at the GroupDefiner nodes and the group-membership information is disseminated to all Gateways, by which they are able to update their MN-to-Group and Group-to-MN mappings, as mentioned previously and will be explained in more detail below.

2.4 Group communication and management

Groups of nodes may be either long-lived/explicit or context-defined. In the former category, they are explicitly defined by the application developer/operator, e.g., nodes belonging to a certain user group, to the same company or administrative domain, or to nodes of the same type. For context-defined groups, the membership of a node is dynamically determined by its most recently updated context data (its ContextUpdate – CxtU). For example, if the context means the "geographic position", then all nodes located within a certain region (e.g., a metropolitan area or within the boundaries of a state), can form a context-defined group. Alternatively, nodes could also be grouped by their current type of connectivity (3G vs 2G), their residual energy level, accelerometer data, local weather condition, or any other dynamic context information. Hence, context-defined group membership has to be continuously updated according to the most recent CxtU sent by the nodes, which is performed by the GroupDefiners in tandem with the Gateways: for each CxtU, the GroupDefiners check whether some membership changed and, if such is the case, disseminate this node's group change to all Gateways, which update their mappings accordingly.

Each GroupDefiner internally consists of a generic CxtU message processing part, and an application-specific, *Group selection module*. The generic part is responsible for reading CxtU messages from the DDS domain, recording the current groups related to the message, and handling the CxtU object to the Group Selection module. This module will execute a specific group-mapping algorithm to determine the group/s that the corresponding producer of the CxtU is a member of and must be implemented accordingly with any application-specific rule.

This split between the generic and specific group membership processing parts has certain advantages: (i) it is possible to deploy several GroupDefiners in the SDDL core, each of which execute a Group selection module that examines a certain type of CxtU object independently of the other modules; and (ii) Group selection modules can be easily exchanged in the GroupDefiner without compromising the remaining function of the SDDL group management and communication capabilities.

2.5 Universal DDS interface and general application topics

The Universal DDS Interface (UDI) is a library that fully abstracts the DDS implementation utilised, promoting the reusability and interoperability of SDDL components. The main goal is to hide away the idiosyncrasies of the APIs of each DDS implementation and simplify the set-up and configuration of DDS entities.

UDI supports the creation of DDS topics (and content-filtered topics), Domain Participants, Publishers, Subscribers, Data Readers and Data Writers, as well as the definition of QoS policies for each such entity, all in a straightforward and uniform way. As mentioned previously, the DDS standard defines 22 possible QoS policies [16,23], but each DDS vendor may have different behaviours and contracts associated with each policy implementation as well as different ways of configuring the corresponding network services, which makes the proper use of QoS of DDS a cumbersome task. Moreover, there are several DDS products that only support DDS setting at build time. Hence, one of our goals in designing UDI was also to simplify this process and to support QoS setting at deployment time. In UDI, therefore, QoS policies are defined by passing a single QoS policy object at the initialisation method, which aggregates the chosen QoS parameter settings for all DDS entities in a single place. This approach bears some similarly to the concept of QoSProvider, present in C++ and Java APIs for DDS. Through UDI, whenever a DDS implementation is to be replaced or added, one needs only to implement the new UDI port to the chosen DDS implementation. UDI is also topic-independent in that it is able to manipulate any DDS topic, not only the SDDL topics. Thus far, we have implemented SDDL's UDI layer for CoreDX DDS[b] and RTI Connext[c].

As already mentioned, all SDDL core components interact through DDS topics. Some of these topics are used for control purposes, e.g., for coordination among Group-Definers, Gateways, and PoA-Manager, while other topics are used for Application messages. For the latter topic, SDDL defines a single and generic Application Topic type that is to be used by the application programmer to create its application topics. The main components of this topic type are a content attribute, which holds any Java-serialised object, and a list of group IDs for the exchanged message. This single generic topic type makes SDDL a general-purpose communication middleware that is completely agnostic to the application-specific classes and that

is responsible only for reliable and efficient message delivery to/from the mobile nodes and for the management of group memberships of the nodes.

2.6 ClientLib

ClientLib, or just CNCLib, is a detached software component of SDDL that must be used to implement the mobile client applications. CNCLib hides most communication protocol details and handles several connectivity issues with the Gateways on the SDDL core network.

Until now, CNCLib has been implemented using only the MR-UDP protocol, described in the previous sections. However, we also plan to map the CNCLib primitives to other protocols, such as HTTP, so that the developer can select the protocol that best suits the developer's application needs, as not all mobile nodes will necessarily have stringent resources and network limitations.

The CNCLib also implements and hides from the application developer all low-level SDDL protocol features, such as the handovers. In this matter, the CNCLib is responsible for handling and managing the PoA-List, deciding and performing both the mandatory and the spontaneous handover. If the application tries to send any information during the short disconnection period between handovers, the CNCLib also buffers packets and sends them as soon as a new connection is available.

When the client application is running in a very unstable network, with frequent temporary disconnections, the CNCLib tries to shield these reconnection attempts from the application so that the mobile client application may behave as if the client had a stable, continuous connection. If a new connection cannot be made, the CNCLib informs the application that there was data that could not be sent to the Gateway. All communication is asynchronous, i.e., the application is informed in a Listener when new messages have been received or when any information could not be sent. For all communication, CNCLib uses a single abstract class *Message* that must be implemented by the application developer.

The CNCLib has also a *server* part, which is used by the Gateways to wait for and handle mobile client connections. Thus, the CNCLib is also responsible for the serialisation and deserialisation of all exchanged data. CNCLib also implements other features that are hidden, such as the reception of and response to *Ping Messages*, which are used by the SDDL to collect statistics about the latency of mobile connections.

For the next version, we are implementing two additional APIs that extend CNCLib with asynchronous communication modes. The first, *Group API*, will offer methods to subscribe to group messages and to send messages to specific groups. The second, the *Pub/Sub API*, will offer a generic content-based publish-subscribe communication mode and allow the application developer to implement applications where any mobile node may subscribe to messages and context updates produced by any other mobile node and which will use the SDDL core as its communication platform.

3 Fleet tracking and management application

SDDL has been deployed in a real-world Fleet Tracking and Management application (InfoPAE Móvel) of a major gas distribution company that operates throughout the entire country of Brazil. Using this application, the company's Operations Center is able to track trajectories of its trucks in real-time, to optimise the trucks' itineraries, to detect and give notice of obstructions or jams on roads and to monitor the vehicle driver's actions (e.g., elapsed time on both planned and involuntary stops). Moreover, it performs simple text messaging with drivers to send them instructions or alerts, both individually as well as to subgroups of the vehicle's drivers, according to the country region they are currently located. For communication with the vehicles, the company uses any of the four Brazilian cellular network operators because one or the other operator(s) better serves each region of the country. Moreover, in each region, there are significant differences in connectivity quality (e.g., 2G vs. 3G) and extension of the wireless coverage. Thus, during a long journey, vehicles may experience several IP address changes and temporary data link disconnections (due to weak coverage or handover latency). Finally, in most cases their 2G/3G connections will be behind firewalls of the cell operators.

Figure 1 shows our application architecture, with all nodes in the SDDL core network (DDS Domain) and our Fleet Tracking and Management application.

3.1 Implementation

Using the SDDL as the middleware to implement this application, the mobile nodes are represented by the company's trucks. Once connected, the mobile client at the vehicle sends up to 20 location updates (probed from the GPS sensor) every 30 seconds to the Gateway. This on-line tracking of all mobile nodes can improve the quality of collaboration among the operator at the Fleet Management Operations Center (FMOC) and the drivers, and among the drivers themselves. Because all participants can be made aware of each other's location (in fact, it could also be other context information about the truck or its environment), it is possible to react immediately to any abnormal situation and perhaps initiate a communication session with the drivers. For example, one could ask a driver why he/she has stopped or is traveling at low speed, thereby receiving information about a traffic jam or an accident, allowing other drivers to choose a different route.

As part of the fleet management system, we implemented another specific element, the Controller. The Controller runs at the FMOC and is used to display, in real-time, the vehicle's position on a map as well as to send unicast, broadcast and groupcast messages to groups of vehicles. In the current version, the Controller is a Java Applet that interacts with a JavaScript to display vehicle positions, groups and text boxes for messaging in a Web browser window.

Figure 3 shows a screenshot of the FMOC Controller (*InfoPAE Móvel Monitor*) browser window, with vehicles (blue icons) with their traces and road problems/alerts (red icons) displayed on the map as well as a "bubble window" for messaging with one specific vehicle (the green icon). On the right hand side, from top to bottom, are a section for editing and sending a message to a group of vehicles (with a group selector), a control panel for measuring round-trip delays to individual vehicles or groups of vehicles, and a window displaying a log of message exchanges.

As the mobile client for this application, we have implemented a prototype using the Android framework (version 2.3). This prototype uses the CNClib in an Android's AsynchTask to connect to a Gateway (the first in the PoA-list) and is capable of sending and receiving simple text messages to/from any other mobile and stationary nodes, including the Controller. Also, using Android's MapView, the prototype displays on a map the current vehicle's position (the green icon), other vehicles' up-to-date positions and traces (blue icons), and road problem/alerts in its vicinity (red icons) see Figure 4 for a screenshot of the client map view.

4 Performance tests and results

Thus far, we have tested our middleware only in lab experiments and not in a real-world Fleet Management application for two reasons. First, our Controller and mobile client are still prototypes and do not implement all the required Vehicle Management functionality. Second, we wanted to test our system with thousands of nodes, and performing such a large-scale deployment of the client software is currently not feasible. Therefore, we used a program to launch and simulate an arbitrary number of concurrent MNs that connect to some Gateways and periodically send their position.

The main goal of the tests was to evaluate SDDL's performance, in terms of communication latencies within the SDDL core network and on the Gateway-mobile links, both of them for unicast, broadcast and groupcast messages from the Controller to the mobile nodes.

We performed two separate tests, one with all participants' nodes and simulated MNs executed in a local area network (LAN) and another with the simulated MNs connected through a remote link on the WAN. The local area test was primarily for evaluating the SDDL

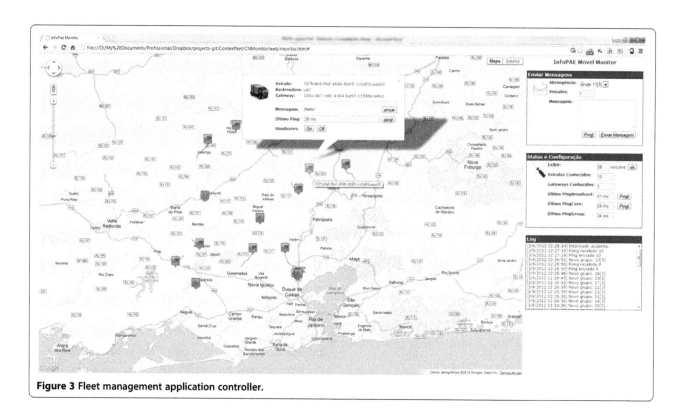

Figure 3 Fleet management application controller.

performance at serving a large number of mobile nodes with a significant amount of data being exchanged, while the wide-area tests showed the reliability of the mobile communications using the MR-UDP protocol, even in the presence of handovers. The PoA-Manager and handovers were active only in the WAN tests.

Although we tested SDDL only with simulated mobile nodes, their communication behaviour is very similar to the expected behaviour of real mobile clients, except for

the lack of mobile-initiated messaging; moreover, these nodes use the same CNCLib/MR-UDP implementations. For example, in the WAN tests we also let the simulated MNs randomly disconnect from their current Gateway and try to connect to another Gateway. Therefore, the simulated MNs did in fact produce quite realistic traffic data, allowing us to measure the system's performance in a high workload scenario, i.e., with a huge volume of data exchanged between the mobile nodes and the

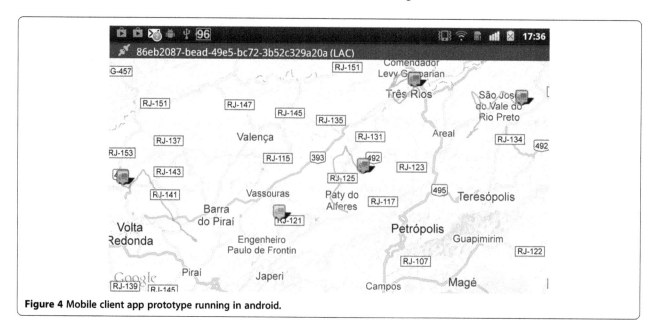

Figure 4 Mobile client app prototype running in android.

SDDL core nodes. Thus, we believe that analysing the system's performance graphs gives a realistic picture of SDDL's scalability and robustness.

4.1 LAN tests

The main goal of the Local Area Network experiments was to evaluate SDDL's performance under a high traffic load of LocationUpdates (i.e., Context updates) generated by thousands of mobile nodes.

4.1.1 Configuration and simulation parameters

Our mobile node simulation program, MN-Simulator, uses a thread pool with a size of 30 to indefinitely execute an arbitrary number of MNs, where each MN is scheduled to periodically send 20 simulated coordinates (pairs latitude, longitude) packed into the ClientLib Message object to one of the Gateways. Thus, the total size of this LocationUpdate (LU) message is approximately 1 KB[d]. In addition to sending LUs, each MN also receives sporadic ping messages from the Controller in the SDDL core and immediately replies with a pong message.

The performance tests were executed with following system configurations and simulation parameters: (a) 2,000, 4,000, 6,000, 8,000 and 10,000 MNs connected to each Gateway; (b) one or two Gateways; (c) LocationUpdate frequencies of 2 LU/min, 4 LU/min and 10 LU/min; and (d) one GroupDefiner.

4.1.2 Experimental setup

To test the communication performance, in each test round we connected all simulated MNs to the Gateways and then sent unicast messages to some MNs, broadcast messages to the Gateways on the DDS domain (Core) and broadcast messages to all MNs. For each type of message we calculated the round trip delay as the difference between the moments the message was sent and the moment the confirmation response was received.

Our hardware test setup comprised 4 computers (virtual and real), 2 of them running Gateways and 2 others running the MN-Simulator. The GroupDefiner was run on one of the simulation machines. All machines were connected through a 10/100 Mbps switch.

We ran experiments with most of the simulation parameters explained in the previous section. However, due to the memory and processing limitations of the machines executing the MN-Simulator, we were able to simulate at most a total of 12,000 MNs performing 10 Location updates per minute.

4.1.3 Testing unicast and broadcast

The results are presented in Figures 5 and 6. All round-trip times are shown in milliseconds. For the sake of better legibility, the subtitles were abbreviated, e.g., LU means Location Updates and 8,000v 2GW means a total of 8,000

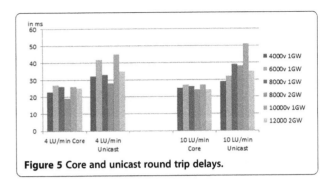

Figure 5 Core and unicast round trip delays.

MNs connected at 2 Gateways (4,000 at each GW). In all experiments, we started to measure the delays only after all MNs were sending their LUs. All results are the mean value of 5 measurements.

As Figure 5 shows, the unicast and core round trip delays are very stable for all test parameters (20–45 ms), which suggests that our system is not yet overloaded. Unicast messages to any MN are delivered quite fast (up to 50 ms), and yet the SDDL core network is still far from saturation (< 20 ms), which means it could handle far more messages. As shown in Figure 6, the broadcast delays are much higher (up to 45 sec), which is expected because all MNs must be contacted individually and their response must be obtained until the total round trip is completed. As mentioned before, we could not send a broadcast message to more than 10,000 MNs connected to a single Gateway because this caused a drop of connections during the broadcast tests. This problem is due to the large bulk of messages being sent out - and the corresponding replies received - nearly simultaneously through a single UDP port. This results in an overload peak on the operating system's UDP buffer and causes several datagrams to be lost, many of them being MR-UDP's Acknowledge and connection control segments. Hence, MR-UDP drops the connections as if the node had lost its network connection.

4.2 WAN tests

To evaluate the performance of the SDDL middleware in a WAN environment with high-latency connections

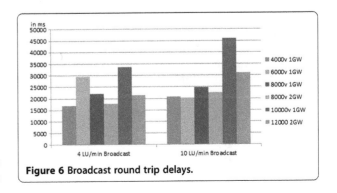

Figure 6 Broadcast round trip delays.

and subject to intermittent connectivity and/or the occurrence of IP address changes (such as those experienced by mobile nodes connected by mobile network providers), we performed the following experiments: we ran several performance tests involving three Gateways and 1 PoA-Manager in our lab and several thousand simulated mobile nodes/vehicles launched in parallel on 4 to 5 remote machines served by different broadband ISP internet connections. We measured the Round-Trip Delay of both unicast and groupcast messages to the MNs. Some experiments also included frequent handovers, both initiated by the mobiles and/or by the PoA-Manager, the latter aiming at load balancing among the Gateways. For all these tests, the LU frequency was every 30 seconds (2 LU/min).

4.2.1 Experimental setup

The experimental setup was as follows. In our laboratory, the three Gateways were executed on separate machines: a Dell PowerEdge server (3.0 GHz, 2× Dual Core), a PowerMac G5 (2.5GHz Quad-core with 8GB RAM), and a PC (CPU Core i5 with 8GB RAM); the PoA-Manager and a GroupDefiner executed on a separate PC. All these machines were connected to a 10/100/1000-Mbps switch. This switch, in turn, was connected to a 10/100-Mbps switch at the router serving the Internet connection of our laboratory. At the remote side, the machines were diverse, but all were connected via wired Ethernet to the ISP modem or router. Before executing the experiment, all home testers measured their effective uplink capacity (which was always within a range of 0.25 to 0.9 Mbps) and downlink capacity (within a range of 1.01 to 9.56 Mbps). We chose not to use a Wi-Fi wireless network, as this would create a less realistic simulation scenario because all simulated MNs would be competing with each other for a single wireless IEEE 802.11 connection, which is not collision free, as opposed to what happens with real-world Edge or 3G connections. However, we emulated the intermittent connectivity of real-world wireless connections by making the simulated MNs randomly change their MR-UDP connections and reconnect to a new Gateway. Additionally, there was very little interference from Internet connection usage by other applications on the remote machines.

4.2.2 Testing unicast and broadcast without handovers

In these experiments, the MN-Simulator program (here denoted by *MS-i*, the MN_simulator program launched at remote/home machine i) initially connected all the simulated MNs to a single Gateway, but immediately after each of them established the MR-UDP connection with this Gateway, it received (only once) a PoA-List of size 3, containing the IP addresses and ports of all three gateways running in our laboratory (which was used for

the handover tests - see section 4.2.4). In this experiment, we turned off the load-balancing function of the PoA-Manager because we wanted to exclusively evaluate the SDDL's performance with mobile-initiated, spontaneous handover, i.e., without any interference/overload caused by mandatory handover requests by the PoA-Manager.

Table 1 shows the round trip delays (RTDs) of the unicast messages for three total amounts of simulated MNs executed at the remote machines. Because the Internet connectivity and the remote machine's capacities were so different, we measured the mean RTD time for each vehicle simulation program separately.

The lower value for the unicast RTDs for 7174 simulated MNSs was most likely caused by a sudden performance boost in the throughput of the ISP up/downlinks at one or more of the remote Internet connections. It also indicates that the increased number of clients does not yet affect the SDDL communication performance. The total number of MNSs is not a multiple of 4 because during the parallel launch and connection of >1000 MNSs to a Gateway some of the MR-UDP connections failed to be established, and our vehicle simulation program was not conceived to retry all failed connections several times.

In this same test run, we also measured the RTDs of a broadcast to, and reply from, all 1000 MNs executed on the 4 home machines, which took only 47.1 seconds. Because the broadcast incurs too great an instantaneous communication load in the MN-Simulator program and their Internet connections, we were only able to execute it for 250 MNs per machine.

4.2.3 Tests with mobile-initiated handovers

To test the performance of SDDL with spontaneous mobile-initiated handovers and with intermittent connectivity of the mobile nodes, we added - just for this experiment - a new message to the system, namely, the Handover Test (HT) message. We also modified the PoA-Manager and the MN-Simulator program accordingly to also perform the following.

Every 3 minutes, each MN decides if it will disconnect from the current Gateway and reconnect to another Gateway, chosen randomly from its PoA-list. This decision is controlled by a handover probability (HO_P), which we varied from 0% to 15%. Whenever an MN starts a handover, it first closes the current MR-UDP connection

Table 1 Round Trip Delays of Unicast to MNs of each home machine (in ms)

Total nr of MNS	MS-1	MS-2	MS-3	MS-4	MS-5	Global mean
1000	108	67.80	70	67.2	N/A	78.25
4123	115.8	86.20	84.4	87	N/A	93.35
7174	98.8	68.60	77.4	67.4	N/A	78.05

and then requests a new MR-UDP connection to the newly chosen Gateway, i.e., for some short period of time (a few ms), the simulated MN is entirely disconnected from any Gateway. Each handover is printed at the terminal console. Each MN also accepts the HT message and increments a global counter, which is also printed at the console.

The purpose of the HT message is to test the reliability of message delivery to the MNs during a handover/disconnection. The message is sent by the PoA-Manager immediately after it receives a "connection closed" message from the corresponding Gateway. Because the mobile node is disconnected, the non-delivered messages are received by the MTD service and later forwarded to the new Gateway where the MN reconnected. Thus, we wanted to check, at each MN-Simulator program, whether the total number of received HT messages equals the total number of performed handovers by the MNs, i.e., whether the MTD service had replayed all the non-delivered unicast messages or if some unicast message had been lost during the handover.

Table 2 shows the mean values of round trip delays (RTDs) of unicast messages for four combinations of total numbers of MNs and handover probability (HO_P), again, presented separately for each home machine.

From this data, we can make two observations: (i) a higher handover probability does not necessarily increase the overall RTD of unicast messages, showing that the retransmissions by the MTD and the disconnection management by the Gateways apparently only affect the message delivery times of the migrating mobile nodes; (ii) for the same handover probability, e.g., 5%, a larger number of total mobile nodes does slightly impact the increase of the overall message RTD.

When comparing the data of Tables 1 and 2 (for approximately 4000 MNs), it is interesting to note that the unicast RTDs are similar and even decreased slightly in the experiments with low-probability mobile-initiated handovers. Again, however, this result could be due to a lucky choice of the "pinged" MNs or a sudden enhancement of the link quality of the remote Internet connections.

There is a natural delay in the delivery of HT messages because the MTD service only resends non-delivered messages to the mobile nodes after the connection establishment is announced by the new Gateway. Because we did not implement the MN-Simulator to stop performing handovers after some time, at the end of the simulation

there was always a gap between the last announced handover and the corresponding delivery of the HT message. This gap obviously increases with the number of MNs and their probability of performing handovers. Table 3 shows the percentage of "missing" HT messages at the end of the simulation for the tests with 1800 and 3979 MNs. However, when examining the output logs of the MN-Simulator, almost all the HT messages (of past handovers) appear to have been delivered. This result raises our confidence that SDDL supports reliable delivery of messages in the presence of handovers between Gateways.

4.2.4 Tests with groupcast messages

The purpose of the groupcast message test was to measure the RTD of groupcast messages (including the corresponding acknowledgements by all group members), for different sizes of groups, where the group members were simulated by MN-Simulator (MS-i) programs executed on the remote machines served by the different ISPs. Because we performed this experiment on a different day and from other remote machines, we named these programs MS-6 to MS-11 to clarify that the RTD times of this and previous experiments cannot be compared. In this experiment, the common ping delay was approximately 25 ms (except for MS-11, which was 444 ms). The down- and uplinks varied between 1.59 and 1.2 Mbps and 0.93 and 0.33 Mbps, respectively. It should be noted that MS-11 was a machine connected in Europe, and therefore, its RTD is much higher than those of the other vehicles executed on the Brazilian machines. For this experiment, we turned off the induced mobile-initiated handover behaviour of the simulated MNs (HO_P=0), i.e., they would only switch to another Gateway if their MR-UDP connection in fact failed.

The group size is approximate, as it was determined by the GroupDefiner using a mod operation (e.g., ×%100) over the least significant byte of the MN-identifier, which is a randomly generated UUID. Thus, in the Gr-10%, the group had approximately 10% of 5795 MNs, and so on. Recall that in all test runs, the SDDL core nodes were also busy processing the LU messages sent every 30 seconds by each MN.

Table 4 shows the mean RTD times of 5 measurements for both the unicast and groupcast communication modes. It also indicates which of the remote machines simulating the mobile nodes actually participated (Yes) in the groupcast experiment. The numbers reveal that the

Table 2 Round trip delays of unicast messages (to each home machine) under different handover probabilities (in MS)

Total nr ot MNs/HO_P	MS-1	MS-2	MS-3	MS-4	MS-5	Global mean
1800/15%	103.6	72	65	61.2	70.2	74.4
3979/15%	93.2	68.2	84	63	73.4	76.36
5812/5%	112.6	79.2	102	70	92.2	91.2
7815/10%	79	58.8	59.6	50.4	334.8	116.52

Table 3 Percentage of "missing" HT messages after stopping the MN-Simulator programs

Total # MNs/HO_P	MS-1	MS-2	MS-3	MS-4	MS-5
1800/15%	2.4	1.7	4.9	3.1	1.5
3979/5%	4.9	5.9	2.5	3.0	6.2

mean RTD time for the estimated 579 and 1358 group members is only 19.7 and 66.4 seconds, respectively. This result suggests that a one-way groupcast message is most likely delivered to all the group members 40-70% of this time. Moreover, although we do not know how many group members were actually executed by MS-11, its longer ping delay certainly contributed to the total increase of the RTD in the Gr-10% experiment. As mentioned in section 4.2.3, we also tested and measured the RTD of a broadcast to 1000 MNs, and the obtained results for 1000 and 1358 deliveries and replies seem to be consistent.

5 Related work

SALES [24] is a middleware for data distribution aimed at large-scale mobile systems. It was designed based on two central concepts: QoC (*Quality of Context*) and CDDLA (*Context Data Distribution Level Agreement*). In a nutshell, QoC is a *Quality of Service* related to context information distribution services, while CDDLA is a quality contract that is established between any data producer and consumer and that is enforced by the middleware. SALES defines a tree-based hierarchical architecture of nodes to balance communication cost, performance and load balancing among the four types of nodes: the *Central Node* (at the root of the tree); the *Base Node*, a stationary node responsible for a network domain; the *Coordinator User Node*, which is responsible for discovering and connecting to (in an ad hoc manner) the *Simple User* nodes. Unlike our work, SALES relies solely on pure UDP for inter-node communication and, hence, does not take advantage of all real-time and QoS support of DDS.

Solar [25] is a middleware for ubiquitous computing that was designed to be scalable in the set of communicating nodes and is based on a self-organising P2P (*Peer-to-Peer*) overlay network. Solar employs a specific programming model called *filter-and-pipe*, where each component (filter) has a set of entry and exit ports and there may be data producers (sources) and consumers (sinks). In the Solar architecture, each node is considered a planet (that may have a number of "satellite

nodes"), and the more nodes are used, the more scalable the system is. This *middleware* uses two transport protocols, DHT Pastry (*Distributed Hash Table*), for Discovery and routing, and TCP, for "inter-planetary communication". Unlike SDDL, which uses the DDS-based core (and the Gateways), to ensure real-time and reliable delivery of data to and from the mobiles, Solar is based on DHT and TCP, which are not suited to mobile networks (TCP) and to low-latency message routing and delivery (DHT).

Apparently, there has been little research and development on DDS-based middleware systems for mobile distributed applications in arbitrary wireless networks. Most DDS studies present comparisons between and benchmarks of different DDS vendors' implementations, such as [26-28], but none of them mention wireless networks or mobile DDS deployments. Among the few works that focus on mobile devices, we found the DDS-based middleware proposed in [4], named DDSS. DDSS includes a specific architectural element that supports mobile nodes and ensures reliable data delivery even for mobile subscribers that switch their wireless access points during system operation, similar to the handovers supported in SDDL. In the proposed architecture, all mobile devices are required to execute a lightweight version of DDS, the Mobile DDS Client, whereas stationary nodes on the fixed communication network run full-fledged DDS nodes and are responsible for the routing and delivery of data to all nodes. Due to DDS connectivity and Firewall/NAT traversal restrictions (unless a VPN is created), all these Mobile DDS Clients must run in a single network domain and rely on stable wireless connectivity. Moreover, the authors present no data about the communication performance over wireless networks, and there is apparently no support for context-defined groups and groupcast communication.

Another DDS-based system targeted at mobile networks is presented in [29]. REVENGE is a DDS-compliant infrastructure for news dispatching among mobile nodes and that is capable of transparently and autonomously balancing the data distribution load in the DDS network. REVENGE implements a P2P routing substrate - deployed on a LAN - that is fault tolerant and self-organising. More specifically, it is able to detect crashed nodes and to reorganise the routing paths from any source node to any mobile sink node. Because all nodes run DDS (mobile nodes have the DDS minimum profile), it has full DDS QoS Policy support. REVENGE has been tested in a

Table 4 Round trip delays of unicast and groupcast messages (in ms)

Vehicles/Mode	Group size	MS-6	MS-7	MS-8	MS-9	MS-10	MS-11	Gr-cast RTD
5794/Unicast	0	100	59.6	58.4	59.2	50	289.4	
5795/Gr-10%	579	Yes	Yes	Yes	Yes	Yes	Yes	19720.60
5430.Gr-25%	1358	Yes	Yes	Yes	Yes	Yes	No	66437.80

wireless network (on a University Campus wireless LAN), but the authors have not shown performance data in situations where the mobile nodes had intermittent wireless connections and suffered IP address changes. For asynchronous communication capabilities at the mobile nodes, this system provides full DDS-based Pub/Sub support, while SDDL implements only a restricted form of group subscription, but which has the advantage of high performance and scalability. Moreover, REVENGE's asynchronous communication depends on mobile nodes' initiative to become a group publisher/subscriber. SDDL asynchronous communication instead supports, in a uniform way, MN-initiated group participation, external MN-agnostic grouping determined by the GroupDefiners, and context-defined groups.

It seems that the main distinguishing feature of SDDL, when compared with the above systems, is that its mobile nodes only need to execute the lightweight MR-UDP protocol, which is platform independent (because it requires only the TCP/IP-protocol stack) and is very resource-efficient. Moreover, because DDS does not perform well with intermittent connectivity and does not natively support Firewall/NAT traversal, the mobile clients of REVENGE and DDSS have to be executed in a single network domain and in wireless networks with strong connectivity guarantees. Table 5 summarises the main differences among the middleware systems.

6 Discussion

The SDDL architecture takes advantage of DDS' powerful data-centric approach, its "broker-free" Peer-to-Peer architecture, rich QoS support, and the highly optimised and scalable RTPS wire protocol to boost its performance. In particular, it is possible to add new DDS nodes without much degrading the overall system's communication performance. SDDL's design was also driven by the desire to be simple, efficient, extensible and generic. This guiding principle can be identified by the following characteristics:

Each type of node has a very specific and simple function, and the overall processing is achieved by the interaction among these simple building blocks. For example, while Gateways are concerned with the reliable communication with MNs, the PoA-Manager handles the mobile-to-Gateway assignment and Gateway load balancing, while GroupDefiners are responsible for tagging vehicles with group information.

SDDL's extensibility is also inherited from DDS, which makes it quite simple to add new nodes to the SDDL core network for inclusion of new processing services.

Table 5 Comparison of middleware systems for mobile communication

Aspect	Sales	Solar	DDSS	Revenge	SDDL
Application	Generic middleware	Generic middleware	Generic middleware	News dissemination	Generic middleware
Communication modes	Pure UDP	Pasty and TCP	Pub/Sub	Pub/Sub	Unicast, Groupcast and Broadcast, Limited form of Pub/Sub on MNs
Fault-tolerance	No	No	No	Active Replication on fixed nodes, and node failure detection allowing data re-routing	Gateway failure through MH handovers, and MR-UDP resilience to node's short disconnections and IP Addr changes
Reliable data delivery to mobile nodes	There is a contact between data producers and consumers	TCP reliability only (not well suited for wireless connection)	Yes	Yes, but no handover support	Yes, MTD service caches non-deliverd messages, and RUDP has internal asks
Software on the mobile node	Just UDP	TCP stack and Pastry protocol	Lightweight DDS node	DDS node with minimum profile	Just the MR-UDP java Library
DDS compliance and QoS support	No	No	Yes, also at the mobile nodes	Yes, also at the mobile nodes	Only in the SDDL core but not on the MNs
Load Balancing	Yes, using a hierarchical (tree)	N/A	N/A	Yes, in the routing substrate	Yes, of the mobile Gateways'load
Wireless deployment/test	Yes, without wireless disconnection tests	Yes, without wireless disconnection tests	Not mentioned	Deployment in campus Wi-Fi network	In a WAN, but simulated disconnection and IP Address changes
Number of MNs	N/A	N/A	N/A	10 source nodes, 10 sink nodes	Several thousands MNs
Context Updates by each MN	N/A	N/A	N/A	N/A	Yes, $\approx$1KB sent every 30 seconds
Total traffic	N/A	N/A	N/A	1000 news/s	>250 1KB-object/s

For example, it is possible to add a logging service that captures all communications on the network and saves them to a database. This service would be completely independent of the rest of the nodes.

Only essential communication support is expected to be running on the mobile nodes. Because a mobile node can be as simple as an embedded processor with limited resources, it is preferable to use an IP-based solution rather than expect more sophisticated communication protocols or middleware to be available on the device. Hence, we built a highly optimised UDP-based communication protocol (MR-UDP) with a small footprint and tangible benefits in regard to communication reliability and Firewall/NAT traversal, which we think is the best way towards a general-purpose connectivity solution. Making this protocol resilient to IP changes and temporary disconnections is a valuable adaptability capability in a mobile applications environment, where network connections are commonly not fully reliable.

No SDDL core node is required to maintain any state about any MN, whether it is its IP address, or its association with groups. This not only simplifies the handovers between Gateways but also facilitates the definition of new sorts of groups that are entirely customisable to the application.

Efficiency and scalability are also supported by the fact that mobile communication issues are decoupled from the processing of their data. Thus far, we have limited ourselves to rather simple context data classification and group definitions, but in the future we plan to experiment with more complex processing of the application messages and context updates. Moreover, the number of Gateways can easily be raised, to handle an increase in the number of nodes or in the generated traffic by the application.

7 Conclusion

In this paper, we presented an inherently distributed communication middleware named the Scalable Data Distribution Layer, which aims to support large numbers of data connections with mobile devices that send location updates many times a minute. Because at its core SDDL uses DDS, it directly inherits several of the OMG standard's benefits, such as data-centric data modelling, real-time and asynchronous event-based communication through the RealTime-PublishSubscribe (RTPS) protocol, powerful subscription filtering and data routing, and a rich set of QoS policies. Thus, the main contributions of SDDL are the following: (i) its optimised extension of real-time communication capabilities with mobile nodes without native DDS support through the use of the highly optimised and IP-address-independent MR-UDP protocol; and (ii) an adaptive and extensible communication middleware supporting mobile node handovers and broadcast and groupcast communication modes, where

the group-defining logic is arbitrary. SDDL is free and can be downloaded from URL www.lac-rio.com/sddl/.

In addition to the Fleet Tracking and Management application described in section 3, more recently we have also used SDDL to develop a second mobile application aimed at supporting vehicle inspection by traffic police. In both cases, tests with several thousands of simulated mobile nodes (sending location updates every 6 seconds) have shown satisfactory performance results, where a group/broadcast communication to more than 1000 nodes happens in less than 1 minute. Of course, it is too early to tell how well this middleware will function when deployed in a real-world setting, which we plan to do soon. As future steps, we intend to work along several lines, such as the following: extend the CNClib with asynchronous communication capabilities (i.e., a content-based Pub/Sub), implement mechanisms and policies for enabling dynamic load balancing among the nodes in the SDDL core network, integrate a secure communications layer, and incorporate autonomic capability into the middleware system, allowing it to become completely adaptive and to support deployment of the middleware as a scalable connectivity service in the cloud.

Endnotes

[a]http://www.lac-rio.com/mr-udp.

[b]CoreDX DDS is a trademark of TwinOaks Computing Inc.

[c]RTI Connext is a trademark of Real Time Innovations (RTI).

[d]Because our current MR-UDP implementation carries 256 Bytes on each UDP packet, each LU is split into at least three UDP packets.

Competing interests
The authors declare that they have no competing interests.

Authors' contributions
All authors read and approved the final manuscript.

References
1. Stojanovic D, Predic B, Antolovic I, et al. (2009) Web information system for transport telematics and fleet management. In: 9th International Conference on Telecommunication in Modern Satellite, Cable, and Broadcasting Services, (TELSIKS '09), pp 314–317
2. Rybicki J, Scheuermann B, Kiess W, Lochert C, Fallahi P, Mauve M (2007) Challenge: Peers onWheels – A Road to New Traffic Information Systems. In: Proceedings of the 13th annual ACM international conference on Mobile computing and networking - MobiCom '07
3. Sibley GT, Rahimi MH, Sukhatme GS (2002) Robomote: a tiny mobile robot platform for large-scale ad-hoc sensor networks. IEEE International Conference on Robotics and Automation (ICRA '02) 2:1143–1148
4. Herms A, Schulze M, Kaiser J, Nett E (2008) Exploiting publish/subscribe communication in wireless mesh networks for industrial scenarios. In: IEEE International Conference on Emerging Technologies and Factory Automation, ETFA 2008, pp 648–655
5. Grossmann M, Bauer M, Honle N, Kappeler U-P, Nicklas D, Schwarz T (2009) Efficiently Managing Context Information for Large-Scale Scenarios. In: Third

IEEE International Conference on Pervasive Computing and Communications (PERCOM '05), pp 331–340

6. Huang Y, Garcia-Molina H (2004) Publish/Subscribe in a Mobile Environment. Wireless Networks 10(6):643–652

7. Castro M, Druschel P, Kermarrec A-M, Rowstron AIT (2002) Scribe: a large-scale and decentralized application-level multicast infrastructure. IEEE J Selected Areas in Communications 20(8):1489–1499

8. Carzaniga A, Rosenblum DS, Wolf AL (2001) Design and evaluation of a wide-area event notification service. ACM Trans Comp Syst 19(3):332–383

9. Terpstra WW, Behnel S, Fiege L, Zeidler A, Buchmann AP (2003) A peer-to-peer approach to content-based publish/subscribe. In: Proceeding of the Second DEBS

10. Pietzuch PR, Bacon JM (2002) Hermes: A distributed event-based middleware architecture. In: Proceedings IEEE 22nd International Conference on IEEE Distributed Computing Systems Workshops, pp 611–618

11. Mahambre SP, Kumar M, Bellur U (2007) A taxonomy of QoS-aware, adaptive event-dissemination middleware. Internet Computing, IEEE 11(4):35–44

12. Corsaro A, Querzoni L, Scipioni S, Piergiovanni ST, Virgillito A (2006) Quality of service in publish/subscribe middleware. Global Data Manag 19:20

13. Esposito C, Cotroneo D, Gokhale A (2009) Reliable publish/subscribe middleware for time-sensitive internet-scale applications. In: Proceedings of the Third ACM International Conference on Distributed Event-Based Systems. ACM

14. OMG (2012) Data Distribution Service for Real-time Systems Specifications. www.omg.org/spec/ (visited on Sept. 28, 2012)

15. Wang N, Schmidt DC, van't Hag H, Corsaro A (2008) Toward an adaptive data distribution service for dynamic large-scale network-centric operation and warfare (NCOW) systems. In: IEEE Military Communications Conference - MILCOM, pp 1–7

16. Pardo-Castellote G, Farabaugh B, Warren R (2005) An Introduction to DDS and Data-Centric Communications. In: Real-Time Innovations

17. Sanchez-Monedero J, Povedano-Molina J, Lopez-Vega JM, Lopez-Soler JM (2011) Bloom filter-based discovery protocol for DDS middleware. J Parallel Distributed Comp 71(10):1305–1317

18. Esposito C (2011) Data Distribution Service (DDS) Limitations for Data Dissemination wrt Large-scale Complex Critical Infrastructures (LCCI). Mobilab Technical Report 100. www.mobilab.unina.it

19. Xu B, Xu B, Linderman M, Madria S, Wolfson O (2010) A Tactical Information Management Middleware for Resource-constrained Mobile P2P Networks. In: Reliable Distributed Systems, 2010 29th IEEE Symposium on. IEEE

20. Baldoni R, Bonomi S, Lodi G, Platania M, Querzoni L (2011) Data dissemination supporting complex event pattern detection. Int J Next Gen Comp 24

21. Endler M, Baptista G, et al. (2011) ContextNet: Context Reasoning and Sharing Middleware for Large-scale Pervasive Collaboration and Social Networking. In: Poster Session, ACM/USENIX Middleware Conference. , Lisbon

22. Malcher M, Aquino J, Fonseca H, et al. (2010) A Middleware Supporting Adaptive and Location-aware Mobile Collaboration. In: Mobile Context Workshop: Capabilities, Challenges and Applications, Adjunct Proceedings of UbiComp 2010. Copenhagen

23. RTI (2011) RTI Data Distribution Service - Comprehensive Summary of QoS Policies. http://community.rti.com/rti-doc/45e/ndds.4.5e/doc/pdf/RTI_DDS_QoS_Reference_Guide.pdf (visited in September 2012)

24. Corradi A, Fanelli M, Foschini L (2010) Adaptive context data distribution with guaranteed quality for mobile environments. In: 2010 5th IEEE International Symposium on Wireless Pervasive Computing (ISWPC), p 8

25. Chen G, Li M, Kotz D (2008) Data-centric middleware for context-aware pervasive computing. Elsevier Pervasive Mobile Comp 4(2):216–253

26. Pongthawornkamol T, Nahrstedt K, Wang G (2007) The Analysis of Publish/Subscribe Systems over Mobile Wireless Ad Hoc Networks. In: 2007 Fourth Annual International Conference on Mobile and Ubiquitous Systems: Networking & Services (MobiQuitous), pp 1–8

27. Esposito C, Russo S, Di Crescenzo D (2008) Performance assessment of OMG compliant data distribution middleware. In: 2008 IEEE International Symposium on Parallel and Distributed Processing, pp 1–8

28. Xiong M, Parsons J, Edmondson J (2010) Evaluating the Performance of Publish/Subscribe Platforms for Information Management in Distributed Real-time and Embedded Systems. http://portals.omg.org/dds/sites/default/files/Evaluating_Performance_Publish_Subscribe_Platforms.pdf

29. Corradi A, Foschini L, Nardelli L (2010) A DDS-compliant infrastructure for fault-tolerant and scalable data dissemination. In: Proceedings of the The IEEE symposium on Computers and Communications (ISCC '10). IEEE Computer Society, Washington, DC, USA, pp 489–495

4

PolyViNE: policy-based virtual network embedding across multiple domains

Fady Samuel[1], Mosharaf Chowdhury[2] and Raouf Boutaba[3,4*]

Abstract

Intra-domain virtual network embedding is a well-studied problem in the network virtualization literature. For most practical purposes, however, virtual networks (VNs) must be provisioned across heterogeneous administrative domains managed by multiple infrastructure providers (InPs).

In this paper, we present PolyViNE, a policy-based inter-domain VN embedding framework that embeds end-to-end VNs in a decentralized manner. PolyViNE introduces a distributed protocol that coordinates the VN embedding process across participating InPs and ensures competitive prices for service providers (SPs), i.e., VN owners, while providing monetary incentives for InPs to participate in the process even under heavy competition. We also present a location-aware VN request forwarding mechanism – basd on a hierarchical addressing scheme (COST) and a location awareness protocol (LAP) – to allow faster embedding. We outline scalability and performance characteristics of PolyViNE through quantitative and qualitative evaluations.

1 Introduction

Network virtualization has gained significant attention in recent years as a means to support multiple coexisting virtual networks (VNs) on top of shared physical infrastructures [1-4]. The first step toward enabling network virtualization is to instantiate such VNs by embedding[a] VN requests onto substrate networks. But the VN embedding problem, with constraints on virtual nodes and virtual links, is known to be $\mathcal{NP}$-hard [5,6]. Several heuristics [5-9] have been proposed to address this problem in the single infrastructure provider (InP) scenario. However, in realistic settings, VNs must be provisioned across heterogeneous administrative domains belonging to multiple InPs to deploy and deliver services end to end.

One of the biggest challenges in end-to-end VN embedding is to organize the InPs under a framework without putting restrictions on their local autonomy. Each InP should be able to embed parts or the whole of a VN request according to its internal administrative policies while maintaining global connectivity through mutual agreements with other InPs.

Moreover, InPs (i.e., network operators) are notoriously known for their secrecy of traffic matrices and topology information. As a result, existing embedding algorithms that assume complete knowledge of the substrate network are not applicable in this scenario. Each InP will have to embed a particular segment of the VN request without any knowledge of how the rest of the VN request has already been mapped or will be mapped.

Finally, there will be constant tussles between service providers (SPs) and InPs on multiple levels:

- Each InP will be interested in getting as much of the deployment as possible put on its equipment, and then optimizing allocation under given constraints. In addition, InPs will be more interested in getting requests for their high-margin equipment while offloading unprofitable work onto their competitors.
- SPs are also interested in getting their requirements satisfied while minimizing their expenditure. Tussles might arise between SPs and InPs when each party selfishly try to optimize their utility functions.

Any inter-domain VN embedding mechanism must enforce proper incentives and mechanisms to address these tussles.

In this paper, we introduce PolyViNE, a policy-based end-to-end VN embedding framework that embeds VNs

*Correspondence: rboutaba@cs.uwaterloo.ca
[3] David R. Cheriton School of Computer Science, University of Waterloo, Waterloo, ON N2L 3G1, Canada
[4] Division of IT Convergence Engineering, Pohang University of Science and Technology (POSTECH), Pohang 790-784, Korea
Full list of author information is available at the end of the article

across multiple InPs in a globally distributed manner while allowing each concerned InP to enforce its local policies. PolyViNE introduces a distributed protocol that coordinates the participating InPs and ensures competitive pricing through repetitive bidding at every step of the embedding process.

We do not claim PolyViNE to be the best or the only way of performing end-to-end VN embedding. However, to the best of our knowledge, this is the first foray into this unexplored domain in the context of network virtualization, and we believe this problem to be absolutely critical in realizing network virtualization for most practical purposes.

The rest of the paper is organized as follows. Section 2 formally defines the inter-domain VN embedding problem. In Section 3 we describe the design choices and the distributed embedding protocol used by PolyViNE, followed by a discussion of its enabling technologies in Section 5. Section 6 and Section 7 respectively provide preliminary quantitative and qualitative evaluations of PolyViNE. We discuss related work in Section 8. Finally, Section 9 concludes the paper with a discussion on possible future work.

2   Problem formulation

The intra-domain VN embedding problem is well-defined in the literature [5-9]. In this section, we formally define the inter-domain VN embedding problem. For simplicity, we avoid intra-domain aspects (e.g., node and link attributes) wherever we see fit. We use the notation introduced here to discuss the details of the PolyViNE protocol in section 3.

2.1   Substrate networks and the underlay

We consider the underlay to be comprised of D substrate networks (Figure 1a), and we model each substrate network controlled by the i-th InP ($1 \leq i \leq D$) as a weighted undirected graph denoted by $G_i^S = (N_i^S, L_i^S)$, where N_i^S is the set of substrate nodes and L_i^S is the set of *intra-domain* substrate links. Each substrate link $l^S(n^S, m^S) \in L_i^S$ between two substrate nodes n^S and m^S is associated with the bandwidth capacity weight value $b(l^S)$ denoting the total amount of bandwidth. Each substrate network has a (centralized or distributed) logical Controller [10] that performs administrative/control functionalities for that InP. $A_i^S (\subset N_i^S)$ denotes the set of border nodes [10] in the i-th InP that connect it to other InPs through *inter-domain* links based on Service Level Agreements (SLAs) to form the underlay. $A_{i,j}^S \subset A_i^S$ denotes the set of border nodes in InP_i that lead to InP_j. Each InP also has a set of policies $\mathcal{P}_i^S$ that is used to take and enforce administrative decisions.

We denote the underlay (shown in Figure 1b) as a graph $G^U = (N^U, L^U)$, where $N^U (= \sum_i A_i^S)$ is the set containing border nodes across all InPs ($1 \leq i \leq D$) and L^U is the set of physical inter-domain links connecting the border nodes between two InPs.

However, the underlay does not have the full connectivity, which is achieved through simple topology abstraction

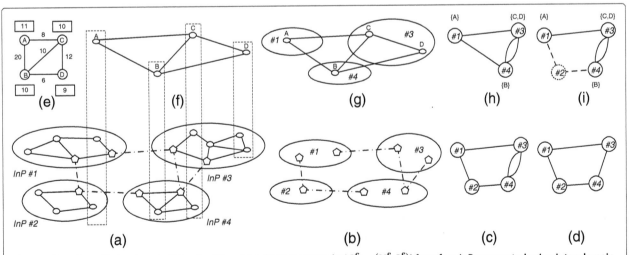

Figure 1 Overview of inter-domain VN embedding: **(a)** substrate networks ($G_i^S = (N_i^S, L_i^S)$) from four InPs connected using inter-domain links; **(b)** the underlay ($G^U = (N^U, L^U)$) consisting of border nodes and inter-domain links; **(c)** the underlay multigraph ($G^W = (N^W, L^W)$) after topology abstraction; **(d)** controller network ($G^C = (N^C, L^C)$) obtained through simplification; **(e)** a single VN request ($G^V = (N^V, E^V)$) with CPU constraints in boxes and bandwidth constraints over links; **(f)** the same VN request (G^V) with location constraints on the virtual nodes shown in vertical boxes covering possible host physical nodes for them; **(g)** the embedded VN request with virtual nodes mapped into three different InPs; **(h)** the meta-VN request ($G_M^V = (N_M^V, L_M^V)$); **(i)** an InP-level view of the embedding (note that, InP #2 has not embedded any virtual node but still it is in the embedding by being in an inter-domain virtual link).

method [11]. All border nodes belonging to a single InP are collapsed to one single node corresponding to that InP (Figure 1c) in this representation resulting in a multigraph $G^W = (N^W, L^W)$, where N^W essentially is the set of InPs in the underlay and $L^W (= L^U)$ is a multiset of inter-domain links that connect the InPs. $G^C = (N^C, L^C)$ is a simple graph (Figure 1d) referring to the controller network [10], where $N^C (= N^W)$ represents the set of Controllers in InPs and L^C is the set of links between Controllers obtained from the multiset L^W.

2.2 VN request

Similar to substrate networks, we model VN requests as weighted undirected graphs and denote a VN request by $G^V = (N^V, E^V)$. We express the requirements on virtual nodes and virtual links in standard terms [6,8]. Figure 1e depicts a VN request with virtual node and link requirements.

Each VN request has an associated non-negative value R^V expressing how far a virtual node $n^V \in N^V$ can be placed from the location specified by $loc(n^V)$ [8], which can be interpreted as the preferred geolocation of that virtual node. Figure 1f shows the substrate nodes within the preferred geolocation for each virtual node using dashed vertical boxes.

2.3 VN assignment

From PolyViNE's point of view, an end-to-end VN assignment is performed on the controller network, G^C.

The VN request $G^V = (N^V, L^V)$ is partitioned into K subgraphs $G_k^V = (N_k^V, L_k^V)$ such that $N^V = \cup_k N_k^V$ and $L^V = (\cup_k L_k^V) \bigcup L_M^V$, where L_M^V is the set of virtual links that will cross domain boundaries. In this version of the PolyViNE protocol, we also consider subsets of L_M^V, $L_{M_{a_i}^{a_j}}^V$ where $L_M^V = \cup_{0 \le i \le k-1} \cup_{i<j} L_{M_{a_i}^{a_j}}^V$. We define $L_{M_{a_i}^{a_j}}^V$ to be the set of all virtual links with a single incident virtual node mapped in InP_{a_j} and another node mapped in InP_{a_l}, $0 \le l \le j$ and an inter-domain path mapping that crosses InP_{a_i}. Thus, $L_{M^{a_j}}^V = \cup_{i \le j} L_{M_{a_i}^{a_j}}^V$ is simply the set of all virtual links crossing inter-domain boundaries with one end mapped InP_{a_j}.

In Figure 1g, $K = 3$: $G_1^V = (\{A\}, \{\})$, $G_2^V = (\{B\}, \{\})$, $G_3^V = (\{C, D\}, \{CD\})$, and $L_M^V = \{AB, AC, BC, BD\}$. Each subgraph G_k^V can be collapsed into a single node to form the meta-VN request $G_M^V = (N_M^V, L_M^V)$ using a transformation function $\mathcal{F} : G_k^V \to N_M^V$ (Figure 1h) for simplicity.

Now we can formally express inter-domain VN embedding as two mappings, $\mathcal{M}_N : N_M^V \to N^C$ that embeds each subgraph to different InP and $\mathcal{M}_L : L_M^V \to L^C$ that embeds inter-domain links in the InP controller network. Figure 1(i) shows a possible InP-level embedding for the

VN request shown in Figure 1(e). Note that, *InP#2* has not embedded any virtual node but is still in the embedding by being in an inter-domain virtual link.

3 PolyViNE overview

In this section, we discuss PolyViNE design decisions, explain its workflow, and describe the distributed protocol that coordinates the PolyViNE embedding process.

3.1 Design choices

We have made the following design choices for PolyViNE aiming toward decentralization of the embedding process, promotion of policy-based decision making, and support for local agility within a flexible global framework.

3.1.1 Decentralized embedding

PolyViNE argues for using a distributed (decentralized) VN embedding solution over a centralized broker-based one. In a centralized solution, the broker will have to know the internal details and mutual agreements between all the InPs to make an informed embedding. However, InPs are traditionally inclined to share as little information as possible with any party. A distributed solution will allow for embedding based only on mutual agreements. Moreover, in a distributed market there will be no single-point-of-failure or no opportunity for a monopolistic authority (e.g., the broker).

3.1.2 Local autonomy with global competition

PolyViNE allows each InP to use its own policies and algorithms to take decisions without any external restrictions. However, it also creates a high level of competition among all the InPs by introducing competitive bidding at every level of distributed VN embedding. Even though each InP is free to make self-serving decisions, they have to provide competitive prices to take part and gain revenue in PolyViNE. To keep track of the behavior of InPs over time, a reputation management mechanism can also be introduced [12,13].

3.1.3 Location-assisted embedding

PolyViNE decision making and embedding process is deeply rooted into the location constraints that come with each VN request. After an InP embeds a part of a VN request, instead of blindly disseminating the rest of the request, it uses geographic constraints as beacons to route the request to other possible providers. PolyViNE aggregates and disseminates location information about how to reach a particular geographical region in the controller network and which InPs might be able to provide virtual resources in that region.

3.2 Workflow summary

PolyViNE is an enabling framework for multi-step distributed embedding of VN requests across InP boundaries. In its simplest form, an SP forwards its VN request to multiple known/trusted InPs; once they reply back with embeddings and corresponding prices, the SP chooses the VN embedding with the lowest price similar to a bidding process.

However, a complete end-to-end VN request may not be mappable by any individual InP. Instead, an InP can embed a part of the request and *outsource* the rest to other InPs in a similar bidding process giving rise to a recursive multi-step bidding mechanism. Not only does such a mechanism keep a VN embedding simple for an SP (since the SP does not need to contact all of the eventual InPs), but it also ensures competitive prices due to bidding at every step.

3.3 Restricting the search space

Through the PolyViNE protocol, when an InP receives a request to map a virtual network, it selects a connected subgraph of the VN to embed, and passes the remaining portion of the VN graph to other InPs. The process is started at the SP where it spawns off k^{SP} instances of the VN request. At each subsequent stage, InP_{a_i} spawns off $k^{InP_{a_i}}$ copies of the remaining portion of the VN request to an appropriate set of InPs determined by LAP.

The search space for all possible virtual network partitionings across the controller network is vast: $O(D^n)$ where D is the number of InPs in the controller network and n is the number of nodes in the virtual network. Thus, it is infeasible to attempt all possible partitionings of a virtual network across all InPs. PolyViNE, instead, takes a best effort approach to mapping virtual networks onto substrate networks by exploring a constant subset of partitionings.

The PolyViNE protocol attempts to navigate InPs for solutions in a breadth-first-like manner, while fixing maximum depth, d, and varying branching factor based on the pricing model discussed in 3.4, giving an upper bound of $O(k^{SP}(k^{InP_{max}})^d)$ visited InPs where $k^{InP_{max}}$ is defined to be the maximum branching factor at participating InPs. As discussed below, the budget for processing is fixed, and effectively, so is $k^{InP_{max}}$.

3.4 Pricing model

The PolyViNE protocol operates under the assumption that every entity in the controller network is behaving in its own best interest, attempting to maximize its profit. Each entity provides a service (embedding reservation) to its predecessor in the recursive process and requests a service from its successors. It then selects the service that provides the best price and rejects the other services. However, when an InP reserves resources for a partial embedding for its predecessor, it incurs an opportunity cost: those reserved resources could have been used to

service another VN request. For simplicity, we assume the opportunity cost is some constant per InP per VN request. Thus, an InP charges its predecessor a processing fee. This has the effect of producing a trade-off between exploration of the space of possible embedding solutions, and price. The more InPs visited and solutions explored, the more processing fees incurred. Thus, a high branching factor (k^{InP}) at an InP can be extremely expensive while a lower branching factor reduces the search space (potentially increasing prices), and increases the chance of failure (not finding a feasible solution to the VN constraints in the search horizon).

In this model, the SP sets an upper bound on the processing fees as a ratio relative to the embedding budget (e.g. 1 : 2 processing fee to embedding fees). For example, an InP may wish to embed a virtual network for a maximum of $5000 and pay no more than an additional $2500 for processing. The processing fee cap implicitly limits the search space. We leave it up to the discretion of the InP to choose how to distribute the processing fee allocation to successors, and how many successors to relay the VN request to (k^{InP}). k^{InP} may, for example, be expressed as a function of the processing fee allocation such that as the allocation grows so does the branching factor.

This model disincentivizes entities (SPs and InPs) from flooding the controller network to search for a cheaper solution. As each InP takes a processing fee, we eventually run out of money in the processing fee allocation, effectively reducing search depth. On the other hand, given a fixed fee allocation, a smaller branching factor increases search depth.

This model also provides InPs an additional incentive to participate in finding an embedding for a given virtual network as it will receive compensation for its work. When an entity sends an *EMBED* message to another entity, it enters a contractual agreement to pay a processing fee up to an upper bound it specifies.

3.5 A running example

To illustrate the details of the PolyViNE protocol, we introduce a simple running example in Figure 2. In this example, an SP issues a VN request (Figure 2a) to InP #1. InP #1 proceeds to map virtual node *A*, and *B* and virtual link *d* in Figure 2 (b)(c). It then forwards the remaining portion of the VN request to InP #2. InP # 2 is unable to map nodes from the VN request, and so it serves as a *relay* InP that may allocate bandwidth resources for virtual links that span multiple domains as need be (links a and c in this example). In turn, InP #2 forwards the remaining portion of the VN request to both InP #3 (Figure 2b) and InP # 4 (Figure 2c). In the recursive process, a sequence of InPs that terminates in failure or ultimately finds a feasible solution that spans that sequence is called a *flow* (see section 4.5). In the example in Figure 2, the solution of the

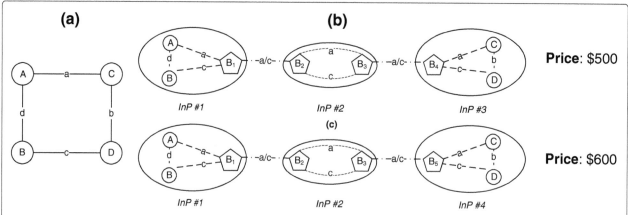

Figure 2 Two mappings and associated prices (b)(c) of a virtual network (a). In the top mapping **(b)**, VN **(a)** is mapped across InP#1, InP#2, and InP#3, while in the bottom mapping **(c)**, the VN is mapped across InP #1, InP #2, and InP #4.

flows in Figures 2 (a) and (b) produce mappings costing $500, and $600, respectively.

3.6 PolyViNE embedding protocol

In order to exchange information between the SP and the InPs, and to organize the distributed embedding process, a communication protocol must be established. We refer to this protocol as the PolyViNE Protocol, which is based on eleven types of messages. These messages are sent and received asynchronously between concerned InPs and the SP to carry out the embedding process from beginning to end. The protocol messages are described in the following:

- **EMBED** *(Req_id, G, M, state_table, budget_ remaining, processing_allocation_remaining, InPSet)*: This message is sent from the SP to InPs to initiate the embedding process of the VN request G with an empty *InPSet*. Upon receipt of this message, an InP_{a_i} will decide whether to process the request, or report failure based on its policies $\mathcal{P}_{a_i}^S$ as well as processing_allocation_remaining. If InP_{a_i} determines that it requires more money to process the message than is allocated by the SP, then it will report failure. If an InP processes the request but later determines that the allocation would go over budget_remaining, it will cancel the reservation, and report failure. An InP also uses this message to outsource the unmapped part of the request after appending itself to *InPSet*, and updating G and the partial embedding M as necessary. Req_id and state_table together uniquely identify a particular instance of the VN request (see section 4.5).
- **EMBED_SUCCESS** *(pred_state_id, M, Price(M), succ_id, InPSet)*: Once an embedding is successfully completed, an InP replies back to its predecessor with a price and M. *pred_state_id* is a unique identifier used to call up the

relevant state stored at the predecessor entity (SP or InP). The *succ_id* is a unique identifier indicating which InP sent the message.
- **EMBED_FAILURE** *(pred_state_id, succ_id, error_desc)*: In case of a failure, an InP replies back with a description outlining the reason of failure using *error_desc*.
- **EMBED_REJECT** *(pred_state_id, pred_id, succ_state_id)*: An InP may reject a mapping provided by one of its successors if its mapping does not meet the predecessor InP's policy, $P^S(\mathcal{M}^S) == FAIL$ or a better mapping has been discovered and chosen or the predecessor InP has itself received an *EMBED_REJECT* message and so it must also recursively reject successors.
- **EMBED_REJECT_ACK** *(pred_state_id, succ_id)*: When an InP is instructed to reject an embedding, it first recursively rejects any partial embeddings by successors, any inter-domain paths leading to it from predecessors, and finally deallocates all resources allocated locally for the given embedding request instance. Once all that has completed, it reports an acknowledgement to the predecessor that issued the *EMBED_REJECT* message.
- **LINK** $\left(pred\_state\_id, succ\_id, succ\_state\_id, L_{M_{a_i}^j}^{V_{a_j}}\right)$:
  Once an InP, InP_{a_j} finishes mapping a subgraph $G_{a_j}^V$, it sends a *LINK* message to each of its predecessors $InP_{a_i}, 0 \leq i \leq j$ to map $L_{M_{a_i}^j}^{V_{a_j}}$ if $L_{M_{a_i}^j}^{V_{a_j}} \neq \emptyset$, the set of virtual links that map to inter-domain paths that pass through InP_{a_i} and end in InP_{a_j}.
- **LINK_SUCCESS** *(pred_id, pred_state_id, succ_state_id)*: Once InP_{a_i} successfully maps $L_{M_{a_i}^j}^{V_{a_j}}$, it reports back the price of the link mapping to InP_{a_j}, along with pred_state_id, a unique identifier used to

call up the latest allocations made at InP_{a_i} for the given VN request instance.

- **LINK_FAILURE** (*pred_id, succ_state_id*): If InP_{a_i} fails to map $L^V_{M^{a_j}_{a_i}}$ due to insufficient resources or policy violations, it reports back *LINK_FAILURE* to InP_{a_j}.

- **LINK_REJECT** (*pred_state_id, succ_id*): If any InP_{a_i} fails to map $L^V_{M^{a_j}_{a_i}}$ or if InP_{a_j}'s partial embedding $\mathcal{M}$ is rejected by an *EMBED_REJECT* message, then InP_{a_j} issues *LINK_REJECT* to all InP_{a_i} requesting they release their reservations for $L^V_{M^{a_j}_{a_i}}$.

- **LINK_REJECT_ACK** (*pred_id, succ_state_id*): Once InP_{a_i} releases $L^V_{M^{a_j}_{a_i}}$, it replies to InP_{a_i} with an acknowledgement for rejecting a successful partial link embedding.

- **EMBED_ACCEPT** (*succ_state_id*): Once an SP decides on an embedding after receiving one or more *EMBED_SUCCESS* messages, it will acknowledge the embedding by directly contacting the InPs involved using this message.

3.7 SP Workflow

Since there is no centralized broker in PolyViNE, each SP must know at least one InP to send the VN request it wants to instantiate. However, sending the request to only one InP can encourage monopolistic behavior and reduce the likelihood of finding a feasible mapping. To create a competitive environment, we argue that an SP should send its VN request to $k^{SP} (\geq 1)$ InPs based on direct contact. Figure 3 depicts an SP sending embedding requests using the *EMBED* message to $k^{SP} = 1$ InPs, for the sake of simplicity. As soon as the receiving InPs have viable embeddings ($\mathcal{M}$) with corresponding prices (*Price* ($\mathcal{M}$)) or they fail, the k^{SP} InPs reply back with *EMBED_SUCCESS* or *EMBED_FAILURE* messages. Once the SP selects an embedding, it proceeds toward instantiating its VN by sending *EMBED_ACCEPT* messages to the InPs involved in the selected embedding and sends *EMBED_REJECT* messages to the InPs involved in unwanted embeddings.

4 InP Workflow

While an SP's workflow is straightforward with a single decision at the end, it shifts much more work to the InPs. An InP has to work through several steps of decision making, organizing, and coordinating between heterogeneous policies to complete the embedding process.

4.1 Local embedding

Upon receiving a VN request, an InP must decide whether to reject or to accept the request. It can reject a VN request outright, in case of possible policy violations or insufficient processing budget provided by the predecessor, returning an *EMBED_FAILURE* message to its predecessor. Even if there are no discernible policy violations, it might still need to reject a VN request if it fails to profitably embed any part of that request or if it fails to find an embedding that meets the budget constraints.

In order to decide which part of a VN request to embed, if at all, the InP can use existing intra-domain VN embedding algorithms [6,8] that can identify conflicting resource requirements in a VN request. This can be done iteratively by looking into the output of the linear programs used in both [6,8] without modifying the actual algorithms presented in those work, and trimming out parts of the virtual network until a feasible solution is found. However, we argue that this heuristic may not be sufficient for high quality or even feasible partial embeddings. In particular, we must ensure that if an InP maps a virtual link, it also maps the two nodes incident to it. We also wish to minimize the number of virtual links that map across multiple domains as inter-domain paths tend to be long and thus are more costly.

In case of a failure, the InP will send back an *EMBED_FAILURE* message (optionally with reasons for the failure). However, sometimes the InP might know of other InPs that it believes will be able to embed part or whole of the VN request. In that case, it will *relay* the VN request forwarding the *EMBED* message to that InP after adding itself to the *InPSet*. In Figure 3, *InP#2* is relaying the VN request *G'* to *InP#3*.

4.2 Reserving inter-domain paths

PolyViNE expects each InP_{a_j} to complete a mapping of all virtual links in the set $L^V_{M^{a_j}}$ prior to forwarding the remainder of the VN request to new participants. This ensures that no additional InPs will be brought in to participate in the mapping before current participants are sure inter-domain paths are feasible between them and satisfy their respective policies.

At a given stage j of the embedding process, InP_{a_j} receives an *EMBED* message that contains an ordered set of InPs participating so far, *InPset* containing $InP_{a_i}, 0 \leq i < j$. For each virtual link, $l^m_k \in L^V_{M^{a_j}}$, InP_{a_j} must identify the predecessor $InP_{a_m} \in InPset, 0 \leq m < j$ mapping the other node incident to l^m_k. Once identified, InP_{a_j} adds each l^m_k to $L^V_{M^{a_j}_{a_i}} \forall m \leq i \leq j$. Subsequently, for each set $L^V_{M^{a_j}_{a_i}} \neq \emptyset$, InP_{a_j} issues *LINK* messages containing that set to each InP_{a_i} instructing it to map the virtual links in $L^V_{M^{a_j}_{a_i}}$ across its domain.

Once InP_{a_i} receives the set $L^V_{M^{a_j}_{a_i}}$, it must decide how to proceed with link mapping. For each virtual link $l^m_k \in$

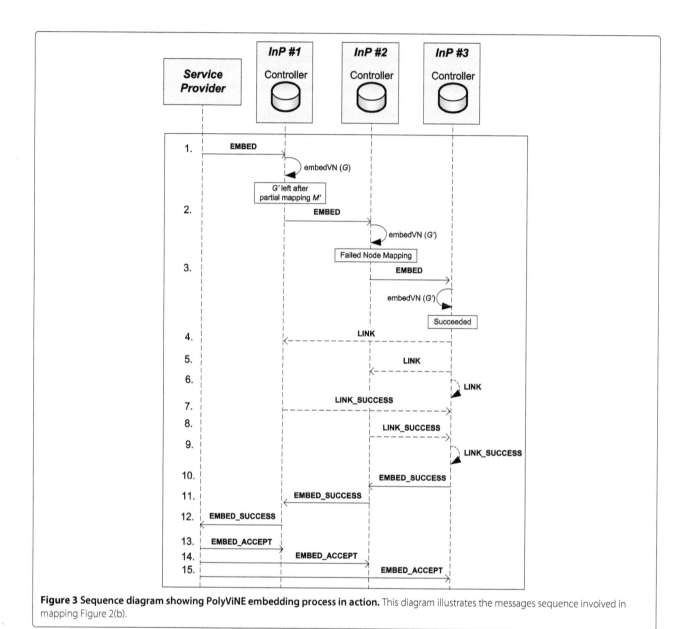

Figure 3 Sequence diagram showing PolyViNE embedding process in action. This diagram illustrates the messages sequence involved in mapping Figure 2(b).

$L^V_{M^{a_j}_{a_i}}$, InP_{a_i} considers its index i in $InPset$ relative to InP_{a_m} in $InPset$:

1. **i = m:** InP_{a_i} must map a path from the virtual node incident to l^m_k in InP_{a_m} to the border node leading to $InP_{a_{m+1}}$.
2. **m < i < j:** InP_{a_i} must map a path from a border node leading to $InP_{a_{i-1}}$ to the border node leading to $InP_{a_{i+1}}$
3. **i = j:** InP_{a_i} must map a path from the border node leading to $InP_{a_{i-1}}$ to the virtual node incident to l^m_k in InP_{a_i}.

If all the virtual links specified by the *LINK* message are mapped successfully by the receiving InP (no policies

are violated and physical resources are available to satisfy the paths), then it responds with a *LINK_SUCCESS* to the sender. Otherwise, the recipient will respond with a *LINK_FAILURE* message to the sender.

An embedding at a given InP is considered successful if and only if at least one node is mapped by the InP and all inter-domain paths are successfully mapped. If one or more predecessor InPs are unable to map inter-domain paths, then the resource reservations must be released. The current InP issues a *LINK_REJECT* message to all InPs that responded with a *LINK_SUCCESS* message. The InP then waits for acknowledgement that resources have been freed through a *LINK_REJECT_ACK* message. Once all pending acknowledgements have been received, the InP releases the resources it allocated locally and issues an *EMBED_FAILURE* message to its direct predecessor (see section 4.9 for more details on roll-back of resource allocations).

4.3 Message complexity

The design of PolyViNE allows for a fairly straightforward analysis of message complexity. If we assume that the implementation of the protocol at each InP does not involve inter-domain paths through new InPs that have not seen the given instance of the VN request, then in the worst case, with n participating InPs, each will visit all predecessors to map virtual links to inter-domain paths. The number of participants is bounded by d. Thus, the message complexity to map a virtual network is $O(min(n, d)^2)$. PolyViNE attempts a total of $O(k^{SP}(k^{InP_{max}})^d)$ mappings (recall section 3.3) giving a total complexity of $O(k^{SP}(k^{InP_{max}})^d min(n, d)^2)$.

4.4 Revisiting our running example

Figure 3 continues our running example by demonstrating the message sequence involved in mapping the VN in Figure 2 (a) corresponding to the flow in Figure 2 (b). A sequence of 15 messages are exchanged:

1. The service provider issues a VN mapping request to InP #1.

2. It performs a partial mapping of the VN request onto its substrate network. The remaining portion of the VN request is forwarded to InP #2.

3. InP #2 fails to map the VN request, and so it *relays* the *EMBED* message to InP #3. Subsequently, InP #3 successfully maps the remaining portion of the request, leaving virtual link to inter-domain path mappings remaining.

4. InP #3 sends a *LINK* message to InP #1 containing the virtual link reference set $L_{M_1^3}^V = \{a, c\}$.

5. InP #3 sends a *LINK* message to InP #2 containing the virtual link reference set $L_{M_2^3}^V = \{a, c\}$.

6. InP #3 sends a *LINK* message to itself containing the virtual link reference set $L_{M_3^3}^V = \{a, c\}$.

7. InP #1 successfully maps paths for the virtual links in $L_{M_1^3}^V = \{a, c\}$ from the substrate node resources reserved for virtual nodes A and B to the B_1 border node. Additionally, it allocates sufficient bandwidth for $L_{M_1^3}^V$ on the B_2B_3 inter-domain link (see Figure 2). It reports back *LINK_SUCCESS* to InP #3 including the total cost of the mapping of $L_{M_1^3}^V$.

8. InP #2 successfully maps paths for the virtual links in $L_{M_2^3}^V = \{a, c\}$ from the B_2 border node to the B_3 border node. Additionally, it allocates sufficient bandwidth for $L_{M_2^3}^V$ on the B_3B_4 inter-domain link (see Figure 2). It reports back *LINK_SUCCESS* to

InP #3 including the total cost of the mapping of $L_{M_2^3}^V$.

9. InP #3 successfully maps paths for the virtual links in $L_{M_3^3}^V = \{a, c\}$ from the B_4 border node to the substrate node resources reserved for virtual nodes C and D. It reports back *LINK_SUCCESS* to itself including the total cost of the mapping of $L_{M_3^3}^V$.

10. InP #3 sees that all participating InPs have reported back *LINK_SUCCESS* and so the VN mapping is complete. It accumulates the prices it received from the *LINK_SUCCESS* messages and adds the cost of its own local mapping to produce a total that it sends back to its predecessor InP #2 within an *EMBED_SUCCESS* message.

11. InP #2 receives InP #3's *EMBED_SUCCESS* message. It compares the price it receives from InP #3 ($300) with that of InP #4 ($400), rejects InP #4's solution, and selects InP #3's solution (see Figure 4). It adds its own local embedding price ($0 in this case, as it did not map any nodes, and the link allocations in InP #2 were accounted for by InP #3's offer) to produce a total that it sends back to InP #1 within an *EMBED_SUCCESS* message.

12. InP #1 receives InP #2's *EMBED_SUCCESS* message. In our example $k^{InP_1} = 1$, and so InP #1 immediately adds the cost of its local mapping ($200) to the price of InP #2's solution ($300). It reports the total price of the mapping ($500) back to the SP.

13. After the solution in Figure 2(c) is rejected, the SP accepts InP #1's mapping, allowing the InP to instantiate and setup virtual machines on substrate nodes.

14. The SP accepts InP #2's mapping, allowing the InP to instantiate and setup virtual machines on substrate nodes.

15. The SP accepts InP #3's mapping, allowing the InP to instantiate and setup virtual machines on substrate nodes.

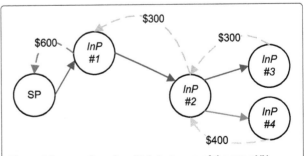

Figure 4 Propagation of multiple instances of the same VN request in the controller network throughout the embedding process. Each InP performs a partial embedding of a request instance and outsources the rest to another InP. The dashed lines demonstrate the back-propagation of accumulated prices toward the SP.

The message sequence corresponding to the solution in Figure 2 (c) would be very similar to the sequence in Figure 3 save for the final few message exchanges. The solution at InP #4 costs more than that at InP #3, and so it will be rejected. In particular, at step 11, InP #4 would receive an *EMBED_REJECT* message from InP #2, and would subsequently issue *LINK_REJECT* messages to each of the participating InPs. InP #4 would wait for *LINK_REJECT_ACK* from the participating InPs, and then will report *EMBED_REJECT_ACK* to its predecessor, InP #2 (see section 4.9 for more details on roll-back of resource allocations).

4.5   Message flows

When an InP receives an *EMBED* message with virtual network G and finds a mapping $\mathcal{M}$ of some subgraph of G, the InP reserves those resources for that particular VN request. The resources are reserved until either the PolyViNE protocol determines that there are no successors that can satisfy the remaining portion of the request or a predecessor has rejected the mapping provided by the current InP. Subsequently, when an InP receives a *LINK* message, it must call up the previous resource allocation associated with the current instance of the virtual network mapping request and bundle any link allocations it performs with the previous resource allocations.

Continuing our running example: In Figure 5, InP #3, and InP #4 both map subgraphs of the VN request issued by the SP. They, then, both independently send *LINK* messages to InP #1 to map inter-domain paths from their respective subgraphs to the subgraph mapped by InP #1.

We define a flow to be an ordered set of InPs visited to map a given virtual network VN_{ij} with a unique identifier i, requested by some service provider, SP_j. It is evident that the flow $f_1^{VN_{ij}} = \{InP\#1, InP\#2, InP\#3\}$ and $f_2^{VN_{ij}} = \{InP1, InP\#2, InP\#4\}$ corresponding to our running example in Figure 2 (b) and (c) respectively are mutually exclusive, as they are two different instances of the same VN request and, ultimately, at most one instance will be accepted by the SP. Thus, while the two instances share the same node embedding state produced by the initial $EMBED_1$ message, their subsequent link allocation state produced by the *LINK* messages are different and independent. Thus, any implementation of PolyViNE must be able to identify flows in order to be able to store and call up the appropriate state specific to that flow. We propose a solution to identify flows and their associated state at an InP. At any point in the embedding process, an InP only sees a prefix of a final InP set. After processing an *EMBED* message, an InP will spawn off k^{InP} mutually exclusive instances of the VN request to map its remaining portion. At this point, the k^{InP} flows diverge but they share a common prefix: the state formed in response to the *EMBED* message.

We propose bundling the allocations performed in response to *EMBED* and *LINK* messages in transactional state objects which we will call *EmbeddingState* objects from this point forward. Allocating an *EmbeddingState* object also reserves an associated unique state identifier, called an *EmbeddingId*, which is used to call up state. *EmbeddingIds* at each InP in the flow so far are bundled in *EMBED* messages in a state table. The state table is simply a mapping from a unique InP identifier (such as an IP address), to an *EmbeddingId* for the latest *EmbeddingState* object for the flow at the given InP.

When a given InP, InP_{a_j} sends a *LINK* message to a predecessor InP_{a_i}, it includes the *EmbeddingId* associated with the flow at InP_{a_i} that it received through *EMBED* message's state table. InP_{a_i} creates a new *EmbeddingState* object, as a child of the previous *EmbeddingState* for that flow, along with a new *EmbeddingId*. When the link allocation successfully completes, InP_{a_i} reports *LINK_SUCCESS* back to InP_{a_j} along with the new *EmbeddingId*. As the PolyViNE embedding process progresses, InPs participating in the process begin to form chains of *EmbeddingState* objects associated with the flow. Flows that share a common prefix may share a prefix of an *EmbeddingState* chain, but diverge at some point, thus forming an *EmbeddingState* tree. Flows that do not share a prefix form disconnected state at any given InP. Thus, for a given InP and a given VN request, PolyViNE state consists of a forest of state trees.

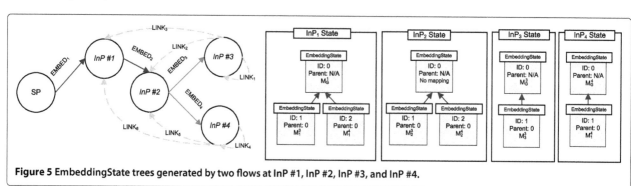

Figure 5 EmbeddingState trees generated by two flows at InP #1, InP #2, InP #3, and InP #4.

In our running example, in Figure 5, the two flows $f_1^{VN_{ij}}$, and $f_2^{VN_{ij}}$ generate four state trees at the four participating InPs. For the sake of brevity, we carefully examine how just InP #1's state tree was formed:

1. When InP #1 maps a part of the VN request VN_{ij}, it allocates an *EmbeddingState* object, stores the mapping $\mathcal{M}_G^1$ with the *EmbeddingId* 0.
2. The mapping $(ID(InP\#1) \rightarrow 0)$ is stored in the state table attached within the message $EMBED_2$.
3. InP #3, and InP #4 send the messages $LINK_3$ and $LINK_6$ respectively to InP #1 with the field $pred\_state\_id = EmbeddingId$ 0 allowing InP #1 to call up the state associated with $\mathcal{M}_G^1$.
4. When InP #1 maps the link allocation, $\mathcal{M}_1^3$, it creates a new *EmbeddingState* object with a InP-level unique *EmbeddingId* 1 as a child to the *EmbeddingState* object housing the $\mathcal{M}_G^1$ mapping. Similarly, when InP #1 maps the link allocation $\mathcal{M}_1^4$, it creates another *EmbeddingState* object attached to the same parent with *EmbeddingId* 2.

    InP #1 responds to InP #3 and InP #4 with $LINK\_SUCCESS$ messages with $pred\_state\_id =$ 1 and 2, respectively.

    When a subsequent message requests state associated with one of the two new *EmbeddingIds*, we are able to disambiguate between the two flows, despite their sharing a common subgraph mapping.

4.6 Resource management

Resource reservation blowup is a major issue in any implementation of PolyViNE. In our implementation of a simulation of the PolyViNE protocol, we quickly realized that in the worst case, the resources allocated in a single InP could grow exponentially as a function of d, the maximum search depth. The total number of flows explored by PolyViNE to find a good inter-domain VN embedding is $O(k^{SP}(k^{InP_{max}})^d)$. In a pathological case, some InP, InP_{a_j} may be involved in as many as $O(k^{SP}(k^{InP_{max}})^d)$ flows. If an InP reserved resources for each flow of a given VN, then we could very quickly end up in a situation where a single, relatively simple VN request drains an InP of all its available resources.

However, we note that for any given VN request, a service provider will ultimately only accept a single flow of the $O(k^{SP}(k^{InP_{max}})^d)$ which will be explored. This means that an InP only needs to reserve sufficient resources for any one such flow per VN request. We denote the capacities on all substrate nodes and links in InP_{a_j}, $C(G_{a_j}^S) = (C(N_{a_j}^S), L(N_{a_j}^S))$ with vectors $C(N_{a_j}^S) = \{C(n_{a_j}^0), C(n_{a_j}^1), ...\}$ for nodes and $C(L_{a_j}^S) = \{C(l_{a_j}^0), C(l_{a_j}^1), ...\}$ for links where each component indicates the maximum capacity of that resource. Each *EmbeddingState* object, $E_{a_j}^k$ at InP_{a_j} with *EmbeddingId* k can be thought to be composed of two resource allocation vectors, one for nodes and one for links, indicating the resources allocated by that state object in addition to its parent state object: $C(E_{a_j}^k) = (C(N_{a_j}^k), C(L_{a_j}^k)) + C(Parent(E_{a_j}^k))$.

The InP then simply applies a component-wise maximum (cmax) of the multiset representing all resource allocation state for a given VN request, VN_{b_i}, $E_{a_j}^{b_i} = \{C(E_{a_j}^k) : \forall \ EmbeddingId \ k \in VN_{b_i}\}$ and reserves those resources. As more allocations are made for VN_{b_i} at InP_{a_j}, the InP updates its $E_{a_j}^{b_i}$ multiset and adjusts its resource reservations accordingly, leaving $C(G_{a_j}^S) - C(E_{a_j}^k)$ resources available for other VN requests. As all the mutually exclusive flows are for the same virtual network, the allocations at any given InP will be relatively similar and so, the component-wise maximum will typically not be much more than those required of any one flow.

The internals of our running example: Let's consider the substrate network of InP #2 in Figure 6 of our running example. Recall from Figure 5, InP #2 has three *EmbeddingIds* (0, 1, and 2) associated with state for VN_{ij}. In Figure 6, we look at the resources allocated by the mappings associated with each of the three *EmbeddingIds*. *EmbeddingId* 0 has no associated resource reservations. *EmbeddingId* 1 and 2 refer to mutually exclusive resources allocated by InP #2 on behalf of InP #3 and InP #4

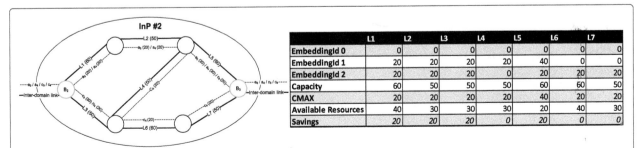

	L1	L2	L3	L4	L5	L6	L7
EmbeddingId 0	0	0	0	0	0	0	0
EmbeddingId 1	20	20	20	20	40	0	0
EmbeddingId 2	20	20	20	0	20	20	20
Capacity	60	50	50	50	60	60	50
CMAX	20	20	20	20	40	20	20
Available Resources	40	30	30	30	20	40	30
Savings	20	20	20	0	20	0	0

Figure 6 A look at the substrate network and resource reservation vectors of InP #2 in our running example.

respectively. Both resource vectors correspond to mappings of virtual links *a*, and *c* from border node B_2 to border node B_3. Note that the two resource vectors correspond to similar, but not identical mappings onto InP #2's substrate network. At most, the SP will accept one of the flows, and so we don't need to allocate resources so that all of the vectors can be satisfied simultaneously. Instead we take the component-wise (i.e. per-resource) maximum resource requirements and reserve that (*CMAX*) vector. Note that the last row of the table in Figure 6 indicates significant resource savings as a result of this technique. Typically, we can expect the savings to grow linearly with the number of flows, enabling much larger search spaces.

4.7   Forwarding

If an InP can only partially embed a VN request, it will have to forward the rest of the request to other InPs in the controller network in order to complete the VN request. An InP should take care to not forward a VN request to another InP already in the *InPSet* to avoid cycles. For example, *InP#1* in Figure 3 is forwarding the unmapped VN request *G'* to *InP#2*. Similar to SPs, InPs also forward the request to $k^{InP} (\geq 1)$ InPs for similar reasons (e.g., competitive prices). While forwarding a request, an InP can prefer to perform a transformation on the VN request in order to hide the details of its mapping (as in Figure 1h). At this point, it can use one of the two possible methods for unmapped VN request forwarding:

- *Recursive forwarding:* In this case, when an InP forwards a VN request, the receiver InP embeds part of it based on its policies and forwards the rest further away to another InP.
- *Iterative forwarding:* In iterative forwarding, the receiver InP return the control back to the sender InP once it is finished with embedding.

In any case, the forwarding decision is a non-trivial one and requires careful consideration. We believe that instead of blindly forwarding based on some heuristics, we can do informed forwarding by utilizing the location constraints attached to all the virtual nodes in a VN request. Details of this forwarding scheme are presented in the next section.

4.8   Back-propagation

The VN request proceeds from one InP to the next, until either the maximum number of participants *d* has been reached, there are no available InPs to send the request to or the VN request has been satisfied completely. In case of a successful embedding of a VN request, the *EMBED_SUCCESS* message carries back the embedding details and corresponding price. At each step of this back-propagation of *EMBED_SUCCESS* and

EMBED_FAILURE messages, the sender InP can select mappings based on internal policies or lower price or some other criteria and rejects the other successful embeddings by issuing *EMBED_REJECT* messages to the appropriate successors.

As VN embeddings follow paths back to the SP, the prices are accumulated and the SP ends up with multiple choices (Figure 4).

4.9   Resource allocation roll-back

Within a single domain, a VN embedding is transactional in nature, as an embedding must be completed as a whole, or not at all. In the multi-domain scenario, each InP is free to map a subgraph of the embedding and so the algorithm used to perform that partial mapping may or may not be transactional (it's up to the discretion of the InP how to implement it). However, from the SP's perspective, the multi-domain scenario is the same as that of the single domain: it expects either a completed embedding reservation or a report of failure. In other words, in a given flow, either all participating InPs succeed in reserving resources or none of them reserve resources. This means that the PolyViNE protocol itself must provide a mechanism to roll-back the work done by other InPs in a given flow once a failure or rejection occurs. An SP is expected to accept only one flow, and reject all other flows. Rejection initiates a roll-back process of all resources allocated for that flow.

Two messages in the protocol can initiate resource allocations within an InP: *EMBED*, and *LINK*. Thus, corresponding roll-back messages must exist in the protocol: *EMBED_REJECT* and *LINK_REJECT*. In order to simplify the implementation of a controller's PolyViNE message handling system and avoid race conditions, associated acknowledgement messages *EMBED_REJECT_ACK* and *LINK_REJECT_ACK* act as barriers to ensure that roll-back occurs in the opposite order to allocation. Note that link allocations corresponding to the set $L^V_{M^{a_j}}$ for a given InP_{a_j} are unordered as there are no dependencies among them. However, state dependencies exist between subgraph allocations on one InP and the next, and so PolyViNE ensures that roll-back occurs in the opposite order to allocation through the *_ACK* messages.

As previously discussed, an InP, InP_{a_j}, will report back *EMBED_FAILURE* in case it fails to map the remaining portion of an embedding. Failure reasons include:

1. The embedding is incomplete at InP_{a_j} and no successors are found or all successors fail for some reason.
2. An InP participating in an inter-domain path allocation on behalf of InP_{a_j} responds back to InP_{a_j} with *LINK_FAILURE*.
3. An embedding solution fails to meet the budget constraints.

4. The processing fee budget has been exhausted.
5. Internal InP policies do not allow the embedding to proceed.

A variation of our running example: To illustrate the roll-back process, we consider a variation of our running example shown in Figure 7. In this variation, we assume that InP #2 is unable to map $L^V_{M^3_2} = \{a, c\}$ or $L^V_{M^4_2} = \{a, c\}$ onto its substrate network. Thus, in step 8, InP #2 reports *LINK_FAILURE* to InP #3 (and InP #4, not shown). In the sequence digram, we see that InP #3 observes that InP #1 and InP #3 were able to map their respective *LINK* requests, but InP #2 was not. As an inter-

domain embedding must either succeed wholly or release all resources across all participating InPs, InP #3 must now begin the roll-back process.

InP #3 issues *LINK_REJECT* messages to InPs #1 and itself (for consistency purposes) with the appropriate *EmbeddingIds* informing them to deallocate their respective allocations for virtual links a and c. InP #1 and InP #3 release their link mappings, and report *LINK_REJECT_ACK* to InP #3 (steps 12-13). Subsequently, InP #3 releases its subgraph embedding for the VN request and reports *EMBED_FAILURE* to its predecessor, InP #2 (step 14). InP #2 also sees that InP #4 has failed. Thus, InP #2 has seen that all its successors fail, and so it must also fail. InP #2 has no subgraph embedding,

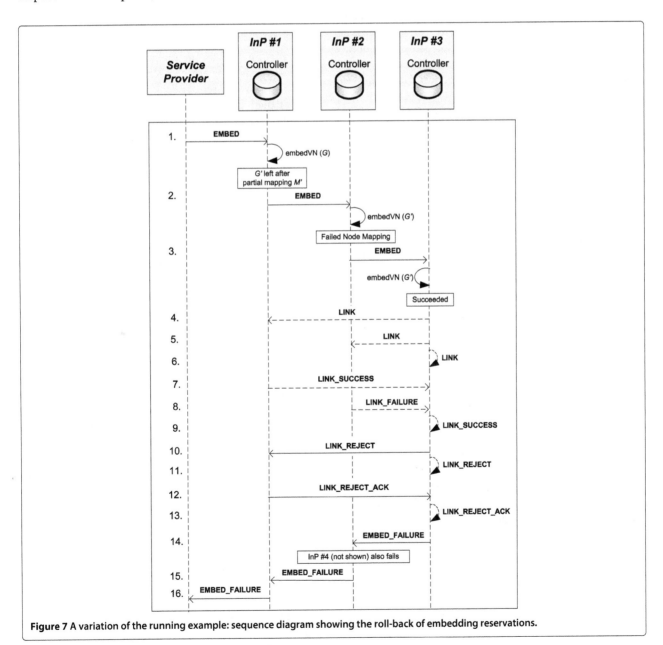

Figure 7 A variation of the running example: sequence diagram showing the roll-back of embedding reservations.

and so it simply reports *EMBED_FAILURE* to its predecessor InP #1 (step 15). InP #1 has only one successor and so it must fail as well. It releases its subgraph embedding for the VN, and reports *EMBED_FAILURE* to the SP.

5   Location aware forwarding

Naïvely an InP can forward a VN request to a set of InPs in the controller network at random. However, this decision is blind to the location requirements of the virtual nodes and the availability of virtual resources at the destination InP to satisfy the constraints for the VN request. This may result in high failure rate or prices well above the fair value. To avoid flooding a VN request or sending it to random InPs which might be unable to meet the constraints of the request, we propose using location constraints associated with unassigned virtual nodes to assist an InP in making this decision. Location constraints of the virtual nodes together with the location information of the underlay will allow informed VN request forwarding in the controller network.

To accommodate such location aware forwarding, we introduce a hierarchical geographic addressing scheme with support for aggregation, named COST. InPs in PolyViNE must associate COST addresses with all the substrate nodes and SPs must express location requirements in terms of COST. Controllers in different InPs publish/disseminate information about the geographic locations of their nodes along with the unit price of their resources. They can then aggregate and disseminate data collected from all neighboring Controllers to build their own knowledge bases of location to InP mappings, each accompanied by path vectors of InPs in the controller network and corresponding prices. We propose Location Awareness Protocol (LAP) to perform this task. Careful readers will notice in the following that COST and LAP are significantly influenced by BGP.

5.1   COST addressing scheme

As outlined in the problem formulation (Section 2), each virtual node in a VN request comes with a permissible geographic region in which it must be embedded. One design question at this point is how to represent and encode the geolocation. We have chosen a hierarchical geolocation representation scheme similar to [14] with the form *Continent.cOuntry.State.ciTy* (hence the name *COST*). Even though in this paper we are using a simple postal address like scheme for simplicity, any hierarchical geolocation representation system will work with PolyViNE.

A virtual node may restrict its location preference to any prefix in this addressing scheme. For example, to restrict a node within Canada, one may assign the address NA.CA.* to a virtual node. This indicates that beyond requiring that the node be mapped within Canada, the SP does not care where in the country it is ultimately mapped.

On the other hand, each substrate node has a complete COST address associated with it. This address indicates within which city lies the given substrate node. If an InP is not willing to share the exact location, it can always choose a higher level address. For example, instead of announcing nodes in Toronto using NA.CA.ON.Toronto, the InP can announce NA.CA.ON.*. However, such announcements can result in receiving of VN requests that it may never be able to satisfy, which will affect its reputation among other InPs.

5.2   Location awareness protocol (LAP)

Location Awareness Protocol (LAP) is a hybrid of Gossip and Publish/Subscribe protocols that assists an InP in making informed decisions about which InPs to forward a VN request to without making policy violations, and thus progressing toward completing the VN embedding. Controllers in different InPs keep track of the geolocations of their internal substrate nodes in COST format and announce availability and prices of available resources to their neighbors using LAP updates in the controller network. This information is aggregated and propagated throughout the controller network to create global view of the resources in the underlay in each Controller's LAP database.

Initially, LAP operates as a path vector based gossip protocol. Every InP in the controller network informs its neighbors of where its nodes are located along with estimated unit prices for its resources on a per location basis. Whenever a Controller receives a LAP update, it updates its LAP database and before announcing updates to its neighbors it adds itself to the path vector. Note that keeping complete paths allows avoiding unnecessary forwarding toward and through InPs that might violate SP's policies or originating InP's policies. InPs can also tune this price to encourage or discourage VN request forwarding to them. In steady-state, each InP should know about all the InPs with nodes in a given geographic region along with price estimations of embedding on their substrate networks. Figure 8 shows an example LAP database.

However, in a rapidly changing environment with continuously fluctuating prices, gossip may not be sufficient to disseminate updated prices in a timely fashion. To reduce the number of failures stemming from staleness of pricing information, we propose extensions to LAP using a Publish/Subscribe mechanism along with its basic gossip protocol. By using this mechanism, any InP will be able to subscribe to announcements of Controllers that are not its direct neighbors. While we leave VN request routing decisions to the discretion of InPs, an InP may use the pricing information to prefer forwarding the VN request to a lower priced InP, all other things being equal.

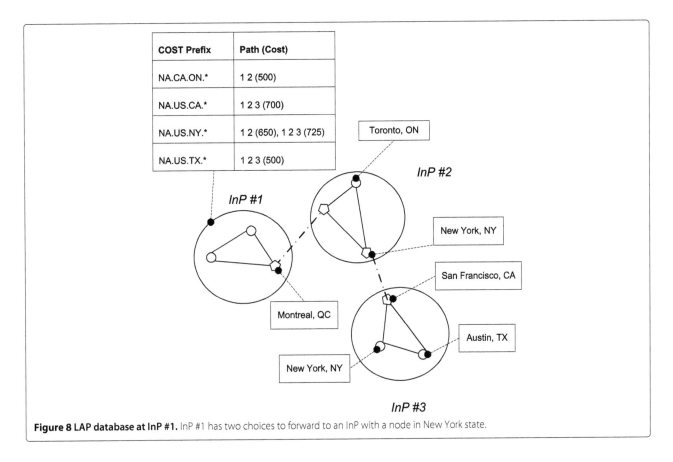

COST Prefix	Path (Cost)
NA.CA.ON.*	1 2 (500)
NA.US.CA.*	1 2 3 (700)
NA.US.NY.*	1 2 (650), 1 2 3 (725)
NA.US.TX.*	1 2 3 (500)

Figure 8 LAP database at InP #1. InP #1 has two choices to forward to an InP with a node in New York state.

The question that remains open to more investigation is why would an InP be honest when announcing pricing estimates? We believe that a reputation metric – indicating long-term accuracy of an InP's pricing estimate to the actual cost of establishing a VN request – is necessary to remedy this situation. We would like to integrate such a reputation metric within LAP to allow dissemination of path vectors attributed with corresponding prices and overall reputation score of the InPs on the paths. An InP will then be able to use pricing and reputation scores to rank multiple paths to a common destination to make a forwarding decision.

6 Numerical evaluation

We have written a 12000 line multi-threaded C++ simulator that allows independent responses from various entities in the controller network. The simulation comprises a complete implementation of the entire set of protocol messages discussed in section 3.6.

We examine four sets of experiments. In our first set of experiments, we look at some of the properties of inter-domain embeddings generated by PolyViNE as the VN request size (node count) is varied. In our second set of experiments, we look at some of the properties of the PolyViNE embeddings as the pricing model attributes are varied (embedding and processing budgets). In our third

set of experiments, we look at properties of PolyViNE embeddings as we vary the maximum number of InPs involved in a mapping. In our last set of experiments, we examine the reliability of the PolyViNE protocol and the cost of embeddings generated in the case of lost or stale LAP information.

Each experiment is run to completion (a VN request has completed) multiple times per data point to produce the averaged results presented here. We found that that variation in tests was very small and so we did not include confidence intervals. Unless otherwise specified, we have used the following settings: For each experiment, we randomly create a controller network with 60 InPs. Each InP network consists of 120 to 150 nodes and 540 to 600 links on average. Each node has a maximum CPU capacity uniformly chosen from 1 to 100 CPU units, and each link has a maximum bandwidth capacity of 100 bandwidth units. Locations of substrate nodes are sampled from a normal distribution with a mean, and variance chosen uniformly from 0 to 255 representing 256 different major cities. InPs with low variance location distributions are effectively local or regional InPs, while high variance InPs have nodes that span the globe. The per unit cost per resource is chosen from a normal distribution with a mean sampled from a prior, per InP, normal distribution (of mean 4, variance 1) and a variance of 1. This means that some InPs will tend to be cheaper than others, on average.

Unless otherwise specified, each VN request has an expected value of 30 nodes, and 120 links (±20%). Each virtual node has a maximum CPU capacity uniformly chosen from 1 to 25, and each virtual link has a maximum bandwidth capacity of 1 to 15, chosen uniformly as well. Locations are chosen uniformly from 256 major cities represented in the controller network.

Each InP charges an *embedding processing fee* of 1 unit (±20%). A maximum InP count per flow (d) is a property of the VN request. Based on this property, an InP estimates the maximum branching factor it can use so that up to d InPs can be involved in a flow and uses that branching factor. Thus, the entire processing budget is always consumed. The processing fees are not refunded if the flow fails.

6.1 Varying VN request size
We begin by varying the number of nodes in a VN request and observing the properties of the embeddings and the success rate of the flows. In each experiment, VN requests have n nodes (where n is varied) and $4n$ links. We also fix $K^{SP} = 7$, maximum InPs per flow to 9, processing budget : embedding budget to 0.75:1, and embedding budget to 25000. The goal of this experiment is to test the limits of PolyViNE's ability to find solutions given a fixed set of resources available to it (Large VN requests relative to InP resources, limited processing and embedding budgets, and thus limited search space). We expect that after a certain point, VN requests will get so large that no mapping will be possible, either because the request hits InP resource limits or it hits budget limits.

In our first experiment in Figure 9, we look at the number of nodes mapped by the first set of InP neighboring the request-generating SP as we vary the VN request size.

Figure 9 demonstrates that the number of nodes mapped by the first-hop InPs grows linearly with the size of the VN request. With small requests, virtually the entire network is mapped by the first InP. As request sizes approach the limits of the resources available at the first-hop InP, the number of nodes mapped by the first-hop InP flattens out at about 35 nodes. When we attempted random VN requests larger than 45 nodes, we found that no solutions are found by the PolyViNE protocol, regardless of the size of the search space.

In our second experiment in Figure 10, we looked at the number of InPs that are involved in a successfully satisfied VN request. In this experiment, we only consider InPs that contribute substrate node resources to the VN mapping, and not InPs that simply reserved bandwidth as *relays*. We see that the the number of InPs involved appears to grow linearly with the size of the VN request but with a very small slope.

In our third experiment in Figure 11, we look at the fraction of successful flows relative to the total number of flows of a VN request. We see that up to 35 nodes, all flows are successful. After 35 nodes the success rate drops dramatically, and after 50 nodes (not shown), it reaches 0.

In our fourth experiment in Figure 12, we look at the the impact on embedding cost as we increase the VN request size. We see a linear relationship between the VN request size and the embedding cost (as is expected), where roughly each node added to a VN request costs about 250 units. Somewhat surprisingly, the higher cost of virtual links mapped across inter-domain paths is not apparent here. This may be due to the relative sparseness of the VN requests we have examined.

6.2 Varying embedding budget and processing fee budget
In this experiment, we vary the embedding budget and processing budget of a VN request and observe

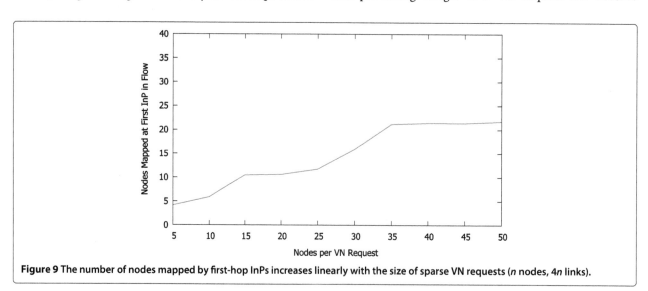

Figure 9 The number of nodes mapped by first-hop InPs increases linearly with the size of sparse VN requests (*n* nodes, 4*n* links).

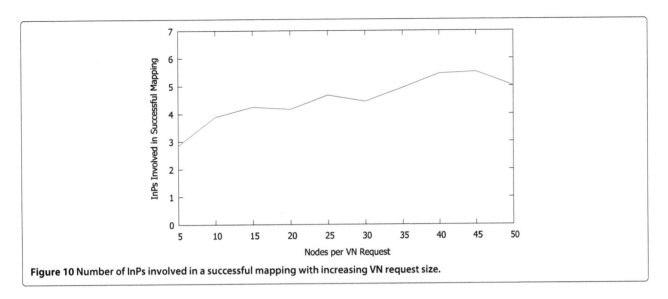

Figure 10 Number of InPs involved in a successful mapping with increasing VN request size.

their impact on the success rate and total embedding cost (embedding + processing). In each experiment, VN requests have 30 nodes and 120 links ($\pm$ 20%). We also fix $K^{SP} = 7$, and maximum InPs per flow to 8.

In our first experiment of this set (Figure 13), we vary both the processing budget and the embedding budget, and observe their impact on the success rate of flows of the VN request. We observe that relatively small changes to the processing budget have little effect on the success rate of a VN request flow, with significant variance up and down as the processing budget increases. This can be attributed to the high cost of increasing k^{InP} at any given InP. Given d, the target maximum number of InPs visited per flow, each InP picks a k^{InP} so that sufficient money remains in the processing budget so that up to d InPs are involved in a flow, if necessary. In other words, for an InP to increase the branching factor k^{InP} by x%, its processing budget must increase by $O((1 + \frac{x}{100})^{d_{remaining}})$

where $d_{remaining}$ is the number of hops remaining to reach the maximum d. Thus, small increases in processing budget will have negligible impact on the search space explored, except in $InP_{a_{d-1}}$ of a given flow.

Budget allocation is distributed at each InP assuming a full n-ary subtree. Thus, at least half of the InPs in the search space are last hop InPs given a fixed search depth. Since processing budget is evenly distributed across all subtrees, to explore more space, the processing budget would need to increase significantly (dependent upon the current average branching factor on the second last hop).

However, we observe a much clearer correlation between the embedding budget and the success rate. A higher embedding budget tends to improve the flow success rate. Also, we see that as we increase the embedding budget, the variation in success rate between processing budgets decreases, suggesting that a larger processing budget does allow for more flows, but most of those new

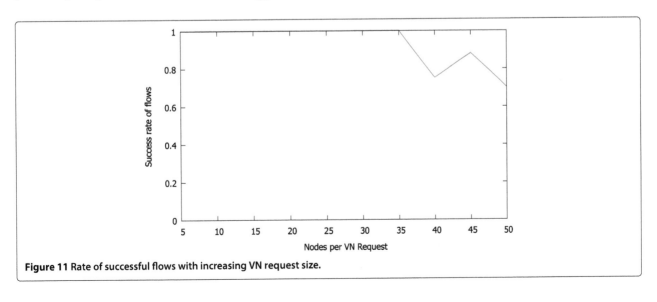

Figure 11 Rate of successful flows with increasing VN request size.

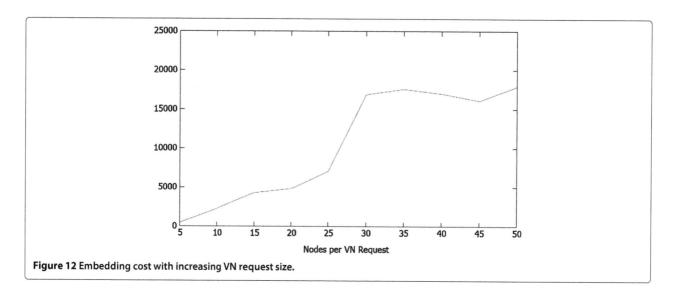

Figure 12 Embedding cost with increasing VN request size.

flows go above the embedding budget. As we increase the embedding budget, fewer of the new flows go over the embedding budget.

In our second experiment of this set (Figure 14), we vary the processing and embedding budgets again but this time, we observe their impact on the total cost of an embedding. We observe a linear growth in total embedding cost as we increase the processing budget and the embedding budget. In our experiments we were unable to find a peak that balances the tradeoff between the processing budget (and hence the size of the search space) and the total embedding cost. Looking at the results in Figure 14 we see that much of the total embedding cost is going into processing fees. As the processing budget is on a per-first-hop InP basis, increasing k^{SP} also increases the processing costs.

In Figure 15, we drop the processing fees, and look at the impact varying the budget and processing fees has on just the embedding cost and not the total cost to the SP. We observe that varying the processing budget has relatively little impact on the cost of the embedding. This supports the argument above that states that a large change to the processing budget is necessary to observe a measurable change to the search space. This suggests that under this pricing model, an SP should pick its processing budget high enough to produce an acceptable success rate, and not to find cheaper solutions.

6.3 Varying maximum InPs per flow

The maximum number of InPs involved in a single flow (d) impacts the size of the search space explored. As d decreases, the branching factor per InP tends to increase.

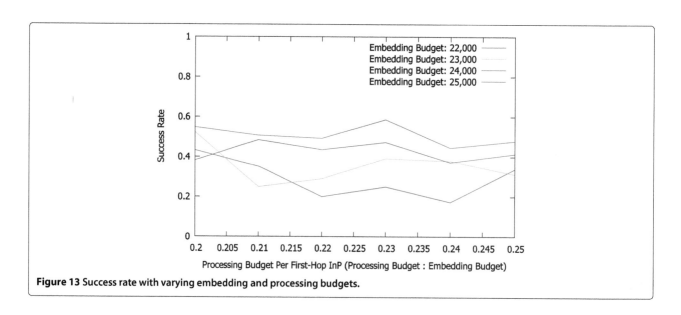

Figure 13 Success rate with varying embedding and processing budgets.

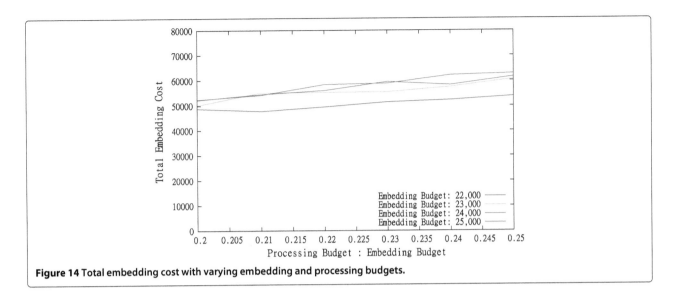

Figure 14 Total embedding cost with varying embedding and processing budgets.

In this experiment, we investigate the tradeoff between increasing the number of flows (k^{InP}) and the maximum number of InPs involved per flow (d) given varying processing budgets ratios (processing budget : embedding budget), and a fixed embedding budget of 25,000.

In the experiment in Figure 16, we see that there is a notable correlation between the maximum number of InPs involved in a flow, and the success rate. Given a fixed processing budget, increasing the maximum number of InPs involved (and thereby decreasing the branching factor k^{InP}) tends to increase the success rate. This is significant because it suggests it may be possible to lower the processing budget without impacting the success rate by increasing the value of d.

In Figure 17, we see there is a very weak correlation between d and the total embedding cost on random graphs.

6.4 Varying LAP update message drop rate

In the final set of experiments, we wish to assess the reliability of the PolyViNE protocol when faced with InPs that have stale LAP information. The propagation rate of LAP data can vary by relationships between InPs and by location and so we wish to ensure that PolyViNE is able to function under a variety of conditions.

In Figure 18, we see that PolyViNE is extremely resilient to dropped LAP update messages. The success rate is largely unimpacted by dropped LAP updates until about 95% of updates are dropped after which, we see a significant drop in success rate of flows. PolyViNE is designed to always forward VN requests to some neighboring InP, even if it cannot find an InP that matches the location constraints of any of the unmapped nodes in the VN request. If an InP cannot map any nodes, it acts as a *relay* and then uses its own LAP data to determine where to forward

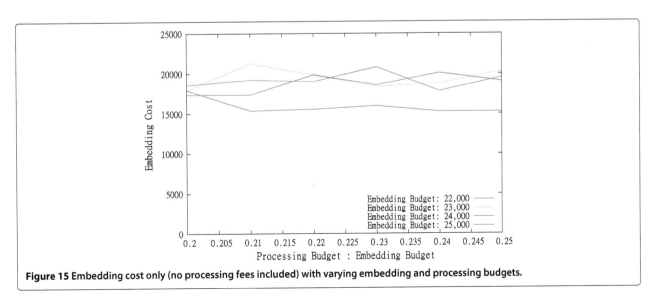

Figure 15 Embedding cost only (no processing fees included) with varying embedding and processing budgets.

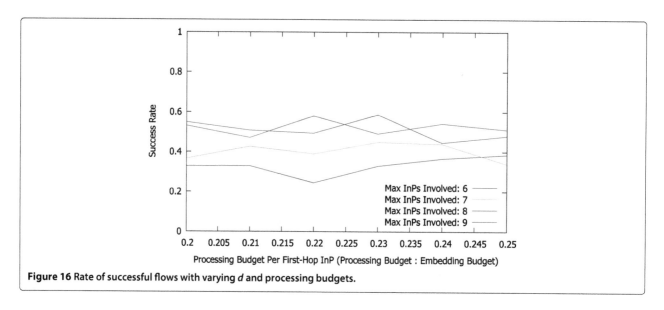

Figure 16 Rate of successful flows with varying *d* and processing budgets.

next. This makes PolyViNE extremely resilient to failing as a result of stale or lost LAP data. However, missing LAP data might affect the quality (cost) of an embedding.

In Figure 19, we delve a bit deeper to see how PolyViNE is so resilient. We observe that the number of flows explored actually **increases** as the drop rate of LAP messages increases (with no changes to the processing budget) This is very counterintuitive. How are we able to explore more flows? Figure 20 sheds some light on this. We see that the number of InPs involved per flow increases as the LAP drop rate increases. This means that each InP is mapping a smaller portion of the VN request, and so the embedding budget allows for more InPs to be involved per flow. Each additional InP spawns off k^{InP} more flows.

In Figure 21, we look at the impact dropped LAP messages have on the embedding cost. Presumably, with less LAP data at every InP, VN request forwarding is effectively

blind. We see that this intuition appears to be correct, after about 80% of LAP updates are dropped. As we lose LAP information, forwarding becomes less informed and so partial mappings are not always done at the cheapest InPs. 80% is also about when we begin to notice additional flows (Figure 19), and so at least some of the increase can be attributed to the additional inter-domain paths required by partitioning the VN across more InPs.

7 Discussion
7.1 Pricing model
The simple pricing model we suggested in this report succeeds in accomplishing the goal of incentivizing InPs to participate in a highly competitive environment and disincentivizing flooding the controller network to find feasible, low-cost embeddings. However, we did not study the practical implications of this pricing model. It may be

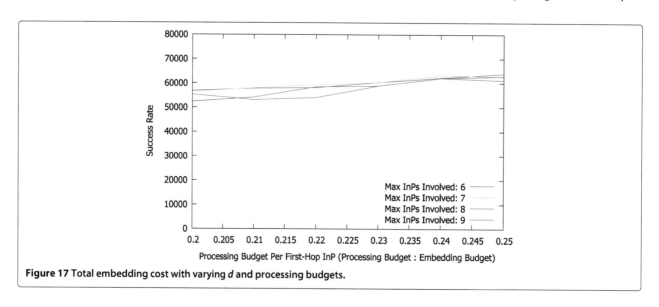

Figure 17 Total embedding cost with varying *d* and processing budgets.

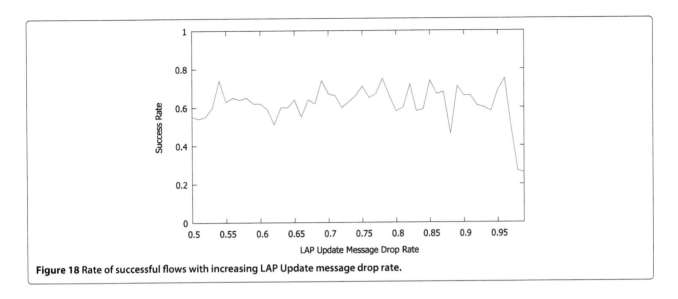

Figure 18 Rate of successful flows with increasing LAP Update message drop rate.

possible for an InP to abuse this model. For example, the dth InP may be able to gouge prices, leaving the predecessor with no option but to accept the higher price. In the future, we will investigate alternative pricing models that will accomplish our primary goals while studying the strengths and weaknesses of each model.

7.2 Scalability

Scalability concerns in PolyViNE come from several fronts: size of the search space, dissemination time of location information, and storage of location and price information among others. As the number of InPs increases in the controller network, the amount of control traffic will increase even with the tweaks proposed in this paper. Moreover, the size of stored location and path information will grow very quickly with more and more InPs joining the controller network. We can limit the number of stored

paths to a certain destination based on some heuristics (e.g., keep only the top M paths and flush the rest after each update), but such loss can result in degraded embedding. Finally, the freshness of the location information is dependent upon the update frequency and the total number of InPs in the controller network.

7.3 Performance

7.3.1 Response time

Recursive processes, by definition, can go on for a long time in the absence of proper terminating conditions resulting in unsuitable response times. Combining iterative mechanism wherever possible and limiting the level of recursion at the expense of search completeness can improve the response time of PolyViNE. However, the question regarding suitable response time depends on the arrival rate and the average life expectancy of VN requests.

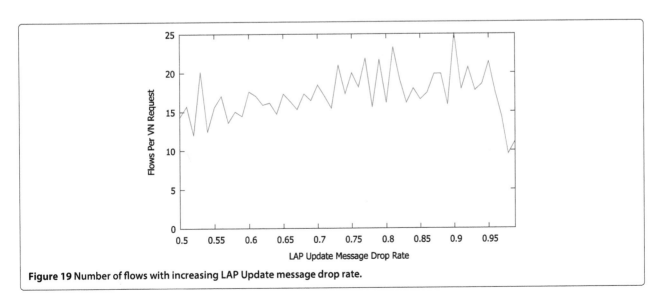

Figure 19 Number of flows with increasing LAP Update message drop rate.

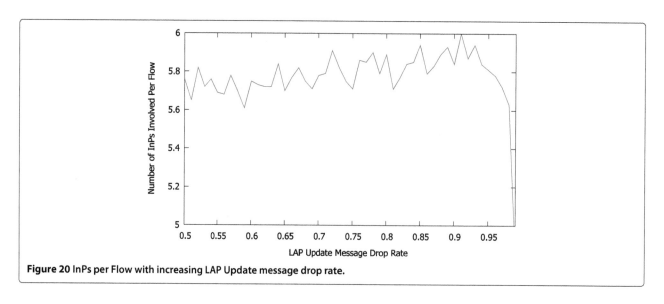

Figure 20 InPs per Flow with increasing LAP Update message drop rate.

7.3.2 Overheads

InPs participating in a PolyViNE embedding will face major computation overheads while trying to map the VN request and minor communication overheads due to relaying of the rest of the request. Since for each VN embedding every InP in each step except for the winning bidder will fail to take part in the embedding, the overheads can be discouraging. We are working toward finding incentives for the InPs to partake in the embedding process.

7.4 Trust and reputation

Since each InP will try to selfishly improve its own performance and will not expose its internal information, InPs can lie to or hide information from each other. From previous studies it is known that it is hard to use mechanism design or game theory to thwart such behaviors in a large

scale distributed system [15]. Our solution against such behavior is the use of competitive bidding at each step of embedding to expose the market price of any leased resource.

7.5 More informed forwarding

PolyViNE currently uses LAP for informed forwarding of VN requests. However, location information is not the only information available to an InP about other InPs. An InP should be capable of "learning" from past experience. That is, it should be able to collect data on previous embeddings, and make more informed decisions in the future based on its observations of the past.

8 Related work

The VN embedding problem, with constraints on both virtual nodes and virtual links, is known to be $\mathcal{NP}$-hard

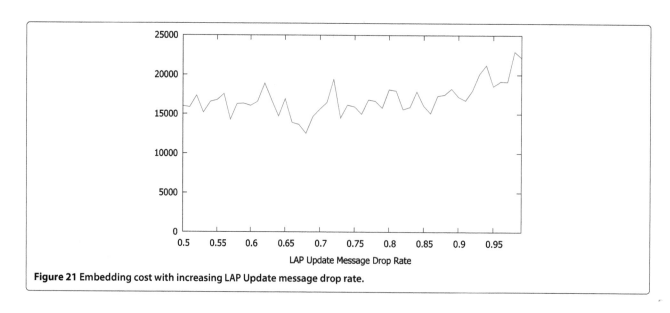

Figure 21 Embedding cost with increasing LAP Update message drop rate.

[5,6]. A number of heuristics have appeared in the literature based on the complete separation of the node mapping and the link mapping phases [5-7]. Existing research has also been restricting the problem space in different dimensions: [5,7] consider the offline version of the problem; [7] ignores node requirements; [5,7] assume infinite capacity in substrate nodes and links to obviate admission control; and [7] focuses on specific VN topologies. Chowdhury et al. [8] proposed a pair of algorithms that provide improved performance through increased correlation between the two phases of VN embedding, while [9] proposed a graph isomorphism-based integrated solution that can take exponential time in the worst case. All these algorithms address VN embedding as an intra-domain problem and take advantage of a centralized embedding entity.

Recently proposed V-Mart [16] framework approaches the inter-domain VN embedding problem using an auction-based model, where the SP performs the partitioning task using heuristics for simplification. As a result, V-Mart cannot enable local and inter-InP policy enforcement and fine-grained resource management.

Unlike inter-domain VN embedding, inter-domain lightpath provisioning [11,17] as well as cross-domain QoS-aware path composition [12,18] are well studied areas. UCLP [17] allows users to dynamically compose, modify, and tear down lightpaths across domain boundaries and over heterogeneous networking technologies (e.g., SONET/SDH, GMPLS etc.). Xiao et al. have shown in [18] that QoS-assured end-to-end path provisioning can be solved by reducing it to the classic k-MCOP (k-Multi Constrained Optimal Path) problem. iREX architecture [12], on the other hand, uses economic market-based mechanisms to automate inter-domain QoS policy enforcement through negotiation between participating domains. PolyViNE is similar to iREX in its allowance of intra-domain policy-enforcement and in using market-based mechanisms, but iREX is concerned about mapping simple paths whereas PolyViNE embeds more complicated VN requests. PeerMart [19] is another auction-based marketplace for resource trading in a network virtualization environment, but it basically deals only with virtual links.

The geographic location representation and related information dissemination protocol proposed in PolyViNE is inspired by the previous proposals of geographic addressing and routing in IPv6 networks [14,20] as well as the predominant global routing protocol in the Internet, BGP [21]. However, unlike these works, PolyViNE does not use the information for addressing or routing purposes; rather it uses the location information to find candidate InPs that will be able to embed part or whole of the remaining unmapped VN request. Moreover, such location information is disseminated between and stored

in Controllers instead of border routers as in BGP or GIRO [14]. The concepts of Controllers in InPs and controller network connecting multiple InPs' Controllers are discussed in the iMark framework [10].

9 Conclusions and future work

In this paper we have formally defined the inter-domain VN embedding problem and presented PolyViNE – a novel policy-based inter-domain VN embedding framework – to address it. PolyViNE allows embedding of end-to-end VNs in a distributed and decentralized manner by promoting global competition in the presence of local autonomy. We have laid down the workflows of InPs and SPs throughout the PolyViNE embedding process and identified the most crucial stage in the InP workflow, VN request forwarding. In this respect, we have proposed a hierarchical addressing system (COST) and a location dissemination protocol (LAP) that jointly allow InPs to make informed forwarding decisions. We have also presented preliminary performance characteristics of PolyViNE through simulation.

In the future we would like to address issues such as pricing models, InP interactions, reputation management, and incentives for InP truthfulness. Relative advantages and disadvantages of contrasting choices (e.g., recursive vs iterative forwarding) in different stages of InP workflow should also be scrutinized. Finally, the scalability, stability, and performance characteristics of PolyViNE require further studies through larger simulations and distributed experiments with a heterogeneous mix of intra-domain VN embedding algorithms and policies.

Another interesting direction of research for this problem would be to model it as a distributed constrained optimization problem (DCOP) and to try to solve that with minimal information exchange between InPs.

10 Endnotes

[a]The words 'embedding', 'mapping', and 'assignment' are used interchangeably throughout this paper.
[b]We will use the terms InP and substrate network interchangeably throughout the rest of this paper.
[c]Each InP uses its own pricing mechanism by which it attaches a price to any embedding it provides.

Competing interests
The authors declare that they have no competing interests.

Authors' contributions
All authors contributed to the idea of inter-domain virtual network embedding. MC and FS proposed and designed the required protocols and algorithms to perform such an embedding. FS wrote the simulator and carried out all the simulation experiments. All authors read and approved the final manuscript.

Acknowledgements
This work was supported in part by the Natural Science and Engineering Council of Canada (NSERC) under the Smart Applications on Virtual Infrastructure (SAVI) Research Network, and in part by the World Class

University (WCU) Program under the Korea Science and Engineering Foundation funded by the Ministry of Education, Science and Technology (Project No. R31-2008-000-10100-0).

Author details

[1]Google Canada Inc., Kitchener, ON, Canada. [2]Computer Science Division, University of California, Berkeley, CA, USA. [3]David R. Cheriton School of Computer Science, University of Waterloo, Waterloo, ON N2L 3G1, Canada. [4]Division of IT Convergence Engineering, Pohang University of Science and Technology (POSTECH), Pohang 790-784, Korea.

References

1. Anderson T, et al. (2005) Overcoming the Internet impasse through virtualization. Computer 38(4): 34–41
2. Turner J, Taylor D (2005) Diversifying the Internet. In IEEE GLOBECOM, St. Louis, MO, USA, pp. 1-6
3. Feamster N, et al. (2007) How to lease the Internet in your spare time. ACM SIGCOMM Computer Communication Review 37: 61–64
4. Chowdhury NMMK, Boutaba R (2010) A survey of network virtualization. Computer Networks 54(5): 862–876
5. Zhu Y, Ammar M (2006) Algorithms for assigning substrate network resources to virtual network components. In IEEE INFOCOM, Barcelona, Spain, pp 1–12
6. Yu M, et al. (2008) Rethinking virtual network embedding: substrate support for path splitting and migration. ACM SIGCOMM CCR 38(2): 17–29
7. Lu J, Turner J (2006) Efficient mapping of virtual networks onto a shared substrate. Tech. Rep. WUCSE-2006-35. Washington University in St. Louis, pp 1-10
8. Chowdhury NMMK, et al. (2009) Virtual network embedding with coordinated node and link mapping. In IEEE INFOCOM, Rio de Janeiro, Brazil, pp 783–791
9. Lischka J, Karl H (2009) A virtual network mapping algorithm based on subgraph isomorphism detection. In ACM SIGCOMM VISA, New Delhi, India, pp 81–88
10. Chowdhury NMMK, et al. (2009) iMark: An identity management framework for network virtualization environment. In IEEE IM, New York, NY, USA, pp. 335–342
11. Liu Q, et al. (2007) Distributed inter-domain lightpath provisioning in the presence of wavelength conversion. Comput Commun 30(18): 3662–3675
12. Yahaya A, et al. (2008) iREX: Efficient automation architecture for the deployment of inter-domain QoS policy. IEEE TNSM 5: 50–64
13. Mekouar L, et al. (2010) Incorporating trust in network virtualization. In IEEE CIT, Bradford, UK, pp 942–947
14. Oliveira R, et al. (2007) Geographically informed inter-domain routing. In IEEE ICNP, Beijing, China, pp 103–112
15. Mahajan R, et al. (2004) Experiences applying game theory to system design. In SIGCOMM PINS, Portland, OR, USA, pp 183–190
16. Zaheer F, et al. (2010) Multi-provider service negotiation and contracting in network virtualization. In IEEE/IFIP NOMS, Osaka, Japan, pp 471–478
17. Boutaba R, et al. (2004) Lightpaths on demand: A Web-services-based management system. IEEE Communications Magazine 42(7): 101–107
18. Xiao J, Boutaba R (2005) QoS-aware service composition and adaptation in autonomic communication. IEEE JSAC 23(12): 2344–2360
19. Hausheer D, Stiller B (2007) Auctions for virtual network environments. In workshop on management of network virtualisation, Brussels, Belgium
20. Hain T (2006) Application and use of the IPv6 provider independent global unicast address format. Internet Draft. (http://tools.ietf.org/html/draft-hain-ipv6-pi-addr-10)
21. Rekhter Y, et al. (2006) A Border Gateway Protocol 4 (BGP-4). RFC 4271 (Draft Standard)

5

Replica placement to mitigate attacks on clouds

Filipe Araujo[1*], Serhiy Boychenko[1], Raul Barbosa[1] and António Casimiro[2]

Abstract

Execution of critical services traditionally requires multiple distinct replicas, supported by independent networks and hardware. To operate properly, these services often depend on the correctness of a fraction of replicas, usually over 2/3 or 1/2. Defying the ideal situation, economical reasons may tempt users to replicate critical services onto a single multi-tenant cloud infrastructure. Since this may expose users to correlated failures, we assess the risks for two kinds of majorities: a conventional one, related to the number of replicas, regardless of the machines where they run; and a second one, related to the physical machines where the replicas run. This latter case may exist in multi-tenant virtualized environments only.

To assess these risks, under crash and Byzantine failures of virtual and physical machines, we resort to theoretical and experimental evaluation. Contrary to what one might expect, we conclude that it is not always favorable to distribute replicas evenly over a fixed number of physical machines. On the contrary, we found cases where they should be as unbalanced as possible. We systematically identify the best defense for each kind of failure and majority to preserve. We then review the most common real-life attacks on clouds and discuss the *a priori* placement of service replicas that minimizes the effects of these attacks.

Keywords: Cloud computing; Fault-Tolerance; Dependability; Virtualization

1 Introduction

To cut costs, companies increasingly outsource information technology to cloud providers. However, with this movement, they lose much of the control they could exert on their most critical services. Popular strategies such as replication may not work well on the cloud, because providers may take advantage of virtualization techniques [1-5] to concentrate some of (or all) the replicas in the same physical machine (PM). Recent research has explored affinities among virtual machines (VMs) to consolidate according to traffic [6,7] or memory pages [8,9], for example. We could think of a cluster of application servers responding to HTTP requests, or a remote storage service [10-12].

Common sense will tell us that one should not use a virtualized infrastructure to run replicas of the same service, because a single fault on a single PM could tear down many replicas at once. Ideally, each new replica should run on a different PM, preferably at distant physical locations, served by different networks, using diverse software, operating systems, and so on. However, the costs and complexity of doing this are enormous and cutting these costs is certainly very tempting for clients. Market offers, like Rackspace's or Microsoft's [13] tend to focus on availability, providing specific advise and Service Level Agreements (SLAs) for more common non-Byzantine faults. Critical Byzantine fault-tolerant (BFT) services have been studied in more academic contexts, including research projects [14-18]. For example, the Archistar project [19] considers a storage system replicated across multiple cloud providers to overcome Byzantine failures. The most well-known system requiring BFT is perhaps Bitcoin [20], although Bitcoin resorts to brute computational force for correctness.

In this paper we consider a setting where clients chose a single cloud provider. They may do this for a number of reasons, being simplicity the most important: it is easier to manage a single cloud contract than three, for example. It is also easier to deploy a service only once, especially in Platform-as-a-Service clouds (PaaS), where

---

*Correspondence: filipius@uc.pt
[1] CISUC, Department of Informatics Engineering, University of Coimbra, Polo II, 3030-290 Coimbra, Portugal
Full list of author information is available at the end of the article

development is closely tied to the provider. Although ideally the client should have different implementations to ensure diversity, this may be difficult to achieve in practice. Replicating data to different providers may also be undesirable, due to the risks involved in such higher exposure. Additionally, as we show in this paper, even when using different providers, the client may need to properly decide the number of replicas to run on each of the providers.

From the point of view of providers, offering BFT services using a small fraction of their resources seems like a very reasonable step. Nevertheless, BFT services have some specificities and may not require features like elasticity. Many BFT protocols assume a fixed number of players and cannot cope with new peers or with the departure of more than a fixed number f of peers (e.g. [21]). To change these settings, the service must stop, before the new group of replicas resumes operation, but this idea may be unreasonable in a critical replicated environment. The cloud provider must therefore provide support for a fixed number of replicas and should ideally allocate these replicas to different servers, availability zones or even regions, to minimize correlated failures.

Given the contradicting goals of consolidating to save money and dispersing to ensure robustness, we focus on a compromise. The provider fixes the number of PMs to a some satisfactory level and then (s)he needs to find the best distribution of VMs (i.e., replicas) by these PMs. We qualitatively try to mitigate the disadvantage of not using more PMs, by giving a single defense to the cloud provider: the distribution of the VMs by the available PMs. Depending on the service, the defender may care for the number of PMs *or* the number of VMs that stand after each failure. In particular, motivated by many consensus-based algorithms, including Byzantine fault-tolerant ones, e.g. [22] or [21], we count the number of attacks that are necessary before the service loses the majority of machines, physical *or* virtual. We also assume that the attacker resources are limited (otherwise, the defense would be helpless). Nevertheless, defining the best defensive strategy for the cloud provider is a complex task, because PMs and VMs may fail in many different ways, from crashes to arbitrary Byzantine failures caused by fragilities in hardware or software.

To determine the best placement of VMs, we consider two fundamental goals, of ensuring a majority of VMs *or* PMs and resisting to a large spectrum of attacks to the infrastructure. These might start and be confined to a single VM, or attacks may spread to other VMs, to the hypervisor, or to the PM hosting the service. Consequences range from a perceived reduction in the quality of service to erroneous responses, due to interferences or complete machine crashes. Attackers may be able to select specific targets, or they might be limited to perform malicious actions over random targets handed by some scheduler of the cloud service. Based on actual evidence of past attacks, we try to model a large spectrum of realistic settings. Based on these settings, we resort to theoretical and experimental analysis to determine the best distribution of VMs against possible attacks. We use a balls and urns and other probabilistic approaches when possible, and experimentally evaluate the remaining cases.

While intuition suggests that we should balance the VMs among the PMs, a deeper analysis shows cases where other options are better. Depending on the kind of attack and majority to keep, the distribution of VMs might be irrelevant or should even be as unbalanced as possible, given the *same* number of PMs. For example, to ensure a majority of PMs, the defender should concentrate the VMs as much as possible: one VM for each but the last PM, and all the remaining VMs in the last PM. This is the best way of restricting the attacker to the smallest possible number of PMs.

Hence, the main contribution of this paper is to determine the appropriate strategy to defend a majority from different types of failures, including Byzantine. This knowledge is important, especially in a setting where migrating VMs can help the cloud provider to consolidate resources in favorable ways. If the provider is not bound to a balanced or extremely unbalanced solution, he may take advantage of traffic correlation to consolidate machines and reduce network traffic, for example. We take our conclusions to real-life attacks and threats hanging over cloud infrastructures. Knowledge of the most common attacks and their consequences lets us break the tie between opposing strategies to place service replicas. This conclusion goes beyond the theoretical and experimental analysis we did in [23]. Our study can be useful both for the cloud provider and for the client, as it tells them what to do or expect from the service. E.g., this may help the provider to create more precise and safer SLAs.

The rest of the paper is organized as follows. Section 2 presents the assumptions of our work. In Section 3 we perform a theoretical analysis regarding the distribution of VMs. Since there is a long and established field using the terms "balls" (VMs) and "urns" (PMs), we often keep these terms. In Section 4 we extend the analysis of the previous section and run Monte Carlo simulations, whenever we are not aware of closed formulas that may help us to find the appropriate distributions. In Section 5 we discuss the best distribution strategies. In Section 6 we go through well-known attacks on clouds and evaluate the effect of this knowledge on the theoretical findings of the previous sections. In Section 7 we conclude the paper.

2 Model

2.1 Failure models

In our analysis we deal with crash failures and Byzantine failures caused by attackers. Crash failures may stop a VM or the entire PM. Byzantine failures may produce these and other arbitrary deviations from the correct service. In this paper we try to consider a representative number of entry points and behaviors for attackers. Attackers may target a specific PM, if they can, or they might depend on some fragility or assignment from the cloud provider, thus being unable to pick their concrete target. We assume the same for VM attacks (limited or unlimited targets). A faulty PM may compromise all its VMs. Conversely, once the attacker controls a VM, he might be able to escalate the attack to control the hypervisor, disturb somehow the PM or co-located VMs ("interference"), or, in the most benign case, he might be limited to shut down the VM.

We consider a service with m PMs and v VMs. Each of the m PMs may run one or more of the v VMs. When appropriate, we consider a balls and urns problem: the urn is a PM; the VMs are the balls. VM failures correspond to drawing a ball from an urn. In some cases, the attacker will put the ball again in the same urn, sometimes he or she will simply remove the ball. For example, consider a cluster of application servers responding to HTTP requests, or a remote storage service [10-12]. Subsequent requests to the service may end up in the same application server, making this a case without removal. Contrary to this, if the attacker may not find the same replica, because he disrupted the previous one, we have removal. This model does not cover all the cases if, for instance, the attacker manages to shut down the entire PM (this would remove all balls from the urn).

2.2 Goal

Depending on the service, we may want to ensure a majority of correct VM *or* PM replicas. Some consensus algorithms, as the one in [22], use special hardware devices, such as a Trusted Platform Module (TPM), to improve the tolerance to Byzantine nodes. To ensure multi-tenancy, sharing the TPM by multiple VMs through virtualization, as in vTPM [24], emerges as a natural step. Therefore, it becomes important to ensure a majority of correct PMs. When we consider crash failures, we assume that the PM is in the group until the last VM crashes.

We assume that, as soon as one VM in the service is under control of the attacker, all co-located VMs and the respective PM might be compromised and out of the majority of correct (physical or virtual) machines. What we do not consider is the case where the attacker manages to create more machines to participate and corrupt the BFT protocol. We consider this kind of attack to be outside the scope of this paper, as this problem is orthogonal to the cloud and exists in BFT protocols in general.

The set of attacks we consider falls into a moderate number of cases. We may have crash and other arbitrary effects, which we refer to as interference and Byzantine, although crashes may have intentional causes. The attacker may or may not be able to pick his or her targets; VMs or PMs may fail; and we may want to preserve VM or PM majority. Overall we have a total of 14 meaningful cases that we discuss throughout the paper and wrap up in Section 5.

3 Theoretical analysis

3.1 Independent VM failures

We start our theoretical analysis by considering that faults are independent: a fault causing the failure of a VM does not affect any other co-located VM. This may be the case of a crash failure. We also assume that to participate in some replicated protocol, the PM needs to have at least one operational VM. The PM becomes unusable as soon as the last VM fails. This could happen if at least one VM is necessary to operate some shared resource, like a TPM, e.g., to sign messages. I.e., given the failure of $n \leq v$ VMs, we can calculate the probability that a PM with v_i VMs fails. We compute this value in Equation 1, for $1 \leq v_i \leq n \leq v$, using the Hypergeometric distribution. $P_i(v_i, n, v)$ is the probability that PM i fails due to the failure of all its v_i VMs. $P_i(v_i, n, v) = 0$, for $n < v_i \leq v$. That is, at least one VM of PM i will survive the n failures.

$$P_i(v_i, n, v) = \frac{\binom{v_i}{v_i}\binom{v - v_i}{n - v_i}}{\binom{v}{n}}$$
$$= \frac{n \times (n - 1) \times \ldots (n - v_i + 1)}{v \times (v - 1) \times \ldots (v - v_i + 1)} \quad (1)$$

Since we assume a fixed number of n crash failures, and a total of v VMs, we analyze the impact of varying v_i and use the notation $P_i(v_i)$. We first show in Equation 2 that for $v_i \in \{1, \ldots, n - 2\}$, $P_i(v_i) - P_i(v_i + 1) > P_i(v_i + 1) - P_i(v_i + 2)$. That is, the marginal gain (in terms of reducing the probability of failure of a PM) achieved by an increment of the number of VMs allocated to one PM decreases as the number of VMs in that PM approaches the number of possible failures, n.

$$P_i(v_i) - P_i(v_i + 1) - P_i(v_i + 1) + P_i(v_i + 2) =$$
$$P_i(v_i) \left(1 - \frac{n - v_i}{v - v_i} - \frac{n - v_i}{v - v_i} + \frac{(n - v_i)(n - v_i - 1)}{(v - v_i)(v - v_i - 1)}\right) =$$
$$P_i(v_i) \cdot$$
$$\cdot \left(1 - \frac{2(n - v_i)(v - v_i - 1) - (n - v_i)(n - v_i - 1)}{(v - v_i)(v - v_i - 1)}\right)$$
$$\geq P_i(v_i) \left(1 - \frac{(n - v_i)(n - v_i - 1)}{(v - v_i)(v - v_i - 1)}\right) \quad (2)$$

Since $v \geq n$, the denominator of the subtrahend is greater or equal than the numerator, which makes the overall expression greater or equal than 0. In Equation 3, we define a new function $Q_i(x)$ that "extends" P_i for the domain $[1, n]$. P_i and Q_i are equal in the domain $\{1, \ldots, n\}$, but Q_i has line segments connecting consecutive points of P_i in $[1, n] \setminus \{1, \ldots, n\}$.

$$Q_i(x) = \begin{cases} P_i(1) + (x-1)(P_i(2) - P_i(1)), 1 \leq x < 2 \\ \cdots \\ P_i(j) + (x-j)(P_i(j+1) - P_i(j)), \\ \qquad\qquad 1 < j \leq x < j+1 < n \\ \cdots \\ P_i(n-1) + (x-n+1)(P_i(n) - P_i(n-1)), \\ \qquad\qquad n-1 \leq x \leq n \end{cases}$$

(3)

From Equation 2, it follows that $Q_i(x)$ is convex in the domain. Now, the number of failed machines can be computed as an expectation $E = \sum_i P_i(v_i) = \sum_i Q_i(v_i)$. From Jensen's inequality:

$$Q\left(\frac{\sum_i v_i}{m}\right) \leq \frac{\sum_i Q_i(v_i)}{m}$$

(4)

where equality occurs when all the v_i's are equal. Since we want to minimize the right side of the equation we should evenly balance the VMs by the PMs (assuming that the division is integer).

3.2 VM failure contaminates other VMs

We now consider Byzantine attacks, where a malicious user may take over all the co-located VMs, once he or she successfully attacks the first one (malware injection, side-channel or protected environment escape attacks). In mathematical terms, we can treat this problem as an urns and balls problem, and use known results, such as [25]. Urns represent a PM, while balls represent the VMs. To distinguish between correct and compromised VMs we may assign colors to balls: white balls represent correct machines, whereas black balls represent compromised machines. The objective of our analysis in this section is to show that there is a proper way of initially distributing white balls, which minimizes the number of urns that end up having black balls as a result of malicious actions successively changing the color of balls from white to black. Our assumption in this particular case is that the previously white ball returns to the same urn as black and the attacker has no option concerning the urn from where it picks a ball. This represents a case where the service is apparently running and the attacker might find the same (possibly compromised) VM.

The option left to the cloud provider is to select a distribution of VMs by the PMs and, in this particular case, we care about the number of urns that do not have black balls, which we denote by the random variable X. $P(X \geq k)$ is the probability that k or more urns have no black balls.

Theorem 1. *Assume that we have v white balls distributed by $1 < m < v$ urns, such that each urn has at least one ball. Assume that the attacker works in successive turns, picking one ball at a time from an urn, and always putting back a black ball in the same urn. The attacker does not select the ball or the urn. $\forall\ k \in \{1, \ldots, m\}$, $P(X \geq k)$ is maximized when $m - 1$ urns have 1 ball, and the remaining urn has the remaining $v - m + 1$ balls.*

Proof. Refer to Figure 1. Note that white urns have only 1 ball, gray urns have at least 1, but less than $v - m + 1$ balls, and black urns have $v - m + 1$ balls. Consider setting A, where only 1 urn has more than 1 ball. I.e., $m - 1$ urns have 1 ball, whereas the last urn in the figure has $v - m + 1$ balls. Setting B represents any other case, with the same number of urns, m, but with a different distribution of balls. Let us match pairwise the urns in setting A with the urns in setting B (original), starting by the 1-ball urns (on the left side of the figure). After this first set of urns, we define another set O, with the urns that have more than 1 ball in B, but only one ball in A. This definition excludes the first urns that have 1 ball in A and B, as well as the last urn of A, which has more than 1 ball. Note that $1 \leq |O| \leq m - 1$.

We now resort to an artificial division of set O in B. We split each one of the $|O|$ urns in B into two other urns: one with 1 ball, and the other with the remaining balls. This makes for a total of $m - 1$ urns with only 1 ball, just like in setting A. The remaining $v - m + 1$ balls are spread over $|O| + 1$ urns (in gray in the "imaginary B"), each having one or more balls. In the rest of our reasoning, we should refer to settings A and "imaginary B", with m and $m + |O|$ urns, respectively. In both cases there are $m - 1$ urns with only 1 ball. We first observe that these urns have exactly the same probability of having a black ball. What about the single black and $|O| + 1$ gray urns in A and "imaginary B", respectively? Since the number of balls is the same, $v - m + 1$, the probability of having one or more black balls is exactly the same in both settings. However, these black balls only "contaminate" (or exist) in a single urn in setting A, whereas in "imaginary B" they may spread over multiple urns. As a consequence, $P(X \geq k)$ in setting A must be the same or greater than in setting B. $\qquad\square$

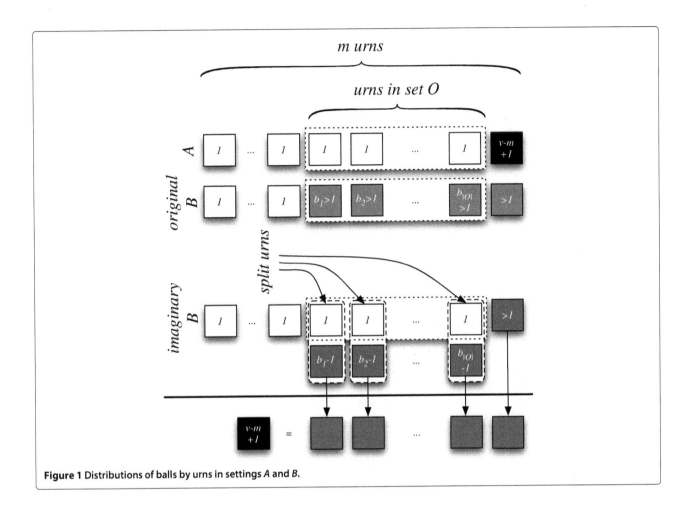

Figure 1 Distributions of balls by urns in settings *A* and *B*.

To calculate $P(X \geq k)$, we can use a result from ([25], Equation (3.5)), which we restate here:

$$P(X \geq k) = \sum_{\mathbf{a}}^{(k)} \left(1 - \sum_{j=1}^{k} p_{a_j}\right)^n -$$

$$- \binom{k}{k-1} \sum_{\mathbf{a}}^{(k+1)} \left(1 - \sum_{j=1}^{k+1} p_{a_j}\right)^n +$$

$$+ \binom{k+1}{k-1} \sum_{\mathbf{a}}^{(k+2)} \left(1 - \sum_{j=1}^{k+2} p_{a_j}\right)^n -$$

$$\cdots$$

$$+ (-1)^{m-k} \binom{m-1}{k-1} \sum_{j=1}^{m} p_j{}^n \qquad (5)$$

The m urns define a set of integers $\{1, 2, \ldots, m\}$. The variable p_j is the probability that we assign a black ball to urn j. From this set, we define subsets with k elements $\{a_1, a_2, \ldots, a_k\}$. $\sum_{\mathbf{a}}^{(k)}$ denotes a summation over all these subsets. Thus, there are $\binom{m}{k}$ terms in this sum. For a better

understanding of this formula, we should realize that summation $\sum_{\mathbf{a}}^{(k)}$ concerns the probability of having k urns without black balls when n black balls have been dropped in the urns. The summation that follows in the formula considers the probability of having $k + 1$ empty for the same n balls and so on.

3.3 Keeping a majority of virtual machines

The next question we consider is the impact of machine failures on the number of VMs that stay alive in a correct state. In many cases, this number might be more important than the number of different PMs where the replicas run. One may ask whether concentrating many VMs in the same (or few) machine(s) could reduce the average number of VMs that survive (other) PM crashes. Interestingly, the answer is *no*. Assume $Z(t)$ to be a random variable that represents the number of VMs that are running at time t. Variable v_i is the number of VMs running on PM i; $Y_i(t)$ is a random variable that assumes the value 0 if PM i is off at time t or 1 if it is on. If we assume that all PMs have the same characteristics, at any given time t, $Y_i(t)$ is the same for all values of i, and we can simply remove the subscript. Equation 6 shows that the distribution of VMs by the PMs is not relevant from the point of view of the average:

$$E[Z(t)] = \sum_{i=1}^{m} v_i \cdot P[Y_i(t) = 1] = P[Y(t) = 1] \, v \qquad (6)$$

However, one should notice that other metrics may be relevant as well. On the few occasions when the most loaded PM fails, much fewer replicas will be available. I.e., the unbalanced setting will most of the time keep a few more VMs running, but sometimes, it will have much less.

4 Experimental evaluation

Since we cannot evaluate all the interesting scenarios using analytical expressions, in this section we partially resort to simulation. To evaluate the likelihood of keeping a majority of correct PMs, we start with $m = 5$ PMs and $v = 10$ VMs in Figure 2. We considered four cases: in one of them, all the machines (urns) have the same probability of receiving an attack (black ball) and this probability remains constant. We call this case "balanced without removal". We also consider the case where a single machine has a probability of 60% of receiving an attack, while the remaining 40% probability is equally distributed among the remaining machines. This corresponds to running 6 VMs in a single *PM*, while the remaining 4 VMs run in the other 4 PMs, in a one-to-one correspondence. To this case we call "unbalanced (60%) without removal". We also consider removals of the VMs once the attacker dominates them. This corresponds to a scenario where the attacker is successively requesting some instance of a service from a limited set. Each time it gets a new instance, the attacker will not get the same, but a new one (e.g., a new VM). These are the two cases with removal.

In the plots without removal, we use Equation 5 to compute the probability that at most 2 out of 5 PMs have black balls, as the number of attacks grows. We can see a clear difference between the balanced and unbalanced cases. The chances of keeping a majority significantly improve for the latter case. For instance, after 5 attacks, there is still more than 40% chances of conserving the majority in the unbalanced case, while in the balanced case, this probability is below 10%. To plot the lines with removal we resorted to Monte Carlo simulation. We show error bars that correspond to a 99% confidence interval of the average, assuming a normal distribution. Since we used 10,000 trials to get these plots, the intervals are very small and the error bars are barely visible. As we expected, removal makes it easier for the attacker to reach a larger number of different PMs, thus negatively affecting the probability of keeping a majority of correct PMs. The four plots of the figure actually depict two extreme pairs of cases: the one without removal approximates a scenario where we have a very large number of VMs, or where the same VM can be handed to the attacker. The pair of lines with removal corresponds to the other extreme case, where we have a small number of VMs (10) for the available PMs (5).

Next, we try a larger number of PMs, $m = 21$, to compare against the smaller set of 5. For this larger set, the advantage of unbalancing the distribution of VMs is even more visible, as we depict in Figure 3. For the case without removal, given by Equation 5, after a little more than 20 attacks, there is nearly no chance that the majority of the PMs is still correct for the balanced option. This takes more than 60 attacks in the case of the unbalanced scenario. The difference in the removal case is also important. Note that in this setting we assumed that the entire PM is compromised once the attacker penetrates the first VM, either because he or she managed to control the

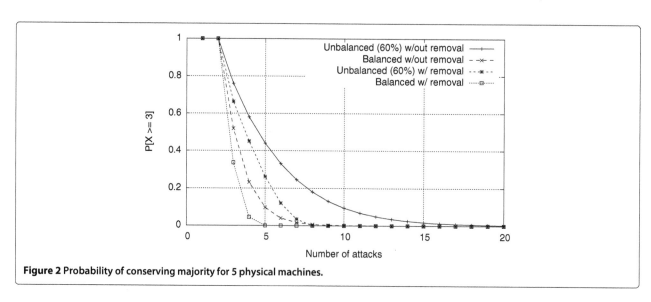

Figure 2 Probability of conserving majority for 5 physical machines.

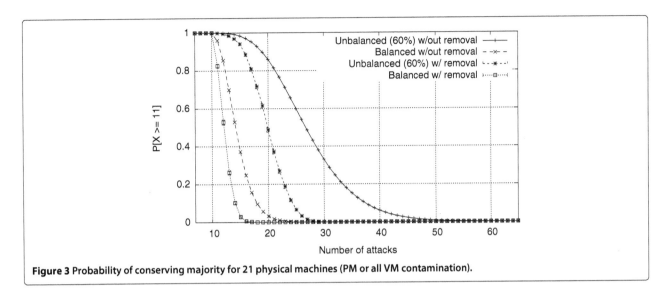

Figure 3 Probability of conserving majority for 21 physical machines (PM or all VM contamination).

hypervisor or because he or she gained control of all the VMs in the same physical machine. Unlike this, in Figure 4 we consider other cases: a 50% and a 0% chance (no contamination) of controlling the service via hypervisor or other machines. We can see that as the chance of dominating the entire service in the PM decreases, balancing becomes increasingly better. This is not surprising, if we think that this case is more similar to crash cases, where the attacker cannot engage more co-located resources in arbitrary behaviors. Hence, by unbalancing the VMs, it becomes more likely that PMs with only one VM are left empty when their single VM fails.

These plots raise the question of determining the number of attacks that it takes until the attacker succeeds in (probabilistically) holding the majority of the machines. We do this evaluation in Figure 5, for the balanced and unbalanced (60%) cases, without removal, for a varying

number of PMs. In both cases, the growth seems to be approximately linear, but the slope is much higher in the unbalanced case, thus making it much more difficult to break.

Finally, in Figure 6 we evaluate the unbalance factor. We use 11 machines and make the balance change from $1/11$ (balanced) to $1 - 1/11 \cong 91\%$ (most unbalanced) in steps of $1/11$. For all these unbalanced factors, we plot the number of attacks until the attacker gets the majority of machines with probability greater than 50%. There is no removal.

5 Placement strategies of the defense

We now identify the best strategies to distribute the VMs by the PMs. Should the defender use a balanced approach or an unbalanced one? We assume that failures render the target unusable either because it crashed or because it

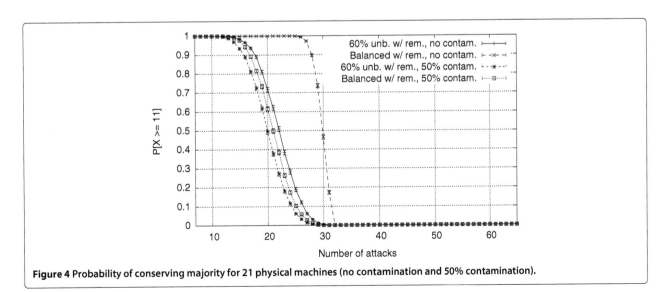

Figure 4 Probability of conserving majority for 21 physical machines (no contamination and 50% contamination).

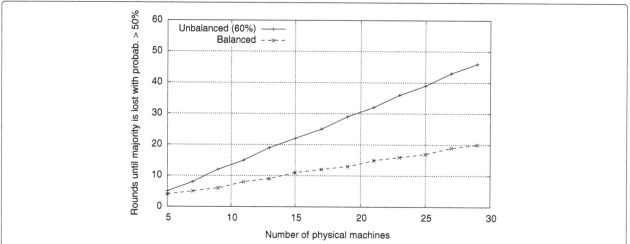

Figure 5 Evaluation of the rounds the attacker needs until it probabilistically gets the majority as a function of the number of physical machines.

ceased to follow the protocol. Then, we consider multiple contamination models: an attack to one VM may or may not become an attack to co-located VMs and PM. We also consider that attacks might be "limited" or "unlimited", to VMs, or directly to the PMs. "Limited" means that the attacker selects a target at random with uniform probability. "Unlimited" is the extreme opposite case, where the attacker may select the target he wants. In the next sections we consider different scenarios of attacks and contamination models. Table 1 shows the best distribution of VMs by PMs for each attack and contamination model.

5.1 Attacks to PMs

In this section we consider attacks to PMs regardless of their source. They could well begin in a VM and escalate

to affect the entire PM. If we assume that the targeted PM disappears from the service or acts incorrectly, the distribution of VMs by the PMs is not relevant for a PM majority. On the other hand, if we consider VM majorities, the distribution of VMs might be relevant. If the attacker can pick his targets ("unlimited" case), it is better to evenly distribute the machines, otherwise the attacker will select PMs with more VMs. If not ("limited" case), the distribution of VMs is irrelevant, as we saw in Section 3.3.

5.2 Attacks contained within VMs

Now, consider VM targets, but assume that the attacker cannot leave the borders of the VM, i.e., the VM might misbehave somehow, but it cannot tamper with other VMs, the PM or any other device related to the service, like a TPM. Crashes are a typical cause for this behavior.

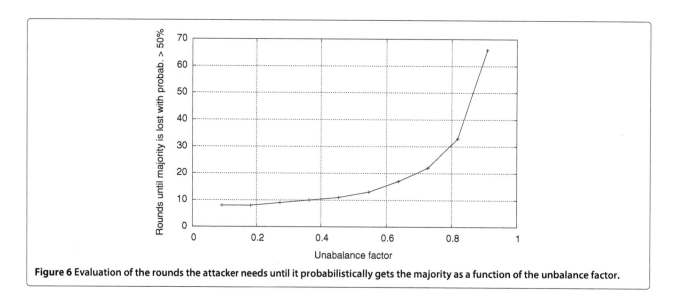

Figure 6 Evaluation of the rounds the attacker needs until it probabilistically gets the majority as a function of the unbalance factor.

Table 1 Distribution of VMs by PMs as a function of the failure and the objective to achieve by the defender

Failure/Objective	PM Majority	VM Majority
Attacks to PMs		
Limited PMs	Irrelevant	Irrelevant
Unlimited PMs	Irrelevant	Balanced
Attacks contained within VMs		
Lim. Crash VMs	Balanced	Irrelevant
Unlim. Crash VMs	Balanced	Irrelevant
Attacks to a VM interfere with the PM service		
Lim. Interf. VMs	Unbalanced	—
Unlim. Interf. VMs	Irrelevant	—
Cross-VM and VM-to-Hypervisor escalation		
Lim. Byzantine VMs	Unbalanced	Balanced
Unlim. Byzantine VMs	Irrelevant	Balanced

In this case, the distribution is irrelevant to keep a majority of VMs, as only one VM is faulty after each successful attack. Keeping a PM majority might be different. If the PM is out of the service when the last VM it holds stops, balancing is better to avoid PMs without VMs.

5.3 Attacks affect the replicated service, but not other VMs or the PM

Now, we assume that attacks to VMs do not cross the frontier of the VM, except to disrupt the service provided by that PM. This corresponds to a case where the corrupted VM manages to control the service, at least sometimes, e.g., by responding first to requests entering the machine. However, this model assumes that the attacker cannot invade other VMs or the PM from the VM (e.g., to shut down other VMs). From the perspective of keeping a majority of VMs, we omit this case from our analysis, because it is similar to the contained VM attacks. For a PM majority, in the "Limited" case, the best thing to do is to unbalance the VMs, as we saw in Sections 3.2 and 4. In the "Unlimited" case, where an attacker can disturb the service in any PM (s)he wants, the distribution is irrelevant. It is interesting to note the striking difference to the case where attacks do not cross VM borders, where we balance the VMs, to ensure that, say, crashes do not leave a PM without VMs. We reviewed a similarly interesting case, where balancing may be a better option in Section 4, Figure 4: as the probability of affecting the service decreases to zero, balancing becomes better.

5.4 Cross-VM or VM-to-hypervisor attacks

We now consider attacks that can cross VM boundaries to take over other VMs (cross-VM) or the PM (VM-to-Hypervisor attack). This case ends up being the same as

the "Unlimited PMs", and thus gets the same distribution. However, it includes some subtleties worth discussing, as it may happen that an attacker is unable to reach arbitrary VMs, but he might end up shutting down the PM or many co-located VMs to reach other VMs and PMs in future interactions. In other words, an attacker with limited access to VMs might end up affecting other co-located VMs, to reach a different set of victims. Although this would not be purely "Unlimited Byzantine", the same distributions (Irrelevant/Balanced) would hold. However, if the attacker cannot improve his chances of reaching arbitrary VMs and is constrained by the provider ("Limited Byzantine VMs"), we have the same case as the "Limited Interference" for the PM majority. For a VM majority we need a Balanced distribution of VMs, or, otherwise, the attacker would have a higher probability of reaching VMs with more co-located VMs.

6 Classification of real attacks

In this section we identify and describe attacks found in the literature that may affect virtualized cloud infrastructures. We categorize real attacks and the resulting failures that we found in the literature, namely described by Jensen *et al.* [26], Zhang *et al.* [27], Gruschka *et al.* [28], and Verizon [29], onto the classes of Table 1. Our analysis intends to support selection and prioritization of the placement strategies, according to the main security concerns and impact of attacks.

6.1 Denial of service

One of the most attractive features of cloud systems is their on-demand provision of computing power for legitimate users. However, this feature may raise serious security problems if it is exploited with the wrong intentions. Attackers may flood a service with requests, inducing the infrastructure, to create countless VMs in response to those requests, thereby exhausting the available hardware resources. This leads to a Denial of Service (DoS), not only on the specific service under attack, but also on other services that share the infrastructure.

There are numerous examples of such attacks on cloud services and providers. The most famous cases are not necessarily connected to models we propose in this paper, but can affect operation of an entire provider. The Spamhaus anti-spam organization and the cloud provider CloudFlare, recently suffered a Distributed Denial of Service (DDoS) attack [30]. By exploiting core Internet infrastructures and open DNS resources, attackers managed to create an attack of great dimension. Although the attack was mitigated and the adversaries were unable to achieve the goal of shutting down the `spamhaus.org` site, they managed to cause delays and outages in some other Internet resources. The work of Domingues *et al.* [31] shows that VMs can actually affect each other, especially when they perform I/O operations, thus opening the door to DoS problems, although cloud providers are evidently reluctant to disclose these cases.

6.2 Malware injection

The malware injection attack consists of installing some malicious service implementation or VM into the cloud. The adversary deceives the cloud system to accept malicious software as a valid instance of the attacked service. Successful invasion allows the infected instance to execute user requests. The effects of malware injection may vary from eavesdropping to completely disabling or changing functionality of the attacked service. Companies like Intel are actively developing solutions against this kind of threat. This is the case of the "Trusted Execution Technology" (TXT).

One of the most notorious injections of malicious software occurred against the Google password system [32]. Vulnerabilities of Internet Explorer 6, which was still used by some workers, allowed hackers to inject malicious software that enabled them to access the company's internal network. Although Google claimed that no passwords were stolen, it is difficult to evaluate all the consequences of the attack.

6.3 Metadata spoofing

In metadata spoofing, attackers modify the Web Services' metadata descriptions. Attackers may modify the syntax and operation of some functions described in the WSDL. Unaware of the fraudulent modification, an unknowing user will invoke functions that execute unexpected operations on the server. A successful attack could allow the adversary to manipulate service operations or even to obtain user credentials, to perform a broader range of attacks.

Although we were not able to find reported cloud-related incidents involving metadata spoofing, we found descriptions of such attacks on web-service based resources. For example, hackers were able to configure administrative settings (without having privileged user access) in an attack to D-Link routers [33], using vulnerabilities of the SOAP-based device control protocol. In some models of the D-Link routers, the attackers were able to execute the SOAP action `GetDeviceSettings` without authentication. This action alone did not allow the adversary to obtain any sensitive data, but it could be used to bypass the authentication requirements for other SOAP actions.

6.4 XML signature wrapping

The XML signature wrapping attack modifies authenticated SOAP messages. Several different variants of this attack exist. In one of the variants, after obtaining the original signed SOAP packet, the attacker moves the message body to a wrapping element inside the SOAP header and creates a new body with a different operation. This may deceive some servers to accept the signature, because the original signed contents still exist inside that wrapping element. However, the new function in the SOAP body of the message may harm the server. As a result, the attacker could execute arbitrary operations on the cloud system as a legitimate user, influencing the availability of the services.

Some studies revealed potential vulnerabilities of cloud providers to XML Signature Wrapping attacks. A group of researchers from the Ruhr-University Bochum demonstrated this fragility in the Amazon Web Services (AWS) [34]. Using this approach, the researchers managed to delete and create new images on the customer's EC2 instance and hijack AWS sessions to get sensitive data, including plaintext passwords. Despite being restricted to AWS, researchers believe that other cloud providers might be affected by the same type of vulnerabilities.

6.5 VM-to-hypervisor attack

The VM-to-Hypervisor attack is based on exploiting security vulnerabilities of the hypervisor. The complexity of the virtualization software may leave some open possibilities for adversaries to escape from the protected environment and gain full access to the hosting physical machine [35]. Consequences of the VM-to-Hypervisor attacks may vary from creation of rogue VMs to complete interruption of the attacked hardware, both of which may compromise multiple services in many different ways.

The media continuously reports privilege escalation vulnerabilities of different virtualization technologies. In a recent case [36], a major vulnerability in the 64-bit Xen hypervisor running 64-bit para-virtualized guests on Intel CPUs was disclosed and patched before any hacker managed to exploit it. Successful attack would allow the adversary to escape from guest status and gain administrative access on the host machine. After breaking the protected environment, the adversary could run arbitrary code in privileged mode, install and run new programs, and create new accounts with administrative rights.

6.6 Cross-VM side-channel attack

The cross-VM side-channel attack consists of taking advantage of information leaks from the system's shared components, such as cache or memory. Timing information in the access to some memory addresses may let the attacker know whether or not data from the address was stored in cache. Several techniques of cache pattern classification, noise reduction and error correction are applied to minimize the search space for cryptographic information. The effect of such attacks varies from eavesdropping to service interruption, depending on the goals of the attacker.

We are not aware of any cloud providers that have been victims of cross-VM side-channel attacks. Nonetheless, a research team managed to collect and reconstruct cryptographic keys from information leaked by the CPU cache. This allowed them to take control over a victim VM [37].

6.7 Hacking

Hacking consists of obtaining illegitimate access to a system by circumventing security mechanisms, either by exploiting security vulnerabilities or by obtaining access credentials. Some of the most common forms of attack include stealing login credentials, brute force attacks, SQL injection and backdoor exploitation. The main goals of hacking generally are data stealing or damaging.

These types of attack have become increasingly common in recent years, as reported by Verizon [29], regarding network infrastructures and data centers. One may expect hacking to be one of the main forms of attack on cloud infrastructures as well, given that the applications running in the cloud make use of common technologies and security mechanisms, and are therefore vulnerable to the same strategies. According to the Verizon study, hacking along with malware injection are the most widespread forms of attack.

6.8 Defending against real attacks

In Table 2 we go through the list of attacks and identify the potential consequences. Since a given attack type can have a range of different effects on a victim, our classification considers the most serious documented consequences of each type of attack. Fortunately, the most serious consequences of attacks are not always the most frequently observed ones. As we shall see, this does not have an impact on the choice of placement strategy regarding PM majorities nor VM majorities.

Based on information about each attack's outcome we assign it to one of the classes listed in Table 1. For example, if the adversary may take full control of one particular PM, he could make it stop, which would be a crash failure. However, since the attacker may also disrupt the service in some other subtler way, we consider this failure as Byzantine instead. After classifying attacks we determine the appropriate defense strategy, taking into account a set of factors explained below.

Let us start with the situations in which resource distribution is irrelevant. Two kinds of attacks share this result: Denial of Service and VM-to-Hypervisor Attacks. The main reason why the distribution is irrelevant in case of a DoS attack has to do with how resources are used with virtualization and cloud computing. Since the physical resources are shared, an attacker, even by targeting one specific VM, may prevent the other co-located VMs from operating properly. In an even more difficult scenario, on-demand resource provisioning may lead to VM instance flooding, congesting the infrastructure of the cloud provider.

While the replica placement strategy for DoS attacks is straightforward, the strategy to defend against VM-to-Hypervisor attacks requires some additional discussion. Although the adversary starts malicious actions from one VM (randomly assigned by the cloud provider), the attack to the target service occurs only when the hypervisor gives in. In fact, intrusion into the target service occurs from a successfully hacked PM (hypervisor). This intrusion method and its potentially serious effects lead us to associate VM-to-Hypervisor attacks with the Limited (Byzantine) PM category, and in this case the placement of VMs for majority preservation is irrelevant. Hence, the first line of Table 3 shows the distribution of replicas as being irrelevant regardless of the kind of majority that is to be assured.

Despite not being necessarily of intentional nature, we include in our analysis VM software faults as one of the causes of VM crashes. This is an interesting case because software faults leading to accidental crashes are quite common. In this case, if we assume that any VM might be affected with uniform probability, the distribution of VMs

Table 2 Classification of the attacks according to the worst consequences documented

Class of Attack	Real Case
Limited PMs	Denial of Service
	VM-to-Hypervisor Attack
Limited Crash VMs	VM Software Faults
Lim. Byzantine VMs	Cross-VM Side-Channel
	XML Signature Wrapping
	Metadata Spoofing
Unlim. PMs/Byzant. VMs	Malware Injection
	Hacking

Table 3 Placement strategies according to attack type and majority goal

PM Maj.	VM Maj.	Real Case
Irrelevant	Irrelevant	Denial of Service
		VM-to-Hypervisor Attack
Balanced	Irrelevant	VM Software Faults
Unbalanced	Balanced	Cross-VM Side-Channel
		XML Signature Wrapping
		Metadata Spoofing
Irrelevant	Balanced	Malware Injection
		Hacking

is only relevant to ensure a PM majority. We do not show PM crashes in the tables, as they would fall in the "Limited PMs" attacks, which we covered already.

We proceed with the discussion of Limited Byzantine VM attacks, where the placement of replicas has great impact on defender's success. There are several characteristics of this attack class corresponding to failures described in Section 6. The analysis of adversary limitations, targets and intrusion consequences lead us to classify XML Signature Wrapping, Metadata Spoofing and Cross-VM Side-Channel as Limited Byzantine VM attacks. Usually the target of these attacks are the VMs hosting the victim's service. The adversary, despite having some information about the victim, does not seem capable of picking the attack starting point and target at will. Nonetheless, a broken service instance may enable the hacker to compromise other service replicas running on the shared resource. The placement strategy in this case greatly depends on the desired majority. When the goal is keeping the majority of VMs, a balanced placement strategy should be adopted, otherwise unbalancing is better.

The classification of Malware Injection and Hacking as Unlimited PMs or Unlimited Byzantine VMs, which ends up being the same, is based on the worst possible consequences achieved by an adversary (partial or total access to the infrastructure). Possible scenarios include exploitation of the same vulnerability in many nodes to start a full scale attack. In the real case we described in Section 6.2, hackers seemed to have accessed the entire intranet of the cloud provider. The analysis performed in Section 5 suggests a balanced placement strategy for Unlimited (Byzantine) PM attacks when VM majority is the goal, whereas the distribution is irrelevant otherwise.

By analyzing Malware Injection and Hacking attacks, along with information provided by the Verizon report [29], the most harmful consequences of these attacks are likely to be uncommon. Although such an attack may provide unlimited access to a cloud infrastructure (e.g., leaked or stolen administration passwords) one may consider that an attacker will in general be more successful in obtaining illegitimate access into a single application and its VMs rather than the whole infrastructure. This would, in fact, suggest that most malware and hacking attacks should be classified as Limited Byzantine VMs.

A careful analysis of the relation between attack types and placement strategies on lines three and four of Table 3 helped us to solve this ambiguous situation. We noted that the replica distribution methods are not contradictory for any of the majorities. When the defender wants to keep a VM majority, both lines suggest a balanced strategy. When the defender's goal is to keep a PM majority under intentional attacks, the irrelevant indications suggest that the unbalanced placement strategy should be used, allowing the defender to protect against a larger fraction of attacks.

7 Conclusion and future perspectives

Clouds are changing the surface of information technologies. As a consequence, the concentration of resources in the same region, network, or even machine poses an evident challenge to designers of dependable systems. In this paper we evaluate the problem of distributing resources over physical machines. We adopt the perspective of the cloud provider that needs to distribute VMs by a given fixed set of PMs. While intuition could perhaps suggest that a balanced distribution of VMs would make a more dependable system for most scenarios, this is not the case.

Based on real evidence of security incidents, the behavior of a defender should consider whether he or she needs to keep a majority of PMs or VMs. Whereas balancing is indeed better for the latter case, unbalancing is the best option for the former. In any case, it is wise to adopt a strategy for placing replicas, rather than leaving the distribution uncontrolled, given that there are relatively few cases in which replica placement may be considered irrelevant.

An interesting perspective for the future is to include probabilities in our analysis. For example, given the probability of having a compromised VM, what is the probability that other co-located VMs might become compromised as well? The same for the hypervisor: given a compromised VM what is the probability that the attack escalates to affect the hypervisor? Standing on figures owned by cloud providers, this may give an idea of the probability that an attack manages to control a majority of VMs or PMs, thus helping providers to select the best defensive strategy.

Competing interests
The authors declare that they have no competing interests.

Authors' contributions
FA carried out the theoretical evaluation in Section 3, the experimental evaluation of Section 4, wrote most part of these sections and contributed in all others. SB carried out most of the research for real attacks. SB and RB were the main contributors to Sections 5 and 6. AC reviewed and rewrote parts of the manuscript. All authors contributed to the conclusions and all authors read and approved the final manuscript.

Acknowledgments
This work has been supported by the FCT, Fundação para a Ciência e a Tecnologia, funded in the scope of Programa Operacional Temático Factores de Competitividade (COMPETE) and Fundo Comunitário Europeu FEDER, through projects EXPL/EEI-ESS/2542/2013, DECAF, An Exploratory Study of Distributed Cloud Application Failures, and CMU-PT/RNQ/0015/2009, TRONE, Trustworthy and Resilient Operations in a Network Environment.

Author details
[1]CISUC, Department of Informatics Engineering, University of Coimbra, Polo II, 3030-290 Coimbra, Portugal. [2]Faculty of Sciences, University of Lisbon, Campo Grande, 1749-016 Lisboa, Portugal.

References

1. Barham P, Dragovic B, Fraser B, Hand S, Harris T, Ho A, Neugebauer R, Pratt I, Warfield A (2003) Xen and the art of virtualization. In: Proceedings of the nineteenth ACM Symposium On Operating Systems Principles, SOSP '03. ACM, New York, pp 164–177
2. Technical White Papers — VMWare. http://www.vmware.com/resources/techresources/. Retrieved on May 6, 2014
3. Papers — Oracle VM VirtualBox. https://www.virtualbox.org/wiki/Papers. Retrieved on May 6, 2014
4. Bellard F (2005) QEMU, a fast and portable dynamic translator. In: Proceedings of the annual conference on USENIX Annual Technical Conference, ATEC '05. USENIX Association, Berkeley, pp 41–41
5. Camargos FL, Girard G, des Ligneris B (2008) Virtualization of Linux servers. In: Proceedings of the Linux symposium. http://ols.fedoraproject.org/OLS/Reprints-2008/camargos-reprint.pdf.
6. Meng X, Isci C, Jeffrey J, Zhang L, Bouillet E, Pendarakis D (2010) Efficient resource provisioning in compute clouds via vm multiplexing. In: Proceedings of the 7th International Conference on Autonomic Computing, ICAC '10. ACM, New York, pp 11–20
7. Sonnek J, Greensky J, Reutiman R, Chandra A (2010) Starling: minimizing communication overhead in virtualized computing platforms using decentralized affinity-aware migration. In: Proceedings of the 2010 39th International Conference on Parallel Processing, ICPP '10. IEEE Computer Society, Washington, DC, pp 228–237
8. Wood T, Tarasuk-Levin G, Shenoy P, Desnoyers P, Cecchet E, Corner MD (2009) Memory buddies: exploiting page sharing for smart colocation in virtualized data centers. In: Proceedings of the 2009 ACM SIGPLAN/SIGOPS International Conference on Virtual Execution Environments, VEE '09. ACM, New York, pp 31–40
9. Gupta D, Lee S, Vrable M, Savage S, Snoeren AC, Varghese G, Voelker GM, Vahdat A (2010) Difference engine: harnessing memory redundancy in virtual machines. Commun ACM 53(10):85–93
10. Heroku | Cloud application platform. http://www.heroku.com. Retrieved on May 6, 2014
11. Ruby On rails and PHP cloud hosting PaaS | Managed rails development | Engine yard platform as a service. http://www.engineyard.com. Retrieved on May 6, 2014
12. Google App Engine — Google Developers. https://developers.google.com/appengine/. Retrieved on May 6, 2014
13. McKeown M, Kommalapati H, Roth J Disaster recovery and high availability for windows azure applications. Web page http://msdn.microsoft.com/en-us/library/windowsazure/dn251004.aspx visited on December 5th 2013
14. Bessani AN, Alchieri EP, Correia M, Fraga JS (2008) DepSpace: a byzantine fault-tolerant coordination service. SIGOPS Oper Syst Rev 42(4):163–176
15. Prieto E, Diaz R, Romano L, Rieke R, Achemlal M (2011) MASSIF: a promising solution to enhance olympic games IT security. In: Georgiadis CK, Jahankhani H, Pimenidis E, Bashroush R, Al-Nemrat A (eds) ICGS3/e-Democracy, volume 99 of Lecture Notes of the Institute for Computer Sciences, Social Informatics and Telecommunications Engineering. Springer, pp 139–147. http://link.springer.com/chapter/10.1007%2F978-3-642-33448-1_20.
16. Bessani A, Cutillo LA, Ramunno G, Schirmer N, Smiraglia P (2013) The TClouds platform: concept, architecture and instantiations. In: Proceedings of the 2nd international workshop on Dependability Issues in Cloud Computing, DISCCO '13. ACM, New York, pp 1:1–1:6
17. SECFUNET - Security for Future Networks - Home. http://www.secfunet.eu. Accessed on 6 May 2014
18. CloudFit. http://cloudfit.di.fc.ul.pt/index.php?title=Public:Main_Page. Accessed on 6 May 2014
19. Slamanig D, Hanser C (2012) On cloud storage and the cloud of clouds approach. In: Internet technology and secured transactions, 2012 international conferece for, pp 649–655. http://ieeexplore.ieee.org/xpl/login.jsp?tp=&arnumber=6470897&url=http%3A%2F%2Fieeexplore.ieee.org%252.
20. Bitcoin - Open source P2P money. http://bitcoin.org/. Accessed on 6 May 2014
21. Castro M, Liskov B (2002) Practical byzantine fault tolerance and proactive recovery. ACM Trans Comput Syst 20(4):398–461
22. Correia M, Veronese GS, Lung LC (2010) Asynchronous Byzantine consensus with $2f+1$ processes. In: Proceedings of the 2010 ACM Symposium on Applied Computing, SAC '10. ACM, New York, pp 475–480
23. Araujo F, Barbosa R, Casimiro A (2012) Replication for dependability on virtualized cloud environments. In: Proceedings of the 10th international workshop on Middleware for Grids, Clouds and e-Science, MGC '12. ACM, New York, pp 2:1–2:6
24. Berger S, Cáceres R, Goldman KA, Perez R, Sailer R, van Doorn L (2006) vTPM: virtualizing the Trusted Platform Module. In: Proceedings of the 15th conference on USENIX security symposium - Volume 15, USENIX-SS'06. USENIX Association, Berkeley
25. Johnson NL, Kotz S (1977) Urn models and their application — an approach to modern discrete probability theory. John Wiley & Sons, New York, Chichester, Brisbane, Toronto
26. Jensen M, Schwenk J, Gruschka N, Iacono LL (2009) On technical security issues in cloud computing. In: Proceedings of the 2009 IEEE International Conference on Cloud Computing, CLOUD '09. IEEE Computer Society, Washington, DC, pp 109–116
27. Zhang Y, Juels A, Reiter MK, Ristenpart T (2012) Cross-VM side channels and their use to extract private keys. In: Proceedings of the 2012 ACM conference on computer and communications security. ACM, New York, pp 305–316
28. Gruschka N, Iacono LL (2009) Vulnerable cloud: SOAP message security validation revisited. In: ICWS, pp 625–631. http://ieeexplore.ieee.org/xpl/login.jsp?tp=&arnumber=5175877&url=http%3A%2F%2Fieeexplore.ieee.org%252.
29. Verizon (2013) Data breach investigations report. http://www.verizonenterprise.com/DBIR/2013/. Retrieved on May 6, 2014
30. CloudFlare blog - The DDoS That Almost Broke the Internet. http://blog.cloudflare.com/the-ddos-that-almost-broke-the-internet. Retrieved on May 6, 2014
31. Domingues P, Araujo F, Silva L (2009) Evaluating the performance and intrusiveness of virtual machines for desktop grid computing. In: Proceedings of the 2009 IEEE International Symposium on Parallel & Distributed Processing, IPDPS '09. IEEE Computer Society, Washington, DC, pp 1–8
32. SFGate.com blog - The Google Attack Scenario Offense and Defense. http://blog.sfgate.com/ybenjamin/2010/04/20/the-google-attack-scenario-offense-and-defense/. Retrieved on May 6, 2014
33. Hacking D-Link Routers With HNAP. http://www.sourcesec.com/Lab/dlink_hnap_captcha.pdf. Retrieved on May 6, 2014
34. Computerworld - Researchers Demo Cloud Security Issue with Amazon AWS Attack. http://www.computerworld.com/s/article/9221208/Researchers_demo_cloud_security_issue_with_Amazon_AWS_attack/. Retrieved on May 6, 2014
35. Szefer J, Keller E, Lee RB, Rexford J (2011) Eliminating the hypervisor attack surface for a more secure cloud. In: Proceedings of the 18th ACM conference on computer and communications security, CCS '11. ACM, New York, pp 401–412
36. InformationWeek - New Virtualization Vulnerability Allows Escape To Hypervisor Attacks. http://www.informationweek.com/security/application-security/new-virtualization-vulnerability-allows/240001996/. Retrieved on May 6, 2014
37. Dark Reading - Researchers Develop Cross-VM Side-Channel Attack. http://www.darkreading.com/attacks-breaches/researchers-develop-cross-vm-side-channel-attack/d/d-id/1138623? Retrieved on May 6, 2014

6

PAMPA in the wild: a real-life evaluation of a lightweight ad-hoc broadcasting family

Christopher Winstanley[1][*], Rajiv Ramdhany[1], François Taïani[2], Barry Porter[1] and Hugo Miranda[3]

Abstract

Broadcast is one of the core building blocks of many services deployed on ad-hoc wireless networks, such as Mobile Ad-Hoc Networks (MANETs) or Wireless Sensor Networks (WSNs). Most broadcast protocols are however only ever evaluated using simulations, which have repeatedly been shown to be unreliable, and potentially misleading. In this paper, we seek to go beyond simulations, and consider the particular case of PAMPA, a promising family of wireless broadcast algorithms for ad-hoc and wireless networks. We report on our efforts to further our experimental understanding of PAMPA, and present the first ever characterisation of the PAMPA family on a real deployment. Here it has to deal with real network problems such as node, message and sending failure. Our experiments show that the standard PAMPA algorithm out-performs all other protocols in the family, with a delivery ratio consistently around 75%, and a retransmission ratio as low as 44%, for a failure-free run. We use this opportunity to reflect on our findings and lessons learnt when moving from simulations to actual experiments[a][b].

1   Introduction

Ad-Hoc wireless networks, such as MANETs (Mobile Ad Hoc Networks) and many WSNs (Wireless Sensor Networks), are self-configuring networks of embedded or mobile devices connected by wireless link. They typically rely heavily on a best-effort message dissemination service, or *broadcast*, as a fundamental building block to implement higher-level services, including routing and service discovery.

The simplest form of ad-hoc broadcast uses flooding, in which every node retransmits the messages it receives. Flooding is simple and generally robust, but wasteful. A number of algorithms have therefore been proposed to improve on flooding, by limiting retransmissions (communication cost) while still trying to reach as many nodes as possible (delivery). These algorithms differ in the policy they use to select retransmitting nodes, but they have in common that most of them avoid explicit control messages, and rely instead on the limited amount of information present on each node to drive retransmissions. They also often use some form of *randomisation* (in timeouts, or in decisions) to overcome the network's

unpredictability. While this approach works, randomisation may unfortunately cause sub-optimal behaviours, such as nodes retransmitting when they should not, or not retransmitting when they should, leading to nodes being missed out, or unnecessary transmissions being triggered.

PAMPA [1] is a lightweight broadcast algorithm that purposely avoids randomisation by combining two known strategies to the problem of ad-hoc broadcast: counting messages, and measuring received signal strength. More specifically, PAMPA first uses the received signal strength of a message as an estimation of the distance to the message's source. PAMPA then uses the estimated distance to order retransmissions, starting at the node that is most distant to the source. Superfluous retransmissions are avoided because nodes closer to the source refrain from retransmitting. PAMPA is a minimalist protocol that does not use control messages; excludes warm-up or calibration phases; and does not assume any particular capabilities on nodes such as location-awareness or directional antennas [2,3]. Overall, PAMPA achieves a per-broadcast delivery rate throughout the network which is close to that of flooding while using far less messages.

Building on PAMPA's insight, a number of variants have been proposed [4] that seek to harden the protocol further. Some of these variants have been shown in simulations to

*Correspondence: c.winstanley@lancs.ac.uk
[1] Lancaster University, Lancaster, UK
Full list of author information is available at the end of the article

provide delivery rates that are even closer to that of simple flooding while still using far less messages. PAMPA and its variants, however, have so far only been tested in simulations, a common approach in wireless protocol research. Although useful to rapidly assess a protocol's behaviour, simulations have frequently been shown to be unreliable in assessing a protocol's real performance [5-7]. The inaccuracy of simulations is further compounded by the fact that most simulation scenarios do not consider node failures. Node failures are however common in real deployments, where wireless sensors or mobile devices may go offline because of a variety of reasons such as mobility, depleted batteries, environmental hazards, hardware faults, and software bugs [8]. This is particular true of wireless systems deployed in aggressive environments such as industrial plants [9], search and rescue operations, or field experiments [10].

In this article, we propose to go beyond simulations for the PAMPA family of protocols, and present an evaluation of a family of algorithms inspired by PAMPA based on a real deployment. Our goal is both to assess PAMPA's actual performance on real scenarios, and to report on our experience in moving from simulated to real experiments. More precisely, our evaluation exercises three aspects of PAMPA in three sets of experiments over real networks containing 7 and 26 nodes: In a first set of experiments we evaluated the effect of different variants proposed to reinforce PAMPA's robustness in sparse topologies. In a second set of experiments, we carried a sensitivity analysis on the position of the broadcasting nodes on a protocol's performance using a simple flooding algorithm as a comparison point. Finally, because node failures are common in wireless sensor networks, we assessed the algorithm's survivability in a last set of experiments in which nodes progressively disappear following an exponential fault model. In such drastic circumstances, PAMPA must adapt to node failures properly, making sure that a broadcasted message gets to its destination even when its choice of propagation paths is limited.

All our experiments show that the PAMPA algorithm used out-performs all other evaluated protocols, with a delivery ratio constantly around 75%, and a retransmission ratio as low as 44% for failure-free runs. Similarly, our experiments with failed nodes show it maintaining a delivery ratio of 70%, even when over one third of the original nodes have failed, well above the delivery ratio of a flooding approach (60%) under the same conditions.

The rest of the article is organised as follows: We first present the challenges involved in implementing a broadcast service for wireless ad-hoc networks, and existing works in this area (Sec. 2). We then introduce PAMPA and its variants (Sec. 3), before moving on to our experimental setup (Sec. 4). Section 5 presents our experimental results, and the lessons we learnt, and Section 6 concludes.

2 Background and related work

Wireless ad-hoc networks are often used in long-term deployments (as in WSNs) where nodes have limited energy resources. The use of naive flooding to disseminate information in such networks is especially costly and can significantly reduce a network's lifetime. More precisely, flooding involves each node re-broadcasting every new packet it receives after a random delay. Although this achieves a good coverage of nodes, its simplistic design consumes non-negligible power, engenders network contention/interferences, and is prone to packet collisions that cannot be detected by the sender [11]. Most broadcast protocols for MANETs/WSNs therefore seek to reduce message retransmissions whilst maintaining a coverage comparable to classic flooding. In doing so, they reduce contention and the chance of collisions, lowering broadcast latencies and saving energy as a result. To optimise on classic flooding, they typically make use of contextual information such as node location or neighbourhood, or rely only on observations of ongoing packet exchanges. Their behaviour is typically *localised* in that each node only uses its local knowledge to decide whether the cost of retransmitting a packet is outweighed by the benefit of reaching new nodes. In the following we review the most common strategies proposed to implement wireless ad-hoc broadcast protocols. We conclude this review with a few comments on the problem of node failures, and on the use of simulations to evaluate wireless protocols.

Location-based protocols use geometric modelling [2,11] to determine the expected additional coverage that is gained by a node by virtue of its position and only allow the node with the maximum expected additional coverage to retransmit. For example, the Six-shot broadcast algorithm [2] relies on geographical coordinates provided by positioning devices on each node, such as GPS.

Alternatively, *efficient flooding* approaches [12-15] restrict message rebroadcast duties to core nodes and achieve the same message delivery ratio at a much lower volume of rebroadcasts. This is typically achieved through the computation of a dominating set of nodes [13] which act as a multicast tree for the wireless ad hoc network. In the dominating set, every node not in the set is adjacent to at least one other node in the set. The main advantage of connected-dominating-set-based broadcast protocols is that it simplifies the rebroadcasting process to the smaller subnetwork generated from the connected dominating set and thus reduces the total overhead of the protocol. For example, in cluster-based routing [16], clusterheads and gateway nodes form a connected dominating set for routing messages from nodes in their respective clusters. The efficiency of this approach depends largely on the process of finding a connected dominating set and the size of the corresponding subnetwork.

Das et al. proposed a number of routing schemes that use the Guha and Khuller's approximation algorithm [17] to calculate a minimum connected dominating set. In [15], Wu et al. suggest an alternative method for minimum connected dominating sets that generates smaller sets within less time. The computation of dominating sets requires neighbouring nodes to exchange their knowledge of local topology. This, of course, necessitates the periodic exchange of explicit control messages for neighbour discovery in a warm-up phase prior to node-set reduction.

The construction of the multicast-tree can also occur at run-time (*self-pruning*). In these *Neighbour Elimination* schemes, each node removes itself from the multicast tree by not retransmitting if all its neighbours are already covered by the retransmission of one of its neighbours. The rebroadcast list at each node is pruned based on its neighbours that were covered by previous transmissions. For example, the Scalable Broadcasting Algorithm (SBA) [12] performs self-pruning at each node receiving a new broadcast message by comparing the sender's neighbours with those of the receiver. Two-hop neighbourhood discovery is periodically undertaken by the exchange of two-hop Hello messages between all peer nodes. Using SBA, a node's retransmission is cancelled if a neighbour's retransmission achieves the same node coverage. This scheme is further improved by the RNG Relay Subset (RRS) protocol [18] which reduces the set of monitored neighbours and thus the quantity of redundant transmissions.

Whilst dominating-set-based and neighbour elimination approaches aim at reducing the number of transmissions to achieve total coverage of the network, another category of broadcasting solutions considers the adjustment of transmission radius and thus, topology control, to obtain a compromise in energy savings and reduction in retransmisions. In *Topological Control* broadcast schemes, node locations (for example, GPS) included in periodically-exchanged HELLO messages, are used to determine the minimum additional transmission power at each node to cover an intended sub-graph of neighbour nodes. A slight increase in transmission power at a node to cover a neighbour node is deemed preferable to having another (closer) node retransmit. The *Broadcast Incremental Power* (BIP) protocol, proposed by Wieselthier, Nguyen and Ephremides [19] uses a topology control algorithm in which a node's relay node (the node covering it) is selected from a set of neighbours such that the additional transmission power required at the chosen relay node is smallest. Topological control algorithms require knowledge of each node's neighbourhood for adjusting its transmission power. A deeper knowledge of nodes' neighbourhood (n-hops) may lead to a more optimal power adjustment in the tree-building process;

but the need for additional HELLO message exchanges inevitably degrades overall performance. Ingelrest and Simplot-Ryl proposed a localized broadcast incremental power protocol [20] where this overhead is limited by having each node applying the BIP algorithm in its k-hop neighbourhood, for moderate values of k (for example, $k=2$).

Contextual information, as used by Location-, Connected-Dominating-Set-based and Topological-Control protocols, is not however always available (or its use desirable). GPS for example, used as a basis for geometric modelling, may be too expensive a requirement for low-cost devices and does not work indoors. Likewise neighbour discovery via Hello messages can be a source of significant overhead, additional contention and collisions. To address these limitations, a range of broadcast protocols have been proposed that do not require any contextual information but instead rely on simple heuristics that have been shown to work well.

For instance, *epidemic protocols* such as *GOSSIP1(p)* [21] use a form of probabilistic flooding in which nodes retransmit a message with some fixed probability p ($p < 1$). To prevent retransmissions from dying out (p is too low), *GOSSIP3(p,k,m)* [21] extends this technique by forcing retransmissions in two cases: *i)* if the message has been travelling for less than k hops, and *ii)* if the number of retransmissions listened by any node after a short delay is lower than a threshold m. Unfortunately static gossip probabilities may render these protocols inefficient in heterogeneous network topologies. A low gossip probability is suitable for a dense network but cause the broadcast to die out in sparser regions. Conversely, a higher probability improves reachability in the sparser regions but is wasteful for denser topologies. The problem is further compounded by the fact that network densities are not usually known a priori. To address this issue, adaptive epidemic protocols such as RAPID [22] and Smart Gossip [3] adapt their retransmission probability to the perceived network density. They assign different gossip probabilities to nodes based on their topological importance; critical nodes broadcast with higher probability. Node densities are evaluated during a warm-up phase through the periodic exchange of messages and neighbour retransmissions count.

Warm-up phases and periodic neighbour discovery can be costly and in the case of volatile networks present the broadcast protocol with outdated neighbour information. Further, as found in [11], if several neighbours around a node were to retransmit the same flooding message, the expected additional coverage, EAC(k), after a host hears the same message k times dramatically decreases. *Counter-based broadcast* protocols therefore restrict the retransmissions in a node's neighbourhood to a predefined threshold. They wait for a random but bounded delay and count the number of duplicate messages received at a node during that time. They then only allow retransmission if the counter does not reach a pre-determined threshold. Counting duplicate messages improves efficiency and is therefore a trait found in many WSN broadcast protocols including PAMPA. On its own, however, counting, like the use of static probability, does not ensure an optimal use of retransmissions. In particular, the problem of selecting suitable thresholds for uneven distributions in network topology remains.

Like counter-based protocols, *distance-based broadcast protocols* [11] use the notion of expected additional coverage to determine the value of a node's retransmission. Instead of counting neighbour retransmissions, they look at the signal strength of these retransmissions to estimate additional coverage. They assume that signal strength (captured from the Received Signal Strength Indicator - RSSI) is an indication of a transmitter's distance to the receiving node. The greater the distance (i.e. the lower the first message's RSSI), the more additional nodes the receiving node can cover with its retransmission. To exploit this notion, distance-based protocols wait for a random but bounded time after the first message reception listening to further retransmissions. If the maximum signal strength of all received retransmissions falls below a certain threshold, the node is allowed to retransmit. Both counter-based and distance-based broadcast protocols use random listening periods which can be counter-productive: nodes of higher topological importance may be preempted from retransmitting if the listening timer of less 'important' nodes in their vicinity expires first.

The most recent research into probabilistic protocols has been looking into coping with node failures. Sensor networks succumb to node failure as nodes often have low power supplies and are prone to errors. In striving to take further account of the underlying network, protocols such as RAPID [22] have been proposed to cope with node failures and varying network densities. RAPID uses corrective deterministic measures to ensure a constant delivery of messages, regardless of the underlying topology. Nodes that miss messages can request them from their neighbours, thus keeping the delivery ratio high. However this can have an adverse effect on the overall efficiency of the protocol. For a node to find out which messages their neighbours have seen, determine which messages they have missed and obtain them from the neighbour, it adds considerable overhead to the protocol's performance.

Although extremely useful to rapidly assess a protocol's behaviour, simulations have repeatedly been shown to be inaccurate in assessing a protocol's real performance [5,6,23,24]. This is because simulations often used simplified models of complex physical phenomena. For instance, the unity disk model—in which nodes have a fix constant transmission range that is free of any interference—has long prevailed in simulations, but is highly unrealistic. In real ad hoc wireless settings, network links are connected intermittently and have dynamic qualities that depend on topographical factors such as building structures and other time-varying factors such as weather and temperature [9]. Radio communication is also affected by fast-time varying interference such as hidden terminals, multi-path effects and gray zones [25]. This time varying environment is not completely controllable and provides a source of non-determinism in the evaluation of broadcast and ad hoc routing protocols. To overcome this inaccuracy, most simulators offer full-fledged propagation models that seek to replicate the imperfections of real radio deployments: imperfect ranges, erroneous links and interferences. These full-fledged models tend unfortunately to be very costly to compute, limiting their use [6]. Current simulators therefore often propose intermediate strategies that seek to balance accuracy against simulation complexity. These strategies however differ from simulator to simulator, making cross-simulator comparisons difficult [24], and any extrapolation of simulation results to real deployments subject to caution, at best [23].

3 PAMPA and its variants

PAMPA [1], which provides the basis for our work, reduces the use for randomisation in wireless ad hoc broadcast protocols by combining both the counting and distance-based strategies. PAMPA has since then been expanded to include hardening mechanisms, in particular in heterogeneous topologies [4], with promising results obtained in simulations.

3.1 Vanilla PAMPA

The basic PAMPA algorithm is shown in Algorithm 1. PAMPA is at its core a counter-based broadcast algorithm, which uses distance (as derived from a transmission's Received Signal Strength Indicator, or RSSI) to calibrate how long a node waits while counting. More precisely, when a node receives a message for the first time, PAMPA apportions a "waiting time" for that node. The waiting time depends on the signal strength at which the message was received (line 8) such that higher RSSI values (i.e. smaller distances) tend to be associated with longer waiting times. During this waiting time a node counts how many retransmissions it receives of that same message. At the end of this waiting time the node makes a decision for that message: if the node heard *less* than a given number n of retransmissions (line 14), the node chooses to retransmit the message itself (line 15), otherwise it does not.

Algorithm 1: The PAMPA Algorithm [1]

```
1 function delay(rssi) begin
2 │   return k*rssi;    /* For some constant k
    │   */
3 end
4 upon receiving(msg) begin
5 │   if msg ∉ messages then
6 │   │   messages ← messages ∪ {msg};
7 │   │   count_msg ← 0;
8 │   │   SetTimer(msg,delay(msg.RSSI));
9 │   else
10 │   │   count_msg ← count_msg + 1;
11 │   end
12 end
13 upon timeout(msg) begin
14 │   if count_msg < n then
15 │   │   Broadcast(msg)
16 │   end
17 end
```

PAMPA intentionally privileges retransmissions performed by the nodes more distant to the source of the previous retransmission as these are the ones expected to provide bigger gains in coverage. The particular value for n is fixed prior to deployment and is chosen based on the desired trade-off between delivery coverage and redundant message overhead (such that lower values of n mean less redundant messaging but potentially lower delivery coverage). However, it should be noted that the relation between n and coverage is not linear given that as retransmissions approximate to the source, so does the probability that the area has been completely covered by one or more previous retransmissions.

For the purpose of counting retransmissions, a "message" is assumed to be uniquely identified in some way; in our implementation this is by way of a monotonically increasing sequence number set by the broadcast source.

3.2 Variants

Although PAMPA is thus more "informed" than other counter-based alternatives, its perception of the local node topology remains limited. In particular, PAMPA is not designed to perform well in heterogeneous topologies where some nodes may perform a key role in the propagation of messages. This is a situation likely to arise in real-world wireless networks, for example when two parts of a network on opposite sides of a river are connected by a small number of sensors deployed over a bridge. To address this problem a number of variants to PAMPA were proposed in [4]. All consist in counting only *some* of the retransmissions (see line 10 of Alg. 1), based on two types of information: (i) the retransmission path just followed by a retransmission (*Common Parenting*), and (ii) the relative position of a retransmission with respect to the original copy of a message (*Dynamic Thresholding*).

Common Parenting looks at the next-before-last hop of a retransmission, which we call its *parent node*. This relationship is illustrated in Figure 1. Common parenting records the parent node of the original message reception, and only counts those retransmissions that have a *different* parent than the original reception. The motivation for this mechanism is that different parent nodes will tend to denote a higher diversity of propagation paths, which is a sign that the message is propagating well and is therefore less likely to need additional retransmissions.

Dynamic Thresholding uses the RSSI to further influence whether or not a message should be retransmitted. It uses a similar approach to distance-based protocols in that it only counts retransmissions that have an RSSI that crosses a particular threshold. However, instead of relying on a fixed threshold, which is difficult to define statically, the dynamic thresholding variant of PAMPA uses the RSSI of the original message reception to set the threshold for observing retransmissions of that message.

Dynamic Thresholding comes in two sub-variants, depending whether only retransmissions with a *lower* (*Thresholding*) or *higher* (*Antithresholding*) RSSI than the original one are counted. Both *Thresholding* and *Antithresholding* have a geometric interpretation: *Thresholding*, in which we count retransmissions with a lower RSSI and therefore estimated greater distance than the original sender, will cause a node C to only count retransmissions from a doughnut area we have termed its *outer-ring* (see Figure 2). By contrast, *Antithresholding*, in which we count retransmissions with a higher RSSI and therefore estimated shorted distance than the original sender, will primarily count retransmissions from a node's *inner-strip* and *forward bubble* on the same figure. In this latter case, note that nodes located between C and R will have a longer delay than C due to the generally higher RSSI that they will observe on the message originally received from R; these nodes are therefore unlikely to retransmit before C.

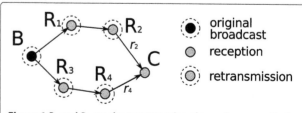

Figure 1 R_1 and R_3 are the parent nodes of r_2 and r_4 respectively.

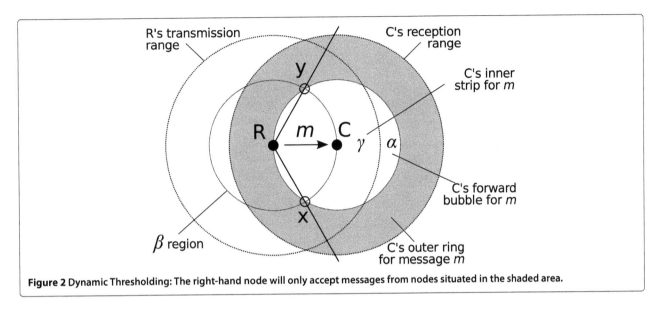

Figure 2 Dynamic Thresholding: The right-hand node will only accept messages from nodes situated in the shaded area.

3.3 A family of protocol variants

The criteria used by Common Parenting and Dynamic Thresholding to filter retransmissions are orthogonal, and can thus be combined to create further variants. This is shown in Figure 3, where the types of retransmissions counted by variants are shown in a 2 × 2 matrix. PAMPA counts all retransmissions, while Common Parenting (CP), Thresholding (TH) and Antithresholding (ATH) only count retransmissions meeting a single criterion (shown as 1's in the figure).

By combining the CP criteria with TH and ATH, one obtains two more protocols, PAMPA-TH/CP and PAMPA-ATH/CP. These are more selective than PAMPA in their counting but less than the original three variants. Another protocol, hereafter named Delayed Flooding (D-Flooding) can be captured in this scheme by simply not counting any retransmission, and retransmitting all messages. D-Flooding differentiates from flooding by replacing the random jitter mechanism used in the latter to reduce collisions by a distance-based delay similar to the one used by PAMPA.

This distance-based delay is expected to improve flooding delivery ratio given that nodes providing a bigger additional coverage will retransmit before the remaining.

4 Experimental setup

Most existing studies of the performance of broadcast protocols use simulations (see, for example [4]). However, even the most detailed simulation models may not capture the particular characteristics of real ad-hoc wireless environments. They may not, for example, include limitations of the radio interface hardware such as limited buffer space, limitations due to the protocol stack implementations, or various random sources of errors in the wireless physical layer such as multipath propagation, radio noise,

asymmetric radio links, and so on. For our real-life evaluation of PAMPA and its variants, we implemented and deployed the algorithms in a live testbed (a WISEBED instance [26]) of sensor mote devices. In particular, we built the algorithms using the component libraries and toolchain of the Lorien OS [27] deployed and executed on TelosB motes. TelosB motes (depicted in Figure 4) are low-power wireless sensor devices, each equipped with a 802.15.4 radio module achieving data rates of up to 250 kbps and an indoor transmission range between 20 m to 30 m.

4.1 Experimental configurations

Our evaluation uses three experimental configurations to examine different aspects of the PAMPA family of protocols in real networks. The first configuration (C1) compares all PAMPA variants head to head against Delayed Flooding. It uses a small wireless network of seven nodes, in which a single source repeatedly broadcast messages. The second configuration (C2) focusses more specifically on PAMPA with no enhancements, and analyses in detail its behaviour over that of Delayed Flooding in a larger network when the source of broadcast rotates among nodes (what we term *node-switching* in the following). Finally, the third configuration (C3) investigates how well PAMPA (with no enhancements) copes with ongoing node failures when compared with the baseline of delayed flooding, in the same network of Configuration C2.

In the version of PAMPA deployed in the testbeds the RSSI is mapped onto waiting time ('msg.delay' in Algorithm 1) by picking a random number between zero and the message's signal strength. This choice was made to account for the coarse nature of RSSI values in current radio hardware (comprised in 0 and 256, with most values falling in the higher end of this range in our experiments),

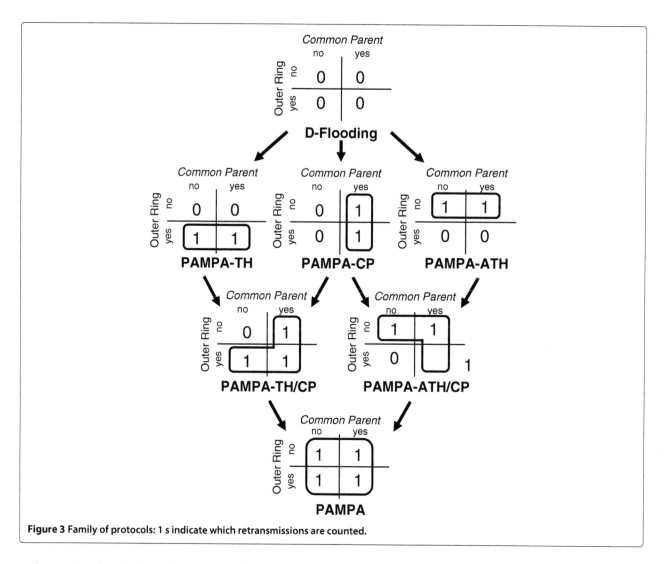

Figure 3 Family of protocols: 1 s indicate which retransmissions are counted.

and minimise the risk for collisions even when most measured RSSI values fall in a small range. For clarity, the reminder of the paper refers to the deployed version of the algorithm as "PAMPA" and uses the term "Vanilla PAMPA" to refer to the baseline version of the algorithm

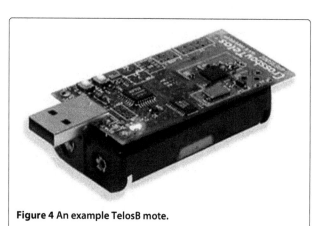

Figure 4 An example TelosB mote.

that was experimented in simulations. In all three configurations, the counting threshold for the number of heard retransmissions is kept fixed and low, at $n = 2$, to keep the messaging overhead low while still providing sufficient redundancy for delivery coverage.

4.2 Selected network topologies

For the C1 experiment, we used a small-scale WSN testbed at Lancaster University containing seven TelosB motes, all running the same variant of the PAMPA algorithm. The TelosB motes belong to an indoor live WSN testbed (part of the WISEBED experimentation facility) and are selected to realise a topology where the notion of 'keyness' of certain nodes is exercised. The layout of the nodes can be seen in Figure 5. Although the 'bridge' topologies tested in simulations [4] are hard to reproduce on the testbed due to the fixed position of nodes, the selection of key nodes (such as Node 3 in Figure 5) allows similar protocol behaviour (for example, overcancellation [4]) to be reproduced. On this topology, Node 1 is unable

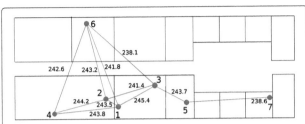

Figure 5 Node layout in the office environment at Lancaster University. Red lines indicate a link between the two nodes with the average RSSI of the link.

to communicate with Node 5 due to environment constraints. This makes Node 3 important to the delivery of messages to Node 5 and Node 7.

For the node switching and node failure experiments (respectively C2 and C3) a larger network testbed was needed. For this another WISEBED network was used in an office environment at the University of Bern. The Bern testbed has 21 nodes placed randomly in different rooms across three different floors (see Figure 6 for a layout of the topology).

Both testbeds are deployed in an 'office' environment, which includes a mixture of brick support, plasterboard separations and glass walls that radio signals must overcome, as well as thick wooden fire doors. The room height is around 2.7m. Most experiments are performed at night

to avoid the added interference of office workers. This set-up allows us to evaluate all protocols under comparable conditions.

4.3 Experimental protocol
The three experiment configurations summarised above are now described in detail to aid in reproducibility. Each configuration is based on the same basic principles with particular alterations according to the characteristics being investigated.

4.3.1 PAMPA variant comparison (C1)
In configuration C1 a particular node (Node 1, Figure 5) in the WSN is selected as the broadcast-originator whose sole responsibility is to broadcast a message every 10 seconds. This node does not attempt to receive or retransmit any messages. The periodic interval of 10 seconds ensures that broadcasts between different experiment runs do not overlap and interfere with each other. Each broadcast message contains a unique identifier (*uid*) in its header that is used by a receiving node to differentiate between multiple messages. This identifier is part of the soft state saved in each node's message log to detect duplicate messages (line 5 of Algorithm 1). Also included in the message log is the RSSI of each message, obtained through a query to the radio module of the TelosB motes for the received message's network parameters. Only the RSSI value of the

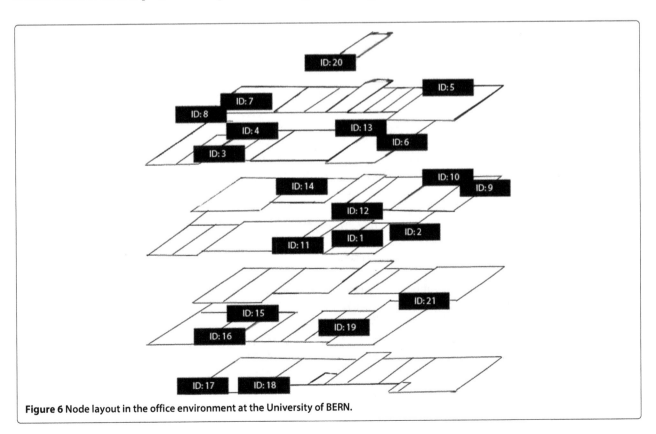

Figure 6 Node layout in the office environment at the University of BERN.

first arriving message is recorded and used as a threshold for the retransmission-based protocols.

4.3.2 Broadcast node switching (C2)

In C2 the broadcast source node is changed after each experiment run. This allows us to analyse how the location of the broadcast node affects the propagation of message and how obstructions in the network's environment affect the performance of each protocol. Broadcast nodes are chosen that would be considered to be clustered in the middle of the network (node ids: 1, 2, 3 and 14 Figure 6) and outliers on the network (node ids: 18, 20 and 21 Figure 6). These nodes are chosen to be broadcast nodes as they give a good indication of whether a broadcasting nodes' position within a network affects the performance of the protocol that is operating within it.

Each combination of a protocol and a source node is evaluated in C2 using 20 experimental runs, with each run comprising 60 individual broadcasts from the same source node. More precisely, each run, which lasts for about 18 minutes, is organised in three phases:

- In the first phase (7–9 minutes), nodes are initialised.
- In the second phase (6–8 minutes), 60 messages are broadcast from the source node and propagated through the network. During this phase, messages are broadcast every 10 seconds from the broadcast source node. This gives each message enough time to disseminate through the network before the next message is broadcast.
- In the third phase (1–5 minutes), the network is finally allowed to cool off to make sure that there are no excess messages on the network when the next run starts.

4.3.3 Node failure (C3)

For C3, the node failure configuration, three sets of experiments are conducted for both PAMPA and Delayed Flooding, which is again used as baseline. Three random nodes (Nodes 4, 10, and 15 in Figure 6) are used as broadcasting nodes. These nodes are spaced evenly around the network on different floors, providing a fair average of how each protocol copes with node failure and not how they are responding to a particular broadcast node. Each set then consists of 20 runs using the same failure model for each, in which nodes are dropped from the network using an exponential decay model. In this failure model, each node has a constant chance of failing per time unit. This corresponds to an adverse network environment, where all nodes are at risk of dying in parallel.

More specifically, we employ the following formula:

The number of surviving nodes at time t is computed to be:

$$N(t) = N(0) \times e^{-\lambda t}$$

where λ is the 'decay constant', and corresponds to the probability for each node to fail per time unit. If the time of failure is larger than the duration of the experiment, the node will not fail during the experiment.

Each experiment has the same node failure model so it shows how well the protocol copes with node failure and not how badly the nodes failed on each particular experiment. The times each node fails was calculated before the experiments took place and the same nodes failed for each run. The failure times were calculated using the algorithm above and are shown in Table 1. The broadcast node never fails as this would completely cease any message propagation on the network (note that on a real deployment of the network the broadcasting node would be changing constantly and so would not be a single point of failure).

4.4 Computed metrics

In each experiment a number of variables are measured to determine the performance of each protocol on the network. These variables are used to calculate two metrics: the *Retransmission Ratio* and the *Delivery Ratio*.

Retransmission Ratio is a key metric for broadcast protocols in WSNs and represents the communication cost paid for each successful delivery of a broadcast. The highest possible retransmission ratio is 1, corresponding to a run where all nodes that receive the message retransmit it. More efficient protocols will have lower retransmission ratios. The retransmission ratio of a run is defined as the average ratio between broadcast deliveries and broadcast retransmissions:

$$\text{The Retransmission Ratio} = \frac{1}{n_{\text{bcasts}}} \sum_{b=1}^{n_{\text{bcasts}}} \frac{\#\text{retransmission}_b}{\#\text{delivery}_b}$$

Table 1 Node failure times

Time since run started (s)	Node failed (id)
66	2
88	5
235	17
265	3
390	16
410	19
448	0
471	9
477	20

where n_{bcasts} is the number of broadcasts (in our experiments, 50), and $\frac{\#\text{retransmission}_b}{\#\text{delivery}_b}$ is the retransmission ratio of broadcast b, i.e. the proportion of nodes that, having received b, retransmit it.

Delivery Ratio is the average proportion of nodes reached by a broadcast on the network. The higher the delivery ratio, the more effective the protocol and the larger the coverage of each broadcast. A delivery ratio of 1 means that every message broadcast across the network was received by every node. More precisely, the delivery ratio is obtained with the following formula:

$$\text{The Delivery Ratio} = \frac{1}{n_{\text{bcasts}}} \sum_{b=1}^{n_{\text{bcasts}}} \frac{\#\text{delivery}_b}{n_{\text{nodes}} - 1}$$

where n_{bcasts} is the number of broadcasts (in our experiments, 50), and $\frac{\#\text{delivery}_b}{n_{\text{nodes}}-1}$ is the delivery ratio of broadcast b, i.e. the proportion of nodes that receive b. Although a high delivery ratio indicates a high degree of coverage of the network nodes by a broadcast protocol, its overall performance can only be determined in combination with the protocol's retransmission ratio.

5 Evaluation results

This section presents the results of our evaluation of the PAMPA suite of protocols based on a real deployment. In doing so, it enables the identification of the most suitable PAMPA variant for a particular deployment scenario.

We also compare our findings with the simulation-based evaluation of vanilla PAMPA and its variants presented in [4]. We have also evaluated the effect of switching the broadcasting node in a network. This observes whether the origin point of a message, or different propagation paths, affects the efficiency and success rate of PAMPA. A further experiment looks at the ability of PAMPA to cope with node failures on the network. We evaluate how it copes when nodes drop out and propagation becomes increasingly difficult. In the comparison, we also factor in

the difference in network topologies, the use of a MAC protocol in the simulation-based study (which is absent in our real deployment), and the random mapping from signal strength to waiting time in our real experiments (while simulations used a deterministic mapping—see Section 4.1).

We re-iterate that maximum node coverage using few retransmissions (i.e. less energy consumption) are the defining traits of the ideal WSN broadcast protocol with the former as the overriding factor.

5.1 PAMPA variant comparison (C1)

Figure 7 and Figure 8 show the delivery ratios and retransmission ratios respectively for each PAMPA variant over 10 experiment runs in C1. In the figures, the box-and-whisker plots give the degree of confidence in and the mean (shown as a cross) of the computed metric values for each broadcast protocol variant. The best performing broadcast protocol in our experimental evaluation is PAMPA, achieving an average delivery ratio of 75% (See Figure 7) at relatively low retransmission cost (only 44%, See Figure 8). It is surprising to find PAMPA achieving an even higher average delivery ratio in this experiment series than D-Flooding (71%). We explain this by observing that, by retransmitting less, PAMPA causes less packet collisions and is therefore able to reach out to more nodes. PAMPA performs markedly *better* than its variants which is in stark contrast to the evaluation results from simulation where the opposite is the case (with the exception of the PAMPA-TH variant). Ellis et al. report vanilla PAMPA achieving delivery ratios higher than 90% in only 37% of 'bridge' topologies selected [4]. We attribute the difference in behaviour of PAMPA in simulation and real deployment to at least three conditions: *1)* the sparser/smaller network topology in our real deployment, *2)* the not inconsequential effects of the aforementioned real-life deployment-level limitations not captured by simulation, and *3)* the changes in the mapping strategies from RSSI to waiting time brought about by practical considerations (Section 4.1).

With regards to node coverage, PAMPA-CP and PAMPA-TH/CP are the second-best performers after PAMPA achieving a healthy average delivery ratios of 0.72 and 0.73 respectively but prove strikingly costlier, posting average retransmission ratios of 0.89 and 0.83 respectively. Clearly, common-parenting curbs overcancellation and produces more retransmissions including those at key nodes. When directional look-ahead is applied to PAMPA-CP, only the retransmissions from nodes in the outer ring (see Figure 2) *and* with no common parents are counted, reducing the wastefulness of common-parenting. This is translated into a reduction of the average retransmission ratio by 0.06. In simulation, by contrast, both PAMPA-CP and PAMPA-TH/CP fared

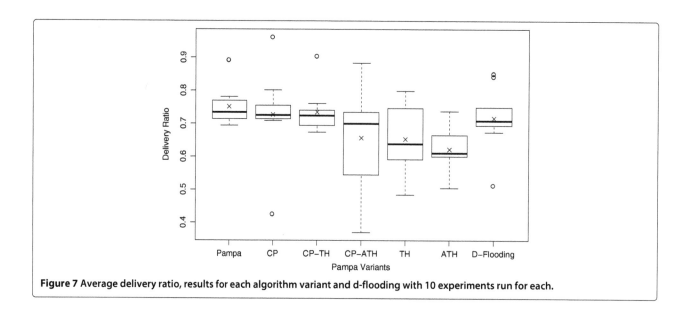

Figure 7 Average delivery ratio, results for each algorithm variant and d-flooding with 10 experiments run for each.

better than PAMPA (the second-worse simulation performer) in terms of node coverage and posted somewhat lower retransmission ratios (0.68 and 0.58 respectively).

The worst performers in our evaluation are the PAMPA-ATH/CP, PAMPA-TH and PAMPA-ATH variants providing modest average delivery ratios (0.65, 0.65 and 0.62 respectively) whilst still incurring high average retransmission ratios (0.8, 0.78 and 0.77, respectively). Considering only the PAMPA-ATH and PAMPA-ATH/CP variants, one can find that the application of common-parenting to PAMPA-ATH curbs overcancellation leading to an improvement in average delivery ratio of 0.03 but incurring an additional retransmission overhead of the same magnitude (0.03). The simulation results for PAMPA-ATH and PAMPA-ATH/CP depict a different picture alto-

gether; they performed consistently better than PAMPA, reducing the average delivery loss of PAMPA by 13–14% approximately.

PAMPA-TH is expected to perform less well than PAMPA in sparse networks where the presence of nodes outside the signal-strength threshold (outer ring) is more likely. As only the retransmissions for these nodes are counted in PAMPA-TH, this leads to higher message drop rates (poorer delivery ratio) in sparser topologies than for PAMPA. This is reflected in our results. In comparison with its simulation results, we find that it performs better in a real deployment than in simulation. The simulated PAMPA-TH exhibited the worst average delivery ratio (node coverage) and the second-most costly retransmission ratio.

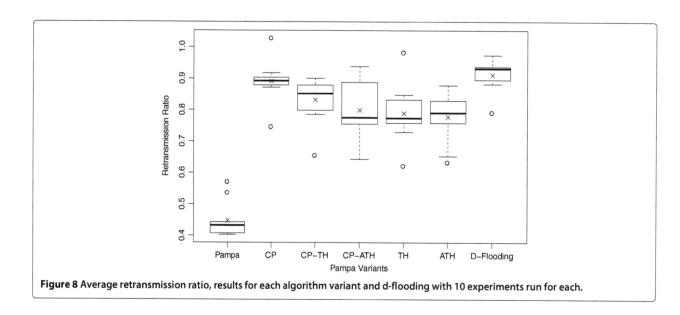

Figure 8 Average retransmission ratio, results for each algorithm variant and d-flooding with 10 experiments run for each.

5.2 Broadcast node switching (C2)

Table 2 and Table 3 show the delivery ratios and retransmission ratios respectively for PAMPA and delayed flooding over 20 broadcast node switching experiment runs (C2). This set of experiments showed that careful choice of a broadcasting node is important. For instance, in the runs where node 20 (Table 3) was the broadcasting node, the performance of each protocol suffers severely.

Node 20 was an outlier to the network, it was positioned very high up in the office environment and struggled to get its initial broadcasts to the first set of nodes. It also shows how different volumes of obstructions can affect the performance of the protocol as the outliers that have to transmit their initial broadcasts through more obstructions than those clustered in a single room. It seems that all of the protocols have an implicit preference to broadcast in a cluster of nodes to obtain a higher delivery ratio, which is consistent with the expected bimodal behaviour of these algorithms [21]. The performance for each protocol increases when nodes are clustered together, for example node 1 and node 2 (Table 3).

D-Flooding again results in high channel contention and packet collisions. This leads to its very poor delivery ratio and shows that a smarter protocol is definitely needed on this type of ad-hoc network. It should be noted that D-Flooding is expected to improve the performance of vanilla flooding as it imposes some order in node retransmissions, in contrast with vanilla flooding where the moment selected by each node for retransmission is exclusively dictated by a random jitter. Wherever the broadcast node resides throughout the network, PAMPA is always the most efficient protocol to use as seen in Table 2. This shows that PAMPA can be applied to a variety of ad-hoc networks with very different properties and still adapt much better than a simple flooding protocol.

These results using node switching on a real network show do not fully agree with simulation-based experiments, and highlight the importance of real deployment, and the potentially large impact of small changes in a protocol's realisation. In the simulations vanilla PAMPA presented around a 50% retransmission ratio, with the results obtained from this set of experiments showing similar results of 48%. However PAMPA's delivery ratio in contrast delivers each message 91% of the time to each node on the network. This was a strong improvement on the simulation results which found vanilla PAMPA to

have a 76% delivery ratio. Beyond the intrinsic differences between PAMPA and vanilla PAMPA, these results are probably also linked to the poor message failure models of our simulations, which do not represent the complex failures experienced in a real network. On one hand this can probably be attributed to the excessive determinism of network simulators, that ignore the effects of walls and multipath on signal propagation. We also think it highlights the importance of node topologies on the performance of individual protocols, and hence the need for realistic topology construction in network simulators.

5.3 Node failure (C3)

Figure 9 and Figure 10 shows the average of delivery and retransmission ratios per minute over the 20 experiment runs on configuration C3. As nodes fail on the network (shown on the Figures by the vertical lines) the graphs display how each of the protocols adapts to the failure of nodes and attempts to keep propagating messages.

PAMPA showed a clear improvement over delayed flooding in this set of experiments. PAMPA's delivery ratio stayed higher than the delayed flooding protocols' throughout the experiment and for all three broadcasting nodes tested. There were a few exceptions to this where the delayed flooding protocol coverage was marginally higher but after around the fifth minute, when more nodes had started to fail, it is clear that PAMPA results are far better.

The delivery ratio clearly decreases as there are less propagation paths for messages to use to reach outlying nodes. Unlike the other protocols, PAMPA shows signs of adapting to the new propagation paths in the network. In future we would like to increase the time between node dropouts to see if the protocol can fully recover and reproduce the same delivery ratio. This would have to be performed on a larger network where there are more propagation paths available.

A further sign that PAMPA adapts to new propagation paths in the network is the retransmission ratio results. It can be seen that as nodes drop out, PAMPA slightly increases its retransmission probability to try and cope with the failure and its corresponding decrease of node density. The protocol gets slightly less efficient after every node failure, however it keeps the delivery ratio much higher than the other protocols.

Table 2 Broadcast node switching retransmission ratios

Protocol	Node#1	Node#2	Node#3	Node#14	Node#18	Node#20	Node#21
PAMPA	0.48	0.46	0.47	0.45	0.48	0.47	0.47
Delayed-flooding	0.99	1	1	1	1	1	1
PAMPA differential	-0.51	-0.54	-0.53	-0.55	-0.52	-0.53	-0.53

Table 3 Broadcast node switching delivery ratios

Protocol	Node#1	Node#2	Node#3	Node#14	Node#18	Node#20	Node#21
PAMPA	0.92	0.91	0.89	0.89	0.9	0.62	0.81
Delayed-flooding	0.67	0.64	0.7	0.68	0.69	0.33	0.63
PAMPA differential	0.25	0.27	0.19	0.21	0.21	0.29	0.18

PAMPA has been shown to adapt very well to a dynamic network and increasingly adverse conditions. PAMPA is a lot more dynamic because of its looser structure and lower data overhead. As PAMPA relies on the current message it has received to make a decision and does not create complex data structures or hierarchies like other protocols (e.g., Multipoint Relaying [21]), it can therefore react quicker to the loss of former propagation paths.

6   Conclusions and lessons learnt

In this paper, we have evaluated the performance of the PAMPA family of broadcast protocols on a real deployment. The results have confirmed PAMPA's strengths: The protocol was able to reach more nodes than a naive flooding strategy (75.2% vs. 71.6%), while incurring much lower retransmissions costs (44.8% vs 90.2%). These results are also in line with earlier simulation results, obtained with different node densities and topologies, in which vanilla

PAMPA achieved a delivery ratio of 77% for a retransmission ratio of 51% [4]. The stateless properties of PAMPA keep it lightweight and dynamic, allowing it to adapt to new and better propagation paths within the network. This article has shown that when a protocol drops redundant messages this will increase the delivery ratio. If a protocol can keep its retransmissions low, it causes less traffic on the network.

The results of the PAMPA variants have been more chequered, however, and different from earlier simulation results in their relative performance to PAMPA. For instance, whereas PAMPA-CP performed better than PAMPA in simulations for a moderate additional cost [4], it performed worse in our real deployment, for a retransmission ratio (89.1%) close to that of flooding.

Several good reasons can explain this divergence: First, as mentioned earlier, simulations only imperfectly reflect reality [5,6], highlighting the need for real deployments.

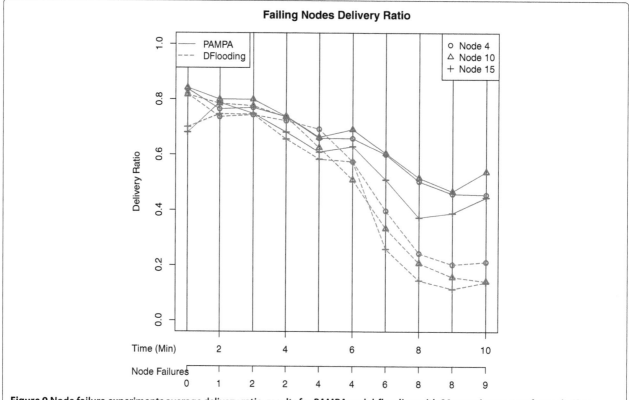

Figure 9 Node failure experiments average delivery ratio, results for PAMPA and d-flooding with 20 experiment runs for each. (One marker represents the average retransmission ratio from that minute in each of experiment runs).

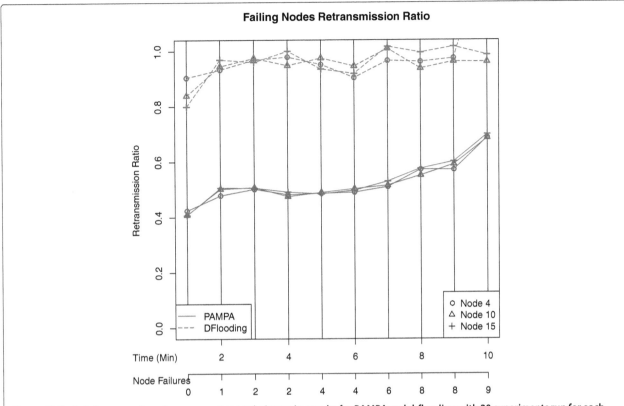

Figure 10 Node failure experiments average retransmission ratio, results for PAMPA and d-flooding with 20 experiments run for each. (One marker represents the average delivery ratio from that minute in each of experiment runs).

Second, but more importantly, earlier simulation results for PAMPA were obtained on large topologies (several hundreds of nodes), which are difficult to compare against the smaller deployments used in this paper. This is particularly important for the CP mechanism, which would be expected to perform better in denser networks with longer and more diverse propagation paths, leading to less retransmissions.

In the future, we would like to better evaluate the impact of a random mapping between RSSI and waiting time. In addition, it would be interesting to look at implementing this small topology in a simulator and seeing whether similar results are achieved. Another reason for this may be the reliance on RSSI to affect the protocol variant's decisions. RSSI is often not accurate enough to determine distances, leading to poor decisions made by the nodes when dropping packets. In further research the hardware should be tested for distance and RSSI measurements and then calibrated accordingly.

This latter point highlights the difficulty in assessing wireless broadcast protocols, and more generally any distributed wireless mechanisms: simulation campaigns tend to focus on large networks to demonstrate scalability, and to benefit from statistical effects (such as the diversity of propagation paths) which are hard to observe at smaller

scales. By contrast, real testbed deployments tend to be much smaller, only involving a few tens of nodes, or less. This experimental discrepancy is probably a reason to focus more on the validity of simulations results, than on their size.

For research in the future this paper has shown that it is important to choose the position of broadcasting nodes within the network carefully. Taking care to place important nodes in clusters of other nodes will result in better coverage for each of the broadcasting nodes' transmissions.

In this context, the fact that the versions of PAMPA obtained very close results both in large simulations and in a small real deployment is a strong indication of PAMPA's robustness, an aspect worth researching further in the future.

In terms of methodology, our results confirm once again the importance of real deployments to evaluate protocols. This somewhat obvious point comes however with a number of caveats: Real deployments are costly, time consuming, and tedious. Although we were able to rely on the infrastructure of the WISEBED testbed [26], failures, in particular of nodes, were frequent, and considerably increased the efforts required to run experiments. The causes of failures were diverse: batteries would get depleted, passers-by would interfere with parts of the infrastructure, the memory of motes would get corrupted. Even without failures, repeating experiments (resetting, re-synchronising, and re-starting each node) made obvious the importance of a powerful management and scripting interface to conduct large numbers of tests in a batch mode, even on a modest network.

The above difficulties in running real experiments, and the importance of these experiments for evaluation, are both key arguments that support the recent efforts made to develop shared wireless testbeds [26,28], an evolution that should provide critical feedback to researchers and practitioners working with wireless distributed networks.

Endnotes
[a]A preliminary version of this paper was published in [29].
[b]All code used is available by emailing the authors at c.winstanley@lancs.ac.uk.

Competing interests
The authors declare that they have no competing interests.

Authors' contributions
CW conducted the experimental work and wrote this article in conjunction with all authors. RR provided supervision on the project and insight into current technologies. FT suggested the original research topic and supervised CW's experimental work. BP provided technical guidance throughout the implementation and experimentation phases, particularly on the use of the software platform and the WSN testbeds. HM participated in the definition of the experiments and on the analysis of the results. All authors contributed equally to the redaction of the paper. All authors read and approved the final manuscript.

Acknowledgements
This work has been partially supported by the European Commission under contract number IST-2008-224460 (WISEBED) and grant agreement number 257992 (SmartSantander). Hugo Miranda was partially supported by Fundação para a Ciência e Tecnologia (FCT) through project PTDC/EIA-EIA/103751/2008 - PATI.

Author details
[1]Lancaster University, Lancaster, UK. [2]University of Rennes 1 - IRISA - ESIR, Rennes, France. [3]Departamento de Informática, Faculdade de Ciências, Universidade de Lisboa, Lisbon, Portugal.

References
1. Miranda H, Leggio S, Rodrigues L, Raatikainen K (2006) A power-aware broadcasting algorithm. In: Procs. of The 17th Annual IEEE Int'l Symposium on Personal, Indoor and Mobile Radio Communications (PIMRC'06). doi:10.1109/PIMRC.2006.254191
2. Garbinato B, Holzer A, Vessaz F (2008) Six-shot broadcast: a context-aware algorithm for efficient message diffusion in MANETs. In: Meersman R, Tari Z (eds) On the Move to Meaningful Internet Systems: OTM 2008, Volume 5331 of LNCS, pp 625–638. http://dx.doi.org/10.1007/978-3-540-88871-0_44.
3. Kyasanur P, Choudhury R, Gupta I (2006) Smart gossip: an adaptive gossip-based broadcasting service for sensor networks. In: IEEE Int Conf. on Mobile Adhoc and Sensor Sys. (MASS'06), pp 91–100. doi:10.1109/MOBHOC.2006.278671
4. Ellis C, Miranda H, Taïani F (2009) Count on me: lightweight ad-hoc broadcasting in heterogeneous topologies. In: Int. Workshop on Middleware for Pervasive Mobile and Embedded Comp., M-PAC'09, pp 1–6. http://doi.acm.org/10.1145/1657127.1657129.
5. Andel T, Yasinsac A (2006) On the credibility of manet simulations. Computer 39(7): 48–54
6. Ben Hamida E, Chelius G, Gorce JM (2009) Impact of the physical layer modeling on the accuracy and scalability of wireless network simulation. Simulation 85(9): 574–588. http://dx.doi.org/10.1177/0037549709106633.
7. Kurkowski S, Camp T, Colagrosso M (2005) MANET simulation studies: the incredibles. SIGMOBILE Mob Comput Commun Rev 9(4): 50–61. http://doi.acm.org/10.1145/1096166.1096174.
8. Szewczyk R, Mainwaring A, Polastre J, Anderson J, Culler D (2004) An analysis of a large scale habitat monitoring application. In: Proceedings of the 2nd International Conference on Embedded Networked Sensor Systems, SenSys '04. ACM, New York, pp 214–226. http://doi.acm.org/10.1145/1031495.1031521.
9. Boano C, Tsiftes N, Voigt T, Brown J, Roedig U (2010) The impact of temperature on outdoor industrial sensornet applications. IEEE Trans Ind Inform 6(3): 451–459
10. Grace P, Hughes D, Porter B, Blair GS, Coulson G, Taiani F (2008) Experiences with open overlays: a middleware approach to network heterogeneity. In: Proceedings of the 3rd ACM SIGOPS/EuroSys European Conference on Computer Systems 2008, Eurosys '08. ACM, New York, pp 123–136. http://doi.acm.org/10.1145/1352592.1352606.
11. Ni SY, Tseng YC, Chen YS, Sheu JP (1999) The broadcast storm problem in a mobile ad hoc network. In: 5th Annual ACM/IEEE Int. Conf. on Mobile Comp. and Networking, MobiCom '99, pp 151–162. http://doi.acm.org/10.1145/313451.313525.
12. Peng W, Lu XC (2000) On the reduction of broadcast redundancy in mobile ad hoc networks. In: 1st ACM Int. Symp. on Mobile Ad Hoc Networking & Computing, MobiHoc '00, pp 129–130. http://dl.acm.org/citation.cfm?id=514151.514171.
13. Das B, Bharghavan V (1997) Routing in ad-hoc networks using minimum connected dominating sets. In: Communications, 1997. ICC '97 Montreal, Towards the Knowledge Millennium. 1997 IEEE International Conference on, Volume 1. IEEE, pp 376–380. doi:10.1109/ICC.1997.605303
14. Qayyum A, Viennot L, Laouiti A (2002) Multipoint relaying for flooding broadcast messages in mobile wireless networks. In: 35th Annual Hawaii Int. Conf. on Sys. Sciences (HICSS'02) - Vol. 9, HICSS '02, p 298. http://dl.acm.org/citation.cfm?id=820747.821299.
15. Wu J, Li H (2001) A dominating-set-based routing scheme in ad hoc wireless networks. Telecommunication Syst 18(1–3): 13–36
16. Krishna P, Chatterjee M, Vaidya NH, Pradhan DK (1995) A cluster-based approach for routing in ad-hoc networks. In: Symposium on Mobile and Location-Independent Computing. USENIX Association, pp 1–10. http://dl.acm.org/citation.cfm?id=646407.692370.
17. Guha S, Khuller S (1998) Approximation algorithms for connected dominating sets. Algorithmica 20(4): 374–387
18. Cartigny J, Ingelrest F, Simplot D (2003) RNG relay subset flooding protocols in mobile ad-hoc networks. Int J Found Comput Sci 14(02): 253–265. http://www.worldscientific.com/doi/abs/10.1142/S0129054103001716.
19. Wieselthier J, Nguyen GD, Ephremides A (2000) On the construction of energy-efficient broadcast and multicast trees in wireless networks. In: INFOCOM 2000. Nineteenth Annual Joint Conference of the IEEE Computer and Communications Societies. Proceedings. IEEE, Volume 2. IEEE, pp 585–594. doi:10.1109/INFCOM.2000.832232
20. Ingelrest F, Simplot-Ryl D (2008) Localized broadcast incremental power protocol for wireless ad hoc networks. Wireless Networks 14(3): 309–319. http://dx.doi.org/10.1007/s11276-006-9817-7.
21. Haas ZJ, Halpern JY, Li L (2006) Gossip-based ad hoc routing. IEEE/ACM Trans Netw 14(3): 479–491. http://dx.doi.org/10.1109/TNET.2006.876186.
22. Drabkin V, Friedman R, Kliot G, Segal M (2007) RAPID: reliable probabilistic dissemination in wireless ad-hoc networks. In: 26th IEEE Int. Symp. on Reliable Dist. Sys. (SRDS 2007), pp 13–22. doi:10.1109/SRDS.2007.9
23. Kotz D, Newport C, Gray RS, Liu J, Yuan Y, Elliott C (2004) Experimental evaluation of wireless simulation assumptions. In: Proc. of the 7th ACM Int. Symp. on Modeling, Analysis and Simulation of Wireless and Mobile Sys., MSWiM '04. ACM, New York, pp 78–82. http://doi.acm.org/10.1145/1023663.1023679.

24. Cavin D, Sasson Y, Schiper A (2002) On the accuracy of MANET simulators. In: 2nd ACM Int. Workshop on Principles of Mobile Comp., POMC '02, pp 38–43. http://doi.acm.org/10.1145/584490.584499.

25. Lundgren H, Lundberg D, Nielsen J, Nordström E, Tschudin C (2002) A large-scale testbed for reproducible ad hoc protocol evaluations. In: Wireless Communications and Networking Conference, 2002. WCNC2002. 2002 IEEE, Volume 1. IEEE, pp 412–418. doi:10.1109/WCNC.2002.993531

26. Coulson G, Porter B, Chatzigiannakis I, Koninis C, Fischer S, Pfisterer D (2012) Flexible experimentation in wireless sensor networks. CACM 55: 82–90. http://doi.acm.org/10.1145/2063176.2063198.

27. Porter B, Roedig U, Coulson G (2011) Type-safe updating for modular WSN software. In: Distributed Computing in Sensor Systems and Workshops (DCOSS), 2011 International Conference on. IEEE, pp 1–8. doi:10.1109/DCOSS.2011.5982140

28. des Roziers CB, Chelius G, Ducrocq T, Fleury E, Fraboulet A, Gallais A, Mitton N, Noël T, Vandaele J (2011) Using SensLAB as a first class scientific tool for large scale wireless sensor network experiments. In: 10th Int IFIP TC 6 Conf. on Networking - Vol. Part I. NETWORKING'11, pp 147–159. http://dl.acm.org/citation.cfm?id=2008780.2008795.

29. Winstanley C, Ramdhany R, Taïani F, Porter B, Miranda H (2012) PAMPA in the wild: a real-life evaluation of a lightweight ad-hoc broadcasting family. In: Proceedings of the 7th International Workshop on Middleware Tools, Services and Run-time Support for Sensor Networks, MidSens '12. ACM, New York, pp 3:1–3:6. http://doi.acm.org/10.1145/2405167.2405170.

Radiator - efficient message propagation in context-aware systems

Pedro Alves[1][*] and Paulo Ferreira[2]

Abstract

Applications such as Facebook, Twitter and Foursquare have brought the mass adoption of personal short messages, distributed in (soft) real-time on the Internet to a large number of users. These messages are complemented with rich contextual information such as the identity, time and location of the person sending the message (e.g., Foursquare has millions of users sharing their location on a regular basis, with almost 1 million updates per day).

Such contextual messages raise serious concerns in terms of scalability and delivery delay; this results not only from their huge number but also because the set of user recipients changes for each message (as their interests continuously change), preventing the use of well-known solutions such as pub-sub and multicast trees. This leads to the use of non-scalable broadcast based solutions or point-to-point messaging.

We propose Radiator, a middleware to assist application programmers implementing efficient context propagation mechanisms within their applications. Based on each user's current context, Radiator continuously adapts each message propagation path and delivery delay, making an efficient use of network bandwidth, arguably the biggest bottleneck in the deployment of large-scale context propagation systems.

Our experimental results demonstrate a 20x reduction on consumed bandwidth without affecting the real-time usefulness of the propagated messages.

Keywords: Context propagation; Scalability; Publish-subscribe; Multicast trees; Peer-to-Peer; Aggregation

1 Introduction

Context-aware systems take into account the user's current context (such as location, time and activity) to enrich the user interaction with the application [1,2]. In the last decade, this topic has seen numerous developments that demonstrate its relevance and usefulness; this trend was further accelerated with the recent widespread availability of powerful mobile devices (such as smartphones) that include a myriad of sensors which enable applications to capture the user environment for a large number of users [3].

Following on this trend, we are watching a radical change in the type of packets that travel on the Internet. Facebook and Twitter (among others) brought the mass adoption of personal short messages or posts, distributed in (soft) real-time to a potentially large number of users[a]. These messages are complemented with rich contextual information such as the identity, time and location of the person sending the message (following the context model devised more than a decade ago [1] among the CSCW community). Context-aware applications were, until recently, created solely in the academic realm and were used by a handful of users. Now, we have very popular applications like: Foursquare [4] which has millions of users sharing their location on a regular basis, with more than 600.000 updates per day [5]; traffic monitoring applications such as Waze [6] which relies on continuous updates with geolocation and accelerometer data from drivers' smartphones; real-time context-aware applications such as Highlight [7] which matches geolocation with social network data to provide "nearby friends" updates in real-time. These are just some examples within the growing group of applications that use the Internet to propagate contextual information among a large number of users.

The huge number of users leads to scalability problems as can be seen in several news articles (e.g., Twitter

*Correspondence: pedro.h.alves@gmail.com
[1]INESC-ID, Technical University of Lisbon, Opensoft, Rua Joshua Benoliel, 1, 4C, 1250 Lisbon, Portugal
Full list of author information is available at the end of the article

admitted that "record traffic" and "unprecedented spikes in activity" led to problems with the site [8]). In addition to the huge number of users and messages exchanged, context propagation creates unique challenges in the realm of distributed systems [9]: it is highly dynamic, does not require user intervention, and has different levels of urgency. We now detail each one of these challenges.

1.1 Highly dynamic

To better understand how dynamic context can be, consider the case of capturing the geolocation of a moving person or the speed at which he is moving. To achieve a reasonable level of accuracy, the system must capture and propagate this information very frequently, probably at least once per minute. Since these systems usually have hundreds of thousands if not millions of users, we are talking about a huge volume of information being sent to the server (assuming a centralized topology which is the case in the vast majority of the commercial applications on this area). Moreover, the server must then be able to propagate this context to whoever may be interested. The problem lies on the dynamics of those interests. For example, if the user is interested in receiving information about friends nearby, there will be a matching rule between his location and the location of his friends. However, if he's moving, and his friends are also moving, the system has to continuously change that matching rule.

For this reason (the dynamics of context), traditional publish-subscribe approaches are unfeasible since they assume a relatively fixed set of matching rules. On these systems, users subscribe to topics (subject-based systems) or predicates (content-based systems) [10]. Then, users feed content into the system (publish) and the system distributes events matching subscribers interest with publisher content. Therefore, developing a "friends nearby" application using publish-subscribe requires each client to continuously change his interests. In fact, every time the user moves, the client application has to send three messages when just one should suffice: (1) publish the current location; (2) unsubscribe from the previous location, and (3) subscribe to the current location. This leads to wasted resources and poor scalability.

Application-level multicast tree approaches [11] fall on the same problem: they assume that distribution rules do not change very frequently. Although they still work on these conditions, the resources wasted by continuously rebuilding the multicast trees lead to poor scalability. For example, the Scribe system [12] relies on the following message types: JOIN, CREATE, LEAVE and MULTICAST. It is easy to see the resemblance with publish-subscribe messages — changing the matching rules implies the propagation of a LEAVE message, a JOIN message and a MULTICAST message (the latter alone should be enough to convey all the information we need, e.g., the new location, in the "friends nearby" application).

1.2 Does not require user intervention

Context propagation does not usually require explicit user intervention — it happens in the background thus increasing the usability and effectiveness of the application [9]. Thus, context-aware applications continuously monitor and propagate the user's context. Moreover, context information is transmitted unattended, i.e., without the user having to explicitly give that command [13]. Contrast that with the kind of traffic we are used to watch until recently. Be it an email, a website or an FTP session, the communication is always deliberately initiated by the user. This has been changing and the immediate consequence of unattended communication is that it will happen a lot more frequently. Humans can only send a small number of messages in a given period of time but computers do not have these limits. To provide the best user experience, these applications will try to propagate their context as much and as often as possible, since they do not have to rely on the user explicitly initiating the communication. This inevitably leads to a huge number of messages being sent to the server at a high rate, thus reducing the system's scalability.

Note that, although smartphone OSs and synchronization tools (e.g., Dropbox) already do non-triggered updates, they are not as prone to scalability issues as context-aware systems. Non-triggered updates on smartphones are typically initiated by the server (e.g., a new version of an installed app is available or a new email has arrived). Synchronization tools are triggered after a human interaction (e.g., editing or copying a file) so they are bound by definition to the number of actions a human can do. Context-aware systems are triggered by changes in the user's context such as his location, speed or heart rate, which can potentially lead to a much larger number of messages than the previous examples.

1.3 Different levels of urgency

Finally, the urgency of context delivery is also highly dynamic. An application that enhances the cellphone's contact list with the current availability of others [14] must propagate context as soon as possible while an application that provides a noise map of the city [15] does not require immediate propagation (specially if it's not the city where the user is currently located). Even within the same application there exists different urgency levels. For example, Cenceme [16] captures users's activity (e.g., dancing at a party with friends) and shares those in the social network. It makes sense to propagate those activities to close friends as fast as possible while acquaintances only receive those updates a few hours later. This behavior resembles traditional relaxed consistency systems [17] with the problematic difference of having some users requiring strong consistency while others tolerate some temporary inconsistencies.

In summary, context-aware applications have the potential to transmit a huge number of messages in a highly dynamic environment therefore raising hard challenges regarding scalability. We argue that current approaches such as publish-subscribe [18,19], multicast trees [11] or gossip-based protocols [20] are not adequate to handle these dynamics, because they assume the matching rules are fixed or change infrequently (therefore changes are too expensive). Also, since such classic approaches do not know how to extract semantic meaning from the exchanged messages, they can't decide what is the most efficient way to distribute those messages — such a burden becomes the application programmer's responsibility.

We propose an adaptable middleware, called Radiator, where context propagation is controlled by functions that, given the context of the recipient, dictate in which conditions a given context message should be propagated. These functions are, by nature, dynamic matching rules which change automatically if the involved clients change their context. Moreover, the retained messages (messages for which the functions have decided that they should not be propagated immediately) are aggregated into single compressed messages that can yield a substantial reduction on the consumed network bandwidth. For this reason, these functions are called *aggregability* functions because they tell whether a message should be aggregated or not, and to which level the aggregation should occur.

It is important to note that the aggregability functions (and therefore the propagation timing) are not only dependent on the message itself but also on the current context of both the sender and the receiver. This is a crucial difference over other generic message propagation approaches: since we know that messages contain the contexts of their senders, we have more information to make decisions about their propagation. Also note that *aggregability* functions are provided by the application programmer. Even though the programmer may take into account the user's input, it is not the user's responsibility to provide such functions.

Finally, we are also able to avoid some limitations of the centralized approach (e.g., less scalability due to resource usage concentration) by allowing a hybrid mechanism: using a centralized approach for defining the message propagation strategy (e.g., deciding whether a message should be retained or propagated) and a peer-to-peer approach for the actual message propagation. Thus, the decision of which clients receive the message and when they do so is still responsibility of the server, but most of the propagation is done through direct connections between the clients following a *p2p* approach, therefore

reducing the outbound network bandwidth needs of the server and increasing scalability.

Moreover, the propagation path is completely dynamic: the set of recipients of each message is continuously changing based on the result of the *aggregability* function. This results in a more efficient use of the available network bandwidth.

In short, this paper makes the following contributions:

- We present a model for context-aware applications that relies on the concept of *aggregability*, a function that tells how aggregated a message can be before being propagated. This function takes into account the current context of both the sender and the receiver, making a more efficient use of the network bandwidth and significantly improving the system scalability.
- We present a hybrid dynamic propagation mechanism, where a server decides if a message should be retained or transmitted (based on the result of the *aggregability* function) and clients communicate directly between them to propagate it.
- We implement and evaluate the scalability of Radiator, a pluggable local middleware and a server that support the above mentioned model, i.e., it supports the hybrid propagation mechanism while still abstracting away from the application programmer the underlying communication and context management.

In the remainder of the paper, we start by describing Radiator's context aggregation model. In Section 3, we present Radiator's architecture and in Section 4 its implementation. Section 5 presents evaluation results of Radiator's implementation and finally, in Sections 6 and 7, we relate Radiator with previous work and draw some conclusions, respectively.

2 Context aggregation model

In this section, we start by explaining the concept of context aggregation and then we describe in detail the model supported by Radiator.

2.1 What is context aggregation?

To help understand the concept of context aggregation, consider a "popular spots" application example. This application shows the most popular spots (e.g., pubs, restaurants, discos) nearby a user's current location, where a popular spot is a place where a large number of users is currently located. The context of those users (in this case, the location) must be propagated to others but it can be grouped before being propagated. In this case, the user does not care about individual context updates given that he only wants to know popular spots, not who's in there. So, instead of propagating N messages, each one saying "user U is now at location L", we can wait until there are N users at location L and only then propagate a **single** message saying "users $U_1..U_N$ are now at location L" or (in case privacy is an issue) "N users are now at location L". In other words, we are delaying the propagation of the first $N - 1$ users' location to improve the efficiency of the system, hence the concept of delayed propagation. Note that the delay does not break user expectations because, for some contextual information, he does not mind receiving it with delay. For example, a spot does not become popular in seconds and it certainly does not stop being so in seconds, so a lag of some minutes is perfectly acceptable between the time when a spot becomes popular and the time a user is informed.

However, if a friend is in one of those spots, the user may no longer tolerate a delay — he may want to receive that information as soon as possible. So, the model has to accommodate multiple delay levels, depending on the user's context (the user's friends are part of his context).

All the messages that are not immediately propagated are said to be retained. The fact that these messages are retained allows the system to aggregate them in the most efficient way possible, thus increasing its scalability. For example, if a group of users share a certain context attribute (e.g., location or interest), we can aggregate their messages based on that attribute. In some cases, this aggregation leads to tremendous decreases in the messages' size, thus increasing the system's scalability (more details in Section 5). Also, the aggregation reduces the cognitive load that users typically suffer when using this kind of applications (caused by the huge number of messages received) [21].

Radiator is a context propagation middleware that combines the concepts of *Delayed Propagation* and *Aggregation* to improve the performance and scalability of context-aware applications. Moreover, these concepts are applied in a completely dynamic manner: each message may be subject to different aggregation levels, depending on the current context of the users involved.

2.2 Model

Context-aware applications start by capturing context in the following form, assuming that P is a person, t a timestamp and A an attribute:

$$Context = (P_1..P_n, \ t_1..t_n, \{A_1..A_n\})$$

This triplet represents the attributes that characterize the situation of P_1 to P_n during the time span between t_1 and t_n, roughly following the context definition coined by Dey in his seminal paper [1]. An attribute can be any name/value pair. For example, an application like CenceMe [16] that shares social activities among a group of friends, might capture context as follows:

```
(("Alice"), 22:30..01:00,{"location":
      "Joe's Pub", "activity":"dancing"})
```

A crucial concept in the Radiator design is the possibility of aggregating multiple contexts into a single one while retaining its basic format. For example, if Alice and Marc are both dancing together at Joe's Pub, their context can be aggregated as follows:

```
(("Alice","Marc"),22:30..01:00,{"location":
      "Joe's", "activity":"dancing"})
```

This context could be further aggregated with other contexts and so on and so forth. The advantages of this aggregation are: (1) it reduces the cognitive load on the user by presenting a summary of what's going on instead of multiple single activities, and (2) it significantly reduces the necessary network bandwidth, specially if combined with a compression algorithm.

Related to aggregation, the Radiator also introduces the concept of *delayed propagation*, based on the principle that some context messages may be temporarily retained before being propagated while still fulfilling user expectations. For example, Paul won't mind receiving a message saying that Alice and Marc are dancing at Joe's Pub with a five minutes delay unless he's just passing nearby, in which case the delay could prevent him from stopping by (when he receives the message he's already too far from the pub). In fact, the urgency level depends on many factors: location, social distance (e.g., if it's a friend or an acquaintance), current activity, mood, etc.

Radiator allows programmers to define the tolerable propagation delay of each message based on the current context of the users involved (sender and recipient). As already mentioned, this is achieved through an *aggregability* function. Let C_S be the current context of sender S and C_R the current context of receiver R. The aggregability function $G(C_S, C_R)$ represents how much aggregated the message must be before being transmitted to R, taking into consideration both C_S and C_R. G returns a tuple in the following format:

$$G(C_S, C_R) \to \{type : value\}, type \in (volume, time, people)$$

The *value* is an integer (or a function returning an integer) representing a threshold of aggregated messages. This threshold may represent a quantity (*volume*), a time range (*time*) or the number of different users contained in the aggregation (*people*). If the type is *time*, context messages will be aggregated until the number of seconds between the oldest and newest retained message is equal or greater than *value*. The types *volume* and *people* are similar in the fact that they represent the maximum number of aggregated messages: *volume* is the number of different messages while *people* represents the number of different senders involved on those messages. For example, if G returns $\{people : 4\}$, the system will aggregate messages until there are four different users involved, before propagating them[b].

Since *value* can be a function, the aggregation threshold can be very dynamic. For example, a certain application may want to immediately propagate a person's context to her friends but aggregate messages up to 40 seconds when they are being propagated to strangers. We could define such function as follows:

$$G(C_S, C_{R_i}) \rightarrow \{volume : 1\} \iff is\_friend(R_i, S)$$

$$G(C_S, C_{R_i}) \rightarrow \{time : 40\} \iff is\_stranger(R_i, S)$$

To better illustrate the generality of the *aggregability* concept, Table 1 shows some examples of aggregability for real-world scenarios. For simple propagation needs, such as traffic monitoring or hazards detection, we define a simple threshold for the maximum delay (1st row) or the number of retained messages (2nd row). Since traffic congestion occurs during a relatively long period of time it can be aggregated within 5 minutes (300 seconds) periods without losing its usefulness and relevance. More interesting scenarios are those in which the aggregation depends on contextual information such as the social distance (3rd and 4th rows), the geographical distance (5th row) or even the number of shares (6th row). This generality is possible because the *aggregability* function takes two arguments: the context of the sender and the context of the receiver. This gives great flexibility to the application programmer who can easily fit the specific requirements of his application into a single function and start benefiting from the Radiator middleware without further effort.

Listing 1 Aggregability function that aggregates messages based on how far the user is from the sender (implemented in Python)

```
def aggregability(Cs, Cr):
return { 'volume' : distance_in_kms
                    (Cs['attributes']['location'],
                     Cr['attributes']['location'])}
```

For example, the *aggregability* function for the scenario #5 (see Table 1) can be implemented in the Python language as shown in Listing 1. C_s represents the context of sender and C_r the context of the recipient. We assume that *distance_in_kms* is a function that returns an integer representing the number of kilometers between two geo-locations. This aggregability function returns a *volume* that depends on that distance, i.e., messages become more aggregated as users become further away from each other.

The effective aggregation of messages is also performed by a function (*aggregation function*). If the developer does not provide any aggregation function, Radiator applies a simple concatenation of the messages to aggregate. To achieve higher compression levels (and therefore reduce network bandwidth), the developer should provide an aggregation function that takes into account the specific needs of his application. Table 2 shows some examples of such functions. In the traffic monitoring case (first row in Table 2), we are concerned about the average traffic speed within a geographical region: if the average speed is near zero, it is reasonable to assume that there is traffic congestion within that particular region.

3   Architecture

The Radiator architecture has two main components (see Figure 1):

1. A **local middleware** that acts as a pluggable component to applications that completely abstracts away the application from the underlying propagation infrastructure;
2. A **server**, to which the local middleware connects, that assumes three responsibilities:

   (a) **Client management** — Keeps track of all the clients (namely their identification and IP address). It also manages the connection with each one of these clients: IP renewal, intermittent connectivity, dead/unreachable client detection, etc. Most importantly, it manages the current context of every client which is crucial to the context aggregation process.
   (b) **Context aggregation** — Applies the aggregability function to every incoming context message, providing both the sender and recipient's contexts. It also manages the list of retained messages and the thresholds at which messages are no longer retained and start being propagated.
   (c) **Context propagation** — Delivers the context messages to all clients triggered by the context aggregation component. The delivery can be done using direct connections to the clients, peer-to-peer propagation between clients, or a combination of both.

We now describe in more detail the key components of the Radiator architecture: *context aggregation* and *context propagation*.

Table 1 Different context propagation scenarios and the corresponding aggregability functions

#	Scenario	Description	Aggregability function
1	Traffic monitoring	Aggregate speedometer and GPS data within 300 second periods	$\{time : 300\}$
2	Road hazards detection	Aggregate vertical accelerometer and GPS data until 5 hazards detected	$\{volume : 5\}$
3	Popular spots + Friends' location	Aggregate location until 10 different people in the same spot but for friends send immediately (non-aggregated)	$\{people : 10\}$ if stranger $\{volume : 1\}$ if friend
4	Facebook likes	Aggregate likes from strangers within 300 seconds periods, likes from friends of friends until there are 5, and likes from direct friends with a maximum delay of 30 seconds	$\{time : 300\}$ if stranger $\{volume : 5\}$ if friend_of_friend $\{time : 30\}$ if friend
5	Friends' location in crowded spaces (concerts, street markets)	Aggregate location based on how far you are from the recipient (further away implies more aggregation)	$\{volume : \texttt{distance}\}$
6	Stock market alerts	Aggregate stock market information during a period of time proportional to the number of shares owned by the recipient (higher number implies less aggregation)	$\{time : 1000/(1 + \texttt{num\_of\_shares})\}$

3.1 Server — context aggregation

The "Context Aggregation" component at the server is responsible for applying an aggregability function to every incoming context message. Depending on the result of the aggregability function, the message may be put on the immediate propagation queue or on a queue associated with the threshold that will trigger the propagation. When one of these queues satisfy the associated threshold (e.g., if the threshold is *volume* : 5, and the associated queue has 5 elements), its items are moved into the immediate propagation queue. Algorithm 1 presents the pseudo-code for this process.

There is a global data structure that stores all the pending messages per client (*pending*). For each received context *C*, the Radiator server calls the algorithm, which may decide, depending on the aggregability function (provided by the application programmer) to append it to the *pending* data structure or return it through the *to_send* variable. The *to_send* variable stores all the messages ready for immediate propagation (line 20) and is passed by the Radiator server to the context propagation component (detailed in the next section).

Note that, as in many context-aware systems, Radiator propagates every message to everyone (albeit some can

Table 2 Different context propagation scenarios and the corresponding aggregation functions (see Table 1 for corresponding scenarios)

#	Scenario	Aggregation function
1	Traffic monitoring	`avg`(speed) by location
2	Road hazards detection	`sum`(hazards) by location
3	Popular spots	`count`(people) by location
4	Facebook likes	`sum`(likes) by object
5	Friends location in crowded spaces	`list`(people) by distance
6	Stock market alerts	`newest`(values) by share

Algorithm 1 Pseudo-code of the context aggregation and propagation process

```
1:  procedure PROPAGATE(in C, in/out pending)
2:      to_send ← NEW_DICTIONARY()
3:      for all recipient ∈ CLIENTS_TABLE do
4:          pending[ recipient].append(C)
5:          pending_queues ← NEW_DICTIONARY()
6:          for all C_pending ∈ pending[ recipient] do
7:              result ← aggregability(C_recipient, C_pending)
8:              pending_queues[ result].append(C_pending)
9:
10:             if result[ "volume"] then
11:                 propagate ←
                    (len(pending_queues[ result] ) >= result[ "volume"])
12:             else if result[ "users"] then
13:                 propagate ←
                    (users(pending_queues[ result] )) >= result[ "users"])
14:             else if result[ "time"] then
15:                 propagate ←
                    (time_range(pending_queues[ result] ) >= result[ "time"])
16:             end if
17:
18:             if propagate then
19:                 C_aggr ← join(pending_queues[ result] )
20:                 to_send[ C_aggr].append(recipient)
21:                 for all c ∈ pending_queues[ result] do
22:                     pending[ recipient].remove(c)
23:                 end for
24:                 pending_queues[ result].clear()
25:             end if
26:         end for
27:     end for return to_send
28: end procedure
```

receive it with delay). In line 3, we can see the beginning of the loop that iterates through all the clients previously registered. For each client (a recipient, in this case), the message to propagate is first appended to its global

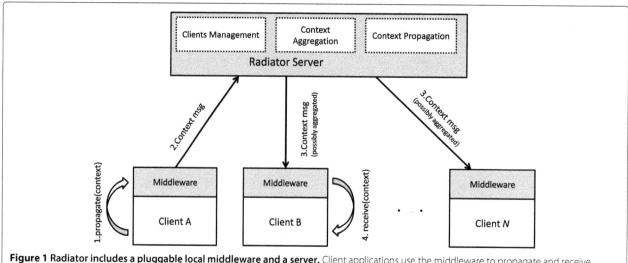

Figure 1 Radiator includes a pluggable local middleware and a server. Client applications use the middleware to propagate and receive context through direct calls. The aggregation/propagation is abstracted away from the application programmer.

pending list. Then, this list is iterated (from the oldest to the newest) while the *aggregability* function is applied to each pending message (line 7). We have to reiterate from the beginning (line 6) because the current context of the recipient may have changed since the last time the *propagate* function was called. That is, the result of applying the *aggregability* function to the same message may change with time so we can never rely on previous results (due to context's dynamic nature). Note that if there is data loss, either the message that was lost is recovered by the underlying network layer or the application deals with that message loss.

In addition, the result of the *aggregability* function may vary with each message in the *pending* list, so we have to group them by result. This is done using the variable *pending_queues*, which stores every result of the *aggregability* function along with the corresponding list of messages (line 8). Lines 10–16 test the different scenarios that can trigger the propagation: reaching the maximum number of retained messages (*volume*), reaching the maximum number of different users (*people*), or reaching the maximum time span since the oldest retained message (*time*).

If one of these thresholds is reached, the *propagate* variable will have the value *True*. In this case, the messages that were retained because of that particular threshold will be aggregated into a single message (line 19). The *join* function has a default behavior: it joins all the users involved into a single set, calculates the global time range based on the difference between the oldest and the newest message in the aggregation, and joins all the attributes into single lists. This behavior can be overridden to achieve more efficient aggregations. For example, if the messages contain geo-location coordinates, the application

programmer may decide to adopt a minimum bounding box approach to condense multiple locations into a single square that contains all the locations. (More examples of aggregation functions can be found in Table 2.)

The aggregated message is then appended to the *to_send* variable (line 20). This variable stores a list of messages for immediate propagation and for each message it stores the list of its recipients. This data structure is optimized for the context propagation component described in Section 3.2. Finally, the messages elected for immediate propagation are removed from the pending queues (lines 21–24).

3.2   Server — context propagation

The "Context Propagation" component at the server is responsible for distributing the context messages (possibly aggregated) to their recipients. Every client will eventually receive all context messages but, depending on the aggregability function, some may receive the messages sooner than others.

The propagation can be done through direct connections from the server to every recipient or through peer-to-peer communication between recipients. In any case, the communication is always initiated by the sender (*push* approach) so there is no need for clients to poll the server or other clients for new messages (causing unnecessary traffic and delays).

The centralized approach, where the server is responsible for pushing messages to every client has the advantage of being simple to implement and allowing clients with network restrictions (e.g., those that are behind a firewall). However, if the number of recipients is large, the server starts suffering from scalability problems, since it has to push the message to everyone.

Radiator introduces an alternative propagation mechanism that is highly dynamic (in the sense, that it automatically adapts itself to the current context of the sender and receiver, which can change very frequently). First, all clients that can communicate directly with other clients (i.e., are not subject to firewall restrictions) send an attribute *p2p_enabled* to the server when they register themselves into the system. Afterwords, for every message ready for propagation, the server checks which of the recipients are *p2p_enabled*. Those that are not *p2p_enabled* receive the message through a direct push as already described. The others are divided into groups of *k* elements (*k* is configurable as a percentage). Each group is processed as a chain of peers through which the message must get through. The message is propagated from the server to the first peer which then propagates to the second peer and so on and so forth. From now on, we will name these groups as *chain of recipients*. So, for each *chain of recipients*, the server sends only one message which is then disseminated directly between the recipients (*p2p propagation*).

Figure 2 shows a possible scenario: there are five recipients for a given message where only one of them is not *p2p_enabled* (Client A). In this case, the chain of recipients size is setup to be 50%. We can see that the server pushes the message directly to client A (not *p2p_enabled*) and divides the remaining recipients in two groups. Then, it pushes the message to client B that should push that message further to client C, that does the same for client D, which must push the message forward to client F. It is obvious from this example that the server must do only 3 pushes instead of 5 if there wasn't any p2p propagation. In fact, the server will always push *N* messages, where (*k* is the *chain of recipients* percentage):

$$N = N_{non\_p2p} + (N_{p2p} * k/100)$$

From this follows that the smaller the *k*, the fewer messages the server has to push although this comes at a cost. The messages must contain the full chain of recipients for each group so, if the group is very large, the chain significantly increases the payload size therefore defeating our main purpose: reducing server outbound bandwidth. However, regarding scalability, this is not significant for two reasons: (1) given that most of the messages are aggregated, the relative weight of the recipients chain generally decreases, since the main payload is much bigger, and (2) compression is highly effective for this chain of recipients (for example, increasing the chain from 10 to 100 recipients only yields a 5× increase in the compressed payload — more details in Section 5).

Note that, due to its dynamic nature, this chain of recipients is very flexible making it specially suitable to highly dynamic conditions such as those usually found in context-aware applications. Since these conditions may vary very frequently, Radiator continuously recalculates the chain of recipients for each message.

If a client is unable to forward the context message to the next in the chain of recipients, it informs the server accordingly. Then, the server tries the next one in the chain. The server will not include the unreachable client in the next propagation to prevent wasting unnecessary resources unless the client shows any sign that it is still alive (e.g., by sending a message to the server).

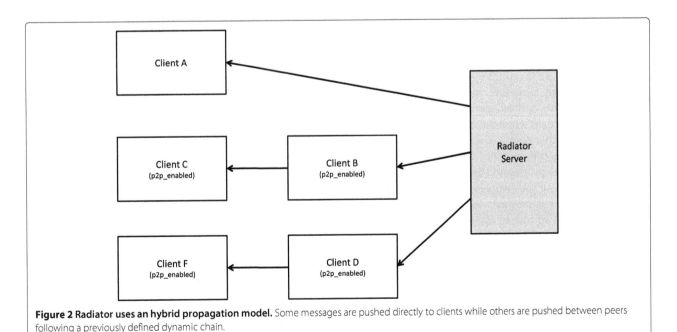

Figure 2 Radiator uses an hybrid propagation model. Some messages are pushed directly to clients while others are pushed between peers following a previously defined dynamic chain.

Even though we included some mechanisms to cope with network data loss such as the one explained above, this is not the focus of the paper for two main reasons: (1) there are well-known distributed systems techniques that deal with this problem that can easily be used within Radiator, and (2) some information that may be lost does not have to be re-sent given its semantics (i.e., it is superseded by the next messages).

4 Implementation

A prototype of Radiator is implemented in Python. The Python language has excellent support for list manipulation and anonymous functions (lambda functions), very useful for defining aggregability functions in a compact form. Its interpreter is also very lightweight (when compared to Java or .NET, for example) which enables experiments where we launch thousands of threads in the same machine. Note that, in order to use Radiator, the client application does not have to be implemented in Python. The Radiator server provides an API through HTTP Web Services which any application can easily use[c].

4.1 API

The local middleware is a pluggable component that runs along the client application and is responsible for abstracting away all the details of context aggregation and propagation. It provides a very simple API with 4 functions:

setup(*server_address*) — Initializes the local middleware and stores the server address that will be used for subsequent API calls. Application programmers must first call this function before using other functions of the API.

register_client(*client_id*, *receive_callback*, *attributes*) — Upon calling this function, the local middleware opens a local HTTP port for receiving messages. It then sends a registration message to the server indicating the *client_id* and the local HTTP port. The server stores this information in a clients' table that will be used to propagate context. The *receive_callback* parameter defines the function that will be called when the client receives a message (see below for further explanation).

Note that from this moment on, the client may start receiving messages propagated by others. It is also able to send messages using the *propagate_context* function (see below). The client is uniquely identified by the pair (ip address, client id) so name collisions are infrequent. If a collision occurs, the function raises an exception and the client application must try again with a different identifier. The *attributes* parameter is optional and is used to inform about specific information related to this client. One of these attributes is the "p2p_enabled" attribute which, as previously described, informs the server that the client is able to connect directly to other peers (either by manual configuration or by testing a connection with a dummy client on well-known location/port).

unregister_client(*client_id*) — It signals that the client is no longer interested in receiving messages propagated by others (e.g., logout). This closes the local HTTP port that was opened to receive incoming messages and sends a message to the server to delete the client from the client's table.

propagate_context(*context*) — The application calls this function whenever it wants to propagate the context associated with a given client to others. The *context* parameter is an object containing a set of clients, a time range and a list of attributes (name/value pairs).

This object is marshalled into JSON format [22] and sent to the server. Depending on the aggregability function, the server may decide to propagate the message immediately or aggregate it with other messages. In any case, this is transparent to the client application — the function returns as soon as it is able to deliver the message to the server.

The application programmer must implement *receive_callback* (the second parameter of the *register_client* function) according to the following interface.

receive_callback(*context*) — This function is called in the client application for every received message. Note that the *context* parameter is an object of the same type of the one sent using *propagate_context*.

Also, the JSON message received from the server is conveniently unmarshalled into an object before invoking the callback. This process occurs asynchronously, following the event-driven paradigm and it is highly convenient for application programmers who want to refresh the application's UI with incoming messages.

4.2 Server — client management

The server keeps a table for each active client. For each client, it stores its identification, IP address and local callback port as well as some attributes that may be sent using the *register_client*. This table is kept in memory for fast access (we opted for storing the table in memory since the volume of data to store for each client is small and the cost of memory is decreasing). If for some reason the server is no longer able to establish a connection or send a message to a client, the client is considered unreachable and is therefore deleted from this table to prevent further wasting of resources. The local middleware can reissue a *register_client* anytime (e.g., if it does not receive any messages for a certain amount of time). If it already exists in the clients' table it will overwrite the previous entry (e.g., it may have new local callback port or a different attribute).

The last context message received for each client is also stored in the table. This effectively represents (possibly with some delay) the current context of each client, which is used by the aggregability function to decide its result.

4.3 Communication protocol

Radiator uses HTTP to communicate between the server and the clients and between clients themselves. Besides being a well-understood widely-adopted protocol, it has several advantages over other protocols: (1) multiple available libraries in many programming languages, (2) works well within security-constrained environments (e.g., behind firewalls), (3) it does not require a permanent connection between the client and the server which would hinder the server's scalability, (4) it supports encryption (HTTPS) and compression (through the *accept-encoding* header).

Our prototype uses a fast and lightweight embeddable web-framework called Bottle [23] in conjunction with Paste [24], a high-performance multi-threaded HTTP middleware.

The connections are accomplished through an HTTP request initiated by the sender (the server or client) to the local TCP port that every recipient opened during its initialization (to receive incoming messages). This port is registered in the clients table, as described in Section 4.2. Note that, by default, all communications are compressed using gzip. The use of the HTTP protocol allows clients behind firewalls, and since the server initiates the connection (push approach) there is no need for clients to poll the server for new messages, causing unnecessary traffic and delays.

4.4 Compression

As already mentioned in Section 2, most of the messages compression results from applying an *aggregation* function to each message. If the developer provides such function, it can achieve high compression levels by taking into account the specific context attributes of his application (e.g., using the average speed instead of individual speed information in a traffic monitoring application).

Besides the *aggregation* function, Radiator also uses standard compression mechanisms (e.g., gzip) to increase the efficiency gains of aggregating multiple messages into one. The HTTP protocol supports compression through the headers *Accept-Encoding* and *Content-Encoding*. There is a negotiation between client and server where the client sends an HTTP Request containing the header Accept-Encoding: gzip and, if the server supports the request compression scheme, responds with a gzip [25] compressed response along with the header Content-Encoding: gzip. Note that this only works for responses — requests are never compressed. Since most of the HTTP

traffic lies on responses, this does not usually constitute a problem.

However, in Radiator, requests make up the biggest slice of traffic, because it follows a push model: clients push context to the server, which then pushes that context to other clients. Also, when a chain of recipients is used (*p2p* propagation), clients push messages between them. The HTTP protocol does allow a *Content-Encoding: gzip* in the request but most of the implementations ignore this header. So, we had to develop: (1) an extension to the standard HTTP python lib that optionally compresses request on the client, and (2) a plugin to handle compressed requests on the server.

5 Evaluation

This section presents results of several experiments to evaluate the scalability of the Radiator implementation. In particular, we measure the tradeoff between network bandwidth consumption and the average propagation time (i.e., the time it takes for a message to go from the sender to the recipient). To study this tradeoff, we take three approaches:

- We evaluate different aggregability functions (using a non-chained approach)
- We evaluate chained (*p2p*) and non-chained (broadcast) message propagation scenarios using the same settings
- We evaluate several chained message propagation scenarios using different *chain of recipients* sizes

5.1 Experimental setup

We developed a traffic monitoring and hazard detection application (scenarios #1 and #2 in Table 1) because it is the kind of context-aware application that usually suffers from the problems outlined on this paper: huge number of messages (e.g., 70.000 cars per day on US expressways [26]) and highly dynamic matching rules (cars in transit are, most of the time, changing their location and speed).

For this experiment, the application produces random context messages (related to traffic information) — we used a standard python random function (within bounds) for each of the context variables: location, speed and number of hazards. Each message contains information about the current location, speed and number of hazards detected by the client. The application then uses the Radiator local middleware to propagate these messages to other clients. The experiment was conducted using 7 machines (each one is a $2\times$ 4-Core Intel Xeon E5506@2.13GHz running Ubuntu 10.04.3) connected through a Gigabit LAN switch. The server runs on a dedicated machine; the other 6 machines run the application (with multiple threads where each thread simulates a client). All these machines have their clocks synchronized using NTP.

Several metrics such as CPU, memory and network bandwidth consumption are captured using the sysstat tool [27]. The average delay between message transmission and reception was also recorded (the average delay between the moment a client sends a message and the moment another client receives the message).

5.2 Aggregation/compression

To measure the impact of the aggregation on the system scalability (as related to the consumed network bandwidth), we launched 60.000 clients (threads) across 6 different machines, each client propagating 1000 messages (each one ranging between 300 and 500 bytes) at 1 msg/sec rate. We experimented with different aggregability/compression settings:

- **Vol: 1 (no gzip)** — Messages are immediately propagated, uncompressed. All other scenarios are performed with compression turned on using gzip (the default settings). We decided to include an uncompressed experiment to understand the impact of compression on the bandwidth.
- **Vol: 1** — Messages are immediately propagated.
- **Vol: 20** — Messages are retained in the server until there are 20 pending messages, which are then propagated in a single message.
- **Vol: 50** — Messages are retained in the server until there are 50 pending messages, which are then propagated in a single message.

We decided to change the volume parameter (as opposed to the time parameter, for example) because it is easier to manipulate. However, as we observed experimentally, changing the time and volume parameters should have the same effect w.r.t. the performance values obtained.

Figure 3 and Table 3 show the results concerning the server outbound bandwidth and average delay (between a client sending a message and another client receiving it), under these settings. As expected, the non compressed scenario is the worse performer in the experiment. We can see in Figure 3 that even without aggregation (*vol 1*), the mere act of compressing achieves a 25% reduction on consumed bandwidth. Aggregating with *vol 20* yields another 8% decrease and with *vol 50* we achieve a substantial reduction of 40% over the non aggregated compressed scenario. This is because, as we aggregate more messages, the compression algorithm becomes more effective because of the increased redundancy [28].

We can also see in Figure 3 that the consumed bandwidth is much more uniform on the unaggregated scenarios, because messages are immediately propagated

(i.e., constant flow of data). On aggregated scenarios, messages are retained in the server and propagated in batches, originating big fluctuations on network usage. Nevertheless, the average consumption is relatively stable (around the values presented in Table 3).

Another important insight from these results is the impact of the different aggregability settings on the average message propagation delay. Table 3 shows that even in the scenario with *vol 1* (where messages are not being retained in the server) there is already a substantial average lag of 42 seconds (between sending and receiving a message) caused by 60.000 clients continuously pushing information and overloading the server's outbound network link. The stress on the network link is key to explaining why the aggregated scenarios (*vol 20* and *vol 50*) actually decrease the lag even though messages are being retained at the server. By sending many fewer messages the server is reducing the stress in the outbound network link and increasing the throughput. In a sense, we can say that under heavy load, it is unavoidable that there will exist message retention on the network link so we might as well retain them at the server. Moreover, Radiator is able to perform this retention without breaking user expectations because, for some contextual information, he does not mind receiving it with delay.

5.3 Hybrid propagation

Even with aggregation, the server outbound bandwidth can easily become the bottleneck on large-scale distributed context-aware systems. We use the same setup (simulating 60.000 clients) to evaluate the hybrid propagation mechanism described in Section 3.2 under different *chain of recipients* sizes. As already mentioned, this size (represented as a percentage) is the maximum number of clients in a group (chain) for which the server sends only one message which is then disseminated directly between them (*p2p propagation*). We tested the following chain sizes (represented by the k parameter described in Section 3.2):

- no chain — server sends messages to every client individually.
- $k = 0.02$ — server sends messages to 5000 groups of 12 clients each.
- $k = 0.05$ — server sends messages to 2000 groups of 30 clients each.
- $k = 1$ — server sends messages to 100 groups of 600 clients each.
- $k = 5$ — server sends messages to 20 groups of 3000 clients each.
- $k = 10$ — server sends messages to 10 groups of 6000 clients each.

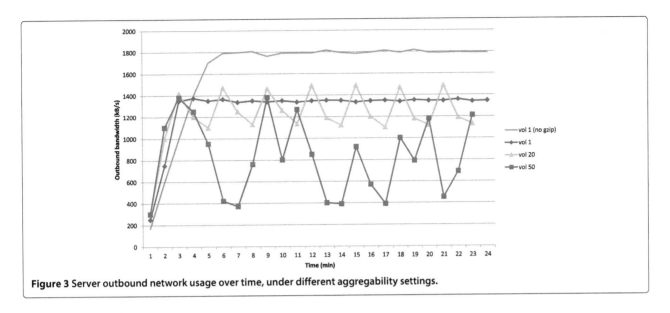

Figure 3 Server outbound network usage over time, under different aggregability settings.

Without lack of generality, to simplify the analysis, we started by conducting the experiment without aggregation (vol 1).

Figure 4 shows the outbound network usage over time (during the experiment) under these chain sizes. Even with a chain size of 0.02% there is already a significant decrease over the no chain scenario (aprox. 26%). Note that, even if the server sends messages to 12× less clients, we incur in the overhead of including all the recipients' IDs and addresses in the message (messages become much bigger). As we increase the chain size, the server outbound bandwidth decreases, since the server send fewer messages. Obviously, the outbound bandwidth consumption on the other (client) machines increases but in a real scenario we expect this not to be a problem since each client will have his own machine/device to run the application.

We can also see that the decrease is logarithmic — the reduction that we get when we go from a chain size of 0,02% to 0,05% is much greater than the reduction we get when we go from 1% to 10%. This is because the cost of including information about the members of the group (increasing the message size) no longer justifies the gain of establishing fewer connections. It is worthy

noting that even though message size increases (due to the inclusion of the recipients chain), this allows a highly dynamic reconfiguration capability of the propagation paths (the propagation path is calculated for each individual message); this solution is better than using a specific protocol (with specific control messages) for the propagation paths reconfiguration (e.g., as in multicast trees — more details in Section 6), specially if it occurs very frequently.

It is also important to understand the impact in the propagation time as we change the sizes of recipients chains. Table 4 shows the average lag in seconds under different sizes of recipients chains. We can observe that there is an increase in the average lag as we go from a non-chained (direct push) model to a chained (p2p) model. This is due to the fact that, in the latter, the messages must travel through the chain of recipients instead of being directly pushed from the server to each recipient. Nevertheless, the average lag only grows 66% (from 42 ms to 70 ms) even though the message has to travel through 60 clients (k=0,1%).

Even propagating the message among 600 clients (k=1%) does not add much to the average lag (76% over the non partitioned scenario, i.e., from 42 ms to 74 ms). This is because this propagation occurs in 6 nodes that do not include the server node (which is the node that is being stressed out with these experiments). Although we do not have yet real-world results, we expect this delay to be even less significant in those conditions, where each node corresponds to a single client. If we grow too much the size of the chain (above 5%), the number of hops the message has to travel starts to severely penalize the average lag and the technique is no longer effective. In this case, a good equilibrium seems to be achieved with a chain size of 1%: the consumed outbound is reduced to 4,4% of the

Table 3 Average outbound network usage (from the server) and lag under different settings

Settings	Avg. outbound bandwidth (kB/s)	Avg. lag (sec)
Vol 1 (no gzip)	1751	41
Vol 1	1324	42
Vol 20	1222	34
Vol 50	797	36

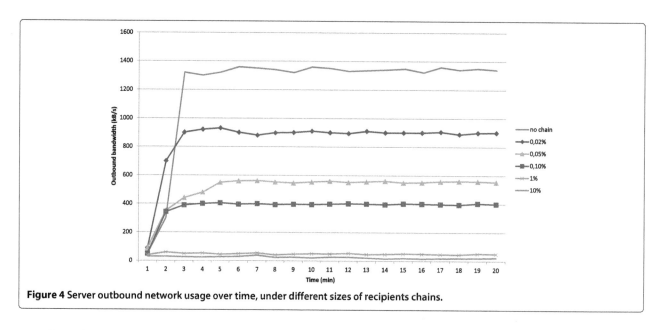

Figure 4 Server outbound network usage over time, under different sizes of recipients chains.

non-chained scenario while the corresponding delay only increases 76%.

Using the chain size of 1% (the one that reached the best compromise between bandwidth and lag), we experimented with different aggregability functions, more specifically, setting different volumes. The results are shown in Table 5. We can see that aggregating messages has the same effect it had in the non chained experiment: the lag decreases from *vol 1* to *vol 20*, and while it increases again with *vol 50*, it remains smaller than the *vol 1* lag. The explanation is the same: since the server is sending many fewer messages (and note that these messages are bigger as they now carry the chain of recipients), the server's network link is less stressed out, allowing a greater throughput.

Although this is a simulated experiment (due to the lack of publicly available real traces), we believe it reflects a real-world scenario of a traffic monitoring application capturing and propagating the location and speed of cars in transit on a medium-sized city. We conducted the experiment with 60.000 nodes which is close to the average number of cars on US expressways, according to USGS data [26].

Table 4 Average lag under different
chain of recipients **sizes (vol 1)**

Chain size	Avg. lag (sec)
No chain	42
0,1%	70
1%	74
5%	223
10%	295

6   Related work

In this section, we review the literature for the usage of aggregation on context-aware systems and some large-scale context propagation techniques.

6.1   Aggregation

The term "aggregation" is usually identified with the inference/reasoning component of typical context-aware systems. Although this component's primary goal is to provide application developers with data on a higher level of abstraction [9], this usually materializes on some kind of semantic aggregation. A classic example is the Activity widget provided by the Context Toolkit [2] that senses the current activity level at a location such as a room, using a microphone. Instead of producing raw audio data captured by the microphone, it provides a high-level attribute "Activity Level" with three possible values: *none, some* or *a lot*. In a sense, we can say that a sample of raw audio data was semantically aggregated into a single attribute.

Another type of aggregation can occur at the distribution stage, when context was already captured and processed, and is now in the process of being sent to the client application. This aggregation consists of gathering into a single large message the content of multiple smaller messages before propagating it. Even though the vast majority of the context-aware frameworks propagate

Table 5 Average lag with chain size 1% under different volumes

Chain size	Settings	Avg. lag (sec)
1%	Vol 1	74
1%	Vol 20	41
1%	Vol 50	53

context in single disaggregated messages [9], recent experiments with aggregation have achieved good results; for example ReConMUC [29] combined a delayed approach with aggregation resulting in a more efficient use of resources on multi-user chat applications; similarly, Dyck [30] referred aggregation as a commonly used technique to improve scalability in network games that could be equally effective on groupware applications. In both cases, we are talking about syntactic aggregation: blindly concatenating single packets into a larger one and possibly compressing it. Although this yields good compression levels for text-based messages, we believe a higher-level semantic aggregation would be much more effective with other types of information (e.g., raw audio or image).

Radiator is able to perform both syntactic and semantic aggregation based on the *aggregation* function implementation. Moreover, since the *aggregation* function is executed on the server, the aggregation can be reused by multiple client applications (e.g., an aggregation of geo-localized messages by city region can be reused by a traffic monitoring and a "popular spots" application).

6.2 Large-scale selective propagation

Even though Radiator is built upon the principle that every client eventually receives every message from other clients (i.e., as in a broadcast system), the propagation can occur at different times and assume different forms (i.e., more or less aggregated) depending on the current context of the users involved. Thus, it makes sense to study current solutions to the large-scale selective propagation problem.

The most popular approach is to rely on a publish-subscribe paradigm. The publish-subscribe paradigm [10] is a loosely coupled form of interaction suitable for large scale settings. It consists of three components: *publishers*, who generate and feed the content into the system; *subscribers*, who receive content based on their interests in a topic or pattern; and an infrastructure that distributes events matching subscriber interests with publishers content. Matching can be done either through a subject-based approach or a content-based approach. Subject-based approaches (e.g., Herald [31]) assume some predefined channels/topics to which both publishers and subscribers can connect. On content-based approaches (e.g., Elvin [19] and Siena [32]), subscribers can issue sophisticated queries or predicates to perform the matching on a message-by-message basis. Note that the publish-subscribe model can be implemented on a centralized topology (e.g., Elvin [19]) or a distributed topology (e.g., [33]).

Content-based matching is usually made at the syntactic level (e.g., exact comparison of keywords) but this requires that publishers and subscribers use the same terminology defeating the decoupling nature of the publish/subscribe approach [34]. Some systems overcome this limitation by performing the matching at the semantic level (e.g., matching different keywords with the same meaning such as *school* and *university*) [35,36]. Radiator does not assume a specific kind of matching — it is up to the developer to implement the *aggregability* function (responsible for matching and aggregating) using the most appropriate techniques for his specific needs. Fulcrum [37] also allows developers to provide their own matching functions but does not provide any solution for delayed propagation - the events are either discarded or propagated immediately.

Even though content-based publish-subscribe systems offer a reasonable level of flexibility and could be used to implement context-aware applications, they lack a very important feature — their predicates are fixed expressions that do not depend on the current context of the publisher or subscriber. For example, a subscriber can't issue a predicate saying "I want to receive messages from users (publishers) who are at most 1 km away from me". His only option is to issue a predicate saying "I want to receive messages from users within a 1 km radius of the coordinates (34.567, 3.566768)" assuming he's currently located in that position; but then, if he's moving, he has to continuously update the predicate. This causes severe scalability problems as the network is flooded with subscribe and unsubscribe messages since each predicate change implies an unsubscribe from the previous predicate and a subscribe to the new predicate.

Berkovsky [38] proposes a context-aware publish-subscribe system that introduces the notion of automatic subscription based on the user's location, personal preferences and interests. The system automatically translates the user's context (which may be changing frequently) into a semantic query to perform the matching. In Radiator, the *aggregability* function is responsible for this translation with two important differences: (1) it may decide to delay its propagation, and (2) it may aggregate multiple events into a single one. These two characteristics are key to the scalability improvements shown in Section 5.

Another approach for selective propagation (or multicast) of messages to multiple recipients is to use structured peer-to-peer (p2p) overlays that support many members with high scalability [11]. In general, all proposals fall into one of two categories: flooding or tree building.

The flooding approach creates a separate overlay network per multicast group. It leverages the routing information already maintained by a group overlay to broadcast messages within that group (e.g., CAN-Multicast [39]). So, for each set of recipients a separate mini-overlay network is constructed, usually a costly operation involving JOIN messages and exchange/splitting of neighborhood tables with the existing nodes. So, once again, this approach does not scale well for frequently changing multicast trees.

The tree approach uses a single overlay and builds a spanning tree for each group, on which the multicast messages for the group are propagated. Some examples of this approach are Bayeux [40] and Scribe [12]. Multicast messages related to a group are propagated through its associated spanning tree. This form of application-level multicast leverages the object location and routing properties of the overlay network to create groups and join groups. For example, Bayeux uses Tapestry's [41] unicast routing to build a multicast tree using 4 message types: JOIN, LEAVE, TREE and PRUNE. A node joins a multicast tree by first sending a JOIN message towards the root node which responds a TREE message towards the joining node. The TREE message sets up the forwarding state at intermediate application-level nodes (in this case acting as routers). The LEAVE/PRUNE messages reverse this operation. Even though this approach scales well for stable multicast trees, the amount of exchanged messages that would be necessary to maintain highly dynamic trees (possibly changing every second) seriously reduces its scalability.

Finally, it is also possible to implement gossip-based multicast [42] by using membership protocols that manage the gossiping strategy, more specifically the nodes to whom gossip messages are sent. Again, the problem with this approach is that membership protocols are not well-suited to dynamic situations where the set of recipients change very frequently. Every time a member joins or leaves, the membership tables must be updated in multiple nodes, generating a lot of traffic.

In short, Radiator does not suffer from the rigidity of these approaches, which either assume a fixed set of matching rules or a set of recipients that does not change very frequently, making them unsuitable for context-aware applications.

6.3 Distributed stream processing systems

Traditional database management systems (DBMS) assume a pull-based model: users submit queries to the system and an answer is returned. In these systems, users play the active role, and the system plays the passive role. In contrast, stream processing systems (SPS) assume a push-based model: data is pushed into the system (as soon as it become available) and it is evaluated in response to detected events. Query answers are then pushed to a waiting user or application [43]. This push-based approach allows real-time processing of events, where query processing is performed directly on incoming messages. Therefore, unlike in DBMS, messages are processed before (or instead of) storing them [44]. Queries are built from a standard set of well-defined operators that accept input streams, transform them in some way and produce one or more output streams. For example, Aurora, a well-known SPS, supports a simple unary operator (Filter), a binary merge operator (Union), a time-bounded windowed sort (WSort), and an aggregation operator (Tumble) [45].

Distributed stream processing systems (DSPS) extend SPS to distribute their operators across multiple machines, providing several benefits: (1) stream processing performance can be scaled to handle increasing input loads; (2) it enables high availability because the machines can monitor and take over for each other when failures occur; and (3) they can take advantage of geographic and administrative distribution that is inherent to certain SPS such as wireless sensor networks [46]. Some examples of DSPS include Medusa [46], Borealis [47] and Stream Mill [48]. More recently there have been proposals for implementing DSPS on Cloud infrastructure such as Stormy [49], taking advantage of its elastic characteristics (i.e., easily adding and removing nodes from the system). Additionally, systems such as Naiad [50] combine DSPS with batch processing techniques, allowing complex incremental computations on streaming data.

DSPS can, and have already been used to, handle message context propagation in distributed systems. However, DSPS are generic systems (they can handle all kinds of data), which is simultaneously their biggest strength and weakness. In fact, since they do not know how to extract semantic meaning from context messages, they can't infer the current context of their users. All the dynamism in Radiator is a consequence of knowing and using the current context of both the sender and recipient, which not only allows more complex propagation scenarios (see Table 1) but also improves scalability in applications where context is frequently changing. To illustrate the last point, take for example how Borealis handles dynamic query modification. If we use Borealis in a context-aware system, every time the user's context changes we have to potentially change the attributes of one or several queries. Borealis supports these changes through a mechanism called control lines [44], which carries messages with revised parameters and functions for the deployed operators. Hence, as in other large-scale selective propagation systems (described in Section 6.2), there is always an overhead associated with transmitting the new parameters. In Radiator, the message itself already carries those parameters, since the current context is implicit in the message.

6.4 Summary

We now summarize the conclusions from this section into Table 6, where we compare the main feature of each system with Radiator.

It is clear from Table 6 that Radiator does not have the limitations of traditional CSCW systems on how

Table 6 Comparison between radiator and the surveyed systems

System	Main feature	How it compares to radiator
Context Toolkit [2]	Inference leads to semantic aggregation	Radiator performs semantic aggregation both at the inference layer and at the distribution layer
ReConMUC [29] and Dyck [30]	Syntactic aggregation at the distribution layer	Radiator is able to perform both syntactic and semantic aggregation at the distribution layer
Content-Based Pub-Sub	Matching is made at syntactic level or at limited semantic level (keywords with the same meaning)	In Radiator, the matching algorithm is more flexible because it can be defined as a function provided by the developer.
Fulcrum [37] (Pub-Sub)	Allows developers to provide matching functions	Radiator also allows events propagation to be delayed.
Berkovsky [38] (Pub-Sub)	Automatic subscription based on user context	Radiator adds to the automatic subscription the possibility of aggregating and delaying messages, improving scalability.
Multi-cast trees	Message propagation using P2P overlays	Radiator does not incur the cost of rebuilding P2P overlays every time the context changes.
DSPs	Efficient push-based propagation of messages	Radiator is able to extract semantic meaning from messages and infer the current context of its users, therefore adapting its propagation characteristics more efficiently.

context data is aggregated since the aggregation is performed by functions defined by the programmer. Aditionally, the aggregability function (equivalent to the matching function in Pub-Sub systems) is also defined by the programmer, allowing Radiator to have much more flexible rules and to take advantage of the current context of its users. Unlike Pub-Sub systems, Radiator also introduces the notion of delayed propagation, improving the applications' scalability. Finally, unlike generic distributed systems approaches (Pub-Sub, Multicast trees, DSPS), Radiator is able to extract semantic meaning from the exchanged messages thus does not need to perform costly "reconfiguration" operations every time the context changes.

7 Conclusions

In this paper, we present Radiator, a dynamic adaptable middleware for efficient distribution of context messages. Unlike current selective message distribution approaches which rely on relatively stable sets of matching rules (the rules that dictate who receives a certain message), our approach relies on functions that, given the current context of sender and receiver, decide under which conditions should a message be distributed.

Moreover, we introduce the concept of propagation based on a chain of recipients that, unlike pub-sub and application-level multicast tree approaches, can quickly react to highly dynamic ever-changing rules. In fact, as our experiments have shown, the chains of recipients can be continuously rebuilt and still achieve significant bandwidth reduction and no penalty on the average propagation time. This is only possible because of our delayed propagation mechanism that, when paired with compressed aggregated messages, makes a much more efficient use of the network bandwidth.

By combining both techniques (aggregation/compression and *chain-based* propagation) we were able to reduce the server's outbound bandwidth $20\times$ (when compared to the usual centralized and non-aggregated approach) without penalizing the average propagation delay in a given scenario (*partition 1%* and *vol 20*).

Regarding future work, we envisage to also use the current clients' context to build more efficient chains of recipients. The system will accept a *chainability* function (similar to the *aggregability* function) that can decide if two clients should belong into the same chain (e.g., based on their network-level proximity). We also plan to experiment parallelizing the context aggregation and propagation algorithm (Algorithm 1), since it can potentially become a bottleneck for systems with many clients.

Endnotes

[a] As of 2012, there are 175 million tweets (Twitter messages) being sent per day and some of these messages are distributed to over 19 million users (the number of followers of Lady Gaga) - http://bit.ly/zOiX8k.

[b] The *people* type can be useful to implement k-Anonymity [51] style privacy mechanisms; the idea is to aggregate as many messages as needed to ensure anonymity. It is out of the scope of this paper to analyze these mechanisms.

[c] The source code for the prototype is available at https://bitbucket.org/anonymousJoe/radiator.

Competing interests
The authors declare that they have no competing interests.

Authors' contributions
Both authors read and approved the final manuscript.

Acknowledgements
This work was partially supported by national funds through FCT, under projects PTDC/EIA-EIA/113993/2009 and PEst-OE/EEI/LA0021/2011.

Author details
[1]INESC-ID, Technical University of Lisbon, Opensoft, Rua Joshua Benoliel, 1, 4C, 1250 Lisbon, Portugal. [2]INESC-ID, IST, Technical University of Lisbon, Rua Alves Redol, 9, 1000 Lisbon, Portugal.

References

1. Dey A, Abowd G (1999) Towards a better understanding of context and context-awareness In: Handheld and ubiquitous computing. Springer, Berlin Heidelberg, pp 304–307. http://link.springer.com/chapter/10.1007/3-540-48157-5_29.
2. Salber D, Dey A, Abowd G (1999) Proceedings of the SIGCHI conference on Human factors in computing systems: the CHI is the limit. ACM, New York, p 441. doi:10.1145/302979.303126, http://portal.acm.org/citation.cfm?id=302979.303126.
3. Capra L, Quercia D (2011) Middleware for social computing: a roadmap. J Internet Serv Appl 3(1): 117–125. doi:10.1007/s13174-011-0045-8, http://www.springerlink.com/index/10.1007/s13174-011-0045-8.
4. Foursquare. http://www.foursquare.com.
5. Foursquare's ups and downs, Foursquare blog. http://blog.foursquare.com/post/607883149/foursquares-ups-and-downs.
6. Waze. http://www.waze.com.
7. Highlight. http://highlig.ht/.
8. Twitter Suffers WORST Month Since October: Here's Why, Huffington Post. http://www.huffingtonpost.com/2010/06/15/twitter-down-time-explain_n_613433.html.
9. Baldauf M, Dustdar S, Rosenberg F (2007) A survey on context-aware systems. Int J Ad Hoc Ubiquitous Comput 2(4): 263. doi:10.1504/IJAHUC.2007.014070, http://www.inderscience.com/link.php?id=14070.
10. Eugster P, Felber P, Guerraoui R, Kermarrec A (2003) The many faces of publish/subscribe. ACM Comput Surv 35(2): 114–131. doi:10.1145/857076.857078, http://portal.acm.org/citation.cfm?doid=857076.857078.
11. Castro M, Jones M, Kermarrec A (2003) An evaluation of scalable application-level multicast built using peer-to-peer overlays. IEEE INFOCOM 2: 1510–1520. http://ieeexplore.ieee.org/xpls/abs_all.jsp?arnumber=1208986.
12. Castro M, Druschel P, Kermarrec A, Rowstron A (2002) SCRIBE: a large-scale and decentralized application-level multicast infrastructure. IEEE J Sel Area Comm 20(8): 1489–1499. http://citeseerx.ist.psu.edu/viewdoc/summary?doi=10.1.1.20.299.
13. Priyantha B, Lymberopoulos D, Liu J (2011) Little rock: enabling energy efficient continuous sensing on mobile phones. IEEE Pervasive Comput 10(2): 12–15
14. Raento M, Oulasvirta a, Petit R, Toivonen H (2005) ContextPhone: a prototyping platform for context-aware mobile applications. IEEE Pervasive Comput 4(2): 51–59. doi:10.1109/MPRV.2005.29, http://ieeexplore.ieee.org/lpdocs/epic03/wrapper.htm?arnumber=1427649.
15. Rana R, Chou C, Kanhere S, Bulusu N, Hu W (2010) Proceedings of the 9th ACM/IEEE international conference on information processing in sensor networks. ACM, pp 105–116. http://dl.acm.org/citation.cfm?id=1791226.
16. Miluzzo E, Lane N, Fodor K, Peterson R, Lu H (2008) 6th ACM conference on Embedded network sensor systems. ACM Press, New York, p 337. doi:10.1145/1460412.1460445, http://portal.acm.org/citation.cfm?id=1460445.
17. Saito Y, Shapiro M (2005) Optimistic replication. ACM Comput Surv 37(1): 42–81. doi:10.1145/1057977.1057980, http://dl.acm.org/citation.cfm?id=1057977.1057980.
18. Mathur A, Hall RW, Jahanian F, Prakash A, Rasmussen C (1995) The publish / subscribe paradigm for scalable group collaboration systems. Ann Arbor 1001(313): 48,109. http://citeseerx.ist.psu.edu/viewdoc/download?doi=10.1.1.53.1487&rep=rep1&type=pdf.
19. Segall B, Arnold D (1997) Elvin has left the building: a publish/subscribe notification service with quenching In: Proceedings of AUUG 1997. Brisbane, September, pp 3–5
20. Allavena A, Demers A, Hopcroft JE (2005) Correctness of a gossip based membership protocol In: Proceedings of the twenty-fourth annual ACM SIGACT-SIGOPS symposium on principles of distributed computing - PODC '05. ACM Press, New York, p 292. doi:10.1145/1073814.1073871, http://dl.acm.org/citation.cfm?id=1073814.1073871.
21. Hudson J, Christensen J, Kellogg W, Erickson T (2002) Proceedings of the SIGCHI conference on human factors in computing systems: changing our world, changing ourselves. ACM, pp 97–104. http://portal.acm.org/citation.cfm?id=503376.503394.
22. Introducing JSON. http://www.json.org/.
23. Bottle: Python Web Framework. http://bottlepy.org/docs/dev/.
24. Python Paste. http://pythonpaste.org/.
25. Deutsch LP (1996) GZIP file format specification version 4.3. http://tools.ietf.org/html/rfc1952.
26. Gruteser M, Grunwald D (2003) Anonymous usage of location-based services through spatial and temporal cloaking In: Proceedings of the 1st international conference on Mobile systems, applications and services - MobiSys '03, pp 31–42. doi:10.1145/1066116.1189037, http://portal.acm.org/citation.cfm?doid=1066116.1189037.
27. Sysstat documentation. http://sebastien.godard.pagesperso-orange.fr/.
28. Shannon CE (1948) A mathematical theory of communication. Bell Syst Tech J 27: 379–423. doi:10.1145/584091.584093, http://dl.acm.org/citation.cfm?id=584093, 9411012.
29. Alves P, Ferreira P (2011) ReConMUC - adaptable consistency requirements for efficient large-scale multi-user chat In: Proceedings of the 2011 ACM conference on computer supported cooperative work. ACM, pp 553–562
30. Dyck J, Gutwin C, Graham T, Pinelle D (2007) Beyond the LAN: techniques from network games for improving groupware performance In: Proceedings of the 2007 international ACM conference on supporting group work. ACM, pp 291–300. http://portal.acm.org/citation.cfm?id=1316669.
31. Cabrera L, Jones M, Theimer M (2001) Herald: achieving a global event notification service In: Proceedings of the eighth workshop on hot topics in operating systems, pp 87–92. doi:10.1109/HOTOS.2001.990066, http://ieeexplore.ieee.org/lpdocs/epic03/wrapper.htm?arnumber=990066.
32. Carzaniga A, Rosenblum D, Wolf A (2000) Achieving scalability and expressiveness in an Internet-scale event notification service In: Proceedings of the nineteenth annual ACM symposium on Principles of distributed computing - PODC '00, pp 219–227. doi:10.1145/343477.343622, http://portal.acm.org/citation.cfm?doid=343477.343622.
33. Tam D, Azimi R, Jacobsen H (2004) Building content-based publish/subscribe systems with distributed hash tables In: Databases, Information Systems, and Peer-to-Peer Computing. Springer, Berlin Heidelberg, pp 138-152. http://www.springerlink.com/index/65HRU54EERAPK0AP.pdf.
34. Burcea I, Petrovic M (2003) I know what you mean: semantic issues in Internet-scale publish/subscribe systems In: Proceedings of the SWDB 2003, pp 51–63. http://arxiv.org/abs/cs/0311047.
35. Petrovic M, Burcea I, Jacobsen H (2003) S-topss: Semantic toronto publish/subscribe system In: Proceedings of the 29th international conference on very large data bases-Volume 29. VLDB Endowment, pp 1101–1104. http://dl.acm.org/citation.cfm?id=1315559.
36. Wang J (2004) A semantic-aware publish/subscribe system with RDF patterns In: Proceedings of the 28th annual international computer software and applications conference, 2004 COMPSAC 2004, pp 141–146. doi:10.1109/CMPSAC.2004.1342818, http://ieeexplore.ieee.org/lpdocs/epic03/wrapper.htm?arnumber=1342818.
37. Boyer R (2005) Fulcrum - an open-implementation approach to internet-scale context-aware publish/subscribe In: 2005 HICSS'05. Proceedings of the 38th Annual Hawaii International Conference on. IEEE, pp 275a–275a. http://ieeexplore.ieee.org/xpls/abs_all.jsp?arnumber=1385802.
38. Berkovsky S, Eytani Y (2005) Semantic platform for context-aware publish/subscribe M-commerce In: Applications and the Internet Workshops, 2005. Saint Workshops 2005. The 2005 Symposium on. IEEE, pp 188–191. http://ieeexplore.ieee.org/xpls/abs_all.jsp?arnumber=1620008.
39. Ratnasamy S, Francis P, Handley M (2001) A scalable content-addressable network In: Proceedings of the 2001 conference on applications, technologies, architectures, and protocols for computer communications. ACM, pp 161–172. http://dl.acm.org/citation.cfm?id=383072.

40. Zhuang S, Zhao B, Joseph A, Katz R (2001) Bayeux: An architecture for scalable and fault-tolerant wide-area data dissemination In: Proceedings of the 11th international workshop on network and OS support for digital audio and video (January). ACM, pp 11–20. http://dl.acm.org/citation.cfm?id=378347.

41. Zhao B, Kubiatowicz J, Joseph A (2001) Tapestry: an infrastructure for fault-tolerant wide-area location and routing (April). http://citeseer.ist.psu.edu/viewdoc/summary?doi=10.1.1.111.1818.

42. Kermarrec A (2007) Gossiping in distributed systems. ACM SIGOPS Oper Syst Rev 41(5): 2–7. doi:10.1145/1317379.1317381, http://dl.acm.org/citation.cfm?id=1317381.

43. Cherniack M, Balakrishnan H, Balazinska M (2003) Scalable distributed stream processing CIDR, vol. 3, pp 257–268. 2003. http://www.eecs.harvard.edu/~mdw/course/cs260r/papers/aurora-cidr03.pdf.

44. Cetintemel U, Abadi D (2006) The Aurora and Borealis Stream Processing Engines In: Data stream management: processing high-speed data streams. Springer-Verlag. http://dumay.info/pdf/StreamProcessor/8.pdf.

45. Carney D, Çetintemel U (2002) Monitoring streams: a new class of data management applications In: Proceedings of the 28th international conference on very large data bases. VLDB Endowment, pp 215–226. http://dl.acm.org/citation.cfm?id=1287389.

46. Balazinska M, Balakrishnan H, Stonebraker M (2004) Load management and high availability in the Medusa distributed stream processing system In: Proceedings of the 2004 ACM SIGMOD international conference on management of data - SIGMOD '04, p 929. doi:10.1145/1007568.1007701, http://portal.acm.org/citation.cfm?doid=1007568.1007701.

47. Ahmad Y, Tatbul N, Xing W, Xing Y, Zdonik S, Berg B, Cetintemel U, Humphrey M, Hwang JH, Jhingran A, Maskey A, Papaemmanouil O, Rasin A (2005) Distributed operation in the Borealis stream processing engine In: Proceedings of the 2005 ACM SIGMOD international conference on management of data - SIGMOD '05, p 882. doi:10.1145/1066157.1066274, http://portal.acm.org/citation.cfm?doid=1066157.1066274.

48. Thakkar H, Mozafari B, Zaniolo C (2008) Designing an inductive data stream management system: the stream mill experience In: Proceedings of the 2nd international workshop on scalable stream processing system. ACM, pp 79–88. http://dl.acm.org/citation.cfm?id=1379286.

49. Loesing S, Hentschel M (2012) Stormy: an elastic and highly available streaming service in the cloud In: Proceedings of the 2012 joint EDBT/ICDT workshops ACM. http://dl.acm.org/citation.cfm?id=2320789.

50. Murray D, McSherry F, Isaacs R (2013) Naiad: a timely dataflow system In: Proceedings of the twenty-fourth ACM symposium on operating systems principles ACM. http://dl.acm.org/citation.cfm?id=2522738.

51. Sweeney L (2002) k-anonymity: a model for protecting privacy. Int J Uncertainty Fuzziness Knowl- Based Syst 10(5): 557–570. http://citeseerx.ist.psu.edu/viewdoc/summary?doi=10.1.1.391.6292.

8

AppaaS: offering mobile applications as a cloud service

Khalid Elgazzar[*], Ali Ejaz and Hossam S Hassanein

Abstract

With the huge number of offerings in the mobile application market, the choice of mobile applications that best fit particular objectives is challenging. Therefore, there is a demand for a platform elevating the momentum of mobile applications that can adapt their behavior according to the user's context. This paper proposes *AppaaS*, a context-aware platform that provides mobile applications *as a service*. AppaaS uses several types of context information including location information, user profile, device profile, user ratings, and time to provision the best relevant mobile applications to such a context. AppaaS supports state preservation, where user-specific data and application status are stored for the user's future reference. Experimental validation demonstrates that AppaaS alleviates the burden on mobile users to find applications that work best for a particular situation. It also enables application providers to dynamically control access to the functionality of their applications. Performance evaluation results show that AppaaS can employ cloud elastic resource provisioning to offer flexible scalability, while satisfying certain QoS constraints. Experimental results also support a conclusion that with little overhead handling context information, AppaaS can bring remarkable benefits to provisioning mobile applications as a service.

Keywords: Mobile applications; Cloud computing; Location-based services; Context-aware; Mobile devices

1 Introduction

Mobile devices have become the most pervasive interface that enables access to information services anywhere, anytime. Nowadays, most business enterprises, governments, and public sectors rely on mobile applications to reach a wider range of customers at their most convenience anytime and anywhere. Recent years have witnessed increasing momentum for mobile applications that can adapt their behavior according to user context. Adaptation to context changes reshapes the application's behavior to support service personalization and offer better user experience. Such context includes location information, user profile, user ratings, device profile, and time.

At the time of writing this paper, *Google Play Store* has over than 1 million apps [1], while *Apple Store* is now the home of over than 900,000 apps [2]. Many of these applications are available from various businesses to benefit their customers and improve their experience. With the ever growing application market, a number of open questions related to context awareness arise. From a user

perspective, how would a user know that there is an application relevant to his/her current location, and how can a user decide on which application to use from the many available choices. From a business perspective, how can businesses control access to their applications while maintaining a high level of mobility and flexibility to their employees or customers. The system proposed in this paper answers these questions.

We propose *AppaaS*, a context-aware platform for mobile application dissemination and control. AppaaS provisions mobile applications as a cloud service on demand with the appropriate access constraints. AppaaS provides a platform where mobile applications providers and users can match offerings with requests. The platform enables providers to customize their offerings and set proper access constraints according to the privileges of users and their context. It also enables users to conveniently find relevant applications to their situation and save the current application state for future reference. The platform handles several types of context information to ensure that selected applications best serve the user requesting the service. The proposed platform offers a user-friendly interface to facilitate the communication

*Correspondence: elgazzar@cs.queensu.ca
School of Computing, Queen's University, Kingston, Canada

between users and the backend server, where all context processing and data storage management occur.

The remainder of this paper is organized as follows. Section 2 presents motivating scenarios. Section 3 provides brief background and outlines related research. Section 4 describes the proposed architecture. In Section 5 we provide the implementation details of our prototype. The platform functionality is validated in Section 6 and a performance evaluation is presented in Section 7. Lastly, Section 8 draws some concluding remarks.

2   Motivating scenarios

To better understand the advantages and functionalities of such a system, consider the following scenarios.

- *Finding the Appropriate Application*: Suppose that Adam walks into a store with his smartphone and is looking for an application by which he can browse through different offers, product catalogues, or find information relative to a specific product of interest. Imagine how convenient this would be to Adam and how beneficial it would be to the store. AppaaS makes this scenario possible. As soon as Adam enters the store's physical space, the store-specific application gets downloaded onto Adam's smartphone, with his consent. As soon as Adam leaves the space, the application preserves its current state (browsed items, shopping cart, etc.) for future reference and gets uninstalled to free up the mobile resources it is holding. If Adam comes back to the same store (or another related store that shares the same application), the application launches back with the last preserved state that is relevant to Adam.

- *User-aware Applications*: Now, suppose Adam and his friend John enter a store where Adam holds a store membership and John does not. As soon as they walk in, Adam gets the application with the membership privileges, giving Adam exclusive access to membership offers, while John gets the application intended for non-member customers, which might have an open access scheme but is limited to the store's physical location. It is also possible that the same application may handle users with different access privileges. AppaaS facilitates such a model which offers great flexibility to business entities.

- *Controlling Application Behavior*: Now let's assume Adam is at work. Adam holds a position that gives him access to confidential data. As soon as Adam enters the workplace premises, AppaaS installs or activates the enterprise application functionality on his mobile device that allows him access to such data. It is possible that enterprises restrict access to their confidential data wherein coffee rooms or break

lounges. Furthermore, enterprises might restrict their business-related mobile applications (or certain functionality) to specific physical places (such as enterprise premises, location of bidders' conference) with variant access privileges according to the user/employee position at workplace.

3   Background & related work

Mobile services that are capable of changing their behavior according to context changes are of particular interest to the provisioning of personalized behaviors [3]. To achieve the desired functionality, such context-aware services typically exploit a combination of several context information, such as location information, user profile, user satisfaction indicators, device features and capabilities, time, etc. [4,5].

Location-based services in ubiquitous computing environments is a rich domain of research [6-9], in which services make use of location information in particular to better provide relevant ubiquitous services. The application of location-based services is popular in many domains such as navigation and traveler services [10,11], shopping and entertainment services (e.g. finding nearby theater), emergency situations (e.g. nearest medical facility), information services [12], and many others [13]. Such services require access to the user's location, which compromises the user's privacy even if several location cloaking techniques are applied [14]. To tackle this challenge, Amoli et al. [14] propose a protocol to preserve privacy in location-based services while satisfying the requirement of accurate location. Similarly, Puttaswamy et at. [15] propose an approach to encrypt location data.

The ultimate objective of AppaaS is to relieve users from having to search and install relevant applications fitting their current situation, especially when there are a huge number of applications in the market. Sharing our objective, Quah et al. [16] propose a mobile application distribution system that retrieves relevant applications based on location information. The system uses the location as the main driver to download mobile applications. Which App? [17] also addresses the same issue in a different way. It proposes a mobile application recommender system that monitors the social interaction and behavior of users to recommend relevant applications accordingly. Toye et al. [18] employ personal information stored on smartphones to customize the behavior of site-specific applications to best fit a particular user. AppaaS shares the same interests of finding relevant applications to a particular context. However AppaaS offers more advantages in managing and controlling the behavior of such applications according to users' access privileges and time constraints. In addition, AppaaS offers the opportunity to preserve the user-specific application state for future reference.

3.1 Context management

Context is any information that can characterize a certain situation relevant to a user including the user itself [19]. Exploiting context information in developing mobile applications opens up new opportunities for a smart generation of applications that dynamically adapt to changing environments and look very personal to the user. Such applications promise a unique user experience. The various context information that AppaaS uses to provide mobile applications as a service are the following.

- Location: The location of mobile user influences what applications users may run on their mobile devices. A user within a certain location might not be aware of relevant application(s) to run in order to get the best service a location might provide. AppaaS employs location information to dispatch the most appropriate application to a user's context. The automatic collection of location information can be obtained in a variety of ways outdoors (e.g. GPS and mobile networks) [20,21], or indoors (e.g. Received Signal Strength techniques) [22,23].

- User Profile: Different users may have different access rights to same applications. For example, within an enterprise different users may have different roles and various job responsibilities, which influence their privilege to access certain information or enterprise-related confidential data. Furthermore, some users could have a variant level of access privilege to such data according to their location or current time. AppaaS exploits such user information in order to assign the user with the proper access rights to an application. Towards this end, AppaaS keeps records of user profiles and credentials.

- Device Profile: AppaaS exploits the device profile in order to identify the appropriate version of a relevant application that fits the device platform. AppaaS takes advantage of communication sessions to collect the device profile information [24].

- User ratings: Web 2.0 and open environments have enabled users to leave feedback and share their consumer experience. User ratings reflect the user perceived quality of service. AppaaS takes advantage of such a feature to choose between applications that provide similar services.

- Time: AppaaS uses time to apply time-based access control over mobile applications. Applications may restrict access to their functionality during certain periods of time. For example, enterprises may allow their employees to access confidential data only during working hours on the premises. AppaaS uses

the server time as a reference while handling time-related constraints to avoid synchronization aspects. The server performs the appropriate time transformation according the user's time zone based on current location information.

3.2 State preservation

State preservation refers to how applications can save their latest status and user-specific data for future access. Mobile applications can manage their own state at different levels. For example, applications may use checkpointing techniques [25,26] to suspend and resume their execution for migration purposes. However, the energy and communication cost of migration is inevitably high for mobile applications. Since most of the mobile environments adopt the concept of the virtual machine (VM) [27] to isolate individual applications, the migration process transfers the whole VM and associated resources. To avoid high migration cost, Hung et al. [28] propose an energy-efficient approach that migrates applications between mobile devices and the cloud resulting in lower overhead. Their approach relies on pre-deployment of mobile applications on the cloud side and then transfer only the application state, by which an application resumes its executions.

Application-independent state preservation of user-specific data remains challenging. Current mobile platforms do not natively support state preservation at any level. However, platforms such as Android offer a generic framework for saving an application's state, in which the platform provides two interfaces *onSaveInstanceState* and *onRestoreInstanceState* for saving and retrieving an application state, respectively. Application developers though need to override these interfaces to handle the application state in a state *Bundle*. The *Bundle* [29] is an Android API for passing data, typically in key-value pairs, between various Android activities. Therefore, AppaaS requires application developers to implement their own algorithms and provide two proprietary APIs to save and restore the user-specific data that impacts the behaviour of their applications. AppaaS then uses these APIs to offer a persistent state preservation.

To better understand how to save an application state, we describe how applications are developed for Android. Android applications are composed of a set of activities. Each activity performs a certain task. Activities are managed by an activity stack, where recent activities reside on top. An Android activity may switch between four essential states [30]: *running, paused, stopped,* and *killed.* An activity is in the *running* state when it is active and running in the foreground of the user's screen. When the activity is out of focus but still alive, the Android platform puts the activity in the *paused* state. In this case the activity maintains all its current state information. When the activity is invisible to the user (put into the background), it means that this activity is in the *stopped* mode. The *onSaveInstanceState* method is called before placing the activity in a background state. Application developers use this method to capture any required user-specific data and pass it to the activity during the *onCreate* event through the *onRestoreInstanceState* interface. The Android system always kills stopped activities first when system memory is required by any other activity. Figure 1 shows the lifecycle of Android application activities and emphasises when the state preservation procedures occur. The rectangle boxes represent the different methods that an Android developer needs to implement to perform operations/functions while activities switch between various states.

4   AppaaS: system architecture

Figure 2 shows an overview of the AppaaS system architecture. The architecture encompasses three main entities, mobile user, space, and AppaaS server. We assume that the user has a smartphone that is capable of running mobile applications, the space is associated with particular mobile applications to better provide a specific service,

and the AppaaS server is hosted on the cloud and is continuously available.

AppaaS maintains a database that stores information about each of the system main entities, namely, users (U), spaces (S), i.e. physical locations, and mobile applications (M). A user $u \in U$ has a set of credentials R_u and an application $m \in M$ has a set of access rights A_m. A user u is granted access to an application m if $R_u \overset{satisfy}{\rightarrow} A_m$. Variations of access rights could be granted to a user according to how the user's credentials satisfy an application's access constraints. Users are identified by their user ID (`user_id`), while applications are identified by a system-generated (`app_id`). Applications are associated with a URL that refers to the application package on their respective market store. Spaces are identified by a numeric location ID (`location_id`) representing a physical location $s \in S$.

Each space $s \in S$ is associated with one or more mobile applications $m \in M$. Once a registered user enters a designated space that is associated with mobile applications, the user's smartphone detects the location and sends the location information to AppaaS context manager for manipulation. AppaaS collects the device profile during communication sessions and retrieves respective context (such as user profile) from the database. AppaaS then checks these various pieces of context information and dispatches the appropriate application to the user's smartphone. AppaaS sends a link to the application of interest, to the user's smartphone, which is then downloaded and installed. If the user has previously used this application, it starts with the last state that the user had left the application with when it was suspended or removed last time. It is worth mentioning that it is possible, according to the provided context, AppaaS returns a response of *"no relevant application fits current context"*, despite that the space has an associated mobile application. This might be because one or more context does not satisfy the access constraints of such an application.

Upon leaving the designated space, the user's smartphone reports that the user is currently outside the space. The AppaaS server reassesses the current context and invokes the *OnExit* procedure to apply prespecified actions set by application providers. These actions include uninstalling or deactivating certain applications. In all cases, the *OnExit* procedure captures the user-specific data and saves it on the server, so that the application can resume with the last user state in the future. Figure 2b illustrates the interactions between the various system entities.

5   Implementation details

We have developed a prototype to test the fundamental functionality of AppaaS. The prototype implements the context and data management on the server side

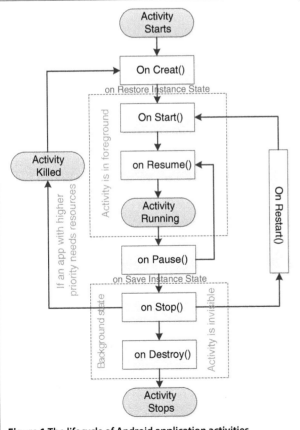

Figure 1 The lifecycle of Android application activities (re-produced from [30]).

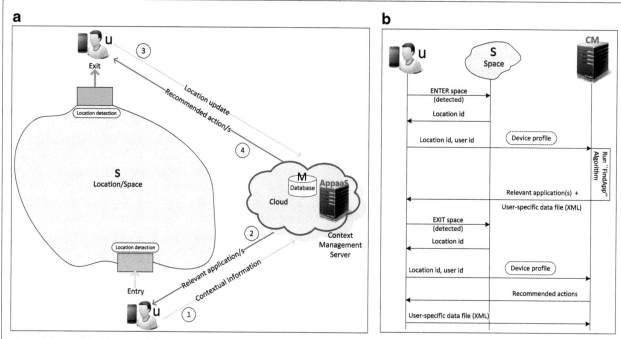

Figure 2 AppaaS Architecture: (a) spatial view of system architecture illustrating different composing entities, (b) logical interactions between various system entities.

while the mobile user interface resides on the mobile device. The user interface is implemented using the latest Android SDK [31]. The server components are responsible for managing the database, handling context information, and dispatching relevant applications along with recommended actions.

5.1 User interface

A user must register with AppaaS to use its functionality. The registration requires the user "name", "email address", and "password". The email address is used as a unique user ID. Once the user is successfully authenticated, AppaaS starts the main process which coordinates between other activities. Figure 3 shows the flow of the main system processes and how they exchange information with one another.

The current version of this prototype identifies location using two Near Field Communication (NFC) RFID tags, one at the space entrance and the other one at the space exit. The entrance tag holds "ENTER:location_id" while the exit tag holds "EXIT:location_id", where location_id represents a numeric value of the location ID. We store the location information on tags in plain text. The user taps the mobile application to scan the location ID. The *NFC scanner* reads the NFC Data Exchange Format (NDEF) message from the RFID tag and reports it to the *Context Manager*, which extracts the locations ID and the user status to query the database for relevant applications and replies with the recommended actions. If

an application is found relevant, the *Downloader* downloads and installs it onto the user's smartphone along with the proper access privileges or function constraints. We remark that the use of RFID to identify space is only an instance and other techniques, including use of beacons are also possible.

The *Context Manager* applies Algorithm 1 to find relevant application to current user's context. The *"match"* function applies Equation 1 to match the user's credentials with the application's access requirements.

$$match(R_u, A_m) = \frac{\sum_{i,j} F(r_{u_i}, a_{m_j})}{i * j} \tag{1}$$

where $r_u \in R_u$ denotes a single user credential and $a_m \in A_m$, denotes a single application's access constraints, i and j are the number of credentials and access constraints, respectively. $F(r_u, a_m)$ represents how much r_u satisfies a_m and it produces values {0,1}. A value of 0 means that if the respective a_m is a constraint at the application level, the application will not be available for the user. If a_m is a constraint at the function level, this functionality will be disabled for the user. Otherwise access is granted. Each relevant application has two scores, relevancy score ($match_m$) and rating score ($rating_m$). For simplicity, we consider the two scores are equally important.

Algorithm 1: Find relevant application(s) to a user's context

---

  Input: user_id, location_id, device_profile, time
  Output: download *url* of relevant application

1 **Function**
    FindApp(user_id,location_id,device_profile,time)

2 Initialize Apps=[] //App collector

3 **if** *location_id has application(s)(M)* **then**

4   **foreach** $m \in M$ **do**

5   Initialize $match_m=0$ //application relevancy score

6   Initialize $rating_m=0$ //application rating score

7   // retrieve application access constraints A_m

8   **if** *m has no absolute time constraints* **then**

9   **if** *m has open-access* **then**

10   // m gets max. score

11          $match_m=1$

12   **end**

13   **else**

14   // retrieve user profile and credentials R_u

15   Initialize $match_m=0$

16   **foreach** $r_u in R_u$ *and* $a_m \in A_m$ **do**

17   // check how much r_u satisfy a_m

18          $match_m = match_m + F(r_u, a_m)$

19   **end**

20   **end**

21   **end**

22    $m = 0.5 * match_m + 0.5 * rating_m$

23   // add m to relevant Apps

24   Apps=Apps + m

25 **end**

26 **end**

27 **if** *Apps is not null* **then**

28   //choose the application with the highest score

29 **end**

30 return *url* //if null means no applicaitons

5.2 State preservation

Figure 4 illustrates an abstract view of how AppaaS handles the state preservation of mobile applications. As we noted earlier, the current implementation of AppaaS assumes that applications provide two proprietary APIs for the sake of state preservation. The *saveState()* API saves the application's current state, where all user-specific data is saved in an XML file format. The *loadState()* API uploads an application state from an XML file when the application launches. Figure 5 shows the lifecycle of AppaaS state preservation. AppaaS invokes the *saveState()* whenever the application stops running (in Android operating environments, this implements the *onStop()* method). The system generates a state bundle

object to save the user-specific parameters. User-specific data is added in a key-value pairs format to a bundle object. This object then is written in an XML file. Each parameter record holds the parameter name, data type, and latest value in memory. The generated XML file is transferred to the server and the context manager updates the database tables or inserts a new record that associates the application ID, user ID, and location ID with a state file name. The state file name is composed of the application ID, user ID and location ID. Listing 1 shows an abstract structure of the state preservation file.

Listing 1 An abstract structure of the application state preservation file in XML format

```xml
<?xml version="1.0" encoding="UTF-8"?>
<application>
        <name> app_name</name>
        <ID> application_id </ID>
</applicaton>

<context>
        <user>
                <ID>user_id </ID>
        </user>
        <location>
                <ID>location_id</ID>
        </location>
</context>

<data>
        <parameter>
          <name>paramter_name</name>
          <type>data_type</type>
          <value>parameter_value</value>
        </paramter>

        <parameter>
          <name>paramter_name</name>
          <type>data_type</type>
          <value>parameter_value</value>
        </paramter>
        .
        .
        .
</data>
```

When a user launches a location-specific application, AppaaS checks if the user has a previous saved state of this particular application at this location. If a match is found in the database, the system retrieves the state file to the user side and uploads it into a state bundle. This bundle is used by onRestoreInstanceState() callback

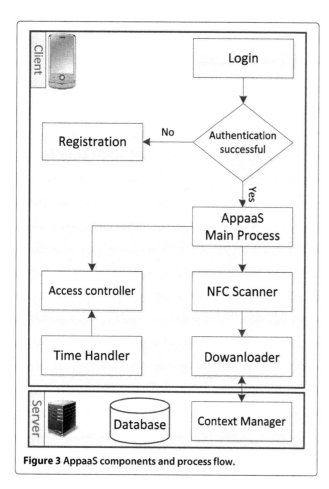

Figure 3 AppaaS components and process flow.

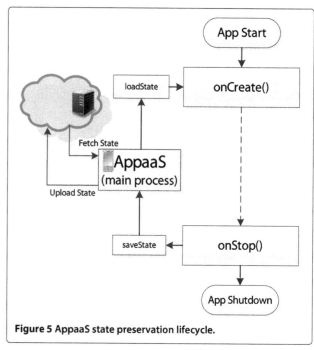

Figure 5 AppaaS state preservation lifecycle.

5.3 AppaaS server-side components

AppaaS system has two components that run on the server: *Database Server* and *Context Manager*. The latter handles context information sent by the user to see if any mobile applications fit this context. The former component (Database server) maintains information about various system entities, users, applications, and a list of registered locations. The database is implemented using MySQL Database Server [32]. It maintains various tables that hold information about each entity such as user profile and credentials, application profile and related access constraints, and location detail which holds information about physical boundaries, associated type of business, working hours, etc. In addition, there are also various database tables that hold the relations between different entities which, for example, relate a certain location to a specific application and users to both locations and applications.

methods during the `onCreate()` to resume the application from where it stopped last time. Although the state file structure is generic, the state information and parameters are application-specific. The current implementation only preserves the last application state and does not keep track of all previous states. It is worth mentioning that AppaaS provides no state preservation support for applications that do not provide appropriate handling of their internal status.

6 Experimental validation

The prototype aims to highlight three aspects of AppaaS functionalities. The first aspect is how AppaaS finds mobile applications which are relevant to a specific context information, in particular user, time, and location. The second aspect demonstrates the ability of AppaaS to customize the application behavior in order to fit certain access rights and constraints. The third aspect shows how AppaaS preserves the application state relevant to a user for future reference.

To demonstrate the first functionality, we define in our prototype some locations and associated these locations

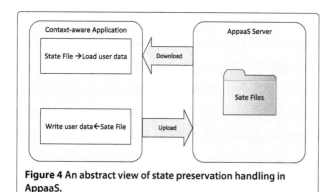

Figure 4 An abstract view of state preservation handling in AppaaS.

with mobile applications. The mobile application packages (.apk) are stored on the AppaaS server with each package associated with a *url* for download purposes. The *id* of one of these registered locations is stored on two RFID tags, one represents the location entrance while the other one holds the NDEF message that denotes the location's exit. To start with the system, a user logs into the AppaaS as shown in Figure 6a. The user then taps the RFID tag that represents the location entrance as shown in Figure 6b. The user's context along with the location information is sent to the context manager for processing. The context manager finds the relevant application that fits this context and sends the download *url* back to the user's device. The *Downloader* at the user's device downloads and installs the application as exhibited in Figure 6c.

AppaaS may also apply access limitations to certain functionalities according to the user's access privileges. To validate the second aspect, we developed *mCalc* to demonstrate how AppaaS implements control over access and preserves the user-specific application sate. The *mCalc* is a proof-of-concept mobile application that implements the basic functionality of a calculator with access restrictions. We have restricted the access to some functions to particular users. Therefore, if an unauthorized user tries to perform these restricted functions, an access denial message appears as illustrated in Figure 6d. At this stage, AppaaS supports control over access for mobile applications that implement embedded policy-control for their functions.

The third aspect that our prototype highlights is the state preservation. We use *mCalc* to test this functionality. We set the application *mCalc* to be accessible by a specific user during two specific time periods, 10:00–11:00 AM and 11:15–11:30 AM. This user logs into the system during the first time period and performs calculations. When first period ends, AppaaS initiates the *saveState* procedure and stops the application *mCalc*. The generated state file is sent to be stored at the context manager. Then, AppaaS invokes the uninstall procedure of *mCalc*. Currently, AppaaS always uninstalls the application whenever the user's authorized time elapses. The same user logs into the system again during the second period of time. When the application downloads onto the user's smartphone, the context server finds that there is a previous state preserved for the user for this application. The context manager sends this state along with the application download *url* to start the application with. In this case the user gets a message during the application launching to choose either to resume the application with the previous state or to initiate a clean start.

7 Performance evaluation

Several experiments are conducted to evaluate the performance of AppaaS including the overall response time, system overhead and footprint, and system scalability. The first experiment investigates the response time of the various system activities such as the user authentication, location identification, and the *OnExit* procedure, in which the system applies certain actions on the current application upon leaving its designated space. The second experiment studies the overhead of state preservation and access constraints. The third experiment explores the system scalability. Each experiment is repeated 10 times and the average of the respective performance parameters is calculated. We remark that confidence intervals were found to be small and hence not reported.

Figure 6 Prototype screenshots: (a) user login screen, (b) location identification using NFC technology, (c) application download to a user's smartphone, (d) mCalc shows access denial message for restricted functionalities.

The AppaaS user interface is installed on a 3G-enabled Samsung I9100 Galaxy II (Dual-core 1.2 GHz Cortex-A9, 1 GB RAM, Super AMOLED Plus 480 x 800 pixels display, 4.3 inches) with a rooted Android 4.0.4 platform. Although we conducted most of our experiments while the smartphone is connected to a WiFi network, the response time of the various activities of AppaaS user interface is evaluated against both 3G and WiFi connectivity for comparison. The server component of AppaaS implements the context manager and storage and is deployed on the Amazon EC2 cloud. We created a pool of instances of virtual machines of the type '*m1.large*' [33] with an EC2 pre-configured image (AMI) of '*Ubuntu Server 12.04 LTS, 64 bit*'. The server maintains the system database, which includes locations and their associated applications. We use two RFID tags to identify the location boundaries, one tag represents the location entrance and the other tag represents the exit.

7.1 Response time

This experiment measures the end-to-end response time, including both communications and processing time, of the various system activities involving communications between the user interface and the back-end server. A user logs into the system with a valid login ID and password. The user authentication module sends a query to the server to validate the user's credentials and checks whether the user has access to the system. When the user taps the location entrance tag, the location identification module reads the location code and sends a query to the system with the location ID and the user status, including whether the user is entering or leaving the location. The server checks if there are applications associated with this location and responds with a list of download links of relevant applications, if found. When the user exits the location, the *OnExit* module sends the location ID, user ID and an exit status to consult the context manager on the appropriate actions to apply on the user's mobile devices, whether to uninstall or deactivate the associated application. The default action of the current prototype upon exiting a location is uninstalling the location-specific application and saving the user current state on the server side. The main reason behind choosing this default action is to prevent the accumulation of outdated or unused applications. However, disabling the application or allowing the user to make the decision are possible options, if the application has an open access.

Figure 7 shows the response time of the three main components of the user interface: the *User Authentication*, *Location Identification*, and *OnExit Action*. This response time is measured for both WiFi and 3G connectivity with a bandwidth of 17.3 MB/sec and 2.5 MB/sec, respectively. Each of these activities sends a query to the server with an average size less than 0.5 KB. The average query time

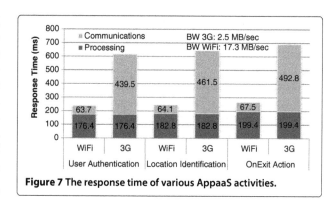

Figure 7 The response time of various AppaaS activities.

on the server side in our case is 145 ms. This time basically depends on the size of the database (10 KB in our case) and the number of concurrent requests. While the processing component of the response time is the same in both cases, the communication component varies significantly. The WiFi connectivity yields a 3-fold better response time than the 3G. This gap between the WiFi and 3G increases with higher data transfer requirements due to communication speed.

The overall download time of selected applications depends on the network conditions and the size of the application package. For example, an application package with a size of 1.9 MB takes about 2.5 Sec on WiFi and 19 Sec on 3G. This time is much higher than all other activities. Frequent application download comes at a high cost on mobile resources, specifically battery power and bandwidth. This leads to a debate on which is better, uninstalling unused applications in order to free up the occupied space and prevent unauthorized access, or deactivating their functionalities and avoid frequent downloads of same applications if used regularly. The tradeoff between overhead and convenience is an issue for future consideration.

7.2 Performance overhead analysis

This experiment investigates the overhead that AppaaS incurs on mobile applications should they implement

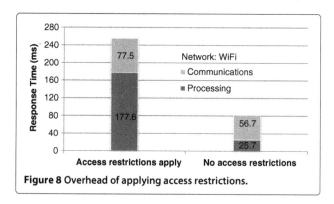

Figure 8 Overhead of applying access restrictions.

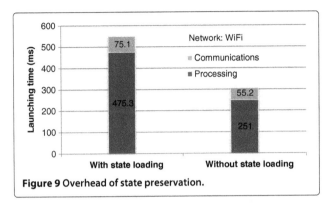

Figure 9 Overhead of state preservation.

access restrictions or launch with a previous state. We employ the *mCalc* to further investigate these aspects since it provides AppaaS with two APIs to capture and restore its internal user state. Figure 8 shows the cost of applying user access control of the mCalc operations. When a user tries to access a certain function of mCalc, AppaaS checks if the user is allowed to perform such an operation or not. AppaaS queries the context manager with the user ID and context. If the user has access to the requested operation, AppaaS sends back a confirmation to the application that the user can perform the operation. Otherwise, the application dispatches a message to the user interface showing that access to the requested functionality is denied. Applying access constraints is performed at the expense of application performance. Figure 9 illustrates another overhead caused by application state preservation. This overhead comes from loading a previous user state, in contrast with starting the same application with no previous state. The size of state file is relatively small in the range of 1 KB. Therefore, fetching this state object from the server side over a reliable network link takes a short time. Such overhead comes with the two benefits: providing users with the appropriate application of a particular location according to the user's

context, and gaining more control over the application behavior according to the user's access rights.

7.3 Scalability

We conduct two experiments to evaluate the scalability of AppaaS. The first experiment tests the scalability when a fixed hardware setting is dedicated to serve incoming requests. In this case, we use only one Amazon EC2 instance of the type *m1.large.* The second experiment shows how AppaaS takes advantage of the cloud computing elastic resource provisioning to accommodate increasing number of users while satisfying certain quality of service (QoS) constraints. In this case, the AppaaS system is served by a pool of cloud server instances. In both cases, we apply a varying stress load to evaluate the performance of AppaaS context manager. We use the WAPT load stress tool [34] to apply various loads (number of users) while measuring the system response time. Figure 10 shows the results of the first experiment. We observe that the response time rapidly increases as the number of incoming requests increase in a nonlinear relation. Although AppaaS context manager can serve a relatively high number of concurrent requests, mobile users might not afford long delays. In such cases, the system administrator may set a threshold value after which the server rejects any upcoming requests to maintain a certain level stability and responsiveness.

In the second experiment, we set a response time threshold of 2 seconds as a QoS measure. This means that when a violation occurs, our cloud setup launches another instance of the type *m1.large* from our pool of VMs. In this case no matter how large the number of requests becomes, the response time does not exceed the prespecified threshold value. Figure 11 shows how AppaaS scales up to accommodate increasing requests, while maintaining the response time below the desired threshold. We observe that the new instance takes up to 60–90 seconds to become active and ready to handle requests. This

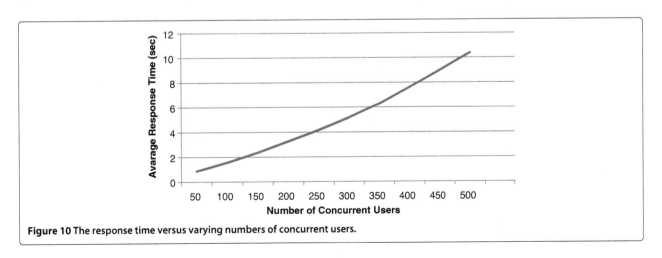

Figure 10 The response time versus varying numbers of concurrent users.

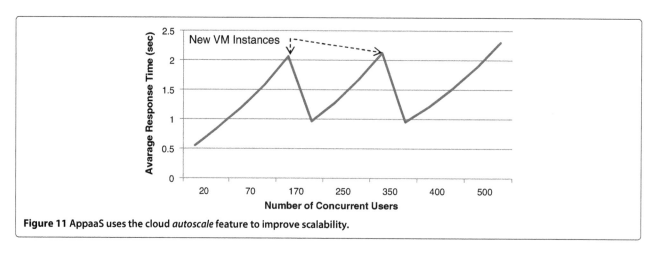

Figure 11 AppaaS uses the cloud *autoscale* feature to improve scalability.

explains why the response time reaches beyond 2 seconds. The EC2 load balancer (ELB) then splits the load between participating instances. Figure 11 also shows that there is a non-negligible overhead incurred by the scheduling of the load balancer, which explains why the response time of $2X$ requests with 2 instances is slightly more than the response time of X requests with a single instance. However, the scheduling overhead is constant and does not increase with further addition of instances.

7.4 AppaaS footprint

Since mobile devices are resource-constrained, mobile applications and services must be highly efficient in resource consumption. The mobile resources of specific concern are CPU cycles, memory, storage, and battery power. These resources indicate how efficient an application is with respect to system resource consumption. In this experiment, we measure the system footprint in terms of memory usage, storage required, and average CPU cycles that are used in cases when AppaaS runs in idle mode (i.e. no activities are performed), and when AppaaS is in active mode (i.e. at least one activity is running). We are concerned with the system footprint at the user side. Table 1 shows the AppaaS system footprint in terms of CPU usage, memory and user application size in both idle and active modes. The energy consumption of the mobile user interface varies according to the running activity and the required data transfer between the interface and the backend server. The lower the data transfer requirements,

the higher the energy efficiency of the system while in active mode. However, AppaaS has a low energy consumption profile in the idle mode, as it consumes on average 350 mj/minute.

8 Conclusion

This paper presents *AppaaS*, a system for provisioning context-aware mobile applications *as a service*. AppaaS uses various context information including location, user information, user ratings, device profile, and time to provide the appropriate mobile applications to such a context. AppaaS also supports access control over application functionality according to users' privileges and access rights. Currently, AppaaS supports this capability only for applications that implement embedded policy control. However, part of our future extension of this research is to provide an application-wrapping capability to enable this feature for applications that lack support for embedded policy control. A prototype is developed to highlight three features of AppaaS, specifically finding the appropriate application to a certain context, controlling access over an application's functions, and preserving the application's state that is relevant to a particular user for future use purposes. Performance evaluation shows that AppaaS can scale up to accommodate increasing number of users while maintaining desired QoS levels. Experimental validation demonstrates that with little overhead, AppaaS can bring benefits to both users and providers of mobile applications with robust and flexible provisioning models.

Competing interests
The authors declare that they have no competing interests.

Authors' contributions
KE proposed the main idea, provided implementation guidance, put the layout of experimental validation and performance evaluation, and drafted the manuscript. AE implemented the prototype and carried out the performance evaluation. HH suggested some modifications on the architecture and recommended the implementation of state preservation. All authors read and approved the final manuscript.

Table 1 AppaaS system footprint in terms of CPU usage, memory, and the size of the user application in both idle mode and active mode

AppaaS (user side)	Avg. CPU usage (%)	Memory usage (MB)	Storage space (KB)
Idle mode	0.00	35.20	96.00
Active mode	6.65	45.96	96.00

Acknowledgments
This research is funded by a grant from the Ontario Ministry of Economic Development and Innovation under the Ontario Research Fund-Research Excellence (ORF-RE) program.

References
1. Google Play Store. https://play.google.com/store?hl=en. Accessed: February, 2013
2. Apple Store. http://store.apple.com/ca. Accessed: February, 2013
3. Toutain F, Bouabdallah A, Zemek R, Daloz C (2011) Interpersonal context-aware communication services. Commun Mag IEEE 49(1): 68–74
4. Elgazzar K, Ejaz A, Hassanein HS (2013) Appaas: Provisioning of context-aware mobile applications as a service In: The IEEE International Conference on Communications (ICC)
5. Elgazzar K, Hassanein H, Martin P (2011) Effective web service discovery in mobile environments In: P2MNETS, The 36th IEEE conference on Local Computer Networks (LCN), pp 697–705
6. Ahn C, Nah Y (2010) Design of location-based web service framework for context-aware applications in ubiquitous environments In: IEEE international conference on sensor networks, ubiquitous, and trustworthy computing (SUTC), pp 426–433
7. Chatterjee L, Mukherjee S, Chattopadhyay M (2011) A personalized mobile application using location based service In: Advances in computer science and education applications, pp 413–419
8. Junglas IA, Watson RT (2008) Location-based services. Commun ACM 51(3): 65–69
9. Mokbel MF, Levandoski JJ (2009) Toward context and preference-aware location-based services In: Proceedings of the 8th ACM international workshop on data engineering for wireless and mobile access, pp 25–32
10. Husain W, Dih LY (2012) A framework of a personalized location-based traveler recommendation system in mobile application. Int J Multimedia Ubiquitous Eng 7(3): 11–18
11. Shi X, Sun T, Shen Y, Li K, Qu W (2010) Tour-guide: providing location-based tourist information on mobile phones In: The IEEE 10th international conference on computer and information technology, pp 2397–2401
12. Stuedi P, Mohomed I, Terry D (2010) Wherestore: location-based data storage for mobile devices interacting with the cloud In: The 1st ACM workshop on mobile cloud computing and services: social networks and beyond, MCS'10, Co-located with ACM MobiSys, pp 1–8
13. Chow CY, Mokbel MF, Liu X (2011) Spatial cloaking for anonymous location-based services in mobile peer-to-peer environments. Geoinformatica 15(2): 351–380
14. Amoli A, Kharrazi M, Jalili R (2010) 2ploc: preserving privacy in location-based services In: The IEEE 2nd international conference on Social Computing (SocialCom), pp 707–712
15. Puttaswamy KPN, Zhao BY (2010) Preserving privacy in location-based mobile social applications In: HotMobile: The 11th workshop on mobile computing systems and applications, pp 1–6
16. Quah JTS, Lim LR (2011) Location based application distribution for android mobile devices In: Proceedings of the IASTED international conference on wireless communications, pp 118–123
17. Costa-Montenegro E, Barragáns-Martínez AB, Rey-López M, Mikic-Fonte F, Peleteiro-Ramallo A (2011) Which app? A recommender system of applications in markets by monitoring users' interaction In: Proceedings of the IEEE International Conference on Consumer Electronics (ICCE), pp 353–354
18. Toye E, Sharp R, Madhavapeddy A, Scott D (2005) Using smart phones to access site-specific services. IEEE Pervasive Comput 4(2): 60–66
19. Dey AK (2001) Understanding and using context. Pers Ubiquitous Comput 5: 4–7
20. Ahn J, Heo J, Lim S, Kim W (2008) A study on the application of patient location data for ubiquitous healthcare system based on lbs In: 10th international conference on advanced communication technology, vol. 3, pp 2140–2143
21. Xin C (2009) Location based service application in mobile phone serious game In: International joint conference on artificial intelligence, pp 50–52
22. Altintas B, Serif T (2012) Indoor location detection with a rss-based short term memory technique (knn-stm) In: IEEE International Conference on Pervasive Computing and Communications Workshops (PERCOM Workshops), pp 794–798
23. Diaz J, de A Maues R, Soares R, Nakamura E, Figueiredo C (2010) Bluepass: an indoor bluetooth-based localization system for mobile applications In: IEEE Symposium on Computers and Communications (ISCC), pp 778–83
24. Al-Masri E, Mahmoud QH (2010) Mobieureka: an approach for enhancing the discovery of mobile web services. Pers Ubiquitous Comput 14: 609–620
25. Biswas S, Neogy S, 2010 A mobility-based checkpointing protocol for mobile computing system. Int J Comput Sci Inf Technol 2(1): 135–151
26. Tuli R, Kumar P (2011) Analysis of recent checkpointing techniques for mobile computing systems. Int J Comput Sci Eng Surv 2(3): 133–141
27. Sevinç PE, Strasser M, Basin D (2007) Securing the distribution and storage of secrets with trusted platform modules In: Proceedings of the 1st IFIP TC6 /WG8.8 /WG11.2 international conference on Information security theory and practices: smart cards, mobile and ubiquitous computing systems. Springer-Verlag, Berlin, Heidelberg, pp 53–66
28. Hung SH, Shih CS, Shieh JP, Lee CP, Huang YH (2012) Executing mobile applications on the cloud: framework and issues. Comput Math Appl 63(2): 573–587
29. Android APIs (Bundle). http://developer.android.com/reference/android/os/Bundle.html. Accessed: August, 2013
30. Android Activity Lifecycle. http://developer.android.com/reference/android/app/Activity.html. Accessed: February, 2013
31. Android SDK. http://developer.android.com/sdk/index.html. Accessed: February, 2013
32. MySQL Database Server. http://www.mysql.com/. Accessed: February, 2013
33. Amazon EC2 Instance Types. http://aws.amazon.com/ec2/instance-types/. Accessed: August, 2013
34. Web Application Testing (WAPT). http://www.loadtestingtool.com. Accessed: February, 2013

9

Quality-of-service in cloud computing: modeling techniques and their applications

Danilo Ardagna[1], Giuliano Casale[2*], Michele Ciavotta[1], Juan F Pérez[2] and Weikun Wang[2]

Abstract

Recent years have seen the massive migration of enterprise applications to the cloud. One of the challenges posed by cloud applications is Quality-of-Service (QoS) management, which is the problem of allocating resources to the application to guarantee a service level along dimensions such as performance, availability and reliability. This paper aims at supporting research in this area by providing a survey of the state of the art of QoS modeling approaches suitable for cloud systems. We also review and classify their early application to some decision-making problems arising in cloud QoS management.

Keywords: Quality of service; Cloud computing; Modeling; QoS management

1 Introduction

Cloud computing has grown in popularity in recent years thanks to technical and economical benefits of the on-demand capacity management model [1]. Many cloud operators are now active on the market, providing a rich offering, including Infrastructure-as-a-Service (IaaS), Platform-as-a-Service (PaaS), and Software-as-a-Service (SaaS) solutions [2]. The cloud technology stack has also become mainstream in enterprise data centers, where private and hybrid cloud architectures are increasingly adopted.

Even though the cloud has greatly simplified the capacity provisioning process, it poses several novel challenges in the area of Quality-of-Service (QoS) management. QoS denotes the levels of performance, reliability, and availability offered by an application and by the platform or infrastructure that hosts it[a]. QoS is fundamental for cloud users, who expect providers to deliver the advertised quality characteristics, and for cloud providers, who need to find the right tradeoffs between QoS levels and operational costs. However, finding optimal tradeoff is a difficult decision problem, often exacerbated by the presence of service level agreements (SLAs) specifying QoS targets and economical penalties associated to SLA violations [3].

While QoS properties have received constant attention well before the advent of cloud computing, performance heterogeneity and resource isolation mechanisms of cloud platforms have significantly complicated QoS analysis, prediction, and assurance. This is prompting several researchers to investigate automated QoS management methods that can leverage the high programmability of hardware and software resources in the cloud [4]. This paper aims at supporting these efforts by providing a survey of the state of the art of QoS modeling approaches applicable to cloud computing and by describing their initial application to cloud resource management.

Scope. Cloud computing is an operation model that integrates many technological advancements of the last decade such as virtualization, web services, and SLA management for enterprise applications. Characterizing cloud systems thus requires using diverse modeling techniques to cope with such technological heterogeneity. Yet, the QoS modeling literature is extensive, making it difficult to have a comprehensive view of the available techniques and their current applications to cloud computing problems.

Methodology. The aim of this survey is to provide an overview of early research works in the cloud QoS modeling space, categorizing contributions according to relevant areas and methods used. Our methodology attempts to maximize coverage of works, as opposed to

*Correspondence: g.casale@imperial.ac.uk
[2]Department of Computing, Imperial College London, 180 Queens Gate, London SW7 2AZ, UK
Full list of author information is available at the end of the article

reviewing specific technical challenges or introducing readers to modeling techniques. In particular, we focus on recent modeling works published from 2006 onwards focusing on QoS in cloud systems. We also discuss some techniques originally developed for modeling and dynamic management in enterprise data centers that have been successively applied in the cloud context. Furthermore, the survey considers QoS modeling techniques for interactive cloud services, such as multi-tier applications. Works focusing on batch applications, such as those based on the MapReduce paradigm, are therefore not surveyed.

Survey Organization. This survey covers research efforts in *workload modeling, system modeling,* and their *applications* to QoS management in the cloud.

- *Workload modeling* involves the assessment or prediction of the arrival rates of requests and of the demand for resources (e.g., CPU requirements) placed by applications on an infrastructure or platform, and the QoS observed in response to such workloads. We review in Section 2 cloud measurement studies that help characterize those properties for specific cloud systems, followed by a review of workload characterizations and inference techniques that can be applied to QoS analysis.

- *System modeling* aims at evaluating the performance of a cloud system, either at design time or at runtime. Models are used to predict the value of specific QoS metrics such as response time, reliability or availability. We survey in Section 3 formalisms and tools employed for these analyses and their current applications to assess the performance of cloud systems.

- *Applications* of QoS models often appear in relation to decision-making problems in system management. Techniques to determine optimized decisions range from simple heuristics to nonlinear programming and meta-heuristics. We survey in Section 4 works on decision making for capacity allocation, load balancing, and admission control including research works that provide solutions for the management of a cloud infrastructure (i.e., from the cloud provider perspective) and resource management techniques for the infrastructure user (e.g., an application provider aiming at minimizing operational expenditure, while providing QoS level guarantees to the end users).

Section 5 concludes the paper and summarizes the key findings.

2 Cloud workload modeling

The definition of accurate workload models is essential to ensure good predictive capability for QoS models. Here, we survey workload characterization studies and related modeling techniques.

2.1 Workload characterization

Deployment environment. Several studies have attempted to characterize the QoS showed by cloud deployment environments through benchmarking. Statistical characterizations of empirical data are useful in QoS modeling to quantify risks without the need to conduct an ad-hoc measurement study. They are vital to estimate realistic values for QoS model parameters, e.g., network bandwidth variance, virtual machine (VM) startup times, start failure probabilities. Observations of performance variability have been reported for different types of VM instances [5-7]. Hardware heterogeneity and VM interference are the primary cause for such variability, which is also visible within VMs of the same instance class. Other works characterize the variability in VM startup times [7,8], which is correlated in particular with operating system image size [8]. Some studies on Amazon EC2 have found high-performance contention in CPU-bound jobs [9] and network performance overheads [10]. A few characterization studies specific to public and private PaaS hosting solutions also appeared in the literature [11,12], together with comparisons of cloud database and storage services [13-16]. Also, a comparison of different providers on a broad set of metrics is presented in [17].

Cloud application workloads. While the above works focus on describing the properties of the cloud deployment environment, users are often faced with the additional problem of describing the characteristics of the workloads processed by a cloud application.

Blackbox forecasting and trend analysis techniques are commonly used to predict web traffic intensity at different timescales. Time series forecasting has been extensively used for web servers for almost two decades. Autoregressive models in particular are quite common in applications and they are already exploited in cloud application modeling, e.g., for auto-scaling [18]. Other common techniques include wavelet-based methods, regression analysis, filtering, Fourier analysis, and kernel-based methods [19].

Recent works in workload modeling that are relevant to cloud computing include [20-22]. Khan et al. [20] uses Hidden Markov Models to capture and predict temporal correlations between workloads of different compute clusters in the cloud. In this paper, the authors propose a method to characterize and predict workloads in cloud environments in order to efficiently provision cloud resources. The authors develop a co-clustering algorithm to find servers that have a similar workload pattern. The pattern is found by studying the performance correlations for applications on different servers. They use hidden Markov models to identify temporal correlations between different clusters and use this information to predict future workload variations. Di et al. [21] defines a Bayesian algorithm for long-term workload prediction and pattern analysis, validating results on data from a Google data center. The authors define nine key features of the workload and use a Bayesian classifier to estimate the posterior probability of each feature. The experiments are based on a large dataset collected from a Google data center with thousands of machines. Gmach et al. [22] applies pattern recognition techniques to data center and cloud workload data. The authors propose a workload demand prediction algorithm based on trend analysis and pattern recognition. This approach aims at finding a way to efficiently use the resource pool to allocate servers to different workloads. The pattern and trend are first analyzed and then synthetic workloads are created to reflect future behaviors of the workload. Zhu and Tung [23] uses a Kalman filter to model the interference caused when deploying applications on virtualized resources. The model accounts for time variations in VM resource usage, and it is used as the basis of a VM consolidation algorithm. The consolidation algorithm is tested and shown to be highly competitive. As the problem of workload modeling is far from trivial, [24] proposes a best practice guide to build empirical models. Important issues are treated, such as the selection of the most relevant data, the modeling technique, and variable-selection procedure. The authors also provide a comparative study that highlights the benefits of different forecasting approaches.

2.2 Workload inference

The ability to quantify resource demands is a pre-requisite to parameterize most QoS models for enterprise applications. Inference is often justified by the overheads of deep monitoring and by the difficulty of tracking execution paths of individual requests [25]. Several works have investigated over the last two decades the problem of estimating, using indirect measurements, the resource demand placed by an application on physical resources, for example CPU requirements. From the perspective of cloud providers and users, inference techniques provide a means to estimate the workload profile of individual VMs running on their infrastructures, taking into account hidden variables due to lack of information.

Regression Techniques. A common workload inference approach involves estimating only the *mean* demand placed by a given type of requests on the resource [26-28]. In [26] a standard model calibration technique is introduced. The technique is based on comparing the performance metrics (e.g., response time, throughput and resource utilization) predicted by a performance model against measurements collected in a controlled experimental environment. Given the lack of control over

the system workload and configuration during operation, techniques of this type may not be applicable to production systems for online model calibration. These methods exploit queueing theory formulas to relate the mean values of a set of performance metrics (e.g., response times, throughputs, or resource utilizations) to a mean demand to be estimated, e.g., CPU demand. Regression techniques can exploit these formulas to obtain demand estimates from system measurements [29-33].

Zhang et al. [32] presents a queueing network model where each queue represents a tier of a web application, which is parameterized by means of a regression-based approximation of the CPU demand of customer transactions. It is shown that such an approximation is effective for modeling different types of workloads whose transaction mix changes over time.

Liu et al. [33] proposes instead service demand estimation from utilization and end-to-end response times: the problem is formulated as quadratic optimization programs based on queueing formulas; results are in good agreement with experimental data. Variants of these regression methods have been developed to cope with problems such as outliers [34], data multi-collinearity [35], online estimation [36], data aging [37], handling of multiple system configurations [38], and automatic definition of request types [39,40].

Kalbasi et al. [35] proposes the Demand Estimation with Confidence (DEC) approach to overcome the problem of multicollinearity in regression methods. DEC can be iteratively applied to improve the estimation accuracy.

Cremonesi et al. [38] proposes an algorithm to estimate the service demands for different system configurations. A time based linear clustering algorithm is used to identify different linear clusters for each service demands. This approach proves to be robust to noisy data. Extensive validation on generated dataset and real data show the effectiveness of the algorithm.

Cremonesi et al. [39] proposes a method based on clustering to estimate the service time. The authors employ density based clustering to obtain clusters of service times and CPU utilizations, and then use a cluster-wise regression algorithm to estimate the service time. A refinement process is conducted between clustering and regression to get accurate clustering results by removing outliers and merging the clusters that fit the same model. This approach proves to be computationally efficient and robust to outliers.

In [36] an on-line resource demand estimation approach is presented. An evaluation of regression techniques Least Squares (LSQ), Least Absolute Deviations (LAD) and Support Vector Regression (SVR) is presented. Experiments with different workloads show the importance of tuning the parameters, thus the authors proposes an online method to tune the regression parameters.

Casale et al. [34] presents an optimization-based inference technique that is formulated as a robust linear regression problem that can be used with both closed and open queueing network performance models. It uses aggregate measurements (i.e., system throughput and utilization of the servers), commonly retrieved from log files, in order to estimate service times.

Pacifici et al. [37] considers the problem of dynamically estimating CPU demands of diverse types of requests using CPU utilization and throughput measurements. The problem is formulated as a multivariate linear regression problem and accounts for multiple effects such as data aging. Also, several works have shown how combining the queueing theoretic formulas used by regression methods with the Kalman filter can enable continuous demand tracking [41,42].

Regression techniques have also been used to correlate the CPU demand placed by a request on multiple servers. For example, linear regression of average utilization measurements against throughput can correctly account for the visit count of requests to each resource [32].

Stepwise linear regression [43] can also be used to identify request flows between application tiers. The knowledge of request flow intensities provides throughputs that can be used in regression techniques.

3 System models

Workload modeling techniques presented in Section 2 are agnostic of the logic that governs a cloud system. Explicit modeling of this logic, or part of it, for QoS prediction can help improving the effectiveness of QoS management.

Several classes of models can be used to model QoS in cloud systems. Here we briefly review queueing models, Petri nets, and other specialized formalisms for reliability evaluation. However, several other classes exist such as stochastic process algebras, stochastic activity networks, stochastic reward nets [44], and models evaluated via probabilistic model checking [45]. A comparison of the pros and cons of some popular stochastic formalisms can be found in [46], where the authors highlight the issue that a given method can perform better on some system model but not on others, making it difficult to make absolute recommendations on the best model to use.

3.1 Performance models

Among the performance models, we survey queueing systems, queueing networks, and layered queueing networks (LQN). While queueing systems are widely used to model single resources subject to contention, queueing networks are able to capture the interaction among a number of resources and/or applications components. LQNs are used to better model key interaction between application mechanisms, such as finite connection pools, admission control mechanisms, or synchronous request calls. Modeling these feature usually require an in-depth knowledge of the application behavior. On the other hand, while closed-form solutions exist for some classes of queueing systems and queueing networks, the solution of other models, including LQNs, rely on numerical methods.

Queueing Systems. Queueing theory is commonly used in system modeling to describe hardware or software resource contention. Several analytical formulas exist, for example to characterize request mean waiting times, or waiting buffer occupancy probabilities in single queueing systems. In cloud computing, analytical queueing formulas are often integrated in optimization programs, where they are repeatedly evaluated across what-if scenarios. Common analytical formulas involve queues with exponential service and arrival times, with a single server ($M/M/1$) or with k servers ($M/M/k$), and queues with generally-distributed service times ($M/G/1$). Scheduling is often assumed to be first-come first-served (FCFS) or processor sharing (PS). In particular, the $M/G/1$ PS queue is a common abstraction used to model a CPU and it has been adopted in many cloud studies [47,48], thanks to its simplicity and the suitability to apply the model to multi-class workloads. For instance, an SLA-aware capacity allocation mechanism for cloud applications is derived in [47] using an $M/G/1$ PS queue as the QoS model. In [48] the authors propose a resource provisioning approach of N-tier cloud web applications by modeling CPU as an $M/G/1$ PS queue. The $M/M/1$ open queue with FCFS scheduling has been used [49-51] to pose constraints on the mean response time of a cloud application. Heterogeneity in customer SLAs is handled in [52] with an $M/M/k/k$ *priority* queue, which is a queue with exponentially distributed inter-arrival times and service times, k servers and no buffer. The authors use this model to investigate rejection probabilities and help dimensioning of cloud data centers. Other works that rely on queueing models to describe cloud resources include [53,54]. The works in [53,54] illustrate the formulation of basic queueing systems in the context of discrete-time control problems for cloud applications, where system properties such as arrival rates can change in time at discrete instants. These works show an example where a non-stationary cloud system is modeled through queueing theory.

Queueing Networks. A queueing network can be described as a collection of queues interacting through request arrivals and departures. Each queue represents either a physical resource (e.g., CPU, network bandwidth, etc) or a software buffer (e.g., admission control, or connection pools). Cloud applications are often tiered and queueing networks can capture the interactions between tiers.

An example of cloud management solutions exploiting queueing network models is [55], where the cloud service center is modeled as an open queueing network of multiclass single-server queues. PS scheduling is assumed at the resources to model CPU sharing. Each layer of queues represents the collection of applications supporting the execution of requests at each tier of the cloud service center. This model is used to provide performance guarantees when defining resource allocation policies in a cloud platform. Also, [56] uses a queueing network to represent a multi-tier application deployed in a cloud platform, and to derive an SLA-aware resource allocation policy. Each node in the network has exponential processing times and a generalized PS policy to approximate the operating system scheduling.

Layered Queueing Networks. Layered queueing networks (LQNs) are an extension of queueing networks to describe layered software architectures. An LQN model of an application can be built automatically from software engineering models expressed using formalisms such as UML or Palladio Component Models (PCM) [57]. Compared to ordinary queueing networks, LQNs provide the ability to describe dependencies arising in a complex workflow of requests and the layering among hardware and software resources that process them. Several evaluation techniques exist for LQNs [58-61].

LQNs have been applied to cloud systems in [62], where the authors explored the impact of the network latency on the system response time for different system deployments. LQNs are here useful to handle the complexity of geo-distributed applications that include both transactional and streaming workloads.

Jung et al. [63] uses an LQN model to predict the performance of the RuBis benchmark application, which is then used as the basis of an optimization algorithm that aims at determining the best replication levels and placement of the application components. While this work is not specific to the cloud, it illustrates the application of LQNs to multi-tier applications that are commonly deployed in such environments.

Bacigalupo et al. [64] investigates a prediction-based cloud resource allocation and management algorithm. LQNs are used to predict the performance of an enterprise application deployed on the cloud with strict SLA requirements based on historical data. The authors also provide a discussion about the pros and cons of LQNs identifying a number of key limitations for their practical use in cloud systems. These include, among others, difficulties in modeling caching, lack of methods to compute percentiles of response times, tradeoff between accuracy and speed. Since then, evaluation techniques for LQNs that allow the computation of response time percentiles have been presented [61].

Hybrid models. Queueing models are also used together with machine learning techniques to achieve the benefits of both approaches. Queueing models use the knowledge of the system topology and infrastructure to provide accurate performance predictions. However, a violation of the model assumptions, such as an unforeseen change in the topology, can invalidate the model predictions. Machine learning algorithms, instead, are more robust with respect to dynamic changes of the system. The drawback is that they adopt a black-box approach, ignoring relevant knowledge of the system that could provide valuable insights into its performance.

Desnoyers et al. [43] studies the relations between workload and resource consumption for cloud web applications. Queueing theory is used to model different components of the system and data mining and machine learning approaches ensure dynamic adaptation of the model to work under system fluctuations. The proposed approach is shown to achieve high accuracy for predicting workload and resource usages.

Thereska et al. [65] proposes a robust performance model architecture focusing on analyzing performance anomalies and localizing the potential source of the discrepancies. The performance models are based on queueing-network models abstracted from the system and enhanced by machine learning algorithms to correlate system workload attributes with performance attributes.

A queueing network approach is taken in [66] to provision resources for data-center applications. As the workload mix is observed to fluctuate over time, the queueing model is enhanced with a clustering algorithm that determines the workload mix. The approach is shown to reduce SLA violations due to under-provisioning in applications subject to to non-stationary workloads.

3.2 Dependability models

Petri nets, Reliability Block Diagrams (RBD), and Fault Trees are probably the most widely known and used formalisms for dependability analysis. Petri nets are a flexible and expressive modeling approach, which allows a general interactions between system components, including synchronization of event firing times. They also find large application also in performance analysis.

RBDs and Fault Trees aim at obtaining the overall system reliability from the reliability of the system components. The interactions between the components focus on how the faulty state of one or more components results in the possible failure of another components.

Petri nets. It has long been recognized the suitability of Petri nets for performance and dependability of computer systems. Petri nets have been extended to consider stochastic transitions, in stochastic Petri nets (SPNs) and generalized SPNs (GSPNs). They have recently enjoyed a resurgence of interest in service-oriented systems to describe service orchestrations [67].

In the context of cloud computing, we have more application examples of Petri nets nets for dependability assessment, than for performance modeling. Applications to cloud QoS modeling include the use of SPNs to evaluate the dependability of a cloud infrastructure [68], considering both reliability and availability. SPNs provide a convenient way in this setting to represent energy flow and cooling in the infrastructure. Wei et al. [69] proposes the use of GSPNs to evaluate the impact of virtualization mechanisms, such as VM consolidation and live migration, on cloud infrastructure dependability. GSPNs are used to provide fine-grained detail on the inner VM behaviors, such as separation of privileged and non-privileged instructions and successive handling by the VM or the VM monitor. Petri nets are here used in combination with other methods, i.e., Reliability Block Diagrams and Fault Trees, for analyzing mean time to failure (MTTF) and mean time between failures (MTBF).

Reliability Block Diagrams. Reliability block diagrams (RBDs) are a popular tool for reliability analysis of complex systems. The system is represented by a set of inter-related blocks, connected by series, parallel, and *k*-out-of-*N* relationships.

In [70], the authors propose a methodology to evaluate data center power infrastructures considering both reliability and cost. RBDs are used to estimate and enforce system reliability. Dantas et al. [71] investigates the benefits of a warm-standby replication mechanism in Eucalyptus cloud computing environments. An RBD is used to evaluate the impact of a redundant cloud architecture on its dependability. A case study shows how the redundant system obtains dependability improvements. Melo et al. [72] uses RBDs to design a rejuvenation mechanism based on live migration, to prevent performance degradation, for a cloud application that has high availability requirements.

Fault Trees. Fault Trees are another formalism for reliability analysis. The system is represented as a tree of inter-related components. If a component fails, it assumes the logical value *true*, and the failure propagation can be studied via the tree structure. In cloud computing, Fault Trees have been used to evaluate dependencies of cloud services and their effect on application reliability [73]. Fault Trees and Markov models are used to evaluate the reliability and availability of fault tolerance mechanisms. Jhawar and Piuri [74] uses Fault Trees and Markov models to evaluate the reliability and availability of a cloud system under different deployment contexts. Based on this evaluation, the authors propose an approach to identify the best mechanisms according to user's requirements. Kiran

et al. [75] presents a methodology to identify, mitigate, and monitor risks in cloud resource provisioning. Fault Trees are used to assess the probability of SLA violations.

3.3 Black-box service models

Service models have been used primarily in optimising web service composition [76], but they are now becoming relevant also in the description of SaaS applications, IaaS resource orchestration, and cloud-based business-process execution. The idea behind the methods reviewed in this section is to describe a service in terms of its response time, assuming the lack of any further information concerning its internal characteristics (e.g., contention level from concurrent requests).

Non-parametric blackbox service models include methods based on deterministic or average execution time values [77-81]. Several works instead adopt a description that includes standard deviations [76,82,83] or finite ranges of variability for the execution times [84,85]. Parametric service models instead assume exponential or Markovian distributions [86,87], Pareto distributions to capture heavy-tailed execution times [88], or general distributions with Laplace transforms [89].

Huang et al. [90] presents a graph-theoretic model for QoS-aware service composition in cloud platforms, explicitly handling network virtualization. Here, the authors explore the QoS-aware service provisioning in cloud platforms by explicitly considering virtual network services. A system model is demonstrated to suitably characterize cloud service provisioning behavior and an exact algorithm is proposed to optimize users' experience under QoS requirements. A comparison with state of the art QoS routing algorithms shows that the proposed algorithm is both cost-effective and lightweight.

Klein et al. [91] considers QoS-aware service composition by handling network latencies. The authors present a network model that allows estimating latencies between locations and propose a genetic algorithm to achieve network-aware and QoS-aware service provisioning.

The work in [92] considers cloud service provisioning from the point of view of an end user. An economic model based on discrete Bayesian Networks is presented to characterize end-users long-term behavior. Then the QoS-aware service composition is solved by Influence Diagrams followed by analytical and simulation experiments.

3.4 Simulation models

Several simulation packages exist for cloud system simulation. Many solutions are based on the CLOUDSIM [93] toolkit that allows the user to set up a simulation model that explicitly considers virtualized cloud resources, potentially located in different data centers, as in the case of hybrid deployments. CLOUDANALYST

[94] is an extension of CLOUDSIM that allows the modeling of geographically-distributed workloads served by applications deployed on a number of virtualized data centers.

EMUSIM [95] builds on top of CLOUDSIM by adding an emulation step leveraging the Automated Emulation Framework (AEF) [96]. Emulation is used to understand the application behavior, extracting profiling information. This information is then used as input for CLOUDSIM, which provides QoS estimates for a given cloud deployment.

Some other tools have been developed to estimate data center energy consumption. For example, GREEN-CLOUD [97], which is an extension of the packet-level simulator NS2 [98], aims at evaluating the energy consumption of the data center resources where the application has been deployed, considering servers, links, and switches.

Similarly, DCSIM [99] is a data center simulation tool focused on dynamic resource management of IaaS infrastructures. Each host can run several VMs, and has a power model to determine the overall data center power consumption.

GROUDSIM [100] is a simulator for scientific applications deployed on large-scale clouds and grids. The simulator is based on events rather than on processes, making it a scalable solution for highly parallelized applications.

Research Challenges A threat to workload inference on IaaS clouds is posed by resource contention by other users, which can systematically result in biased readings of performance metrics. While some bias components can be filtered out (for example using the CPU steal metric available on Amazon EC2 virtual machines), contention on resources such as cache, memory bandwidth, network, or storage, is harder or even impossible to monitor for the final user. Research is needed in this domain to understand the impact of such contention bias on demand estimation.

Major complications arise in workload inference on PaaS clouds, where infrastructure-level metrics such as CPU utilization are normally unavailable to the users. This is a major complication for regression methods which all depend on mean CPU utilization measurements. Methods based on statistical distributions do not require CPU utilization, but they are still in their infancy. More work and validations on PaaS data are required to mature such techniques.

4 Applications

A prominent application of QoS models is optimal decision-making for cloud system management. Problem areas covered in this section include capacity allocation, load balancing, and admission control. Several other relevant decision problems exist in cloud computing, e.g., pricing [101], resource bidding [102], and provider-side energy management [103].

We classify works in three areas using, for comparability, a taxonomy similar to the one appearing in the software engineering survey of Aleti et al. [104], which also covers design-time optimization studies, but does not focus on cloud computing. Our classification dimensions follow from these questions:

Perspective: is the study focusing on the perspective of the infrastructure user or or on the perspective of the provider?

Dimensionality: is the study optimizing a single or multiple objective functions?

Solution: is the presented solution centralized or distributed?

Strategy: is the optimization problem tackled by an exact or approximate technique?

Time-scale: is the time-scale for the performed adaptations, which can be short (seconds), medium (minutes), or long (hours/days)?

Discipline: is the management approach based on control theory, machine learning or operations research (i.e., optimization, game theory, bio-inspired algorithms)?

Table 1 provides a taxonomy of the papers reviewed in the next sections, organized according to the above criteria. Few remarks are needed to clarify the methodology used to classify the papers:

- In the *Perspective* dimension, a public PaaS or SaaS service built on top of a public IaaS offering is classified as a user-side perspective.
- Under *Dimensionality*, we treat studies that weight multiple criteria into a single objective as Multi-Objective methods.

Finally, the following observations on the *Discipline* dimensions must also be made.

- *Control theory* has the advantage of guaranteeing the stability of the system upon workload changes by modeling the transient behavior and adjusting system configurations within a transitory period [143].
- *Machine learning* techniques, instead, use learning mechanisms to capture the behavior of the system without any explicit performance or traffic model and with little built-in system knowledge. Nevertheless, training sessions tend to extend over several hours [144] and retraining is required for evolving workloads.
- *Operations research* approaches are designed with the aim of optimizing the degree of user satisfaction. The goals, in fact, are expressed in terms of user-level QoS

Table 1 Decision-making in the cloud - a taxonomy

Category	Value	Application		
		Capacity allocation	Admission control	Load balancing
Perspective	Infrastructure user	[47] [105][106] [107] [108] [109] [110] [111] [112] [113] [114] [115] [116] [117]	[118] [116] [119]	[120] [47] [105] [107] [121] [122] [123]
	Infrastructure provider	[55] [124] [49] [125] [126] [52] [56] [127] [128] [129] [130] [131] [54] [132] [18] [133] [134] [135] [136] [137] [138] [51] [23]	[49] [131] [130] [139] [140] [124] [52]	[50] [141] [132] [134]
Dimensionality	Single-Objective	[55] [47] [106] [132] [49] [105] [108] [126] [56] [127] [128] [109] [130] [110] [111] [112] [113] [114] [115] [134] [116] [135] [136] [138] [51] [23] [129]	[49] [116] [130] [119] [118] [139] [140]	[120] [122] [105] [132] [134] [47] [123] [141] [50]
	Multi-Objective	[125] [52] [137] [133] [124] [107] [131] [18] [117]	[52] [124] [131]	[121] [107]
Solution	Centralized	[124] [49] [108] [125] [126] [56] [132] [127] [128] [130] [131] [110] [111] [112] [18] [133] [113] [114] [115] [134] [116] [135] [137] [138] [52] [136] [23] [129] [51] [117]	[124] [49] [142] [52] [131] [116] [130] [119] [118] [139] [140]	[120] [122] [50] [132] [121] [141] [134]
	Decentralized	[47] [105] [106] [109] [107] [55] [54]		[47] [105] [107] [123]
Strategy	Exact	[52] [131] [116] [108] [49] [113] [114] [115] [51]	[52] [49] [142] [131] [116]	[122]
	Approximate	[47] [105] [132] [124] [106] [130] [109] [108] [23] [129] [125] [126] [56] [110] [111] [112] [18] [138] [133] [135] [134] [137] [127] [107] [55] [54] [136] [117]	[124] [130] [119] [118] [139] [140]	[50] [120] [105] [132] [47] [107] [123] [121] [141] [134]
Timescale	Short	[47] [105] [52] [128] [54] [113] [115]	[142] [49] [52] [139] [140]	[120] [122] [47] [105] [141]
	Medium	[124] [49] [47] [132] [52] [131] [109] [108] [125] [126] [56] [129] [110] [111] [112] [18] [138] [106] [133] [134] [137] [127] [107] [55] [54] [130] [136] [51] [23] [114] [117]	[124] [131] [52] [130] [119]	[47] [132] [107] [123] [134] [121]
	Long	[116] [108] [111] [135] [55]	[116] [118]	[50]
Discipline	Control Theory	[54] [126] [110] [112] [114]		
	Machine Learning	[110] [134] [23]	[140]	[134]
	Operations Research	[124] [49] [47] [52] [128] [130] [131] [116] [109] [108] [132] [125] [56] [129] [110] [111] [18] [106] [136] [138] [133] [135] [137] [127] [107] [55] [115] [113] [117] [51]	[124] [49] [142] [52] [119] [139] [116] [131] [130] [141]	[120] [122] [132] [47] [107] [123] [121] [50]

metrics. Typically, this approach consists of a performance model embedded within an optimization program, which is solved either globally, locally, or heuristically.

4.1 Capacity allocation

4.1.1 Infrastructure-provider capacity allocation

The capacity allocation problem arising at the provider side involves deciding the optimal placement of running applications on a suitable number of VMs, which in turn has to be executed on appropriate physical servers. The rationale is to assign resource shares trying to minimize management costs (formed mainly by costs associated with energy consumption), while guaranteeing the fulfilment of SLAs stipulated with the customers. Bin packing is a common modeling abstraction [51], but its NP-hardness calls for heuristic solutions. In [127] the capacity allocation problem is solved by means of a dynamic algorithm, since static allocation policies and pricing usually lead to inefficient resource sharing, poor utilization, waste of resources and revenue loss when demands and workloads are time varying. The paper presents a Minimum Cost Maximum Flow (MCMF) algorithm and compares it against a modified Bin-Packing formulation; the MCMF algorithm exhibits very good performance and scalability properties. An autoregressive process is used to predict the fluctuating incoming demand.

In [137], autoscaling is modeled as a modified Class Constrained Bin Packing problem. An auto-scaling algorithm is provided that automatically classifies incoming requests. Moreover, it improves the placement of application instances by putting idle machines into standby mode and reducing the number of running instances in condition of light load.

Tang et al. [133] proposes a fast heuristic solution for VM placement over a very large number of servers in a IaaS data center to equally balance the CPU load among physical machines, taking into account also memory requirements of running applications.

In [125] is proposed a framework for VM deployment and reconfiguration optimization, with the aim at increasing profits of IaaS providers. The authors reduce costs considering the balance of multi-dimensional resources utilization and building up an optimization method for resource allocation; as far as reconfiguration is concerned, they propose a strategy for VM adjustment based on time-division multiplex and on VM live migration.

In [55] a VM placement problem for a PaaS is solved at multiple time-scales through a hierarchical optimization framework. Authors in [132] provide a solution for traffic-aware VM placement minimizing also network latencies among deployed applications. The work presents a two-tier approximate algorithm able to successfully solve very large problem instances. Moreover, a formulation for the considered problem is presented and its hardness is proven.

A capacity allocation problem is also studied in [136], in which a game-theoretic method is used to find approximated solutions for a resource allocation problem in the presence of tasks with multiple dependent subtasks. The initial solution is spawned by a binary integer programming method; then, evolutionary algorithms are designed to achieve a final optimized solution, which minimizes efficiency losses of participants.

Goudarzi et al. [56] provides a solution method for a multi-dimensional capacity allocation problem in a IaaS system, while guaranteeing SLA requirements to customers running multi-tiers applications. An improved solution is obtained starting from an initial configuration based on an upper bound; then, a force-directed search is adopted to increase the total profit. Moreover, a closed-form formula for calculating the average response time of a request and a unified framework to manage different levels of SLAs are provided.

Zaman et al. [138] considers an online mechanism for computing resource allocation to VMs subject to limited information. The algorithm evaluates allocation and revenues as the users place requests to the system. Furthermore, the authors prove that their approach is incentive compatible; they also report extensive simulation experiments.

Wang et al. [135] considers capacity allocation subject to two pricing models, a pay-as-you-go offering and periodic auctions. An optimal capacity segmentation strategy is formulated as a Markov decision process, which is then used to maximize revenues. The authors propose also a faster near-optimal algorithm, proven to asymptotically approach the optimal solution, and show a significantly lower complexity with respect to the optimal method.

Roy et al. [18] proposes a model-predictive resource allocation algorithm that auto-scales VMs, with the aim of optimizing the utility of the application over a limited prediction horizon. Empirical results demonstrate that the proposed method satisfies application QoS requirements, while minimizing operational costs.

Dutta et al. [126] develops a resource manager that uses a combination of horizontal and vertical scaling to optimize both resource usage and the reconfiguration cost. Finally, the solution is tested using real production traces.

Zhu et al. [23] builds a VM consolidation algorithm that makes use of an inference model that considers the effect of co-located VMs to predict QoS metrics. In this method, the workload is modeled by means of a Kalman filter, while the resource usage profile is estimated with a Hidden Markov Model. The proposed method is tested against SPECWeb2005.

Hwang et al. [129] also considers the VM consolidation problem by modeling the VM resource demands as a set of correlated random variables. The result is a multi-capacity stochastic bin packing problem, which is solved by means of a simple, scalable yet effective heuristic.

He et al. [128] uses a multivariate probabilistic model to schedule VMs among physical machines in order to improve resource utilization. This approach also considers migration costs, and the multi-dimensional nature of the VM resource requirements (e.g., CPU, memory, and network).

Finally, in [134] a framework that automatically reconfigures the storage system in response to fluctuations in the workload is presented. The framework makes use of a performance model of the system obtained through statistical machine learning. Such model is embedded into an effective Model-Predictive Control algorithm.

4.1.2 Infrastructure-user capacity allocation

From the user perspective, capacity allocation arises in IaaS and PaaS scenarios where the user is in charge with the control of the number of VMs or application containers running in the system. In this context the user is generally a SaaS provider, which wants to maximize her revenues providing a service that meets a certain QoS. Then, the problem to be addressed is to determine the minimum number of VMs or containers needed to fulfill the target QoS, pursuing the best trade-off between cost and performance.

From the user side, capacity allocation is often implemented through auto-scaling policies. Mao and Humphrey [111] defines an auto-scaling mechanism to guarantee the execution of all jobs within given deadlines. The solution accounts for workload burstinesses and delayed instance acquisition. This approach is compared against other techniques and it shows cost savings from 9.8% to 40.4%. Maggio et al. [110] compares several approaches for decision-making, as part of an autonomic framework that allocates resources to a software application.

Patikirikorala et al. [112] proposes a multi-model control-based framework to deal with the highly nonlinear nature of software systems. An extensible meta-model and a class library with an initial set of five models are developed. Finally, the presented approach is endorsed against fixed and adaptive control schemes by means of a campaign of experiments.

In [108] an optimal resource provisioning algorithm is derived to deal with the uncertainty of resource advance-reservation. The algorithm reduces resources under- and over-provisioning by minimizing the total cost for a customer during a certain time horizon. The solution methods are based on the Bender decomposition approach to divide the problem into sub-problems, which can be solved in parallel, and an approximation algorithm to solve problems with a large set of scenarios.

On-demand and reserved resources are considered in the model proposed in [107] to define a bio-inspired self-adapting solution for cloud resource provisioning with the aim of minimizing the number of required virtual machines while meeting SLAs.

A decentralized probabilistic algorithm is also described in [106], which focuses on federated clouds. The proposed solution has the aim to take advantage of a Cloud federation to avoid the dependence on a single provider, while still minimizing the amount of used resources to maintain a good QoS level for customers. The solution provides an effective decentralized algorithm for deploying massively scalable services and it is suitable for all the situations in which a centralized solution is not feasible.

Ali-Eldin et al. [114] aims at dynamic resource provisioning exploiting horizontal elasticity. Two adaptive hybrid controllers, including both reactive and proactive actions, are employed to decide the number of VMs for a cloud service to meet the SLAs. The future demand is predicted by a queueing-network model.

A key-value store is presented in [115] to meet low-latency Service Level Objectives (SLOs). The proposed middleware achieves high scalability by using replication, providing more predictable response times. An analytical model, based on queueing theory, is presented to describe the relation between the number of replicas and the service level, e.g., the percentage of requests processed according to SLOs.

A capacity allocation problem in presented in [113] that exploits both horizontal and vertical elasticity. An integer linear problem is used to calculate an optimized new configuration able to deal with the current workload. However, reconfiguration is executed if the associated overhead cost calculated on a expected stability duration is lower than a certain minimum benefit defined by a human decision maker.

In [117] two multi-objective customer-driven SLA-based resource provisioning algorithms are proposed. The objectives are the minimization of both resource and penalty costs, as well as minimizing SLA violations. The proposed algorithms consider customer profiles and quality parameters to cope with dynamic workloads and heterogeneous cloud resources.

Finally, a profile-based approach for scalability is described in [109], the authors propose a solution based on the definition of platform-independent profiles, which enable the automation of setup and scaling of application servers in order to achieve a just-in-time scalability of the execution environment, as demonstrated with a case study presented in the paper.

4.2 Load balancing
4.2.1 Infrastructure-provider load balancing

Request load-balancing is an increasingly supported feature of cloud offerings. A load balancer dispatches requests from users to servers according to a load dispatching policy. Policies differ for the decision approach and for the amount of information they use. Research work has focused on policies that are either simple to implement, and thus minimize overheads, or that offer some optimality guarantees, typically proven by analytical models.

The research literature has investigated both centralized and decentralized load balancing mechanisms for providers.

Among centralized approaches, [122] introduces an offline optimization problem for geographical load balancing among data centers, explicitly considering SLAs and dynamic electricity prices. This is complemented with an online algorithm to handle the uncertainty in electricity prices. The proposed algorithm is compared against a greedy heuristic method and it shows significant cost savings (around 20-30%).

A load balancer is presented in [50] to assign VMs among geographically-distributed data centers considering predictions on workload, energy prices, and renewable energy generation capacities. Two complementary methods are proposed: an offline deterministic optimization method to be used at design time and an online VM placement, migration and geographical load balancing algorithm for runtime. The authors studied the behavior of both online and offline algorithms by means of a simulation campaign. The results demonstrate that online version of the algorithm performs 8% worse than the offline one because it deals with incomplete information. On the other hand, the analysis also shows that turning on the geographical load balancing has a strong impact on quality of the solutions (between 27% and 40%) of the online algorithm.

Spicuglia et al. [141] proposes an online load balancing policy that considers the inherent VM heterogeneity found in cloud resources. The load balancer uses the number of outstanding requests and the inter-departure times in each VM to dispatch requests to the VM with the shortest expected response time. The authors demonstrate that their solution is able to improve the variance and percentiles of response times with respect to a built-in policy of the Apache web server.

Decentralized methods are considered in [107], which proposes a self-organizing approach to provide robust and scalable solutions for service deployment, resource provisioning, and load balancing in a cloud infrastructure. The algorithm developed has the additional benefit to leverage Cloud elasticity to allocate and deallocate resources to help services to respect contractual SLAs.

Another example is the cost minimization mechanism for data-intensive service provisioning proposed in [121]. Such mechanism uses biological evolution concepts to manage data application services and to produce optimal composition and load balancing solutions. A multiobjective genetic algorithm is described in detail but a systematic experimental campaign is planned as future work.

4.2.2 Infrastructure-user load balancing

In the studies considered in the previous section, the load balancer is installed and managed transparently by the cloud provider. In some cases, the user can decide to install its own load balancer for a cloud application. This may be helpful, for instance, to jointly tackle capacity allocation and load balancing.

For example, [47] considers a joint optimization problem on multiple IaaS service centers. A non-linear model for the capacity allocation and load redirection of multiple request classes is proposed and solved by decomposition. A comparison against a set of heuristics from the literature and an oracle with perfect knowledge about the future load shows that the proposed algorithm overcomes the heuristic approaches, without penalizing SLAs and it is able to produce results that are close to the global optimum. Anselmi and Casale [120] provides a simple heuristic for user-side load-balancing under connection pooling that is validated against an IaaS cloud dataset. The main result is that the presented approach is able to provide tight guarantees on the optimality gap and experimental results show that it is at the same time accurate and fast.

Hybrid clouds are considered in [116]. The authors formulate an optimization problem faced by a cloud procurement endpoint (a module responsible for provisioning resources from public cloud providers), where heavy workloads are tackled by relying on public clouds. They present a linear integer program to minimize the resource cost, and evaluate how the solution scales with the different problem parameters.

In [123] a structured peer-to-peer network, based on distributed hash tables, is proposed to support service discovery, self-management, and load-balancing of cloud applications. The effectiveness of the peer-to-peer approach is demonstrated through a set of experiments executed on Amazon EC2.

Finally, [105] proposes an adaptive approach for component replication of cloud applications, aiming at finding a cost-effective placement and load balancing. This is a distributed method based on an economic multiagent model that achieves high application availability guaranteeing at the same time service availability under failures.

4.3 Admission control
4.3.1 Infrastructure-provider admission control

Admission control is an overload protection mechanism that rejects requests under peak workload conditions to prevent QoS degradation. A lot of work has been done in the last decade for optimal admission control in web servers and multi-tier applications. The basic idea is to predict the value of a specific QoS metric and if such value grows above a certain threshold, the admission controller rejects all new sessions favoring the service of requests from already admitted sessions.

In cloud computing, several works on admission control have emerged in IaaS. Khazaei et al. [130] develops an analytical model for resource provisioning, virtual machine deployment, and pool management. This model predicts service delay, task rejection probability, and steady-state distribution of server pools.

The availability of resources and admission control is also discussed in [131]. The work uses a probabilistic approach to find an optimized allocation of services on virtualized physical resources. The main requirement of this system is the horizontal elasticity. In fact, the probability of requesting more resources for a service is at the basis of the formulated optimization model, that constitutes a probabilistic admission control test.

Almeida et al. [49] proposes a joint admission control and capacity allocation algorithm for virtualized IaaS systems minimizing the data center energy costs and the penalty incurred for request rejections and SLA violations. SLAs are expressed in terms of the tail distribution of application response times.

Agostinho et al. [124] optimizes the allocation and scheduling of VMs in federated clouds using a genetic algorithm. The solution is composed by two parts: First, servers selection in a data-center is performed by using a search based bio-inspired technique; then, data centers are selected within the cloud federation by using a shortest path algorithm, according to the available bandwidth of links connecting the domains. The aim of the paper is to exploit resources in domains with low allocation costs and, at the same time, achieve better network performance among cloud nodes.

Ellens et al. [52] allows service providers to reserve a certain amount of resources exclusively for some customers, according to SLAs. The proposed framework helps to stipulate a realistic SLA with customers and supports dynamic load shedding and capacity provisioning by considering a queueing model with multiple priority classes. The main performance metric being optimized is the rejection probability, which has to guarantee the value stipulated in the SLA.

The work in [139] proposes an admission control protocol to prevent over-utilization of system resources, classifying applications based on resource quality requirements. It uses an open multi-class queueing network to support a QoS-aware admission control on heterogeneous resources to increase system throughput.

In order to control overload in Database-as-a-Service (DaaS) environments, [140] proposes a profit-aware admission control policy. It first uses nonlinear regression to predict the probability for a query to meet its requirement, and then decides whether the query should be admitted to the database system or not.

4.3.2 Infrastructure-user admission control

From the cloud-user perspective, the admission control mechanism is used as an extreme overload mechanism, helpful when additional resources are obtained with some significant delay. For example, during a cloud burst (i.e., when part of the application traffic is redirected from a private to a public data center to cope with a traffic intensity that surpasses the capacity of the private infrastructure), if the public cloud resources are not provided timely, one can decide to drop new incoming request to preserve the QoS for users already in the system (or at least part of them, e.g., *gold customers*), avoiding application performance degradation.

Three different admission control and scheduling algorithms are proposed in [119] to effectively exploiting public cloud resources. The paper takes the perspective of a SaaS provider with the aim of maximizing the profit by minimizing cost and improving customer satisfaction levels.

Leitner et al. [118] introduces a client-side admission control method to schedule requests among VMs, looking at minimizing the cost of application, SLA violations and IaaS resources.

5 Discussion and conclusion

In recent years, cloud computing has matured from an early-stage solution to a mainstream operational model for enterprise applications. However, the diversity of technologies used in cloud systems makes it difficult to analyze their QoS and, from the provider perspective, to offer service-level guarantees. We have surveyed current approaches in workload and system modeling and early applications to cloud QoS management.

From this survey, a number of insights arise on the current state of the art:

- The number of works that apply white-box system modeling techniques is quite limited in QoS management, albeit popular in the software performance engineering community. This effectively creates a divide between the knowledge that can be made available for an application by its designers and the techniques used to manage it. A research question is whether the availability of more detailed information about application internals can provide significant advantages in QoS management. Indeed, a trade-off exists between available information, QoS model complexity, computational cost of decision-making, and accuracy of predictions. This trade-off requires further investigation by the research community.
- Gray-box models that emphasize resource consumption modeling are currently prevalent in QoS management studies. However, description of performance is often quite basic and associated with mean resource

requirements of the applications. However, the cloud measurement studies in Section 2.1 have identified performance variability as a major issue in today's offerings, calling for more comprehensive models that can describe also the variability in CPU requirements, in addition to mean requirements. Such extension has been explored in black-box system models (e.g., QoS in web services), but it is far less understood in white-box and gray-box modeling.

- Quite surprisingly, we have found a limited amount of work specific to workload analysis and inference techniques in the cloud. Most of the techniques used for traffic forecasting, resource consumption estimation, and anomaly detection have received little or no validation in a cloud environment. As such, it remains to establish the robustness of current techniques to noisy measurements typical of multi-tenant cloud environments.

- Another observation arising from our survey is that the literature is rich in works focusing on IaaS systems, often deployed on Amazon EC2, at present the market leader in this segment.

- If we consider the resource management mechanisms for applications QoS enforcement provided by public clouds, they are quite simplistic if compared to current research proposals. Indeed, such mechanisms are mainly *reactive* and are triggered by thresholds violations (related to response times, as in Google App Engine, or CPU utilization or other low level infrastructure metrics, as in Amazon EC2.) Vice versa, integrating workload characterisation, system models and resource management solutions, *pro-active* systems, may help to prevent QoS degradation. The development of research prototypes that are transferable in commercial solutions seems to remain an open point.

- Finally, in cloud systems an important role is played by resource pricing models. There is a growing interest towards understanding better cloud spot markets, where bidding strategies are developed for procuring computing resources. Approaches are currently being proposed to automate dynamic pricing and cloud resources selection. We expect that, in upcoming years, these models will play a bigger role than today in capacity allocation frameworks.

Summarizing, this survey shows that the literature has already a significant number of works in cloud QoS management, but their focus leaves open several research opportunities in the areas discussed above.

Endnote

a Throughout this paper, we mainly focus on QoS aspects pertaining to performance, reliability and availability. Broader descriptions of QoS are possible (e.g., to include security) but they are not contemplated in the present survey.

Competing interests
The authors declare that they have no competing interests.

Authors' contributions
All authors read and approved the final manuscript.

Acknowledgment
The research reported in this article is partially supported by the European Commission grant FP7-ICT-2011-8-318484 (MODAClouds, www.modaclouds.eu).

Author details
[1] Dipartimento di Elettronica, Informazione, e Bioingegneria Politecnico di Milano, Piazza Leonardo da Vinci 32, Milan 20133, Italy. [2] Department of Computing, Imperial College London, 180 Queens Gate, London SW7 2AZ, UK.

References
1. Armbrust M, Fox A, Griffith R, Joseph AD, Katz R, Konwinski A, Lee G, Patterson D, Rabkin A, Stoica I, Zaharia M (2010) A view of cloud computing. Commun ACM 53(4):50–58
2. Zhang Q, Cheng L, Boutaba R (2010) Cloud computing: state-of-the-art and research challenges. J Internet Serv Appl 1(1):7–18
3. Ardagna D, Panicucci B, Trubian M, Zhang L (2012) Energy-aware autonomic resource allocation in multitier virtualized environments. IEEE Trans Serv Comput 5(1):2–19
4. Petcu D, 0 Macariu G, Panica S, Craciun C (2013) Portable cloud applications - from theory to practice. Future Generation Comput Syst 29(6):1417–1430
5. Farley B, Juels A, Varadarajan V, Ristenpart T, Bowers KD, Swift MM (2012) More for your money: Exploiting performance heterogeneity in public clouds. In: Proceedings of the 2012 Third ACM Symposium on Cloud Computing, SoCC '12, San Jose, CA, USA, pp 1–14
6. Ou Z, Zhuang H, Nurminen JK, Ylä-Jääski A, Hui P (2012) Exploiting hardware heterogeneity within the same instance type of amazon ec2. In: Proceedings of the 4th USENIX Conference on Hot Topics in Cloud Ccomputing, HotCloud'12, Boston, MA, USA, pp 4–4
7. Schad J, Dittrich J, Quiané-Ruiz J-A (2010) Runtime measurements in the cloud: Observing, analyzing, and reducing variance. Proc VLDB Endowment 3(1–2):460–471
8. Mao M, Humphrey M (2012) A performance study on the VM startup time in the cloud. In: Proceedinngs of the 2012 IEEE Fifth International Conference on Cloud Computing, CLOUD '12, Honolulu, HI, USA, pp 423–430
9. Xu Y, Musgrave Z, Noble B, Bailey M (2013) Bobtail: Avoiding long tails in the cloud. In: Proceedings of the 10th USENIX Conference on Networked Systems Design and Implementation, NSDI '13, Lombard, IL, USA, pp 329–342
10. Wang G, Ng TSE (2010) The impact of virtualization on network performance of amazon ec2 data center. In: Proceedings of the 29th Conference on Information Communications, INFOCOM'10, San Diego, CA, USA, pp 1163–1171
11. Hill Z, Li J, Mao M, Ruiz-Alvarez A, Humphrey M (2011) Early observations on the performance of Windows Azure. Sci Program 19(2–3):121–132
12. Li Z, O'Brien L, Ranjan R, Zhang M (2013) Early observations on performance of Google compute engine for scientific computing. In: Proceedings of the 2013 IEEE 5th International Conference on Cloud Computing Technology and Science, volume 1 of CloudCom 2013, Bristol, United Kingdom, pp 1–8
13. Drago I, Mellia M, Munafo MM, Sperotto A, Sadre R, Pras A (2012) Inside Dropbox: understanding personal cloud storage services. In: Proceedings of the 2012 ACM Conference on Internet Measurement Conference, IMC '12, Boston, MA, USA, pp 481–494

14. Kossmann D, Kraska T, Loesing S (2010) An evaluation of alternative architectures for transaction processing in the cloud. In: Proceedings of the 2010 ACM SIGMOD International Conference on Management of Data, SIGMOD '10, Indianapolis, IN, USA, pp 579–590

15. Wada H, Fekete A, Zhao L, Lee K, Liu A (2011) Data consistency properties and the trade-offs in commercial cloud storage: the consumers' perspective. In: Proceedings of the 5th Biennial Conference on Innovative Data Systems Research, CIDR 2011, Asilomar, CA, USA, pp 134–143

16. Liu S, Huang X, Fu H, Yang G (2013) Understanding data characteristics and access patterns in a cloud storage system. In: Proceedings of the 2013 13th IEEE/ACM International Symposium on Cluster, Cloud and Grid Computing, CCGrid 2013, Delft, Nederlands, pp 327–334

17. Li A, Yang X, Kandula S, Zhang M (2010) Cloudcmp: comparing public cloud providers. In: Proceedings of the 10th ACM SIGCOMM conference on Internet measurement. ACM, pp 1–14

18. Roy N, Dubey A, Gokhale A (2011) Efficient autoscaling in the cloud using predictive models for workload forecasting. In: Proceedings of the 2011 IEEE International Conference on Cloud Computing, CLOUD '11, Washington, DC, USA, pp 500–507

19. Gasquet C, Witomski P (1999) Fourier analysis and applications: filtering, numerical computation, wavelets, volume 30 of Texts in applied mathematics. Springer, New York, USA

20. Khan A, Yan X, Shu T, Anerousis N (2012) Workload characterization and prediction in the cloud: A multiple time series approach. In: Proceedings of the 2012 IEEE Network Operations and Management Symposium, NOMS 2012, Maui, HI, USA, pp 1287–1294

21. Di S, Kondo D, Walfredo C (2012) Host load prediction in a google compute cloud with a Bayesian model. In: Proceedings of the International Conference for High Performance Computing, Networking, Storage and Analysis, SC12, Salt Lake City, Utah,USA, pp 1–11

22. Gmach D, Rolia J, Cherkasova L, Kemper A (2007) Workload analysis and demand prediction of enterprise data center applications. In: Proceedings of the 2007 IEEE 10th International Symposium on Workload Characterization, IISWC '07, Boston, MA, USA, pp 171–180

23. Zhu Q, Tung T (2012) A performance interference model for managing consolidated workloads in QoS-aware clouds. In: Proceedings of the 2012 IEEE Fifth International Conference on Cloud Computing, CLOUD '12, Honolulu, HI, USA, pp 170–179

24. Hoffmann GA, Trivedi KS, Malek M (2007) A best practice guide to resource forecasting for computing systems. IEEE Trans Reliability 56(4):615–628

25. Anandkumar A, Bisdikian C, Agrawal D (2008) Tracking in a spaghetti bowl: Monitoring transactions using footprints. In: Proceedings of the 2008 ACM SIGMETRICS International Conference on Measurement and Modeling of Computer Systems. ACM Press, Annapolis, Maryland, USA, pp 133–144

26. Menascé D, Almeida V, Dowdy L (1994) Capacity planning and performance modeling: from mainframes to client-server systems. Prentice-Hall, Inc. NJ, USA

27. Rolia J, Vetland V (1995) Parameter estimation for performance models of distributed application systems. In: In Proc. of CASCON. IBM Press, Toronto, Ontario, Canada, p 54

28. Rolia J, Vetland V (1998) Correlating resource demand information with ARM data for application services. In: Proceedings of the 1st international workshop on Software and performance. ACM, Santa Fe, New Mexico, USA, pp 219–230

29. Liu Y, Gorton I, Fekete A (2005) Design-level performance prediction of component-based applications. IEEE Trans Softw Eng 31(11):928–941

30. Sutton CA, Jordan MI (2008) Probabilistic inference in queueing networks. In: Proceedings of the 3rd conference on Tackling computer systems problems with machine learning techniques. USENIX Association, Berkeley, CA, US, p 6

31. Sutton CA, Jordan MI (2010) Inference and learning in networks of queues. In: International Conference on Artificial Intelligence and Statistics, Sardinia, Italy, pp 796–803

32. Zhang Q, Cherkasova L, Smirni E (2007) A regression-based analytic model for dynamic resource provisioning of multi-tier applications. In: Proc. of the 4th ICAC Conference, Jacksonville, Florida, USA, pp 27–27

33. Liu Z, Wynter L, Xia C, Zhang F (2006) Parameter inference of queueing models for it systems using end-to-end measurements. Perform Eval 63(1):36–60

34. Casale G, Cremonesi P, Turrin R (2008) Robust workload estimation in queueing network performance models. In Proc. of Euromicro PDP:183–187

35. Kalbasi A, Krishnamurthy D, Rolia J, Dawson S (2012) DEC: Service demand estimation with confidence. IEEE Trans Softw Eng 38(3):561–578

36. Kalbasi A, Krishnamurthy D, Rolia J, Richter M (2011) MODE: Mix driven on-line resource demand estimation. In: Proceedings of the 7th International Conference on Network and Services Management. International Federation for Information Processing, pp 1–9

37. Pacifici G, Segmuller W, Spreitzer M, Tantawi A (2008) CPU demand for web serving: Measurement analysis and dynamic estimation. Perform Eval 65(6):531–553

38. Cremonesi P, Sansottera A (2012) Indirect estimation of service demands in the presence of structural changes. In: Proceedings of Quantitative Evaluation of Systems (QEST). IEEE, London, UK, pp 249–259

39. Cremonesi P, Dhyani K, Sansottera A (2010) Service time estimation with a refinement enhanced hybrid clustering algorithm. In: Analytical and Stochastic Modeling Techniques and Applications. Springer, pp 291–305

40. Sharma AB, Bhagwan R, Choudhury M, Golubchik L, Govindan R, Voelker GM (2008) Automatic request categorization in internet services. ACM SIGMETRICS Perform Eval Rev 36(2):16–25

41. Wu X, Woodside M (2008) A calibration framework for capturing and calibrating software performance models. In: Computer Performance Engineering. Springer, pp 32–47

42. Zheng T, Woodside CM, Litoiu M (2008) Performance model estimation and tracking using optimal filters. IEEE Trans Softw Eng 34(3):391–406

43. Desnoyers P, Wood T, Shenoy PJ, Singh R, Patil S, Vin HM (2012) Modellus: Automated modeling of complex internet data center applications. TWEB 6(2):8

44. Longo F, Ghosh R, Naik VK, Trivedi KS (2011) A scalable availability model for Infrastructure-as-a-Service cloud. In: Proceedings of the 2011 IEEE/IFIP 41st International Conference on Dependable Systems Networks, DSN 2011, Hong Kong, China, pp 335–346

45. Calinescu R, Ghezzi C, Kwiatkowska MZ, Mirandola R (2012) Self-adaptive software needs quantitative verification at runtime. Commun ACM 55(9):69–77

46. Chung M-Y, Ciardo G, Donatelli S, He N, Plateau B, Stewart W, Sulaiman E, Yu J (2004) Comparison of structural formalisms for modeling large markov models. In: Parallel and Distributed Processing Symposium, 2004 Proceedings. 18th International, Santa Fe, New Mexico, USA, p 196

47. Ardagna D, Casolari S, Colajanni M, Panicucci B (2012) Dual time-scale distributed capacity allocation and load redirect algorithms for cloud systems. J Parallel Distributed Comput 72(6):796–808

48. Xiong P, Wang Z, Malkowski S, Wang Q, Jayasinghe D, Pu C (2011) Economical and robust provisioning of n-tier cloud workloads: A multi-level control approach. In: Proceedings of the 31st IEEE International Conference on Distributed Computing Systems (ICDCS), Minneapolis, Minnesota, USA, pp 571–580

49. Almeida J, Almeida V, Ardagna D, Cunha I, Francalanci C, Trubian M (2010) Joint admission control and resource allocation in virtualized servers. J Parallel Distributed Comput 70(4):344–362

50. Goudarzi H, Pedram M (2013) Geographical load balancing for online service applications in distributed datacenters. In: Proceedings of the 2013 IEEE Sixth International Conference on Cloud Computing, CLOUD '13, Santa Clara, CA, USA, pp 351–358

51. Zhang Q, Zhu Q, Zhani MF, Boutaba R (2012) Dynamic service placement in geographically distributed clouds. In: Proceedings of the 2012 IEEE 32Nd International Conference on Distributed Computing Systems, ICDCS '12, Macau, China, pp 526–535

52. Ellens W, Zivkovic M, Akkerboom J, Litjens R, van den Berg H (2012) Performance of cloud computing centers with multiple priority classes. In: Proceedings of the 2012 IEEE 5th International Conference on Cloud Computing, CLOUD '12, Honolulu, HI, USA, pp 245–252

53. Kusic D, Kandasamy N (2006) Risk-aware limited lookahead control for dynamic resource provisioning in enterprise computing systems. In: Proceedings of the 2006 IEEE International Conference on Autonomic Computing, ICAC '06, Dublin, Ireland, pp 74–83

54. Kusic D, Kephart JO, Hanson JE, Kandasamy N, Jiang G (2009) Power and performance management of virtualized computing environments via lookahead control. Cluster Comput 12(1):1–15

55. Addis B, Ardagna D, Panicucci B, Squillante MS, Zhang L (2013) A hierarchical approach for the resource management of very large cloud platforms. IEEE Trans Dependable Secure Comput 10(5):253–272

56. Goudarzi H, Pedram M (2011) Multi-dimensional sla-based resource allocation for multi-tier cloud computing systems. In: Proceedings of the 2011 IEEE 4th International Conference on Cloud Computing, CLOUD '11, Washington, DC, USA, pp 324–331

57. Becker S, Koziolek H, Reussner R (2009) The Palladio component model for model-driven performance prediction. J Syst Softw 82(1):3–22

58. Franks G, Al-Omari T, Woodside CM, Das O, Derisavi S (2009) Enhanced modeling and solution of layered queueing networks. IEEE Trans Softw Eng 35(2):148–161

59. Omari T, Franks G, Woodside M, Pan A (2007) Efficient performance models for layered server systems with replicated servers and parallel behaviour. J Syst Softw 80(4):510–527

60. Tribastone M (2013) A fluid model for layered queueing networks. IEEE Trans Softw Eng 39(6):744–756

61. Pérez JF, Casale G (2013) Assessing sla compliance from palladio component models. In: Proceedings of the 2013 15th International Symposium on Symbolic and Numeric Algorithms for Scientific Computing, SYNASC '13, Timisoara, Romania, pp 409–416

62. Faisal A, Petriu D, Woodside M (2013) Network latency impact on performance of software deployed across multiple clouds. In: Proceedings of the 2013 Conference of the Center for Advanced Studies on Collaborative Research, CASCON '13, Ontario, Canada, pp 216–229

63. Jung G, Joshi KR, Hiltunen MA, Schlichting RD, Pu C (2008) Generating adaptation policies for multi-tier applications in consolidated server environments. In: Autonomic Computing, 2008 ICAC'08. International Conference on. IEEE, Chicago, IL, USA, pp 23–32

64. Bacigalupo D, van Hemert J, Chen X, Usmani A, Chester A, He L Dillenberger D, Wills G, Gilbert L, Jarvis S (2011) Managing dynamic enterprise and urgent workloads on clouds using layered queuing and historical performance models. Simul Model Prac Theory 19:1479–1495

65. Thereska E, Ganger GR (2008) IRONmodel: Robust performance models in the wild. ACM SIGMETRICS Perform Eval Rev 36(1):253–264

66. Singh R, Sharma U, Cecchet E, Shenoy P (2010) Autonomic mix-aware provisioning for non-stationary data center workloads. In: Proceedings of the 7th ACM international conference on Autonomic computing, Washington, DC, USA, pp 21–30

67. Brogi A, Corfini S, Iardella S (2009) From OWL-S descriptions to Petri nets. In: Service-Oriented Computing - ICSOC 2007 Workshops, volume 4907 of Lecture Notes in Computer Science. Springer-Verlag, Vienna, Austria, pp 427–438

68. Callou G, Maciel P, Tutsch D, Araujo J (2011) Models for dependability and sustainability analysis of data center cooling architectures. In: Proceedings of the 2011 Symposium on Theory of Modeling & Simulation: DEVS Integrative M&S Symposium, TMS-DEVS '11, Boston, MA, USA, pp 274–281

69. Wei B, Lin C, Kong X (2011) Dependability modeling and analysis for the virtual data center of cloud computing. In: Proceedings of the 2011 IEEE 13th International Conference on High Performance Computing and Communications, HPCC 2011, Bamff, Canada, pp 784–789

70. Figueiredo J, Maciel P, Callou G, Tavares E, Sousa E, Silva B (2011) Estimating reliability importance and total cost of acquisition for data center power infrastructures. In: Proceedings of the 2011 IEEE International Conference on Systems, Man, and Cybernetics, SMC 2011, Anchorage, AK, USA, pp 421–426

71. Dantas J, Matos R, Araujo J, Maciel P (2012) An availability model for eucalyptus platform: An analysis of warm-standy replication mechanism. In: Proceedings of the 2012 IEEE International Conference on Systems, Man, and Cybernetics, SMC 2012, Seoul, Korea, pp 1664–1669

72. Melo M, Maciel P, Araujo J, Matos R, Araujo C (2013) Availability study on cloud computing environments: Live migration as a rejuvenation mechanism. In: Proceedings of the 2013 IEEE/IFIP 43rd International Conference on Dependable Systems and Networks, DSN 2013, Hong Kong, China, pp 1–6

73. Ford B (2012) Icebergs in the clouds: The other risks of cloud computing. In: Proceedings of the 2012 4th USENIX Conference on Hot Topics in Cloud Computing, HotCloud'12, Boston, MA, USA, pp 2–2

74. Jhawar R, Piuri V (2012) Fault tolerance management in IaaS clouds. In: Proceedings of 2012 IEEE First AESS European Conference on Satellite Telecommunications, ESTEL 2012, Rome, Italy, pp 1–6

75. Kiran M, Jiang M, Armstrong DJ, Djemame K (2011) Towards a service lifecycle based methodology for risk assessment in cloud computing. In: Proceedings of the 2011 IEEE Ninth International Conference on Dependable, Autonomic and Secure Computing, DASC 2011, Sydney, NSW, Australia, pp 449–456

76. Ardagna D, Pernici B (2007) Adaptive service composition in flexible processes. IEEE Trans Softw Eng 33(6):369–384

77. Ben Mabrouk N, Beauche S, Kuznetsova E, Georgantas N, Issarny V (2009) QoS-aware service composition in dynamic service oriented environments. In: Proceedings of the 10th ACM/IFIP/USENIX International Conference on Middleware, Middleware '09, Urbanna, Il, USA, pp 1–20

78. Alrifai M, Skoutas D, Risse T (2010) Selecting skyline services for QoS-based web service composition. In: Proceedings of the 19th International Conference on World Wide Web, WWW '10, Raleigh, NC, USA, pp 11–20

79. El Haddad J, Manouvrier M, Rukoz M (2010) TQoS: Transactional and QoS-aware selection algorithm for automatic web service composition. IEEE Trans Serv Comput 3(1):73–85

80. Cardellini V, Casalicchio E, Grassi V, Mirandola R (2006) A framework for optimal service selection in broker-based architectures with multiple QoS classes. In: Proceedings of the 2006 IEEE Services Computing Workshops, SCW '06, Chicago, IL, USA, pp 105–112

81. Jiang D, Pierre G, Chi C-H (2010) Autonomous resource provisioning for multi-service web applications. In: Proceedings of the 2010 19th International Conference on World Wide Web, WWW '10, Raleigh, NC, USA, pp 471–480

82. Yu T, Zhang Y, Lin K-J (2007) Efficient algorithms for web services selection with end-to-end QoS constraints. ACM Trans Web 1(1):6

83. Stein S, Payne TR, Jennings NR (2009) Flexible provisioning of web service workflows. ACM Trans Internet Technol 9(1):1–45

84. Comuzzi M, Pernici B (2009) A framework for qos-based web service contracting. ACM Trans Web 3(3):1–52

85. Schuller D, Polyvyanyy A, García-Bañuelos L, Schulte S (2011) Optimization of complex qos-aware service compositions. In: Proceedings of the 2011 9th International Conference on Service-Oriented Computing, ICSOC'11, Paphos, Cyprus, pp 452–466

86. Clark A, Gilmore S, Tribastone M (2009) Quantitative analysis of web services using srmc. In: Formal Methods for Web Services, volume 5569 of Lecture Notes in Computer Science. Springer, Berlin Heidelberg, pp 296–339

87. Reinecke P, Wolter K (2008) Phase-type approximations for message transmission times in web services reliable messaging. In: Proceedings of the 2008 SPEC International Workshop on Performance Evaluation: Metrics, Models and Benchmarks, SIPEW '08 Boston, MA, USA, Darmstadt, Germany, pp 191–207

88. Haddad S, Mokdad L, Youcef S (2010) Response time of BPEL4WS constructors. In: Proceedings of the 2010 IEEE Symposium on Computers and Communications, ISCC'10, Riccione, Italy, pp 695–700

89. Menascé DA, Casalicchio E, Dubey VK (2010) On optimal service selection in service oriented architectures. Perform Eval 67(8):659–675

90. Huang J, Liu Y, Duan Q (2012) Service provisioning in virtualization-based cloud computing: Modeling and optimization. In: Proceedings of 2012 IEEE Global Communications Conference, GLOBECOM 2012, Anaheim, CA, USA, pp 1710–1715

91. Klein A, Ishikawa F, Honiden S (2012) Towards network-aware service composition in the cloud. In: Proceedings of the 21st International Conference on World Wide Web, WWW '12, Lyon, France, pp 959–968

92. Ye Z, Bouguettaya A, Zhou X (2012) QoS-aware cloud service composition based on economic models. In: Proceedings of the 10th International Conference on Service-Oriented Computing, ICSOC'12, Shanghai, China, pp 111–126

93. Calheiros RN, Ranjan R, Beloglazov A, De Rose CAF, Buyya R (2011) Cloudsim: a toolkit for modeling and simulation of cloud computing environments and evaluation of resource provisioning algorithms. Software–Pract Exp 41(1):23–50

94. Wickremasinghe B, Calheiros RN, Buyya R (2010) CloudAnalyst: A cloudsim-based visual modeller for analysing cloud computing environments and applications. In: Proceedings of the 2010 24th IEEE International Conference on Advanced Information Networking and Applications, AINA 2010, Perth, Australia, pp 446–452

95. Calheiros RN, Netto MAS, De Rose CAF, Buyya R (2013) Emusim: an integrated emulation and simulation environment for modeling,

evaluation, validation of performance of cloud computing applications. Software–Pract Exp 43:595–612

96. Calheiros RN, Buyya R, De Rose CAF (2010) Building an automated and self-configurable emulation testbed for grid applications. Software–Pract Exp 40:405–429

97. Kliazovich D, Bouvry P, Khan SU (2010) GreenCloud: A packet-level simulator of energy-aware cloud computing data centers. In: Proceedings of the 2010 IEEE Global Telecommunications Conference, GLOBECOM 2010, Miami, FL, USA, pp 1–5

98. The Network Simulator - NS. (http://www.isi.edu/nsnam/ns/)

99. Keller G, Tighe M, Lutfiyya H, Bauer M (2012) DCSim: A data centre simulation tool. In: Proceedings of 2012 8th international conference on Network and service management, and 2012 workshop on systems virtualiztion management, CNSM-SVM 2012, Las Vegas, NV, USA, pp 385–392

100. Ostermann S, Plankensteiner K, Prodan R, Fahringer T (2011) Groudsim: An event-based simulation framework for computational grids and clouds. In: Proceedings of the 2010 Conference on Parallel Processing, Euro-Par 2010, Ischia, Italy, pp 305–313

101. Wang H, Jing Q, Chen R, He B, Qian Z, Zhou L (2010) Distributed systems meet economics: pricing in the cloud. In: Proceedings of the 2nd USENIX conference on Hot topics in cloud computing, HotCloud'10, Boston, MA, USA, pp 6–6

102. Sowmya K, Sundarraj RP (2012) Strategic bidding for cloud resources under dynamic pricing schemes. In: Proceedings of 2012 International Symposium on Cloud and Services Computing, ISCOS 2012, Mangalore, India, pp 25–30

103. Beloglazov A, Buyya R, Lee YC, Zomaya AY (2011) A taxonomy and survey of energy-efficient data centers and cloud computing systems. Adv Comput 82:47–111

104. Aleti A, Buhnova B, Grunske L, Koziolek A, Meedeniya I (2013) Software architecture optimization methods: A systematic literature review. IEEE Trans Softw Eng 39(5):658–683

105. Bonvin N, Papaioannou T, Aberer K (2010) An economic approach for scalable and highly-available distributed applications. In: Proceedings of the 2010 IEEE 3rd International Conference on Cloud Computing, CLOUD '10, Miami, FL, USA, pp 498–505

106. Calcavecchia NM, Caprarescu BA, Di Nitto E, Dubois DJ, Petcu D (2012) DEPAS: A decentralized probabilistic algorithm for auto-scaling. Computing 94(8–10)

107. Caprarescu BA, Calcavecchia NM, Di Nitto E, Dubois DJ (2012) Sos cloud: Self-organizing services in the cloud. In: Bio-Inspired Models of Network, Information, and Computing Systems, volume 87 of Lecture Notes of the Institute for Computer Sciences, Social Informatics and Telecommunications Engineering. Springer, Berlin Heidelberg, pp 48–55

108. Chaisiri S, Lee B-S, Niyato D (2012) Optimization of resource provisioning cost in cloud computing. IEEE Trans Serv Comput 5(2):164–177

109. Jie Y, Jie Q, Ying L (2009) A profile-based approach to just-in-time scalability for cloud applications. In: Proceedings of the 2009 IEEE International Conference on Cloud Computing, CLOUD '09, Bangalore, India, pp 9–16

110. Maggio M, Hoffmann H, Santambrogio MD, Agarwal A, Leva A (2011) A comparison of autonomic decision making techniques. Technical Report MIT-CSAIL-TR-2011-019, Massachusetts Institute of Technology. USA, Massachusetts

111. Mao M, Humphrey M (2011) Auto-scaling to minimize cost and meet application deadlines in cloud workflows. In: Proceedings of the 2011 International Conference for High Performance Computing, Networking, Storage and Analysis, SC '11, Seattle, WA, USA, pp 1–12

112. Patikirikorala T, Colman A, Han J, Wang L (2011) A multi-model framework to implement self-managing control systems for qos management. In: Proceedings of the 6th International Symposium on Software Engineering for Adaptive and Self-Managing Systems, SEAMS '11, Honolulu, HI, USA, pp 218–227

113. Sedaghat M, Hernandez-Rodriguez F, Elmroth E (2013) A virtual machine re-packing approach to the horizontal vs. vertical elasticity trade-off for cloud autoscaling. In: Proceedings of the 2013 ACM Cloud and Autonomic Computing Conference, CAC '13, Miami, FL, USA, pp 6:1–6:10

114. Ali-Eldin A, Tordsson J, Elmroth E (2012) An adaptive hybrid elasticity controller for cloud infrastructures. In IEEE Network Operations and Management Symposium (NOMS):204–212

115. Stewart C, Chakrabarti A, Griffith R (2013) Zoolander: Efficiently meeting very strict, low-latency slos. In Proceedings of the 10th International Conference on Autonomic Computing (ICAC):265–277

116. Van den, Bossche R, Vanmechelen K, Broeckhove J (2010) Cost-optimal scheduling in hybrid iaas clouds for deadline constrained workloads. In: Proceedings of the 2010 IEEE 3rd International Conference on Cloud Computing, CLOUD'10, Miami, FL, USA, pp 228–235

117. Wu L, Garg SK, Versteeg S, Buyya R (2013) SLA-based resource provisioning for hosted software as a service applications in cloud computing environments. IEEE Trans Serv Comput 99:1

118. Leitner P, Hummer W, Satzger B, Inzinger C, Dustdar S (2012) Cost-efficient and application sla-aware client side request scheduling in an infrastructure-as-a-service cloud. In: Proceedings of the 2012 IEEE 5th International Conference on Cloud Computing, CLOUD '12, Honolulu, HI, USA, pp 213–220

119. Wu L, Garg SK, Buyya R (2012) SLA-based admission control for a software-as-a-service provider in cloud computing environments. J Comput Syst Sci 78(5):1280–1299

120. Anselmi J, Casale G (2013) Heavy-traffic revenue maximization in parallel multiclass queues. Perform Eval 70(10):806–821

121. Wang L, Shen J (2012) Towards bio-inspired cost minimisation for data-intensive service provision. In: Proceedings of the 2012 IEEE First International Conference on Services Economics, SE 2012, Honolulu, HI, USA, pp 16–23

122. Adnan MA, Sugihara R, Gupta RK (2012) Energy efficient geographical load balancing via dynamic deferral of workload. In: Proceedings of the 2012 IEEE Fifth International Conference on Cloud Computing, CLOUD '12, Honolulu, HI, USA, pp 188–195

123. Ranjan R, Zhao L, Wu X, Liu A, Quiroz A, Parashar M (2010) Peer-to-peer cloud provisioning: Service discovery and load-balancing. In: Cloud Computing, Computer Communications and Networks. Springer, London, pp 195–217

124. Agostinho L, Feliciano G, Olivi L, Cardozo E, Guimaraes E (2011) A bio-inspired approach to provisioning of virtual resources in federated clouds. In: Proceedings of the 2011 IEEE Ninth International Conference on Dependable, Autonomic and Secure Computing, DASC 2011, Sydney, NSW, Australia, pp 598–604

125. Chen W, Qiao X, Wei J, Huang T (2012) A profit-aware virtual machine deployment optimization framework for cloud platform providers. In: Proceedings of the 2012 IEEE Fift International Conference on Cloud Computing, CLOUD '12, Honolulu, HI, USA, pp 17–24

126. Dutta S, Gera S, Verma A, Viswanathan B (2012) Smartscale: Automatic application scaling in enterprise clouds. In: Proceedings of the 2012 IEEE 5th International Conference on Cloud Computing, CLOUD '12, Honolulu, HI, USA, pp 221–228

127. Hadji M, Zeghlache D (2012) Minimum cost maximum flow algorithm for dynamic resource allocation in clouds. In: Proceedings of the 2012 IEEE 5th International Conference on Cloud Computing, CLOUD '12, Honolulu, HI, USA, pp 876–882

128. He S, Guo L, Ghanem M, Guo Y (2012) Improving resource utilisation in the cloud environment using multivariate probabilistic models. In: Proceedings of the 2012 IEEE 5th International Conference on Cloud Computing, CLOUD '12, Honolulu, HI, USA, pp 574–581

129. Hwang I, Pedram M (2013) Hierarchical virtual machine consolidation in a cloud computing system. In: Proceedings of the 2013 IEEE Sixth International Conference on Cloud Computing, CLOUD '13, Santa Clara, CA, USA, pp 196–203

130. Khazaei H, Misic J, Misic V, Rashwand S (2013) Analysis of a pool management scheme for cloud computing centers. IEEE Trans Parallel Distributed Syst 24(5):849–861

131. Konstanteli K, Cucinotta T, Psychas K, Varvarigou T (2012) Admission control for elastic cloud services. In: Proceedings of the 2012 IEEE 5th International Conference on Cloud Computing, CLOUD '12, Honolulu, HI, USA, pp 41–48

132. Meng X, Pappas V, Zhang L (2010) Improving the scalability of data center networks with traffic-aware virtual machine placement. In: Proceedings of the 29th Conference on Information Communications, INFOCOM'10, San Diego, CA, USA, pp 1154–1162

133. Tang C, Steinder M, Spreitzer M, Pacifici G (2007) A scalable application placement controller for enterprise data centers. In: Proceedings of the 16th International Conference on World Wide Web, WWW '07, Banff, Canada, pp 331–340

134. Trushkowsky B, Bodík P, Fox A, Franklin MJ, Jordan MI, Patterson DA (2011) The SCADS director: Scaling a distributed storage system under stringent performance requirements. In: Proceedings of the 9th USENIX Conference on File and Stroage Technologies, FAST'11, San Jose, CA, USA, pp 12–12

135. Wang W, Li B, Liang B (2012) Towards optimal capacity segmentation with hybrid cloud pricing. In: Proceedings of the 2012 IEEE 32nd International Conference on Distributed Computing Systems, ICDCS 2012, Macau, China, pp 425–434

136. Wei G, Vasilakos AV, Zheng Y, Xiong N (2010) A game-theoretic method of fair resource allocation for cloud computing services. J Supercomput 54(2):252–269

137. Xiao Z, Chen Q, Luo H (2014) Automatic scaling of internet applications for cloud computing services. IEEE Trans Comput 63(5):1111–1123

138. Zaman S, Grosu D (2012) An online mechanism for dynamic vm provisioning and allocation in clouds. In: Proceedings of the 2012 IEEE 5th International Conference on Cloud Computing, CLOUD '12, Honolulu, HI, USA, pp 253–260

139. Delimitrou C, Bambos N, Kozyrakis C (2013) QoS-aware admission control in heterogeneous datacenters. In: Proceedings of the 2013 10th International Conference on Autonomic Computing, ICAC ÁŢ13, San Jose, CA, USA, pp 291–296

140. Xiong P, Chi Y, Zhu S, Tatemura J, Pu C, Hacigümüş H (2011) Activesla: A profit-oriented admission control framework for database-as-a-service providers. In: Proceedings of the 2nd ACM Symposium on Cloud Computing, SOCC '11, Cascais, Portugal, pp 1–14

141. Spicuglia S, Chen LY, Binder W (2013) Join the best queue: Reducing performance variability in heterogeneous systems. In: Proceedings of the 2013 IEEE Sixth International Conference on Cloud Computing, CLOUD '13, Santa Clara, CA, USA, pp 139–146

142. Huang DT, Niyato D, Wang P (2012) Optimal admission control policy for mobile cloud computing hotspot with cloudlet. In: Proceedings of the 2012 IEEE Wireless Communications and Networking Conference, WCNC 2012, Paris, France, pp 3145–3149

143. Padala P, Shin KG, Zhu X, Uysal M, Wang Z, Singhal S, Merchant A, Salem K (2007) Adaptive control of virtualized resources in utility computing environments. In: Proceedings of the 2Nd ACM SIGOPS/EuroSys European Conference on Computer Systems 2007, EuroSys'07, Lisbon, Portugal, pp 289–302

144. Kephart J, Chan H, Das R, Levine D, Tesauro G, Rawson F, Lefurgy C (2007) Coordinating multiple autonomic managers to achieve specified power-performance tradeoffs. In: Proceedings of the Fourth International Conference on Autonomic Computing, ICAC '07, Jacksonville, FL, USA, pp 24–24

10

On middleware for emerging health services

Jatinder Singh[*] and Jean M Bacon

Abstract

Healthcare concerns have become diverse, ranging from acute and chronic conditions to lifestyle, wellbeing and the prevention of illness. Increasingly, individuals are taking responsibility for monitoring their own conditions. Healthcare technologies are increasingly used not only for administration, but also in specialist treatments and many forms of monitoring, including when a person is mobile. As well as formal interactions with professional carers and results from specialist procedures, care may involve ad hoc interactions with an individual's community. Together, these yield a wealth of data relevant in different contexts. Unfortunately, many existing healthcare systems are inflexible, single-purpose, and self-contained, so that we cannot fully realise their potential. We believe that a framework for flexible interoperability of healthcare-relevant components is crucial, in a time of increasing need from an ageing population. We present a vision of *pervasive, preventative and personalised healthcare*. To achieve this we believe that the application logic embodied in components should be separated from the policy that specifies where and how they should be used—which may be in ways not contemplated by their original designers. Middleware should therefore provide a framework that supports not only traditional communication among components but also dynamic reconfiguration of components in response to circumstances that arise, with the management and enforcement of high-level policy integrated with the middleware. By this means, functionality for patients, carers and health administrators can be customised and provided as, when and where required.

This paper explores middleware requirements and challenges arising from technology- and population-driven developments in healthcare provision. We describe the specific requirements that middleware must address, and present some practical steps towards addressing these from the initial stages of a middleware (SBUS).

Keywords: Healthcare; e-health; Assisted living; Middleware; Management; Policy enforcement; Dynamic reconfiguration; Event-based systems; Pervasive computing; Security; Privacy; Internet of things; SBUS

1 Introduction

With the world's ageing population, there is an increased burden on healthcare resources [1]. As such, there is a global push to improve the efficiencies and effectiveness of health care services. The goal is to improve patient outcomes, alleviate chronic conditions, and more generally improve an individual's quality of life [2]. This in turn reduces healthcare expenditure, as there is less reliance on more costly health services [3].

Traditionally, healthcare provision focuses on acute issues. These are significant, highly symptomatic, health concerns that often require urgent treatment, such as a heart attack or stroke. Such incidents are often serious, greatly impacting a patient's life, and consume significant health resources. Health services are evolving to take a more on-going, preventative approach to care [4]. This involves risk management, taking active steps to mitigate potential health concerns. These steps can be clinical interventions, such as medication or periodic diagnostic tests, as well as lifestyle factors, such as exercise, diet, stress-levels, and so forth.

Information is the key to improving health and wellbeing [5]. Clearly, better informed practitioners give a better quality of care. Technological advances, such as sensors and monitoring technologies, means that there is increasingly more data available than ever before. The more data that medical professionals have access to, for example on a patient's physiology, lifestyle, other medical interventions, the more effective advice and treatment regimes can be. This enables care to be better customised to the individual and their circumstances, and also contributes to improving general care standards

*Correspondence: jatinder.singh@cl.cam.ac.uk
Computer Laboratory, University of Cambridge, Cambridge, UK

by providing input into case-studies, best practices and medical research.

Information is relevant not only to the medical professional. An explicit goal of emerging care models is to empower patients to take control of their health, well-being and any conditions that they may have [6]. Therefore, as more data becomes available, it is important for patients, and their care community (e.g. family members, social carers) to be better informed, since more understanding of their conditions and risks can help to reduce risk and lead to positive change.

Information technology already plays an important role in healthcare, though the focus so far has predominantly been to support the acute-based approach to care. Thus, IT systems tend to concern clinical aspects, providing health-enterprise services, such as management tools, patient administration and health records (to various degrees), or a particular diagnostic capability[a]. Many of these systems are bespoke; only for specific purposes, and operate in vertical silos. If interoperable, there tends only to be integration with other local systems (cf. across care units) or the major systems– often an expensive undertaking and therefore driven by management concerns, rather than focusing on more flexible care pathways.

The way forward is to realise the vision of *personalised, preventative care* [7]. This involves a more holistic approach, where healthcare not only occurs within the traditional, clinical space, but also informally through patients and their care community in an on-going, day-to-day manner. Technology is central to this vision. With respect to data, sensor technologies are increasingly providing rich streams of information giving valuable insight into a person's daily activities, progress and well-being. Advances in communication technologies enable interactions at a distance (remote care), and improvements in connectivity footprints provide the means for patients to be 'continually online' for monitoring. The uptake of mobile devices by both patients and medical professionals promises their increasing familiarity with technology [8], providing a highly personal mechanism that can be leveraged to communicate, inform, alert and monitor. From the clinical perspective, this will lead to better informed care, more efficient use of carer time, and improvements in the speed and quality of response. Continuous monitoring of environmental and physiological state provides rich datasets to aid diagnosis through analysis of risks, traits and trends. Monitoring can be extended to provide alerts of detected conditions, for reminders, etc. This is important for patients and their care communities, to give them insight, feedback support and reinforcement of their care goals. As well as providing rich data for clinical use, to customise care and diagnosis, this data is also useful for medical research.

There are systems for remote care (telecare) and self-monitoring[b]. However, these tend to be bespoke, closed systems, designed for specific conditions or exclusive concerns, such as raising particular alerts, or diabetes management. While a step in the right direction, to properly realise the goal of preventative care more integrated, flexible approaches are required. The systems should be able to deal with the idiosyncrasies of individual patients, their care needs, their support networks and their care team, and capable of leveraging a range of different health systems, services and data as appropriate.

The vision for a system environment should therefore be *pervasive healthcare* [9], rather than a number of specific systems (integrated to various degrees). That is, a number of systems—including applications, services, sensors, and so forth—should come together, seamlessly, when and where relevant, as appropriate for each individual. Data drives health and well-being processes, enabling tailored interactions across clinical and more informal and/or personal systems. Care efficiencies are improved, as integrated systems and improved communications help the movement away from the environment of manual, human-initiated actions.

Pervasive healthcare imposes significant challenges for supporting infrastructure. Firstly, in such an environment, it will be less clear which systems are health related; heart-rate sensors are obviously relevant but, for some people, lack of phone communication could indicate depression. The availability and relevance of different systems will vary between individuals. Each user, clinical or otherwise, is different, they will vary in how, when and why they use particular systems. Further, security and privacy concerns pervade, given the sensitivity of personal/health information. However, such sensitivity may depend on context.

Perhaps most importantly, system developers will not be able to envisage all the circumstances in which their systems may be used. Therefore, these concerns can no longer all be encoded in application logic. Indeed, this has led to today's vertical silos and interoperability problems. Useful functionality comes not from single systems, but by coordinating systems in various ways.

Middleware provides a layer of abstraction that mediates between applications and network infrastructures [10]. Often described as *systems-glue*, middleware is crucial in supporting this emerging healthcare because middleware operates *across systems*, to assist communication and management. The challenges of pervasive healthcare means that middleware, in addition to its traditional role of enabling interoperability, must be more active in controlling systems and driving interactions between them, when and where appropriate, in order to meet user-defined goals. Policy, representing an individual's (patient and/or carer) requirements, is crucial; defined outside application-logic, it operates to orchestrate and reconfigure system components to meet particular goals. The purpose is to allow people (and their carers) to customise how and when various systems are used, and how their data is handled, in order to best manage patients' health and well-being.

This paper explores the impact of this emerging healthcare vision and the requirements this model imposes on supporting infrastructure. We begin by describing the evolution of healthcare provision (§2), and the resulting systems requirements (§3), before emphasising the importance of policy for enabling dynamic management across system components (§4). We then explore areas of systems research, and consider their fit within the broader healthcare vision (§5). The SBUS middleware is introduced as proof of concept to practically illustrate the types of capabilities required by emerging health infrastructure (§6). Policy enforcement specifics are then explored (§7), and we conclude with a summary of open challenges (§8).

2 The evolution of care

The burden on health resources is ever increasing, given the world's ageing population [1]. The majority of care services relate to *chronic* conditions. These are on-going, long-term health conditions or diseases, such as heart disease, cancer, diabetes, etc. The World Health Organization shows that 75% of the total population will develop one chronic condition and 50% two or more conditions [2]. As people live longer, the number of people living with chronic health conditions is increasing. Chronic conditions, particularly when improperly managed, can lead to acute episodes requiring urgent medical attention.

The worldwide goal is to improve people's health, well-being and quality of life, and at the same time, reduce the burden on health resources. *Preventative care* fundamentally involves taking active steps to reduce the risk of developing acute and chronic conditions, and also improving the management of chronic conditions (and/or the factors that can lead to chronic conditions). In addition to clinical aspects, such as diagnostic services and medication, lifestyle factors, such as smoking, alcohol intake, exercise and diet directly impact many aspects of health. Lifestyle management can often limit the onset and exacerbation of both acute and chronic conditions.

It is clear that such an evolution in the care paradigm would lead to more informal care practices; that is, managing aspects of health and well-being outside the formal, traditional clinical space. In general terms, this entails: a) establishing a patient support network, including professional and informal carers (friends, community and family), b) assisting with everyday activities, c) ongoing observation to indicate any improvement or deterioration in condition(s), d) educating and informing patients on how to 'help themselves', and e) enabling

(formal) interventions when and where required. This approach would lead to a much wider coverage by healthcare services.

2.1 Healthcare systems

Currently, a vast number of systems underpin clinical health services. In formal care environments, such as a hospital ward or a surgical theatre, the system components relating to care tend to be standardised, used for a particular purpose. Some are more general, enterprise-level systems such as electronic health records, designed to improve communication between medical professionals.

Others are more specialist, e.g. monitoring a particular set of vital signs or the treatment flow of a particular condition. Many of these systems operate standalone, or have few, specific interactions with major services, such as National Care Records or the patient administration systems (PAS) in the UK[c]. From the clinical perspective, the lack of integrated technologies means much inefficiency: actions and interventions are manually initiated, e.g. doctors must log-on and switch between many different systems, and communication is typically synchronous (pagers that require follow-up phone calls), requiring staff to be available and reachable. Preventative care adds another dimension to the healthcare technology landscape; it requires systems to be *patient-centric*, rather than enterprise-centric, that can be customised to the user—be they the patient or carer.

Technology can enable a more holistic approach to health, in which a wide variety of systems, sensors and applications come together, when and where appropriate, to achieve particular care-related outcomes. Some of these will be person-centric, providing monitoring of aspects of health, lifestyle and well-being, to give information and feedback to enable positive change. Others, aimed at medical practitioners, will facilitate their communication with others, direct access to monitoring devices, and support their interactions with more formal care systems. However, it seems that information flows should not be partitioned between clinical and informal. Rather, the line between the formal and informal care processes blurs, as person-centric systems may interact with more formal systems, when and where necessary.

Such a vision is realistic. Monitoring and communications technology have developed to the extent that they are potentially exploitable in large-scale, widespread healthcare. At the same time, people (patients and medical professionals) are becoming increasingly familiar with and accepting of a wide range of technologies [8,11]. Thus, there is scope for more mobile communications and sensor technologies to help support this vision of pervasive healthcare. There are UK Government initiatives to support assisted living developments via the

Technology Strategy Board[12] and the UK Research Councils' Healthcare Technology theme [13]. The EU proposes to continue its Ambient Assisted Living Joint Programme (AALJP) [14].

However, there are significant barriers that must be overcome[d]. Most current systems, enterprise and diagnostic, including research systems, still operate in vertical silos, with little interoperability except between major systems. These limited interactions tend to be specified as part of the procurement contract. This will become more of an issue moving forward, where a plethora of new systems will become relevant to providing care. Even initial movements towards supporting informal care processes suffer from the same issues: concerning a single standalone application or closed service, focusing on a particular aspect of care, e.g. a monitoring infrastructure for a specific condition or a "panic button". It is said that a panic button service tends to restrict the movement of the elderly who are afraid of falling to its 50 metre range. This greatly impacts quality of life. Enabling such a person seamlessly to raise an alarm when inside the home or when out and about is the vision of an integrated service.

To realise pervasive healthcare, system components need to operate across application-level boundaries, to enable wide-ranging and customisable health and well-being services — which can seamlessly include assisted-living, formal and informal care processes. Interactions may occur across administrative domains, e.g. to include doctors, insurance companies, and so forth. Further, the same system components or services can be used for different purposes. For instance, heart rate data can be useful for the patient when exercising, for a General Practitioner (GP) for diagnosis, and for a paramedic in an emergency. Also, systems designed for other purposes could be integrated for certain individuals to provide health-relevant data, e.g. an application monitoring television viewing habits might have been designed for targeted advertising purposes, but can also contribute to a view on psychological well-being.

We now explore the specific requirements that the emerging care model imposes on supporting infrastructure.

3 Healthcare infrastructure requirements

As argued in §1, information underpins the emerging care model since information can be used and combined for a range of purposes. This leads to appropriate, timely interventions to achieve better health and well-being. Thus, from a systems-perspective, requirements concern data: production, consumption, communication and management. As technology becomes increasingly pervasive, there will be a rapid growth in the number of data sources/sinks (forming the *components* of systems and services). The use of these components will vary depending on user preferences and environmental context. Some will be relevant to clinical concerns, some will relate to patients and/or informal aspects, and some will be useful for both. Thus, the infrastructure that supports care must facilitate and provide data availability across a highly variable range of applications and services, as well as providing mechanisms for dynamic and flexible management.

Much of the responsibility for managing these concerns falls on middleware. By mediating the communications between system components, middleware "glues" them together. At present, most middleware focuses on enabling communication at the request of applications. Indeed, middleware abstracts various communication specifics but typically, applications still control how and when they connect to and interact with peers, brokers or services. In this section, we show how the emerging care environment extends this traditional role of middleware to include the dynamic composition of systems to support requirements in real-time.

3.1 Supporting data sources and monitoring

Healthcare is data driven; the more informed medical professionals, patients and their care community, the better the outcomes. *Big data* will become increasingly important to healthcare, where data and analytics can lead to improved diagnoses, decision making, treatments, and responses [15].

Monitoring people and their environments is central to the vision of personalised, preventative care. Sensing technologies will operate to generate rich representations of an individual's physiological state, and also to generate information concerning physical environments (which might relate to a static location, such as a particular room in a house, or the current location of a mobile user). This data can be filtered, aggregated and interpreted, thus driving positive steps for managing and improving health and well-being.

There are a wide range of data sources that can be used for patient monitoring. Data representing different aspects of state will be produced by various user devices, such as mobile phones, body and environmental sensors/actuators, as well as online services, databases, etc. The information used may include location, movement, ECG, environmental context (e.g., noise levels, temperature, weather, pollen levels, etc.), inference of social context, messages, calendar events, and many more. In addition, there are also knowledgebase sources aimed at the general public, such as NHS Direct [16], WebMD [17], etc., that can help determine the relevance of particular information, how to interpret results, and the appropriate interventions to take.

Note that personal and mobile technologies have specific data management and communication concerns, different from those of standard clinical systems (which tend to reduce to standard enterprise systems, often client-server). Further, each data source may be relevant to meeting a number of different care goals; ECG sensors and pulse-rate monitor outputs can be used by individuals, their GPs and paramedics under different circumstances. As argued in §2, a wealth of data not designed for specific health purposes is available and relevant for some individuals, such as (changes in) phone or TV usage.

Thus, it is particularly important that systems do not function within a single vertical silo or product ecosystem, whether through technical constraints (e.g. only operating with other products by the same producers) or functionality (e.g. only operating with other systems with the aim of targeting a particular goal). Each individual will differ on the systems they use, as determined by their conditions, care budget, physical environment, care community, etc. System components should be able to address a range of concerns, operating across products, services and management domains. As Figure 1 illustrates, middleware can integrate a wide range of systems and services.

Clearly some of these concerns align to those of the *internet of things* (IoT) [18], in which a myriad of devices, many representing everyday objects, are available online. This is because a vast number of data sources, sinks and services have the potential to be relevant to health and well-being. Indeed, the supporting infrastructure explored in this paper can certainly be used in a wider IoT-context; however, given the inherently stringent requirements of healthcare, the management and control capabilities of the infrastructure will be above and beyond the connectivity and interaction concerns of most IoT application scenarios.

Requirement 1. *Future healthcare requires a generic middleware capable of supporting current and future technology and the types of data produced.*

3.2 Supporting multiple communication paradigms

It is clear that healthcare is data driven. In a preventative care environment, pervasive systems offer functionality by means of system components *interacting*, exchanging data to realise system functionality. The supporting infrastructure must therefore be sufficiently flexible to support interoperability across a range of components in different scenarios. This imposes a number of considerations for the supporting middleware.

Firstly, the middleware must support a number of *interaction paradigms* (data exchange patterns). The vast majority of health-focused systems, like most systems in general, operate in a request/reply or Remote Procedure Call (RPC) manner. RPC interactions are important, for instance, to query a patient record, access a historical log of heart rate data to aid diagnosis, or to perform particular processing operations (e.g. calculating BMI). However, the emerging care environment will necessarily involve live data streams, the natural form of monitored data. Such data will be analysed to detect significant incidents and raise alerts, e.g. recognising a fall or a heart-attack and raising an alarm. Supporting infrastructure must therefore be able to support the range of interaction paradigms.

Given healthcare is data driven, it naturally maps to an event-based approach. An *event* can be defined as a data-rich encapsulation of some occurrence. Events can operate in a RPC manner, by one event encapsulating the request and another the response, and within a stream representing an individual data point. Events can also encapsulate a higher level of meaning and/or context. An event-based model makes sense for an emerging care environment, as it can represent everything from an alert (perceived emergency), data reading (e.g. clinical result, ECG sensor reading), health-record query/response, as well as more benign, system-relevant occurrences, such as a person entering a hospital, changing their privacy preferences, etc. The communication of events can greatly improve care efficiency, by reducing the need and reliance on manual, human-initiated actions.

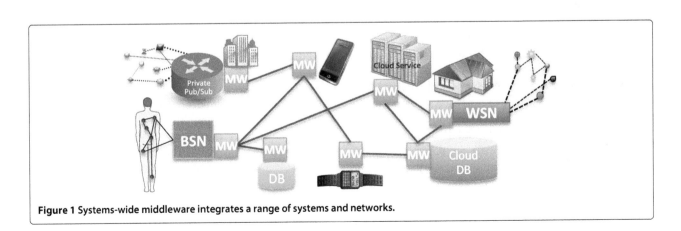

Figure 1 Systems-wide middleware integrates a range of systems and networks.

Events can also pave the way for flexible interaction paradigms. For instance, some components, particularly user-facing applications, will actively drive their interactions with others, e.g. a patient accessing their record entails a query to a particular server. Events can represent the connection, query, processing and/or response. This (RPC) is the predominant form of interaction today. Other components are passive, e.g. a body-sensor system focusing on producing vital-sign data, having no concern as to potential consumers.

It is clear that service discovery is a critical issue for infrastructure that aims to support the emerging care environment. In order to break the application silos prevalent in healthcare, it must be possible to discover the relevant data sources and sinks with which to interact dynamically, at runtime. This is particularly important in a pervasive healthcare scenario, as many interactions are not predetermined, but rather the relevant system components and forms of interaction are dictated by user preference and the particular circumstances. Thus, unlike much of today's communication which involves interactions with particular addresses, there must also be mechanisms for finding components based on the data they serve (and other attributes).

Event-based modelling also assists service discovery. If events are typed, it means service discovery (and hence interactions) are based on *the data they provide*, rather than a specific address and/or particular known systems. Further, type systems pave the way for further description of events and data that a particular component handles, as well as details about the component itself. This facilitates more formal descriptions, the semantics of which can assist in managing dynamism and heterogeneity [19].

Requirement 2. *Future healthcare requires a middleware capable of supporting a wide variety of communication patterns. Event-based middleware is most appropriate.*

3.3 Security-aware middleware

Health data information is inherently sensitive. Such concerns are exacerbated in pervasive computing environments, as these involve extremely detailed physiological and environmental data.

The current approach of encoding security policy within systems themselves is inadequate, as each system will vary in its definitions, capabilities, protection measures, etc. First, this hinders both usability and accountability leading to different login credentials for different systems, which many NHS doctors rightly complain about and often subvert by sharing sessions between users or taping passwords to machines. Secondly, the governance capabilities of one system might vary greatly from that of another.

Further, having security policy encoded in several systems for local enforcement, often repeated and represented in different ways, increases complexity and leads to mistakes. Therefore, governance regimes must apply *across* a range of technologies and locations.

Middleware deals with interactions, across systems. By making the middleware security aware, it means that governance policy can be generalised across a range of applications. For instance, the same policy can apply to a doctor's access to a Patient Record System, Hospital Administration System and a patient's live data-feed.

Therefore, it is important that middleware provides the mechanisms for enabling security. Specifically, this concerns: a) when and how components may communicate, b) the prevention of eavesdropping, c) information flow management, d) service discovery, e) audit.

The first entails access control policies, which can set up the privileges to enable connections, as well as actively intervene with respect to an interaction, e.g. forcing or closing connections when appropriate. To support this, components must be identifiable so correct privileges can be defined. It is important that the infrastructure supports encryption, to protect information in transit. Information flow management means having the ability to trace where information has flowed from and to where, and also to set certain constraints on its flow at runtime (e.g. it must not pass certain boundaries, or must touch certain systems before flowing to others)–see [20]. Sometimes uncovering the mere existence of a service associated with a patient may be damaging, e.g. services relating to sexual health; and as pervasive health will involve many personal services (surrounding an individual user), it is likely that many of these should be hidden from others. Thus, service discovery processes must also have the possibility of being regulated. Finally, audit gives visibility, which not only enables the ability to unpick the past, but also provides a normative form of behaviour control (the knowledge of being watched can prevent misuse). Audit is crucial to supporting governance in the health services. Such concerns are particularly important in this pervasive environment, as interactions will occur ad hoc, with potentially any source.

Requirement 3. *Future healthcare requires security-capable middleware.*

3.4 Supporting dynamic reconfiguration and adaptation

We have described how the emerging care environment entails many different system components interacting with each other in various ways, to achieve various outcomes. A rigid workflow is no longer an option and systems must be configured to meet individuals' needs. Further, it will not be possible to predetermine all the required components and interactions when tailoring to individuals. Thus, the role and functionality of middleware must be extended to include mechanisms to drive and control the interactions between components dynamically. To achieve this, it must be possible to specify and enforce, at the middleware level, how and when interactions should occur.

In practical terms, this means that there must be a mechanism for the middleware to reconfigure systems at runtime, adapting to circumstances as they occur. Given that middleware provides communication, this means the ability to manage runtime interactions. The key is the ability to control connections between components. At present, most middleware leaves this to the applications, as discussed above.

Enabling runtime connection management brings much flexibility; for example, to control the properties of an interaction (i.e. who is talking to whom), perhaps they should interact with someone else, perhaps some change in context implies a different set of interactions should take place, in addition to lower-level concerns, e.g. component failure. Initiating (or ceasing) an interaction is one aspect of this. Reconfiguration is also highly relevant to security, as it also involves changing the properties of the components themselves. Security policy will certainly be dynamic, and thus the system must be able to manage components and their interactions to properly effect this properly — a simple example may be "nobody may access my location information except in an emergency, when my doctor can". This means the location component must be able to enforce such a constraint (either directly, or by being 'told' what to do) as appropriate.

Such scenarios involve components relying on others to initiate and manage interactions on their behalf. Middleware must therefore support both direct and third-party initiated interactions. The latter is particularly important, bringing flexibility as it allows interactions to be managed outside component application-logic.

In summary, middleware for the emerging care environment must not only support the interoperability between systems, but also the means to drive those interactions, and reconfigure the system as appropriate to the circumstances. However, middleware provides merely the mechanism. It is *policy* that will manage and define these orchestrations, coordinating between the various components, often across application and administrative boundaries, when and where appropriate in order to meet particular functionality goals.

Requirement 4. *Future healthcare requires a middleware capable of effecting dynamic reconfiguration of system components in response to event-driven policy.*

The next section focuses on how policy can be expressed and enforced to meet this requirement.

4   The role of policy

Policy-based systems operate to effect some change (by taking actions) in response to particular happenings or circumstances. It is the role of policy to express these circumstances and actions.

Traditionally, the policy used by middleware targets network management, resource allocation and/or quality of service e.g. dealing with node failure, or allocating sufficient resources as requested by an application. However, as technology becomes increasingly pervasive and connected, it is important that policy encapsulates higher-level concerns, to bring about user-level goals. The emerging healthcare environment takes advantage of functionality coming from a number of different systems, used in different ways, by different people.

The focus is no longer solely on managing resources to serve a particular application requirement, but also on managing ranges of system components across application boundaries. More specifically, policy can trigger, or regulate user/application actions or behaviour, or react/respond to data generation and inference. Such actions are aspects of *coordination*, operating to mediate and orchestrate components to meet high-level functional goals. Coordination may include *actively* generating data or starting/stopping an interaction e.g. emergency action is to send an alert message to paramedics, and to set up a voice connection to a relative. Coordination may also enable (or prevent) some *potential* interaction, e.g. authorising a carer to access sensor devices when visiting a home.

Effecting such coordination requires the means to control components from *outside their application logic*. That is, enabling reconfigurations initiated by third-parties. This means that it is no longer the individual components that must manage and enforce policy, but rather, the components can be instructed (by those who are 'policy aware') to take specific actions to meet user goals. This is key to enabling systems to be user-driven, to coordinate component use to meet specific, individual concerns. It also allows new functional possibilities, where system components can be used/reused in various ways, not envisaged by the original developers. Clearly, this becomes increasingly important in a pervasive health environment which needs to account for individual preferences, user mobility entailing interactions in completely new environments, and the fact that care interventions are event-based - requiring response on certain happenings. All of these could result in different component compositions and interactions in different circumstances.

In summary, policy in a middleware context represents user specified goals and functional concerns, meeting these by operating to **a) bring functionality**, and **b) regulate/control** within and across applications, by reconfiguring the system/environment.

Figure 2 shows a policy-based reconfiguration for an emergency situation concerning an elderly male patient. In the general case, some of the patient's data is streamed to his phone to provide feedback on his current state. Data is also stored persistently to assist in diagnosis and prognosis. In an emergency situation, policy exists to bring help. This entails alerting his wife and the emergency services (A&E) of the incident; sending vital signs streams directly to A&E so they have a better indication of the situation and progression; and relaxing privilege constraints on various data sources to enable those providing help to access data that may assist.

4.1 Context and events

Context is crucial to policy enforcement; policy combined with context determines when various systems are brought together. Since the emerging care environment is user-centric, the infrastructure and environment must be tailored to individuals. Patients (with help from their support network), informal carers and medical professionals will all have preferences as to how the services supporting them are managed and controlled. These preferences form the *policy* that manages and governs systems environments.

In a pervasive care environment, context can be derived from many aspects: treatment/intervention regimes, prac-

titioner interactions, feedback from physiological (e.g. heart rate, movement) and environmental (e.g. location, pollution levels) sensors, interactions with clinical services (e.g. querying electronic health records), etc.

Policy is context-sensitive, e.g. a patient may say that nobody can access their location, except in an emergency, or "only my treating doctor can access my vital-signs data"; or a practitioner may only access clinical systems when they are physically present in a hospital ward.

Policy actions are tied to context, where changes in context lead to defined responses. For example, the results from a laboratory test will define a particular care pathway (treatment plan); detection of some anomaly leads to referral to a specialist. A timer might remind a patient to take medication, a doctor leaving a ward or going "off duty" might lose certain access rights, an alert might be sent on detection that someone has fallen, a doctor querying a health record must be authorised and audited.

As established above, healthcare is data driven, and thus is amenable to an *event-driven* systems approach. Information can generally be broken down into particular events (occurrences) that individually, or in aggregate, through event composition, represent some significant change in state. For example, an event might represent a single occurrence, such as someone entering a ward, taking a reading, taking medication, leaving home; or can be

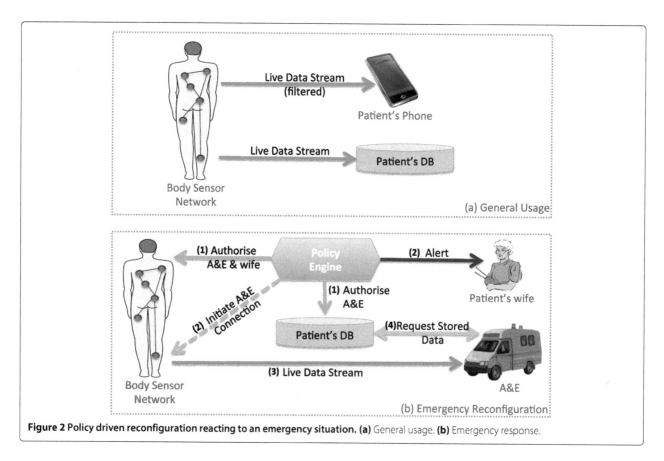

Figure 2 Policy driven reconfiguration reacting to an emergency situation. **(a)** General usage. **(b)** Emergency response.

composed with other events to represent some higher-level event, e.g. a significant rise in heart rate with a drop in blood pressure could mean a blood-loss event, or leaving home without taking medication should result in an extra reminder. Events can also represent concerns at various levels, e.g. systems level concerns such as a loss of connectivity, or higher-level concerns, such as a user action (e.g. pressing a panic button, initiating a query, entering a hospital). Policy rules can be defined to respond to these events, by dictating the components that could or should interact and the associated security and governance concerns.

In Figure 2, the reconfiguration is triggered by an emergency. This could be represented by a single event that may have been derived through analysis of the underlying sources, e.g. a rapid accelerometer change followed by some period without subsequent movement (GPS, indoor positioning) suggests a serious fall.

We have argued that an event-based representation of context is particularly suitable for emerging healthcare. Firstly, events facilitate a response. Aside from the more complex examples listed, in an environment where information is sensitive, even the most basic happenings (data access, sensor samples) can require some sort of response, such as being stored persistently or logged. Events provide well-defined hooks enabling response actions to occur. Secondly, an event-based approach facilitates context awareness in the middleware. Middleware concerns data communication, while events encapsulate data (e.g. a message can neatly encapsulate the data for an occurrence); thus rather than merely managing the conduit, the middleware can be active with respect to the data it handles.

4.2   Policy actions and engines

We have identified three general types of policy action relevant to healthcare middleware. These are:

> **Reconfiguration:** Taking a configuration action, such as initiating/removing a connection or changing the privilege of particular components.
> **Event production:** Generating an event to transfer some information, e.g. to raise an alert, inform of some happening, or simply respond to a query.
> **Policy Management:** Policies are contextual, thus a change in state might change the set of active (applicable) policies; e.g. a set of restrictive privacy policies may be relaxed in a medical emergency, making more components visible to an entity.

To effect these actions, a) the communications support in the middleware must allow, through the appropriate hooks and interfaces, reconfigurations to be initiated by third-parties, external to the application logic of the

components being affected; b) the components enforcing policy should be integrated into the same middleware, in order to receive events (context) to evaluate policy rules, produce new events, and so forth.

To manage policy, there is a requirement for system components that are dedicated to managing the policy process. *Policy engines* are services that encapsulate, and enforce, a set of policies. Policies often take the form of *Event-Condition-Action (ECA)* rules [21]. A policy engine will watch for particular events corresponding to its rule-set. On the occurrence of these events (which may be composite), the action selected by the policy rule will be executed. Some events might trigger a change in the active rules, while others might produce events, or issue the middleware with particular reconfiguration operations for particular components.

Figure 2 shows these actions. Event production policy enables the alerting of the patient's wife (step 2). The reconfiguration alters privileges on the database and sensor network (step 1), so that the wife can access sensor information (such as her husband's location) and A&E has the ability to access both the live sensor information, and the patient database in case historical information is relevant. A connection is then automatically established between the sensor network and A&E (step 3) so that A&E is immediately made aware of the patient's current state and ongoing progression. More generally, policy exists to relax privileges in an emergency situation to aid response; thus the policy engine will deactivate some of the more restrictive policies (not illustrated in the figure). A&E may then, manually, query the database for any relevant historical data (step 4), made possible by the earlier privilege reconfiguration (step 1).

4.3   Taking a policy-driven approach

So far, we have seen the following advantages from taking a policy driven approach. Firstly, it can break down vertical application silos. Operating outside application logic, and across system boundaries, it allows for more functionality and flexibility, enabling components to be used and reused in ways not previously possible. It allows for fine-grained personalisation and customisation, responsive to a range of different circumstances. Such functionality is crucial for systems supporting emerging care services.

In addition, this approach greatly reduces the burden on application/service developers, and the likelihood of errors. This is because developers need not account for individual users' requirements by having some mechanism for them to specify and encapsulate their preferences, and then, only from the concerns foreseen by the developers. Also, the burden of maintaining the details of all potential contexts in which components can operate is removed from developers. This facilitates component use/reuse, paving the way for new components to be integrated with minimal configuration. Otherwise, developers would need to enumerate all possible circumstances in which particular systems might be used, including the specifics of the operating environment, such as nearby components and interaction protocols.

The use of policy engines means fewer policy definition/enforcement points, which can simplify management. The alternative, of having each application maintain and enforce its own policy leads to policy gaps and inflexibility since systems will be limited in the policy functionality they provide. In practice, components would only provide for specified policy that they deem relevant. Further, trying to encapsulate cross-system functionality in each application itself is not only impractical, but is prone to errors, particularly as different applications may have different mechanisms for accounting for preferences. All of this is a major concern in healthcare where governance is central.

There will be a number of policy engines operating simultaneously within various environments. Issues of conflict arising from competing engines poses a significant challenge, and requires careful consideration. However, the scope and reach of the policy engines can lead to a natural resolution. In practice, a policy engine should only effect actions on components that authorise it to do so, which models the real-world in the sense that only those who 'own' an entity can control it. This inherently limits the scope for conflict. For example, there may be a policy engine managing a hospital ward, and one on a doctor's phone. The ward's engine will set the baseline for interaction, e.g. who can access the various monitoring equipment, whereas the doctor's engine will reflect the doctor's individual preferences regarding when it connects to particular components within the ward. Having an engine that encapsulates policy aids policy management. The alternative is to have policy fragmented among different components, using and limited by the expression mechanism of each.

Given that policy entails some components controlling others, trust becomes an issue. To function effectively, there needs to be the ability to regulate who can access, and reconfigure, particular components in specified circumstances. And such regulation must, itself, be dynamically reconfigurable. Further, there is often the requirement for audit, not only of the actions taken but also the policy applied. Such concerns will vary depending on the circumstances and environment. Indeed, issues of trust can be encoded in policy, which if the middleware supplies appropriate security/governance mechanisms, can be implemented through similar mechanisms to effect control over management processes.

Overhead is another concern of policy-based systems. Given that policy enforcement involves rule evaluation, based on particular events (communicated by data flows),

which also involve reconfigurations, there will naturally be some impact on performance. However, this must be considered with respect to the flexibility of the approach. We explore this more in §7.3.

4.4 Policy summary

Middleware is required that enables policy to coordinate the components in the system. Policy-enforcing middleware allows control *across components*, irrespective of their individual logic. This is crucial as it enables user goals to drive the system, bringing components together in particular circumstances to meet users' requirements. It enables components to be used/reused for a number of purposes, facilitates personalisation/customisation, and naturally helps to group related policy through dedicated policy components.

From the middleware perspective, this approach moves middleware beyond its traditional role of enabling communication. Instead, it provides the ability for components to be managed by third parties, and means that middleware can actively drive *how* and *when* communication occurs.

This is important for emerging healthcare, which requires a pervasive systems environment. A policy-driven approach allows flexible functionality, operating across systems, tailored to individuals, in order to effect a range of health-related goals.

5 Moving towards the vision

So far, we have outlined the requirements that the emerging model of healthcare imposes on supporting infrastructure, arguing for a policy-based middleware with dynamic, third-party initiated reconfigurability. There is no single solution or approach that addresses all these challenges. However, there has been work in a number of areas that provides a solid foundation on which to build. Rather than providing an exhaustive literature review, we instead highlight general areas of relevant systems research and their fit within the broader vision of pervasive health.

We have reached these requirements for future middleware through focussing on the healthcare domain. It is interesting to note the overlap with work on generic requirements for emerging middleware, as explored in FOME (Future of Middleware) [22]. For the healthcare domain we concur with the findings of FOME for future complex and dependable systems and our work begins to address the highlighted challenges, in a targeted manner—see §6.

5.1 Service composition and adaptive middleware

Reconfigurable middleware is an area of much research. Middleware that allows configuration and customisation is generally termed *adaptive* (see [23]) or *reflective* (see [24]). Such middleware exposes the current system configuration and state to enable reconfiguration based on inspection. Reconfigurations may come from applications themselves, or involve managing lower-level concerns (e.g. the network) to fulfil application resource or quality of service requirements. Work in this area clearly relevant to pervasive healthcare, reconfiguring lower-level systems concerns to meet application requirements. However, there is also the need for higher-level controls through policy, not only to serve application requirements, but to work within and across a range of applications to meet users' functional goals.

Related is *service composition* middleware (SC) (see [25]), which combines services to provide particular functionality. This involves taking an application-level task (request) and mapping it to a combination of services [26]. SC considers resource allocation and task distribution and ordering in response to application-specific requests or goals. Again, SC is highly relevant, however healthcare requires the means to *directly control* system components. In a general policy-based middleware, meeting the goals of service composition is only one of the targets that policy could address.

Given the trend towards the internet of things, some recent work considers service composition at scale [27]. Certainly, over time the line will blur between infrastructure for supporting care, and that for more general concerns; however, for the moment, the nature of healthcare imposes specific requirements that must be directly accounted for (§3.1).

Work in this area is ongoing. The authors of [28] are concerned with dependable systems and highlight "better coordination facilities" as a topic for future research. The six research challenges for middleware for future complex systems addressed in [29] include "deriving valid, high-performance configurations of highly configurable infrastructure platforms" and "static configuration and dynamic reconfiguration".

5.2 Sensor networks

Sensor networks (SNs) are well researched, with much literature focusing on networking, addressing the constraints imposed by devices and the operating environment. A lot of work takes place in the context of wireless sensor networks [30], and to a lesser extent body sensor networks [31]. The focus is low-level, considering sensor nodes/devices and their specifics, including data acquisition, resource management (power, memory, and other hardware constraints), node placement, failures, routing protocols, code migration/deployment, etc. [30,32]. *Data aggregation* [33] concerns how and when to aggregate and fuse data across nodes to improve efficiency and data richness. Some recent work considers network abstractions and virtualisations [34,35]. Sensors provide much important data for pervasive healthcare. It is, however,

explicitly recognised that sensor networks must be integrated into a broader system infrastructure [32,35]. Thus, middleware aiming to support emerging healthcare must be able to incorporate (or interface with) a range of sensors and sensor networks (see requirement 1, §3.1). This not only allows sensor data to be processed and consumed throughout the system, but also allows policy to influence sensor network behaviour, such as prioritising the data flows that pertain to an emergency situation.

Generally, our insight is that for future health services, it is not just the infrastructure and resources underlying applications and services that must be configured and managed, but also the applications and services themselves, in terms of how and when they (inter)operate. Configuration at this higher-level is encapsulated by user-defined policy — which can operate across applications, as well as manage lower-level concerns on behalf of applications. The work in adaptive, reflective and SC systems is of direct relevance to the latter, and provides useful insight into realising the former.

5.3 Policy-based systems

There is work that considers high-level policy enforcement [36]. However, these policy models typically involve imposing a particular structure on the environment; for instance, defining entities as managed objects e.g. the *self-managed cells* of *Ponder2* [37], the grouping of agents with trusted controllers [38], and/or other constraints, e.g. a particular form of interaction [39-41] (see §5.5). Clearly, policy specification and enforcement specifics are relevant; however, the nature of pervasive healthcare requires systems to be open and flexible. Thus, any policy-based middleware must deliberately avoid imposing modelling, design or communication constraints such that any structuring is dictated by user and usage requirements.

Reasoning about policy is difficult, especially about consistency when policy is decentralised. A formalism is proposed in [35] which allows for reasoning about access control, especially relating to emergency management.

5.4 Representing context

Policy is contextual, in that it is enforced in particular circumstances. It follows that richer representations of state entail more flexible policy. There are a number of contextual/reasoning models that enable complex state representations [42,43], which in pervasive environments often involve combining and processing data across many underlying sources. Richer and complex state models provide the means for more powerful, granular and expressive policy rules, which allows for policy that better represents particular healthcare concerns. If the context model is well structured, it enables analysis and reasoning over policy behaviours, useful for determining operational semantics, potential policy (or contextual) errors or omissions—which one can imagine would be most useful for health services.

Managing context in emerging systems is difficult, due to its inherent dynamic and heterogenous nature. An ontological approach presents a promising way forward [19], as it enables modelling of context, message types, namespaces, etc. based on semantic meaning. This can assist managing dynamism and reconfigurablity, for example the ability to dynamically negotiate a method for system interoperability at runtime [44]. Such work directly supports the policy driven approach we advocate, as policy will impose the constraints and circumstances for facilitating an interaction, in addition to enabling direct interventions to trigger system changes. However, managing semantics is not without its challenges [45], for example agreeing a common vocabulary/coding scheme. This is a longstanding problem even in the more specialist clinical care domain [46]; such concerns will likely be exacerbated by integrating informal care scenarios.

5.5 Communication specifics

Regarding communication (see requirement 2, §3.2), the design and optimisation of interaction paradigms, such as RPC and pub/sub (see [47]) have been well researched. However, we see that much healthcare infrastructure accounts only for a single form of interaction, often RPC. It is important that the supporting middleware enables *both* request-reply and stream-based communication, which is important to serving a range of application requirements.

With respect to communication, there is some work that considers integrating policy into pub/sub infrastructure [40,41,48], for enforcement throughout a broker network. Pub/sub, however, is inappropriate as the sole means of communication for emerging healthcare, as it provides only for stream-based interactions (request-reply is cumbersome), and the layer of indirection (event-bus) favours anonymous interactions through a shared communication channel, which is inappropriate for healthcare as it raises identity, security and policy enforcement concerns.

6 SBUS: Middleware towards this aim

Having argued the need for a policy-based approach, we now introduce *SBUS* [49], a middleware designed and developed to support the requirements of emerging healthcare. SBUS provides an open systems framework for securely reconfigurable components. Its main contribution lies in its support for policy-driven reconfiguration of components, and management of their interactions, with fully decentralised management. This enables policy to represent high-level concerns, to operate across applications to achieve users' functional goals.

Here, we present SBUS as a proof-of-concept to indicate of the concepts, considerations, and design processes for a policy-based approach.[e] The focus is on policy for directly controlling components and their interactions; in moving to wider solutions, such functionality will complement other work, e.g. that concerning contextual representation.

In order to indicate the practicalities of policy-driven healthcare infrastructure, we now provide an overview of SBUS functionality, and follow by describing the means for policy enforcement.

6.1 SBUS architecture (requirement 1, §3.1)

SBUS aims to provide the mechanisms for building and managing complex systems environments. As such, there is deliberately no particular structure imposed on system design. Its design aim is openness and flexibility, to provide the building blocks to enable any structuring required by the user, of applications or the operating environment.

In line with this, and to account for the variability and requirements of the emerging care environment, the architecture allows incorporation of other systems, such as closed or proprietary networks, wireless and body sensor networks and other systems that manage device and resource constraints in specific operating environments. This, of course, requires *gateway* components to export data outside the subnet's environment (see Figure 1). Closed or proprietary sensor networks usually provide this gateway functionality [32].

6.2 Communication (requirements 1, §3.1 and 2, §3.2)

SBUS is a data-centric communications middleware. Data is encapsulated within a *message* of a specific type. A messaging approach suits healthcare, as a message can neatly encapsulate details of an event.

The basic unit in SBUS is a *component*: an SBUS-enabled process (i.e. an application, service, or part thereof) that uses the middleware to manage its communication. Each component has a number of *endpoints*, which can be thought of as typed communication ports. The endpoints of different components are connected *(mapped)* together to enable communication (Figure 3).

Each endpoint is associated with a schema (in *LITMUS* [50]) describing the message type(s) it handles. Communication is type safe, the middleware ensuring that mappings only occur between compatible endpoints, i.e. that schema and interaction modes agree, and messages correspond to the schema for that mapping. Type identifiers (hashes) are encoded to make messages self identifying, removing the need for a central type authority. Content-based filters can be imposed on mappings to control message flows.

It is important for healthcare applications that the infrastructure supports a range of interaction paradigms.

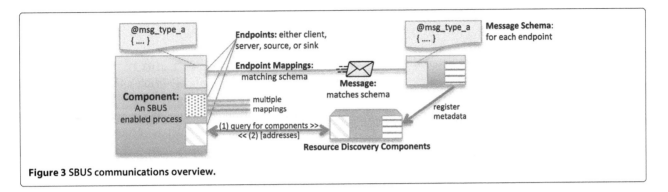

Figure 3 SBUS communications overview.

Thus, SBUS was designed to support client/server *and* stream-based interactions. An endpoint takes an *interaction mode*: either a *client* (the query issuer) or *server* (returning a result); or for stream communications, either a *source* (producer) or *sink* (consumer). Figure 4 illustrates the directly supported interaction paradigms. Mappings only occur between endpoints with corresponding types and interaction modes, i.e. sources with sinks (possibly one-to-many), or clients with servers.

Communication is naturally peer-to-peer and thus the infrastructure is inherently decentralised. Again, this is to provide the building blocks; more complex interaction models can be built where required. For instance, it is simple to implement pub/sub (event-bus) functionality and message-queue brokers to enable indirect and asynchronous communication. Such flexibility is important in supporting pervasive healthcare.

6.2.1 Resource discovery

We have described how resource discovery is a significant concern for emerging healthcare, due to the variability of the computing environment. Components (including policy engines) must be able to find dynamically the appropriate components to interact with, when and where necessary.

For a connection, one requires the network address of the component with which to interact. *Resource Discovery Components* (RDCs) assist by maintaining a directory of active (registered) components in the environment. A component registers with an RDC so it is discoverable by others. The RDC provides a lookup service returning the addresses for components who match a query, somewhat similar to DNS. Components register their *metadata* with RDCs—each describing itself, its functionality, and data handled—thus enabling powerful lookup queries.

The lookup query constraints tend towards two categories:

> **Identity:** Concerns component specifics, such as its class (named-type), instance-name, author, owner, or public key (i.e. when seeking one specific component).
> **Data:** Concerns the data that the component offers, based on endpoint types, interaction modes, etc.

The purpose of the lookup queries is to facilitate the *flexible* discovery of relevant components at runtime, based on the data they serve, aspects of their identity, or some combination thereof. Thus such constraints can apply in combination. The constraints are encapsulated within a mapping operation, so that rather than connection requests necessarily being address-based, they can also be metadata-based. Such queries could look for a component with a particular name (of a particular public key), or any component serving a particular video data, or a component owned by 'Ward 1' that serves patient administration data, etc.

For further flexibility, we have also explored *schema negotiation*, which aims to enable communication bet-

Paradigm:	one-shot	push-stream	rpc	conversation	pull-stream
Endpoints:	source / sink	source / sink	client / server	client / server	sink / source

Figure 4 SBUS interaction paradigms, encapsulating both stream and client-server based interactions.

ween components whose endpoint type schemas only partially match (see [49] for details). This involves discovery query operators that compare of the endpoint type structures of a potential connection, to determine whether a connection can be agreed. If so, SBUS will automatically convert incoming messages into the format the component expects.

This represents only our initial steps regarding negotiation[f], requiring guidance of the attributes to negotiate. The ability to take account of event semantics enables more powerful, automated interoperability functionality [19]. However, as our initial focus is on SBUS specifics, our approach is an attempt to balance the advantages of strong typing with the flexibility required for dealing with different environments. Such functionality is useful for policy designers who have some knowledge about the components needing to interact; allowing communication that would not otherwise be possible[g]. This is not unrealistic, as there may be some knowledge of the components that could interact; for instance, a user buying new sensor kit, or a hospital by way of procurement.

There may be any number of RDCs in an operating environment. RDCs may be federated and replicate information, e.g. across a national health service. Others may operate within a specific scope, dealing only with a particular set of components, such as those in a patient's house. Again, it is important not to impose any structure on the operating environment; but rather to allow any structuring to come from user requirements. For instance, there may be a number of RDCs in the same environment, several cooperating to manage the lower-level concerns for components of a large-scale distributed application, and one to handle the user-facing services.

The location of an RDC must be known/discoverable: perhaps by running at a well-known address; infrastructure providing the address on connection (e.g. through DHCP options at a low-level, or a policy-engine at a higher level); or by prior knowledge if deliberately obscured. A component maintains a list of RDCs with which it interacts, which is changeable at runtime.

SBUS is decentralised, RDCs exist only to aid interactions. Discovery without RDCs is through *inspection*, where a component is probed to retrieve information via its endpoints and connected peers, enabling service discovery by trawling a connectivity graph. This is useful when an RDC is unavailable, or inappropriate.

To reiterate, SBUS aims to provide a number of different discovery capabilities that can be leveraged as appropriate, in an attempt to address the inherent variability of the emerging systems environment.

SBUS also provides mechanisms to manage disconnections and failures, the technical specifics are given in [49]. We mention this as dynamic reconfiguration around failures are crucial for pervasive health, for example, in

providing a seamless/continuous service to the sick and vulnerable.

6.3 Security (requirement 3, of §3.3)

The SBUS security model enables the protection and control of middleware operations. These complement application-specific security mechanisms, e.g. clinician log-on services, or biometric protection for mobile devices.

6.3.1 Transmission

Given SBUS is peer-to-peer, control is intuitive because communication is directed. This differs from an event-bus approach where a shared communication channel potentially allows many components to see the same message. To protect the data (messages) and metadata (e.g. protocol state) from eavesdropping at lower network layers, *Transport Layer Security (TLS)* [51] is used. Before any SBUS communication, components exchange certificates, which after validation are used to create a secure communication channel.

6.3.2 Access Control

Each component maintains an *access control list (ACL)* for each endpoint describing the components that may connect. A mapping is established only if each peer authorises the other.

All privileges can be dynamically changed; when this occurs, all mappings are examined to determine whether they remain authorised—if not, the connection is closed.

Access control policy is defined for a component by its class (self-described type), instance name and/or public key. This enables a range of specificity, allowing security policy and component discovery queries to apply to a particular component, or a group. Coupling component identity to certificates enables strong authentication, which is important to ensure that the access control policy is applied to the correct components.

The result is a regulated namespace, which is appropriate for healthcare; e.g. if the name of the component should encapsulate a patient-ID, instance names must be governed. This is important in environments such as healthcare where data is inherently sensitive. If components do not specify a certificate, and thus cannot be authenticated, by default they may only interact with remote endpoints without access control constraints (world-readable).

Of course, the ACL can be extended to incorporate other component metadata or even other authentication systems.

Filtering: There are cases where a particular component should only receive *some* of the messages emitted from an endpoint. To effect this, filters can be imposed (by parties external to the communication) on a mapping to select the messages transmitted. In this way, the filter acts as an authorisation rule evaluated in the context of each message, based on its content.

Protecting discovery: There will be instances where even the existence of a component may be sensitive, e.g. services relating to sexual health. A component can avoid being discovered, by electing (or being told) not to register with an RDC. However, this may preclude important interactions. An RDC maintains access control policy to dictate the components that may register and query, which is useful where an RDC is responsible for a particular grouping. However, more flexible, granular controls are also required. As such, the local RDC mirrors (where appropriate) the ACLs of its registered components. These are used to filter the results of a discovery query, so that only details of accessible components are returned by a query.

Discovery by inspection can reveal sensitive information. For this, SBUS provides two forms of control. First, a component maintains access control policy restricting the components that may inspect it. Secondly, a component can dictate whether its existence is revealed to others in an inspection operation.

Though *security by obscurity*, these measures help prevent inadvertent discovery of services, providing an extra hurdle for the malicious. Of course, the access control regime still protects the data and component metadata even if an address is known.

6.4 Reconfiguration (requirement 4, §3.4)

Runtime reconfiguration is crucial to supporting emerging health services, and was the fundamental concern in designing SBUS. Table 1 presents some key functions of the SBUS reconfiguration API, which a component uses to change its state. SBUS ensures that all related operations are performed, e.g. that removing a privilege closes connections that are no longer authorised, and that the RDC is informed of the privilege change.

Table 1 SBUS reconfiguration functions

`map(map_params)`	Establishes a mapping between endpoints.
`unmap(map_params)`	Terminates a mapping.
`divert(divert_params)`	Moves an endpoint's mapping(s) to another component.
`subscribe(filter)`	Changes a mapping's content-based filter(s).
`privilege(ac_policy)`	Alters an endpoint(s)' access control policy.
`rdc_address(addresses)`	Changes the RDC(s) that a component uses.

6.4.1 *Third-party initiated reconfiguration*

A key contribution of SBUS is that it enables third-party initiated, or remote reconfiguration, where a component effectively 'invokes' the SBUS operations of another. This makes it possible to instruct components on how and when to behave; e.g. to map or unmap, update privileges, apply filters, etc.

Such functionality is implemented through *control* messages. Each component has a set of default control endpoints that directly correspond to the reconfiguration API (Table 1). If a component receives a control message, it will perform the relevant operation according to the control message's parameters; this is equivalent to self-invocation of the operation. The security mechanisms ensure that control messages are only acted on when issued by appropriately trusted peers.

Figure 5 illustrates a component instructing another to undertake a mapping (step 1). Here the control message forces an RDC query (step 2), though passing the network address avoids this step. The component, as instructed, then establishes the mapping (step 3).

It is this capability that enables powerful and flexible policy enforcement. Further, as any component can influence another, it allows decentralised control. Such an approach is crucial to realising the vision of pervasive healthcare (for example, it underpins the functionality of Figure 2). This is because it enables application-independent support, where data and components may be used for a number of purposes; at a high-level to meet user and application-level goals, as well as at the system level, for service composition, connection management, etc.

7 Policy enforcement

Policy encodes particular goals. Its role is to regulate, coordinate, control and manage a system, by performing actions in the particular circumstances. It is SBUS' third-party reconfiguration capability that paves the way for application-independent and cross-application policy enforcement. That is, policy actions achieve health-related goals through executing SBUS reconfiguration operations.

In §4 we described the general categories of policy actions relevant to care, which in SBUS include: *reconfiguration*, involving the management of components, e.g. altering mappings, privileges, and filters; *messaging*—generating and transmitting new events and alerts; and *policy management* selecting (or de/activating) the applicable ruleset.

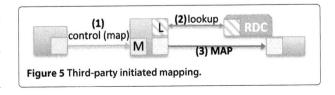

Figure 5 Third-party initiated mapping.

SBUS provides the mechanism for any component to (potentially) affect another. This means, for example, a distributed application can control its components as it deems appropriate. However, as discussed in §4, to assist in managing complex environments and interactions, and to deal with cross-application concerns, it is useful to have components dedicated to policy specifics.

To explore policy enforcement, we implemented two policy engines that aim at different environments. One approach was to integrate policy engine functionality into a relational database, the other more lightweight, designed to run on a mobile device. The reasoning was to demonstrate a powerful, expressive policy engine, suitable for managing the components belonging to a particular systems environment such as a hospital, surgery or patient's home; while the mobile policy engine encapsulates an individual's preferences, to govern the interactions between their mobile device and components in their surroundings.

Both approaches defined policy in ECA rules, where each rule embodies a specific action, to be applied in response to a particular happening. Thus, high-level policy is encoded, and the response automatically effected, through a set of rules.

7.1 Database policy engine

Databases are highly amenable to policy enforcement capabilities. Firstly, databases operate across applications, enabling indirect and asynchronous communication between components. More importantly, systems require persistence. Coupling policy enforcing capabilities with databases allows policy to leverage the rich representation of state and context encapsulated within the datastore.

We built policy engine functionality into a database by first making the database an SBUS component (see [49]). Relations were defined between endpoints and table schemata, so that a database tuple converts (in a type-safe manner) to an SBUS message and vice-versa to enable the sending and receiving of messages. Policy rules were then implemented as database *triggers* (ECA rules), where the enforcement conditions referenced tables—perhaps corresponding to an endpoint (incoming message), or a more complex state representation. The database rules engine would then enforce these on the relevant happening, taking the defined action which could include creating and transmitting a message, altering the triggers to change the active policy set, updating state representations by updating/persisting data, or effecting a reconfiguration through sending SBUS control messages.

Initially, the database policy engine was developed for managing particular environments, for instance, to control interactions between systems (and people) perhaps within a hospital, particular ward, or patient home. This is because a database requires a server, and thus is part of a relatively fixed infrastructure. However, with the increase in the availability and prevalence of cloud services, such an engine could also facilitate policy enforcement at a number of locations.

7.2 Mobility: lightweight engines

Some components are mobile, moving between different operating environments and infrastructures; e.g. from leaving a car to entering a hospital. Policy engines can enforce user preferences to manage and govern the interactions with the particular environment, e.g. automatically connecting a nurse to a patient's vital-signs sensor when entering their home.

We implemented a lightweight policy engine on Android to manage the interactions between components on the device in its physical environment. Developed as a service component, it maintains a simple rules engine, where rules can be defined to execute on particular events. Though the engine could respond to any event, our focus was changes in location. On moving to a new environment, as determined by OS-events (e.g. connecting to a new network) or higher-level event definitions (e.g. sensor-data indicating a location change), the service automatically applies rules to manage and dis/connect components (typically those on the device with those in physical proximity) as appropriate.

7.3 Policy considerations

Since policy actions are triggered by changes in state, a policy engine needs the ability to detect, or be told of, state changes relevant to the policies it is responsible for enforcing. Our approach leverages the existing messaging capability to also provide both the representation of context (as events) and policy actions (as messages and reconfiguration instructions through control messages). Such an approach precludes the need to implement any specific policy layers, or particular constraints over the infrastructure and its design. Policy engines are components like any other and render the middleware policy and context aware.

The event processing capabilities of the middleware directly impact the flexibility and expressiveness of the policy rules. That is, a system only capable of dealing with primitive events is far more limited than one employing *composite events* [52] or other context modelling techniques [42] that can correlate and compose events within and across message streams. Such capabilities may be built into policy engines, and/or implemented in other components (such as sensor gateways) that report the relevant state transitions to policy engines.

Without event semantics, higher-level components would need to understand and interpret the data. Reasoning over events and event flows facilitates data transformation and informed choices, e.g. in service discovery. As §5.4 mentions, while the role of semantics is clear, it remains an ongoing challenge in healthcare. Interoperability is difficult, even between the two prominent clinical coding schemes [53]: HL7 [54], and SNOMED [55]. There are groups dedicated to such issues, including OpenEHR [56] (see also [57]), and Integrating the Healthcare Enterprise [58], though these focus on the clinical perspective. Issues of semantics compound in the pervasive health environment, given the enormous range of potential components, interactions, and usage scenarios.

Policy conflict is a concern, particularly in an environment with dynamically changing users and services, and with numerous policy engines. We have previously considered issues of conflict detection and resolution for trigger-based policy [59]. Thus far we have encountered few conflicts primarily because in practice, there will be a number of policy engines (operating within different scopes)—likely linked to component/infrastructure ownership—each having specific concerns. For instance, a policy engine might manage the components in an hospital ward; policies relating to that ward will be centrally defined. Similarly, a user will have their own policies that dictate how the local components (on their phone) interact with an environment; e.g. a doctor may wish to interact with components in a ward, but this will only be with those components that the environment (here, the ward's policy engine) authorises.

Note that our focus thus far has been generic, providing the mechanism for policy enforcement that is capable of effecting a wide range of goals. Further work is required to explore effective mechanisms (interfaces) for users to author policy. In practice, policy authoring and rule derivation will necessarily be determined by the applications being targeted, depending on likely users, components, etc. For more on policy specification issues, see [60].

There is generally a tradeoff between flexibility and efficiency. Thus, one intuitively expects policy enforcement to entail performance overheads. This is because such an approach involves policy engines, and the associated monitoring of state changes, evaluating policies and taking relevant actions. Firstly, it is important to note that healthcare presents an environment that operates at human speed. Therefore, in many situations, any degree of automatic response will be more than adequate, especially given the status-quo in which interventions tend to be manual, with little automated assistance, e.g. using a pager or telephone.

We explored some overheads with respect to policy enforcement—see [49] for details of the experiments—which indicate the practicality of policy-based coordination, and third-party initiated reconfiguration. We found

for a particular scenario involving the database policy engine, that the overheads of policy enforcement were lost in the network variability when clients components connected through a particular wireless network; with a small statistically significant overhead (~5 ms out of a ~35 ms operation) for the same scenario where components connected through a particular Ethernet network. This is important, given wireless networks will be a predominant medium for communication in pervasive care environments. Our Android implementation, for a particular scenario, was significantly slower at rule evaluation for a particular scenario (~75 ms to enforce a policy, cf. ~12.5 ms for the database policy engine).

We mention these results as they indicate that performance will depend on the underlying infrastructure, and that policy may not necessarily introduce a tangible overhead. Ultimately, any timing information will vary according to the implementation and the environment: depending on factors such as the physical infrastructure, OS (e.g. Android), network load, cross-traffic, database size, message sizes/frequency, number of rules, users and components, etc.

Such factors must be considered by those designing for emerging care environments, if their system has specific performance requirements. For example, systems that require a particular service level, e.g. a pacemaker system, may be better developed as a bespoke, closed system to ensure the performance necessary for safety. Interfaces (or gateways) can still provide for integration of the specialist system with the general systems environment, for non time-critical operations (e.g. parameter tweaking). However, many health interventions occur minutes or even hours after incident detection; certainly, an automated response is a movement in the right direction. Indeed, our particular experiments resulted in subsecond functionality (see [49]), which opens up real healthcare possibilities.

The focus of our policy work is to bring together systems in a more general manner, focusing on flexibility and adaptability to bring functionality and efficiencies previously not available.

8 Summary and concluding remarks

Healthcare is undergoing an evolution, driven and supported by the health profession, government initiatives and technological innovation. The healthcare systems environment will thus involve an increasing number of applications, systems and services. Users, be they clinical, informal carers or patients, will leverage these in various ways, to provide a number of different health outcomes relevant to their preferences and circumstances.

Information, communication and management capabilities underpin the vision of pervasive, preventative and personalised healthcare. In this paper we have presented and discussed the requirements for middleware to support this. We see the open challenges as follows:

1. The need to incorporate existing and future sensor technologies into a generic system architecture.
2. The need to move towards an open systems approach by developing applications without embedded policy and predefined interactions.
3. The need to support policy authoring on behalf of many categories of individuals.
4. The need to develop an event-based middleware architecture to achieve:

   - Response to changes in people's and environmental contexts.
   - Support for a wide range of communication patterns.
   - Support for policy engines as middleware service components.
   - Support for policy-driven, dynamic reconfiguration of components by third parties, when authorised.
   - Support for security and privacy.

Our work on the SBUS middleware infrastructure and policy engines demonstrates the feasibility of this open systems approach. This moves beyond providing 'systems-level-glue' to actively driving new functional possibilities through high-level, user-specified preferences, thus making the vision of pervasive, preventative and personalised healthcare a real possibility.

Endnotes

[a] See http://systems.hscic.gov.uk (21 Mar 2014) for a flavour of the many systems in use by the National Health Service (UK).

[b] For background information and examples, see [61] and [62].

[c] For specifics, see http://systems.hscic.gov.uk (21 Mar 2014).

[d] See [63] for a roadmap of general issues concerning assisted living.

[e] See [49] for further technical details on SBUS.

[f] See [64] for a survey of various techniques.

[g] By policy designers we mean those who manage the environment or user preferences and/or system deployment—not general application developers.

Competing interests
The authors declare that they have no competing interests.

Authors' contributions
This article represents our work and experience over many years in infrastructure for supporting health services. Both authors contributed with respect to the concepts, technical work and text provided in this paper, and both have read and approved the final manuscript.

Acknowledgements
We acknowledge the support of the UK Technology Strategy Board and the Engineering and Physical Sciences Research Council for the PAL project, grant TP/AN072C, 2009-12.

References

1. World Health Organisation, US National Institute of Aging (2011) Global health and ageing. http://www.who.int/ageing/publications/global_health/en/. Accessed 30 Apr 2014
2. Department of Health, (UK) (2004) Improving Chronic Disease Management. http://webarchive.nationalarchives.gov.uk/+/www.dh.gov.uk/en/Publicationsandstatistics/Bulletins/GPbulletin/Browsable/DH_4842264. Accessed 30 Apr 2014
3. World Health Organisation (2002) Innovative Care for Chronic Conditions. http://www.who.int/diabetes/publications/icccreport/en/. Accessed 30 Apr 2014
4. Department of Health, (UK) (2009) NHS 2010–2015: from good to great. Preventative, people-centred, productive. http://webarchive.nationalarchives.gov.uk/+/www.dh.gov.uk/en/publicationsandstatistics/publications/publicationspolicyandguidance/dh_109876. Accessed 30 Apr 2014
5. Hersh WR (2002) Medical informatics: improving health care through information. J Am Med Assoc 288(16): 1955–1958
6. Department of Health (2006) Supporting people with long term conditions to self care. http://webarchive.nationalarchives.gov.uk/+/dh.gov.uk/en/publicationsandstatistics/publications/publicationspolicyandguidance/dh_4130725. Accessed 30 Apr 2014
7. European Science Foundation (2012) Personalised Medicine for the European Citizen. http://www.esf.org/coordinating-research/forward-looks/biomedical-sciences-med/current-forward-looks-in-biomedical-sciences/personalised-medicine-for-the-european-citizen.html. Accessed 30 Apr 2014
8. Franko OI, Tirrell TF (2012) Smartphone app use among medical providers in ACGME training programs. J Med Syst 36(5): 3135–3139
9. Mihailidis A, Bardram JE (2010) Pervasive Computing in Healthcare. CRC Press, FL, USA
10. Bernstein PA (1996) Middleware: a model for distributed system services. Commun ACM 39(2): 86–98
11. Payne KFB, Wharrad H, Watts K (2012) Smartphone and medical related app use among medical students and junior doctors in the United Kingdom (UK): a regional survey. BMC Med Inform Decis Mak 12: 121
12. Healthcare Technology Strategy Board. http://www.innovateuk.org/healthcare. Accessed 21 Mar 2014
13. EPSRC Research Portfolio Themes. http://www.epsrc.ac.uk/research/ourportfolio/themes. Accessed 21 Mar 2014
14. Ambient Assisted Living JointProgramme Europe. http://www.aal-europe.eu. Accessed 21 Mar 2014
15. Groves P, Kayyali B, Knott D, Van Kuiken S (2013) The Big, Data Revolution in Healthcare: Accelerating Value and Innovation. McKinsey Global Institute, New York
16. NHS Direct. http://webarchive.nationalarchives.gov.uk/20140220132333/http:/www.nhsdirect.nhs.uk/. Accessed 21 Mar 2014
17. WebMDmobile. http://www.webmd.com. Accessed 21 Mar 2014
18. Mattern F, Floerkemeier C (2010) From the internet of computers to the internet of things In: From Active, Data Management to Event-Based Systems and More. Springer, Berlin, Heidelberg, pp 242–259
19. Blair GS, Bennaceur A, Georgantas N, Grace P, Issarny V, Nundloll V, Paolucci M (2011) The Role of Ontologies in Emergent Middleware: Supporting Interoperability in Complex Distributed Systems In: ACM/IFIP/USENIX Middleware 2011, LNCS 7049. Springer, Berlin, Heidelberg, pp 410–430
20. Bacon J, Eyers D, Pasquier T, Singh J, Papagiannis I, Pietzuch P (2014) Information flow control for secure cloud computing, Vol. 11
21. Chakravarthy S (1995) Early active database efforts: a capsule summary. IEEE Trans Knowl Data Eng 7(6): 1008–1010
22. Issarny V, Blair G (2012) Guest editorial: special issue on the future of middleware (FOME'11). J Internet Serv Appl 3(1): 1–4

23. Sadjadi SM, McKinley PK (2003) A survey of adaptive middleware. Michigan State University Report MSU-CSE-03-35

24. Kon F, Costa F, Blair G, Campbell RH (2002) The case for reflective middleware. Commun ACM 45(6): 33–38

25. Ibrahim N, Le Mouël F (2009) A survey on service composition middleware in pervasive environments. Int J Comput Sci Issues 1: 1–12

26. Kalasapur S, Kumar M, Shirazi B (2007) Dynamic service composition in pervasive computing. IEEE Trans Parallel Distr Syst 18(7): 907–918

27. Ben Hamida A, Kon F, Ansaldi Oliva G, Dos Santos CEM, Lorré J-P, Autili M, De Angelis G, Zarras A, Georgantas N, Issarny V, Bertolino A (2012) The Future Internet. Springer, Berlin, Heidelberg. Chap. An Integrated Development and Runtime Environment for the Future Internet

28. Little M, Shrivastava S (2012) Another look at the middleware for dependable distributed computing. J Internet Serv Appl 3(1): 95–105

29. White J, Dougherty B, Schantz R, Schmidt DC, Porter A, Corsaro A (2012) R&D challenges and solutions for highly complex distributed systems: a middleware perspective. J Internet Serv Appl 3(1): 5–13

30. Akyildiz IF, Su W, Sankarasubramaniam Y, Cayirci E (2002) Wireless sensor networks: a survey. Comput Network 38(4): 393–422

31. Chen M, Gonzalez S, Vasilakos A, Cao H, Leung VC (2011) Body area networks: a survey. Mobile Network Appl 16(2): 171–193

32. Wang M, Cao J, Li J, Das SK (2008) Middleware for wireless sensor networks: a survey. J Comput Sci Technol 23(3): 305–326

33. Rajagopalan R, Varshney PK (2006) Data aggregation techniques in sensor networks: a survey. IEEE Commun Surv Tutorials 8: 48–63

34. Leontiadis I, Efstratiou C, Mascolo C, Crowcroft J (2012) Senshare: Transforming sensor networks into multi-application sensing infrastructures In: European Conference on, Wireless Sensor Networks. Springer, Berlin, Heidelberg, pp 65–81

35. Marinovic S, Craven R, Ma J, Dulay N (2011) Rumpole: a flexible break-glass access control model In: Proceedings of the 16th, ACM Symposium on Access Control Models and Technologies (SACMAT), pp 73–82

36. Sloman M (1994) Policy driven management for distributed systems. J Netw Syst Manag 2: 333–360. Kluwer

37. Twidle K, Lupu E, Dulay N, Sloman M (2008) Ponder2 - A policy environment for autonomous pervasive systems. IEEE Symposium on, Policy for Distributed Systems and Networks (Policy'08): 245–246

38. Minsky NH, Ungureanu V (2000) Law-governed interaction. ACM Trans Softw Eng Methodologies 9(3): 273–305

39. Matthys N, Huygens C, Hughes D, Ueyama J, Michiels S, Joosen W (2010) Policy-driven tailoring of sensor networks In: Sensor Systems and Software, S-CUBE'10. Springer, Berlin, Heidelberg, pp 20–35

40. Singh J, Eyers DM, Bacon J (2011) Disclosure control in multi-domain publish/subscribe systems In: ACM 5th International, Conference on Distributed Event-Based Systems, DEBS'11. ACM, New York, pp 159–170

41. Wun A, Jacobsen H-A (2007) A policy management framework for content-based publish/subscribe In: ACM/IFIP/USENIX Middleware 2007, Springer, LNCS 4834, pp 368–388

42. Bettini C, Brdiczka O, Henricksen K, Indulska J, Nicklas D, Ranganathan A, Riboni D (2010) A survey of context modelling and reasoning techniques. Pervasive Mobile Comput 6(2): 161–180

43. Baldauf M, Dustdar S, Rosenberg F (2007) A survey on context-aware systems. Int J Ad, Hoc Ubiquitous Comput 2(4): 263–277

44. Bennaceur A, Blair G, Chauvel F, Gang H, Georgantas N, Grace P, Howar F, Inverardi P, Issarny V, Paolucci M, Pathak A, Spalazzese R, Steffen B, Souville B (2010) Towards an architecture for runtime interoperability In: Leveraging applications of formal methods, verification, and validation. Lecture Notes in Computer Science, LNCS 6416. Springer, Berlin, Heidelberg, pp 206–220

45. Paolucci M, Souville B (2012) Data interoperability in the future of middleware. J Internet Serv Appl 3(1): 127–131

46. Campbell JR, Carpenter P, Sneiderman C, Cohn S, Chute CG, Warren J (1997) Phase II evaluation of clinical coding schemes: completeness, taxonomy, mapping, definitions, and clarity. J Am Med Inform Assoc 4(3): 238–251

47. Mühl G, Fiege L, Pietzuch P (2006) Distributed event-based systems. Springer, New York

48. Singh J, Vargas L, Bacon J, Moody K (2008) Policy-based information sharing in publish/subscribe middleware In: IEEE 9th Symposium on Policy for Distributed Systems and Networks, Policy'08. IEEE Computer Society, Palisades, pp 137–144

49. Singh J, Bacon J (2014) SBUS: a generic, policy-enforcing middleware for open pervasive systems. University of Cambridge Computer Laboratory Technical Report (TR 850)

50. Ingram D (2009) Reconfigurable middleware for high availability sensor systems. ACM, New York

51. Dierks T, Allen C (1999) The TLS Protocol (RF 2246). Internet Engineering Task Force

52. Chakravarthy S, Krishnaprasad V, Anwar E, Kim S-K (1994) Composite events for active databases: Semantics, contexts and detection In: Very Large, Data Bases, VLDB'94. Morgan Kaufmann, Burlington, MA, USA, pp 606–617

53. Benson T (2012) Why interoperability is hard In: Principles of Health Interoperability HL7 and SNOMED. Health Information Technology Standards. Springer, London, pp 21–32

54. Health Level 7 International. http://www.hl7.org. Accessed 21 Mar 2014

55. International Health Terminology Standards Development Organisation. http://www.ihtsdo.org/snomed-ct. Accessed 21 Mar 2014

56. openEHR. http://www.openehr.org. Accessed 21 Mar 2014

57. Garde S, Knaup P, Hovenga EJ, Heard S (2007) Towards semantic interoperability for electronic health records–domain knowledge governance for open ehr archetypes. Methods Inf Med 46(3): 332–343

58. Integrating the Healthcare Enterprise. http://www.ihe.net/. Accessed 21 Mar 2014

59. Singh J (2009) Controlling the dissemination and disclosure of healthcare events. PhD thesis, University of Cambridge Computer Laboratory Technical Report (TR 770)

60. Reeder RW, Karat C-M, Karat J, Brodie C (2007) Usability challenges in security and privacy policy-authoring interfaces In: Proceedings of the 11th, IFIP TC 13 International Conference on Human-computer Interaction - Volume Part, II. INTERACT'07. Springer, Berlin, Heidelberg, pp 141–155

61. Baum P, Abadie F (2012) Strategic intelligence monitor on personal health systems phase 2, market developments - remote patient monitoring and treatment, telecare, fitness/wellness and mhealth. JRC-IPTS Working Papers JRC71141, Institute for Prospective and Technological Studies, Joint Research Centre, European Commission

62. Rashidi P, Mihailidis A (2013) A survey on ambient-assisted living tools for older adults. J Biomed Health Informatics, IEEE, USA 17(3): 579–590

63. Next Generation European Ambient Assisted Living Innovation Alliance (2013) AALIANCE2 Roadmap. http://www.aaliance2.eu/archive-files. Accessed 30 Apr 2014

64. Haslhofer B, Klas W (2010) A survey of techniques for achieving metadata interoperability. ACM Comput Surv 42(2): 1–37

Fluχ: a quality-driven dataflow model for data intensive computing

Sérgio Esteves[*], João Nuno Silva and Luís Veiga[*]

Abstract

Today, there is a growing need for organizations to continuously analyze and process large waves of incoming data from the Internet. Such data processing schemes are often governed by complex dataflow systems, which are deployed atop highly-scalable infrastructures that need to manage data efficiently in order to enhance performance and alleviate costs.

Current workflow management systems enforce strict temporal synchronization among the various processing steps; however, this is not the most desirable functioning in a large number of scenarios. For example, considering dataflows that continuously analyze data upon the insertion/update of new entries in a data store, it would be wise to assess the level of modifications in data, before the trigger of the dataflow, that would minimize the number of executions (processing steps), reducing overhead and augmenting performance, while maintaining the dataflow processing results within certain coverage and freshness limit.

Towards this end, we introduce the notion of Quality-of-Data (QoD), which describes the level of modifications necessary on a data store to trigger processing steps, and thus conveying in the level of performance specified through data requirements. Also, this notion can be specially beneficial in cloud computing, where a dataflow computing service (SaaS) may provide certain QoD levels for different budgets.

In this article we propose *Fluχ*, a novel dataflow model, with framework and programming library support, for orchestrating data-based processing steps, over a NoSQL data store, whose triggering is based on the evaluation and dynamic enforcement of QoD constraints that are defined (and possibly adjusted automatically) for different sets of data. With *Fluχ* we demonstrate how dataflows can be leveraged to respond to quality boundaries that bring controlled and augmented performance, rationalization of resources, and task prioritization.

Keywords: Dataflow, Workflow, Quality-of-Data, Data store, NoSQL

1 Introduction

Current times have been witnessing an increase of massively scale web applications capable of handling extremely large data sets throughout the Internet. These data-intensive applications are owned by organizations, with cutting edge performance and scalability requirements, whose success lies in the capability of analyzing and processing terabytes of incoming data feeds on a daily-basis. Such data processing computations are often governed by complex dataflows, since they allow better expressiveness and maintainability than low-level data processing (e.g., java map-reduce code).

---

[*]Correspondence: sesteves@gsd.inesc-id.pt; luis.veiga@inesc-id.pt
Instituto Superior Técnico - UTL / INESC-ID Lisboa Distributed Systems Group
Rua Alves Redol, 9, 1000-029 Lisboa, Portugal

Dataflows (or data processing workflows) can be represented as directed acyclic graphs (DAGs) that express the dependencies between computations and data. These computations, or processing steps, can potentially be decoupled from object location, inter-object communication, synchronization and scheduling; hence, being highly flexible on supporting parallel scalable and distributed computation. The data is either transferred directly from one processing step to another using intermediate files or via a shared storage system, such as a distributed file system or a database (which is our target in this particular work).

Another extensive use of dataflows has been for continuous and incremental processing. Here, vast amounts of raw data are continuously fed, as input, to cross an incremental processing pipeline in order to be transformed into final structured and refined data. Examples include data aggregation in databases, web crawlers, data mining, and others from many different scientific domains, like sky surveys, forecasting, RNA-sequencing, or seismology [1-5].

The software infrastructure to setup, execute and monitor dataflows is commonly referred to as Workflow Management System (WMS). Generally, WMSs either enforce strict temporal synchronization across the various input, intermediate and output data sets (i.e., following the SDF computing model [6]), or leave the temporal logic in the programmer hands, who have often to explicitly program non-synchronous behavior to meet application latency and prioritization requirements. For example, processing news documents faster than others in a web indexing system; or, in the astronomy domain, processing images, collected from ground-based telescopes, of objects that are closer to Earth first, and only then images that do not require immediate attention. Moreover, these systems do not account with the volume of data that arrives on each dataflow step, which could and should be used to reason about their performance impact on the system. Precisely, executing a processing step each time a small fragment of data arrives can have a great impact on performance, as opposed to executing only when a certain substantial quantity of new data is available. Such issues are addressed in this work with a data quality-driven model based on the notion of what we call Quality-of-Data.

Informally, we define Quality-of-Data (QoD) as the ability to provide different priority to different data sets, users or dataflows, or to guarantee a certain level of performance of a dataflow. These guarantees can be enforced, for example, based on data size, number of hits in a certain data store object, or delay inclusion. High QoD should not be confused with high level of performance, but instead it conveys in the capability of strictly complying with QoD constraints defined over data sets.

With the QoD concept,[a] we are thus able to define and apply temporal semantics to dataflows based on the volume and importance of the data communicated between processing steps. Moreover, relying on QoD we can augment the throughput of the dataflow and reduce the number of its executions while keeping the results within acceptable limits. Also, this concept is particularly interesting in (public) cloud computing, where a dataflow service (SaaS) may provide different QoD levels for different budgets. Therefore, this work can also give a contribute to the new studies addressing the cost and performance of deploying dataflows in the cloud (e.g., [7]).

Given the current envisagement, we propose a novel dataflow model, with framework and programming library support, for orchestrating data-based computation

stages (actions), over a NoSQL data store, whose triggering is based on the evaluation and dynamic enforcement of QoD constraints that are defined, and possibly adjusted automatically, for different sets of data. With this framework, named *Fluχ*, we enable the setup of dataflows whose execution is guided and controlled to comply with certain QoD requirements, delivering thus: controlled performance (i.e., improved or degraded); rationalization of resource usage; execution prioritization based on relative importance of data; and augmented throughput between processing steps.

We implemented *Fluχ* using an existing WMS, that was adapted to enforce our model and triggering semantics, and adopted, as the underlying data store, the HBase tabular storage [8]. Our results show that *Fluχ* is able to: i) ensure result convergence, hence showing that the QoD model does not introduce significant errors, ii) save significant computational resources by avoiding wasteful repetitive execution of dataflow steps, and iii) consequently, reduce machine load and improve resource efficiency, in cluster and cloud infrastructures, for equivalent levels of data *value* provided to, and as perceived by, decision makers.

Shortcomings of state-of-the-art solutions include (to the best of our knowledge): i) lack of tools to enable transparent asynchronous behavior in workflow systems; ii) no support for dataflows to share data through highly-scalable cloud-like databases; iii) lack of integration, in mostly loosely-coupled environments, between the workflow management and the underlying intermediate data (which is seen as opaque); and iv) no quality of service, and of data, is enforced (at least in a flexible manner).

The remainder of this article is organized as follows. Section 2 presents the *Fluχ* dataflow model based on the QoD notion. Section 3 describes an archetypal meta-architecture of the *Fluχ* middleware framework, and Section 4 offers its relevant implementation aspects. Then, Section 5 presents a performance evaluation, and Section 6 reviews related work. Finally, we draw all appropriate conclusions in Section 7.

2 Abstract dataflow model

In this section we describe the *Fluχ* dataflow model which was specially designed to address large-scale and data-intensive scenarios that need to continuously and incrementally process very large sets of data while maintaining strong requirements about the quality of service and data provided. Moreover, our model implies that the underlying data, shared among processing steps, should be done via tabular data stores; whereas most workflow models rely on files to store and share the data, which cannot achieve the same scalability and flexibility.

Our dataflow model can be expressed as a directed acyclic graph (DAG), where each node represents a processing step (designated here by *action*) that must perform changes in a data store; and the edges between actions represent dependencies, meaning that an action needs the output of another action to get executed (naturally, these dependencies need to be decoupled from WMS implementation so that the same actions can be combined in different ways). More precisely, each action A, in a dataflow D, is executed only after all actions A' preceding A (denoted $A' \prec_D A$) in D have been executed at least once (elaborated hereafter). In addition, actions can be divided in: input actions, which are supplied with data from external sources; intermediate actions, which receive data from other actions; and output actions, whose generated data is read by external consumers.

Unlike the other typical models, our approach takes a step further: the end of execution of a node A does not mean that the successor nodes A' (denoted $A' \succ_D A$), that depend on A, will be immediately triggered (like it usually happens). Instead, successor nodes should be triggered as soon as A has finished its execution and has also performed a sufficient level of changes in the data store that comply with certain QoD requirements (which can cause a node being executed multiple times with the successor nodes being triggered only once). If such changes do not occur in a given time frame, successor nodes would eventually be triggered. Hence, the QoD requirements evaluate the volume of data input fed to an action that is worth its execution. This is the key difference and novelty of our approach that breaks through the SDF (synchronous data-flow) computing model.

The amount of data changes (QoD) necessary to trigger an action, denoted by κ, is specified using multidimensional vectors that associate QoD constraints with data object containers, such as a column or group of columns in a table of a given column-oriented database. κ bounds the maximum level of changes through numeric scalar vectors defined for each of the following orthogonal dimensions: time (θ), sequence (σ), and value (v).

Time Specifies the maximum time an action can be on hold (without being triggered) since its last execution occurred. Considering $\theta(o)$ provides the time (e.g., seconds) passed since the last execution of a certain action that is dependent on the availability of data in the object container o, this time constraint κ_θ enforces that $\theta(o) < \kappa_\theta$ at any given time.

Sequence Specifies the number of still unapplied updates to an object container object container o upon which, the action that depends on o is triggered. Considering $\sigma(o)$ indicates the number of applied updates over o, this sequence constraint κ_σ enforces that $\sigma(o) < \kappa_\sigma$ at any given time.

Value Specifies the maximum relative divergence between the updated state of an object container o and its initial state, or against a constant (e.g., top value), since the last execution of an action dependent on o. Considering $v(o)$ provides that difference (e.g., in percentage), this value constraint κ_v enforces that $v(o) < \kappa_v$ at any given time. It captures the impact or importance of updates in the last state.

These constraints are used to trigger the execution of actions. When they are reached, the action is executed (or scheduled to be executed). Access to the object containers is not blocked but update counters are still maintained in synch. Only if specified (and it is not required for the intended applications in this paper), will the constraints, when reached, block access to the data containers, preventing further updates until the action is re-executed.

The QoD bound κ, associated with an object container o, is reached when any of its vectors has been reached, i.e., $\theta(o) \geq \kappa_\theta \vee \sigma(o) \geq \kappa_\sigma \vee v(o) \geq \kappa_v$. Also, grouped containers (e.g., a column and a row) are treated as single containers, in the sense that modifications performed on any of the grouped objects change the same κ.

Moreover, the triggering of an action can depend on the updates performed on multiple database object containers, each of which possibly associated with a different κ. Hence, it is necessary to combine all associated constraints to produce a single binary outcome, deciding whether or not the action should be triggered. To address this, we provide a QoD specification algebra with the two logical operators *and* and *or* ($\wedge$ and $\vee$) that can be used between any pair of QoD bounds. The *and* operator requires that every associated QoD bound κ should be reached in order to trigger an associated action; while the *or* requires that at least one κ should be reached for the triggering of the action. Following the classical semantics, the operator *and* has precedence over operator *or*. For example, an action A can be associated with the expression $\kappa_1 \vee \kappa_2 \wedge \kappa_3$, which causes the triggering of A when κ_1 is reached, or κ_2 and κ_3 have been both reached.

Furthermore, we also allow a unique definition for the combination of all κ bounds, instead of individually specifying operators for every pair of bounds. The pre-built available definitions are:

all ($\forall$) An action is triggered *iff* all associated κ bounds are reached.
at-least-one ($\exists_1$) An action is triggered *iff* at least on associated κ is reached.
majority ($\lceil (n+1)/2 \rceil$) An action is triggered *iff* the majority of associated κ bounds are reached (e.g., 2 of 3 bounds, or 3 of 4 bounds, are reached).

These definitions are, afterwards, automatically unfolded in regular expressions containing *and* and *or* operators.

2.1 Prototypical example

Figure 1 depicts a simple and partial example dataflow of a typical web crawler, which serves as motivation and familiar prototypical example to introduce dataflows. Step *A* crawls documents over the web and stores their text on stable storage, either in a file system or as an opaque object in a database (e.g., no-SQL), along with some metadata extracted from the document contents, HTTP response headers, or derived from some preprocessing based on title words, URL, or tags. Depending on the class of the accessed pages, their content is stored in different tables: one for the news items, other for the remaining static pages.

Steps *B* and *C* are similar in function, in the sense that they process existing documents, generating word counts of the words present in the document, along with the URL containing them. The difference being that step *B* processes specifically only those documents identified or marked as containing news-related content in the previous step.

Since news pages change more frequency and are more relevant, *B* has stricter QoD requirements, and therefore is processed faster (i.e., activated more often). Its divergence bounds are lower, meaning that it will take less time (200 vs 300 seconds), fewer new documents crawled (100 vs 500), and/or fewer modifications on new versions of crawled documents (10% vs 20% of contents), in order to activate it.

Finally, in step *D*, all the information generated by the previous executions of steps *B* and *C* is joined and the inverted index (*word* ↦ {*list of URLs*}, for each word) is generated.

This whole process could be performed resorting to Map-Reduce programs but, as we describe in Section 6, since Map-Reduce programs are becoming increasingly larger and more complex, their reuse can be leveraged chaining them into workflows, reducing development effort. In Section 5 we will address a more elaborate example.

3 Architecture

In this section we present the architecture and design choices of the *Fluχ* middleware framework that is capable of managing dataflows following the model described in the previous section (Section 2). The *Fluχ* framework, is designed to be tightly coupled with a large-scale (NoSQL) data store, enabling the construction of quality-driven dataflows in which the triggering of processing steps (actions) may be delayed, but still complying with QoD requirements defined over the stored data.

This framework may be particularly useful in public cloud platforms where it can be offered as a Software-as-a-Service (SaaS) in which the QoD requirements are defined according to certain budgets; i.e., small budgets would have stricter QoD constraints, and large budgets looser QoD constraints.

Figure 2 shows a distributed network architecture in the cloud whereby a dataflow is set up to be executed upon a cluster of machines connected through a local network. More precisely, a coordinator machine, running a WMS with *Fluχ*, allocates the dataflow actions to available worker nodes and the input/output data is communicated between actions via a shared cloud tabular data store. In this particular work we abstract from the details of scheduling and running actions in parallel; our focus here is that actions share input, intermediate, and output data through a distributed cloud database (instead of intermediate files, like it usually happens).

Figure 3 depicts an archetypal meta-architecture of the *Fluχ* middleware framework, which operates in the middle of a dataflow manager and an underlying non-relational tabular storage. Actions of a dataflow run on top of the dataflow manager and they must share data through the underlying storage. These actions may consist

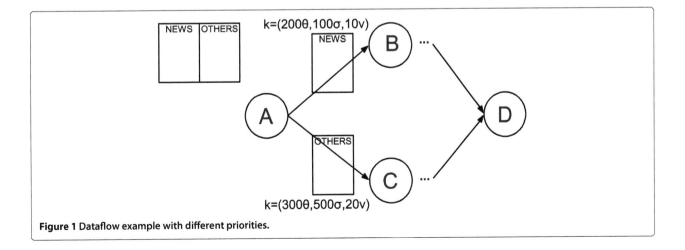

Figure 1 Dataflow example with different priorities.

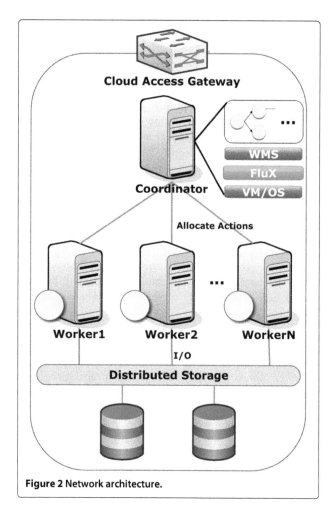

Figure 2 Network architecture.

of Java applications, scripts expressed through high-level languages for data analysis (e.g., Apache Pig [9]), map-reduce jobs, as well as other out-of-the-box solutions. The components outlined with no solid line dash are optional meta-components for the adaptation of *Fluχ*.

The framework can operate either with its own provided simple WMS, or with an existing dataflow manager by means of the WMS Adaptation Component (colored in red). This inherent dependency of our framework with a WMS concerns mainly to the triggering notifications. With our WMS, we simply use a provided API through which *Fluχ* signals the triggering of actions. While using an existing WMS, we need to change its source and provide an adaptation component that controls the triggering of actions upon request.

Since *Fluχ* needs to be aware of the data modifications performed by actions in the underlying database, we contemplate three different solutions, regarding the adaptation of database libraries, that can be derived from the meta-architecture. The components colored in gray within the middleware are the core components and should be included by every derived solution; and the components colored in blue represent the three different alternatives for the adaptation, which are described as follows.

Application Libraries This solution consists of adapting application libraries, referenced in actions, that are used to interact directly with the data store via its client API. It is a bit intrusive in the sense that applications need to be modified, albeit we intend to provide tools so that this process may be completely automatized.

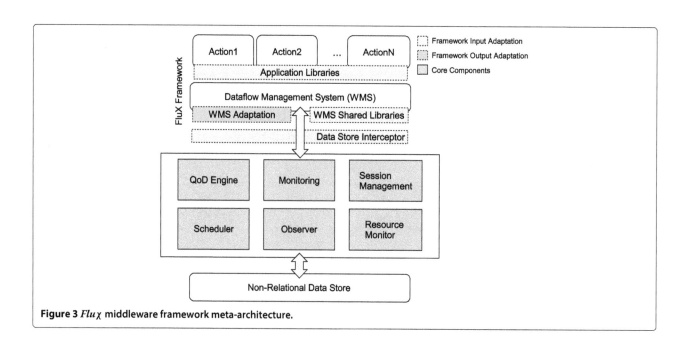

Figure 3 *Fluχ* middleware framework meta-architecture.

WMS Shared Libraries This alternative is on a lower layer and works for actions that need to access the database through WMS shared libraries (e.g., pig scripts or any other high-level language that must be compiled by the WMS). It provides transparency to actions, that do not need to be modified to work with *Fluχ*.

Data Store Interceptor This solution functions as a proxy that implements the underlying database communication protocol and intercepts the calls from the applications or WMS directed to the database; hence, achieving full transparency regarding action code. Applications may only interact with the data store via this proxy, and therefore they should define as the database entry-point the address of the proxy (probably in the form of URL).

Next, we describe the responsibilities and purpose of each of the components present in the *Fluχ* framework.

Monitoring This component analyzes all requests directed to the database. It uses information about update requests to maintain the current state of control data regarding the quality-of-data; and also collects statistics regarding access patterns to stored data (mainly read operations) in order to automatically adjust the QoD levels, in the view of the improvement of the overall system performance.

Session Management It manages the configurations of the QoD constraints, over data objects, through the meta-data that is provided, along with the dataflow specification, and defined for each different dataflow. A dataflow specification is then derived to the target WMS.

QoD Engine It maintains data structures and control meta-data which are used to evaluate and decide when to trigger next actions, obeying to QoD specifications.

Scheduler This component verifies the time constraints over the data. When the time for triggering of successor actions expires, the Scheduler notifies the QoD Engine component in order to clear the associated QoD state and notify the WMS to execute the next processing steps.

Observer It provides mechanisms to scan the data store for modifications in case the updates performed do not go through the Monitoring component.

Resource Monitor This component is responsible for monitoring the resource utilization and load of the machines allocated to execute dataflows. It informs the QoD Engine about the computation loads at runtime in order to automatically tune the QoD constraints.

3.1 Session management, metadata and dataflow isolation

Dataflow specification schemas need to be provided to register dataflows with the *Fluχ* framework. They should contain the description of the dataflow graph where each action must explicitly specify the underlying database object containers (e.g., table, column, or row) it depends and the relative QoD requirements necessary to the action triggering. Precisely, one QoD bound, κ, can be provided either for single database containers associated or for groups of object containers (e.g., several columns covered by the same κ); these two ways of associate κ imply different QoD evaluation and enforcement.

QoD constraints (time, sequence, and value) can be specified as either single values or intervals of values. The former guarantees always the same quality degree, while the latter is used for dynamic adjustment at runtime: each interval relies on two numerical scalars that are used for specifying the minimum and maximum QoD bounds respectively, and the QoD Engine component adjusts κ within the interval as needed. If no bound is associated with an action A, then it is assumed that A should be triggered right after the execution of its precedent actions (i.e., strict temporal synchronism). After dataflow registration, the underlying database schema is extended to incorporate the metadata related with the QoD bound and QoD control state. Specifically, it is necessary to have maps that given a dataflow, an action node, and a database object container, return the quality bound and current state.

It may happen that database object containers, associated with actions of a certain dataflow, can be being written by other dataflows or external applications (and thus changing the triggering semantics). To disentangle such conflicts, we consider three isolation modes through which our framework can be configured:

Normal Mode It relies on an optimistic approach in which it is assumed that nothing changes the database containers besides the dataflows. In this case, different dataflows will share the same QoD state; i.e., whenever data is changed on a DBMS object container, the QoD state of all actions associated with that object are changed irrespective of which active dataflow has caused the modifications.

Observer Mode This (pessimistic) mode assumes that dataflows are not the only entities performing changes on database objects. Therefore, it resorts to observers to scan the objects to detect modifications, since it is not guaranteed that every update passes through the Monitoring component.

Isolation Mode In this mode each dataflow should only work with its own inputted data and have its own QoD state irrespective of how many dataflows or external processes are also writing to the same DBMS objects. This mode implies the creation of a notify column (described hereafter) per each dataflow.

Since database object containers are likely to receive a vast volume of data items (e.g., a column with millions of keys being written), it could be very inefficient for observers to scan the whole columns and find those that have been changed. Therefore, we resort to a notification mechanism where each updated item in a container needs to write an entry in an auxiliary data structure. For example, every key written in a certain column would have to also write a timestamp in a special column (notify column); and, thus, the scans will only cover that notify column, which is much more efficient in a column-oriented NoSQL data store.

3.2 Evaluation and enforcement of quality-of-data bounds

The QoD state of a database object container o, for an action A, is updated every time an update is perceived by $Flux$ through the Monitoring and Observer components. Upon such event, it is necessary to identify the action A' that made the update ($A' \prec A$) and the affected object container, o, which is sent by the client libraries; this, in order to retrieve the quality bound and current state associated through the metadata. Then, given A' and o, we can find all successor actions of A', including A, that are dependent on the updates performed on o, and thus update their QoD state (i.e., the state of each successor action depending on o). Specifically, we need to increment all of the associated vectors σ and re-compute the ratio *modified keys/total keys*, hold in all v vectors. Afterwards, the QoD state of a pair (action, object) needs to be compared against its relative QoD reference bound (i.e., the maximum level of changes allowed, κ).

The evaluation of the quality vectors σ and v, to decide if an action A should be triggered or not, may take place at one of the following times: a) every time a write operation is performed by a precedent action of A; b) every time a precedent action finishes completely its execution; or c) periodically between a given time frame. These options can be combined together; e.g., it might be of use to combine option c) with a) or b), for the case where precedent actions of A take very long periods of time in performing computations and generating output. Despite option a) being the most accurate, it is the least efficient, especially when dealing with large bursts of updates.

To evaluate the time constraint, θ, $Flux$ uses timers to check periodically (e.g., every second) if there is any timestamp in θ about to expire (i.e., a QoD bound that is almost reached). Specifically, references to actions are held in a list ordered ascending by time of expiration, which is the time of last execution of a dependent action plus θ. In effect, the Scheduler component starts from the first element of the list checking if timestamps are older or equal than current time. As the list is ordered, the Scheduler has only to fail one check to ignore the rest of the list; e.g., if the check on the first element fails (its timestamp has not expired yet), the Scheduler does not need to check the remaining elements of the list.

As described in Section 2, the possible various QoD states, associated with an action, can be combined using provided operators. If no operators or mode are provided, the mode *all* is used, enforcing that every single associated QoD bound should be reached in order to trigger the relative action. If any limit is reached and an action is initiated, all QoD state vectors associated with that action are reset: θ receives a new timestamp, σ and v go to zero.

3.3 Dynamic adjustment of quality-of-data constraints

As previously mentioned, users may also specify intervals of values on the QoD vectors (instead of single values), and let the framework automatically adjust the quality constraints (within the intervals), hence varying the level of data modifications necessary to trigger successor actions, while preventing excessive load and error accumulation. This adjustment, performed by the QoD Engine component, is driven by two factors: i) the frequency of recent write operations to data items, during a given time frame; and ii) the current availability of computer resources and relative capabilities.

As for the former factor, we relax the QoD bound upon many consecutive updates, in an attempt to reduce the inherent overhead of triggering a given action an excessive number of times; i.e., we try to feed an action with as much data as possible within the upper boundary, as we anticipate further new input, instead of triggering that action with smaller subsets of that same data; hence, increasing throughput and resource efficiency. Conversely, we restrict the bound when updates are becoming less frequent and more spaced in time to increase the speed and reduce latency of the pipeline and dataflow processing steps.

The other factor, adjustment based on resource availability, consists of monitoring (based on a library abstracting system calls from different operating systems) at runtime the computing resources such as CPU, memory and disk usage, and determine, based on reference values, if each machine (or weighted for all in a set of allocated machines) is, or is not, fully utilized in order to decrease, or increase, the dataflow processing speed; i.e., if a machine (or a the set of machines) is underutilized the QoD bound is restricted to augment the overall dataflow performance; otherwise, if a machine is overloaded, the QoD bound is relaxed. This adjustment is performed in a progressive manner to avoid jitters.

These two factors can be entwined in the following way. Assuming the outcome of the assessment of each factor is either: *restrict*, *relax*, or *none*; if one factor decides *relax* and the other decides *restrict*, then no action is taken (i.e., factors disagree). If one factor decides *relax* or *restrict* and the other decides *none*, then the resulting bound is *relaxed* or *restricted* respectively. Otherwise, the factors agree and the adjustment is made in accordance with the outcome (*relax*, *restrict*, or *none*).

For not-so-expert users, we also provide a mechanism to automatically and dynamically adjust the QoD constraints. Users have only to specify the *significance factor*, i.e., the percentage of changes in the dataflow output (or against a reference) that would be meaningful and *significant* to decision-makers. For example, an air-sampling smoke detector should only issue a signal to a fire alarm system if the concentration of micro particles of combustion found is high enough (or *significant*); e.g., the fire alarm should not be triggered by the smoke of a simple cigar.

In this mode, vector element θ is simply set to a default constant. Figure 4 shows how the sequence constraint (σ) is adjusted, by successive approximation and assessment, ensuring that the target *significance* is met at the output of the final step. This, by inferring, backwards along the dataflow, the maximum QoD at each step that still achieves it.

First, the σ constraint in all steps, besides the first, is initialized to 1, meaning that every time a step completes its execution, performing at least 1 update, all its successors are triggered (like in the SDF model). The *qodSeqUpdate* method is called upon a wave of incoming data over the steps that have not been adjusted yet (checked through the *qodComplete* boolean). First (lines 13-18), σ is doubled until the amount of variation in the output (*currentDelta*) goes above the significance factor (*targetDelta*). This variation is calculated by summing the differences (in absolute value) between current and previous row's values and dividing by the sum of all previous values. The goal is to make *currentDelta* and *targetDelta* to match or be within a given small ε (method *isEqualWithinEpsilon*).

After this first stage to find the maximum, σ starts to converge to the optimal value, thereby decreasing its value when *currentDelta* is greater than *targetDelta*, and increasing when it is lower (lines 28-31). If they match (lines 21-27) - in reality within a given ε, the optimal value of σ was found, and the *qodSeqUpdate* is called recursively for the predecessor step (if any), thereby setting its *targetDelta* to the *currentInDelta* (i.e., the current amount of variation in the input of the current step).

Applying this mechanism to the σ constraint is sufficient for dataflows where output variation across waves is mostly stable (not necessarily linearly dependent), given the number of updates to the input. When this relationship does not hold, the dynamic adjustment mechanism targets the ν constraint instead, using an analogous approach to Figure 4. This way, it attempts to determine the maximum magnitude of the modifications made at the input of each step, regardless of the actual number of updates, that would still not produce any relevant change in the significance of the dataflow output results.

4 Implementation

In this section we present the relevant implementation details of a developed prototype, as a proof of concept, with the architecture aforementioned to demonstrate the advantages of our dataflow model when deployed as a WMS for high-performance and large-scale data stores.

4.1 Adopted technology

Starting from the top layer, and to avoid reimplementing basic workflow capabilities, we have implemented our model using Oozie, [10] which is a Java open-source workflow coordination system to manage Apache Hadoop [11] jobs. Hence, we adapted the Oozie triggering semantics, by replacing the time-based and data detection triggering mechanisms, with a notification scheme that is interfaced with the *Fluχ* framework process through Java RMI. In general, Oozie only has to notify when an action finishes its execution, and *Fluχ* only has to signal the triggering

```
1  private void init(List<Step> steps) {
2    for(s : steps) {
3      s.setSeq(1);
4      s.setQoDComplete(false);
5      s.setState(0);
6    }
7  }
8
9  private void qodSeqUpdate(Step step) {
10   double currentDelta = step
11     .getCurrentOutDelta();
12   double targetDelta = step.getTargetDelta();
13   if(step.getState() == 0) {
14     if(currentDelta < targetDelta)
15       step.setSeq(step.getSeq() * 2);
16     else
17       step.setState(1);
18   }
19   if(step.getState() == 1) {
20     int mid = Math.abs(step.getSeq() - step.
         getPreviousSeq()) / 2;
21     if(isEqualWithinEpsilon(currentDelta,
         targetDelta)) {
22       step.setQoDComplete(true);
23       if(step.previousStep() != null) {
24         step.previousStep().setTargetDelta(
25           step.getCurrentInDelta());
26         qodSeqUpdate(step.previousStep());
27       }
28     } else if(currentDelta < targetDelta)
29       step.setSeq(step.getSeq() + mid);
30     else if(currentDelta > targetDelta)
31       step.setSeq(step.getSeq() - mid);
32   }
33 }
```

Figure 4 QoD dynamic adjustment.

of a certain action; naturally, these notifications share the same action identifiers.

As for the lower layer, and although the framework can be adapted to work with other non-relational data stores, in the scope of this particular work, our target is BigTable [12] open-source Java clone, HBase [8], which we used as an instance of the underlying storage. This database system is a sparse, multi-dimensional sorted map, indexed by row, column (includes family and qualifier), and timestamp; the mapped values are simply an uninterpreted array of bytes. It is column-oriented, meaning that most queries only involve a few columns in a wide range, thus significantly reducing I/O. Moreover, these databases scale to billions of rows and millions of columns, while ensuring that write and read performance remain constant.

Finally, *Fluχ* was also built in Java, and uses, i.a., the Saxon http://saxon.sourceforge.net/ XPath engine to read and process XML configurations files (e.g., the dataflow description); and the SIGAR http://support.hyperic.com/display/SIGAR/Home library for monitoring resource usage and machine loads. For efficiency, we followed the solution of adapting the HBase client libraries used by Java classes, representing the type of actions we tried at evaluation stage.

4.2 Library support and API

In order to intercept the updates performed by actions, we adapted the HBase client libraries by extending the implementation of some of their classes while maintaining their original APIs. http://hbase.apache.org/apidocs/overview-summary.html Namely, the implementation of the classes *Configuration.java*, *HBaseConfiguration.java*, and *HTable.java*, were modified to intercept every update performed on HBase, especially *put* and *delete* operations, and send the needed parameters (like action, operation, table, and column identifiers) to the *Fluχ* framework.

Applications need therefore only to be slightly modified to use our API. Specifically, only the import declarations of the HBase packages need to be changed to *Fluχ* packages, since our API is practically the same. To ease such process, we provide tools that automatically modify all the necessary import declarations, thereby patching the java bytecode at loading time.

4.3 Definition of dataflows with QoD bounds

The QoD constraints, referring to the maximum degree of data modifications, are specified along with standard Oozie XML schemas (version 0.2), and given to the *Fluχ* middleware with an associated dataflow description. Specifically, we introduced in the respective XSD the new element *qod*, which can be used inside the element *action*. Inside *qod*, it is necessary to indicate the data object containers associated, i.e., using the elements *table*, *column*,

row, or *group*. Each of these elements must specify the three constraints time (a decimal indicating the number of seconds), sequence (an integer), and value (an integer indicating the percentage of modifications), that are combined through the method defined in the qod attribute *combine*. Additionally, the element *group* groups object containers, which are specified through the element *item*, that should be handled at the same QoD degree. Next, we present an example, in Figure 5, omitting some details for readability purposes.

These particular dataflow descriptions are then automatically adapted to the regular Oozie schema (i.e., without the QoD elements) and fed to the Oozie manager.

```
<workflow-app name="sample-wf"
       xmlns="uri:oozie:workflow:0.1">
    ...
   <action name="myfirstjavajob">
     <java>
         <job-tracker>foo:9001</job-tracker>
         <name-node>bar:9000</name-node>
         <prepare>
            <delete path="${jobOutput}"/>
         </prepare>
         <configuration>
            <property>
               <name>mapred.queue.name</name>
               <value>default</value>
            </property>
         </configuration>
         <main-class>org.apache.oozie.
            MyFirstMainClass</main-class>
         <java-opts> -Dblah </java-opts>
         <arg>argument1</arg>
         <arg>argument2</arg>
     </java>
     <qod>
         <column id="column0">
            <time>600</time>
            <sequence>2000</sequence>
            <value>40</value>
         </column>
     </qod>
     <ok to="mysecondjavajob"/>
     <error to="errorcleanup"/>
   </action>
   <action name="mysecondjavajob">
     <java>
         ...
     </java>
     <qod combine="all">
         <column id="column1">
            <time>300</time>
            <sequence>1000</sequence>
            <value>20</value>
         </column>
         <group>
            <item type="column" id="column2" />
            <item type="row" id="123" />
            <time>600</time>
            <sequence>5000</sequence>
            <value>60</value>
         </group>
     </qod>
     <ok to="end"/>
     <error to="fail"/>
   </action>
   <kill name="fail">
     <message>Java failed, error message
         [${wf:errorMessage(wf:lastErrorNode())}]
     </message>
   </kill>
   <end name="end"/>
</workflow-app>
```

Figure 5 *Fluχ* dataflow description.

Hence, our framework controls the upper workflow management system and it is not necessary to perform additional configurations on such external systems (i.e., all configurations must go through *Fluχ*). Nevertheless, we envision in the future for a more general dataflow description, where it can be, afterwards, automatically adapted to a range of popular WMSs.

5 Evaluation

This section presents the evaluation of the *Fluχ* framework and its benefits when compared with the regular DAG semantics (i.e., SDF with no QoD enforcement). More precisely, and attending to our objectives, we analyze the gains of *Fluχ* with dataflows for continuous and incremental processing in terms of: i) result convergence, as the dataflow execution pipeline advances; ii) error coverage; and iii) machine loads and resource usage through the amount of executions performed/saved. All tests were conducted using 6 machines with an Intel Core i7-2600K CPU at 3.40GHz, 11926MB of available RAM memory, and HDD 7200RPM SATA 6Gb/s 32MB cache, connected by 1 Gigabit LAN.

5.1 Prototypical scenario

For evaluating our model and framework we relied on a dataflow, for continuous and incremental processing, that expresses a simulation of a prototypical scenario inspired by the calculation the Air Quality Health Index (AQHI), www.ec.gc.ca/cas-aqhi/ used in Canada. It captures the potential human health risk from air pollution in a certain geographic area, typically a city, while allowing for more localized information. More specifically, the incoming data fed to this dataflow is obtained through several detectors equally distributed over an area of 10000 square units. Each detector comprises three sensors to gauge the amount of Ozone (O_3), Particulate Matter ($PM_{2.5}$) and Nitrogen Dioxide (NO_2). In effect, each sensor corresponds to a different generating function, following a distribution with smooth variations across space (i.e., realistic while exactness not relevant for our purposes), which

will provide the necessary data to the dataflow. These generating functions return a value from 0 to 100, where 0 and 100 are, respectively, the minimum and maximum known values of O_3, $PM_{2.5}$ or NO_2. At the end, in the final step of the dataflow, the index is generated, thereby producing a number that is mapped into a class of health risk: low (1-3), moderate (4-6), high (7-10), and very high (above 10).

Figure 6 illustrates the dataflow with the associated QoD vectors and the main HBase columns (some columns were omitted for readability purposes) that comprise the object containers in which the processing steps' triggering depends on. k specifies i) the maximum time, in seconds, the action can be on hold; ii) the minimum amount, in percentage, of changes necessary to the triggering (e.g., 20% associated to step C means that this action will be triggered when at least 20% of the detectors have been changed by step B; and iii) the maximum accepted divergence, in units.

We describe each processing step in the following.

Step A: This step continuously feeds data to the dataflow by reading sensors from detectors that perceive changes in the atmosphere (i.e., randomly chosen in practice) to simulate asynchronous and deferred arrival of update sensory data. The values from each sensor are written in three columns (each row is a different detector) which are grouped as a single object container with one associated k.

Step B: Calculates the combined concentration (of pollution) of the three sensors for each detector whose values were changed in the previous step. Every single calculated value (a number from 0 to 100 also) is written on column *concentration*.

Step C: Processes the concentrations of small areas, called zones, encircled by the previously changed detectors. These zones can be seen as small squares within the overall considered area and comprise the adjacent detectors (until a distance of two in every direction). The concentration of a zone is given by a simple

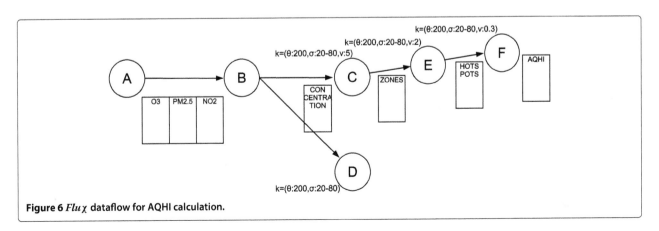

Figure 6 *Fluχ* dataflow for AQHI calculation.

multiplicative model of the concentration of each comprising detector.

Step D: Calculates the concentration of points of the city between detectors, thereby averaging the concentration perceived by surrounding detectors; and plots a chart containing a representation of the concentrations throughout the whole probed area, for displaying purposes, and reference of concentration and air quality risk indicator in localized areas of a city (as traditionally, red and darker means higher risk, while green and lighter yellow means reduced risk). This step can be executed in parallel with Step E.

Step E: Analyzes the previous stored zones and respective concentrations in order to detect hotspots; i.e., zones where the overall concentration is above a certain reference. Zones deemed as hotspots are stored in column *hotspots* for further analyzation.

Step F: Performs final reasoning about the hotspots detected, thereby combining, through a simple additive model, the amount (in percentage) of hotspots identified with the average concentration of pollution (O_3, $PM_{2.5}$ and NO_2) on all hotspots. Then, the AQHI index is produced and stored for each wave of incoming data.

We conducted the evaluation for 2500 (50×50) to 40000 (200×200) detectors with 1 to 6 nodes and averaged the results over several runs to reduce noise. We simulated this experiment as though we were analyzing the pollution of a city for a week, with a wave of incoming data (from changed detectors) fed to the dataflow at each hour, which performs 168 waves in total (24 hours per 7 days). Also, we used distributions of pollution with 3 different tendencies in the generating functions (mimicking the sensors): increasing over time, decreasing over time, and globally uniform over time. Following, we analyze the

most important aspects of correctness and performance, for all the steps with QoD enforcement in the AQHI dataflow.

5.2 Step C analysis

Through Figure 7 we may see the pollution concentration, on average of all zones, per each wave, while varying the QoD sequence vector, σ, in 20, 40, 60 and 80% of changed detectors (new data), and comparing against the concentration without using QoD. As depicted, the zone concentration on average with QoD converges to the concentration without QoD. It takes more time (or waves) to converge as we increase the minimum percentage of detectors detecting changes (σ). In this particular trial, the tendency configured on the generating functions was to increase the pollution as the number of waves increase. Our trials allow us to show that the differences between values calculated with and without QoD are always representatively small and bounded. Moreover, our other trials also show that the values of concentration with and without QoD mostly converge, i.e. differences are diminishing. This confirms the initial motivation that it would waste resources, for most purposes, to execute the dataflow completely for each wave, as the increase in output accuracy may be deemed as not significant, or relevant.

Figure 8 shows the maximum deviation (or error) of the concentration calculated, in relation to the pollution observed with no QoD, when varying σ from 10 to 100%, meaning triggering execution only when there is new input for all sensors. The maximum error always stays below our defined threshold (vector v) and the error increases with a linearly tendency as the waves or number of changed detectors increase. Despite, some noise and jitters (introduced by the variation of hundreds or thousands of sensors), the linear trend is clearly observable.

Through Figure 9 we can see that the number of executions decreases in an almost linear fashion as the

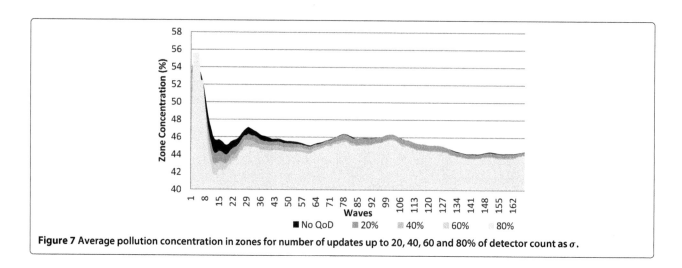

Figure 7 Average pollution concentration in zones for number of updates up to 20, 40, 60 and 80% of detector count as σ.

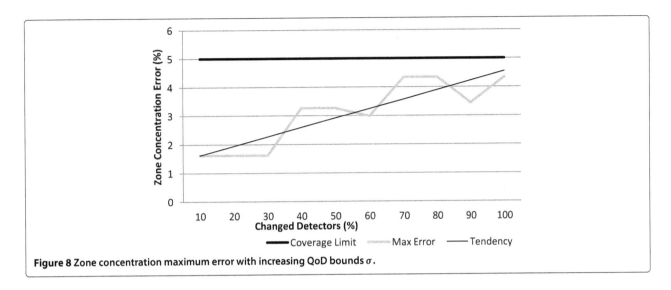

Figure 8 Zone concentration maximum error with increasing QoD bounds σ.

allowed percentage of changed detectors (σ) increases. The number of step executions performed without QoD is naturally equal to the number of waves, 168, corresponding to the 100%. When σ was 25% we saved about 20% of 168 executions (i.e., fewer 33 executions than using regular DAG semantics); and for 80% of detected changes we only performed 80 executions (48%). The machine loads and resource utilization were naturally proportional to the savings presented here.

5.3 Step D analysis
We present the graphs generated during a day (24 samples) using regular DAG semantics and contrast them against the *Fluχ* model with QoD, for 20, 40, 60 and 80% of variation in vector σ.

Without QoD, Figure 10 illustrates the evolution of the concentration of pollution in the city during a day. Areas colored in shades of green represent safer zones with lower pollution concentrations (low health risk);

yellow areas represent medium pollution concentration (moderate health risk); and colors ranging from orange to red indicate hotspots (high and very high health risk).

Figure 11 presents a similar matrix on the left and a difference matrix on the right. The former illustrates the evolution of pollution, but enforcing QoD, which means that not all 24 samples are generated, and thus there are repeated samples (i.e., during 2 or more hours the samples can be equal). The latter shows the differences between the repeated samples and the original ones (generated for each hour without QoD) with a maximum error of 5%, representing the darkest areas. Hence, brighter areas mean that the differences were minimal.

Figure 11a depicts a matrix with tiles generated when 20% of detectors have perceived changes. The divergence was minimal: only the 5th not-updated tile was darker (above 2.5% of difference) as at that hour the pollution had already decreased.

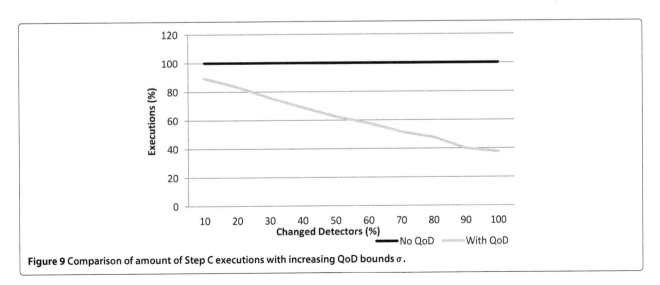

Figure 9 Comparison of amount of Step C executions with increasing QoD bounds σ.

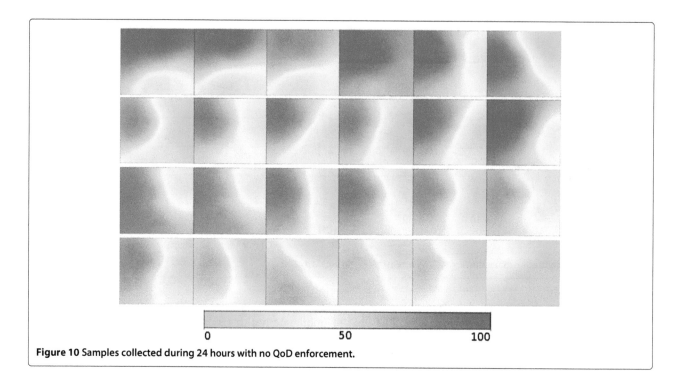

Figure 10 Samples collected during 24 hours with no QoD enforcement.

In Figure 11b, 40% of changed detectors are needed in order to generate new and updated tiles. The black and white matrix shows slightly darker tiles than the previous trial (Figure 11a) for the first hours of the day. Again, the levels of pollution at that hour were decreasing. When dealing with the opposite situation, levels increasing, the vector v component comes to place and guarantees that a strong variation on pollution (above 5%) concentrations will cause the graph to be re-generated.

Through Figure 11c we can see that the generated tiles follow the same tendency of becoming darker as σ augments. The difference matrix shows moderate variations in the tiles per hour, however notice that more than a half of the detectors have perceived changes (this hints that it might not be the most appropriate value of σ for a real environment).

Finally, with a σ of 80% (Figure 11d) more error was introduced, but still within the acceptable limit of 5%. The contiguous black and white tiles do not show much difference in their color, but, instead, on the location of the pollution concentrations; meaning that there is not much variation in the overall concentration levels of pollution and that the pollution is flowing from area to area.

To conclude, we can see that for higher levels of changed detectors (60 and 80%) the differences and errors are higher, but this higher divergence on some tiles happened due to the levels of pollution being greater with QoD than with the original tiles calculated without QoD (and not the opposite, which would be more dangerous). Notwithstanding, black and white graphs in general were brighter

and thus acceptable (especially for realistic and lower levels of σ), supporting the intuitive notion and our arguments that the dataflow does not need to be recalculated every time a single, or a few, changes occur.

5.4 Step E analysis

Now using uniform distributions to generate the pollution concentrations, we may observe, through the charts of Figure 12, that the most divergence of concentration in hotspots, between using QoD and no QoD, occurs when σ is 40 and 60% (i.e., the percentage of minimum changes necessary in the concentration of zones to trigger step E). The concentrations are very close with and without QoD for 20% of σ due to the small oscillations and peaks of the generated values. As for the 80%, the error is also smaller, since there are even less oscillations; i.e., the average is more stabilized as step E is executed fewer times.

Figure 13 shows in percentage the number of hotspots for each wave when varying σ for 20, 40, 60 and 80% of sensors. As the previous figures show, the most divergence happens in the waves leading to the middle of the sequence in the graph (waves 35-85) for the same reasons explained.

Figure 14 shows that the maximum deviation error follows an order 2 polynomial tendency, and therefore we will have, for an uniform distribution of pollution, higher errors when the percentage of changed zones are set in the middle of the range (unlike when pollution is increasing or decreasing, as afore demonstrated). Furthermore, when step E was triggered, it was never due to the error

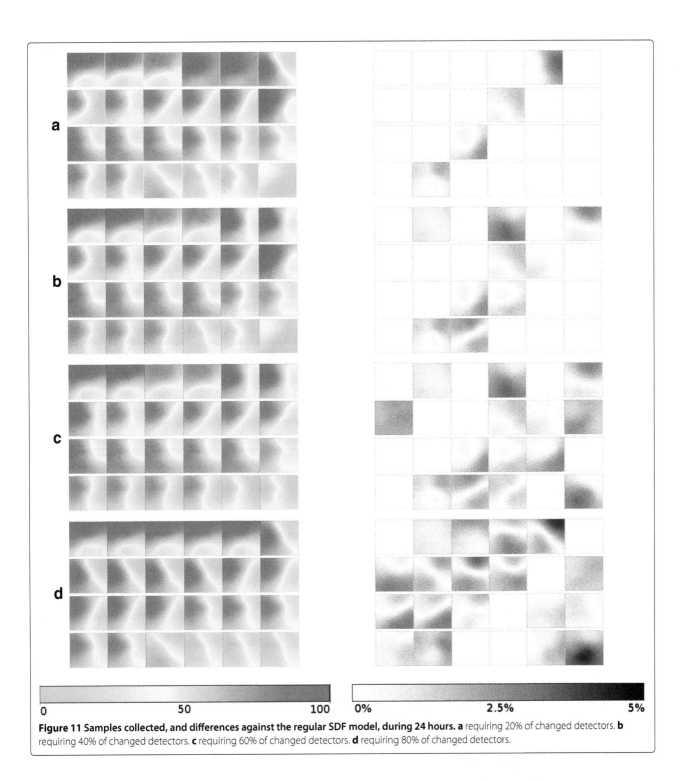

Figure 11 Samples collected, and differences against the regular SDF model, during 24 hours. a requiring 20% of changed detectors. **b** requiring 40% of changed detectors. **c** requiring 60% of changed detectors. **d** requiring 80% of changed detectors.

being greater than v, 2, which happened due to the regular tendency in the concentration distribution.

In Figure 15 we may see the impact in the percentage of executions when combining the QoD of steps C and E (i.e., minimum percentage of changes in zones and detectors). For this particular trial, step E: i) presents an improvement, almost linear, in the number of executions when no QoD is enforced on step C; and ii) only improves starting from 75% when QoD is enforced for the detectors. In a dataflow with pipeline processing, like the one considered, it is natural that the QoD of previous or upstream steps influence the executions of current and downstream steps in the pipeline, since the inputted data is derived from upstream, i.e., from the beginning of the processing.

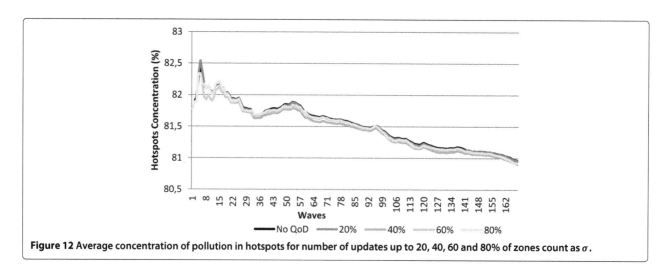

Figure 12 Average concentration of pollution in hotspots for number of updates up to 20, 40, 60 and 80% of zones count as σ.

5.5   Step F analysis

Since the Air Quality Health Index is a single discrete scalar value, we observe a step plot represented by the lines of the chart depicted in Figure 16, where we compared the accumulated average of the index with and without QoD for levels of changes in the number of hotspots (σ) of 20, 40, 60, and 80%. Due to the uniform distribution of pollution used, the lines are roughly parallel starting on the 18th wave, and, as the σ increases, the QoD lines become further distant from the *No QoD* line, meaning an increasing on the deviation of the index. Nevertheless, this deviation reaches our coverage limit of 0.3 (ν) roughly from 60% of σ and therefore the divergence of the lines corresponding to 60 and 80% is much smaller. Moreover, the step effect is higher for greater values of σ, so the index is steady until σ or ν are reached.

Through Figure 17 we may see that the error increases with the percentage of changed hotspots and roughly follows a linear tendency. This increase is more abrupt from 20 to 60%, also showing the impact that ν had on the index values; i.e., the increase was smaller from 60%.

We fixed the QoD of the previous steps in the dataflow and analyzed the gains in terms of executions of step F (Figure 18). A great quantity of executions were saved, even for 20% of changed hotspots where about 70% of the total executions without any QoD (i.e., 168 executions) were spared. At 80% of changed hotspots, only about 5% of the total executions were performed with an error not greater than 0.3. It is natural that, as we go through the actions of the pipeline, the number of executions with QoD is reduced, since the noise from the raw data injected in the dataflow is funnelled through the processing chain into more refined and structured data.

5.6   Overall analysis

Figure 19 shows the running time of a complete cycle of 168 waves with different loads (2500, 10000, 22500, and 40000 detectors) for 1 to 6 nodes. As the number of nodes increases we may see that the time remains roughly constant, showing that our model with HBase can achieve scalability, and almost practically constant access times. We stress that these are only exemplificative: real

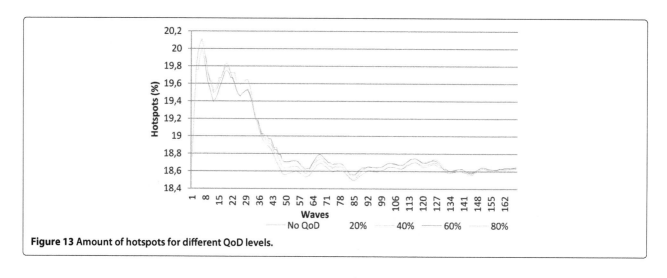

Figure 13 Amount of hotspots for different QoD levels.

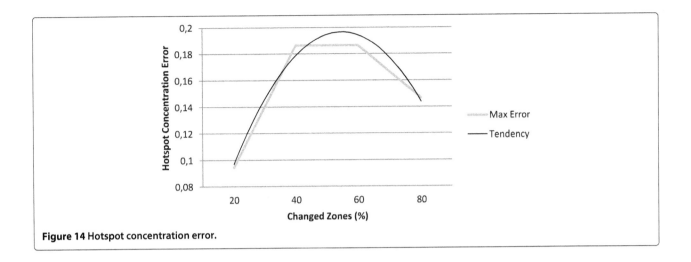

Figure 14 Hotspot concentration error.

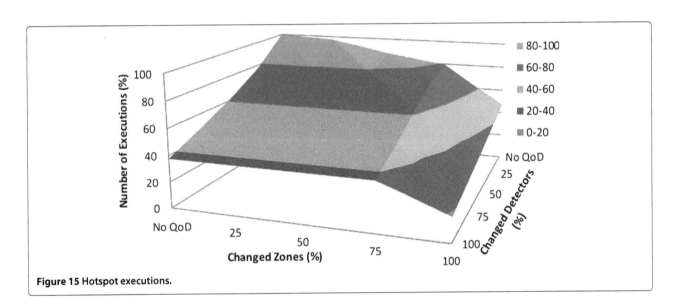

Figure 15 Hotspot executions.

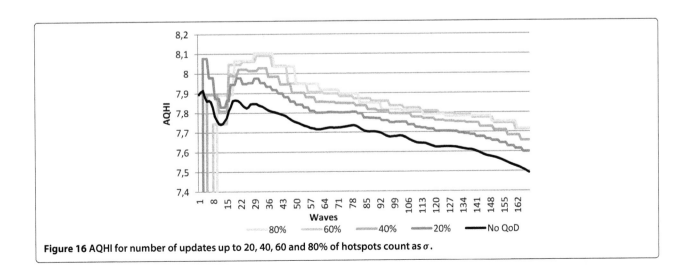

Figure 16 AQHI for number of updates up to 20, 40, 60 and 80% of hotspots count as σ.

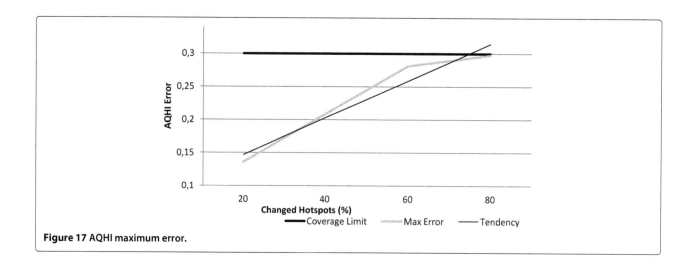

Figure 17 AQHI maximum error.

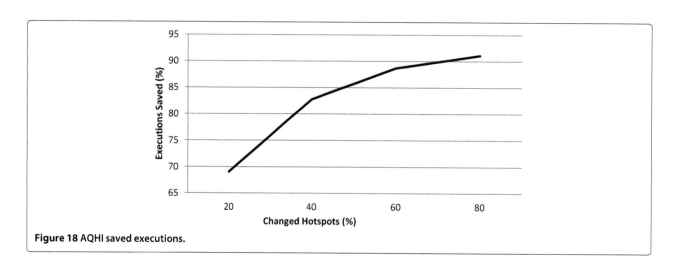

Figure 18 AQHI saved executions.

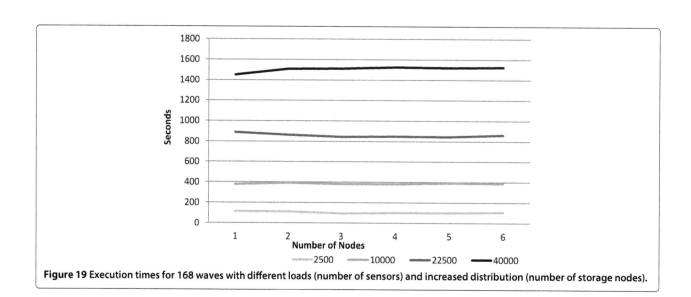

Figure 19 Execution times for 168 waves with different loads (number of sensors) and increased distribution (number of storage nodes).

life calculations for each wave may involve greater computational effort both due to complexity and to higher sampling rates; possibly, many other dataflows may be also being executed in a shared infrastructure. Thus, gains in real life settings may be more significant.

In Figure 20, the average load of tasks during a cycle of 168 waves is shown when σ is 25, 50, 75, and 100%, as the cluster increases in size from 1 to 6 nodes. The total tasks are calculated by multiplying the executed dataflow's tasks (6) by the total number of waves (168). Tasks executions are scheduled across the cluster worker nodes by following a round-robin scheduling, hence saved executions will tend to adhere to this distribution as well. In fact, the average load observed is naturally in line with what would result from dividing the total number of tasks by the number of nodes in the cluster. We can see that i) the gains with QoD are higher for higher ratios of *tasks / number_of_nodes*, and ii) the loads converge, in absolute values, as the number of nodes increases. More importantly, we assessed the load balancing across the cluster, and observed, as depicted in Figure 21 that, for all QoD levels, the load across the 6 nodes in the cluster is very evenly distributed around the average values. Achieving resource savings by avoiding dataflow executions and ensuring load balance across the cluster, combined, allow the system to scale effectively.

Through Figure 22 we may see the variation of the output error as waves go by. This error, which comes from postponing the triggering of actions, corresponds to the deviation of the output that should have been modified having the dataflow been completely executed; i.e., this error is calculated by summing the differences (in absolute value) between current and previous row's values and dividing by the sum of all previous values. Also due to the restrictions on ν, the steps are triggered when greater variations in magnitude occur and, therefore, the maximum

error observed never goes above 25%, for the QoD range of values that we used in σ. Decision-makers should settle for a percentage of error that they can tolerate, i.e, up to a value that carries enough *significance* for the given activity, and depending on how critical it is, and their systems are. Notwithstanding, we consider an error up to 15% as quite acceptable for most monitoring activities, given the extensive gains in saved resources. Note that on average the error stayed under that mark.

5.7 Discussion

The results and patterns observed, for the executions of the AQHI dataflow with different QoD divergence bounds, corroborate the intuitive notion that most of the times, just because there is new data available, it would be neither necessary nor useful to re-execute the dataflow as the final results would suffer little or no difference, thus wasting resources and computational power. This also happens with other tests we performed with fire risk analysis in forests, and social impact of companies in blog references.

The problem with ad-hoc approaches is that the user is left with an all-or-nothing approach, or to simply define periodical (guessing) execution. With QoD, dataflow users and developers can define, with a sound model and approach, the precise conditions when they consider each individual step of a dataflow should be re-executed due to changes in its input being considered as relevant. Furthermore, we can improve resource efficiency in a predictable way as savings are proportional to the percentage of avoided re-executions.

6   Related work

In this section we review relevant solutions, within the current state of the art, that intersect the main topics approached in this work. First, we describe general and

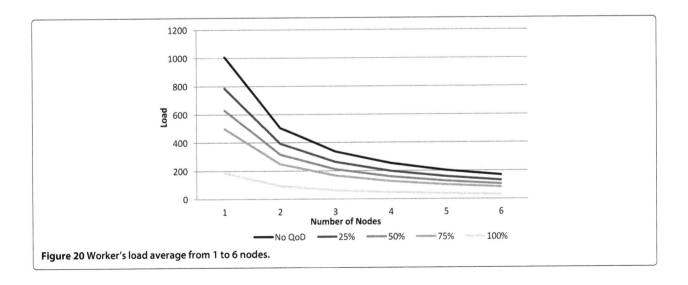

Figure 20 Worker's load average from 1 to 6 nodes.

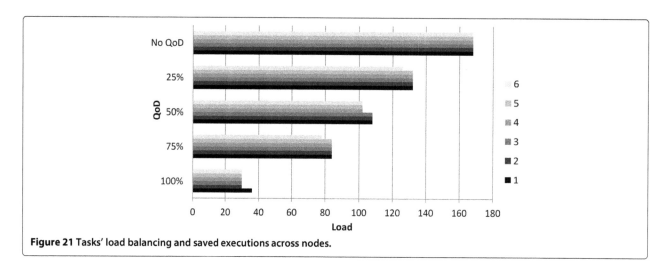

Figure 21 Tasks' load balancing and saved executions across nodes.

e-science data/workflow systems. Next, we focus on solutions for incremental processing.

6.1 Workflow systems

DAGMan [13] is one of the early workflow languages in e-science. It interprets and manages text descriptions of jobs comprising directed acyclic graphs (DAGs). DAGMan accounts for job dependencies, allows pre- and post-processing scripts for each vertex and reissues failed jobs. Being a meta-scheduler, it relies on the Condor workload management system (which is centralized) for scheduling and does not represent data as a first-class entity. Still, DAGMan is very popular due to its integration with Condor.

Taverna [14], part of the myGrid project, is heavily used in bioinformatics. It is a workflow management system with interoperability support for a multitude of execution environments and data formats. Data sources and data links are considered as first entities in the dataflow language. Execution can be placed remotely on a large list of resources but without cross-site distribution and no QoD is enforced.

Triana [15] is a decade proven visual programming environment, focusing on minimum effort, that allows users to compose applications from programming components (drawn from a large library on text, signal and image processing) by drag and drop into a workspace, and connecting them in a workflow graph.

Pegasus [16] is a long running project that extends DAGMan in order to allow mapping of workflows of jobs to remote clusters, and cloud computing infrastructures. It maps jobs on distributed resources and from the description of computation tasks, it performs necessary data transfers (required files) among sites. Pegasus aims at optimizing workflow performance and reliability by scheduling to appropriate resources but there are no

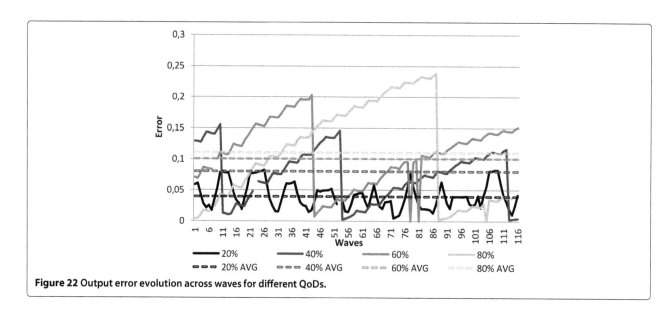

Figure 22 Output error evolution across waves for different QoDs.

QoD guarantees on continuous processing or data flow, and no data sharing.

Dryad [17] executes DAGs explicitly created via an imperative API. It includes composition of operators/ operations and enabled new ones to be defined, allowing for graph and vertex merger. It allows the construction of computation pipelines spanning across a cluster. It has been integrated with LINQ data query capabilities in .NET languages as C#, SQL and others. It has support for channels of shared mutable data.

Kepler [18] is a solution for managing scientific workflows. It was designed to help scientists and other non-expert computer users to create, execute, and share models and analyses, thereby including a set of features for reducing the inherent complexity of deploying workflows in various computing environments (e.g., in the Grid).

Our work is akin, and can be regarded as an advance, to the support for conditional workflows [19], supported by Triana and Kepler, but absent in dominant approaches such as Pegasus and DAGMan. First, they target mainly grid computing and not dataflows manipulating cloud storage. Second, in the approaches supporting conditional workflows, the conditions to be evaluated need to be expressed explicitly in the workflow, i.e. almost programmatically, and are usually actual functional decisions required at execution time. These are inserted in order to take independent paths of execution in a workflow depending on some shared state. We do not require workflow designers to *pollute* workflow descriptions with numerous conditional nodes assessing QoS or QoD criteria, they need only be expressed declaratively, outside the dataflow. Thus, the same dataflow description can be instantiated multiple times, and by different users, with different QoD criteria. Still, our approach does not forbid the usage of conditional nodes, it simply does not mandate it. Moreover, the enforcement of quality criteria is automated, based on information gathered from the cloud storage when data objects are updated. In essence, the conditional behavior of executing dataflow steps only when relevant new input is available, is completely declarative, automated and driven by goal-like criteria, instead of explicit, replicated across every node describing steps, and evaluated by manually developed, and opaque, code.

6.2 Incremental processing

MapReduce [20] is inspired by the map and reduce primitives in functional programming. Computation is divided into two sequential phases. The first is a mapping phase, which operates over each element in the input and produces a set of intermediate key/value pairs. A reduce phase follows where all values sharing the same key are processed and aggregated based on some application level logic. This allows for automatic parallelization. MapReduce is used in large clusters to analyze in parallel huge data sets in domains such as web log and graph analysis. It automatically partitions input data, schedules execution across the cluster, and handles nodes failures. It is batch-oriented so changes in input require full execution from scratch. While allowing custom functions for input partitioning, comparisons, and preliminary key/ value reduce, executed locally by combiners, MapReduce still forces programmers to obey a strict model different of those used for application logic. Though, the automatic parallelization and fault-tolerance features have drawn an enthusiastic community that has developed a complete open-source port of the original proprietary system in Hadoop [11]. Like Oozie, a few other workflow managers have arisen for Hadoop, such as Azkaban, http://sna-projects.com/azkaban/ Cascading, http://www.cascading.org and Fluxua. https://github.com/pranab/fluxua.

MapReduce is a powerful abstraction for simple tasks, e.g. word counting, that have to be applied to colossal amounts of data. This was its initial purpose: reverse index creation and page rankings, essentially weighted sums. More modern functionality such as supporting online social networks and data analytics are extremely cumbersome to code as a giant set of interdependent MapReduce programs. Reusability is thus very limited. To amend this, the Apache Pig platform [9] eases creation of data analysis programs. The Pig Latin language combines imperative-like script language (foreach, load, store) with SQL-like operators (group, filter). Scripts are compiled into Java programs linked to Map Reduce libraries. An example of productivity and reusability is a word counting script with 6 lines of code. The Hive [21] warehouse reinstates fully declarative SQL-like languages (HiveQL) over data in tables (stored as files in an HDFS directory). Queries are compiled into MapReduce jobs to be executed on Hadoop. SCOPE [22] takes a similar approach to scripting but targeting Dryad [17] for its execution engine.

HyMR [23] is a hybrid MapReduce workflow system that combines Hadoop and Twister [24] to enable efficient processing of iterative data analysis applications. It points out the inability of Hadoop to directly support iterative parallel applications, thereby requiring a driver program to orchestrate application iterations (each piped as a separate MapReduce job). This, however, has drawbacks, such as forcing the user to manually set the number of iterations (making it impossible for a program to ensure convergence to a given condition), and the re-scheduling overhead of mapping and reduce tasks on every application iteration. Twister, by its turn, allows iterative applications to run without any of those problems. However, it requires intermediate output files to be transferred from one node to another, instead of using and benefiting from a shared distributed file system, such as HDFS from Hadoop, with fault tolerance mechanisms. HyMR, therefore, combines Twister and Hadoop to take the best of each and support iterative programs. We also share data ultimately through Hadoop, albeit at a higher semantic level with HBase noSQL storage; however there is no performance reasoning about the data semantics and output impact in HyMR.

To avoid recreating web indexes from scratch after each web crawl, as most sites change slowly, Google Percolator [25] does incremental processing on top of BigTable, replacing batch processing of MapReduce. It provides row and table-wide transactions, snapshot isolation, with locks stored in special Bigtable columns. Observers allow programmers to monitor columns. Notify columns are set when rows are updated, with several threads scanning them. Applications are sets of custom-coded observers. At most one transaction is run when a column is modified, but several updates may be fed to the same transaction. Timestamps allow identifying new rows since last execution. Although it scales better than MapReduce, it has 30-fold resource overhead over traditional RDBMS. Nova [26] is similar but has no latency goals, accumulating many new inputs and processing them lazily for throughput. Moreover, Nova provides data processing abstraction through Pig Latin; and supports stateful continuous processing of evolving data sets.

Yahoo CBP [27] aims at greater expressiveness by expressing incremental processing as dataflows with explicit mention when computation stages are stateless or stateful. Input is split by determining membership in frames of new records (e.g., 1 hour epoch), allowing grouping input to reduce messaging. Thus, as a result of a partial web crawl, a new input frame is processed. For stateful stages, translator functions combine data from new frame with existing state. CBP provides primitives for explicit control flow and synchronize execution of multiple inputs. It requires an extended MapReduce implementation and some explicit programming when a QoD-enabled dataflow.

InCoop [28] aims at transparently detecting the repeated execution of the same task (code and input data) and retrieve from cache the results of previous executions. It allows simply restarting jobs from scratch when new data is available. Most re-computation is prevented and cached results used instead. Map, combine, and reduce phase results are stored and memoized. A new memorization-aware scheduler is used to repeat tasks where cached output is already stored, reducing data transfers that still cause overhead even if re-computation is avoided. Content-based splitting minimizes number of reprocessed partitions. Somehow like *Fluχ*, this project attempts to reduce the number of executions of processing steps; however, it implies that the input/output datasets are repeated or intersected among each other.

Nectar [29] for Dryad links data and the computation that generated it as unified hybrid cacheable element. When data is unused for long, it is removed and replaced by the computation that produced it to be rerun later if needed. On Dryad programs reruns, Nectar replaces results partially, or totally, with cached data. Dryad programs need to be enhanced with cache management calls that check and update the cache server. Cached results and modified programs are managed in a central store. Cacheable elements include sub-expressions, and DAGs shared by different processes operating on the same data. Like InCoop, Nectar is advantageous only for scenarios where input/output is repeated, whereas the QoD model fits a broader range of scenarios.

In [30], it is presented a formal programming and scheduling model for defining temporal asynchrony in workflows (motivated by the need of low-latency processing of critical data). The workflow vertices consist of operators, that process data, and data channels, which are pathways through which data flows between operators. These operators have signatures that describe the types and consistency of the blocks (which are the atomic units of data) accepted as input and returned as output. Data channels have a representation of time to a relation snapshot, with an interval of validity, which are used to enforce consistency invariants. These constraints, types of blocks permitted on output, freshness, and consistency bounds, are then used by the scheduler which produces minimal-cost execution plans. This project shares our goals of exploring and providing non ad-hoc solutions for introducing asynchronous behavior in workflows, however, it does not account with the volume, relevance or impact of modifications of the data given as input for each workflow step.

7 Conclusion

In this article we presented *Fluχ*, a novel dataflow model with framework and library support, for data-intensive computing, capable of orchestrating different data-based computation steps, while enforcing quality constraints over the data shared among those steps. With *Fluχ*, we aim at enhancing the workflow and dataflow paradigms with quality-of-service notions, expressed by constrains over the divergence of data and the bounds on input data, that should trigger re-execution of a computational step, and update of its output. We call this enforcement quality-of-data (QoD).

Such quality-of-data enforcement is thus used to guide, and to some extent, autonomously schedule the execution and triggering semantics of dataflows. This allows achieving controlled performance and high resource efficiency, flexibility and elasticity, which is essential in today's cloud-like environments. Such properties are increasingly more relevant nowadays, where data is digitally flowing all over the world, throughout the Internet: ranging from smartphones to desktops, and where a single click or tap on an application may generate large streams of information, that need to be properly, and resource efficiently, processed in support of keeping up the pace in the innovation space.

The *Fluχ* model and supporting framework and library were implemented and found both easy to integrate with existing WMS infrastructures, as well as with currently popular cloud tabular storage (HBase) for scalability. To demonstrate *Fluχ* feasibility, usefulness, and efficiency, the assessment of *Fluχ* was centered on a realistic prototypical example of intensive data processing, addressing the evaluation of air quality, pollution and health risks, for a city based on sensory data, gathered asynchronously, from thousands of sensors. The evaluation of *Fluχ* revolved around three fundamental criteria: i) result convergence, showing that using QoD divergence bounding criteria does not introduce significant errors in results; ii) execution overhead, showing that we are able to avoid large numbers of multiple repetitive executions of dataflow steps; and iii) that due to the aforementioned, we reduce machine load, e.g., in cluster, grid or cloud infrastructures, as well as improving resource usage efficiency for the same level of data *value* generated by the dataflows.

Therefore, we find *Fluχ* a compelling effort, within the current state of the art, to improve dataflows execution, in a performance-improved, resource efficient and correct manner and, thus, deliver higher QoS to end-users and drive costs of operation down.

Endnote

[a]*Quality-of-Data* is a novel concept, akin to SLA, different from *data quality*, that traditionally refers to other issues such as internal data correctness, semantic coherence, data adherence to real-life sources, or data appropriateness for managerial and business decisions.

Competing interests
The authors declare that they have no competing interests.

Authors' contributions
All authors read and approved the final manuscript.

Acknowledgements
This work was partially funded by FCT under projects PTDC/EIA-EIA/102250/2008, PTDC/EIA-EIA/108963/2008, and PEst-OE/EEI/LA0021/2011, and PhD grant SFRH/BD/80099/2011. We also would like to thank the anonymous reviewers who greatly contributed to the betterment of this work.

References

1. Ahrens J, Hendrickson B, Long G, Miller S, Ross R, Williams D (2011) Data-intensive science in the us doe: Case studies and future challenges. Comput Sci Eng 13(6): 14–24. doi:10.1109/MCSE.2011.77
2. Deelman E, Callaghan S, Field E, Francoeur H, Graves R, Gupta N, Gupta V, Jordan TH, Kesselman C, Maechling P, Mehringer J, Mehta G, Okaya D, Vahi K, Zhao L (2006) Managing large-scale workflow execution from resource provisioning to provenance tracking: The cybershake example. In: Proceedings of the Second IEEE International Conference on e-Science and Grid Computing, E-SCIENCE '06. IEEE Computer Society, Washington, p 14. doi:10.1109/E-SCIENCE.2006.99
3. Falgout J (2011) Dataflow programming: Handling huge loads without adding complexity the basic concepts of dataflow programming. Dr. Dobb's. http://www.drdobbs.com/database/dataflow-programming-handling-huge-data/231400148
4. Livny J, Teonadi H, Livny M, Waldor MK (2008) High-Throughput, kingdom-wide prediction and annotation of bacterial non-coding RNAs. PLoS ONE 3(9): e3197+. doi:10.1371/journal.pone.0003197
5. York DG, et al. (2000) The sloan digital sky survey: Technical summary. Astronomical J 120(3): 1579
6. Ludäscher B, Altintas I, Bowers S, Cummings J, Critchlow T, Deelman E, Roure DD, Freire J, Goble C, Jones M, Klasky S, McPhillips T, Podhorszki N, Silva C, Taylor I, Vouk M (2009) Scientific process automation and workflow management. In: Shoshani A Rotem D (eds). Scientific Data Management, Computational Science Series, chap. 13. CRC press, Boca raton. http://www.crcpress.com/product/isbn/9781420069808
7. Juve G, Deelman E, Berriman GB, Berman BP, Maechling P (2012) An evaluation of the cost and performance of scientific workflows on amazon ec2. J Grid Comput 10(1): 5–21
8. George L (2011) HBase: The Definitive Guide, 1edn. O'Reilly Media, Sebastopol. http://shop.oreilly.com/product/0636920014348.do#
9. Olston C, Reed B, Srivastava U, Kumar R, Tomkins A (2008) Pig latin: a not-so-foreign language for data processing. In: Proceedings of the 2008 ACM SIGMOD international conference on Management of data. SIGMOD '08. ACM, New York, pp. 1099–1110. doi:10.1145/1376616.1376726
10. The Apache Software Foundation (2013) Apache Oozie Workflow Scheduler for Hadoop. http://oozie.apache.org/
11. White T (2009) Hadoop: The Definitive Guide, 1st edn. O'Reilly Media, Inc., Sebastopol. http://shop.oreilly.com/product/0636920021773.do
12. Chang F, Dean J, Ghemawat S, Hsieh WC, Wallach DA, Burrows M, Chandra T, Fikes A, Gruber RE (2006) Bigtable: a distributed storage system for structured data. In: Proceedings of the 7th USENIX Symposium on Operating Systems Design and Implementation - Volume 7. OSDI '06. USENIX Association, Berkeley, pp. 15–15
13. Couvares P, Kosar T, Roy A, Weber J, Wenger K (2007) Workflow management in condor. In: Taylor IJ, Deelman E, Gannon DB, Shields M (eds). Workflows for e-Science. Springer, London, pp. 357–375
14. Missier P, Soiland-Reyes S, Owen S, Tan W, Nenadic A, Dunlop I, Williams A, Oinn T, Goble CA (2010) Taverna, reloaded. In: SSDBM. Springer-Verlag Berlin, Heidelberg, pp. 471–481
15. Taylor I, Shields M, Wang I, Harrison A (2007) The Triana workflow environment: architecture and applications. In: Taylor I, Deelman E, Gannon D, Shields M (eds). Workflows for e-Science. Springer, New York, Secaucus, pp. 320–339
16. Lee K, Paton NW, Sakellariou R, Deelman E, Fernandes AAA, Mehta G (2009) Adaptive workflow processing and execution in pegasus. Concurr Comput: Pract Exper 21(16): 1965–1981. doi:10.1002/cpe.v21:16
17. Isard M, Budiu M, Yu Y, Birrell A, Fetterly D (2007) Dryad: distributed data-parallel programs from sequential building blocks. In: Proceedings of the 2nd ACM SIGOPS/EuroSys European Conference on Computer Systems 2007, EuroSys '07. ACM, New York, pp. 59–72. doi:10.1145/1272996.1273005
18. Altintas I, Berkley C, Jaeger E, Jones M, Ludäscher B, Mock S (2004) Kepler: An extensible system for design and execution of scientific workflows. Sci Stat Database Manag Int Conf 0(423). http://ieeexplore.ieee.org/xpl/articleDetails.jsp?arnumber=1311241
19. Bahsi EM, Ceyhan E, Kosar T (2007) Conditional workflow management: A survey and analysis. Sci Program 15(4): 283–297
20. Dean J, Ghemawat S (2004) Mapreduce: simplified data processing on large clusters. In: Proceedings of the 6th conference on Symposium on Opearting Systems Design & Implementation - Volume 6, OSDI'04. USENIX Association, Berkeley, pp. 10–10
21. Thusoo A, Sarma JS, Jain N, Shao Z, Chakka P, Anthony S, Liu H, Wyckoff P, Murthy R (2009) Hive- a warehousing solution over a map-reduce framework. In: IN VLDB '09: Proceedings of the vldb endowment. Very Large Data Base Endowment Inc., USA, pp. 1626–1629
22. Chaiken R, Jenkins B, Larson PA, Ramsey B, Shakib D, Weaver S, Zhou J (2008) Scope: easy and efficient parallel processing of massive data sets. Proc VLDB Endow 1(2): 1265–1276. http://dl.acm.org/citation.cfm?id=1454166

23. Ruan Y, Guo Z, Zhou Y, Qiu J, Fox G (2012) Hymr: a hybrid mapreduce workflow system. Tech. rep., Indiana University, Bloomington, IN

24. Ekanayake J, Li H, Zhang B, Gunarathne T, Bae SH, Qiu J, Fox G (2010) Twister: a runtime for iterative mapreduce. In: Proceedings of the 19th ACM International Symposium on High Performance Distributed Computing, HPDC '10. ACM, New York, pp. 810–818. doi:10.1145/1851476.1851593

25. Peng D, Dabek F (2010) Large-scale incremental processing using distributed transactions and notifications. In: Proceedings of the 9th USENIX conference on Operating systems design and implementation, OSDI'10. USENIX Association, Berkeley, pp. 1–15

26. Olston C, Chiou G, Chitnis L, Liu F, Han Y, Larsson M, Neumann A, Rao VB, Sankarasubramanian V, Seth S, Tian C, ZiCornell T, Wang X (2011) Nova: continuous pig/hadoop workflows. In: Proceedings of the 2011 international conference on Management of data, SIGMOD '11. ACM, New York, pp. 1081–1090. doi:10.1145/1989323.1989439

27. Logothetis D, Olston C, Reed B, Webb KC, Yocum K (2010) Stateful bulk processing for incremental analytics. In: Proceedings of the 1st ACM symposium on Cloud computing, SoCC '10. ACM, New York, pp. 51–62. doi:10.1145/1807128.1807138

28. Bhatotia P, Wieder A, Rodrigues R, Acar UA, Pasquin R (2011) Incoop: Mapreduce for incremental computations. In: Proceedings of the 2nd ACM Symposium on Cloud Computing, SOCC '11. ACM, New York, pp. 7:1–7:14. doi:10.1145/2038916.2038923

29. Gunda PK, Ravindranath L, Thekkath CA, Yu Y, Zhuang L (2010) Nectar: automatic management of data and computation in datacenters. In: Proceedings of the 9th USENIX conference on Operating systems design and implementation, OSDI'10. USENIX Association, Berkeley, pp. 1–8

30. Olston C (2011) Modeling and scheduling asynchronous incremental workflows. Tech. rep., Yahoo! Research

12

PaaSHopper: Policy-driven middleware for multi-PaaS environments

Stefan Walraven[*†], Dimitri Van Landuyt[†], Ansar Rafique[†], Bert Lagaisse[†] and Wouter Joosen[†]

Abstract

Offering Software-as-a-Service (SaaS) applications on top of a Platform-as-a-Service (PaaS) platform is a promising strategy as the SaaS provider does not need to acquire and maintain private cloud infrastructure, and it enables him/her to enjoy the benefits of cloud scalability and flexiblity as well. However, as this entails losing some control over the application and its data, SaaS providers are in practice reluctant to migrate to a PaaS platform entirely. To alleviate such concerns of vendor lock-in, the concept of a multi-cloud involves integrating and combining multiple cloud environments, private as well as public, but also involving multiple providers and different technologies. This has the added benefit that it further improves overall availability, flexibility and scalability. Current support for multi-cloud applications however is limited.

This paper presents PaaSHopper, a middleware platform for developing and operating multi-tenant SaaS applications in a multi-PaaS environment. It enables the SaaS provider to have fine-grained control over the execution of applications and the storage of application data, while offering the tenant some degrees of customization and self-service as well. Driven by stakeholder-specific policies, the middleware dynamically decides which requests and tasks are executed in a particular part of the multi-PaaS environment. We validated this work in the context of four realistic SaaS application cases on top of a multi-cloud consisting of a local JBoss Application Server cluster, Google App Engine, and Red Hat OpenShift.

Keywords: Multi-cloud; PaaS; Policy-driven adaptation; Middleware; Portability

1 Introduction

Cloud computing enables the on-demand delivery of ICT solutions as online services, covering software applications, system software, and hardware infrastructure [1-3]. High flexibility and scalability benefits are gained by allowing these services to be provisioned rapidly upon customer request. The cloud computing paradigm includes three cloud service delivery models [1,3]: (i) Infrastructure as a Service (IaaS), for example Amazon EC2 [4], delivers fundamental computing resources, such as processing, storage and network capacity, as a service, (ii) Platform as a Service (PaaS) provides a higher-level application development and hosting platform, for example Google App Engine (GAE) [5], and (iii) Software as a Service (SaaS) delivers software applications as online, on-demand services, e.g. Salesforce CRM [6].

In this paper, we focus on the PaaS delivery model. PaaS is a promising development and deployment platform for enterprise SaaS applications [7,8], as it allows the SaaS provider him- or herself to enjoy the cloud benefits of high availability, on-demand scalability, and pay-per-use cost models without having to acquire and manage the underpinning cloud infrastructure.

However, several concerns still withhold the general adoption of this strategy [9-11]. By building SaaS applications on top of a PaaS platform, the SaaS provider partially loses control over his/her applications and data. Especially for core business applications, many SaaS providers prefer their own private cloud or data center, but this requires large investments and has a capacity that is limited in practice. In addition, depending on a single PaaS provider comes with the non-negligible risks of provider and technology lock-in as well as limited availability [12-14]. In addition, SaaS providers typically adopt a multi-tenant architecture [15,16] to achieve economies of scale: a single application instance is shared by many different customer

*Correspondence: stefan.walraven@cs.kuleuven.be
[†]Equal Contributors
iMinds-DistriNet, KU Leuven, Celestijnenlaan 200A, 3001 Leuven, Belgium

organizations (tenants), each in turn servicing their own end users. High operational cost efficiency is achieved by sharing the same resources among multiple customer organizations. In practice however, multi-tenancy requires even more flexibility and scalability to address the fluctuating number of (active) tenants and to support all variations of the respective tenant requirements at once.

To address these disadvantages, there is a growing interest in multi-cloud solutions [17]. We define a *multi-cloud* as a composition of multiple cloud environments with as purpose to improve availability and flexibility, and to avoid vendor lock-in. A hybrid cloud is a multi-cloud that consists of at least a public and a private cloud environment, thus combining the unlimited capacity of public clouds with the increased control of private clouds into an integrated system. However, current support for multi-cloud applications is still fairly limited.

In this paper, we focus on the key challenges faced by the SaaS provider when deploying SaaS applications in a multi-PaaS environment:

1. *Heterogeneity in development and deployment platform:* In essence, the current PaaS platforms offer a lot of similar architectural concepts towards application developers, but typically via vendor-specific solutions using different programming languages and supporting technologies [7]. This heterogeneity hinders portability and interoperability of SaaS applications across different PaaS platforms.
2. *Flexible and (re)configurable decisions that need to be supported:* There are large differences in the trust relationship between the customers and the different (public) cloud providers. This requires smart and fine-grained control (up to the tenant level) over the execution of multi-tenant applications and storage of data across multi-PaaS environments.

This paper presents PaaSHopper, a policy-driven middleware that addresses the above-mentioned challenges by (i) offering a PaaS abstraction layer to increase portability and interoperability of application components over different PaaS platforms and providers, and (ii) facilitating flexible, reconfigurable deployment and execution, driven by policies that express stakeholder-specific constraints such as geographical location, security, and workload.

A first version of the PaaSHopper middleware architecture has been presented in previous work [18,19]. In contrast, this paper introduces an extensive motivation based on four different SaaS application cases, all based on our analysis of industrial SaaS applications. In addition, the middleware architecture

has been extended and the validation strengthened. This paper also provides an extensive discussion of the PaaSHopper middleware and the remaining open challenges.

The remainder of this paper is structured as follows. Section 2 introduces several multi-cloud scenarios from four realistic SaaS application cases, and identifies the challenges that are addressed in this paper. Section 3 elaborates on the architecture of the PaaSHopper middleware with respect to portability, interoperability, and policy-driven execution and storage. Section 4 validates the middleware based on a prototype implementation. In Section 5, we discuss the work and identify the open challenges ahead. Section 6 discusses related work and Section 7 concludes the paper.

2 Motivation

The motivation for this paper is based on our experience with a number of multi-cloud applications, obtained in the context of several applied research projects in collaboration with industrial SaaS providers. In Section 2.1, we discuss a set of realistic cases of SaaS applications in multi-cloud environments, from which we derive in Section 2.2 the key challenges for multi-cloud applications.

2.1 Multi-cloud application cases

The following cases present a number of the deployment and operation aspects of four multi-tenant SaaS applications, while illustrating the benefits of multi-cloud environments. Each of these applications have different properties and requirements with respect to execution and storage.

Application #1: Document processing as a service. This multi-tenant SaaS application delivers B2B document processing facilities to a wide range of companies (see also [20]). It supports the business-specific generation, the archival and the delivery of large sets of customized digital documents. This SaaS application is deployed on top of a hybrid cloud solution, consisting of a private cloud platform that is managed by the SaaS provider, and a public cloud offering that is used as a spillover to address peaks in the processing load. The storage of the documents occurs at the same location in the hybrid cloud as the processing.

However, the various types of data and documents (e.g. invoices, payslips, medical reports and leaflets) have different requirements with respect to confidentiality. For example, invoices may only be processed and stored in a cloud environment where certain security requirements are guaranteed (encrypted communication and storage), while there are no such constraints for generating leaflets. In addition, the SaaS provider aims to maximally utilize his/her on-premise infrastructure.

Application #2: Log management as a service. This B2B cloud offering integrates with the on-premise infrastructure of the different tenants: a local agent collects and aggregates the logs of the applications and infrastructure, and sends them to the log management service. This service performs complex analysis activities on the collected logs (e.g. detection of suspicious activities) and heavily relies on scalable storage. To ensure the necessary availability and scalability, the SaaS provider deploys the application in a multi-cloud environment consisting of a number of geographically distributed private data centers.

As the log management service is a data-driven application, the analysis activities should occur near the storage location to avoid the (expensive) migration of large data sets. In addition, tenant-specific constraints are applicable to the geographical placement of the data. For example, a financial company requires that the data may only be stored in a data center in the same country, or even using a dedicated storage infrastructure to ensure strict isolation.

Application #3: Medical image processing as a service. In this application, medical images from different hospitals are processed and stored online as part of the electronic health record (EHR). The SaaS provider uses a multi-cloud solution to distribute and replicate the data over multiple data centers. These data centers can be managed by external (certified) companies, but are in practice not part of a public cloud offering.

Typically, medical images are large files and subject to strict rules with respect to privacy. As a consequence, different hospitals have different requirements with respect to the processing and storage of these medical images, especially driven by governmental rules. For example, European medical data should be stored within Europe, or even more strict, a specific tenant can require that the data may not be stored in a data center that is hosted by a US company, even if it is located in Europe.

Application #4: Simulation processing as a service. This enterprise SaaS offering provides services to perform simulations and optimizations of engineering processes for companies in the automotive and aerospace industry. After the simulation process, the results should be presented to the respective tenants. The amount of data sent throughout this application is limited (e.g. input parameters and end results), but the simulations and optimizations are CPU-intensive. Therefore, a hybrid cloud solution is used to outsource the processing to the public cloud.

However, the input data as well as the simulation results can be highly confidential, for example information about new prototypes, thus putting restrictions on the storage. In this case, processing could be allowed in the public cloud, but the results should be stored in the private cloud.

Similar to the first application, the SaaS provider also aims to maximally use his/her on-premise infrastructure for processing before doing a spill-over.

2.2 Challenges

Based on the application cases presented above, we have identified the following challenges to support the development and deployment of SaaS applications in multi-PaaS environments:

- *Portability and interoperability across different PaaS platforms:* There is a large variety in PaaS platforms, possibly supporting different programming languages and technologies. Even when only considering Java-based platforms, differences exist in terms of development API and deployment: each platform offers its own vendor-specific solution for interfacing with the platform itself as well as with its cloud services, such as scalable storage and background workers (for asynchronous execution) [7,21,22]. Moreover, not every platform supports the same cloud services. This heterogeneity hinders the portability and interoperability of SaaS applications across different PaaS platforms, and thus also the deployment in multi-PaaS environments.

- *Fine-grained control over execution and storage:* Tenants can impose constraints concerning the geographical location of the processing and/or storage of their data, security, available cloud services, etc. Furthermore, SaaS providers want to ensure availability and address peak loads, but also want to limit the use of (more expensive) external cloud infrastructure. Therefore, there should be support to manage and enforce these co-existing stakeholder-specific requirements within the shared SaaS application and across different cloud environments. This enforcement should not only occur for incoming requests and data, but potentially for any interaction between the different application components as well as cloud services.

3 Policy-driven middleware for multi-cloud platforms

This section presents *PaaSHopper*, a policy-driven middleware framework that enables SaaS providers as well as individual tenants to have fine-grained control over the execution and operation of the multi-tenant SaaS application in dynamic multi-PaaS environments. The PaaSHopper middleware consists of two subsystems (see Figure 1) to address the respective challenges in Section 2.2: (i) an *abstraction layer* to tackle the portability and interoperability requirements, and (ii) a *policy-driven execution layer* to control the execution and storage. The constraints and rules of the different stakeholders are

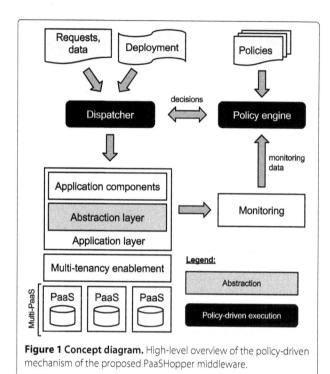

Figure 1 Concept diagram. High-level overview of the policy-driven mechanism of the proposed PaaSHopper middleware.

specified in *policies*. Driven by these different co-existing policies and in collaboration with the policy engine, a dispatcher selects at run time the appropriate application components, which are distributed over multiple (heterogeneous) PaaS offerings, to process requests and data (cf. Figure 1).

Furthermore, a multi-tenancy enablement layer (see Figures 1 and 2) offers basic *multi-tenancy* support by managing the current tenant context and by facilitating the tenant-aware isolation of application data, configurations and policies. Some PaaS platforms already offer built-in support for tenant-aware data isolation, e.g. Google App Engine (GAE) [5]. In addition, the PaaSHopper middleware ensures that the specific tenant context is passed with every invocation throughout the distributed application. This way, the middleware platform offers built-in support for creating multi-tenant applications.

The next subsections elaborate on the architecture of the middleware framework (see Figure 2), providing more details on the common abstractions offered by the abstraction layer, the cross-cloud interaction managed by the dispatcher, and the policy-driven execution. This is an open and versatile architecture, as it supports different implementations and deployments, depending on the application type and the specific nature of the multi-cloud environment.

3.1 Common abstraction for PaaS platforms

The abstraction layer (see (a) and (b) in Figure 2) is responsible for application portability across the

heterogeneous multi-PaaS environment. The core of this layer offers a uniform API to the application components for interaction with the PaaSHopper middleware as well as with the underpinning PaaS platform(s). More specifically, the `AbstractPaaSPlatform` component represents the application container of the execution environment, while the `PaaSService` components provide interfaces to each of the supported cloud services (e.g. scalable storage).

An application component interacts with `Abstract-PaaSPlatform` to retrieve references to these `PaaSServices` or other application components. A `CallContext` object is associated to each invocation. It contains all relevant information regarding the user and the current tenant (see Figure 3). The passing of a `CallContext` is imposed by the distributed nature of the middleware: there is no single application run-time environment or single main memory in a multi-cloud where information about the current active tenant can be stored. Explicitly passing `CallContext` simplifies the design and implementation and enables us to keep the different services stateless. Furthermore, the usage of this `CallContext` object in combination of web service standards (e.g. SOAP or REST) ensures interoperability between application components across different PaaS platforms.

For each of the different PaaS platforms, portability drivers are required to provide an implementation for the common abstraction. These drivers ensure the correct mapping to the vendor-specific APIs, for example in the form of a data access middleware for storage services. Optionally, a driver can provide a full implementation of a PaaS service that is not natively supported by the underpinning platform. Obviously, the appropriate drivers have to be deployed together with the implementation of the application to ensure proper execution.

In [19], we have defined and evaluated such a uniform API for three common PaaS services, including structured storage (NoSQL), blob storage, and asynchronous task execution. However, this solution can easily be interchanged by creating or configuring different drivers with other existing abstractions, for example Hibernate OGM [23] or Impetus Kundera [24] as data access middleware.

3.2 Cross-cloud interaction

The `Dispatcher` (see (c) in Figure 2) ensures the transparent interaction between the different application components that are distributed over the multi-PaaS environment. `AbstractPaaSPlatform` relies on the `Dispatcher` to select the appropriate component instance. However, in order to select an instance of a particular component and to interact with it, the dispatcher

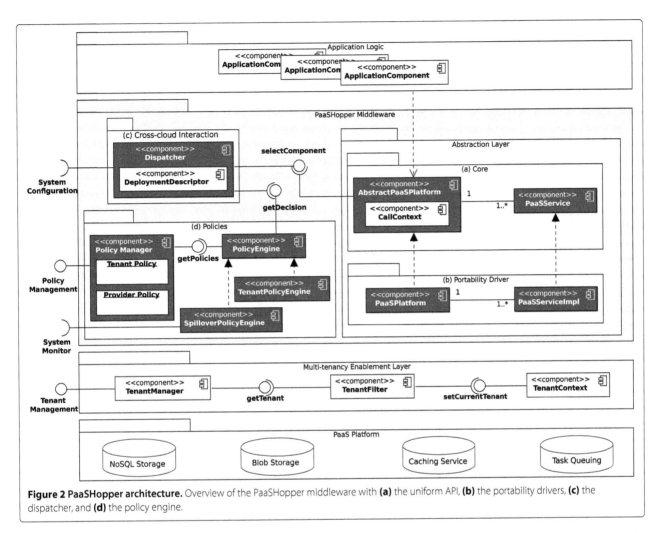

Figure 2 PaaSHopper architecture. Overview of the PaaSHopper middleware with **(a)** the uniform API, **(b)** the portability drivers, **(c)** the dispatcher, and **(d)** the policy engine.

requires an up-to-date overview of the deployment of the entire application across the multi-PaaS environment (i.e. the deployment descriptor). After an instance is selected, it is returned to the application that can start invoking operations on it. The returned component

instance is either a local instance or a proxy to a remote instance, as shown in Figure 4.

The *deployment descriptor* is a configuration artifact that specifies (i) the different PaaS platforms and their properties (e.g. private versus public cloud offering), and (ii) the deployment of all the available local and remote instances for each component interface, i.e. mapping of an instance to one of the PaaS platforms and how to access it, including metadata (e.g. description, tags). The SaaS provider can specify additional domain- and application-specific properties and corresponding values to reflect the characteristics of the different cloud platforms, for example with respect to security.

3.3 Policy-driven execution and storage
The core functionality of the PaaSHopper middleware is offering fine-grained control over the execution of a tenant's request using policies. These policies describe the constraints and rules of the different stakeholders in a declarative way, extracting them from the application code in a modular and reusable way. Based on the different

Figure 3 Call context. `CallContext` interface.

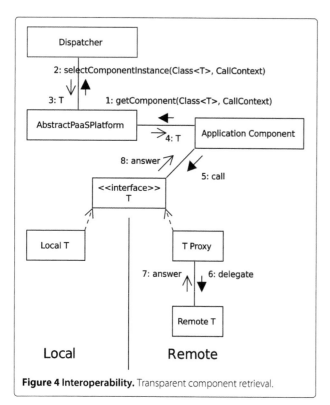

Figure 4 Interoperability. Transparent component retrieval.

Listing 1 Grammar of a tenant policy in BNF notation

```
1   <policy> ::= <component−info >,
2                <message−info >,
3                <constraints >
4   <component−info > ::=
5       Component = <interface −name>
6   <message−info > ::=
7       MessageType = <string >
8       | MessageType = not <string >
9   <constraints > ::=
10      <constraint > (',' <constraint >)∗
11      | (<constraints > and <constraint >)
12      | (<constraints > or <constraint >)
13  <constraint > ::=
14      <location −info >
15      | <access−info >
16      | <provider−info >
17      | <property>
18  <location −info > ::=
19      Location = <location >
20      | Location = not <location >
21  <location > ::= <string > | '∗'
22  <access−info > ::= Access = <access >
23  <access> ::= Public | Private | '∗'
24  <provider−info > ::=
25      Provider {
26          [Company = <company−name >,]
27          [HQ = <string > | not <string >,]
28      }
29  <property> ::=
30      <provider−property> = <value >
```

tenant- and provider-specific policies, the middleware decides where in the multi-cloud a task will be executed or data will be stored. Thus, the execution flow of the multi-cloud application has to continuously adapt based on the context.

Policy types. The PaaSHopper middleware currently supports two types of policies: tenant policies and spill-over policies. A *tenant policy* defines all tenant-specific constraints. These policies are automatically isolated from each other due to our multi-tenant data store abstraction. A tenant policy is coupled to the type of the message (e.g. confidential messages) that is sent to the requested component (and which is indicated by the messageType field in the CallContext, as illustrated in Figure 3). For each message type, the tenant policy can list several constraints to which the receiving component must comply. Listing 1 defines the grammar for describing tenant policies that are currently supported.

The second policy is the *spill-over policy* and is specified by the SaaS provider. Such a policy specifies a configurable threshold for the current workload and enables the PaaSHopper middleware to dynamically decide where a task needs to be executed, either on-premise or remotely, based on the load information retrieved from the overall system monitor. When the load is low, the on-premise utilization is maximized by executing all tasks locally. When the load surpasses the configured threshold, the policy engine tries to force a remote execution.

Policy evaluation. In the current middleware architecture (see (d) in Figure 2), the dispatcher relies on a PolicyEngine to select an instance of a requested component depending upon the constraints specified in the applicable policies and the context (e.g. the associated CallContext and the current load). The policy engine filters the set of all possible component instances that are matched by the different policies. The first component instance that complies to all imposed constraints is returned via the dispatcher to the AbstractPaaS-Platform component (cf. Figure 4). A unique priority integer value is assigned to each policy. This priority value is used when two policies output conflicting constraints, for example when a tenant policy requires local execution but the spill-over policy forces remote execution due to the high load. In that case the policy with the highest priority overrules the other policy. In the middleware this ensures that only tenant requests that are allowed to execute on a public cloud, are delegated when the load is high.

As multi-tenancy enables multiple tenants to use the SaaS application simultaneously, it is important to make the application components stateless and to evaluate the policies on a per call basis, i.e. at each interaction. This implies that requested instances cannot be stored within the member variables of an application component. While experimenting with the use of (traditional) dependency injection [25] techniques to inject the selected component in the client component as a member variable, it became clear to us that when executing a tenant call this often led to concurrency control issues. Dependencies thus need to be re-resolved for each call, as different policies apply for different tenants. For example, in [26] we also required a tenant-aware dependency injector to enable tenant-specific customization of SaaS applications.

SaaS providers can also implement their own control mechanisms. The `CallContext` contains much relevant information that enables other control mechanisms to be implemented (see Figure 3). For example, an application can implement a user policy that allow to define individual policies on a per end user (of tenants) basis. Furthermore, a custom implementation of a policy engine can be provided and inserted into the dispatcher to support custom component selection.

4 Validation

Based on our analysis of the application cases presented in Section 2.1, we extracted a set of three common multi-cloud scenarios: (i) enforcing constraints of tenants and other stakeholders with respect to where data can be processed and/or stored (all applications), (ii) spill-over to the public cloud driven by provider-specific rules (cf. applications #1 and #4), and (iii) migration to other PaaS platforms to replace current providers or to expand the multi-cloud environment (all applications).

To validate the PaaSHopper middleware in the context of these scenarios, we adopted a prototype-driven approach: we implemented a prototype of the document processing application on top of the PaaSHopper middleware (Section 4.1). As the document processing application covers all these multi-cloud scenarios (Sections 4.2 till 4.4), this prototype is representative to illustrate the practical feasibility and applicability of the middleware for the four application cases.

4.1 Prototype

We have developed a Java prototype of the PaaSHopper middleware and an implementation of the document processing application, called CloudPost. This CloudPost implementation consists of a set of services that are executed in a workflow, such as a templating service, a PDF rendering service and a delivery service.

As underpinning multi-PaaS environment, we used (i) a local JBoss AS 7 cluster with a MongoDB database (representing the private cloud), (ii) Google App Engine (GAE) [5] with its datastore, and (iii) Red Hat OpenShift [27] using a Apache Tomcat 7 gear extended with a MongoDB gear for storage. As part of the abstraction layer of the PaaSHopper middleware, we implemented portability drivers for each of these platforms, offering multi-cloud support for three common PaaS services (i.e. structured storage, blob storage and asynchronous task execution). The abstraction layer is deployed on each PaaS platform, combined with the appropriate portability drivers, in order to support the deployment of the Cloud-Post application on top of this heterogeneous multi-cloud.

As the public PaaS offerings are not necessarily used (only during high load), the entry point of the application as well as the dispatcher are deployed in the private cloud only.

Furthermore, the CloudPost provider has to define the multi-cloud environment in the deployment descriptor (see Listing 2). The PaaSHopper middleware allows the provider to specify the properties of the different PaaS platforms. For example, the private cloud provides secure communication (lines 12–13 in Listing 2), OpenShift offers both secure communication and encrypted storage (lines 38–39 in Listing 2), and GAE supports none of these properties (lines 25–26 in Listing 2). This metadata allows the `PolicyEngine` to reason about these platforms.

Listing 2 First part of the deployment descriptor, specifying the different PaaS platforms in the multi-cloud and their respective properties.

```
1   <?xml version = ''1.0'' encoding = ''UTF-8''?>
2   <multicloud>
3     <cloudenv id = ''local''>
4       <name>JBoss AS 7</name>
5       <hosted>private</hosted>
6       <location>Belgium</location>
7       <provider>
8         <company>CloudPost</company>
9         <hq>Belgium</hq>
10      </provider>
11      <properties>
12        <secureComm>true</secureComm>
13        <encrypted>false</encrypted>
14      </properties>
15    </cloudenv>
16    <cloudenv id = ''GAE''>
17      <name>Google App Engine</name>
18      <hosted>public</hosted>
19      <location>US</location>
20      <provider>
21        <company>Google</company>
22        <hq>US</hq>
23      </provider>
24      <properties>
25        <secureComm>false</secureComm>
26        <encrypted>false</encrypted>
27      </properties>
28    </cloudenv>
29    <cloudenv id = ''OpenShift''>
30      <name>Red Hat OpenShift</name>
31      <hosted>public</hosted>
32      <location>EU</location>
33      <provider>
34        <company>Red Hat</company>
35        <hq>US</hq>
36      </provider>
37      <properties>
38        <secureComm>true</secureComm>
39        <encrypted>true</encrypted>
40      </properties>
41    </cloudenv>
42  </multicloud>
43  <components>
44    ...
45  </components>
```

4.2 Scenario #1: Enforcing tenant-specific constraints

Potential tenants of the CloudPost system are *supermarkets* that send targeted advertisements or leaflets to their customers, *utility companies* that send out personal invoices, and *hospitals* that want to deliver the medical reports to the doctors or patients. Although these tenants have roughly the same functional requirements (i.e. generating and delivering digitalized documents), they have different non-functional requirements, for example regarding security.

Assuming that the document generation service is deployed on each PaaS platform of the multi-cloud environment (see Listing 3), then a tenant can constrain (via policies) which instance of this application component will be used for processing his requests. Such a tenant policy specifies the required properties of a certain application component. For example, the policy in Figure 4 specifies that, for a confidential document type, the document generation service must provide encrypted storage and secure communicaton, or must run in a private cloud. Tenants can further define other document types (that are mapped to message types in the middleware) and specify constraints for each type.

Listing 3 Second part of the deployment descriptor, specifying one private and two public versions of an application component.

```
1  <?xml version=''1.0'' encoding=''UTF-8''?>
2  <multicloud>
3    ...
4  </multicloud>
5  <components>
6    <component id=''Doc1''>
7      <interface>cloudpost.service.DocumentService</
            interface>
8      <description>
9        Generation and storage of documents in
              private cloud
10     </description>
11     <implementation>
12       cloudpost.document.generation.
              DocumentServiceImpl
13     </implementation>
14     <cloud>local</cloud>
15   </component>
16   <component id=''Doc2''>
17     <interface>cloudpost.service.DocumentService</
            interface>
18     <description>
19       Generation and storage of documents on
              Google AppEngine
20     </description>
21     <implementation>remote</implementation>
22     <url>
23       http://cloudpost-gae.appspot.com/remote/
              docservice
24     </url>
25     <cloud>GAE</cloud>
26   </component>
27   <component id=''Doc3''>
28     <interface>cloudpost.service.DocumentService</
            interface>
29     <description>
30       Generation and storage of documents on
              OpenShift
31     </description>
32     <implementation>remote</implementation>
33     <url>
34       http://cloudpost.openshift.com/docservice
35     </url>
36     <cloud>OpenShift</cloud>
37   </component>
38  </components>
```

Listing 4 Example of a tenant policy for confidential documents. Confidential documents should be processed in private clouds, or on an external location that supports encrypted storage and ensures secure communication.

```
1  Component =
2    cloudpost.service.DocumentService,
3  MessageType = confidential,
4    Location = *,
5    Access = Private
6    or
7  (Encrypted = true and SecureComm = true)
```

In case of the log management and medical image processing services, the location where data is stored and the PaaS provider are important properties (e.g. lines 6–10 in Listing 2). For example, some banks require that a private cloud is used in the same country as where the bank is located. This can easily be enforced using tenant policies that specify constraints on location and by assigning the appropriate message types to the requests and/or data. This way, tenants keep control over their data in a fine-grained way, while the SaaS provider can still benefit from the flexibility and scalability of a multi-cloud environment.

4.3 Scenario #2: Dynamically controlling spill-over

The CloudPost provider aims to maximally utilize his/her own private data center. Therefore, the provider specifies a load threshold using a spill-over policy. As long as the load in the private cloud is lower than this threshold, all incoming requests are processed by the local instance of the document generation service (i.e. component "Doc1" in Listing 3).

However, the processing of documents is often of a recurring nature, e.g. processing payslips and invoices at the end of the month, typically in the form of large document batches. The private data center of CloudPost thus faces high peaks in loads at the end of the month. To address these peak loads, the public PaaS platforms are used as spill-over. Evidently, also the decision which documents to process in the public cloud, depends on the applicable tenant policies, for example non-confidential documents (like advertising) will be generated in the public cloud, and confidential documents in public clouds that offer encrypted storage or in the private cloud.

4.4 Scenario #3: Migrating to other PaaS providers

The CloudPost provider does not want to be completely dependent on the current three PaaS providers. Therefore, he regularly evaluates new PaaS offerings, for example with respect to cost, security properties, availability and performance guarantees, etc. When one of the current PaaS providers in the multi-cloud becomes too expensive or a better alternative is available, then the PaaSHopper middleware enables the CloudPost provider to easily replace the PaaS platforms that are part of the multi-cloud. Similarly, the multi-cloud can be extended with additional PaaS offerings, for example when a tenant has a feature request that is unsupported by the current platforms.

More specifically, the SaaS provider should only update the part of the deployment descriptor that defines the multi-cloud environment (cf. Listing 2), and the PaaSHopper middleware will automatically adapt to the new environment. As the measurements of the migration overhead in [19] show, the abstraction layer enables the migration of the CloudPost application to different PaaS platforms without any impact on the application code. All code changes are contained within the portability drivers. This means that to support a new PaaS platform in the multi-cloud, merely the appropriate portability drivers have to be installed. Furthermore, no policy changes are required, as the policies only use properties to specify constraints and do not refer to specific PaaS platforms. Finally, this adaptation occurs instantaneous as the policy evaluation is applied at the fine-grained level of requests.

4.5 Concluding remarks

The validation shows (i) that the abstraction layer of the PaaSHopper middleware supports the migration of the document processing application across multiple PaaS platforms, without any code modification (at the application level), and (ii) the effectiveness of using policies to control the execution and storage in a fine-grained way and in correspondence to the different stakeholder-specific requirements.

Although the validation focuses on a single, representative application (i.e. document processing), we did analyse the feasibility and applicability of the middleware for the four application cases presented in Section 2.1. Moreover, the complexity of this work lies in the middleware and the validation demonstrates that it supports the deployment of the document processing application on top of quite different PaaS offerings (i.e. JBoss AS, GAE [5] and OpenShift [27]).

However, further validation and improvement of the PaaSHopper middleware is required to verify its effectiveness and extensibility in the context of different SaaS applications as well as different PaaS platforms and their provided services (especially storage). For example, we did not cover interactive applications, but we believe that the proposed approach is still viable, with the dispatcher acting as a policy-driven load balancer for all incoming requests. Similarly, the expressiveness of the policies should be further evaluated.

Section 3 presented the open and versatile architecture of the PaaSHopper middleware. The document processing prototype validates only one deployment instance of this architecture, with a single dispatcher deployed in the private cloud. We believe that this is the most common deployment of the PaaSHopper middleware, but it is certainly worth to investigate the potential benefits and/or issues of having multiple dispatchers and policy engines within a multi-cloud environment.

5 Discussion

This section discusses the strengths and limitations of the current PaaSHopper middleware. Based on this discussion and our experience with this middleware in the different SaaS application cases, we itemize a set of open challenges and directions for future work.

5.1 Reconfigurable policy evaluation

The PaaSHopper middleware is able to control the processing and/or storage of data in a fine-grained way by enforcing policies on any interaction between the different application components. However, as indicated by the application cases in Section 2, there exist different types of SaaS applications, such as data-driven, computationally-intensive or combinations. Furthermore, the different stakeholders can specify policies with respect to the location of processing, the location of storage, the load etc. Depending on the application type, it is not always desirable to intercept each interaction for policy evaluation. This not only leads to a performance overhead because of the additional (possibly remote) policy evaluation, but in data-driven applications such as medical image processssing, this can lead to sending back and forth large data sets between different cloud offerings.

In the current prototype, this problem is solved by logically grouping different application components as one entry in the deployment descriptor. For example, we specified that the document generation service includes the generation as well as the storage of the generated documents. This ensures that the policies apply to both processing and storage, and thus prevents that input data is sent to a public PaaS platform for generation and then sent back to the private cloud for storage. However, this requires the SaaS provider to adapt the granularity of the components or services, and it limits the flexibility.

Alternatively, the PaaSHopper middleware could be extended to enable the reconfiguration of the interception points for policy evaluation. This requires an application model that defines the dependencies between the different application components. When set to limit the amount of interactions across the multi-cloud environment (e.g. data-driven application), the policy engine can take all dependencies into account for incoming requests and make a single decision on where the entire execution will take place. Only when necessary, the policy evaluation occurs at every interaction, for example for the simulation processing application, where the data traffic is limited and processing may occur in the public cloud.

5.2 Dynamic deployment specification

The PaaSHopper middleware supports different types of policies based on a potentially large variety of properties. In addition, the SaaS provider can further extend (i) the specification of the PaaS platforms in the deployment descriptor with domain- and application-specific properties, and (ii) the middleware with custom policy engines to support new types of policies. In the current prototype, these properties are considered to be static.

However, we can think of several interesting multi-cloud scenarios that involve dynamic cloud properties, such as performance, availability and cost. These properties can change over time and also vary depending on the type of operation. The use of dynamic properties also requires more expressive policies to take into account the cost and performance of the different PaaS offerings.

To support these dynamic cloud properties, the deployment specification has to be updated at run time. This requires, as depicted in Figure 5, the integration of the PaaSHopper middleware with cloud management services to form a control loop. This enables the middleware (i) to continuously monitor the application as well as the underpinning PaaS environment(s), (ii) to use this monitoring data to improve decision making, and (iii) to dynamically reconfigure and (re)deploy the SaaS application across the multi-cloud environment (e.g. in case of a spill-over or migration to another PaaS offering) if necessary, instead of a static assignment as is currently the case in our prototype. The configuration management service then has to send the up-to-date deployment view to the dispatcher. With such a control loop, the PaaSHopper middleware actually becomes a cloud broker.

5.3 Retrieving data in multi-cloud

Our experience with the deployment of the different application cases in a multi-cloud environment revealed a major challenge with respect to locating and querying data. When an application wants to access data that is previously stored, it has to know where it is stored in the multi-cloud environment. Moreover, to prevent unnecessary data traffic, access to the data should preferably occur on the same cloud platform. This problem arises especially in dynamic multi-cloud environments, for example with spill-over scenarios: during the spill-over data is stored using a public cloud storage service, but afterwards all execution should occur locally in the private cloud.

Depending on the application type and the amount of data, different solutions are possible. For example, in the case of the document processing application, an application-level index of all documents can be

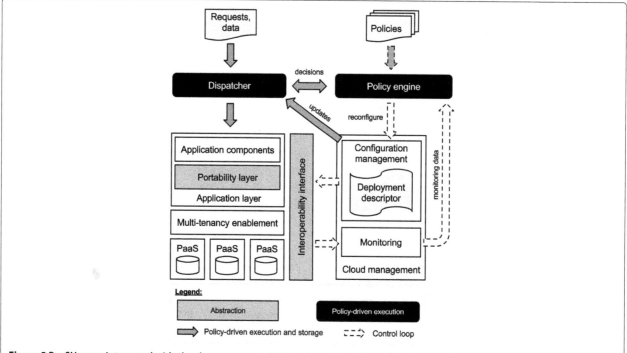

Figure 5 PaaSHopper integrated with cloud management. High-level overview of the policy-driven PaaSHopper middleware, including the integration with cloud management services such as monitoring and configuration management.

maintained. Furthermore, data can regularly be migrated to aggregate the data of the same tenant. However, an index is not appropriate for the log management service, as this application involves a continuous input stream of small log entries and the analysis of all log entries (i.e. the full data set). As this application case uses a set of private data centers, the policy engine of the PaaSHopper middleware could be used to ensure that the logs of the same tenant are stored at the same location, and that the analysis is performed where the data is stored.

5.4 Portability and interoperability

In previous work [7], we identified three categories of PaaS platforms with respect to SaaS development. The first and second category contain the PaaS platforms that support traditional programming models and aim to match the APIs of enterprise application servers and middleware platforms (e.g. Cloud-Foundry [28], OpenShift [27] and GAE [5]). However, these platforms still use vendor-specific solutions, especially for typical cloud services such as scalable storage, which hinders portability. The third category consists of metadata-driven PaaS platforms. These platforms use a higher-level composition and configuration interface, and lack any compatibility with common programming models.

The PaaSHopper middleware is aimed at (Java-based) PaaS platforms of the first and second category, and offers an abstraction layer to address the heterogeneity and to support migration. Evidently, the appropriate portability drivers should be present. Indirectly, the middleware also supports IaaS offerings through the use of application servers.

As exemplified by the different application cases, the PaaSHopper middleware does not put any constraints on the types of applications that are supported. However, to enable fine-grained control of the execution, the application should be decomposable into *modular and loosely-coupled* software artifacts (e.g. components, services). This way, the PaaSHopper middleware can intercept the incoming requests as well as the invocations between the different components or services within the application, and dynamically adapt the composition driven by the policies that are applicable. Such an application model is commonly supported, for example by component-based software development (CBSD) [29], aspect-oriented software development (AOSD) [30], dependency injection [25], and service-oriented computing (SOC) [31,32].

Finally, interoperability is not only a concern with respect to the interaction between the different application components across the heterogeneous multi-PaaS environment. When integrating with cloud management services such as monitoring and configuration management, interoperability of these services with the different PaaS platforms is also required. With the large variety of management APIs of these platforms, there is a need for a uniform interface (and accompanying implementations) to address the heterogeneity and to support the management of multi-cloud environments, as indicated by Figure 5. This is certainly an open challenge.

5.5 Versatility of the PaaSHopper middleware

This paper presents a generic middleware framework in the sense that it provides a versatile architecture that supports different implementations and deployments, depending on the application type and the specific nature of the multi-cloud environment.

One of these supported customizations is related to the deployment of the dispatcher. For example, the document processing application is deployed in a dynamic multi-cloud environment: the public cloud environments are only used when the load on the on-premise infrastructure is high. Therefore, the entry point for the application is deployed in the private cloud only. Consequently, we decided to use one dispatcher, which is also deployed in the private cloud. A similar deployment is recommended for the simulation processing case (cf. application #4).

However, in the case of the log management service or medical image processing (cf. applications #2 and #3), the different cloud environments are always used (i.e. a static multi-cloud environment), so it is possible to have multiple entry points and then it might be recommended to have a dispatcher in every data center to limit the latency overhead. In future work, we will investigate the impact of multiple dispatchers within a multi-cloud environment on the operation of the PaaSHopper middleware as well as the application.

A second customization lies in the optional usage of the abstraction layer. The proposed abstraction layer can be interchanged with other solutions for cloud portability (cf. Section 3.1) or can even be omitted. The latter is especially relevant when the PaaS platforms in the multi-cloud environment offer the same or technologically compatible APIs.

6 Related work

This section discusses three domains of related work: a) multi-cloud support, b) policy-driven middleware, and c) cloud brokerage.

6.1 Multi-cloud support

Mietzner et al. [33] focus on cloud application portability, using an extension to the service component architecture (SCA) with variability descriptors and multi-tenancy patterns. However, SCA applications can only be executed in an SCA application environment, whereas our work focuses on PaaS platforms, which typically do not support SCA. Moreover, their focus is on multi-tenant customization, packaging, and deployment migration obstacles, while this work presents a policy-driven middleware that offers a common PaaS API in order to facilitate flexible, reconfigurable deployment and execution of SaaS applications in multi-PaaS environments.

Paraiso et al. [11] present a so-called federated multi-cloud PaaS infrastructure that enables the deployment of service component architecture (SCA) applications on heterogeneous PaaS and IaaS offerings. This federated PaaS infrastructure relies on their own FraSCAti execution environment for SCA applications. Furthermore, it supports the dynamic reconfiguration of component bindings and the addition of components and services, but this happens globally for all tenants. In contrast, we focus on a technology-agnostic approach without the need of a SCA execution environment, and the PaaSHopper middleware supports dynamic reconfiguration on a per-tenant basis and is driven by co-existing policies that express the stakeholder-specific constraints.

Cunha et al. [34] proposed a middleware architecture that facilitates dynamic deployment, registration and portability of services across different PaaS providers, and enables developers to create and expose services using a cloud-based service delivery platform within a service-oriented architecture (SOA). Although, the authors also focus on portability and application migration, there are still significant differences with our work: (i) their focus is on SOA applications, while the PaaSHopper middleware does not put any constraints on the application model, (ii) the authors acknowledge the need for a uniform PaaS API, but do not make any concrete suggestions whereas we have implemented a common abstraction layer for three heterogeneous PaaS platforms, and (iii) their solution does not enable the different stakeholders to control the execution of the deployed applications.

Another related solution is provided by the European mOSAIC project [35], where an independent PaaS platform API is developed to provide support for heterogeneous hybrid clouds. The developed API uses a driver architecture and can be deployed on top of heterogeneous hybrid PaaS platforms. We applied a similar approach for the abstraction layer, but with different focus. While they have focused on a PaaS API for task automation, the PaaSHopper middleware offers a uniform API for three common cloud services, including structured storage (NoSQL), blob storage and asynchronous task execution. Moreover, the focus of our work is on providing the different stakeholders more control over the execution of multi-tenant SaaS applications in multi-PaaS environments.

DRACO [36] is a new PaaS platform that is inspired by FCAPS, the ISO telecommunications management network model. It is built on top of an IaaS layer and can be utilized by other SaaS applications or PaaS platforms. The focus of DRACO is (i) to address issues concerning PaaS management such as fault tolerance, configuration, accounting, performance, and security, and (ii) to provide a platform for the development of algorithms that require parallel processing and a considerable amount of computation in the cloud. In contrast, we solve application-level issues and provide portability and interoperability support across existing PaaS environments in order to support fine-grained control of execution and storage.

Kaviani et al. [37] have proposed a cross-tier partitioning approach to support developers making the trade-off between performance and cost in hybrid clouds. The focus is on optimizing the partitioning of both the application- and data-tier of web applications across hybrid IaaS deployments driven by application profiles, while taking into account that sensitive data may not be moved to the public cloud. In contrast, the PaaSHopper middleware does not rely on profiling to make decisions, but enforces at run time the different tenant- and provider-specific policies on the different interactions. Furthermore, we assume that the SaaS provider has already invested in a private cloud and wants to maximally utilize this on-premise infrastructure. However, the work by Kaviani et al. can be used to extend the PaaSHopper middleware, for example to limit the costs and performance overhead because of data traffic (as discussed in Section 5).

Petcu et al. [22] have conducted a survey on the state of the art with respect to portability of applications that consume cloud services. The paper provides a taxonomy for cloud portability, an overview of the latest solutions, and it identifies the open challenges. The use of abstraction layers and adapters to hide the differences and to expose a uniform API, cf. our approach, is one of the common solutions they identified to address the portability issue. Kolb et al. [38] have defined a model that describes the current PaaS offerings, and they clustered a set of core properties into a PaaS profile in order to support the comparison and portability matching of PaaS offerings based on application dependencies and capabilities.

6.2 Policy-driven middleware

Policy-driven middleware is commonly used in the context of service compositions to support customizaton and dynamic selection of web services, for example [39,40]. These policy-driven adaptations are required to keep fulfilling the QoS requirements of the applications. In the PaaSHopper middleware, however, policies are used to constrain the deployment and execution of multi-cloud applications based on the properties of the underpinning platforms. Furthermore, the focus is on keeping control over the applications and the data, and less on QoS.

In [41], the authors design a middleware that supports the development of multi-tenant SOA applications. In such applications both tenants and application providers can define policies. The middleware uses a message dispatch mechanism in order to guide incoming request messages to the right service instance as indicated by the global and tenant-specific policies. The relevant policies are processed in two steps. In the first step, all the global policies are applied, and in the second step tenant-specific policies are taken into account. This paper, however, focuses on the use of policies in a multi-cloud context, thus containing multiple run-time environments. These policies are then used to select a PaaS platform within the multi-cloud. Furthermore, the PaaSHopper middleware supports more complex policies that relate to the active tenant as well as the current message type.

6.3 Cloud brokerage

Several European research projects tackle challenges with respect to cloud brokerage, for example OPTIMIS [42] and MODAClouds [43]. The focus of OPTIMIS is on optimal placement of virtual machines (VMs) in multi-cloud environments driven by cost, energy efficiency, QoS, etc., and also involves SLA negotiation and creation. MODAClouds aims to support cross-cloud portability and to automatically (re)configure the deployment of applications on multi-clouds to ensure the QoS. The goal of the latter project is certainly related to this work. Although the PaaSHopper middleware is not a cloud broker, it does provide several complementary solutions to the MODAClouds project, for example an abstraction layer to support the cross-cloud migration of multi-tenant SaaS applications, and a policy-driven middleware layer to control the processing and storage of data in a fine-grained way.

7 Conclusion

Multi-cloud deployment has the potential of solving many problems that enterprises currently face with cloud computing. Especially in the area of multi-tenant SaaS applications, there is a large potential in leveraging not one, but many different underpinning PaaS platforms, each potentially having different properties in terms of cost, performance, availability, security, etc.

To realize this potential however, complex middleware support is required to deal with issues of portability and interoperability and to provide the different stakeholders (tenant, SaaS provider, etc.) with fine-grained control on the deployment, execution and operation of the SaaS offering on top of multiple PaaS platforms.

This paper presents such a middleware architecture for exploiting SaaS applications in a multi-PaaS environment. This middleware offers on the one hand a PaaS abstraction layer that ensures portability accross different PaaS platforms, while on the other hand it offers policy-based control mechanisms to influence its execution. These policies are based on expressive abstractions and as such allow defining key non-functional requirements such as constraints about the geographical deployment location, security constraints, etc.

Although the presented middleware is a first step in the development of middleware systems that deal with the complexity and heterogeneity inherent to hybrid and multi-cloud environments, many research opportunities are left open. In future work, we plan to investigate additional adaptation support to dynamically (un)deploy components on the appropriate public platforms and enabling more expressive policies based on more dynamic cloud properties such as cost, performance, etc.

Competing interests
The authors declare that they have no competing interests.

Authors' contributions
SW has been in charge of defining the PaaSHopper middleware and drafting the manuscript. Further refinement was conducted in collaboration with DVL. The validation was conducted by AR. BL and WJ have participated in the initial design of the middleware, and have contributed significantly to the positioning of the work. All authors have read and approved the final manuscript.

Acknowledgements
We would like to thank Tom Desair for the initial implementation of the PaaSHopper middleware as part of his master thesis. This research is partially funded by the Research Fund KU Leuven (project GOA/14/003 - ADDIS), the FWO project iSPEC and by the iMinds DMS2 project, which is co-funded by iMinds (Interdisciplinary Institute for Technology), a research institute founded by the Flemish Government. Companies and organizations involved in the project are Agfa Healthcare, Luciad, UP-nxt and Verizon Terremark, with project support of IWT (government agency for Innovation by Science and Technology).

References
1. Mell P, Grance T (2011) The nist definition of cloud computing. Special publication 800-145, National Institute of Standards and Technology (NIST). http://csrc.nist.gov/publications/nistpubs/800-145/SP800-145.pdf
2. Armbrust M, Fox A, Griffith R, Joseph AD, Katz R, Konwinski A, Lee G, Patterson D, Rabkin A, Stoica I, Zaharia M (2010) A view of cloud computing. Commun ACM 53(4):50–58. doi:10.1145/1721654.1721672
3. Zhang Q, Cheng L, Boutaba R (2010) Cloud computing: State-of-the-art and research challenges. J Internet Serv Appl 1(1):7–18. doi:10.1007/s13174-010-0007-6
4. Amazon Web Services LLC Amazon Elastic Compute Cloud (Amazon EC2). http://aws.amazon.com/ec2/. [Last visited on November 24, 2014]
5. Google Inc. Google App Engine. https://cloud.google.com/appengine/docs. [Last visited on November 24, 2014]
6. Salesforce.com Inc. Salesforce CRM. http://www.salesforce.com/. [Last visited on November 24, 2014]
7. Walraven S, Truyen E, Joosen W (2014) Comparing PaaS offerings in light of SaaS development. Computing 96(8):669–724. doi:10.1007/s00607-013-0346-9
8. Mueller D (2014) It's 2014 and PaaS is eating the world. https://www.openshift.com/blogs/its-2014-and-paas-is-eating-the-world
9. Leavitt N (2009) Is cloud computing really ready for prime time? Computer 42(1):15–20. doi:10.1109/MC.2009.20

10. Marston S, Li Z, Bandyopadhyay S, Zhang J, Ghalsasi A (2011) Cloud computing — the business perspective. Decis Support Syst 51(1):176–189. doi:10.1016/j.dss.2010.12.006

11. Paraiso F, Haderer N, Merle P, Rouvoy R, Seinturier L (2012) A federated multi-cloud PaaS infrastructure. In: CLOUD '12: IEEE 5th International Conference on Cloud Computing. IEEE. pp 392–399. doi:10.1109/CLOUD.2012.79

12. Whittaker Z (2012) Amazon cloud down; reddit, github, other major sites affected. ZDNet.com. http://www.zdnet.com/article/amazon-cloud-down-reddit-github-other-major-sites-affected/. [Last visited on November 24, 2014]

13. Takahashi D (2011) Amazon's outage in third day: debate over cloud computing's future begins. VentureBeat. http://venturebeat.com/2011/04/23/amazonsoutage-in-third-day-debate-over-cloud-computings-future-begins/. [Last visited on November 24, 2014]

14. Bilton N (2012) Amazon web services knocked offline by storms. The New York Times (Bits). http://bits.blogs.nytimes.com/2012/06/30/amazon-web-services-knocked-offline-by-storms/. [Last visited on November 24, 2014]

15. Chong F, Carraro G (2006) Architecture strategies for catching the long tail. Microsoft Corporation. http://msdn.microsoft.com/en-us/library/aa479069.aspx

16. Guo CJ, Sun W, Huang Y, Wang ZH, Gao B (2007) A framework for native multi-tenancy application development and management. In: CEC/EEE '07: 9th IEEE International Conference on E-Commerce Technology and 4th IEEE International Conference on Enterprise Computing, E-Commerce, and E-Services. IEEE. pp 551–558. doi:10.1109/CEC-EEE.2007.4

17. Leavitt N (2013) Hybrid clouds move to the forefront. Computer 46(5):15–18. doi:10.1109/MC.2013.168

18. Desair T, Joosen W, Lagaisse B, Rafique A, Walraven S (2013) Policy-driven middleware for heterogeneous, hybrid cloud platforms. In: ARM '13: Proceedings of the 12th International Workshop on Adaptive and Reflective Middleware. ACM, New York, NY, USA. pp 7–12. doi:10.1145/2541583.2541585

19. Rafique A, Walraven S, Lagaisse B, Desair T, Joosen W (2014) Towards portability and interoperability support in middleware for hybrid clouds. In: CrossCloud '14: Proceedings of the 1st IEEE INFOCOM CrossCloud Workshop. IEEE. pp 7–12. doi:10.1109/INFCOMW.2014.6849160

20. Decat M, Bogaerts J, Lagaisse B, Joosen W (2014) The e-document case study: Functional analysis and access control requirements. CW Reports 654. https://lirias.kuleuven.be/handle/123456789/440202

21. Petcu D (2011) Portability and interoperability between clouds: Challenges and case study. In: ServiceWave '11: Towards a Service-Based Internet. Springer, Berlin, Heidelberg. pp 62–74. doi:10.1007/978-3-642-24755-2_6

22. Petcu D, Vasilakos AV (2014) Portability in clouds: Approaches and research opportunities. Scalable Comput Pract Exp 15(3):251–270. doi:10.12694/scpe.v15i3.1019

23. Red Hat Inc. Hibernate Object/Grid Mapper (OGM). http://hibernate.org/ogm/. [Last visited on November 24, 2014]

24. Impetus Technologies Inc. Kundera: Object-datastore mapping library for NoSQL datastores. https://github.com/impetus-opensource/Kundera. [Last visited on November 24, 2014]

25. Fowler M (2004) Inversion of control containers and the dependency injection pattern. http://martinfowler.com/articles/injection.html

26. Walraven S, Truyen E, Joosen W (2011) A middleware layer for flexible and cost-efficient multi-tenant applications. In: Middleware '11: Proceedings of the 12th ACM/IFIP/USENIX International Conference on Middleware. Springer, Berlin, Heidelberg. pp 370–389. doi:10.1007/978-3-642-25821-3_19

27. Red Hat Inc. Red Hat OpenShift. https://www.openshift.com/. [Last visited on November 24, 2014]

28. VMware Inc. Cloud Foundry. http://www.cloudfoundry.org/. [Last visited on November 24, 2014]

29. Szyperski C (2002) Component software - beyond object-oriented programming. 2nd edn. Addison-Wesley/ACM Press, Boston, MA, USA

30. Filman RE, Elrad T, Clarke S, Akşit M (2004) Aspect-oriented Software Development. 1st edn. Addison-Wesley Professional, Boston, MA, USA

31. Papazoglou MP (2003) Service-oriented computing: Concepts, characteristics and directions. In: WISE '03: Proceedings of the Fourth International Conference on Web Information Systems Engineering. IEEE. pp 3–12. doi:10.1109/WISE.2003.1254461

32. Huhns MN, Singh MP (2005) Service-oriented computing: Key concepts and principles. IEEE Internet Computing 9(1):75–81. doi:10.1109/MIC.2005.21

33. Mietzner R, Leymann F, Papazoglou MP (2008) Defining composite configurable SaaS application packages using SCA, variability descriptors and multi-tenancy patterns. In: ICIW '08: 3rd International Conference on Internet and Web Applications and Services. IEEE. pp 156–161. doi:10.1109/ICIW.2008.68

34. Cunha D, Neves P, Sousa PNMd (2012) Interoperability and portability of cloud service enablers in a PaaS environment. In: CLOSER '12: Proceedings of the 2nd International Conference on Cloud Computing and Services Science. SciTePress. pp 432–437. doi:10.5220/0003959204320437

35. Petcu D, Macariu G, Panica S, Crăciun C (2013) Portable cloud applications - from theory to practice. Future Generation Comput Syst 29(6):1417–1430. doi:10.1016/j.future.2012.01.009

36. Celesti A, Peditto N, Verboso F, Villari M, Puliafito A (2013) DRACO PaaS: A distributed resilient adaptable cloud oriented platform. In: IPDPSW '13: IEEE 27th International Parallel and Distributed Processing Symposium Workshops PhD Forum. IEEE. pp 1490–1497. doi:10.1109/IPDPSW.2013.266

37. Kaviani N, Wohlstadter E, Lea R (2013) Cross-tier application and data partitioning of web applications for hybrid cloud deployment. In: Middleware '13: Proceedings of the ACM/IFIP/USENIX 14th International Middleware Conference. Springer, Berlin, Heidelberg. pp 226–246. doi:10.1007/978-3-642-45065-5_12

38. Kolb S, Wirtz G (2014) Towards application portability in Platform as a Service. In: SOSE '14: Proceedings of the 8th IEEE International Symposium on Service-Oriented System Engineering. IEEE. pp 218–229. doi:10.1109/SOSE.2014.26

39. Wohlstadter E, Tai S, Mikalsen T, Rouvellou I, Devanbu P (2004) GlueQoS: Middleware to sweeten quality-of-service policy interactions. In: ICSE '04: Proceedings of the 26th International Conference on Software Engineering. IEEE Computer Society, Washington, DC, USA. pp 189–199. doi:10.1109/ICSE.2004.1317441

40. Erradi A, Maheshwari P, Tosic V (2006) Policy-driven middleware for self-adaptation of web services compositions. In: Middleware '06: ACM/IFIP/USENIX 7th International Middleware Conference. Springer, Berling, Heidelberg. pp 62–80. doi:10.1007/11925071_4

41. Azeez A, Perera S, Gamage D, Linton R, Siriwardana P, Leelaratne D, Weerawarana S, Fremantle P (2010) Multi-tenant SOA middleware for cloud computing. In: CLOUD '10: IEEE International Conference on Cloud Computing. IEEE Computer Society, Washington, DC, USA. pp 458–465. doi:10.1109/CLOUD.2010.50

42. Ferrer AJ, Hernández F, Tordsson J, Elmroth E, Ali-Eldin A, Zsigri C, Sirvent R, Guitart J, Badia RM, Djemame K, Ziegler W, Dimitrakos T, Nair SK, Kousiouris G, Konstanteli K, Varvarigou T, Hudzia B, Kipp A, Wesner S, Corrales M, Forgó N, Sharif T, Sheridan C (2012) OPTIMIS: A holistic approach to cloud service provisioning. Future Generation Comput Syst 28(1):66–77. doi:10.1016/j.future.2011.05.022

43. Ardagna D, Di Nitto E, Mohagheghi P, Mosser S, Ballagny C, D'Andria F, Casale G, Matthews P, Nechifor CS, Petcu D, Gericke A, Sheridan C (2012) MODAClouds: A model-driven approach for the design and execution of applications on multiple clouds. In: MiSE '12: ICSE Workshop on Modeling in Software Engineering. IEEE. pp 50–56. doi:10.1109/MISE.2012.6226014

13

Partitioning of web applications for hybrid cloud deployment

Nima Kaviani, Eric Wohlstadter[*] and Rodger Lea

Abstract

Hybrid cloud deployment offers flexibility in trade-offs between the cost-savings/scalability of the public cloud and control over data resources provided at a private premise. However, this flexibility comes at the expense of complexity in distributing a system over these two locations. For multi-tier web applications, this challenge manifests itself primarily in the partitioning of application- and database-tiers. While there is existing research that focuses on either application-tier or data-tier partitioning, we show that optimized partitioning of web applications benefits from both tiers being considered simultaneously. We present our research on a new cross-tier partitioning approach to help developers make effective trade-offs between performance and cost in a hybrid cloud deployment. The general approach primarily benefits from two technical improvements to integer-programming based application partitioning. First, an asymmetric cost-model for optimizing data transfer in environments where ingress and egress data-transfer have differing costs, such as in many infrastructure as a service platforms. Second, a new encoding of database query plans as integer programs, to enable simultaneous optimization of code and data placement in a hybrid cloud environment. In two case studies the approach results in up to 54% reduction in monetary costs compared to a premise only deployment and 56% improvement in response time compared to a naive partitioning where the application-tier is deployed in the public cloud and the data-tier is on private infrastructure.

Keywords: Cloud computing; Hybrid cloud; Middleware; Application partitioning; Optimization

1 Introduction

While there are advantages to deploying Web applications on public cloud infrastructure, many companies wish to retain control over specific resources [1] by keeping them at a private premise. As a result, hybrid cloud computing has become a popular architecture where systems are built to take advantage of both public and private infrastructure to meet different requirements. However, architecting an efficient distributed system across these locations requires significant effort. An effective partitioning should not only guarantee that privacy constraints and performance objectives are met, but also should deliver on one of the primary reasons for using the public cloud, a cheaper deployment.

In this paper we focus on partitioning of OLTP-style web applications. Such applications are an important target for a hybrid architecture due to their popularity.

Web applications follow the well known multi-tier architecture, generally consisting of tiers such as: client-tier, application-tier (serving dynamic web content), and back-end data-tier. When considering how to partition applications for these multi-tier web applications in a hybrid cloud environment, we are faced with a spectrum of choices. This spectrum ranges from a simplistic, or naive approach which simply keeps data on-premise and moves code in the public cloud, through a more sophisticated partition that splits code between premise and cloud but retains all data on premise, up to a fully integrated approach where both data and code are partitioned across public and private infrastructure, see Figure 1.

In our work, we have explored this spectrum as we have attempted to develop a partitioning approach and associated framework that exploits the unique characteristics of hybrid cloud infrastructure. In particular we began our work by looking into a simpler approach that focused on code partitioning. Although there have been

---

* Correspondence: wohlstad@gmail.com
University of British Columbia, 201-2366 Main Mall, Vancouver V6T 1Z4, Canada

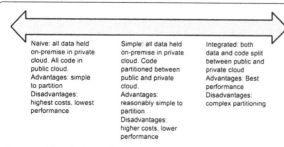

Figure 1 The choices when considering partitioning for hybrid cloud infrastructure.

several projects that have explored code partitioning for hybrid cloud, such as CloneCloud [2], Cloudward Bound [3], work by Leymann et al. [4], and our own work on Manticore [5], we realised that the unique characteristics of cloud business models offered an interesting optimization that we wished to exploit. Specifically, we attempted to explore the *asymmetric* nature of cloud communication costs (where costs of sending data to the public cloud are less than the cost of retrieving data from the public cloud) with a goal of incorporating these factors into the partitioning algorithm. This work, described in detail in Section 3, led to measurable improvements in both cost and performance, but equally highlighted the need for a more integrated approach that partitioned both code and data - an approach we refer to as *cross-tier partitioning*.

Cross-tier partitioning acknowledges that the data flow between the different tiers in a multi-tier application is tightly coupled. The application-tier can make several queries during its execution, passing information to and from different queries; an example is discussed in Section 2. Even though developers follow best practices to ensure the source code for the business logic and the data access layer are loosely coupled, this loose coupling does not apply to the data-flow. The data-flow crosscuts application- and data-tiers requiring an optimization that considers the two simultaneously. Such an optimization should avoid, whenever possible, the latency and bandwidth requirements imposed by distributing such data-flow.

Any attempt to partition code that does not take account of this data flow is unlikely to offer significant cost and performance benefits however, cross-tier partitioning is challenging because it requires an analysis that simultaneously reasons about the execution of application-tier code and data-tier queries. On the one hand, previous work on partitioning of code is not applicable to database queries because it does not account for modeling of query execution plans. On the other hand, existing work on data partitioning does not account for the data-flow or execution footprint of

the application-tier [6]. To capture a representation for cross-tier optimization, our contribution in this paper includes a new approach for modeling dependencies across both tiers as a combined *binary integer program* (*BIP*) [7].

Building on our initial work on asymmetric code partitioning, we have addressed the challenges of cross-tier code and data partitioning by developing a generalized framework that analyzes both code and data usage in a web application, and then converts the data into a BIP problem. The BIP is fed to an off-the-shelf optimizer whose output yields suggestions for placement of application- and data-tier components to either public cloud or private premise. Using proper tooling and middleware, a new system can now be distributed across the hybrid architecture using the optimized placement suggestions. We provide the first approach for partitioning which integrates models of both application-tier and data-tier execution.

In the rest of this paper we first describe a motivating scenario (Section 2), based on the Apache day trader benchmark, which we use throughout the paper to clarify the requirements and operations of our approach to partitioning. Using this, we explain our approach to application-tier (or code) partitioning (Section 3) and provide details of our initial attempts to develop a comprehensive tool for code partitioning. As mentioned above, we exploited the asymmetric nature and cost of cloud communications, i.e. data sent into the public cloud is cheaper than data sent from the public cloud to private premises, to drive code partitioning decisions and so improve application run costs. While we were able to achieve cost benefits using this asymmetric approach to application-tier partitioning, our analysis indicated that we also needed to consider data partitioning, specifically tightly integrated data partitioning with our application (or code) partitioning. This led us to expand our code partitioning approach with data partitioning and this work is reported in Section 4. Following on from this, we briefly explain in Section 5 our tool implementation and then in Section 6 provide an evaluation of our tool. Section 7 describes related work and finally in section 8 we summarize and discuss future work.

2 Motivating scenario and approach

As a motivating example, assume a company plans to take its on-premise trading software system and deploy it to a hybrid architecture. We use Apache DayTrader [8], a benchmark emulating the behaviour of a stock trading system, to express this scenario. DayTrader implements business logic in the application- tier as different *request types*, for example, allowing users to login (*doLogin*), view/update their account information (*doAccount & doAccountUpdate*), etc. At the data-tier it consists of tables storing data for *account, accountprofile, holding, quote*, etc. Let us further assume that, as part of company regulations, user information (*account & accountprofile*) must remain on-premise.

We will use this example to illustrate our initial work on code partitioning which, as highlighted above, led to improvements in performance as we moved parts of the code to the cloud and exploited its lower costs. Intuitively, by forcing certain data tables (*account & accountprofile*) to remain on premise, then code that manipulates these data elements is likely to remain on premise so that it stays close to the associated data and that communication times (and costs) do not become excessive. The diagram below, Figure 2(a), shows the call-tree of function execution in the application-tier as well as data-tier query plans at the leaves. In the figure, we see three categories of components: (i) data on premise shown as black nodes, (ii) functions on premise as gray nodes, and (iii) functions in the cloud as white nodes.

As can be seen in Figure 2a, because, in our initial approach, we are unable to partition data, we pin data to premise (account and holding) and so as expected, this forces significant amounts of code to stay on premise. However, as can also be seen from Figure 2a, some code can be moved to the cloud and our initial investigation (reported in section 3) explores what flexibility we had in this placement and the resulting performance and cost trade-offs.

In contrast, once we have the flexibility to address both code and data partitioning we have a more sophisticated tool available and so can explore moving data to the cloud, which obviously, will also have an affect on code placement. Figure 2b shows the output of our

cross-tier partitioning for *doLogin*. The figure shows the call-tree of function execution in the application-tier as well as data-tier query plans at the leaves. In the figure, we see four categories of components: (i) data on premise shown as black nodes, (ii) a new category of data in the cloud as square nodes, (iii) functions on premise as gray nodes, and (iv) functions in the cloud as white nodes.

As can be seen, once we have the ability to partition data and move some of it, in Figure 2b Holdings, to the cloud, we are then able to move significantly more code to the cloud and so exploit its benefits. We explain the details of this in section 4.

2.1 Overall methodology

To address application tier and data tier partitioning, we follow the methodology shown in Figure 3. The application is initially profiled by measuring execution time on a reference machine and collecting the data exchanges between software functions and data entities. Using this profile information, a dependency graph is developed which weaves application-tier and data-tier dependencies into a single cohesive dependency graph. The graph can then be analyzed to examine the effects of applying different cost models and placement constraints. Finally, the dependency graph can be converted into an optimization problem that captures requirements both at the application-tier and data-tier and then solved using binary integer linear programming (BIP) to partition the application.

3 Application-tier partitioning

Our initial work focused on application-tier partitioning and attempted to exploit aspects of cloud infrastructure

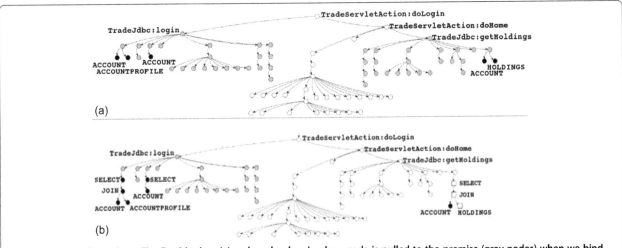

Figure 2 Code-only vs. Cross-Tier Partitioning: (a) code-only, showing how code is pulled to the premise (gray nodes) when we bind database tables to the premise (black nodes) (b) cross-tier, with data on premise (black nodes), data in the cloud (square nodes), functions on premise (gray nodes), and functions in the cloud (white nodes).

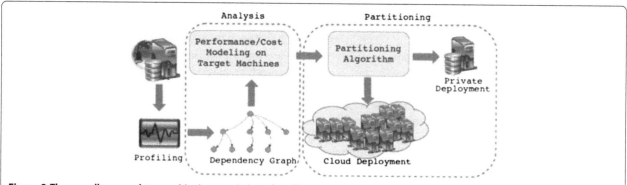

Figure 3 The overall approach to partitioning consisting of profiling, building a dependency graph of the application and then partitioning the application.

in such a way as to improve the code partitioning algorithm. In particular, we wanted to understand if the asymmetric nature of cloud communication costs (i.e. in-bound data costs do not equal out-bound data costs), could be exploited to improve partitioning where one goal is to reduce overall execution costs of the application. To achieve this goal, we provide a new formulation of application partitioning as a binary integer programming optimization problem. This process consists of three high-level steps described above, (i) profiling, (ii) analysis, (iii) generating the BIP constraints and objective function.

3.1 Application profiling and analysis

Our process for application partitioning starts by taking an existing web application and applying instrumentation to its binaries. The software is then exercised on representative workloads, using the instrumentation to collect data on measured CPU usage and frequency of execution for software functions as well as data exchange between them. This work builds on our previous work where we explore online profiling of live execution in a cloud setting [9]. In that work, we showed how to provide low-overhead profiling of live application deployment using sampling. This allows profiles to account for popularity observed during usage by real customers. This log of profiling information will be converted to the relevant variables and costs of a BIP.

The log of profile data is converted to a graph model before being converted to a BIP, as shown in Figure 3. Let $App(V,E)$ represent a model of the application, where $forall\ v \in V$, v corresponds to a function execution in the application. Next, $e(u, v) \in E$ is a directed edge from u to v in the function call graph for the profiled application. Figure 2(a) and (b) show the visual graphical representation of $App(V,E)$ which is produced by our tool for visualization by software developers. For each $v \in V$ we define $exec(v)$ to represent the average profiled cost of

executing v on-premise and $exec'(v)$ to represent the average profiled cost of executing v in the cloud. We also define $latency(u, v)$ to represent the latency cost on $e(u, v)$ and calculate the communication cost $comm(u, v)$ for $e(u, v)$ as follows:

$$comm(u, v) = latency(u, v) + d(u, v) \times commCost \quad (3.1)$$

Where $commCost$ is the cloud charges for each byte of data transfer, and $d(u, v)$ represents the bytes of data exchange along $e(u, v)$.

3.2 BIP constraints and objective

Binary Integer Programming has been utilized previously for partitioning of applications (although not leveraging an asymmetric data exchange model or a cross-tier partitioning). A binary integer program consists of the following:

- Binary variables: A set of binary variables $x_1, x_2, \dots x_n \in \{0,1\}$.
- Constraints: A set of linear constraints between variables where each constraint has the form: $c_1x_1 + c_2x_2 + \dots + c_nx_n \{\leq,=,\geq\} c_m$ where c_i are all constants
- Objective
  A linear expression to minimize or maximize: $cost_1x_1 + cost_2x_2 + \dots + cost_nx_n$, with each $cost_i$ being the cost charged to the model when $x_i = 1$.

The job of a BIP optimizer is to choose the set of values for the binary variables which minimize/maximize this expression. For this purpose we convert our model of application profiling to a BIP and use an existing off-the-shelf BIP solver to optimize for placement of functions on either the public cloud or private premise.

For every node u in the dependency graph we consider a variable $x(u)$ in the BIP formulation, where the set s

refers to entities placed on-premise and the set t refers to entities placed in the cloud.

$$x(u) \in \{0, 1\}$$
$$\forall x(u) \in s,\ x(u) = 0$$
$$\forall x(u) \in t,\ x(t) = 1$$

$$(3.2)$$

With all the above constraints, the following objective can then be defined:

$$min\left(\sum_{u \in V}(x(u) \times exec'(u) + (1-x(u)) \times exec(u)) + \sum_{(u,v) \in E}(x(u)-x(v))^2 \times comm(u,v)\right)$$

$$(3.3)$$

where the quadratic expression in the objective function can be relaxed by making the expansion suggested in [10].

$$\forall(u,v) \in E\ e(u,v) \geq 0,\ e(u,v) \leq 1$$
$$\forall(u,v) \in E\ e'(u,v) \geq 0,\ e'(u,v) \leq 1$$
$$\forall(u,v) \in E\ x(u)-x(v) + e(u,v) \geq 0$$
$$\forall(u,v) \in E\ x(v)-x(u) + e'(u,v) \geq 0$$

$$(3.4)$$

This expansion introduces auxiliary variables $e(u,v)$ for each edge in the original model; these new variables are used for emulating the constraints of a quadratic function by a combination of linear functions and don't directly map to the system being modeled. Their interpretation is described further below. Now the objective function of Equation 3.3 is converted to the following formulation. We refer to the objective of Equation 3.5 as *Symmetric IP* as it does not distinguish between inbound and outbound communication costs:

$$min\left(\sum_{u \in V}(x(u) \times exec'(u) + (1-x(u)) \times exec(u)) + \sum_{(u,v) \in E}(e(u,v) + e'(u,v)) \times comm(u,v)\right)$$

$$(3.5)$$

Interpreting this equation, $e(u,v)$ and $e'(u,v)$ will be 0 if both $x(u)$ and $x(v)$ are assigned to the same host but $e(u,v)$ will be 0 and $e'(u,v)$ will be 1 if $x(u)$ is assigned to t and $x(v)$ is assigned to s. Otherwise $e(u,v)$ will be 1 and $e'(u,v)$ will be 0 if $x(u)$ is on s and $x(v)$ is on t. An immediate benefit of being able to determine module placements in relation to one another is the ability to formulate the asymmetric data exchange charges for a cloud deployment into the partitioning problem. Benefiting from the expansion in Equation 3.4, we can add public cloud's asymmetric

billing charges to the communication cost of Equation 3.1 as follows:

$$comm'(u,v) = (e(u,v) + e'(u,v)) \times latency(u,v)$$
$$+ async(u,v) \times cloudCommCost$$
$$\times e'(u,v) + async(v,u)$$
$$\times premiseCommCost \times e(u,v)$$

$$(3.6)$$

where $async(u,v)$ stands for quantity of data transfer from cloud to the premise with $x(u)$ being in the cloud and $x(v)$ being on-premise, and $async(v,u)$ represents quantity of data transfer from premise to the cloud where $x(u)$ is on-premise and $x(v)$ is in the cloud. We also calculate the monetary cost for $latency(u,v)$ based on the formulation provided in our previous work which allows the tool user to tune the cost to match the specific deployment situation. Essentially the user just provides a weighted parameter to penalize optimization solutions which increase the average request latency, further details are described in [5]. The above formulation, combined with separation of outgoing and ingoing data to a function during application profiling leads to a more accurate cost optimization of the target software service for a hybrid deployment. Following the changes above, the objective function of Equation 3.5 can be updated by replacing $(e(u,v) + e'(u,v)) \times comm(u,v)$ with $comm'(u,v)$. In our evaluations, we refer to this new IP formulation as the *Asymmetric IP*.

As a concrete example of how the asymmetric algorithm works within the context of DayTrader, we provide an example in Figure 4 of part of the code partitioning suggested by the asymmetric algorithm when applied to DayTrader'-sApp(V,E). Figure 4 shows a piece for the request type *doAccount*. Assuming that the *accountprofile* database table is constrained to stay on-premise, in a symmetric partitioning algorithm separating *getAccountData* from *doAccount* (7 ~ KB of data exchange) is preferred over cutting *executeQuery* (13 ~ KB of data exchange). In an asymmetric partitioning however, the algorithm will assign no costs to the edges going to the cloud. For this reason, cutting *executeQuery* to be pushed to the premise has equivalent cost overhead (1 ~ KB) compared to cutting *getAccountData*. However, there is a gain in cutting *executeQuery* in that by pushing only this method to the premise, all other function nodes (black nodes) can be placed in the cloud, benefiting from more scalable and cheaper resources.

3.3 Asymmetric vs. symmetric partitioning

We evaluated our asymmetric partitioning on the aforementioned DayTrader application (cf. Section 2). Recall that for this part of the research, we consider all data to be deployed on the private premise but code can be split between public cloud and private premise. Later, in Section 4, we extend this to both code and data partitioning.

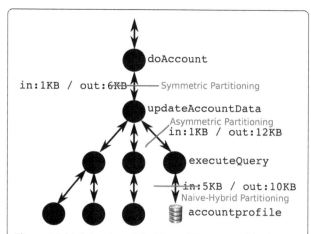

Figure 4 A high-level model of how different partitioning algorithms would choose the placement of code and data components between the public and the private cloud. For each of the three lines, code elements and database tables falling below the line are considered to be placed on premise and all the other elements are placed in the public cloud.

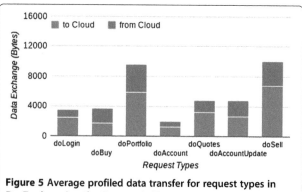

Figure 5 Average profiled data transfer for request types in DayTrader using the Symmetric IP.

We used the following setup for the evaluation: for the premise machines, we used two 3.5 GHz dual core machines with 8.0 GB of memory, one as the application server and another as our database server. Both machines were located at our lab in Vancouver, and were connected through a 100 Mb/sec data link. For the cloud machines, we used an extra large EC2 instance with 8 EC2 Compute Units and 7.0 GB of memory as our application server and another extra large instance as our database server. Both machines were leased from Amazon's US West region (Oregon) and were connected by a 1 Gb/sec data link. We use Jetty as the Web server and Oracle 11 g Express Edition as the database servers. We measured the round-trip latency between the cloud and our lab to be 15 milliseconds. Our intention for choosing these setups is to create an environment where the cloud offers the faster and more scalable environment. To generate load for the deployments, we launched simulated clients from a 3.0 GHz quad core machine with 8 GB of memory located in our lab in Vancouver.

Figures 5 and 6 show the results of data exchange for symmetric versus asymmetric partitioning algorithms. From the data, we can see two main results. First, considering each bar as a whole (ignoring the breakdown of each bar into its two components) and comparing the same request between the two figures (e.g. doLogin, Figure 5 vs. doLogin, Figure 6), we can notice the difference of aggregate data exchange for the two approaches. Here we see that in some cases, the aggregate data exchange is greater for the symmetric approach but in other cases it is greater for the asymmetric approach. However, there is a clear trend for asymmetric to be greater. On average over all the requests, asymmetric partitioning increases the overall amount of

data going from the premise to the cloud by a factor of 82%. However, when we breakdown the aggregate data exchange into two components (ingoing and outgoing), we can see an advantage of the asymmetric approach.

This second result of Figures 5 and 6 can be seen by comparing the ratio of ingoing and outgoing data for each request type. Here we see the asymmetric algorithm reduces the overall amount of data going from the cloud to the premise (red part of the chart). This can be a major factor when charges associated with data going from the cloud to the premise are more expensive than charges for data going from the premise to the cloud. On average over the request types, asymmetric partitioning reduces the overall amount of data going from the cloud to the premise by a factor of 52%. As we see in the next experiment, this can play a role in decreasing the total cost of deployment.

Figures 7 and 8 show the overall average request processing time for each request type when using symmetric compared to asymmetric partitioning. Each bar is broken down into two components: average time spent processing the request in the cloud and average time spent processing the request on premise. Again we see two results, that somewhat mirror the two results from Figures 5 and 6. First, again considering each bar as a whole, the total request processing time in each case is similar. In some

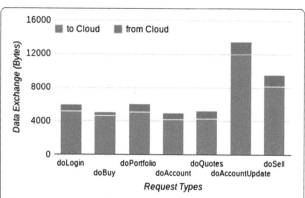

Figure 6 Average profiled data transfer for request types in DayTrader using the Asymmetric IP.

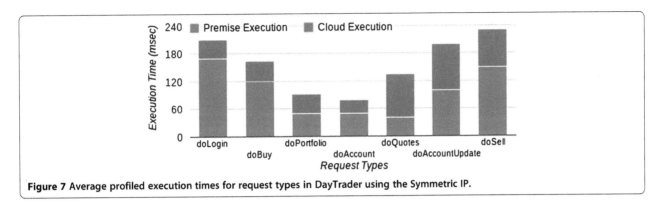

Figure 7 Average profiled execution times for request types in DayTrader using the Symmetric IP.

cases, the total processing time is greater for the symmetric approach but in other cases it is greater for the asymmetric approach. However, the asymmetric partitioning allows for more of the code to be moved to the cloud (with its associated cheaper resources for deployment costs) and so the overall cost of execution is also reduced.

This second result of Figures 7 and 8 can be seen by comparing ratio of cloud processing time and premise processing time for each request. We see that asymmetric partitioning increases the overall usage of cloud resources. Overall, asymmetric partitioning moves an additional 49% of execution time for an application to the cloud. With cloud resources being the cheaper resources, this will translate to cost savings for charges associated to CPU resources.

From the results of these experiments, we saw the significant effect that asymmetric partitioning had in enabling more code to be pushed to the cloud by the optimizer. This is because costs of data transfer to the code running on the public cloud are less expensive than data coming from the public cloud. However, while closely examining the resulting partitioning in our visualization we noticed a common case where some code was rarely ever pushed to the public cloud, making automated partitioning less effective. This case always occurred for code which was tightly coupled to some persistent data which we assumed was always stored on premise. This phenomenon is

illustrated well by the function nodes in Figure 2(a) which are rooted at the function TradeJdbc:getHoldings. Based on this observation we were motivated to investigate the potential of extending our approach to scenarios where persistent data could be distributed across both the public cloud and private premise. Next in Section 5, we augment the asymmetric code partitioning approach with this cross-tier, code and data partitioning.

4 Data-tier partitioning

The technical details of extending application-tier partitioning to integrate the data-tier are motivated by four requirements: (i) weighing the benefits of distributing queries, (ii) comparing the trade-offs between join orders, (iii) taking into account intra-request data-dependencies and (iv) providing a query execution model comparable to application-tier function execution. In this section, we first further motivate cross-tier partitioning by describing each of these points, then we cover the technical details for the steps of partitioning as they relate to the data-tier. Data in our system can be partitioned at the granularity of tables. We choose this granularity for two reasons: (i) it allows us to transparently partition applications using a lightweight middleware on top of an existing distributed database (we used Oracle in our experiments), (ii) tables are already a natural unit of security isolation for existing RDBMS controls. Transparently partitioning row-level or column-level

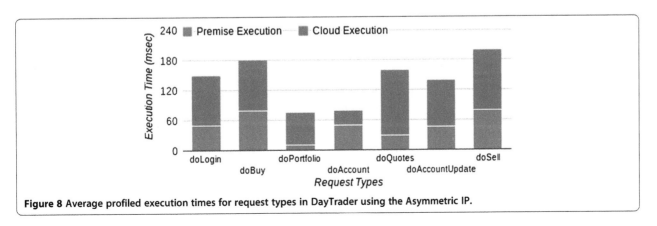

Figure 8 Average profiled execution times for request types in DayTrader using the Asymmetric IP.

data would not be difficult from the perspective of our BIP model, but it would require additional sophistication in our middleware or a special-purpose database. We focus on a data-tier implemented with a traditional SQL database. While some web application workloads can benefit from the use of alternative NoSQL techniques, we chose to focus initially on SQL due to its generality and widespread adoption.

First, as described in Section 2, placing more of the less-sensitive data in the cloud will allow for the corresponding code from the application-tier to also be placed in the cloud, thus increasing the overall efficiency of the deployment and reducing data transfer. However, this can result in splitting the set of tables used in a query across public and private locations. For our DayTrader example, each user can have many stocks in her holding which makes the holding table quite large. As shown in Figure 2, splitting the join operation can push the holdings table to the cloud (square nodes) and eliminate the traffic of moving its data to the cloud. This splitting also maintains our constraint to have the privacy sensitive account table on the private premise. An effective modeling of the data-tier needs to help the BIP optimizer reason about the trade-offs of distributing such queries across the hybrid architecture.

Second, the order that tables are joined can have an effect not only on traditional processing time but also on round-trip latency. We use a running example throughout this section of the query shown in Figure 9, with two different join orders, left and right. If the query results are processed in the public cloud where the holding table is in the cloud and *account* and *accountprofile* are stored on the private premise, then the plan on the left will incur two-round trips from the public to private locations for distributed processing. On the other hand, the query on the right only requires one round-trip. Modeling the data-tier should help the BIP optimizer reason about the cost of execution plans for different placements of tables.

Third, some application requests execute more than one query. In these cases, it may be beneficial to partition functions to group execution with data at a single location. Such grouping helps to eliminate latency overhead otherwise needed to move data to the location where the application-tier code executes. An example of this is

shown in Figure 2(b), where a sub-tree of function executions for *TradeJdbc:login* is labeled as "private" (gray nodes). By pushing this sub-tree to the private premise, the computation needed for working over *account* and *accountprofile* data in the two queries under *TradeJdbc: login* can be completed at the premise without multiple round-trips between locations.

Fourth, since the trade-offs on function placement depend on the placement of data and vice-versa, we need a model that can reason simultaneously about both application-tier function execution and query plan execution. Thus the model for the data-tier should be compatible for integration with an approach to application partitioning such as the one described in Section 3.

4.1 Database profiling with explain plan

Having motivated the need for a model of query execution to incorporate the data-tier in a cross-tier partitioning, we now explore the details. Figure 10 shows an extended version of Figure 3 in which we have broken out the code and data parts of the 3 phase process, (i) profiling, (ii) analysis, (iii) generating the BIP constraints and objective function. For data, the overall process is as follows. We first profile query execution using Explain Plan. This information is used to collect statistics for query plan operators by interrogating the database for different join orders (Section 4.2). The statistics are then used to generate both BIP constraints (Section 4.3) and a BIP objective function (Section 4.4). Finally, these constraints and objective are combined with that from the application-tier to encode a cross-tier partitioning model for a BIP solver.

Profiling information is available for query execution through the Explain Plan SQL command. Given a particular query, this command provides a tree- structured result set detailing the execution of the query. We use a custom JDBC driver wrapper to collect information on the execution of queries. During application profiling (cf. Section 3) whenever a query is issued by the application-tier, our JDBC wrapper intercepts the query and collects the plan for its execution. The plan returned by the database contains the following information:

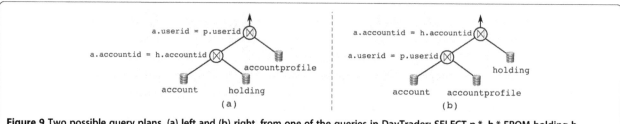

Figure 9 Two possible query plans, (a) left and (b) right, from one of the queries in DayTrader: SELECT p.*, h.* FROM holding h, accountprofile p, account a WHERE h.accountid = a.accountid AND a.userid = p.userid AND h.quote_symbol = ? AND a.ccountid = ?.

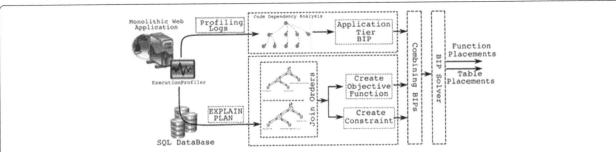

Figure 10 The overall process of applying cross-tier partitioning to a monolithic web application (process flows from left to right). The top of the figure shows the process of application partitioning through code dependency analysis and generating the application-tier IP. The bottom of the figure shows data partitioning through analyzing data access patterns and creating objective functions and dependency constraints. The two IP models are then combined and passed to an off-the-shelf IP solver to provide the solution to the optimization problem.

1. *type(op)*: Each node in the query plan is an operator such as a join, table access, selection (i.e. filter), sort, etc. To simplify presentation of the technical details, we assume that each operator is either a join or a table access. Other operators are handled by our implementation but they don't add extra complexity compared to a join operator. For example, in Figure 9, the selection (i.e. filter) operators are elided. We leverage the database's own cost model directly by recording from the provided plan how much each operator costs. Hence, we don't need to evaluate different operator implementations to evaluate their costs. On the other hand, we do need to handle joins specially because table placement is greatly affected by their ordering.

2. *cpu(op)*: This statistic gives the expected time of execution for a specific operator. In general, we assume that the execution of a request in a hybrid web application will be dominated by the CPU processing of the application- tier and the network latency. So in many cases, this statistic is negligible. However, we include it to detect the odd case of expensive query operations which can benefit from executing on the public cloud.

3. *size(op)*: This statistic captures the expected number of bytes output by an operator which is equal to the expected number of rows times the size of each retrieved row. From the perspective of the plan tree-structure, this is the data which flows from a child operator to its parent.

4. *predicates(joinOp)*: Each join operator combines two inputs based on a set of predicates which relate those inputs. We use these predicates to determine if alternative join orders are possible for a query. When profiling the application, the profiler observes and collects execution statistics only for plans that get executed but not for alternative join orders. However, the optimal plan executed by the database engine in a distributed hybrid deployment can be different from the one observed during profiling. In

order to make the BIP partitioner aware of alternative orders, we have extended our JDBC wrapper to consult the database engine and examine the alternatives by utilizing a combination of Explain Plan and join order hints. Our motivation is to leverage the already existing cost model from a production database for cost estimation of local operator processing, while still covering the space of all query plans. The profiler also captures which sets of tables are accessed together as part of an atomic transaction. This information is used to model additional costs of applying a two-phase commit protocol, should the tables get partitioned.

4.2 Join order enumeration

We need to encode enough information in the BIP so it can reason over all possible plans. Otherwise, the BIP optimizer would mistakenly assume that the plan executed during our initial profiling is the only one possible. For example, during initial profiling on a single host, we may only observe the left plan from Figure 5. However, in the example scenario, we saw that the right plan introduces fewer round-trips across a hybrid architecture. We need to make sure the right plan is accounted for when deciding about table placement. Our strategy to collect the necessary information for all plans consists of two steps: (i) gather statistics for all operators in all plans irrespective of how they are joined, and (ii) encode BIP constraints about how the operators from step (i) can be joined. Here we describe step 1 and then describe step 2 in the next subsection. The novelty of our approach is that instead of optimizing to a specific join order in isolation of the structure of application-tier execution, we encode the possible orders together with the BIP of the application-tier as a combined BIP.

As is commonly the case in production databases, we assume a query plan to be left-deep. In a left-deep query plan, a join takes two inputs: one from a single base relation (i.e. table) providing immediate input (referred to as the "inner relation"); and another one potentially derived as an intermediate result from a different set of relations (the "outer relation"). The identity of the inner relation and the set of tables comprising the outer relation uniquely determine the estimated best cost for an individual join operator. This is true regardless of the in which the outer relation was derived [11]. For convenience in our presentation, we call this information the operator's id, because we use it to represent an operator in the BIP. For example, the root operator in Figure 9a takes *accountProfile* as an inner input and *{holding, account}* as an outer input. The operator's id is then *{(holding, account), accountProfile}*. We will refer to the union of these two inputs as a join set (the set of tables joined by that operator). For example, the join set of the aforementioned operator is *{holding, account, accountProfile}*. Notably, while the join sets for the roots of Figure 9a & b are the same, Figure 9b's root node has the operator id *{(accountProfile, account), holding}* allowing us to differentiate the operators in our BIP formulation. Our task in this section is to collect statistics for the possible join operators with unique ids.

Most databases provide the capability for developers to provide hints to the query optimizer in order to force certain joins. For example in Oracle, a developer can use the hint *LEADING(X, Y, Z, ...)*. This tells the optimizer to create a plan where X and Y are joined first, then their intermediate result is joined with Z, etc. We use this capability to extract statistics for all join orders.

Algorithm 1 takes as input a query observed during profiling. In line 2, we extract the set of all tables referenced in the query. Next, we start collecting operator statistics for joins over two tables and progressively expand the size through each iteration of the loop on line 3. The table t, selected for each iteration of line 4 can be considered as the inner input of a join. Then, on line 5 we loop through all sets of tables of size i which don't contain t. On line 6, we verify if t is joinable with the set S by making sure that at least one table in the set S shares a join (access) predicate with t. This set forms the outer input to a join. Finally, on line 7, we collect statistics for this join operator by forcing the database to explain a plan in which the join order is prefixed by the outer input set, followed by the inner input relation. We record the information for each operator by associating it with its id. For example, consider Figure 4 as the input Q to Algorithm 1.

In a particular iteration of line 5, i might be chosen as 2 and t as *accountProfile*. Since *accountProfile* has a predicate shared with account, S could be chosen as the set of size 2: *{account, holdings}*. Now on line 6, *explainPlanWithLeadingTables({account, holdings}, accountProfile)* will get called and the statistics for the join operator with the corresponding id will get recorded.

The bottom-up structure of the algorithm follows similarly to the classic dynamic programming algorithm for query optimization [11]. However, in our case we make calls into the database to extract costs by leveraging Explain Plan and the LEADING hint. The complexity of Algorithm 1 is $O(2n)$ (where n is the number of tables); which is the same as the classic algorithm for query optimization [11], so our approach scales in a similar fashion. Even though this is exponential, OLTP queries typically don't operate on over more than ten tables.

4.3 BIP constraints

Now that we know the statistics for all operators with a unique id, we need to instruct the BIP how they can be composed. Our general strategy is to model each query plan operator, *op*, as a binary variable in a BIP. The variable will take on the value 1 if the operator is part of the query plan which minimizes the objective of the BIP and 0 otherwise. Each possible join set is also modeled as a variable. Constraints are used to create a connection between operators that create a join set and operators that consume a join set (cf. Table 1). The optimizer will choose a plan having the least cost given both the optimizer's choice of table placement and function execution placement (for the application-tier). Each operator also has associated variables op_{cloud} and $op_{premise}$ which indicate the placement of the operator. Table placement is controlled by each table's associated table access operators. The values of these variables for operators in the same query plan will allow us to model the communication costs associated with distributed queries.

```
1 Function collectOperatorStats(Q)
2        tables ← getTables(Q);
3        for i ← 1 to |tables| do
4              foreach t ∈ tables do
5                    foreach S ∈ Pi (tables − {t}) do
6                          if isJoinable(S, t) then
7                                explainPlanWithLeadingRelations(S, t);
```

```
Function createConstraints(joinSet)

2        ops ← getOperatorsForJoinSet(joinSet);

3        genChoice(joinSet, ops);

4        foreach op ∈ ops do

5                inputs ← getInputs(op);

6                genInputConstraint(op, inputs);

7                if sizeof(left(inputs)) > 0 then

8                        createConstraints(left(inputs));
```

Our algorithm to formulate these composition constraints makes use of two helper functions as shown in Table 1, namely *genChoice* and *genInputConstraint*. When these functions are called by our algorithms, they append the generated constraint to the BIP that was already built for the application-tier. The first function, *genChoice*, encodes that a particular join set may be derived by multiple possible join operators (e.g., *{holding, account, accountprofile}* could be derived by either of the root nodes in Figure 9). The second function, *genInputConstraint*, encodes that a particular join operator takes as inputs the join sets of its two children. It ensures that if *op* is selected, both its children's join sets (in_{left} and in_{right}) are selected as well, constraining which subtrees of the execution plan can appear under this operator. The "≥" inequality in Table 1 helps to encode the boolean logic $op \rightarrow in_{left} \wedge in_{right}$.

Starting with the final output join set of a query, Algorithm 2 recursively generates these constraints encoding choices between join operators and how parent operators are connected to their children. It starts on line 2 by calling a function to retrieve all operator ids which could produce that join set (these operators were all collected during the execution of Algorithm 1). It passes this information to *genChoice* on line 3. On line 4, we loop over all these operator ids, decomposing each into its two inputs on line 5. This information is then passed to *genInputConstraint*. Finally on line 7, we test for the base case of

a table access operator. If we have not hit the base case, then the left input becomes the join set for recursion on line 8.

4.4 BIP objective

Creating the optimization objective function consists of two parts: (i) determining the costs associated with the execution of individual operators, and (ii) creating a mathematical formulation of those costs. The magnitude of the execution cost for each operator and the communication cost between operators that are split across the network are computed using a similar cost model to previous work [12]. This accounts for the variation between local execution and distributed execution in that the latter will make use of a semi-join optimization to reduce costs (i.e. input data to a distributed join operator will transmit only the columns needed to collect matching rows). We extend the previous cost model to account for possible transaction delays. We assume that if the tables involved in an atomic transaction are split across the cloud and the private premise, by default the transaction will be resolved using the two-phase commit protocol.

Performance overhead from atomic two-phase distributed transactions comes primarily from two sources: protocol overhead and lock contention. Protocol overhead is caused by the latency of prepare and commit messages in a database's two-phase commit protocol. Lock contention is caused by queuing delay which increases as transactions over common table rows become blocked. We provide two alternatives to account for such overhead:

– For some transactions, lock contention is negligible. This is because the application semantics don't induce sharing of table rows between multiple user sessions. For example, in DayTrader, although

Table 1 Constraint generation functions

Function	genChoice(joinSet, {op₁... opₙ})
Generated constraint	$op_1 + ... + op_n = joinSet$
Description	ajoinSet is produced by one and only one of the operators $op_1... op_n$
Function	genInputConstraint(op, {in_left, in_right})
Generated constraint	$-2 \times op + in_{left} + in_{right} \geq 0$
Description	If op is 1, then variables representing its left and right inputs (in_{left} and in_{right}) must both be 1

Table 2 Functions for generating objective helper constraints

Function	genAtMostOneLocation(op)
Generated constraint	$op_{cloud} + op_{premise} = op$
Description	If the variable representing op is 1, then either the variable representing it being placed in the cloud is 1 or the variable representing it being place in the premise is 1
Function	genSeparated(op₁, op₂)
Generated constraint	$op_{1, cloud} + op_{2, premise} - cut_{op1, op2} \leq 1$
	$op_{1, premise} + op_{2, cloud} - cut_{op1, op2} \leq 1$
Description	If the variables representing the locations of two operators are different, then the variable $cut_{op1, op2}$ is 1

Table 3 Functions for generating objective function

Function	genExecutionCost(op)
Generated objective component	$op_{cloud} \times execCost_{cloud}(op) + op_{premise} \times execCost_{premise}(op)$
Description	If the variable representing op deployed in the cloud/premise is 1, then charge the associated cost of executing it in the cloud/premise respectively
Function	genCommCost(op_1, op_2)
Generated objective component	$cut_{op1, op2} \times commCost(op_1, op_2)$
Description	If $cut_{op1, op2}$ for two operators op_1 and op_2 was set to 1, then charge their cost of communication

Account and Holdings tables are involved in an atomic transaction, specific rows of these tables are only ever accessed by a single user concurrently. In such cases we charge the cost of two extra round-trips between the cloud and the private premise to the objective function, one to prepare the remote site for the transaction and another to commit it.

- For cases where lock contention is expected to be considerable, developers can request that certain tables be co-located in any partitioning suggested by our tool. This prevents locking for transactions over those tables to be delayed by network latency. Since such decisions require knowledge of application semantics that are difficult to infer automatically, our tool provides an interactive visualization of partitioning results, as shown in Figure 2(a) and (b). This allows developers to work through different "what-if" scenarios of table co-location constraints and the resulting suggested partitioning.

Next, we need to encode information on CPU and data transmission costs into the objective function. In addition to generating a BIP objective, we will need some additional constraints that ensure the calculated objective is actually feasible. Table 2 shows functions to generate these constraints. The first constraint specifies that if an operator is included as part of a chosen query plan (its associated id variable is set to 1), then either the auxiliary variable op_{cloud} or $op_{premise}$ will have to be 1 but not both. This enforces a single placement location for op. The second builds on the first and toggles the auxiliary variable $cut_{op1,op2}$ when op_{1cloud} and $op_{2premise}$ are 1, or when $op_{1premise}$ and op_{2cloud} are 1.

The objective function itself is generated using two functions in Table 3. The first possibly charges to the objective function either the execution cost of the operator on the cloud infrastructure or on the premise infrastructure. Note that it will never charge both due to the constraints of Table 2. The second function charges the communication cost between two operators if the associated cut variable was set to 1. In the case that there is no communication between two operators this cost is simply 0.

Algorithm 3 takes a join set as input and follows a similar structure to Algorithm 2. The outer loop on line 3, iterates over each operator that could produce the particular join set.

```
1  Function createObjFunction(joinSet)
2       ops ← getOperatorsForJoinSet(joinSet);
3   foreach op ∈ ops do
4           genAtMostOneLocation(op);
5           genExecutionCost(op);
6           inputs ← getInputs(op);
7       foreach input ∈ inputs do
8               foreach childOp ∈ getOperatorsForJoinSet(input) do
9                       genSeparated(op, childOp);
10                      genCommCost(op, childOp);
11          if sizeof(left(inputs)) > 0 then
12                  createObjFunction(left(inputs));
```

It generates the location constraints on line 4 and the execution cost component to the objective function on line 5. Next, on line 7, it iterates over the two inputs to the operator. For each, it extracts the operators that could produce that input (line 8) and generates the communication constraint and objective function component. Finally, if the left input is not a base relation (line 11), it recurses using the left input now as the next join set.

Having appended the constraints and objective components associated with query execution to the application-tier BIP, we make a connection between the two by encoding the dependency between each function that executes a query and the possible root operators for the associated query plan.

5 Implementation

We have implemented our cross-tier partitioning as a framework. It conducts profiling, partitioning, and distribution of web applications which have their business logic implemented in Java. Besides the profiling data, the analyzer also accepts a declarative XML policy and cost parameters. The cost parameters encode the monetary costs charged by a chosen cloud infrastructure provider and expected environmental parameters such as available bandwidth and network latency. The declarative policy allows for specification of database table placement and co-location constraints. In general we consider the placement of privacy sensitive data to be the primary consideration for partitioning decisions. However, developers may wish to monitor and constrain the placement of function executions that operate over this sensitive data. For this purpose we rely on existing work using taint tracking [13] which we have integrated into our profiler.

For partitioning, we use the off-the-shelf integer programming solver *lp_solve* [14] to solve the discussed BIP optimization problem. The results lead to generating a distribution plan describing which entities need to be separated from one another (cut-points). A cut-point may separate functions from one an- other, functions from data, and data from one another. Separation of code and data is achievable by accessing the database engine through the database driver. Separating inter-code or inter-data dependencies requires extra middleware.

For functions, we have developed a bytecode rewriting engine as well as an HTTP based remote call library that takes the partitioning plan generated by the analyzer, injects remote call code at each cut-point, and serializes data between the two locations. This remote call instrumentation is essentially a simplified version of J-Orchestra [15] implemented over HTTP (but is not yet as complete as the original J-Orchestra work). In order to allow for distribution of data entities, we have taken advantage of Oracle's distributed database management system (DDBMS). This allows for tables remote to a local Oracle DBMS, to be identified and queried for data through the local Oracle DBMS. This is possible by providing a database link (@dblink) between the local and the remote DBMS systems. Once a bidirectional dblink is established, the two databases can execute SQL statements targeting tables from one another. This allows us to use the distribution plan from our analyzer system to perform vertical sharding at the level of database tables. Note that the distributed query engine acts on the deployment of a system after a decision about the placement of tables has been made by our partitioning algorithm. We have provided an Eclipse plugin implementation of the analyzer framework available online [16].

6 Evaluation

Now we evaluate our complete cross-tier partitioning on two different applications: DayTrader [8] (cf. Section 2) and RUBiS [17]. RUBiS implements the functionality of an auctioning Web site. Both applications have already been used in evaluating previous cloud computing research [17,18]. We can have 9 possible deployment variations with each of the data-tier and the application tier being (i) on the private premise, (ii) on the public cloud, or (iii) partitioned for hybrid deployment. Out of all the placements we eliminate the 3 that place all data in the cloud as it contradicts the constraints to have privacy sensitive information on-premise. Also, we consider deployments with only data partitioned as a subset of deployments with both code and data partitioned, and thus do not provide separate deployments for them. The remaining four models deployed for evaluations were as follows: (i) both code and data are deployed to the premise (Private-Premise); (ii) data is on-premise and code is in the cloud (Naive-Hybrid); (iii) data is on-premise and code is partitioned (Split-Code); and (iv) both data and code are partitioned (Cross-Tier).

For both DayTrader and RUBiS, we consider privacy incentives to be the reason behind constraining placement for some database tables. As such, when partitioning data, we constrain tables storing user information (*account* and *accountprofile* for DayTrader and users for RUBiS) to be placed on-premise. The remaining tables are allowed to be flexibly placed on-premise or in the cloud.

The details of machine and network setup are the same as described in Section 3.3, so we don't repeat them here. In the rest of this section we provide the following evaluation results for the four deployments described above: execution times (Section 6.1), expected monetary deployment costs (Section 6.2), and scalability under varying load (Section 6.3).

6.1 Evaluation of performance

We measured the execution time across all business logic functionality in DayTrader and RUBiS under a load of 100 requests per second, for ten minutes. By execution time we mean the elapsed wall clock time from the beginning to the end of each servlet execution. Figure 11 shows those with largest average execution times. We model a situation where CPU resources are not under significant load. As shown in Figure 11, execution time in cross-tier partitioning is significantly better than any other model of hybrid deployment and is closely comparable to a non-distributed private premise deployment. As an example, execution time for DayTrader's doLogin under Cross-Tier deployment is 50% faster than Naïve-Hybrid while *doLogin's* time for Cross-Tier is only 5% slower compared to Private-Premise (i.e., the lowest bar in the graph). It can also be seen that, for *doLogin*, Cross-Tier has 25% better execution time compared to Split-Code, showing the effectiveness of cross-tier partitioning compared to partitioning only at the application-tier.

Similarly for other business logic functionality, we note that cross-tier partitioning achieves considerable performance improvements when compared to other distributed deployment models. It results in performance measures broadly similar to a full premise deployment. For the case of DayTrader - across all business logic functionality of Figure 11a - Cross-Tier results in an overall performance improvement of 56% compared to

Naïve-Hybrid and a performance improvement of around 45% compared to Split-Code. We observed similar performance improvements for RUBiS. Cross-Tier RUBiS performs 28.3% better - across all business logic functionality of Figure 11b - compared to its Naive-Hybrid, and 15.2% better compared to Split-Code. Based on the results, cross-tier partitioning provides more flexibility for moving function execution to the cloud and can significantly increase performance for a hybrid deployment of an application.

6.2 Evaluation of deployment costs

For computing monetary costs of deployments, we use parameters taken from the advertised Amazon EC2 service where the cost of an extra large EC2 instance is $0.48/hour and the cost of data transfer is $0.12/GB. To evaluate deployment costs, we apply these machine and data transfer costs to the performance results from Section 6.1, scale the ten minute deployment times to one month, and gradually change the ratio of premise-to-cloud deployment costs to assess the effects of varying cost of private premise on the overall deployment costs. As these input parameters are changed, we re-run the new inputs through our tool, deploy the generated source code partitions from the tool as separate Java "war" archives, and run each experiment.

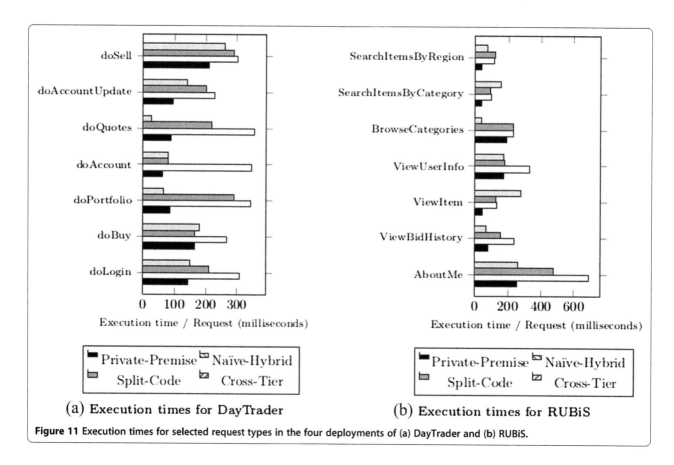

(a) Execution times for DayTrader

(b) Execution times for RUBiS

Figure 11 Execution times for selected request types in the four deployments of (a) DayTrader and (b) RUBiS.

As shown in both graphs, a Private-Premise deployment of web applications results in rapid cost increases, rendering such deployments inefficient. In contrast, all partitioned deployments of the applications result in more optimal deployments with Cross-Tier being the most efficient. For a cloud cost 80% cheaper than the private-premise cost (5 times ratio), DayTrader's Cross-Tier is 20.4% cheaper than Private-Premise and 11.8% cheaper than Naive-Hybrid and Split-Code deployments. RUBiS achieves even better cost savings with Cross-Tier being 54% cheaper than Private-Premise and 29% cheaper than Naive-Hybrid and Split-Code. As shown in Figure 12a, in cases where only code is partitioned, a gradual increase in costs for machines on-premise eventually results in the algorithm pushing more code to the cloud to the point where all code is in the cloud and all data is on-premise. In such a situation Split-Code eventually converges to Naive-Hybrid; i.e., pushing all the code to the cloud. Similarly, Cross-Tier will finally stabilize. However since in Cross-Tier part of the data is also moved to the cloud, the overall cost is lower than Naive-Hybrid and Split-Code.

6.3 Evaluation of scalability

We also performed scalability analyses for both DayTrader and RUBiS to see how different placement choices affect application throughput. DayTrader comes with a random client workload generator that dispatches requests to all available functionality on DayTrader. On the other hand, RUBiS has a client simulator designed to operate either in the browsing mode or the buy mode.

For both DayTrader and RUBiS we used a range of 10 to 1000 client threads to send requests to the applications in 5 minute intervals with 1 minute ramp-up. For RUBiS, we used the client in buy mode. Results are shown in Figure 13. As the figure shows, for both applications, after the number of requests reaches a certain threshold, Private-Premise becomes overloaded. For Naive-Hybrid and Split-Code, the applications progressively provide better throughput. However, due to the significant bottleneck when accessing the data, both deployments maintain a consistent but rather low throughput during their executions. Finally, Cross-Tier achieved the best scalability. With a big portion of the data in the cloud, the underlying resources for both code and data can scale to reach a much better overall throughput for the applications. Despite having part of the data on the private premise, due to its small size the database machine on premise gets congested at a slower rate and the deployment can keep a high throughput.

7 Related work

Our research bridges the two areas of application and database partitioning but differs from previous work in that it uses a new BIP formulation that considers both areas. Our focus is not on providing all of the many

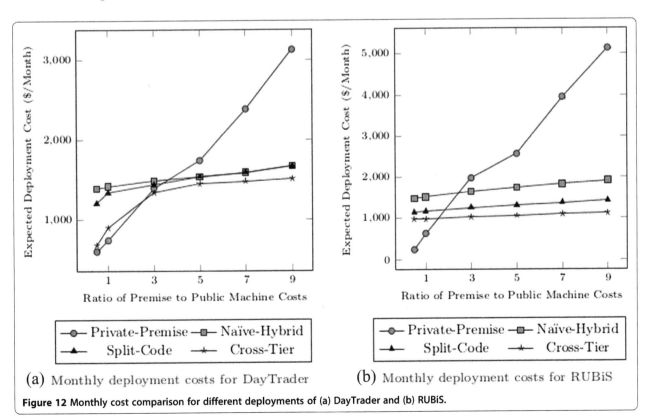

(a) Monthly deployment costs for DayTrader   (b) Monthly deployment costs for RUBiS

Figure 12 Monthly cost comparison for different deployments of (a) DayTrader and (b) RUBiS.

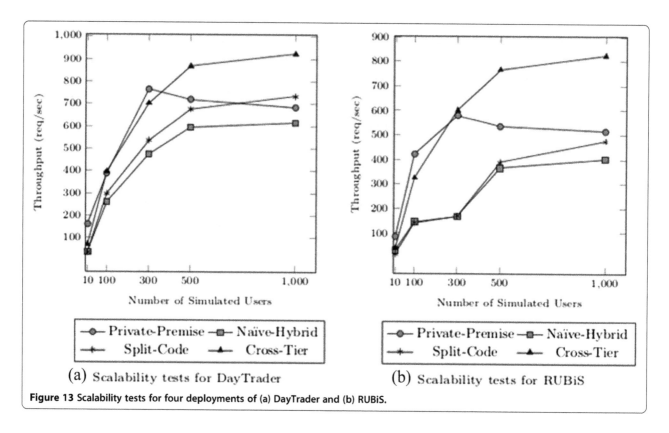

(a) Scalability tests for DayTrader   (b) Scalability tests for RUBiS

Figure 13 Scalability tests for four deployments of (a) DayTrader and (b) RUBiS.

features provided by every previous project either on application partitioning or database partitioning. Instead, we have focused on providing a new interface between the two using our combined BIP. We describe the differences in more detail by first describing some related work in application partitioning and then database partitioning.

Application Partitioning: Coign [19] is an example of classic application partitioning research which provides partitioning of Microsoft COM components. Other work focuses specifically on partitioning of web/mobile applications such as Swift [20], Hilda [21], and AlfredO [22]. However that work is focused on partitioning the application-tier in order to off-load computation from the server-side to a client. That work does not handle partitioning of the data-tier.

Minimizing cost and improving performance for deployment of software services has also been the focus of cloud computing research [23]. While approaches like Volley [24] reduce network traffic by relocating data, others like CloneCloud [2], CloudwardBound[3], and our own Manticore [5] improve performance through relocation of server components. Even though Volley examines data dependencies and CloneCloud, Cloudward Bound, and Manticore examine component or code dependencies, none of these approaches combine code and data dependencies to drive their partitioning and distribution decisions. In this paper, we demonstrated

how combining code and data dependencies can provide a richer model that better supports cross-tier partitioning for web application in a hybrid architecture.

Database Partitioning: Database partitioning is generally divided into horizontal partitioning and vertical partitioning [25]. In horizontal partitioning, the rows of some tables are split across multiple hosts. A common motivation is for load-balancing the database workload across multiple database manager instances [26,27]. In vertical partitioning, some columns of the database are split into groups which are commonly accessed together, improving access locality [9]. Unlike traditional horizontal or vertical partitioning, our partitioning of data works at the granularity of entire tables. This is because our motivation is not only performance based but is motivated by policies on the management of data resources in the hybrid architecture. The granularity of logical tables aligns more naturally than columns with common business policies and access controls. That being said, we believe if motivated by the right use-case, our technical approach could likely be extended for column-level partitioning as well.

8 Limitations, future work, and conclusion

While our approach simplifies manual reasoning for hybrid cloud partitioning, it requires some input from a developer. First, we require a representative workload for profiling. Second, a developer may need to provide input about the impact that atomic transactions have on partitioning. After partitioning, a developer may also want to consider changes to the implementation to handle some transactions in an alternative fashion, e.g. providing forward compensation. Also as noted, our current implementation and experience is limited to Java-based web applications and SQL-based databases.

In future work we plan to support a more loosely coupled service-oriented architecture for partitioning applications. Our current implementation of data-tier partitioning relies on leveraging the distributed query engine from a production database. In some environments, relying on a homogeneous integration of data by the underlying platform may not be realistic. We are currently working to automatically generate REST interfaces to integrate data between the public cloud and private premise rather than relying on a SQL layer.

In this paper we have demonstrated that combining code and data dependency models can lead to cheaper and better performing hybrid deployment of Web applications. Our initial approach considered only code partitioning but different from previous approaches it was sensitive to the ingress or egress flow of data to/from the public cloud. Our initial evaluation showed this to be promising but still limited since placement of data was fixed at the private premise. By extending this approach to cross-tier partitioning we demonstrated further improvement. In particular, our evaluation showed that for our evaluated applications, combined code and data partitioning can achieve up to 56% performance improvement compared to a naive partitioning of code and data between the cloud and the premise and a more than 40% performance improvement compared to when only code is partitioned (see Section 6.1). Similarly, for deployment costs, we showed that combining code and data can provide up to 54% expected cost savings compared to a fully premise deployment and almost 30% expected savings compared to a naively partitioned deployment of code and data or a deployment where only code is partitioned (cf. Section 6.2).

Competing interests
The authors declare that they have no competing interests.

Authors' contributions
NK participated in the study design and carried out the experimental work on both application and data tier partitioning, developed the experimental setup and gathered all data from the experiments. EW helped formulate the original study design, participated in the design of the approach to both application and data tier partitioning and analysis of both data sets. RL helped formulated the original study design, participated in the design of the asymmetric/symmetric approach and in the analysis of the both data sets. All authors participated in writing the manuscript and final approval.

References

1. Armbrust A, Fox A, Griffith R, Joseph AD, Katz RH, Konwinski A, Lee G, Patterson DA, Rabkin A, Stoica I, Zaharia M (2009) Above the Clouds: A Berkeley View of Cloud Computing., Technical Report UCB/EECS-2009-28, UC Berkeley

2. Chun BG, Ihm S, Maniatis P, Naik M, Patti A (2011) Clonecloud: Elastic Execution Between Mobile Device and Cloud, Proceeding of EuroSys., p 301, doi:10.1145/1966445.1966473

3. Hajjat M, Sun X, Sung YWE, Maltz D, Rao S, Sripanidkulchai K, Tawarmalani M (2010) Cloudward Bound: Planning for Beneficial Migration of Enterprise Applications to the Cloud. In: Proc. of SIGCOMM., p 243, doi:10.1145/1851275.1851212

4. Leymann F, Fehling C, Mietzner R, Nowak A, Dustdar S (2011) Moving applications to the cloud: an approach based on application model enrichment. J Cooperative Information Systems 20(3):307–356

5. Kaviani N, Wohlstadter E, Lea R (2012) Manticore: A Framework for Partitioning of Software Services for Hybrid Cloud, Proceedings of IEEE CloudCom., p 333, doi:10.1109/CloudCom.2012.6427541

6. Khadilkar V, Kantarcioglu M, Thuraisingham B (2011) Risk-Aware Data Processing in Hybrid Clouds, Technical report, University of Texas at Dallas

7. Schrijver A (1998) Theory of Linear and Integer Programming. Wiley & Sons, Hoboken, NJ

8. DayTrader 3.0.0. http://svn.apache.org/repos/asf/geronimo/daytrader/tags/daytrader-parent-3.0.0/. Accessed 23 Jun 2014.

9. Kaviani N, Wohlstadter E, Lea R (2011) Profiling-as-a-Service: Adaptive Scalable Resource Profiling for the Cloud in the Cloud. In: Proceedings of the 9th international conference on Service-Oriented Computing (ICSOC'11)., doi:10.1007/978-3-642-25535-9_11

10. Newton R, Toledo S, Girod L, Balakrishnan H, Madden S (2009) Wishbone: Profile-based Partitioning for Sensornet Applications. In: Proceedings of NSDI., p 395

11. Selinger G, Astrahan M, Chamberlin D, Lorie R, Price T (1979) Access Path Selection in a Relational Database Management System. In: SIGMOD., p 23, doi:10.1145/582095.582099

12. Yu CT, Chang CC (1984) Distributed Query Processing, Computer Survey

13. Chin E, Wagner D (2009) Proceeding of ACM workshop. on Secure Web Services., p 3, doi:10.1145/1655121.1655125

14. Berkelar M, Dirks J (2014) lp_solve Linear Programming solver., http://lpsolve.sourceforge.net/. Accessed 23 Jun 2014

15. Tilevich E, Smaragdakis Y (2002) J-Orchestra: Automatic Java Application Partitioning. Proceedings of ECOOP, p 178–204. Springer-Verlag

16. Kaviani N (2014) Manticore. http://nima.magic.ubc.ca/manticore. Accessed 23 Jun 2014

17. OW2 Consortium (2008) RUBiS: Rice University Bidding System. http://rubis.ow2.org/. Accessed 23 Jun 2014

18. Stewart C, Leventi M, Shen K (2008) Empirical Examination of a Collaborative web Application, Proceedings of IISWC., p 90, doi:10.1109/IISWC.2008.4636094

19. Hunt G, Scott M (1999) The Coign Automatic Distributed Partitioning System, Proceedings of OSDI., p 252, doi:10.1109/EDOC.1998.723260

20. Chong S, Liu J, Myers A, Qi X, Vikram K, Zheng L, Zheng X (2009) Building secure web applications with automatic partitioning. J Communications ACM 52(2):79

21. Yang F, Shanmugasundaram J, Riedewald M, Gehrke J (2007) Hilda: A High-Level Language for Data-Driven web Applications. In: WWW., p 341

22. Rellermeyer R, Riva O, Alonso G (2008) AlfredO: An Architecture for Flexible Interaction With Electronic Devices. In: Middleware., pp 22–41, doi:10.1007/978-3-540-89856-6_2

23. Ko SY, Jeon K, Morales E (2011) The HybrEx Model for Confidentiality and Privacy in Cloud Computing, Proceedings of HotCloud, USENIX

24. Agarwal S, Dunagan J, Jain N, Saroiu S, Wolman A (2010) Volley: Automated Data Placement for Geo-Distributed Cloud Services, Proceedings of NSDI, p 17

25. Pavlo A, Curino C, Zdonik S (2012) Skew-Aware Automatic Database Partitioning in Shared-Nothing, Parallel Oltp Systems, Proceedings of SIGMOD., p 61, doi:10.1145/2213836.2213844

26. Abadi DJ, Marcus A, Madden SR, Hollenbach K (2009) Sw-store: a vertically partitioned dbms for semantic web data management. VLDB J 18(2):385, doi:10.1007/s00778-008-0125-y

27. Garcia-Molina H, Salem K (1987) Sagas, Proceeding of SIGMOD., p 249, doi:10.1145/38714.38742

Dioptase: a distributed data streaming middleware for the future web of things

Benjamin Billet[*] and Valérie Issarny

Abstract

The Internet of Things (IoT) is a promising concept toward pervasive computing as it may radically change the way people interact with the physical world, by connecting sensors to the Internet and, at a higher level, to the Web, thereby enacting a Web of Things (WoT). One of the challenges raised by the WoT is the in-network continuous processing of data streams presented by Things, which must be investigated urgently because it affects the future data models of the IoT, and is critical regarding the scalability and the sustainability required by the IoT. This cross-cutting concern has been previously studied in the context of Wireless Sensor Networks (WSN) given the focus on the acquisition and in-network processing of sensed data. However, proposed solutions feature various proprietary and highly specialized technologies that are difficult to integrate and complex to use, which represents a hurdle to their wide deployment. At the other end of the spectrum, cloud-based solutions introduce a too high energy cost for the envisioned IoT scale, considering the energy cost of communication over computation. There is thus a need for a distributed middleware solution for data stream management that leverages existing WSN work, while integrating it with today's Web technologies in order to support the required flexibility and the interoperability of the IoT. Toward that goal, this paper introduces *Dioptase*, a lightweight Data Stream Management System for the WoT, which aims to integrate the Things and their streams into today's Web by presenting sensors and actuators as Web services. The middleware specifically provides a way to describe complex fully-distributed stream-based mashups and to deploy them dynamically, at any time, as task graphs, over available Things of the network, including resource-constrained ones.

Keywords: Data stream management system; Internet of things; Streaming; Middleware

1 Introduction

The Internet of Things (IoT) is a promising concept toward pervasive computing and one of the major paradigm shifts that the computing era is facing today [1]. In the IoT, everyday objects, the "Things", get networked so that they can cooperate autonomously, and allow humans to interact with the physical world as simply as they do with the virtual world [2,3]. However, the IoT paradigm raises tremendous challenges, including the ability to perform continuous processing of data streams presented by Things. Data stream management is indeed a cross-cutting concern for the IoT [4], which must be studied urgently because it affects the future data models of the IoT. Specifically, applications aimed at the IoT have to manage data acquired from the physical world and

thus deal with the consumption of continuous data that evolve over time, as opposed to consuming data of the traditional Internet that are primarily discrete. Hence, in the IoT, data become volatile since they are useful only when they are produced and processed, while requests become persistent since they are permanently executed.

The continuous processing of sensed data has been extensively studied in the context of Wireless Sensor and Actuator Networks (WSAN) given the focus on the acquisition of data from the physical world. This has resulted in the introduction of dedicated Data Stream Management Systems (DSMS), which are, in the case of WSANs, tools to manage and process streams across a sensor network [5]. Historically, DSMSs were part of relational database research, as extension of Data Base Management Systems (DBMS), establishing a theoretical background for data stream management. In contrast to DBMS, WSAN research focuses on very low-power

*Correspondence: benjamin.billet@inria.fr
MiMove Project-Team, Inria Paris-Rocquencourt, Rocquencourt, France

devices and emphasizes in-network processing in order to save energy and increase the lifetime of the networks [4], as one exchanged bit is sometimes equivalent to 1000 CPU cycles [6]. WSAN-based DSMSs thus adapt formal algebras and data models of DBMSs [4,7], while featuring custom operations for continuous stream processing as well as probabilistic operators [8,9] that are designed to reduce the device's processing load (CPU, memory and energy) and correct the errors that occur within mobile and distributed sensing environments (transient errors). Still, WSAN-based DSMSs are facing major challenges which prevent them from being used directly in the IoT:

1. They are characterized by various levels of in-network processing, with the use of fully or partially centralized approaches based on a single or many collection points. The systematic use of proxies in WSANs to solve resource constraints is indeed a bottleneck and a threat to the scaling up aim, a mandatory criterion of the IoT.

2. They introduce many proprietary technologies (from both network and development perspectives) which can be used only in specific sensor networks and are difficult to use for developers who are not expert in the domain [2,4]. As a solution, given that today's Web connects smoothly a huge number of highly heterogeneous devices [10], Web-based DSMSs for the IoT promote interoperability, standardization and openness by using Web-based techniques and methods that enable stream management [11], making the IoT part of the greater Future Internet as a Web of Things (WoT). However, existing approaches do not suit well the energy- and resource-efficiency requirements of resource-constrained Things, because of the overhead associated with Web technologies that makes them working only on the most powerful Things [3], or "smart Things" (typically smartphones or plug computers).

3. Due to the limited resources of the devices, WSAN-based DSMSs are dedicated to specific tasks composed from a fixed set of operations (e.g., relational operators). As a result, it is either not possible, or at least very difficult, for developers to apply new operators once the network has been deployed. The developer can only compose a fixed set of existing operators provided by the DSMS. This is not appropriate for dynamic and large networks like the IoT, which is expected to run various contextual tasks that are not predefined.

Most of the above problems are related to the resource constraints of the existing sensor technologies. However, moderately powerful Things, or "average Things", are emerging, pioneered by sensor technologies like Imote2 [12] and Sun SPOT [13]. These devices are likely to expand drastically in the near future while their cost will decrease, as more and more IoT appliances are expected to be released by the industrial world [14]. Typically, this class of devices can accommodate Web technologies provided the technologies are adequately revisited, knowing that only a subset of these technologies are useful for implementing Web services in order to achieve the Web of Things (WoT) vision. Hence, we argue that WSAN- and Web-based techniques need to be integrated within a fully-distributed streaming middleware that is able to run directly onto every type of average and smart Things. As a benefit, the IoT will be more interoperable, each Thing will be more autonomous and the need of proxies will be mitigated.

Toward this end, this paper introduces a customizable distributed DSMS middleware, called *Dioptase*, whose contributions are as follows:

- *Dioptase* adds flexibility to state of the art DSMS solutions for resource-constrained devices, by introducing a high-level application model that can map any IoT/WoT application onto the entities of the network (sensors, actuators, users, services, databases, etc.). In this model, each Thing is abstracted as a generic device that can be dynamically assigned communication, storage and computation tasks according to its available resources, enabling the applications to be directly executed in the network without any proxy (in-network processing).

- *Dioptase* features a customizable middleware architecture that is versatile enough to be deployed on a large class of Things that vary significantly in terms of resource availability (e.g., sensors, smartphones or plug computers), provided these Things are able to communicate directly through the Internet infrastructure (typically the average Things that use 6LoWPAN) [15]. Unlike WSAN-based DSMSs that target specific sensor networks, *Dioptase* enable developers to use the same middleware on moderately powerful sensors (e.g. Sun SPOT), smartphones, personal computers, servers and the cloud.

- From a technical perspective, the flexibility of *Dioptase* is based on a lightweight domain-specific language (DSL) designed to express continuous processing tasks. The DSL syntax is specifically optimized to be interpreted on the huge number of average Things that are more powerful than small sensors but very limited compared to smart Things. This mechanism enables the dynamic deployment of tasks in isolated sandboxes which are naturally safer than arbitrary binary-code deployment [16,17]. As a benefit, developers can build applications composed of tasks deployed in the network at any time, using standard Web services. To achieve this, *Dioptase* features relevant optimizations of Web technologies (small Web server, subset of protocols, compression, etc.) and leverages advanced stream management techniques (in-network processing, approximation and dynamic reconfiguration).

As detailed in the following, *Dioptase* makes it possible: (i) to integrate the Things with today's Web by exposing sensors and actuators as Web services, (ii) to manage physical data as streams, and (iii) to use any Thing as a generic pool of resources that can process streams by running tasks that are provided by developers over time. The rest of this paper is organized as follows: Section 2 first discusses the role of proxies in WSANs and reviews related work in the area of streaming solutions for WSANs and IoT/WoT, highlighting required capabilities for data streaming middleware in the future IoT/WoT context. Section 3 then presents the *Dioptase* application model for the WoT, which allows the design of mashups[a] that compose the streams flowing in the WoT. Following, Section 4 describes the architectural design of the *Dioptase* middleware together with its implementation, while Section 5 provides an evaluation of *Dioptase* for both average and smart Things. Finally, Section 6 draws some conclusions and sketches our perspectives for future work.

2   Background

Our work is motivated by the two following main goals:

- We want to make Things able to execute complex tasks that are not predefined at the Things' deployment time so as to enable developers to use the WoT as a pool of generic resources, without unneeded intermediaries (proxies, gateways, base stations, etc.). The role of such intermediaries is specifically discussed in Section 2.1.
- We want to integrate the work done on data streaming for wireless sensor networks with the Web in order to actually achieve the Web of Things (WoT) vision [18], which has led us to base our research on the work on data streaming as part of the Web and of WSANs. Existing DSMSs for WSANs are presented in Section 2.2 with their related advantages and drawbacks.

Our solution specifically lies in enabling stream-oriented mashups that may be dynamically deployed and reconfigured, which suits well the real-world use cases that are commonly presented in the IoT/WoT literature and highlights the increased autonomy of Things (e.g., see [2]).

2.1   Intermediaries in WSANs

Usually, a WSAN is composed of (i) several motes equipped with one or more sensors and a wireless interface, and (ii) more powerful devices, typically fixed and continuously-powered, that embed actuators [4]. In addition, a WSAN leverages proxies, gateways or base stations for carrying out collection and computation tasks, as well as communication with other networks, such as the Internet. Nowadays, the above intermediaries are not anymore required for communication between motes and the Internet, thanks to the standardized stack composed of IEEE802.15.4 and 6LoWPAN, which is intended to replace proprietary communication proxies (application level) by standardized IP routers (network level) [15]. As a benefit, motes have an IPv6 address, or an equivalent made of the network identifier and a small address, and can communicate directly with the Internet.

Regarding data collection, proxies are still needed in order to enhance the sensor network capabilities, e.g., for implementing heavy computation (offloading), centralized management and task deployment, caching and security/privacy (access control, key management, etc.). However, offloading data collection and processing to proxies is energy-consuming due to the wireless communication, which holds for any wireless device, including smartphones [6,19]. Similarly, cloud-based stream processing is quite popular today, and there are some attempts to use it with sensor networks and IoT: cloud of sensors, cloud-based IoT, cloud-assisted remote sensing, etc [20,21]. However, the same problems arise regarding communication costs, availability (specifically for mobile Things with sparse connectivity), latency and privacy.

As a solution to the above problems, it has been proposed to let the sensor network performs as much in-network processing as possible before sending anything to a proxy or the cloud, in order to: (i) reduce the amount of transferred data and (ii) make use of the motes at their full potential. For example, structural health monitoring is a case where a huge amount of measurements is produced quickly because of the vibration sensors. These types of sensors are very sensitive and detect a lot of 3-axis accelerations, saturating the network and exhausting the sensors' batteries. In such a case, pre-aggregation, pre-filtering and compression can be performed within the motes instead of the base station [22].

Consequently, in our opinion, centralized intermediaries (proxies, surrogates, cloudlets and the cloud) should be leveraged primarily for heavy computation, while in-network processing should be favored for common and simple tasks (filtering, merging, etc.) as well as for complex tasks when powerful/specialized enough Things are available. To this end, *Dioptase* is intended to avoid reliance on those intermediaries whenever possible, by running on devices that support 6LoWPAN or IPv6 and communicate directly with the Internet. Nevertheless, in cases where intermediaries are needed, *Dioptase* can be deployed on them and run as a middleware layer for deploying tasks dynamically and managing data streams.

2.2 DSMSs for WSANs

The work most related to ours may then be classified into three major families of DSMSs for WSANs, which are respectively based on: (i) the relational model, (ii) macro-programming and (iii) Web services.

We also identify related work on supporting the construction of mashups in the WoT although focused on the exchange of discrete data like Actinium [23], COMPOSE [24], Eywa [25] and the Thin Server architecture [26]. However, these solutions consider Things as passive data providers and shift the computation logic into powerful servers or into the cloud. As we said before, in our opinion, centralization is not suitable for the WoT from a scaling up perspective, even in the cloud, as it weakens the entire network and increases the overall energy consumption.

Relational DSMSs extend the relational model by adding concepts that are necessary to handle data streams and persistent queries, together with the stream-oriented version of the relational operators (e.g., selection or union). The sensor network is then managed as a large database that can be queried using a SQL-like language, with some specific operations. The database may further be distributed (each node runs a part of the query), centralized (a powerful node collects all the data and applies queries) or partially centralized (with many powerful nodes) [27]. From a practical perspective, queries are translated into query plans that are distributed in the network. State of the art DSMSs primarily differ with respect to: the expressiveness of the query language, the associated algebra, and assumptions made about the underlying networking architecture. A well-known DSMS is *TinyDB* [28], which exposes the sensed data as a relation (i.e., table) on which it is possible to apply queries over the sensed values as well as the metadata associated with the sensors. During the handling of queries, all the nodes execute the queries that are distributed in the network and the results of each query get aggregated as they traverse the routing tree maintained by the system. In the same vein, *Cougar* [29] acts as a database of sensors where the query plans are provided to proxies that take care of activating the relevant sensors and applying the operations on the collected data. *MaD-WiSe* [30] offers a runtime system for queries that is fully distributed, and each sensor may directly execute part of a query plan and then deal with sensor-specific tasks. *Borealis* [31], previously *Aurora*, uses data stream diagrams, which express the combination of relational operators over the streams received by

the system. From a theoretical perspective, various systems propose custom extensions to the relational model as well as custom implementations of the relational operators. For instance, *STREAM* [32] distinguishes streams from relations, where the latter can be handled by classical relational operators. New operators then deal with translation from stream to relations (typically using windows), and vice versa (using streamers). *EQL* [33] moves a step forward, by enabling the developers to express composite queries in a very concise way, in order to detect and track complex events which involves various types of sensors (e.g., gas leak). Other proposals [7-9,34] deal with issues as diverse as blocking and non-blocking operators, windows, stream approximation, and various optimizations.

State-of-the-art WSAN-based DSMSs suffer from proprietary protocols and technologies specifically designed to handle the characteristics of resource-constrained devices. As a consequence, proxies are often used to collect, process and present sensed data on the Internet, creating (i) an unwanted bottleneck, (ii) a single point of failure and (iii) an increased energy consumption if no proper in-network processing technique is used. To alleviate such effects, a DSMS for the WoT should include a middleware layer designed to run directly on Things without any intermediary (except for conversions at physical and link levels), given that modern device classes are emerging and allows more flexible data stream management based on the use of Web technologies. In addition, such middleware must reuse and extends the rich theoretical background of relational DSMSs, especially the data models proposed to describe streams and the non-blocking operators initially designed for WSANs.

Macroprogramming-based DSMSs enable users to express tasks over the WSAN using a DSL instead of a query language. The resulting tasks, or macroprograms, are compiled into microprograms to be run on the networked nodes, hence easing the developer's work who no longer has to bother with the decomposition and further distribution of the macroprograms. Macroprogramming-based DSMSs are overall similar to classical macroprogramming approaches aimed at WSAN. However, they feature additional primitives and mechanisms oriented toward stream management. For instance, Regiment [35] introduces a functional language that enables programming the WSAN and manipulating the streams that flow in the network. As for Semantic Streams [36], it defines a declarative language based on Prolog, which features data structures to handle streams, together with mechanisms to reason about the semantics of sensors. For instance, the system is able to compose or adapt data according to the available sensors and the given request.

As outlined above, existing macroprogramming-based DSMSs follow a static approach where the macroprograms are compiled into microprograms that are deployed once for all. Specific techniques can be used to dynamically update the network: (i) dynamic reconfiguration and (ii) dynamic deployment. However, the former techniques usually assume that the tasks are already implemented on the devices [37], while the latter techniques usually support binary deployment (e.g., Deluge [16]). Instead, a DSMS for the WoT must provide a high-level of dynamicity by making possible to change both the global and the local behaviors of the network at any time. To this end, the developers should be provided a way to represent WoT applications as abstract programs that are distributed dynamically in the actual network. In addition, sandboxes should be used to increase the overall reliability, as an attacker can benefit from arbitrary binary deployment to deploy malicious code on any open device.

Service-oriented DSMSs aim to integrate with classical service-oriented architectures, thereby taking advantages of the existing infrastructure (interaction and discovery protocols, registries, service composition based on orchestration or choreography, etc.). Similarly to database-oriented relational DSMSs, the simplest service-oriented DSMSs are centralized with a unique point of data collection [11,38,39], or semi-distributed based on a set of data collection points [40,41]. However, these DSMSs focus mainly on the problem of presenting streams as services, without reusing the existing and valuable theoretical work from WSANs. In practice, these approaches are based on well-known Web service technologies. For RESTful services, some studies use specific mechanisms of the HTTP protocol, like *Web hooks*, *long polling* and *HTTP streaming* [11]. As for SOAP services, some work extends the SOAP architecture by adding new *message exchange patterns* (MEP) designed for stream communication (e.g., the capability for a service to receive multiple requests and produce multiple responses in parallel when invoked) [42]. Usually, sensors are presented as Web resources, identified by URIs [11,38,41]. The paradigms used to broadcast streams vary from one solution to another. *Stream Feeds* [38] uses pull requests to gather historical data and push requests to receive new data issued by the sensors. *RMS* [11] goes a step further by building upon a topic-based pub/sub infrastructure, while *WebPlug* [41] uses an infrastructure based on pollers that periodically check the state of resources.

Integrating data stream management into service-oriented architectures is a logical evolution of sensor networks, as Web technologies provide a greater flexibility, ease of use and interoperability compared to existing WSNs technologies. The proposed solutions, in particular, enable Things to communicate through the Internet and expose their resources as standardized Web services. As simple as the present Web, these services can be used to build mashups that interact with the physical world. However, existing solutions are limited by their scope. Indeed, much research is focusing on how to present streams as Web services, and neglects many complex aspects like continuous processing of streams (merging, filtering, adaptation, approximation, etc.). Reusing theoretical and practical foundations that were established by the two other families of DSMSs is a crucial step to enable the IoT to take advantage of WSAN capabilities together with the flexibility, the reliability and the interoperability of the Web, which guided the design of the *Dioptase* application model and supporting middleware toward the WoT vision.

3 The dioptase application model for the WoT

The *Dioptase* application model for the WoT allows developers to easily build mashups able to manage, process and compose streams produced within networks of Things. This model is oriented toward the high-level description and distribution of stream-based mashups as components over the network, enabling the dynamic deployment of these components over resource-constrained Things.

3.1 Dioptase component model

As illustrated by the WSAN work, we identify four high-level roles that each Thing may play, usually in combination, depending on its resources: (i) A *production* role where the Thing presents sensor data as streams, (ii) a *processing* role where the Thing continuously processes streams, (iii) a *consumption* role where the Thing acquires streams and drives actuators, and (iv) a *storage* role where the Thing saves data extracted from streams (in its memory, or persistently).

A *Dioptase mashup* is thus composed of distributed components, called *atomic components*, derived from the above roles: *producer*, *processor*, *consumer* and *storage*. These components interact (are connected) by continuously exchanging data as *streams*. The mashup can then be easily described as an acyclic directed graph (VL, EL) where the nodes $vl_i \in VL$ are producers (sources), processors, consumers (sinks) and storages, and the edges of the graph, $el_j \in EL$, are streams that link components together.

The mashup graph is equivalent to the query plan that can be found in DSMSs that present sensor networks as databases. However, query plans are strongly coupled to the query language capabilities that are limited w.r.t. the set of operations that can be executed. In contrast, the high-level nature of the *Dioptase* components makes it possible to easily represent any element of a WoT application as components that produce and consume streams. For example, end-users, GUI and actuators can be abstracted as consumers while sensors, databases, crowd-sensors and any other type of data source (e.g., a

Web service that gives information about the weather) can be abstracted as producers. In addition, processors may implement any type of continuous computation, or *task*. This flexibility allows the representation of mashups that can describe complex tasks for a wide variety of entities (sensors, actuators, servers, users, services, etc.).

As an illustration, Figure 1(a) presents an example of a simple mashup that analyzes outdoor light in order to control an indoor lighting system. In this mashup, a producer ① reads the light value and another producer ② monitors the lighting system state. These data are acquired by a processor ③ that produces an event stream for the lighting system ④. At the same time, the light measurements are saved by a storage ⑤ and are consumed by the lighting control application ⑥ that presents historical values to the administrator.

We call this graph a *logical mashup graph* because it describes the tasks that the network has to perform. This graph is provided by the developer either directly or expressed as a query that is translated into a mashup graph. Using information provided by a discovery system (e.g., registry or distributed protocol [43]) that is aware of Things' locations and available resources, the logical mashup graph is automatically converted into a *physical mashup graph* (VP, EP), were each $vp_i \in VP$ is a pair (vl, n) that maps a component vl onto a host device n, as depicted in Figure 1(b). In particular, depending on its capabilities, a Thing can be assigned either a single component or an entire subgraph. The problem of computing the physical mashup graph from the logical mashup graph is a variation of the *task mapping problem*, where a set of communicating tasks with several properties (constraints, requirements, resource consumption,

etc.) have to be mapped to a set of connected nodes given their characteristics (location, hardware capabilities, etc.). Task mapping within *Dioptase* is beyond the scope of this paper, and the interested reader is referred to [44] for relevant baseline together with [45] for a specific *Dioptase* solution.

In our component model, each component defines some *input ports* for the consumption of streams, depending on the component type, and at most one *output port* where new stream items are produced. Provided the data types specified for the input and output streams match, any output port can be connected to any input port through a one-to-one connection. Theoretically, stream communication between components can be achieved in three ways: (i) *pull*, where a consumer requests a producer to send the data stream, (ii) *push*, where a producer requests a consumer to process its data, and (iii) *hybrid*, which allows the two previous modes. The choice of either mode is not important from a functional perspective and defines only which component should initiate the transmission. In our work, we consider that a consumer must be autonomous and does not have to process an unwanted stream. As a consequence, the data exchange between two components is pull-based, as a component always decides how to connect its input ports.

3.2 Data stream

According to the literature [5,32,46], a *stream* is a sequence of discrete items that are linked by some properties (e.g., same source, same type, time coupling, etc.). The size of this sequence is theoretically infinite and it is not possible to know its end *a priori*. In *Dioptase*, each *stream*

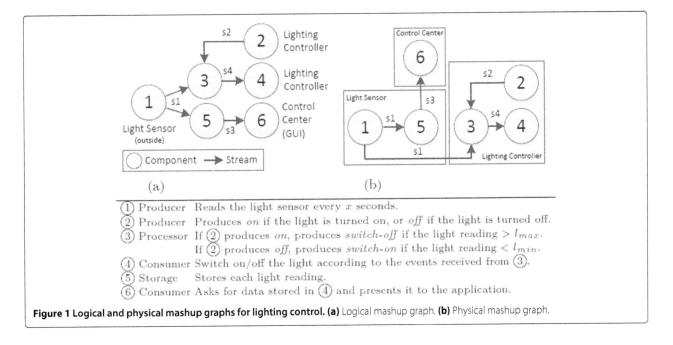

(a)   (b)

① Producer   Reads the light sensor every x seconds.
② Producer   Produces *on* if the light is turned on, or *off* if the light is turned off.
③ Processor   If ② produces *on*, produces *switch-off* if the light reading $> l_{max}$.
             If ② produces *off*, produces *switch-on* if the light reading $< l_{min}$.
④ Consumer   Switch on/off the light according to the events received from ③.
⑤ Storage   Stores each light reading.
⑥ Consumer   Asks for data stored in ④ and presents it to the application.

Figure 1 Logical and physical mashup graphs for lighting control. (a) Logical mashup graph. **(b)** Physical mashup graph.

item is a tuple associated with a *timestamp* that can be explicit, if generated with the tuple, or implicit, if defined when the tuple is received [5,32,46]. Then, as for relations in relational databases, a *Dioptase* stream adheres to a *schema* that defines the *attributes* of each tuple. In addition, the *Dioptase* schema is intended to take into account semantic aspects of the sensed data and the characteristics of the data source. In practice, the schema is composed of:

- The *Semantic concept* of the attribute (e.g., temperature or pressure), which helps Things to reason about the produced data in order to, e.g., compose them automatically (e.g., kinetic energy = $\frac{1}{2} \times$ mass $\times$ speed^2) or select the most relevant algorithms for approximation, prediction or interpolation.
- The *Concrete type* of the attribute, i.e., the data type. The most simple types are integer, real or boolean, but more complex types can be considered, like image or audio/video sequence.
- *Metadata* that are specific to the semantic concept, and make the system more adaptable. For example, the *unit of measurement* can be used to adapt automatically to requests that involve different units for the same semantic concept (e.g., kelvin, celsius and farenheit for temperature).

The properties defined in the schema can be defined using a standard vocabulary in order to reason automatically about these data, according to external knowledge provided by the developers. For example, the unit and semantic type can refer to ontologies of physical concepts and related models (prediction, interpolation or error models) [47].

The connection between a component's output port to the input port of another component is established through a *connector*, i.e., a software component that manages the transport, adaptation and presentation of the data as streams, between two components. We introduce two types of connectors for stream transportation in *Dioptase*: *local connector* and *remote connector*. The former manages connections between two components that are running on the same Thing and optimizes communication accordingly, while the latter acquires data from a component that is running on another Thing.

Various specializations of the remote connector may be envisioned, notably for interfacing the *Dioptase* middleware with other data stream management systems, sensor networks (e.g., a CoAP connector) [15] or existing services (e.g., a meteorological database). This remains an area for further extension of the *Dioptase* middleware, while our current middleware implementation supports HTTP-based streaming (polling, hooks and websockets [48,49]).

3.3 Stream processing

Stream-based communication requires dedicated support for data processing. Indeed, as streams are unbounded, it is not feasible to store the entire stream before applying any operation. Although some operations are naturally non-blocking, i.e., able to produce tuples without detecting the end of input streams (e.g., set intersection), some other operations are unable to produce any item before the acquisition of the entire streams (e.g., set difference) [50]. The current *Dioptase* middleware handles blocking operations using windows, although this is not detailed in the paper; the interested reader may refer to [46] for classical windowing techniques. Concerning non-blocking operations, traditional WSAN-based DSMSs fix the set of operations that can be applied (typically relational operators). However, this is too restrictive, especially in light of the increasing capabilities of Things. Instead, the developers should be provided means to dynamically specify complex tasks for execution by Things. Hence, *Dioptase* introduces the processor components, which perform non-blocking processing.

Thanks to processor components, Things are able to perform any computation over data streams that is not necessarily defined at the time the Things are deployed. Specifically, a processor executes a given task, i.e., a sequence of operations, over one or more streams, where the task may be provided at any time. A task can be either *compiled* (directly implemented on the Thing by the developer, using the platform's native language) or *interpreted*, i.e., described in a lightweight DSL, which is directly interpreted by the middleware. While the *Dioptase* DSL, called *DiSPL* (Dioptase Stream Processing Language), supports generic-purpose structures (control flow statements), specific primitives are provided to manipulate data streams (e.g., read/write into streams or build new stream items) and atomic components (e.g., create new storages or migrate a processor). As a benefit, *DiSPL* enables the developer to describe a wide range of complex tasks and dynamically send them to any known Thing, at any time. Technical details about *DiSPL* to describe interpreted tasks are provided in the next Section.

Compiled tasks are less flexible than interpreted ones, but they are more efficient (native code) and are useful to implement the library of common processing tasks (e.g., compute an average value, count the number of items) which we refer to as *operators*. These operators are often used in practice by developers and it is better to express them as compiled tasks in order to improve the efficiency of WoT applications. In addition, *Dioptase* includes various packages of operators dedicated to approximation (e.g., linear prediction [51], sampling), correction and compression of sensed data.

The lifecycle of a processor is divided in three steps: (i) deployment of the processor and initialization of the required resources (global variables, parameters, libraries, etc.), (ii) processing of each new stream item, and (iii) termination of the component that frees all the resources previously initialized. As shown in Figure 2, these three steps are described by corresponding sections in the task: *initialization logic*, *work logic* and *finalization logic*. Each step is allowed to read and write data into the *internal state* maintained by the processor, which is a structure that can be serialized and moved into another Thing if necessary.

In order to reason about the types of data a task can produce or consume, each task is characterized by a *contract*. This contract defines the schemas of the input and output streams that are compatible with the task and its operations. At deployment time, these information are used by the processor to instantiate its ports and the related schemas. The following JSON snippet presents an example of contract for a simple operator that counts the tuples (any type) of a single input stream: for each stream item read from the input stream, the operator increments its internal counter and writes the value of this counter in its output stream. Accordingly, the contract expresses that the output stream is composed of single-valued items (attribute name is *count*) that do not have semantic type and unit.

```
"operator": "dioptase.count",
"inputs": {
  "main": {
      "type": "any",
      "scope": "tuple"
  }
},
"output": {
    "count": {
        "semantic": "none",
        "unit": "none",
        "concrete": "integer"
    }
}
}
```

However, in some cases, the output schema must be built dynamically at deployment-time by the task, based on the actual schemas of the input streams. For example, the output schema could be identical to one of the input schema, or the output schema could be composed from some attributes of each input schemas. The following JSON snippet presents an example of contract for an inner join operator on two input streams. This operator admits a string parameter (called *attribute*) used for performing the join on one attribute of the input schemas.

```
"operator": "dioptase.join",
"inputs": {
    "input1": {
        "type": "any",
        "scope": "tuple"
    },
    "input2": {
        "type": "any",
        "scope": "tuple"
    }
},
"output": "dynamic",
"params": {
    "attribute": {
        "type": "string"
    }
}
}
```

4   Dioptase architecture and design

Figure 3 depicts, from a high-level perspective, the *Dioptase* middleware architecture supporting the dynamic deployment of distributed mashups within the WoT. First, to manage the specifics of different classes of Things and platforms, Thing-specific low-level functionalities are separated into *Drivers*. These drivers are loaded when the middleware starts and are used by other modules. Drivers have to be implemented for each class of Things and provide, in particular, the communication routines, the access to the Thing's sensors and actuators and the storage management functions.

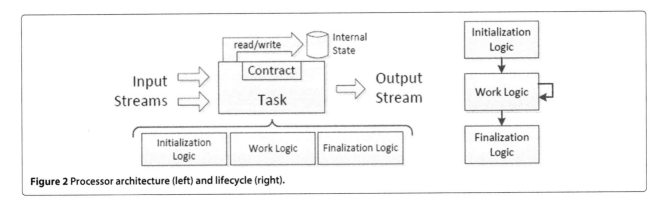

Figure 2 Processor architecture (left) and lifecycle (right).

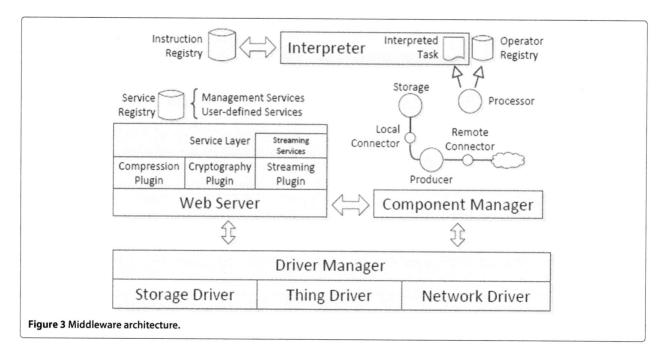

Figure 3 Middleware architecture.

At run-time, the *Component Manager* runs the components that are deployed on the Thing. These components produce and consume streams, locally and remotely, through the connectors that manage data transport. The processors run the tasks that are either provided by developers or obtained from a standard operator library (e.g., selection, join, sort). Non-predefined tasks are deployed at run-time and are described using the *DiSPL* DSL that is run by the embedded *Interpreter*.

Network communication is carried out through Web services that expose the resources of the Thing (access to streams and metadata, manage components, settings, etc.). For this purpose, the middleware embeds a lightweight all-in-one *Web client/server* optimized to run with few resources. The services are written in native code and are directly compiled with the middleware. Their implementations are well-decoupled from the Web server and, instead of the costly TCP transport protocol, Web services protocols for resource-constrained devices can be used, such as CoAP or HTTPU (HTTP over UDP) [52].

Precisely, only a subset of HTTP is useful to implement a Web service [52] and, consequently, our small HTTP implementation supports only a limited set of requests (GET/POST only), headers, MIME types, encodings (UTF-8 only), languages and mechanisms. Similarly, lightweight formats are used whenever possible (binary serialization or JSON) for describing services parameters and responses' content. Basically, only simple requests/responses are supported, with the smallest set of mandatory HTTP headers. For the Thing with higher capabilities, additional HTTP standard functions, like *Compression* (e.g., gzip, deflate) or *Cryptography* (e.g., SSL, TLS), are

provided as *Plugins* that can be enabled or disabled according to the Thing's resources. Compression is particularly interesting, as it can reduce drastically the amount of exchanged data and the energy consumption [22].

All the components presented in Figure 3 are intended to be deployed directly on the Thing. However, in order to run on a large number of Things and to handle the hardware heterogeneity of Things (heterogeneous resources, specific capabilities, etc.), *Dioptase* is highly modular and can be adapted to the resources of the Things. Concretely, the middleware deployment consists of two steps: *customization* and *deployment*. Customization of the middleware consists into removing irrelevant modules (e.g., compression/cryptography plugins or the interpreter component) and adding or implementing new modules based on the specific capabilities of the Thing (e.g., hardware video decoding). For example, during this phase, the Thing's owner may implement new operators and register them in the standard library, for future usage. Similarly, the *DiSPL* DSL can be extended by defining additional packages of instructions (e.g., a wrapper for a library deployed onto the Thing). Ultimately, the customized middleware is deployed onto the Thing and connected to the network.

In fact, customizing the middleware is rather straightforward, as the modules are clearly identified. Nevertheless, even if it has to be done only once, this operation can be time-consuming. Fortunately, a great deal of it can be simplified, by providing pre-packaged and preconfigured versions of *Dioptase* built for specific classes of Things (depending on their hardware resources). Regarding the development of Thing-specific components (e.g., supporting a video decoding chip), widely used libraries can be shared between developers or, in the future, provided by the vendors.

4.1 Middleware services

Dioptase is a service-oriented middleware that exposes the Thing's resources (sensors, actuators, components and streams) as services, and more specifically RESTful services because of performance constraints [52]. The main middleware services are the *streaming services* that enable access to streams, and the *management services* which are used to manage and control the Thing and the middleware modules.

Streaming Services are implemented using two different techniques supported by the web server's streaming plugin: (i) *HTTP streaming*, where the connection is never closed and each item is sent as chunks in the HTTP response, and (ii) *Web hooks*, which establish a callback service in the client in order to enable the server to send new items as HTTP requests. We use both techniques because of their respective advantages and drawbacks. On the one hand, HTTP streaming implies maintaining a TCP connection and Web hooks lead to a large overhead (request headers) [11]. As a consequence, if the stream's data rate (i.e., stream items per second) is high, HTTP streaming is more efficient as it introduces a constant overhead (the TCP connection) independently of the number of stream items. On the other hand, if the data rate is low, Web hooks are more suitable because they avoid the use of an infinite connection.

Access to a stream is done in two steps: *access request* and *streaming*. The first step consists in calling the service stream as a regular RESTful service with the desired streaming method (HTTP streaming or Web hooks) as a parameter. The second step is different according to the method: in the case of HTTP streaming, the data are embedded in the response and, in the case of Web hooks, the callback service is invoked for each new stream item. To illustrate this two step process, Appendices A and B present an example of a simple stream of light values, accessed over HTTP streaming and Web hooks.

This behavior is abstracted by using the remote connector, which manages these low-level aspects by opening or closing callback services transparently. However, if it is not possible to directly access a Thing through the network (e.g., because of NAT), using a proxy is mandatory and Web hooks communication is disabled. This problem, which is related to some networks (e.g., LAN, 3G), will be alleviated in the future because of the use of IPv6 that solves the addressing problem. As a benefit, NAT mechanisms will disappear [53], enabling each Thing to be accessed directly through a public address.

Management services enable developers and other Things to control the components that are running on the middleware and to deploy new ones, as shown in Table 1 that summarizes the usual services and their parameters. For example, a new processor can be deployed by providing a task and a set of streams to use as inputs. These streams are identified by a specific URI that describes local and remote streams (e.g., *dioptase://localhost/stream-name, dioptase://server:port/stream-name*). Then, the middleware deploys the processor, instantiates each connector according to the given stream URI and starts the execution in accordance with the lifecycle presented earlier. In addition, at deployment time, a processor or a producer can be asked to save a history of their output streams that can be queried later. Once deployed, a processor can be stopped and removed, as well as any other component. As an example of task deployment, Appendix C presents a deployment request over HTTP for an interpreted processor that consumes two streams and executes a given *DiSPL* program.

Deploying a storage component is a similar operation, provided the storage type is supported by the Thing. At present, the *Dioptase* prototype supports three types of storage: (i) memory storage (fixed or extensible), (ii) file storage, and (iii) database storage (for embedded databases). Unlike producer and processor components, storages have a memory of past states that can be queried *a posteriori*. A storage component can produce a stream only when it receives a query that expresses some constraints that can be temporal (items between two timestamps, items older than x, etc.), volumetric (the x last items) or a combination of them. The complying results are presented as a new stream that ends when the last item is sent. Each storage type supports these constraints, but some storages can accept specific parameters (e.g., the database storage can handle a SQL query directly).

Similarly, actuators are presented as Web services and are based on the information provided by the *Thing Driver* about the physical actions that the Thing is able to perform. Each action can receive specific typed parameters that compose an *actuation contract* which defines the name and the type of each parameter, and the type of the returned result if any.

Other services can be used to access the Thing's metadata about the embedded sensors and actuators, the Thing's capabilities (e.g., hardware, location, load, energy level, operator library), and the components that are currently deployed (e.g., input/output schemas and load).

4.2 Dioptase stream processing language (DiSPL)

As already mentioned, non-blocking operations are executed by processors, which are components dedicated to the execution of (i) *compiled tasks* that are linked to the middleware during the customization phase, and (ii)

Table 1 Common *Dioptase* services and their parameters

Service path	Description and parameters
/streams	Access to a stream. *id=<stream id>, mode=stream|hook,* **hook=<hook name> (if mode=hook)*
/thing/properties	Get the properties of the Thing: sensors, actuators, supported storage types and metadata. **sensors=true|false, *actuators=true|false,* **storages=true|false, *metadata=true|false*
/thing/sensors	Get identifiers, units, semantic/concrete types and metadata of one or all the sensors. **id=<sensor id>*
/thing/actuators	Get identifiers and parameters (names, types, metadata) of one or all the actuators. **id=<actuator id>*
/thing/operators	Get identifiers and contracts (name/type of inputs, number of inputs) of one or all the compiled operators. **id=<operator id>*
/thing/actuate	Executes one of the actuation service. *id=<actuator id>, service=<service name>,* *actuator-specific parameters (key/value)*
/components/running	Get the name and the input/output stream URIs of deployed components (producer, processor, storage).
/components/remove	Stop and destroy a component. *id=<component id>*
/processors	Get identifiers and input/output streams schemas of one or all the processors, possibly in extended form (logic, state, schemas). *id*=<processor id>, *extended=true|false*
/processors/state	Get the content of the internal state of a processor. *id=<processor id>*
/processors/new	Deploy a new processor and starts it. *id=<processor id>, code=<source code> or* *operator=<operator id>, inputs=<URIs>,* **state=<start state>, *history=true|false,* **h-size=<history size>, operator-specific* *parameters (key/value)*
/processors/history	Get a processor history as a stream. *id=<processor id>, *t-start=<timestamp>,* **t-end=<timestamp>|now, *nb=<nb of* *items>*
/processors/migrate	Migrate a processor to another device. *id=<processor id>, to=<URI>,* **forget-state=true|false*
/producers	Get identifiers, sensor names and output streams schemas of one or all the producers. **id=<processor id>*
/producers/new	Deploy a new producer. *id=<producer id>, sensor=<sensor id>,* **sampling=<sampling rate>*
/storages	Get identifiers, types and input/output schemas of one or all the storages. **id=<storage id>*
/storages/new	Deploy a new storage. *id=<storage id>, type=<storage type>,* *storage-specific parameters (key/value)*

Legend: **xxx* = optional parameter   *<yyy>* = any value   *a\|b\|c* = parameter value can be *a*, *b* or *c*.

interpreted tasks that are described using the *DiSPL* DSL and deployed during the execution. This makes it possible to build logical and physical mashup graphs that use both compiled and interpreted tasks. Using the management services presented in the previous section, the developer is able to ask any known Thing to create a processor that executes either (i) a compiled task by providing its identifier, or (ii) an interpreted task by providing the *DiSPL* source code of the task.

The literature in stream processing already features languages like IBM SPL [54] but, in our case, the programs are intended to be interpreted directly onto the Things, as opposed to resource-rich servers. As a consequence, we introduce a new stream processing language, designed to be parsed efficiently by resource-constrained devices. Our language is based on the properties and the syntax of the functional language Scheme [55], which we chose for its simplicity and flexibility; S-Expressions have a very small grammar. The core of the language remains the same (variable definition, conditions, arithmetic and boolean expressions, etc.) but without λ-calculus support, which is not essential to describe continuous processing tasks, and increases the resources consumption of the interpreter. The general-purpose nature of the language makes feasible the description of a wide range of complex customized tasks, enhanced by various primitives dedicated to stream management. In addition, other instructions are related to the Thing management and includes the ability to create and deploy new components, connect components' ports and monitor the Things' resources (memory, CPU load, battery). As an example, the following snippet of *DiSPL* code shows the implementation of a simple *COUNT* program that uses instructions for reading the new incoming stream items (*getNewItems*), build new stream items (*item*), and write data into the output stream (*write*). Please note that a larger example is given in Appendix D, which consists in the implementation of a Bloom Filter [56] using *DiSPL*.

```
;initialization section
init:
  ;creates a global variable for counting

    (define count 0)

;work section
work:
  ;gets the set of new items
  (define diff (getNewItems "inStream"))
  (if (> (size diff) 0)
    ;computes the new total
    ((set count (+ count (size diff)))
    ;writes the total into the output stream
    (write (item (now) "count" count)))
  )
```

As shown in Figure 4, interpreted tasks rely on a dedicated *parser*, which converts the source code into an *abstract syntax tree* (AST). Then, the processor sends the AST to the *interpreter* which builds an *execution context* for the given task. This context is used to store information like local variables or the call stack. Driven by the processor, the interpreter runs each section of the task and stores the global variables into the internal state of the component (i.e., the set of variables that are required to restore a component). Finally, the interpreter is monitored by a watchdog that collects information about the running task (execution time, consumed memory and CPU, etc.). This watchdog can kill any processor when resources are low, according to some policies provided by the user or the administrator of the Thing.

5 Experimental results

In order to evaluate our system, we implemented a prototype[b] of *Dioptase* in Java and deployed it onto devices with heterogeneous capabilities. The choice of Java is motivated by (i) the advances in porting the Java Virtual Machine to small sensors [57], (ii) the existence of all-in-one Java sensors, such as Sun SPOT, and (iii) the huge number of operating systems that supports Java, enabling us to work directly with a wide range of devices (computers, smartphones, embedded systems, etc.).

The experiments presented in this section have two goals. First, we want to show that the customization phase enables the use of the *Dioptase* middleware on heterogeneous Things in order to serve HTTP streams with suitable performances relative to available resources. Second, we aim to analyze the overhead due to the code interpretation mechanism, by comparing the consumption of resources by compiled and interpreted tasks, respectively.

During our experiments, we focused on two Things: a *Galaxy Nexus* and an *Oracle Sun SPOT*. The Galaxy Nexus is a smartphone that we consider representative of today's smart Things, i.e., a very powerful and mobile Thing [3]. The device embeds a dual-core 1.2 GHz CPU (ARM Cortex-A9), one gigabyte of memory, and it runs with the Android 4.2.2 "Jelly Bean" operating system. Sun SPOTs are wireless motes developed by Sun Microsystems (today Oracle) that embed a small Java

Micro Edition virtual machine called Squawk. The Sun SPOT v6 integrates a 400 MHz CPU (AT91SAM9G20) and one megabyte of memory. These motes are a perfect example of averagely powerful Things (or *average Things* for short) that, from our perspective, will compose the future IoT/WoT (average power, but modern execution environment) and that are targeted by our middleware. The same customized middleware ($\sim$209 KB) is deployed on both the Spot and the phone and embeds all the modules, except the compression and cryptography plugins that are not used during the experiments.

5.1 Stream serving experiment

Our first experiment analyzes the ability of the *Dioptase* middleware to efficiently serve streams. Toward that end, a producer is deployed on the Thing and acquires data from the embedded light sensor. Every 500 milliseconds, the producer performs a new measurement and sends it ($\sim$100 B/s) to each consumer connected to the component. Each consumer is deployed on a standard computer and, because the Spot and the phone have very different capabilities, the number of clients is different between the experiments. All the experiments generate raw data directly into the devices' storages (the phone and the Spot embed two flash storages of respectively 16 GB and 4 MB). These data are retrieved and processed *a posteriori*. Before the beginning of the experiment, time informations are broadcasted (UDP) to synchronize the internal clock of each device; time error is less than ten milliseconds.

As depicted in Figure 5, communication between clients and the Spot is done through a base station that is used as a router between the Ethernet network and the radio IEEE 802.15.4 network. The experiment is run in two phases: (i) every 2 seconds, the client opens a new connection to the Spot, with a limit of 10 connections, then (ii) every 40 seconds, the client opens 10 new connections in order to stress the device. The connection's opening time, the time interval between two messages (jitter), and the time between the production and reception of a light measurement (including the transmission time and the middleware processing time) are collected. Figure 6 presents the average time used to open a connection and the latency between the production and the consumption

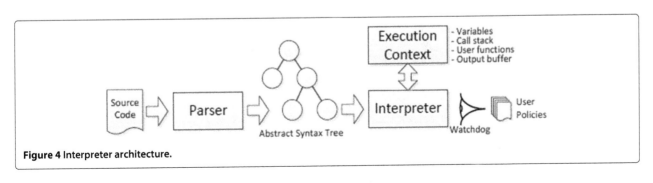

Figure 4 Interpreter architecture.

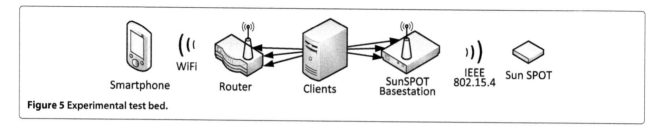

Figure 5 Experimental test bed.

of a stream item. Figure 7 shows the latency between two stream items. Ideally, this time should stay close to the production interval time (i.e., 500 ms).

The phone experiment is done through a direct WiFi 802.11 g connection (access point). The same data as in the previous experiment are collected. However, the connection's opening phases are slightly different to take into account the higher capability of the phone. The experiment starts with 100 established connections and, every 20 seconds, 100 new connections are opened with a limit of 1000. Figures 8 and 9 show the same information as the previous Spot experiment. Unlike with Spots, it is possible to read data about CPU and memory consumption, using the system files */proc/stat* and */proc/meminfo*. Figure 10 presents these measures, acquired every 5 seconds (this long duration was chosen in order to avoid influencing the other readings).

As expected, the devices resources decrease as the number of connections increases, up to a critical threshold that is clearly visible in Figure 6. After around 40 connections, the latency increases significantly (packet loss and resent many times) and, as a consequence of the Thing's overload, the jitter grows quickly (Figure 7). For smart Things, we can see that even with 1000 connections, network and resource usage stay stable, as shown in Figure 8. These results on smart Things are very encouraging, with regard to Web-based DSMSs' performances [11,38], which makes *Dioptase* a good solution for data streaming, with the benefit of advanced stream processing capabilities.

Assessing the performances of our middleware against other DSMSs is actually extremely difficult as the classes of Things and the criteria considered in other work are very different. *Dioptase* is designed to run on average Things, provides an in-network interpretation mechanism, and presents sensed data as embedded streaming Web services. These features are unique and cannot be compared to existing DSMSs. WSAN-based DSMSs typically focus on energy consumption for tiny Things but not on the ability to handle many heterogeneous parallel tasks. In contrast, Web-based DSMSs focus on smart Things, powerful servers, desktop computers or even the cloud. As a consequence, average Things provide inferior performances, in terms of simultaneous connections and processing speed.

Still, it is worth highlighting that the capability for an average Thing to serve around 30 streams of two measurements per second with a limited latency (< 500 ms) is, in absolute terms, suitable for most of the envisioned IoT/WoT scenarios [2]. For example, let us consider the scenario of the SmartPark project [58], where informations about parking space availability are collected in order to synchronize and guide the drivers toward free parking spots. Specifically, each vehicle is equipped with a wireless communication device and exchanges informations with the Things (presence sensors) that are deployed at each parking spot. In this case, if each of these Things handles 30 streams, as shown in our performance experiments, it

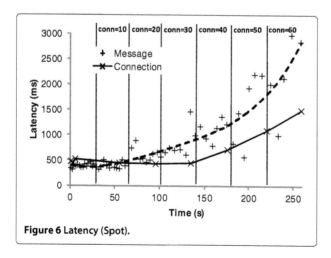

Figure 6 Latency (Spot).

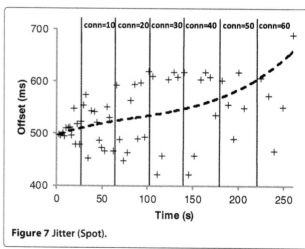

Figure 7 Jitter (Spot).

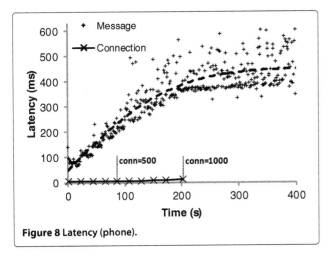

Figure 8 Latency (phone).

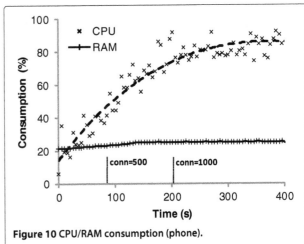

Figure 10 CPU/RAM consumption (phone).

enables the entire parking network to manage and process thousands of streams (which is clearly more than necessary for this scenario). In addition, as in WSAN work, limiting the amount of data exchanged between Things is a goal of the IoT due to the energy constraints. In-network processing, compression and approximation are therefore used to ensure that only strictly useful data are exchanged by Things, alleviating the need for many simultaneous data streams.

5.2 Stream processing experiment

Our second experiment assesses the capability of *Dioptase* to support dynamic deployment of tasks, by evaluating the resource consumption of processors for compiled and interpreted tasks. The chosen task is a hash-based pipelined inner join [59], which is applied many times in parallel on two light streams produced by two different sensors: the light sensor local to the Thing, and a light sensor available from another Spot. As in the first set of experiments, the producer reads the light sensors every 500 ms.

The pipelined inner join requires a memory space that grows proportionally to the size of the input streams. The operator is implemented using one hash table per stream. When a new item x is received from an input stream, the operator checks if it is present in the tables of the other streams. If it is, the item is written in the output stream and stored in the related table.

The Spot experiment is run in two steps, both for compiled and interpreted joins: (i) every 5 seconds a new processor is deployed, with a limit of 5 processors, then (ii) 10 new processors are deployed every 40 seconds. As we said before, we can not acquire the memory and CPU consumption on Spots and, as a consequence, we measure only the time spent by each processor to run its work section. This time is an image of the real resource consumption, as it increases if the memory and the CPU are overloaded. Figure 11 shows the average execution time, and the experiment is stopped when the Thing load becomes too high (after around one hundred processors).

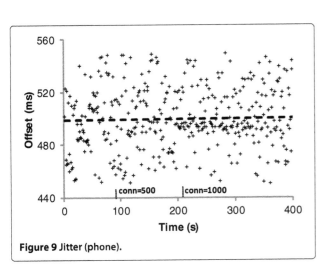

Figure 9 Jitter (phone).

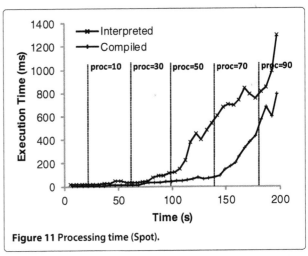

Figure 11 Processing time (Spot).

The phone experiment starts with 10 processors and, every 10 seconds, 10 new processors are deployed. When the Thing reaches 100 processors, 100 new processors are deployed every 10 seconds. Like the previous one, this experiment is run for compiled and interpreted joins. In addition to the execution time presented in Figure 12, we get information about resource consumption shown in Figures 13 (interpreted) and 14 (compiled).

Interpreted joins are of course more expensive than compiled ones, because of the depth-first search of the AST. The figures show that the interpreted join consumes approximately twice as much CPU as the compiled join. However, the execution on the phone is very efficient, with a pretty low difference between the two operators (approximately forty microseconds in the worst case, where some peaks are a consequence of the garbage collector). On the Spot, the Thing is overloaded with 60 interpreted joins and 90 compiled joins. These results are not a CPU problem, which is oversized for these types of operations, but a problem of memory, which is quickly full (especially because of the AST that requires more space than the hash tables).

The results obtained are satisfying, but are also difficult to compare to other DSMSs as, to the best of our knowledge, other DSMSs for constrained devices do not manage fully-dynamic tasks. The pipelined inner join is an expensive operation that consumes CPU and memory continuously, far more than other operations like counting or filtering that are computed in constant time and space. Relatively to the scenarios presented in [2], the *Dioptase* ability to run around sixty complex interpreted operations (respectively ninety compiled ones) in parallel on a single resource-constrained Thing is perfectly compatible with the needs of the IoT/WoT.

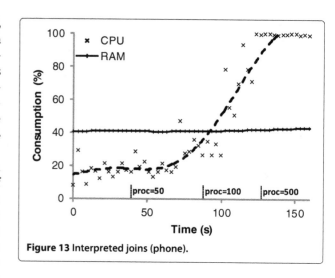

Figure 13 Interpreted joins (phone).

6 Conclusion

The IoT and related WoT are expected to become significant enablers of pervasive computing given the interaction with the physical world that they promote. However, numerous obstacles must be overcome by judiciously combining the knowledge acquired from the various visions involved rather than trying to reinvent the wheel.

In this paper, we presented *Dioptase*, a middleware that aims at simplifying building complex mashups based on the multiple data sources of the WoT. *Dioptase* makes it possible to integrate Things, even averagely powerful ones, with the Web and enables them to produce, process and store data streams dynamically. Each Thing, and by extension the entire network, is then seen as a consistent entity, dedicated to the (complex) processing of sensed data, and able to dynamically run tasks written in a DSL called *DiSPL*. This language aims to be simple, but flexible enough to describe such advanced operations and, for interoperability concerns, we plan to write converters from state-of-the-art stream processing languages like SPL [54] or C-SPARQL [60]. We demonstrated that

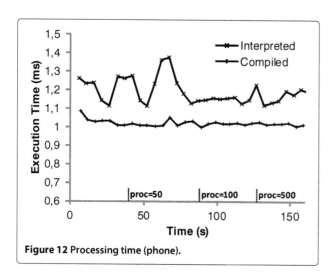

Figure 12 Processing time (phone).

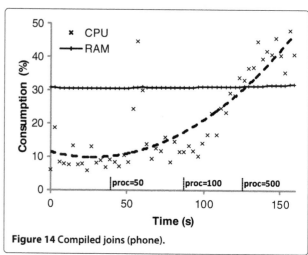

Figure 14 Compiled joins (phone).

the *Dioptase* middleware can avoid the systematic use of centralized or partially centralized infrastructures, which are commonly used in WSAN-based DSMSs. In addition, we have shown that *Dioptase* is efficient enough to be deployed on average Things w.r.t. the IoT/WoT needs and use cases, and enables these Things to be integrated in the Web despite the additional complexity of data streaming communication.

Dioptase remains a work in progress. Our work can be first improved in a technical way, especially by enhancing the efficiency of the interpreter or integrating other continuous operators. However, we are more interested in dealing with many other IoT/WoT research problems. First, making each Thing an entity of generic processing is a first step toward simplifying the deployment and the distribution of applications within the WoT networks. The next step is to study how to manage security in this context of dynamic deployment, to avoid making the WoT a wide area of chaos. Access control, encryption, identification/authentication and trust management are the security aspects that must be studied in the future, reusing the existing state of the art technologies for security and privacy [1,2]. The problems of integrating the semantic Web and enabling Things to collaborate and use public and shared knowledge (ontologies, knowledge base) are still active areas of research, as well as adaptation to unknown cases (overloaded network, breakdowns, transient errors, etc.). We plan, for example, to enable Things to automatically delegate, adapt and split their own tasks according to their environment, their load, their available resources and their capabilities. Finally, small Things must not be ignored in the IoT, of which they are a significant part. Since a lot of Things are mobile, average and smart Things can act opportunistically as gateways and proxies for very resource-limited Things (e.g., RFID chips or small embedded sensors). By presenting small Things as resources of average and smart Things, we want to enable developers to transparently query resource-limited Things in a similar way they query smart Things. In addition, we are working on a prototype of *Dioptase* for the Contiki [61] operating system, in order to integrate more devices to our research.

Endnotes

[a] In web development, a mashup is an application that composes data and services from many sources, using open programming interfaces. Some examples can be seen on http://www.programmableweb.com/mashups (last access: 10-14-2014).

[b] We are finalizing the prototype for release. The current version is made available to reviewers at http://www.rocq.inria.fr/arles/index.php/component/content/article/248 (last access: 10-14-2014). The source code is password-protected: *dioptase_inria_rev*.

Appendix

A Example of streams (access request and streaming) over HTTP, using the HTTP streaming technique

```
GET /streams?id=light-
stream&mode=stream HTTP/1.1\r\n
...\r\n\r\n
HTTP/1.1 200 OK\r\n
Transfer-Encoding: chunked\r\n
Content-Type: application/x-www-form-
urlencoded\r\n
...\r\n\r\n
17\r\n
t=566175600&light=226.3\r\n
18\r\n
t=566177500&light=201.08\r\n
...
```

This is a network dump of the HTTP request (lines 1-2) sent to a producer by a consumer to acquire a stream called "light-stream", and the resulting HTTP response (lines 3-11) where the stream items are written as they are produced.

Specifically, the request contains a parameter *mode=stream*, indicating that the consumer wants to receive the stream items using the HTTP streaming technique. Accordingly, the HTTP response is then configured to use chunks (line 4) and the streams items are written as chunks in the response while they are produced: lines 7-8 and 9-10 are two stream items (*t* is the timestamp and *light* is the attribute name), written as HTTP chunks. The HTTP response is not closed by the server until the stream reaches its end.

B Example of streams (access request and streaming) over HTTP, using the Web hooks technique

```
GET /streams?id=light-
stream&mode=hook&hook=hook1 HTTP/1.1\r\n
...\r\n\r\n
HTTP/1.1 200 OK\r\n
...

GET /hooks/hook-name?
t=566175600&light=226.3 HTTP/1.1\r\n
...\r\n\r\n
HTTP/1.1 200 OK\r\n
...

GET /hooks/hook-name?
t=566177500&light=201.08 HTTP/1.1\r\n
...\r\n\r\n
HTTP/1.1 200 OK\r\n
...
```

This is a network dump of the HTTP request (lines 1-2) sent to a producer by a consumer to acquire a stream called "light-stream", and the resulting HTTP response (lines 3-4). While the stream items are produced, they are pushed by the producer to the consumer as HTTP request-response (lines 6-8 and 11-13).

Specifically, the first request contains a parameter *mode=hook*, indicating that the consumer wants a stream using the Web hooks technique. This request indicates to the producer that the Web hook to use for sending back the stream items is called "hook1". Then, for each stream item produced into the stream, the producer sends an HTTP request to the consumer, using the hook name (*/hooks/hook1* is the callback URI of the consumer): lines 6-8 and 11-13 are two stream items, encoded in the URI query string (*t* is the timestamp and *light* is the attribute name).

C Example of deployment of an interpreted processor through HTTP services.

```
POST /processors/new HTTP/1.1\r\n
Content-Type: multipart/form-data;
boundary=fyrdm2\r\n
...\r\n\r\n

--fyrdm2\r\n
Content-Disposition: form-data;
name="id"\r\n\r\n

processor-name\r\n
--fyrdm2\r\n
Content-Disposition: form-data;
name="code"\r\n\r\n

<some DiSPL code>\r\n
--fyrdm2\r\n
Content-Disposition: form-data;
name="inputs"\r\n\r\n

dioptase://localhost/aLocalStream\r\n
dioptase://173.194.34.24:9000/
anotherStream\r\n

--fyrdm2--\r\n\r\n

HTTP/1.1 200 OK\r\n
...
```

This is a network dump of the HTTP request (lines 1-20) sent to a *Dioptase* instance by a developer to deploy an interpreted processor called "processor-name" with a given piece of *DiSPL* code that consumes two streams, and the resulting HTTP response (lines 22-23).

Specifically, the parameters are encoded in the *multipart/form-data* MIME format (line 2), which is the common format for high-length parameters [62]. The processor name is defined at lines 5-8, the *DiSPL* code at lines 9-13 and the URIs of the input streams that must be consumed by the processor are defined at lines 14-18. Given these URIs, the operation will specifically consume a local stream, produced by an operation already deployed on the Thing, and a remote stream currently produced by another Thing (173.194.34.24).

D Bloom Filter implementation using DiSPL

```
init:
  (define bitsetSize 32)
  (define bitset
  (bitword bitsetSize false))
  (define nbBuckets 8)
  (define nbItems 0)

work:
  ; first, update the Bloom filter
  ; with the next pending item
  (define item
    (getNextItem "itemStream"))
  (if (notnull item)
    ((define hash (murmur3 128 2 item))
    (for 0 to nbBuckets
      ((define index (%
        (abs (+
        (get hash 0)
        (* i (get hash 1)))))
      bitsetSize))
    (set bitset index true))
  )
  (increment nbItems 1)

  ; write the probability of false
  ; positive into the corresponding
  ; output
  (define p (pow
    (- 1 (exp (*
    (- nbBuckets)
    (/ nbItems bitsetSize)))))
    nbBuckets))
  (write "probaStream"
    (item (now) "proba" p)))
  )

  ; second, perform the presence test
  ; if a new item has to be checked
  (define request
    (getNextItem "requestStream"))
```

```
(if (notnull request)
  ((define hash
    (murmur3 128 2 request))
  (define present true)
  (for 0 to nbBuckets
    ((define index (%
      (abs (+
        (get hash 0)
        (* i (get hash 1))))
      bitsetSize))
    (if (not (get bitset index))
      ((set present false)
      (break))
    ))
  )
  (if present
    (write request)
  ))
)
```

Competing interests

VI is member of the JISA editorial board. In addition, we may have conflicts of interests with the following members of the board: Gordon Blair, Fabio Kon, Serge Fdida, Gang Huang, Michel Hurfin, Wouter Joosen, Tiziana T Margaria-Steffen.

Authors' contributions

In the context of his PhD, BB conducted the research, developed the prototype and performed the experiments. VI provided a continuous scientific feedback, was involved in the revision process and participated in the design of the experiments. Both authors read and approved the final manuscript.

Acknowledgements

VI and BB are employed by Inria, the french national institute for research in computer science.

References

1. Gubbi J, Buyya R, Marusic S, Palaniswami M (2013) Internet of things (IoT): A vision, architectural elements, and future directions. Future Generation Comput Syst 29(7):1645–1660
2. Atzori L, Iera A, Morabito G (2010) The internet of things: a survey. Comput Netw 54(15)
3. Teixeira T, Hachem S, Issarny V, Georgantas N (2011) Service oriented middleware for the Internet of Things: A perspective. In: Proc. of the 4th European conference on Towards a service-based internet, ServiceWave '11. Springer, Berlin
4. Mottola L, Picco GP (2011) Programming wireless sensor networks: Fundamental concepts and state of the art. ACM Comput Surv 43(3):19:1–19:51
5. Garofalakis M, Gehrke J, Rastogi R (2007) Data stream management: processing high-speed data streams (data-centric systems and applications). Springer, New York
6. da Silva Neves PAC, Rodrigues JJPC (2010) Internet protocol over wireless sensor networks, from myth to reality. J Commun 5(3):189–196
7. Golab L, Özsu MT (2010) Data stream management. Synthesis Lectures on Data Management, vol. 2. Morgan & Claypool, San Rafael
8. Dezfuli MG, Haghjoo MS (2012) Probabilistic querying over uncertain data streams. Int J Uncertainty Fuzziness Knowledge-Based Syst 20(05)
9. Dezfuli M, Haghjoo M (2012) Xtream: a system for continuous querying over uncertain data streams. In: Scalable Uncertainty Management. Springer, Berlin
10. Guinard D, Trifa V (2009) Towards the web of things: web mashups for embedded devices. In: Proc. of the 18th International World Wide Web Conferences, WWW '09. ACM, New York
11. Trifa V, Guinard D, Davidovski V, Kamilaris A, Delchev I (2010) Web messaging for open and scalable distributed sensing applications. In: Proc. of the 10th international conference on Web engineering. Springer, Berlin
12. Crossbow Imote2.Builder. http://www.xbow.jp/Imote2.Builder_kit.pdf. Accessed 14 Oct 2014
13. Sun SPOT World – Program The World! http://www.sunspotworld.com. Accessed 14 Oct 2014
14. Business Adapts to a New Style of Computer. http://www.technologyreview.com/news/527356/business-adapts-to-a-new-style-of-computer. Accessed 14 Oct 2014
15. Ishaq I, Carels D, Teklemariam GK, Hoebeke J, Abeele FVd, Poorter ED, Moerman I, Demeester P (2013) IETF standardization in the field of the internet of things (IoT): a survey. J Sensor Actuator Netw 2(2)
16. Hui JW, Culler D (2004) The dynamic behavior of a data dissemination protocol for network programming at scale. In: Proc. of the 2nd International Conference on Embedded Networked Sensor Systems, SenSys '04. ACM, New York
17. Leontiadis I, Efstratiou C, Mascolo C, Crowcroft J (2012) SenShare: Transforming sensor networks into multi-application sensing infrastructures. In: Wireless Sensor Networks. Springer, Berlin
18. Corredor Pérez I, Bernardos Barbolla AM (2014) Exploring major architectural aspects of the web of things. In: Mukhopadhyay SC (ed) Internet of Things. Springer, Berlin
19. Carroll A, Heiser G (2010) An analysis of power consumption in a smartphone. In: USENIX annual technical conference, USENIX '10. USENIX Association, Berkeley
20. Rao B, Saluia P, Sharma N, Mittal A, Sharma S (2012) Cloud computing for Internet of Things amp; sensing based applications. In: Proc. of the 6th International Conference on Sensing Technology, ICST '12. IEEE, New York
21. Mohapatra S, Majhi B, Patnaik S (2014) Sensor cloud: the scalable architecture for future generation computing. Springer, India
22. Xu N, Rangwala S, Chintalapudi KK, Ganesan D, Broad A, Govindan R, Estrin D (2004) A wireless sensor network for structural monitoring. In: Proc. of the 2nd International Conference on Embedded Networked Sensor Systems, SenSys '04. ACM, New York
23. Kovatsch M, Lanter M, Duquennoy S (2012) Actinium: a RESTful runtime container for scriptable internet of things applications. In: Proc. of the 3rd International Conference on the Internet of Things, IOT '12. IEEE, New York
24. Pérez JL, Villalba A, Carrera D, Larizgoitia I, Trifa V (2014) The COMPOSE API for the internet of things. In: Proc. of the Companion Publication of the 23rd International Conference on World Wide Web Companion, WWW Companion '14. ACM, New York
25. Demirbas M, Yilmaz Y, Bulut M (2013) Eywa: Crowdsourced and cloudsourced omniscience. In: Proc. of the 11th International Conference on Pervasive Computing and Communications Workshops, PerCom '13. IEEE, New York
26. Kovatsch M, Mayer S, Ostermaier B (2012) Moving application logic from the firmware to the cloud: towards the thin server architecture for the internet of things. In: Proc. of the 6th International Conference on Innovative Mobile and Internet Services in Ubiquitous Computing, IMIS '12. IEEE, Washington
27. Hadim S, Mohamed N (2006) Middleware: middleware challenges and approaches for wireless sensor networks. Distributed Syst Online 7(3)
28. Madden SR, Franklin MJ, Hellerstein JM, Hong W (2005) TinyDB: an acquisitional query processing system for sensor networks. ACM Trans Database Syst 30:122–173
29. Yao Y, Gehrke J (2002) The cougar approach to in-network query processing in sensor networks. ACM SIGMOD Record 31(3): 9–18
30. Amato G, Chessa S, Vairo C (2010) MaD-WiSe: a distributed stream management system for wireless sensor networks. Software: Pract Exp 40(5):431–451
31. Abadi DJ, Ahmad Y, Balazinska M, Cetintemel U, Cherniack M, Hwang JH, Lindner W, Maskey AS, Rasin A, Ryvkina E, Tatbul N, Xing Y, Zdonik S (2005) The design of the Borealis stream processing engine. In: Proc. of the Conference on Innovative Data Systems Research, CIDR '05. pp 277–289

32. Arasu A, Babcock B, Babu S, Cieslewicz J, Datar M, Ito K, Motwani R, Srivastava U, Widom J (2004) STREAM: The Stanford data stream management system. Tech. rep., Stanford InfoLab, Stanford

33. Amato G, Chessa S, Gennaro C, Vairo C (2014) Querying moving events in wireless sensor networks. Pervasive and Mobile Computing (in press)

34. Le-Phuoc D, Xavier Parreira J, Hauswirth M (2012) Linked stream data processing. In: Reasoning Web. Semantic Technologies for Advanced Query Answering. Springer, Berlin

35. Newton R, Morrisett G, Welsh M (2007) The regiment macroprogramming system. In: Proc. of the 6th international conference on Information processing in sensor networks. IPSN '07. ACM, New York

36. Whitehouse K, Zhao F, Liu J (2006) Semantic streams: a framework for composable semantic interpretation of sensor data. In: Proc. of the 3rd European conference on Wireless Sensor Networks. Springer, Berlin

37. Szczodrak M, Gnawali O, Carloni L (2013) Dynamic reconfiguration of wireless sensor networks to support heterogeneous applications. In: Proc. of the 9th International Conference on Distributed Computing in Sensor Systems, DCOSS '13. IEEE, Washington

38. Dickerson R, Lu J, Lu J, Whitehouse K (2008) Stream feeds: an abstraction for the world wide sensor web. In: The Internet of Things. Springer, Berlin

39. Grosky W, Kansal A, Nath S, Liu J, Zhao F (2007) SenseWeb: An infrastructure for shared sensing. IEEE Multimedia 14(4):8–13

40. Le-Phuoc D, Nguyen-Mau HQ, Parreira JX, Hauswirth M (2012) A middleware framework for scalable management of linked streams. Web Semantics: Sci Serv Agents World Wide Web 16:42–51

41. Ostermaier B, Schlup F, Römer K (2010) WebPlug: A framework for the web of things. In: Proc. of the 8th International Conference on Pervasive Computing and Communications Workshops, PERCOM '10. IEEE, New York

42. Lam G, Rossiter D (2012) A web service framework supporting multimedia streaming. IEEE Trans Serv Comput PrePrints 99:400–413

43. Hachem S, Pathak A, Issarny V (2013) Probabilistic registration for large-scale mobile participatory sensing. In: Proc. of the 13th International Conference on Pervasive Computing and Communications, PERCOM '13. IEEE, New York

44. Sahu PK, Chattopadhyay S (2013) A survey on application mapping strategies for Network-on-Chip design. J Syst Arch 59:60–76

45. Billet B, Issarny V (2014) From task graphs to concrete actions: a new task mapping algorithm for the future internet of things. In: Proc. of the the 11th IEEE International Conference on Mobile Ad hoc and Sensor Systems, MASS '14. IEEE, New York

46. Golab L, Özsu MT (2003) Issues in data stream management. ACM SIGMOD Record 32(2):5–14

47. Hachem S, Teixeira T, Issarny V (2011) Ontologies for the internet of things. In: Proc. of the 8th Middleware Doctoral Symposium, Middleware '11. ACM, New York

48. Loreto S, Saint-Andre P, Salsano S, Wilkins G (2011) RFC 6202 - Known issues and best practices for the use of long polling and streaming in bidirectional. http://tools.ietf.org/html/rfc6202. Accessed 06 Jun 2014

49. Fette I, Melnikov A (2011) RFC 6455 - The websocket protocol. http://tools.ietf.org/html/rfc6455. Accessed 06 Jun 2014

50. Law YN, Wang H, Zaniolo C (2004) Query languages and data models for database sequences and data streams. In: Proc. of the 13th international conference on Very Large Data Bases, VLDB '04. VLDB Endow, USA

51. Raza U, Camerra A, Murphy A, Palpanas T, Picco G (2012) What does model-driven data acquisition really achieve in wireless sensor networks? In: Proc. of the International Conference on Pervasive Computing and Communications, PerCom '12. IEEE, New York

52. Duquennoy S, Grimaud G, Vandewalle JJ (2009) The web of things: interconnecting devices with high usability and performance. In: Proc. of the International Conference on Embedded Software and Systems, ICESS '09. IEEE, New York

53. Mitzel D (2000) RFC 3002: Overview of 2000 IAB wireless internetworking workshop. http://tools.ietf.org/html/rfc3002. Accessed 06 Jun 2014

54. (2012) IBM streams processing language specification. http://pic.dhe.ibm.com/infocenter/streams/v2r0/topic/com.ibm.swg.im.infosphere.streams.product.doc/doc/IBMInfoSphereStreams-SPLLanguageSpecification.pdf . Accessed 06 Jun 2014

55. Sperber M, Dybvig RK, Flatt M, Van Straaten A, Findler R, Matthews J (2009) Revised report on the algorithmic language scheme. J Funct Program:19

56. Kirsch A, Mitzenmacher M (2008) Less hashing, same performance: building a better bloom filter. Random Struct Algorithms 33(2):187–218

57. Maye O, Maaser M (2013) Comparing java virtual machines for sensor nodes. In: Grid and Pervasive Computing. Springer, Berlin

58. SmartPark – Parking Made Easy. http://smartpark.epfl.ch. Accessed 14 Oct 2014

59. Wilschut A, Apers PMG (1990) Pipelining in query execution. In: Proc. of the International Conference on Databases, Parallel Architectures and Their Applications, PARBASE '90. IEEE, New York

60. Barbieri DF, Braga D, Ceri S, Valle ED, Grossniklaus M (2010) C-SPARQL: A continous query language for RDF data streams. Int J Semantic Comput:4

61. Contiki: The Open Source OS for the Internet of Things. http://www.contiki-os.org. Accessed 14 Oct 2014

62. Masinter L (1998) RFC 2388: Returning Values from Forms: multipart/form-data. http://tools.ietf.org/html/rfc2388. Accessed 06 Jun 2014

Mapping virtual networks onto substrate networks

Gustavo P Alkmim[1*], Daniel M Batista[2] and Nelson LS da Fonseca[1]

Abstract

Network virtualization is a promising technique for building the Internet of the future since it enables the low cost introduction of new features into network elements. An open issue in such virtualization is how to effect an efficient mapping of virtual network elements onto those of the existing physical network, also called the substrate network. Mapping is an NP-hard problem and existing solutions ignore various real network characteristics in order to solve the problem in a reasonable time frame. This paper introduces new algorithms to solve this problem based on 0–1 integer linear programming, algorithms based on a whole new set of network parameters not taken into account by previous proposals. Approximative algorithms proposed here allow the mapping of virtual networks on large network substrates. Simulation experiments give evidence of the efficiency of the proposed algorithms.

Keywords: Virtual networks, Mapping, Future internet

1 Introduction

The minimalism approach of the architecture of the Internet specific network has enabled its global spread. One consequence of this simplicity, known as the ossification of the Internet, has been the impossibility to provide missing features in the original design. These limitations has prevented the development of many possible applications and services, although various attempts have been made to provide some of the features missing in its design [1].

These attempts to overcome the original limitations include various new mechanisms proposed to promote the evolution of the Internet [2,3]. Those based on network virtualization allow the definition of virtual networks composed of virtual routers and links; these are then hosted by routers and links of the real network called "substrate network". Network virtualization permits the coexistence of various protocol stacks and architectures on a single substrate, without the need to modify the actual physical network. Moreover, this approach imposes no restrictions on the protocols and architectures involved.

One of the main issues in network virtualization is the efficient mapping of virtual networks onto the substrate network [4,5]. This mapping determines the allocation of routers and links of the virtual network onto the routers and links of the substrate network. However, the search for the optimal mapping of virtual networks is an NP-hard problem [6].

Various solutions have been proposed for this problem [1,4,5,7]. However, most of them assume certain restrictions to make the problem tractable, such as the consideration that requests for virtual network establishment be previously known [1,7] or that the substrate capacity be infinite [1,8] and on network topology restricted [7].

This paper proposes a novel solution to the mapping problem to helps to overcome such limitations which imposes fewer restrictions than previous proposals. Our proposal does not consider previous knowledge of virtual network requests; but rather considers that the substrate has a finite capacity, although no specific network topology is assumed. It considers more realistic scenarios and, hence, can handle a large number of parameters that impact on the complexity of a solution.

The proposed algorithms require the presence of repositories of software images containing the software and protocols required by virtual networks. These images are used to instantiate the virtual routers on real routers, as illustrated in Figure 1. Since all images must be transferred from the repository to the real router prior to the

*Correspondence: alkmim@lrc.ic.unicamp.br
[1] State University of Campinas, Campinas, Brazil
Full list of author information is available at the end of the article

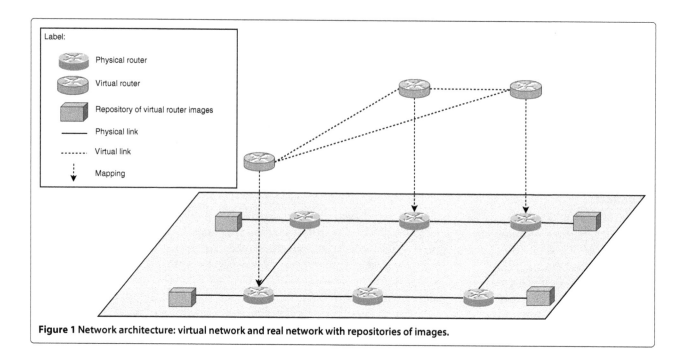

Figure 1 Network architecture: virtual network and real network with repositories of images.

operation of the virtual network, an adequate mapping algorithm must select the image and the path the image transfer should take.

The algorithms proposed here are based on integer linear programming (ILP) formulations designed to minimize the total amount of bandwidth allocated to each virtual network. One of the algorithms is slow but provides optimal solutions, while the others are designed to decrease the run time. Relaxation Techniques for ILP formulations are employed by these approximative algorithms.

The proposed algorithms are efficient since they can provide solutions in a reasonable time frame. The results show that their execution time is acceptable for various scenarios with different virtual networks requirements. The approximative algorithms also produce a reasonable probability of blocking requests in the establishment of virtual network. The algorithms introduced here differ from those in our preliminary investigation [9] in that a two step formulation has been adopted which reduces memory demands thus allowing solutions involving large network substrates with as much as 400 routers.

The paper is organized as follows: Section "Motivation" illustrates the need for a more detailed modelling of the problem. Section "Related work" summarizes related work. Section "Proposed algorithms" introduces the six proposed algorithms. Section "Performance evaluation" presents the performance evaluation of the algorithms and Section "Conclusions and future work" presents the conclusions and suggestions for future work.

2 Motivation

The formulation proposed here models various characteristics of existing operational networks. One of the most important is link delays, which impact on the time needed to instantiate a virtual network, that is, a requirement of service providers. Another important issue is the characteristics of the physical routers.

In general, the algorithms presented in the literature [4] attempt to minimize the amount of resources allocated to requests from virtual networks, but fail to consider the need for transferring image files prior to the instantiation of virtual routers. The following example illustrates the importance of considering link delays and the time for transferring images from the image repository to the physical routers. Figure 2 shows a substrate network with routers, identified as **R1** to **R6**; each router has a different number of processing elements (cores). The available bandwidths of links **E1** to **E5** are labelled in the figure. A repository of images is connected to the router **R4** by the link **E6**. This repository stores the image file **I1** which size is 12.5MB. Each virtual router in the virtual network shown in Figure 3 has two cores and uses the same image **I1**. Moreover, the virtual network must be instantiated in at most 100 seconds.

The router **R1** has no resources available for the allocation of a virtual router since it has a single core and a virtual router requires two cores. Thus, if the transfer of images is ignored, the virtual network using routers (**R2,R5**) and link **E4** or routers (**R2,R6**) and link **E5** would be instantiated. As a result of such mapping the required image would be transferred to the physical routers via the

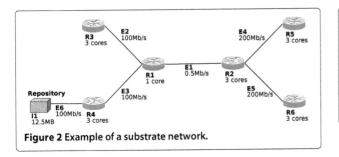

Figure 2 Example of a substrate network.

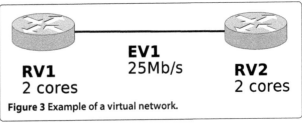

Figure 3 Example of a virtual network.

link **E1**, which has an available bandwidth of only 0.5Mb/s. Thus requiring 404.5 seconds for the transfer, four times as long as the time limit to instantiate the virtual network. Even the use of multicast routing would only reduce this to 202.5 seconds, i.e. twice the limit.

However, the use of the algorithms proposed in this paper would lead to the use of routers (**R3**, **R4**) and links (**E2**, **E3**), since the approach introduced here considers the transfer delay of images and the image transfer would take only four seconds, i.e. much less than the time permitted.

3 Related work

This section summarizes major existing proposals for network virtualization.

The "Cabo" solution [3] is composed of two layers managed by separate providers with infrastructure providers responsible for controlling the elements in the physical layer, and service providers for the provision of network services in the application layer. The approach presented here, however, considers the existence of an additional layer managed by the connectivity providers.

This three-layer architecture is based on the Cabernet architecture [10], which was designed to eliminate some of the limitations in the deployment of virtual services in Wide Area Networks (WAN). This elimination results from by making the infrastructure transparent to the services provider.

The initial design of the Underlay Fused with Overlays (UFO) architecture is first presented in [11]. This solution is also limited to two layers, with the underlay notifying the overlay about changes in network resources. The overlay receives notifications and, in order to increase efficiency and scalability of the virtual networks, can propose routing changes in the underlay. The mapping algorithms in the presented paper can be used in conjunction with the UFO architecture.

In [12], the algorithm Assign was introduced for solving the network testbed mapping problem. This algorithm assumes that a substrate node can only be used by a single request which can lead to under-utilization of the cores of the substrate nodes. Such assumption is not used by the formulations introduced in the present paper, allowing an optimized use of resources. Moreover, the present paper

considers the transfer of software images which is neither considered in [12] nor by the Application Component Placement problem [13].

In most of the existing proposals [4-7], the resources considered are limited to bandwidth and routers processing capacity. Some papers [14] do suggest the inclusion of other characteristics as a topic for future work; nonetheless, no solution has yet been published. Our proposal has been able to make several realistic assumptions about resource availability, memory available, the number of processing elements of routers, and the time required to instantiate a virtual router. Our work differ by that in [15] by the modelling of repositories of images in the substrate.

A multi-commodity flow approach was adopted in [16] to maximize the number of virtual networks that could be accommodated on a single substrate network. The substrate has access nodes, which serve as sources and destinations for all traffic, and the core nodes are responsible for the routing of packets. A request for virtual network establishment consists of a list of access nodes of the substrate, as well as of a traffic matrix that represents the amount of traffic transferred between the access nodes listed. Although network capacity is considered, the processing capacity of the nodes is ignored. Furthermore, this approach assumes that the demands of a request are small compared to the available capacity of the network. Unlike [16], algorithms proposed here take into consideration various other characteristics, and no restrictions are imposed on the demands of virtual networks. Another difference is that the algorithm in [16] considers only the edge nodes of the virtual network. The algorithm in [7] is similar to that in [16], except that it is uses a mixed integer quadratic problems branch and bound approach [17] to map the requests.

The network in [5] supports path splitting and path migration, thus allowing the solution to be found in polynomial time. In path splitting, a single virtual link can be mapped onto more than one physical path in the substrate whereas Path migration allows a virtual link to be remapped offline to adapt a solution in the face of changes in resource availability. Although the algorithm in [5] runs in a very short time, it does not consider many of the realistic parameters involved e.g, software images, link delay and the size of images.

In several studies [5,6], the mapping of virtual links is separated from the mapping of virtual routers. Two algorithms were proposed in [4] to integrate the steps, called Deterministic Embedding VN (D-Vine) and Randomized Embedding VN (R-Vine). In the algorithms presented in this paper, however, routers and links can be mapped simultaneously.

In [6], a distributed algorithm to map virtual networks was introduced to balance the load among all routers in the substrate. The experiments presented in [6] show that such as distributed algorithm can generate a large number of control messages which can cause long delays and high overhead for network operation. The algorithms presented here do not overload the network with such messages.

There are various aspects that make the solution of the problem of mapping virtual networks very challenging [5]. The first is the large number of router characteristics. The second is that given resources limitations, there is a need for admission control. The third is the fact that requests for virtual network establishment cannot be foreseen and usually have a time limit for instantiation. The final reason is the diversity of topologies in the Internet. The algorithms presented in this paper address all of these issues except the proposed admission control.

Table 1 compares the characteristics of the algorithms proposed in this paper with those of the existing algorithms summarized in this section. The columns of the table list some of the characteristics that should be considered by an ideal mapping algorithm, while the rows represent the characteristics of the algorithms presented in the literature.

Table 1 shows that the number of router processing cores and the bandwidth of the links is being considered by the most of the algorithms. However, our work is unique since it considers: sets of images with different sizes, the time required to instantiate virtual routers, the locations of the repository in which images are stored and the available memory of the physical routers. Restrictions on the usage of physical routers by virtual routers (locality restriction) is rarely accounted for, although it is quite important. Other characteristics such as link delay and the time threshold for instantiations of virtual networks are neglected by all previous papers. Therefore, our algorithms significantly improve the state of the art for mapping virtual networks onto substrate networks, since they provide a more realistic assessment of operational networks.

Our work does not impose any alignment constraints between virtual topologies and physical topologies. It is possible that the topology of physical routers and links allocated to a virtual network will be the same of that of the requested virtual network, but this happens only if the topology is the one which minimizes the bandwidth allocated. Moreover, such an alignment is not necessary to guarantee the QoS requirements of the application,

Table 1 Comparison of the algorithms

Reference	Number of processing cores	Bandwidth	Locality restrictions	Images for the virtual routers
[16]	no	yes	no	no
[5]	yes	yes	no	no
[4]	yes	yes	yes	no
[6]	yes	yes	no	no
[7]	no	yes	no	no
[15]	yes	yes	no	no
Our proposal	yes	yes	yes	yes

Reference	Link delay	Available memory / size of images	Locality of repository of images	Instantiation time
[16]	no	no	no	no
[5]	no	no	no	no
[4]	yes	no	no	no
[6]	no	no	no	no
[7]	no	no	no	no
[15]	no	no	no	no
Our proposal	yes	yes	yes	yes

which are indeed assured by the constraints of the mapping problem.

4 Proposed algorithms

The algorithms in this paper model requests dynamically arriving for virtual network establishment on network substrates. Each request specifies the topology of the virtual network, the resources demanded by the virtual network elements, and the QoS requirements, which include a time limit to instantiate it.

The proposed algorithms are based on 0-1 ILP formulations. One algorithm, called the Optimal algorithm, uses the exact solution of the formulations to define the mappings. The other algorithms, called approximated algorithms, employ relaxation techniques to reduce the time needed to find a solution for the formulations. Before presenting the algorithms, we will present the ILP formulations. This formulation differs from that in our previous work [9] since a two step approach has been introduced which reduce memory demands.

The following notation is used for the formulations of the problem:

- $N \subset \mathbb{Z}$ is the set of physical routers;
- $F \subset \mathbb{Z}$ is the set of physical links, with the physical link (n_1, n_2) connecting two physical routers n_1 and $n_2 \in N$;
- $M \subset \mathbb{Z}$ is the set of virtual routers;
- $V \subset \mathbb{Z}$ is the set of virtual links with the virtual link (m_1, m_2) connecting two virtual routers m_1 and $m_2 \in M$;
- $I \subset \mathbb{Z}$ is the set of images stored in the repository. Each image corresponds to a file with an operating system and a specific set of software ready to be instantiated in a physical router;
- $A \subset \mathbb{N}$ is the set of the number of available cores in the physical routers; $A(n), n \in N$, gives the number of cores of router n;
- $P \subset \mathbb{N}$ is the set of the number of cores requested by the virtual routers; $P(m), m \in M$, gives the number of cores required by the virtual router m to be instantiated;
- $C \subset \mathbb{R}$ is the set of values of the available bandwidth in the physical links; $C(f), f \in F$, gives the available bandwidth in the link f;
- $Q \subset \mathbb{R}$ is the set of bandwidth values requested by the virtual links; $Q(v), v \in V$, gives the bandwidth required by the virtual link v;
- $D \subset \mathbb{R}$ is the set of values of delays in the physical links; $D(f), f \in F$, gives the delay in link f;
- $K \subset \mathbb{R}$ is the set of values of maximum delay allowed on a virtual link; $K(v), v \in V$, represents the maximum delay allowed on the virtual link v;

- $L_{n,m} \in \{0, 1\}$ are the binary values that establish restrictions on locations. If the virtual router m can be mapped onto the physical router n, the value of the variable is 1. Otherwise, it is 0. This variable is useful for imposing policy restrictions related to the geographical location of routers.
- $R_{n,i} \in \{0, 1\}$ are the binary values that provide details about the location where images are stored. If the image i is located in a repository with a direct link dedicated to the physical router n, the value of the variable is 1. Otherwise, it is 0;
- $E_{m,i} \in \{0, 1\}$ are the binary values related to software restrictions. If the image i contains all the software requirements required by the virtual router m (operating system, protocol stacks, kernel modules and others), the value of the variable is 1. Otherwise, it is 0;
- $B \subset \mathbb{R}$ is the set of values that represents the memory available in the physical routers; $B(n), n \in N$, represents the memory available in the router n;
- $G \subset \mathbb{R}$ is the set of image sizes; $G(i), i \in I$, represents the size of the image i;
- $S \in \mathbb{R}$ is the time limit for instantiation of the VN;
- $T_{n,i} \in \mathbb{R}$ represents the time the physical router n takes to boot the image i;

The substrate network is represented by a graph (N, F) in which the physical routers are modelled as the vertices of the graph and the physical links as the edges. Similarly, the virtual network is represented by the graph (M, V).

Requests must specify the maximum delay allowed in the virtual network links (D and K), since this information affects the performance of network applications. The specific image to each virtual router must be defined because various configurations can exist (I and $E_{m,i}$). The content of each repository must be known ($R_{n,i}$) because this affects the path chosen to transfer the images. The size of the images should be considered because the routers have limited storage capacity (B and G). Moreover, it is important to consider that clients can have specific policies that prevent the utilization of certain physical routers ($L_{n,m}$). Furthermore, the maximum time acceptable for the instantiation of the VN must be considered (S, D, K and $T_{n,i}$). To our knowledge, parameters related to transfer and the instantiation of software images (I, $E_{m,i}$, $R_{n,i}$, B, G and $T_{n,i}$) have never been taken into consideration in previous mapping algorithms proposed in the literature.

The solution to the problem is given by the binary variables:

- $X_{n,m,i}$: if the virtual router m is mapped onto the physical router n using the image i then this value is 1; otherwise, its value is 0;

- $Y_{n,u,w}$: if the physical path used by the virtual link w includes the physical link (n, u), this value is 1; otherwise, it is 0;
- $Z_{n,u,m}$: if the physical link (n, u) is used to transfer the image requested by the virtual router m, this value is 1; otherwise, it is 0.

4.1   ILP formulations

All the algorithms proposed in this paper are based on two ILP formulations that must be sequentially executed. The first (ILP-Mapping) searches for the solution of the problem of mapping routers and links of VNs onto routers and links of the substrate. The second (ILP-Image) searches for routes in the substrate for transferring images from the repositories to the nodes in the substrate which will host the virtual nodes. The employment of two ILPs reduces the time needed to find solutions when compared to the execution time needed for our previous formulation, which try to find routes and allocate physical routers and links in a single ILP [9]. The reduction in execution time is mainly due to the reduction of the search space.

The ILP-Mapping algorithm is formulated as follows:
Minimize $\sum_{n \in N} \sum_{u \in N} \sum_{w \in V} Y_{n,u,w} \times Q(w)$ subject to the following 11 constraints:

$$\sum_{n \in N} \sum_{i \in I} X_{n,m,i} = 1 \tag{C1}$$
$$\forall m \in M$$

$$\sum_{m \in M} \sum_{i \in I} X_{n,m,i} \leq 1 \tag{C2}$$
$$\forall n \in N$$

$$\sum_{m \in M} \sum_{i \in I} P(m) \times X_{n,m,i} \leq A(n) \tag{C3}$$
$$\forall n \in N$$

$$X_{n,m,i} = 0 \tag{C4}$$
$$\forall n \in N, \forall m \in M, \forall i \in I | L_{n,m} = 0 \text{ or} E_{m,i} = 0$$

$$\sum_{w \in V} Y_{n,u,w} \times Q(w) \leq C(w') \tag{C5}$$
$$\forall w' = (n, u) \in F$$

$$\sum_{n \in N} \sum_{u \in N} Y_{n,u,w} \times D(n, u) \leq K(w) \tag{C6}$$
$$\forall w \in V, (n, u) \in F$$

$$\sum_{m \in M} \sum_{i \in I} X_{n,m,i} \times G(i) \leq B(n) \tag{C7}$$
$$\forall n \in N$$

$$Y_{n,u,w} = 0 \tag{C8}$$
$$\forall n, u \in N, \forall w \in V | (n, u) \notin F$$

$$\sum_{u \in N} Y_{n,u,w} - \sum_{u \in N} Y_{u,n,w} = \tag{C9}$$
$$\sum_{i \in I} X_{n,m,i} - \sum_{i \in I} X_{n,a,i}$$
$$\forall w = (m, a) \in V, \forall n \in N$$

$$X_{n,m,i} \in \{0, 1\} \tag{C10}$$
$$\forall n \in N, \forall m \in M, \forall i \in I$$

$$Y_{n,u,w} \in \{0, 1\} \tag{C11}$$
$$\forall n, u \in N, \forall w \in V$$

The objective function of the ILP-Mapping algorithm minimizes the bandwidth allocated to requests for the establishment of a virtual network. By doing so, the formulation maximizes the bandwidth available for future requests.

The constraint (C1) establishes that each virtual router is allocated to a single physical router and that a single image is used to instantiate it. Constraint (C2) limits the number of virtual routers that can be allocated on a physical router per request, with only a single virtual router can be allocated to a given physical router per request. The constraint (C9) ensures that the set of physical links on which a virtual link is mapped constitutes a valid path. This constraint compares the in-degree and the out-degree of each physical router n. The constraints (C3) and (C7) express the limitations of the physical routers related to the number of cores and the amount of memory, respectively.

The constraint (C4) guarantees that the virtual routers will be instantiated using images that satisfy all software requirements as well as any geographic location defined by the client requesting the VN.

The constraints (C5) and (C6) express the limitations of the physical links. The constraint (C6) establishes that the total delay in the physical path allocated to a virtual link does not exceed the delay threshold requested for that virtual link. Constraint (C8) guarantees that only existing physical links can be used in the mapping of virtual links.

Constraints (C10) and (C11) define the domains of the variables as {0,1}, i.e., the variables are binary. If the value of these variables is 1, a router (or link) is allocated to a virtual router (or link). Otherwise, it is zero.

After the solution of the ILP-Mapping is found, the values of $X_{n,m,i}$ are used as input for the second formulation, entitled the ILP-Image formulation.

The ILP-Image is formulated as follows:

Minimize $\displaystyle\sum_{m \in M} \sum_{n \in N} \sum_{u \in N | (n,u) \in F} Z_{n,u,m} \times D(n,u) + $

$\dfrac{Z_{n,u,m} \times G(i | X_{v,m,i}=1)}{C(n,u)}$ subject to the following 3 constraints:

$$\sum_{m \in M} Z_{n,u,m} = 0 \qquad\qquad (C12)$$

$$\forall n, u \in N | (u,u) \notin F$$

$$\sum_{v \in N} Z_{u,v,m} - \sum_{v \in N} Z_{v,u,m} = \qquad (C13)$$

$$X_{n,m,i} \times R_{u,i} - X_{n,m,i} \times (1 - \lceil \frac{|u-n|}{\alpha} \rceil)$$

$$\forall m \in M, \forall i \in I, \forall n, u \in N, \alpha = |N|$$

$$Z_{n,u,m} \in \{0,1\} \qquad\qquad (C14)$$

$$\forall n, u \in N, \forall m \in M$$

The objective function of the ILP-Image minimizes the time required to instantiate a VN. The time needed to instantiate each virtual router is the sum of the times required to transfer the image and to boot the operating system of the image. We assume here that two or more images can be transferred simultaneously on the same physical link.

Constraint $(C12)$ guarantees that (u,v) will be used in the mapping only if it is a physical link in the substrate. The constraint $(C13)$ establishes that the set of physical links allocated for the transfer of an image consists of a valid path in the substrate network. Constraint $(C14)$ defines the domain of the variables.

The following subsections present the proposed algorithms. Subsection "Optimal algorithm" presents the algorithm that execute the implementation of the ILPs exactly as shown in this subsection. This algorithm is called the Optimal algorithm. Subsection "Root approximative algorithm" presents the Root Approximative algorithm which limits the search for a solution at an earlier stage than does the Optimal algorithm. Subsection "Algorithms based on relaxed versions of ILPs" presents four approximative algorithms based on relaxation technique. Relaxed versions of ILPs tend to find solutions faster than the original formulation of the problem. The approximative algorithms are called the Random Approximative algorithm, the Deterministic Approximative algorithm, Iterative Random Approximative algorithm and Iterative Deterministic Approximative algorithm. They differ from the algorithm employed to round off the real variable values to binary ones.

4.2 Optimal algorithm

The Optimal algorithm implements the two ILP formulations exactly as shown in Subsection "ILP formulations". To find the solution to the problem, it uses the Branch and Cut technique [18] which builds a tree with the root corresponding to the solution of a relaxed formulation of the original ILP and each node to a solution of the relaxed ILP formulation.

The search for the solution starts at the root of the tree and as long as an integer variable is associated with a fractional value in relaxed version, new constraints (cuts) to the formulation are added reducing the search space (adjusted polyhedron). The addition of new constraints branches on a fractional variable creating two new nodes (sub-problems) in the search tree.

The Optimal algorithm traverses all the nodes of the search tree. It is possible either to establish deadlines for execution time of the traversal or to establish stopping criteria based on the position of the node in the tree.

In our formulation, the ILP-Mapping formulation traverses all the nodes of the tree and returns a solution that minimizes the allocated bandwidth. The ILP-Image formulation solution also traverses all nodes and minimizes the VN instantiation time. The Optimal algorithm for solving the ILP formulations is presented in Algorithm 1.

Algorithm 1. Optimal algorithm
    Data: Substrate network γ with characteristics α, virtual network δ with characteristics β.
    Result: Mapping of δ on γ and on the physical paths θ used to transfer the images.
1:   Define γ, α, δ and β as input of the ILP-Mapping;
2:   Traverse the entire search tree of the ILP-Mapping and obtain the values of $X_{n,m,i}$ and $Y_{n,u,w}$ variables related to the best solution found;
3:   **if** ILP-Image does not find any solution **then**
4:     Block the request;
5:   **end if**
6:   **else**
7:     Define $\gamma, \alpha, \delta, \beta$ and $X_{n,m,i}$ variables as input to the ILP-Image;
8:     Traverse the entire search tree of the ILP-Mapping and obtain the values of $X_{n,m,i}$ and $Y_{n,u,w}$ variables related to the best solution found;
9:     **if** ILP-Image does not find any solution **then**
10:      Block the request;
11:     **end if**
12:     **else**
13:      Return the mapping of δ on γ using the values of the variables $X_{n,m,i}$ and $Y_{n,u,w}$;
14:      Return the paths θ using the values of the variables $Z_{n,u,m}$.
15:     **end if**
16: **end if**

The Optimal algorithm solves ILP formulations (lines 2 and 8) by passing the characteristics of both the virtual network and the substrate network (lines 1 and 7), and returns the mapping of virtual routers and links (lines 13 and 14) onto the substrate network. If no feasible solution is found, the request for VN establishment is rejected (lines 3, 4, 9 and 10).

Table 2 Characteristics of the algorithms based on the use of relaxed versions of the ILPs

Algorithm	# of times ILP-Mapping is executed	# of times ILP-Image is executed	Definition of variables
RAA	2	1	Draw considering probabilities
DAA	2	1	Higher value
IRAA	$|M| + |V|$	$|M|$	Draw considering probabilities
IDAA	$|M| + |V|$	$|M|$	Higher value

In the remainder of this paper, the Optimal algorithm will be referred as Opt.

4.3 Root approximative algorithm

Preliminary experiments with the Opt algorithm showed that it takes too long to find solutions involving substrates with more than 100 routers. This motivated us to implement an approximative algorithm, called the Root Approximative algorithm. This algorithm stops the traversal at the root of the tree. By doing that, a reduction on execution time is expected in comparison with the time required by the Opt algorithm. Such a criterion was derived from the observation that several solutions for the optimal problem are obtained at the root of the tree.

The Root Approximative algorithm differs from the Opt algorithm in solution to lines 2 and 8, which are respectively replaced by:

- **Line 2**: Stop the search for solutions to the ILP-Mapping at the root of the search tree and obtain the values of variables $X_{n,m,i}$ and $Y_{n,u,w}$;
- **Line 8**: Stop the search for solutions to the ILP-Image at the root of the search tree and obtain the values of variables $Z_{n,u,m}$.

In the remainder of this paper, the Root Approximative algorithm will be referred as Root.

4.4 Algorithms based on relaxed versions of ILPs

In addition to the Root algorithm, four other approximative algorithms are proposed. These algorithms relax integer constraints of the two ILP formulations in an attempt to reduce execution time. This relaxation replaces the constraints $(C11)$, $(C12)$ and $(C14)$, by the constraints $(C11')$, $(C12')$ and $(C14')$, given below:

$$X_{n,m,i} \in \mathbb{R}_{[0,1]} \tag{C11'}$$
$$\forall n \in N, \forall m \in M, \forall i \in I$$

$$Y_{n,u,w} \in \mathbb{R}_{[0,1]} \tag{C12'}$$
$$\forall n, u \in N, \forall w \in V$$

$$Z_{n,u,m} \in \mathbb{R}_{[0,1]} \tag{C14'}$$
$$\forall n, u \in N, \forall m \in M$$

These new constraints modify the domain of decision variables from $\{0, 1\}$ to $\mathbb{R}_{[0,1]}$, so after finding the solution to the relaxed version of the ILP, it is necessary to round off fractional values to binary ones. The four algorithms differ in relation to the method implemented for this rounding off.

Each of the four algorithms consists of three steps: node mapping, link mapping and definition of paths for transfer of the required images. For each step two procedures defines: how to round the real values off to binary ones and when such rounding off should take place. In node mapping, the first procedure defines which variable will be rounded off to 1 since only one $X_{n,m,i}$ can be set to 1 for each virtual node m. The second procedure determines whether or not all the other variables values should be rounded off to 1. There are two options for each of these

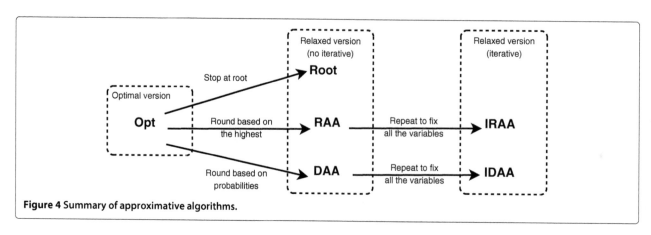

Figure 4 Summary of approximative algorithms.

Table 3 Types of virtual networks

Type	# of virtual routers	# of cores	Bandwidth (uniformly distributed)
1	5	2	100Mbps–200Mbps
2	8	3	200Mbps–300Mbps
3	10	6	300Mbps–400Mbps

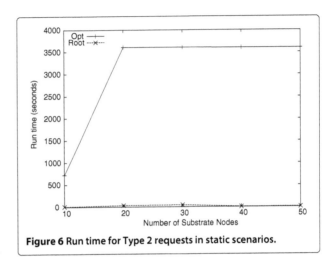

Figure 6 Run time for Type 2 requests in static scenarios.

two procedures with their combinations defining the four different algorithms proposed.

4.4.1 How to round off variables

The rounding off of real numbers can be either deterministic or random. In deterministic, the highest real value for a virtual node is rounded off to 1. In random algorithms, a random number is drawn and if this is lower than the value of the real variable, then the real value is rounded off to 1.

Such procedure is also employed for the Y and Z variables.

4.4.2 When to round off variables

After the execution of the relaxed ILP, another decision must be made. It is possible either to round all the X variables associated with all the virtual nodes at once or to round off only the X variables related to a specific virtual node, and then run the relaxed ILP as for each X variables. The same procedure applies to the Y and Z variables.

The option that round off all the variables at once implies two executions of the relaxed version of the ILP-Mapping. For the first, the value of the X variables are set and later used as input for setting the values of the Y variables. After the values of X and Y variables are set, the relaxed version of the ILP-Image is executed once to find the values of the Z variables. This is the procedure adopted by the non-iterative algorithms, i. e., the

Deterministic Approximative Algorithm (DDA) and the Random Approximative Algorithm (RAA).

The other way is to set the value of a single variable after each execution of the relaxed ILP. In this case, the ILP-Mapping must be executed $|M|$ times to round off all X variables and another $|V|$ times to round off all the Y variables. The relaxed version of the ILP-Image must then be executed $|M|$ times to round all Z variables. This option is employed in the **Iterative** Deterministic Approximative Algorithm (IDAA) and in the **Iterative** Random Approximative Algorithm (IRAA). Table 2 summarizes the main characteristics of the four approximative algorithms proposed and Figure 4 illustrates the differences between all the algorithms presented in this section.

5 Performance evaluation

This section assesses the efficiency of the proposed mapping algorithms. Numerical examples presented in this section compare the performance of the algorithms in both static and dynamic scenarios. The static scenario

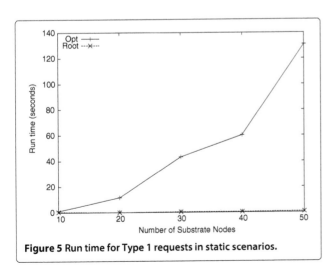

Figure 5 Run time for Type 1 requests in static scenarios.

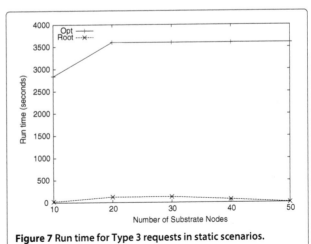

Figure 7 Run time for Type 3 requests in static scenarios.

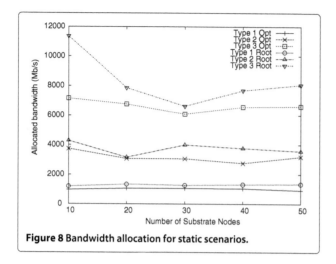

Figure 8 Bandwidth allocation for static scenarios.

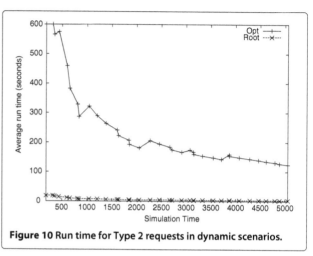

Figure 10 Run time for Type 2 requests in dynamic scenarios.

involves only the mapping of a single request. The dynamic scenarios involves requests arrive during a certain time interval, with the availability of resources in the substrate network varying over time. The algorithms were evaluated in terms of run time, the amount of bandwidth allocated to the virtual networks requests, and the blocking probability. A description of the experimental setup is followed by a comparison of the Opt and Root algorithms and another of the performance of the approximative algorithms. Comparisons with existing algorithms [4,19] were not performed, since these do not consider all of the parameters considered by the algorithms presented here.

5.1   Experimental setup

All the algorithms and the simulator were implemented in C++ with the linear program formulations implemented using the CPLEX optimization library version 12.0. All programs were executed on a computer running the operating system Debian GNU/Linux Squeeze. The computer

was equipped with two Intel Xeon 2.27GHz processors each one with 6 cores capable of running 12 simultaneous threads and 40GB of RAM.

The configuration for the scenarios considered:

- Number of routers in the substrate network: 10 to 50. Using this variation, it is possible to evaluate the performance of the algorithms as a function of the number of physical routers. Moreover, for dynamic scenarios, the number of nodes in the substrate varied from 10 to 400 for the evaluation of the scalability of the approximative algorithms.
- Number of routers with attached image repositories set to 3. This value was experimentally found by the authors to avoid a large number of infeasible allocations;
- Number of cores available in the physical routers set to 6, which is the actual number found in real routers [20];
- Available bandwidth in real links determined by a uniform distribution between 1Gbps and 10Gbps,

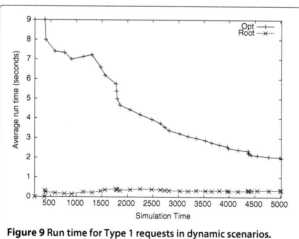

Figure 9 Run time for Type 1 requests in dynamic scenarios.

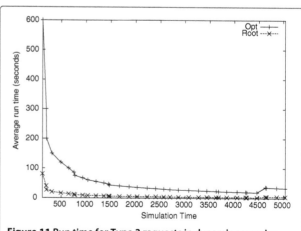

Figure 11 Run time for Type 3 requests in dynamic scenarios.

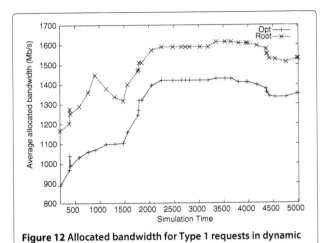

Figure 12 Allocated bandwidth for Type 1 requests in dynamic scenarios.

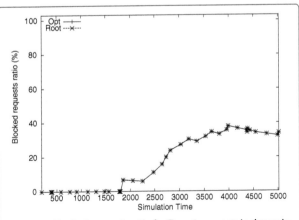

Figure 14 Allocated bandwidth for Type 3 requests in dynamic scenarios.

which is the interval common in substrate networks [21];

- Available memory in the physical routers set to 512MB; this number was based on the actual amount of flash memory in existing real routers [22];
- Size of images set to 128MB. This value was based on the amount of flash memory recommended for use of the software defined in [23], which is an operating system for routers;
- Time needed to boot an image in a physical router set to 10 seconds;
- Time threshold to instantiate each virtual network set to 100 seconds;
- Type of request: Type 1, Type 2 and Type 3. This depends on the number of resources required. Table 3 describes the requirements for each type of virtual network. They differ in terms of the number of requested virtual routers, the number of cores to instantiate each virtual router and in the guaranteed

bandwidth per virtual link being requested. Requests are not known a priory; they are randomly generated in the ranges defined in the Table 3. The bandwidth demands for each request is defined in run time.

Both the topology of the substrate networks and that of the virtual networks were randomly generated by using the topology generator BRITE [24], with the BA-2 [25] algorithm, a method that generates network topologies similar to those found on the Internet. For the substrate network, the link delays were the values given by BRITE. Since the requested delay of the links of the virtual networks must be greater than those of the links of the substrate network, these were defined by multiplying the value returned by BRITE by a random number derived from a uniform distribution. For Type 1 virtual networks, the delay was calculated as the value given by BRITE multiplied by a number up to 15. For Type 2 virtual networks, the delay was calculated to be the value returned by

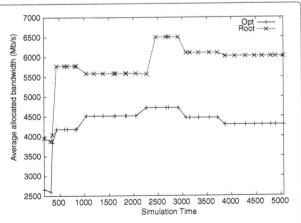

Figure 13 Allocated bandwidth for Type 2 requests in dynamic scenarios.

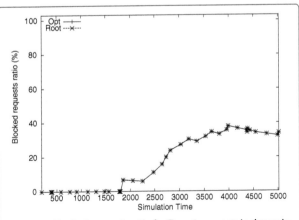

Figure 15 Blocked requests ratio for Type 1 requests in dynamic scenarios.

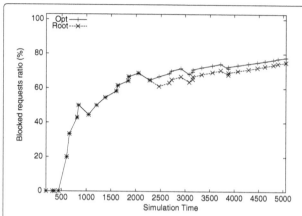

Figure 16 Blocked requests ratio for Type 2 requests in dynamic scenarios.

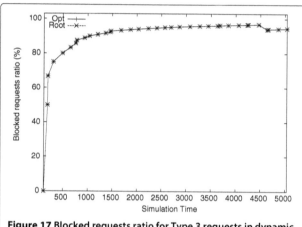

Figure 17 Blocked requests ratio for Type 3 requests in dynamic scenarios.

BRITE multiplied by a number up to 10. For Type 3 virtual networks, the delay was the value returned by BRITE multiplied by a number up to 5.

5.2 Optimal and root approximative algorithms

5.2.1 Static scenarios

The static scenarios involved only a single request, since the aim was to evaluate the differences between the proposed algorithms. The mapping of each request deals with an unallocated substrate. In this way, restrictions due to previous allocation have no impact on the difference of performance of the algorithms.

Results are reported as a function of the substrate size to evaluate the impact of it on the solution derived. The execution time of the Opt algorithm is limited to 3600 seconds. Each point in the graphs corresponds to the mean derived from five different requests.

Figures 5 and 6 plot the execution time of the algorithms as a function of the number of physical routers for requests of Type 1 and 2, respectively. For requests of type 1 (Figure 5) the execution time of the Root algorithm is less than that of the Opt algorithm with the execution time of the Opt algorithm increasing much faster than that of the Root algorithm as a function of the number of physical routers because of the increase in the search space. While the execution time of the Opt algorithm is 131 seconds for substrates with 50 nodes, the execution time of Root algorithm is less than 1 second. For requests of Type 2 which involve greater demands than do those of Type 1, while Root algorithm demands are still 6.4 seconds, the Opt demands 725.8 seconds for substrates with 10 nodes. Opt reaches the threshold for the execution time for substrates with only 20 nodes. For requests of Type 3 (Figure 7) the same trend is found although the execution time of the Opt algorithm was 2841 seconds for substrates with only 10 nodes.

Figure 8 plots the bandwidth allocated by the algorithms as a function of the number of physical routers. The Root algorithm always allocates more bandwidth than does Opt algorithm since only a limited number of solutions are evaluated. However, for requests of Type 1 the difference is quite small. For more demanding type of requests, these difference increases. For requests of Type 2, the maximum difference is 36.18%, while for Type 3 requests it is 58.91%.

These results show that the Root algorithm is more attractive than the Opt algorithm. The shorter run time of the Root algorithm and the similar bandwidth allocation justify the choice of the Root algorithm for the mapping on substrate with more than 30 nodes.

5.2.2 Dynamic scenarios

In the dynamic scenarios, several requests are included in each configuration of the network, so that the algorithms can be evaluated as the availability of the network changes as a function of time. The different sequence of resource allocations produced by different algorithms leads to different resource availability scenarios which implies different probabilities of success in the acceptance a request.

Simulation of each scenario took 5000 seconds. The arrival time and the duration of requests were defined randomly, on the basis of an exponential distribution with means of 100 and 2000 seconds, respectively.

Figures 9, 10 and 11 present the execution time of the algorithms for the three types of requests as a function of time. The execution time decreases along the simulation since resources are allocated and the search space shrink, as a consequence, the run time. Requests of Type 1 require low execution times since this type of requests can be easily accommodated. Although initially the difference is large, the execution time for the Opt algorithm is not

Table 4 Summary-dynamic scenarios

	Opt		
Type	Average run time (s)	Average allocated bandwidth (Mbps)	Average blocking rate
1	4.48	1282.73	17.43%
2	245.80	4311.06	55.15%
3	71.77	6052.83	88.08%
	Root		
Type	Average run time (s)	Average allocated bandwidth (Mbps)	Average blocking rate
1	0.30	1491.63	17.43%
2	6.46	5775.64	55.10%
3	9.84	6387.78	88.08%

that long. For requests of Type 2, differences in execution time are quite significant, being of the order of 600 seconds. For requests of Type 3 the differences are also large when the substrate is largely available, although the difference diminishes as the substrate becomes saturated. The average reductions in run time when using the Root algorithm were 99.93%, 99.97% and 99.86% for types 1, 2 and 3, respectively.

Figures 12, 13 and 14 show the bandwidth allocation per request. For requests of Type 1, the allocated bandwidth increases as the availability of resource decreases but reaches an almost constant value as the substrate occupancy tends to saturation. The greatest difference in bandwidth allocation was of 35.45%. The state of saturation is reached much faster as the demands of requests increases. For requests of Type 2 the maximum difference was in the order of 48.87%, while for Type 3, requests the bandwidth allocated per request by the Opt algorithm and Root algorithm was almost constant, equal to **6088** Mbps and **6424** Mbps, respectively.

Figures 15, 16 and 17 present results for the blocking ratio. As resources are allocated, their availability decreases leading to an increase in the probability of blocking. Requests of Type 2 and 3 saturate the substrate more quickly than do those of Type 1. The blocking rates for the two algorithms are very similar in despite of the difference of bandwidth allocated per request. This can be explained by the reduction of availability of physical routers leading to similar blocking ratio regardless of the savings in bandwidth.

Table 4 summarizes the results obtained in the dynamic scenario. Although the Root algorithm allocates in average 16.29%, 33.97% and 5.53% more bandwidth per request than does the Opt algorithm, these difference have no impact on the blocking ratio. In addition to yielding the same blocking ratio, the Root algorithm reduced the average run time in 99.93%, 99.97% and 99.86%, for types 1, 2 and 3, respectively. These results reinforce the advantage of the adoption of the Root algorithm given its reduced computational demand.

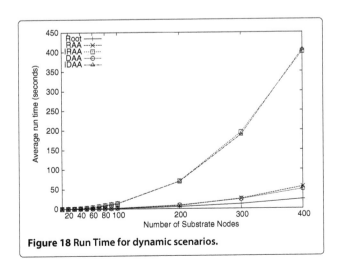

Figure 18 Run Time for dynamic scenarios.

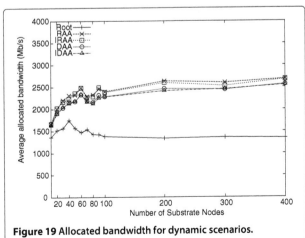

Figure 19 Allocated bandwidth for dynamic scenarios.

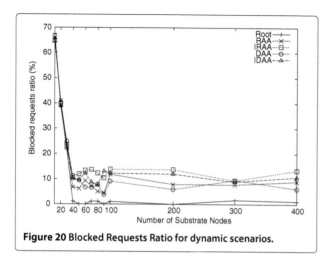

Figure 20 Blocked Requests Ratio for dynamic scenarios.

5.3 Approximative algorithms

The results produced by the approximative algorithms introduced in "Algorithms based on relaxed versions of ILPs" were compared to those yielded by the Root algorithm. In order to evaluate the growth in computational demands and the quality of the solution with an increase on the number of nodes in the substrate, the number of nodes in the substrate was up to 400 and the results are shown as a function of the number of nodes in the substrate.

Figure 18 shows that the average run time of the iterative algorithms (IRAA, IDAA) grows exponentially as a function of the number of nodes in the substrate and is ten times greater than that of the other approximative algorithms and twenty times greater than that of the Root algorithm for substrates with 400 nodes.

The iterative approximative algorithms allocate more bandwidth than do the other approximative algorithms and roughly 44.42% more than the Root algorithm (Figure 19). Moreover, the Root algorithm produces blocking ratio 8.93% lower than the other approximative algorithms as can be seen in Figure 20.

Table 5 summarizes the results found for the approximative algorithms. These results makes clear that the Root algorithm outperforms all other approximative algorithms. For instance, it requires 51.25 seconds less to run,

on average, than does the IRAA and produces blocking ratio almost 8.93% lower.

6 Conclusions and future work

Mapping virtual networks onto networks substrates is a crucial step for processing of VN services. therefore efficient mapping algorithms are of paramount for network virtualization.

This paper introduced six novel algorithms based on 0-1 ILP: one optimal and five approximative algorithms. These algorithms can be easily integrated to admission control mechanisms. They differ from previous proposals by the consideration of a large number of characteristics existing in real networks. It was shown via numerical examples that the Root algorithm demands considerably less computational time than the Opt algorithm and the iterative approximative algorithms. Such demand allows the adoption of Root algorithm for admission control in real time. It gives similar blocking ratio as does the Opt algorithm, and lower ratios than those of by the other approximative algorithms.

For future work, we intend to modify the formulation to consider the migration of virtual elements (routers and links), so that the algorithms potential migrations of VNs can be suggested. Formulations for the mapping problem considering path splitting are under development. We intent to verify results derived in a testbed for further validation.

Acknowledgements
This research was partially financed by Fundação de Amparo à Pesquisa do Estado de São Paulo (FAPESP), process 2010/03422-5.

Author details
[1]State University of Campinas, Campinas, Brazil. [2]University of São Paulo, São Paulo, Brazil.

Table 5 Numerical Comparisons (Average values)

	Type 1		
Algorithm	Run time (s)	Bandwidth (Mbps)	Blocked requests
Root	3.57	1314.57	10.40%
RAA	7.27	1816.10	15.79%
DAA	6.75	1706.33	15.97%
IRAA	54.82	1898.53	19.33%
IDAA	54.94	1827.07	17.86%

References
1. Zhu Y, Ammar M (2006) Algorithms for assigning substrate network resources to virtual network components. In: IEEE INFOCOM, 1–12. INFOCOM 2006. 25th IEEE International Conference on Computer Communications. Proceedings, Barcelona, Spain,
2. Bless R, Hübsch C, Mies S, Waldhorst O (2008) The Underlay Abstraction in the Spontaneous Virtual Networks (SpoVNet) Architecture. In: Next Generation Internet Networks (NGI 2008), 115–122. Next Generation Internet Networks, 2008. NGI 2008, Krakow, Poland,
3. Feamster N, Gao L, Rexford J (2007) How to lease the internet in your spare time. SIGCOMM Comput Commun Rev 37(1): 61–64
4. Chowdhury N, Rahman M, Boutaba R (2009) Virtual Network Embedding with Coordinated Node and Link Mapping. In: IEEE INFOCOM, 783–791. INFOCOM 2009. 28th IEEE International Conference on Computer Communications. Proceedings, Rio de Janeiro, Brazil,
5. Yu M, Yi Y, Rexford J, Chiang M (2008) Rethinking virtual network embedding: substrate support for path splitting and migration. SIGCOMM Comput Commun Rev 38(2): 17–29
6. Houidi I, Louati W, Zeghlache D (2008) A distributed and autonomic virtual network mapping framework. In: ICAS '08, 241–247. Autonomic and Autonomous Systems, 2008. ICAS 2008, Gosier, Guadeloupe,

7. Lu J, Turner J (2006) Efficient mapping of virtual networks onto a shared substrate. Tech. Rep. W0UCSE-2006-35. Washington University , Washington, USA. http://www.arl.wustl.edu/~jst/pubs/wucse2006-35. pdf. Accessed at 12/20/2010

8. Fan J, Ammar MH (2006) Dynamic topology configuration in service overlay networks: a study of reconfiguration policies. In: IEE INFOCOM, 1–12. INFOCOM 2006. 25th IEEE International Conference on Computer Communications. Proceedings, Barcelona, Spain,

9. Alkmim GP, Batista DM, Fonseca NLS (2011) Optimal mapping of virtual networks 2011. GLOBECOM '11. IEEE. In: Global Telecommunications Conference. Global Telecommunications Conference (GLOBECOM 2011), Houston, USA

10. Zhu Y, Zhang-Shen R, Rangarajan S, Rexford J (2008) Cabernet: Connectivity Architecture for Better Network Services. In: ACM CoNEXT '08, 64:1–64:6. CoNEXT '08 Proceedings of the 2008 ACM CoNEXT, New York, USA,

11. Zhu Y, Bavier A, Feamster N, Rangarajan S, Rexford J (2008) UFO: a resilient layered routing architecture. SIGCOMM Comput Commun Rev 38(5): 59–62

12. Ricci R, Alfeld C, Lepreau J (2003) A solver for the network testbed mapping problem. SIGCOMM Comput Commun Rev 33(2): 65–81

13. Zhu X, Santos C, Beyer D, Ward J, Singhal S (2008) Automated application component placement in data centers using mathematical programming. Int J Netw Manag 18: 467–483. [http://dx.doi.org/10.1002/nem.707]

14. Padala P, Shin KG, Zhu X, Uysal M, Wang Z, Singhal S, Merchant A, Salem K (2007) Adaptive control of virtualized resources in utility computing environments. In: ACM EuroSys '07, 289–302

15. Botero J, Hesselbach X, Fischer A, de Meer H (2011) Optimal mapping of virtual networks with hidden hops. Telecommunication Systems 51: 1–10. doi:10.1007/s11235-011-9437-0

16. Szeto W, Iraqi Y, Boutaba R (2003) A multi-commodity flow based approach to virtual network resource allocation. In: Global Telecommunications Conference, 2003, 3004–3008. GLOBECOM '03. vol 6. IEEE, San Francisco, USA,

17. Fletcher R, Leyffer S (1998) A mixed integer quadratic programming package . http://www.mcs.anl.gov/~leyffer/solvers.html. Accessed at 02/22/2011

18. Gomory RE (1958) Outline of an algorithm for integer solutions to linear programs. Bull Am Soc 64: 275–278

19. Lischka J, Karl H (2009) A virtual network mapping algorithm based on subgraph isomorphism detection. In: ACM VISA '09, 81–88. CM SIGCOMM 2009, Barcelona, Spain,

20. Cisco Systems (2010) Cisco Multiprocessor WAN Application Mode [Cisco Catalyst 6500 Series Switches]. http://www.cisco.com/en/US/prod/ collateral/modules/ps5510/ product_data_sheet0900aecd800f8965_ps708_Products_Data_Sheet.html. Accessed at 12/20/2010

21. RNP (2011) RNP Backbone map. http://www.rnp.br/en/backbone/index. php. Accessed at 09/19/2011

22. Cisco Systems (2011) Cisco 7200 Series Routers Overview [Cisco 7200 Series Routers]. http://www.cisco.com/en/US/prod/collateral/routers/ ps341/product_data_sheet09186a008008872b.html. Accessed at 09/19/2011

23. Cisco Systems (2011) Download Software. http://www.cisco.com/cisco/ software/release.html?mdfid=278807391&flowid=956&softwareid= 280805680&release=12.4.2-XB11&rellifecycle=GD&relind=AVAILABLE& reltype=latest. Accessed at 09/19/2011

24. Medina A, Lakhina A, Matta I, Byers J (2011) Brite. http://www.cs.bu.edu/ brite/. Accessed at 09/19/2011

25. Albert R, Barabási AL (2000) Topology of Evolving Networks: Local Events and Universality. Phys Rev Lett 85(24): 5234–5237

Permissions

All chapters in this book were first published in JISA, by Springer; hereby published with permission under the Creative Commons Attribution License or equivalent. Every chapter published in this book has been scrutinized by our experts. Their significance has been extensively debated. The topics covered herein carry significant findings which will fuel the growth of the discipline. They may even be implemented as practical applications or may be referred to as a beginning point for another development.

The contributors of this book come from diverse backgrounds, making this book a truly international effort. This book will bring forth new frontiers with its revolutionizing research information and detailed analysis of the nascent developments around the world.

We would like to thank all the contributing authors for lending their expertise to make the book truly unique. They have played a crucial role in the development of this book. Without their invaluable contributions this book wouldn't have been possible. They have made vital efforts to compile up to date information on the varied aspects of this subject to make this book a valuable addition to the collection of many professionals and students.

This book was conceptualized with the vision of imparting up-to-date information and advanced data in this field. To ensure the same, a matchless editorial board was set up. Every individual on the board went through rigorous rounds of assessment to prove their worth. After which they invested a large part of their time researching and compiling the most relevant data for our readers.

The editorial board has been involved in producing this book since its inception. They have spent rigorous hours researching and exploring the diverse topics which have resulted in the successful publishing of this book. They have passed on their knowledge of decades through this book. To expedite this challenging task, the publisher supported the team at every step. A small team of assistant editors was also appointed to further simplify the editing procedure and attain best results for the readers.

Apart from the editorial board, the designing team has also invested a significant amount of their time in understanding the subject and creating the most relevant covers. They scrutinized every image to scout for the most suitable representation of the subject and create an appropriate cover for the book.

The publishing team has been an ardent support to the editorial, designing and production team. Their endless efforts to recruit the best for this project, has resulted in the accomplishment of this book. They are a veteran in the field of academics and their pool of knowledge is as vast as their experience in printing. Their expertise and guidance has proved useful at every step. Their uncompromising quality standards have made this book an exceptional effort. Their encouragement from time to time has been an inspiration for everyone.

The publisher and the editorial board hope that this book will prove to be a valuable piece of knowledge for researchers, students, practitioners and scholars across the globe.

List of Contributors

Rajiv Ranjan
CSIRO ICT Centre, Canberra, Australia

Karan Mitra
CSIRO ICT Centre, Canberra, Australia

Dimitrios Georgakopoulos
CSIRO ICT Centre, Canberra, Australia

Ahmed Mihoob
School of Computing Science, Newcastle University, Newcastle upon Tyne, NE1 7RU, UK

Carlos Molina-Jimenez
School of Computing Science, Newcastle University, Newcastle upon Tyne, NE1 7RU, UK

Santosh Shrivastava
School of Computing Science, Newcastle University, Newcastle upon Tyne, NE1 7RU, UK

Lincoln David
Department of Informatics, Pontifícia Universidade Católica do Rio de Janeiro (PUC-Rio), Rio de Janeiro, Brazil

Rafael Vasconcelos
Department of Informatics, Pontifícia Universidade Católica do Rio de Janeiro (PUC-Rio), Rio de Janeiro, Brazil

Lucas Alves
Department of Informatics, Pontifícia Universidade Católica do Rio de Janeiro (PUC-Rio), Rio de Janeiro, Brazil

Rafael André
Department of Informatics, Pontifícia Universidade Católica do Rio de Janeiro (PUC-Rio), Rio de Janeiro, Brazil

Markus Endler
Department of Informatics, Pontifícia Universidade Católica do Rio de Janeiro (PUC-Rio), Rio de Janeiro, Brazil

Fady Samuel
Google Canada Inc., Kitchener, ON, Canada

Mosharaf Chowdhury
Computer Science Division, University of California, Berkeley, CA, USA

Raouf Boutaba
David R. Cheriton School of Computer Science, University of Waterloo, Waterloo, ON N2L 3G1, Canada
Division of IT Convergence Engineering, Pohang University of Science and Technology (POSTECH), Pohang 790-784, Korea

Filipe Araujo
CISUC, Department of Informatics Engineering, University of Coimbra, Polo II, 3030-290 Coimbra, Portugal

Serhiy Boychenko
CISUC, Department of Informatics Engineering, University of Coimbra, Polo II, 3030-290 Coimbra, Portugal

Raul Barbosa
CISUC, Department of Informatics Engineering, University of Coimbra, Polo II, 3030-290 Coimbra, Portugal

António Casimiro
Faculty of Sciences, University of Lisbon, Campo Grande, 1749-016 Lisboa, Portugal

Christopher Winstanley
Lancaster University, Lancaster, UK

Rajiv Ramdhany
Lancaster University, Lancaster, UK

François Taïani
University of Rennes 1 - IRISA - ESIR, Rennes, France

Barry Porter
Lancaster University, Lancaster, UK

Hugo Miranda
Departamento de Informática, Faculdade de Ciências, Universidade de Lisboa, Lisbon, Portugal

Pedro Alves
INESC-ID, Technical University of Lisbon, Opensoft, Rua Joshua Benoliel, 1, 4C, 1250 Lisbon, Portugal

Paulo Ferreira
INESC-ID, Technical University of Lisbon, Opensoft, Rua Joshua Benoliel, 1, 4C, 1250 Lisbon, Portugal

Khalid Elgazzar
School of Computing, Queen's University, Kingston, Canada

Ali Ejaz
School of Computing, Queen's University, Kingston, Canada

Hossam S Hassanein
School of Computing, Queen's University, Kingston, Canada

Danilo Ardagna
1Dipartimento di Elettronica, Informazione, e Bioingegneria Politecnico di Milano, Piazza Leonardo da Vinci 32, Milan 20133, Italy

Giuliano Casal
Department of Computing, Imperial College London, 180 Queens Gate, London SW7 2AZ, UK

Michele Ciavotta
Dipartimento di Elettronica, Informazione, e Bioingegneria Politecnico di Milano, Piazza Leonardo da Vinci 32, Milan 20133, Italy

Juan F Pérez
Department of Computing, Imperial College London, 180 Queens Gate, London SW7 2AZ, UK

Weikun Wang
Department of Computing, Imperial College London, 180 Queens Gate, London SW7 2AZ, UK

Jatinder Singh
Computer Laboratory, University of Cambridge, Cambridge, UK

Jean M Bacon
Computer Laboratory, University of Cambridge, Cambridge, UK

Sérgio Esteves
Instituto Superior Técnico - UTL / INESC-ID Lisboa Distributed Systems Group Rua Alves Redol, 9, 1000-029 Lisboa, Portugal

João Nuno Silva
Instituto Superior Técnico - UTL / INESC-ID Lisboa Distributed Systems Group Rua Alves Redol, 9, 1000-029 Lisboa, Portugal

Luís Veiga
Instituto Superior Técnico - UTL / INESC-ID Lisboa Distributed Systems Group Rua Alves Redol, 9, 1000-029 Lisboa, Portugal

Stefan Walraven
Equal Contributors iMinds-DistriNet, KU Leuven, Celestijnenlaan 200A, 3001 Leuven, Belgium

Dimitri Van Landuyt
Equal Contributors iMinds-DistriNet, KU Leuven, Celestijnenlaan 200A, 3001 Leuven, Belgium

Ansar Rafique
Equal Contributors iMinds-DistriNet, KU Leuven, Celestijnenlaan 200A, 3001 Leuven, Belgium

Bert Lagaisse
Equal Contributors iMinds-DistriNet, KU Leuven, Celestijnenlaan 200A, 3001 Leuven, Belgium

Wouter Joosen
Equal Contributors iMinds-DistriNet, KU Leuven, Celestijnenlaan 200A, 3001 Leuven, Belgium

Nima Kaviani,
University of British Columbia, 201-2366 Main Mall, Vancouver V6T 1Z4, Canada

Eric Wohlstadter
University of British Columbia, 201-2366 Main Mall, Vancouver V6T 1Z4, Canada

Rodger Lea
University of British Columbia, 201-2366 Main Mall, Vancouver V6T 1Z4, Canada

Benjamin Billet
MiMove Project-Team, Inria Paris-Rocquencourt, Rocquencourt, France

Valérie Issarny
MiMove Project-Team, Inria Paris-Rocquencourt, Rocquencourt, France

Gustavo P Alkmim
State University of Campinas, Campinas, Brazil

Daniel M Batista
University of São Paulo, São Paulo, Brazil

Nelson LS da Fonseca
State University of Campinas, Campinas, Brazil

Printed in the USA
CPSIA information can be obtained
at www.ICGtesting.com
JSHW051430221024
72173JS00006B/1425